# Preface

The *Sixth Workshop on Distributed Algorithms* (WDAG 92) took place on November 2-4, 1992 in Haifa, Israel. WDAG is intended to provide a forum for researchers and other parties interested in distributed algorithms and their applications. The aim is to present recent research results, explore directions for future research, and identify common fundamental techniques that serve as building blocks in many distributed algorithms. WDAG 92 follows five successful workshops in Ottawa (1985, proceedings published by Carleton University Press), Amsterdam (1987, see Lecture Notes in Computer Science (LNCS) 312), Nice (1989, LNCS 392), Bari (1990, LNCS 484) and Delphi (1991, LNCS 579).

Papers were solicited describing original results in all areas of distributed algorithms and their applications, including distributed graph algorithms, distributed combinatorial algorithms, design of network protocols, routing and flow control, communication complexity, fault-tolerant distributed algorithms, distributed data structures, distributed database techniques, replica control protocols, distributed optimization algorithms, mechanisms for safety and security in distributed systems, and protocols for real-time distributed systems.

The 24 papers were selected by the Program Committee from 38 submitted papers. The selection was based on perceived originality and quality. The selection process was carried out via email, using a scoring analysis program (courtesy of Robert Schapire, of AT&T). It is expected that the authors will prepare extended versions of the papers appearing in this proceedings, to be submitted for refereed publication in one of the scientific journals. The Program Committee wishes to thank all who submitted papers for consideration.

The Program Committee consisted of

| | |
|---|---|
| L. Bougé (ENS Lyon) | A. Segall (*co-chair*, Technion) |
| D. Dolev (Hebrew U. and IBM Almaden) | P. Spirakis (CTI and Patras U.) |
| S. Kutten (IBM) | G. Tel (Utrecht U.) |
| M. Merritt (AT&T) | S. Toueg (Cornell U.) |
| N. Santoro (Carleton U.) | J. Welch (U. of North Carolina) |
| A. Schiper (EPF Lausanne) | S. Zaks (*co-chair*, Technion). |

We wish to express our gratitude to all members of the Program Committee for their cooperation and to the referees who assisted them (see appendix for list).

We wish to thank the Department of Computer Science, Technion for placing at our disposal the best professional assistance it can offer. Judith Tamari did an excellent job in organizing the conference and putting the proceedings together, and Aythan Avior - in handling the computer work and adapting the scoring analysis program to WDAG needs. Our deepest thanks go to them both. We would also like to thank David Cohen of the *S. Neaman Institute* for his experienced help and advice.

The *S. Neaman Institute* selected WDAG 92 as the first workshop to receive sponsorship under the newly-established program to support scientific meetings related to research carried out at the Technion. On behalf of all Workshop participants and the entire Distributed Algorithms scientific community, the Workshop Steering Committee and Co-Chairmen would like to express their deep appreciation to the *S. Neaman Institute* for this support.

Haifa, November 1992                                    Adrian Segall
                                                        Shmuel Zaks

# Lecture Notes in Computer S

Edited by G. Goos and J. Hartmanis

Advisory Board: W. Brauer   D. Grie

A. Segall    S. Zaks (Eds.)

# Distributed Algorithms

6th International Workshop, WDAG '92
Haifa, Israel, November 2–4, 1992
Proceedings

Springer-Verlag

Berlin Heidelberg New York
London Paris Tokyo
Hong Kong Barcelona
Budapest

Series Editors

Gerhard Goos
Universität Karlsruhe
Postfach 69 80
Vincenz-Priessnitz-Straße 1
W-7500 Karlsruhe, FRG

Juris Hartmanis
Cornell University
Department of Computer Science
5149 Upson Hall
Ithaca, NY 14853, USA


Volume Editors

Adrian Segall
Shmuel Zaks
Department of Computer Science, Israel Institute of Technology
Technion, Haifa 32000, Israel


CR Subject Classification (1991): F.1, D.1.3, F.2.2, C.2.2, C.2.4, D.4.4-5


ISBN 3-540-56188-9 Springer-Verlag Berlin Heidelberg New York
ISBN 0-387-56188-9 Springer-Verlag New York Berlin Heidelberg

Typesetting: Camera ready by author/editor
Printing and binding: Druckhaus Beltz, Hemsbach/Bergstr.
45/3140-543210 - Printed on acid-free paper

# The S. Neaman Institute
# for Advanced Studies in Science and Technology

The Samuel Neaman Institute for Advanced Studies in Science and Technology is an independent public-policy research institute, established in 1978 to assist in the search for solutions to national problems in science and technology, education, economy and industry, and social development. As an interdisciplinary think-tank, the institute draws on the faculty and staff of Technion, other institutions and scientists in Israel, and specialists abroad. The Institute serves as a bridge between academia and decision makers through research, workshops and publications.

The Institute pursues a policy of inquiry and analysis designed to identify significant public policy problems, to determine possible courses of action to deal with the problems, and to evaluate the consequences of the identified courses of action.

As an independent not-for-profit research organization, the Institute does not advocate any specific policy or embrace any particular social philosophy. As befits a democratic society, the choices among policy alternatives are the prerogative and responsibility of the elected representatives of the citizenry. The Samuel Neaman Institute endeavors to contribute to a climate of informed choice.

The Institute undertakes sponsored advanced research, formulates invitational workshops, implements continuing education activities on topics of significance for the development of the State of Israel, and maintains a publications program for the dissemination of research and workshop findings. Specific topics for research may be initiated by the Institute, researchers, government agencies, foundations, industry or other concerned institutions. Each research program undertaken by the Institute is designed to be a significant scholarly study worthy of publication and public attention.

# Table of Contents

# Sparser: A paradigm for running distributed algorithms

Yehuda Afek[1,2] and Moty Ricklin[1]

[1] Computer Science Department, Tel-Aviv University, Ramat-Aviv 69978 Israel.
[2] AT&T Bell Laboratories, 600 Mountain Avenue, Murray Hill, NJ 07974.

**Abstract.** This paper introduces a transformer for improving the communication complexity of several classes of distributed algorithms. The transformer takes a distributed algorithm whose message complexity is $O(f \cdot m)$ and produces a new distributed algorithm for the same problem with $O(f \cdot n \log n + m \log n)$ message complexity, where $n$ and $m$ are the total number of nodes and links in the network, and $f$ is an arbitrary function of $n$ and $m$.

Applying our paradigm to the standard *all shortest paths algorithm* [15, 16, 22] yields a new algorithm which solves the problem in $O(n^2 \log n)$ messages (The previous best that we know of is $O(m \cdot n)$ messages). When applied to the $O(m \cdot polylogn)$ breadth-first search algorithm of Awerbuch and Peleg [8] our paradigm yields an $O(m + n \cdot polylogn)$ messages algorithm.

## 1 introduction

One way to run a distributed algorithm is to collect all its inputs to one node, run a sequential algorithm on all the inputs at this node, and then distribute the outputs to the nodes. For many applications this is inefficient, since the message complexity of such a process is usually bounded by $\Theta(nm)$ messages, where $n$ and $m$ are the total number of nodes and links in the network. For most applications, truly distributed algorithms which keep the inputs and outputs of every node only at that node, are more efficient. In this paper we observe that an intermediate combination of the two approaches yields distributed algorithms that are sometimes more efficient than any of the two extremes.

The idea of our technique is to use a particular partition of the network into subsets of nodes, and select a center in each set. Each center simulates the algorithm execution on behalf of each node in its set. That is, messages sent in the original algorithm between pairs of nodes in the same set are eliminated. On the other hand, a message sent from a node in one set to a node in another set, is now sent from the center of the first set to the center of the other set. The algorithm is based on the existence of a partition such that the intra cluster communication, and the radius of every cluster, are small. The existence of a suitable partition was constructively proved by Awerbuch and Peleg in [21, 10].

The main contribution of this paper is a distributed algorithms transformer that reduces the message complexity of many distributed algorithms from $O(f \cdot$

$m$) to $O(f \cdot n \log n + m \log n)$ message complexity, where $f$ is an arbitrary function of $n$ and $m$. Perhaps one of the most prominent examples where such a technique might be useful is the all pairs shortest paths problem. A distributed algorithm to solve this problem is repeatedly executed all the time in the ARPANET and in other networks (ARPANET [19] and others e.g. [18]). In this problem a routing table at each node, with one entry for each other node in the network is computed. Node $u$'s entry in node $v$'s table contains the length of the shortest path from $v$ to $u$ and the name of the first link on this path. This information is used in order to rout data messages between nodes.

Though the worst case message complexity ($O(mn)$) of the all pairs shortest paths problem has not been improved for several years, this fundamental task has been the subject of many papers [15, 19, 18, 14, 20, 16, 22, 11, 23]. This paper produces an $O(n^2 \log n)$ messages distributed algorithm for the all pairs shortest paths problem (from scratch, i.e., including the construction of the sparse partition).

Another immediate corollary of this paper is a $O(E + n \log^4 n)$ messages BFS algorithm by executing the $O(E \cdot \log^3 n)$ messages algorithm of Awerbuch and Peleg [8] in our framework. The message complexity of BFS has drawn considerable attention in recent years; In 1982 Gallager gave an $O(n^2)$ messages algorithm [16], in 1985 Awerbuch and Gallager gave an $O(E^\epsilon)$ messages algorithm [6], and in an earlier draft of this paper we have presented an $O(E\sqrt{\log n} + n^\epsilon)$ messages algorithm [3]. A break through in the message complexity of BFS has been recently reported by Awerbuch and Peleg in their elegant work [8] where an $O(E \cdot \log^3 n)$ messages algorithm is given. Being aware of our technique Awerbuch and Peleg have also pointed out in [8] that the combination of [3] and [8] gives an $O(E + n \log^4 n)$ messages algorithm.

Furthermore, as suggested by our paper, once such a partition exists in the network other algorithms could be run more efficiently, e.g. the DFS in $O(n \log n)$ messages, by applying our technique to the algorithm of [5].

We believe that the above discussion shows that the sparser technique belongs to the set of elementary tools in distributed computing, such as the snapshot [12], the termination detection of diffusing computation [13] the synchronizer [4, 9], the resource controller [2], and the reset procedure [1], which are used as building blocks in the design and implementation of other algorithms.

The rest of the paper is organized as follows: Section 1.2 gives an overview, Section 2 describes the sparser, which is the structure over which the simulation is performed, and in Section 3 the basic simulation technique is presented. In Section 4 extensions of the technique are presented.

## 1.1 Relation to other works

Our work uses a particular partition from the sparse graph partitions of [10] and combines it with a simple new idea: let the centers of clusters in the partition do the work for all the nodes in their cluster (computation and communication). It is important to note that most known partitions (e.g. synchronizer $\gamma$, and [7]) would not yield any savings in the communication complexity with the above idea.

Our usage of the sparse graph partition is somewhat different from the applications introduced by Awerbuch and Peleg [10, 9] for tracking mobile users, constructing compact routing tables, and synchronizer. Technically all their applications use the partitioning to localize global information in a hierarchical way.

A seemingly similar idea was presented in [7], where a network is partitioned into clusters and a problem is solved by first solving it in the subnetwork of each cluster and then piecing together the partial solutions. This is in contrast to our technique where the centers of the clusters continuously communicate and cooperatively solve the problem in a distributed manner. Moreover, [7] is geared towards reducing the locality of a given problem while we are concerned with the message complexity of distributed algorithms.

## 1.2   Overview

The central idea in this paper is to execute distributed algorithms by communicating only between the nodes of a subset of the nodes. That is, to partition the network into a number of subsets of nodes, each with a distinguished central node, and establish a simple path connecting the two central nodes of each pair of neighboring subsets. To run the algorithm each central node executes the algorithm for each node in its subset. Whenever a message is sent from a node in one subset to a subset of the nodes in another subset, that message is sent between the corresponding centers. Thus the cost of sending a message from one node to all its neighbors is bounded by the number of subsets in which the node has neighbors, times the distance between two centers.

In order for the execution of a distributed algorithm to be communication efficient, the partition should have special properties. Roughly speaking, the sum over all nodes $v$, of the number of subsets in which $v$ has neighbors, should be small (e.g. $O(n)$), and second, the radius of the connected graph spanning each subset must also be small (e.g. $O(\log n)$). The next section defines the structure of such a partition, and the section after specifies the simulation technique more precisely.

## 2   The sparser

Following [21, 10] we give in this section some necessary basic notations.

Let $G = (V, E)$ be an undirected graph. For two vertices $u, w \in V$, let $dist(u, v)$ denote the number of links on a shortest path from $u$ to $v$ in G. Define the radius of a graph to be

$$Rad(G) = min_{u \in V}(max_{v \in V} dist(u, v))). \qquad (1)$$

For a set of vertices $U$ the *neighborhood* of $U$ is

$$\Gamma(U) = U \cup \{v | (v, u) \in E \wedge u \in U\}. \qquad (2)$$

Given a set of vertices $C \subset V$, let $G(C)$ denote the subgraph induced by $C$ in $G$. A **cluster** is a set $C \subset V$ such that $G(C)$ is connected. A set $\mathcal{P}$ is a **partition** of $V$ if $\mathcal{P}$ is a set of pairwise disjoint nonempty sets and $\cup \mathcal{P} = V$. The elements of a partition are called **cells**. For a node $v \in V$ we define $\Delta_v(\mathcal{P})$, the degree of $v$ relative to $\mathcal{P}$, to be the number of cells in $\mathcal{P}$ which are at distance 1 or less from $v$. Formally:

$$\Delta_v(\mathcal{P}) = |\{P | v \in \Gamma(P), P \in \mathcal{P}\}|. \tag{3}$$

Let the **density** [21] of a partition $\mathcal{P}$ be:

$$dens(\mathcal{P}) = \sum_{P \in \mathcal{P}} |\Gamma(P)| \left( = \sum_{v \in V} \Delta_v(\mathcal{P}) \right). \tag{4}$$

**Definition 1.** A **sparser** is a pair $(\mathcal{C}, \mathcal{P})$ where $\mathcal{C}$ is a collection of clusters $\{C_1, C_2, \ldots, C_k\}$ and, $\mathcal{P}$ is a partition $\{P_1, P_2, \ldots, P_k\}$ of $V$, such that: $\forall i \in \{1, \ldots, k\}\{P_i \subseteq C_i \wedge (\forall j \neq i)(P_j \not\subseteq C_i)\}$. That is, each cell of $\mathcal{P}$ is covered by exactly one cluster of $\mathcal{C}$.

The **density** and **radius** of a sparser $(\mathcal{C}, \mathcal{P})$ are defined as follows:

$$dens(\mathcal{C}, \mathcal{P}) = dens(\mathcal{P}) \tag{5}$$

$$Rad(\mathcal{C}, \mathcal{P}) = max_{C \in \mathcal{C}}(Rad(G(C))) \tag{6}$$

A sparser whose density is $d$ and radius $r$ is an $(r, d)$-sparser.

**Constructing the sparser:** Awerbuch and Peleg gave a sequential algorithm for constructing a $(z, n^{1+1/z})$-sparser, $z$ integer [10, 21]. Extending this algorithm to a distributed algorithm with message complexity $O(m + n \cdot z)$ is straightforward using the standard DFS and BFS techniques. Moreover, the distributed implementation readily produces the following additional structures: distinguishes a center in each cluster and constructs a breadth-first search tree spanning each cluster, rooted at the center. Each pair of neighboring cells selects one inter-cell link, called the *preferred link*. The collection of breadth-first search trees and the preferred links is the structure spanning the network that is used by our simulation to pass messages between centers (similar to synchronizer $\gamma$ in [4]). All of this is achieved with the same message complexity, $O(m + n \cdot z)$.

## 3 The simulation technique

Assuming that an $(r, d)$-sparser $(\mathcal{C}, \mathcal{P})$ is given in the network, the sparser simulation technique proceeds in three major steps: First, collect the topological information of all the nodes in each cell in $\mathcal{P}$ to the center of the cluster that covers the cell. This information includes the identity of all the cells that are incident to nodes in the cell and the links leading to these cells. Second, simulate the algorithm by exchanging messages between the center nodes. Third, the outputs of the algorithm are distributed by the center of each cell to nodes in the cell along the breadth-first search tree. The crucial step is the second step in which centers have to exchange messages on behalf of their nodes. The first step requires $O(rm)$ messages since information about $m$ links is sent to distance $r$ (assuming the topological information dominates the size of the input data to the algorithm). If the size of the output of the algorithm at each node is at most $O(y \log n)$ bits, then the third phase, the output distribution phase, costs $O(yrn)$ messages. [3]

To describe the simulation let us define a cycle of computation for an asynchronous distributed algorithm. A distributed asynchronous algorithm proceeds at each node in cycles of three steps; (1) *message receipt*, (2) *local computation of a new local state*, and (3) *message transmission to a subset of the neighbors*. (Some cycles might consist only of steps 1 and 2.)

Lemma 3 considers asynchronous distributed algorithms in which nodes in the third step of each cycle send either the same message to all their neighbors, or a message to only one neighbor, or no message at all. Call such distributed algorithms *type $\alpha$ distributed algorithms*. (Lemma 10 is Section 5 consideres more general classes of algorithms).

**Definition 2.** The *cycle complexity* of an asynchronous algorithm $A$, is the maximum, over all the nodes, of the number of cycles a node goes through during the execution of the algorithm, in the worst case.

Consider a message $M$ of a type $\alpha$ algorithm $A$ that is sent from node $v$ to node $u$. In the $(\mathcal{C}, \mathcal{P})$ sparser simulation of $A$, if $v$ and $u$ are in the same cell then no message has to be sent by the simulation. If however $v \in P_1$ and $u \in P_2$, $P_1, P_2 \in \mathcal{P}$, then $C_1$'s center $c_1$, sends the message to the preferred link that connects $P_1$ with $P_2$. Then the message is sent over the preferred link and through the parent links of the breadth-first search tree of $P_2$ to $c_2$. Since algorithm $A$ is of type $\alpha$ then $M$ is either sent to all the neighbors of $v$ in $P_2$ or to exactly one. In either case this information can be coded in the message from $c_1$ to $c_2$ in at most $\log n$ bits.

**Lemma 3.** *Given a network with an $(r, d)$-sparser and a $K$ cycle complexity distributed algorithm $A$ of type $\alpha$, then $A$ can be run in the network in $O(mr + Kdr + yrn)$ messages, where $y \log n$ is the size of the output of the algorithm at each node in bits.*

**Proof:** The term $O(yrn)$ is the cost of distributing the outputs of $A$ to the nodes. The term $O(mr)$ is the cost of collecting the topology of the neighborhood of each cell to the center of the cell.

In each cycle of computation at node $v$ the simulation sends at most $2r + 1$ messages for each neighboring cell of $v$. Thus at most $\sum_v \Delta_v(\mathcal{P}) \cdot (2r+1)$ messages are sent, per cycle, resulting in a total of $O(Kdr)$ over the entire run of the algorithm. $\square$

---

[3] If the algorithm produces outputs at the nodes several times during a run then $O(yrn \log n)$ small messages might be necessary.

*Example 1.* Consider the following algorithm for the all pairs shortest paths algorithm, which is also given in [15, 16, 22]. Each node starts by sending its identity to all its neighbors. When a node receives the identity of all its neighbors, it marks them to be in distance one from it, and starts the second step. In the $i$'th step every node builds a message which consists of all the nodes which it marked to be in distance $i-1$ from it, and sends the message to all its neighbors. The node waits until it receives all the messages sent by its neighbors during their $i$'th step, mark the nodes which it receives their identities for the first time, to be in distance $i$ from it, and passes to the next step. A node terminates when it receives no new identities in an entire round. Segall in [22], gave a correctness proof for this algorithm. Note that for this algorithm both cycle complexity, and the size of the output at each node are $O(n)$.

Using a $(\log n, n)$-sparser (by setting $z = \log n$) and Lemma 3 we get a $O(n^2 \cdot \log n)$ messages distributed algorithm to solve the all shortest paths problem. (The algorithm to construct a $(\log n, n)$-sparser costs $O(n \log n + m)$ messages).

Since the simulated all shortest path algorithm works as well in the weighted case, i.e. when each link has a real length in each direction, also our algorithm solves the weighted problem with the same communication complexity. (The length corresponds to the queue length in the entry to the link [19], however the messages of the algorithm do not incur this delay because they are of the highest priority). That is, each $O(\log n)$ bits message of the shortest paths algorithm still incur one unit of cost. In this case, in the $i$th step node $v$ sends to all its neighbors the $i$-th closest node to $v$.

**Corollary 4.** *The upper bound on the message complexity of the (weighted and unweighted) all pairs shortest paths problem is $O(n^2 \log n)$ messages (each message is of size $O(\log n)$ bits).*

Another example is to apply the technique to the BFS algorithm of [8] which results in:

**Corollary 5.** *The upper bound on the message complexity of the BFS problem is $O(E + n \log^4 n)$ messages.*

## 4 Generalizations

Although Lemma 1 applies only to a certain class of algorithms a similar result can be derived to a much wider class. Lemma 10 in the sequel applies to any algorithm that in step 3 of the computation cycle sends the same message from a node to any subset of its neighbors.

Lemma 3 relied on the following fact about distributed algorithms of type $\alpha$: whenever a node sends a message to a subset of its neighbors, the information about the destinations of the message can be coded in no more than $O(\log n)$ bits. To enable a generalization of Lemma 3 we relax this assumption by introducing two modifications in algorithms in which nodes send a message to an arbitrary subset of their neighbors, as follows: First, whenever a node makes a "relevant" change in its local state it sends a message to this effect to all its neighbors (where "relevant" is defined in the sequel). Second, each message that is sent to a subset of the neighbors is now sent to all the neighbors. Knowing the local state of the sender, each neighbor determines whether the message was addressed to it or not.

Let us define things more formally. Let $A$ be a distributed protocol, and let $S(A)$ be the set of local states of the protocol at some node. We define a relation, $\propto$, on $S(A)$, such that $s_1 \propto s_2$ if for every possible message $M$, each node upon receiving $M$ sends exactly the same set of messages, in both states $s_1$, and $s_2$. Obviously, $\propto$ divides $S(A)$ into equivalence classes. During a run of a distributed protocol at node $v$, we define the *relevant state* of $v$ to be the equivalence class into which the internal state of $v$ belongs, under the relation $\propto$.

**Definition 6.** The *state complexity* of an asynchronous algorithm $A$, is the maximum, over all the nodes, of the number of times a node changes its relevant state (i.e. changes the equivalence class) during the execution of the algorithm, in the worst case.

In many distributed algorithms the following pattern of communication, called *local-polls*, that consists of three phases occurs several times: first a node sends the same message to a subset of its neighbors, then, in the second phase, each neighbor that receives the message responds with a reply, and in the third phase, the originating node collects all the replies and continues with its computation. Usually the replies are called acknowledgments.

Informally, we define the *weak-cycle* complexity of a distributed algorithm to be the cycle complexity of the algorithm discounting the cycles in which a node sends only a response message as part of a local poll pattern of communication. The motivation for this definition is that in many algorithms the cycle complexity is high due to acknowledgment type of messages. Applying Lemma 3 to these algorithms would result in no savings in the message complexity.

Again, let us define these notions more formally. Let $A$ be a distributed protocol, and let $v$ be a node in the network.

**Definition 7.** We say that a message $M$ sent from node $u$ to $v$ is an *acknowledgment*, if the cycle in which $M$ has been sent was initiated by a message received from $v$, and $M$ was the only message sent during this cycle.

We say that a cycle is a *real* cycle if the messages that were sent during the cycle were not acknowledgments and were sent to more than one neighbor.

**Definition 8.** The *weak cycle complexity* of an asynchronous algorithm $A$, is the maximum, over all the nodes, of the number of real cycles a node goes through during the execution of the algorithm, in the worst case.

**Definition 9.** The cycles in which a node sends a message to only one neighbor are called *trivial cycles*, and the *trivial cycle complexity* is the total number of such cycles in the network during the execution of the algorithm.

In order to transform algorithm $A$ into an $\alpha$ type, apply to it the following three changes (assuming FIFO discipline on the links):

1. Any change in the relevant state of a node in step 2 of the computation cycle is broadcast by the node to all its neighbors, before step 3 is performed. Thus, whenever a node $u$ receives a message $M$ from node $v$, the relevant state of $v$ at the time $M$ was sent is available at $u$.

2. Replace each response message (acknowledgment) by the same fixed-size pre-determined standard response message. (The standard response is a fixed message with $O(1)$ bits that is recognized as such). Upon receiving the standard response, each node can compute the real response from the relevant-state information of the neighbor, that it has last received.

3. Any message that is sent by a node $v$ in $A$ to a subset of the neighbors is sent to all the neighbors of $v$. Since the neighbors know the relevant state of $v$ at the time that the message was sent, each will be able to determine whether the message was addressed to it, or not.

**Lemma 10.** *Given a network with an $(r,d)$-sparser and a distributed algorithm $A$ with $K$ weak cycle complexity, and $t$ trivial cycle complexity which was modified as discussed above, then $A$ can be run in the network in $O(mr + (K+s)dr + tr + yrn)$ messages where $y \log n$ is the size of the output of the algorithm at each node in bits, and $s$ is the state complexity of $A$ (assuming that the value of the relevant state of a node can be transmitted with $\log n$ bits).*

**Proof:** Apply Lemma 3 to the modified algorithm $A$. In any local-poll the responses from all the neighbors of a node that are in one cell are sent as one message from the center of the cell to the corresponding neighboring cell center. That is, when a leader of a cluster receives a message which was sent to nodes in its cluster, it checks to see whether any of these nodes have to respond with an acknowledgment. If yes, it sends back only one copy of the standard response message.

Recall that in a trivial cycle at node $v$ exactly one message is sent from node $v$. Since such a message could in general go over a path of length $r$ in the simulation, the total complexity due to the trivial cycles is $tr$. □

*Example 2.* Consider the Depth First Search algorithm presented in [5]. The trivial cycle complexity $t$, of that algorithm is n. The weak cycle complexity $s$, of that algorithm is 2, and its state complexity is also 2. Thus, if a $(\log n, n)$-sparser already exists in the network the DFS algorithm can be run in $O(n \log n)$ messages.

Once a sparser is given in the network, the message complexity of any algorithm is determined by its three parameteres: trivial cycle complexity, real cycle complexity, and state complexity. E.g. the MST algorithm of [17] has a trivial cycle complexity $O(n \log n)$, real cycle complexity $O(\log n)$ and state complexity $O(\log n)$.

*Acknowledgments:* We thank Baruch Awerbuch and David Peleg for helpful discussions. In particular, David brought to our attention [21] in early 1989, and Baruch pointed out that the standard shortest paths algorithm works as well in the weighted case. We would also like to thank Mike Merritt and Mike Saks for helpful discussions.

# References

1. Y. Afek, B. Awerbuch, and E. Gafni. Applying static network protocols to dynamic networks. In *Proc. of the 28th IEEE Annual Symp. on Foundation of Computer Science*, pages 358–370, October 1987.
2. Y. Afek, B. Awerbuch, S. Plotkin, and M. Saks. Local management of a global resource in a communication network. In *Proc. of the 28th IEEE Annual Symp. on Foundation of Computer Science*, pages 347–357, October 1987.
3. Y. Afek and M. Ricklin. Sparser: A paradigm for running distributed algorithms. Extended abstract submitted to FOCS-90, April 1990.
4. B. Awerbuch. Complexity of network synchronization. *Journal of the ACM*, 32(4):804–823, October 1985.
5. B. Awerbuch. A new distributed depth-first-search algorithm. *Information Processing Letters*, 20(3):147–150, April 1985.
6. B. Awerbuch and R. Gallager. Distributed bfs algorithms. In *Proc. of the 26th IEEE Annual Symp. on Foundation of Computer Science*, October 1985.
7. B. Awerbuch, A. Goldberg, M. Luby, and S. Plotkin. Network decomposition and locality in distributed computation. In *Proc. of the 30th IEEE Annual Symp. on Foundation of Computer Science*, pages 364–369, October 1989.
8. B. Awerbuch and D. Peleg. Efficient distributed construction of sparse covers. Technical report, Weizman Institute of Science, Dep. of Computer Science, July 1990.
9. B. Awerbuch and D. Peleg. Network synchronization with polylogarithmic overhead. In *Proc. of the 31st IEEE Annual Symp. on Foundation of Computer Science*, October 1990.
10. B. Awerbuch and D. Peleg. Sparse partitions. In *Proc. of the 31st IEEE Annual Symp. on Foundation of Computer Science*, October 1990.
11. D. P. Bertsekas and R. G. Gallager. *Data Networks*. Prantice Hall, 1987.
12. K. M. Chandy and L. Lamport. Distributed snapshots: Determining global states of distributed systems. *ACM Trans. on Computer Systems*, 3(1):63–75, January 1985.
13. W. Dijkstra and C. S. Scholten. Termination detection for diffusing computations. *Information Processing Letters*, 11-1:1–4, August 1980.
14. A. Ephremides. *The routing problem in Computer Networks*. Springer Verlag, 1986.
15. R. G. Gallager. A shortest path routing algorithm with automatic resynch. Unpublished note, March 1976.
16. R. G. Gallager. Distributed minimum hop algorithms. Technical Report LIDS-P-1175, M.I.T. Lab for Information and Decision Systems, January 1982.
17. R. G. Gallager, P. A. Humblet, and P. M. Spira. A distributed algorithm for minimum weight spanning trees. *ACM Trans. Program. Lang. Syst.*, 5:66–77, January 1983.

18. J. Jaffe and F. Moss. A responsive distributed routing protocol. *IEEE Trans. on Communication*, COM-30(7, part II):1758–1762, July 1982.

19. J. M. McQuillan, I. Richer, and E. C. Rosen. The new routing algorithm for the arpanet. *IEEE Trans. on Communication*, COM-28(5), May 1980.

20. U. Pape. Implementation and efficiency of moor-algorithms for the shortest route problem. *Mathematical Programming*, 7:212–222, 1974.

21. D. Peleg. Sparse graph partitions. Technical Report CS89-01, Dep. of Applied Math. The Weizmann Institute, Rehovot, Israel, February 1989.

22. A. Segall. Distributed network protocols. *IEEE Trans. on Information Theory*, IT-29(1), January 1983.

23. J. M. Spinelli. Broadcasting topology and routing information in computer networks. Master's thesis, MIT, March 1986.

# Closed Schedulers:
# Constructions and Applications to Consensus Protocols

Ronit Lubitch & Shlomo Moran

Dept. of Computer Science, Technion, Haifa 32000, Israel

**Abstract.** Analyzing distributed protocols in various models often involves a careful analysis of the set of *admissible runs*, for which the protocols should behave correctly. In particular, the admissible runs assumed by a $t$-resilient protocol are runs which are fair for all but at most $t$ processors. In this paper we define *closed* sets of runs, and suggest a technique to prove impossibility results for $t$-resilient protocols, by restricting the corresponding sets of admissible runs to smaller sets, which are closed, as follows:

For each protocol $PR$ and for each initial configuration $c$, the set of admissible runs of $PR$ which start from $c$ defines a tree in a natural way: the root of the tree is the empty run, and each vertex in it denotes a finite prefix of an admissible run; a vertex $u$ in the tree has a son $v$ iff $v$ is also a prefix of an admissible run, which extends $u$ by one atomic step.

The tree of admissible runs described above may contain infinite paths which are not admissible runs. A set of admissible runs is *closed* if for every possible initial configuration $c$, each path in the tree of admissible runs starting from $c$ is also an admissible run. Closed sets of runs have the simple combinatorial structure of the set of paths of an infinite tree, which makes them easier to analyze.

We introduce a unified method for constructing closed sets of admissible runs by using a model-independent construction of closed *schedulers*. We use this construction to provide unified proofs of impossibility results in various models of asynchronous computations. One of our results generalizes a known impossibility result in a non-trivial way.

## 1   Introduction

A distributed decision task is a distributed task in which every processor eventually makes an irreversible decision step. One of the more challenging problems in distributed computing is the characterization of the decision tasks that can be solved in the presence of crash (fail stop) failures, under which a processor may stop participating in the protocol prematurely. A protocol that solves such a task in the presence of at most $t$ crash failures is called $t$-resilient. A general characterization of tasks that can be solved in the presence of $t$ crash failures is known only for the case $t = 1$ [2]. In spite of the large number of papers published in this area, our understanding of $t$-resilient protocols for $t > 1$ is still quite limited. For instance, for each $t \geq 2$, it is not yet known whether there are $t$-resilient protocols for the *renaming* task with $n + t - 1$ new names [1], or for the *$k$-set consensus* task with $k = t$ [3].

The difficulty of this problem does not seem to depend on the specific model of computation studied (i.e., shared memory or message passing), but more on the inherent difficulty of coordination between processors in a totally asynchronous environment, and in particular on the impossibility to distinguish between faulty processors and processors which are very slow, but in working order. Consequently, it is possible to have a $t$-resilient protocol for a given task, with the following unpleasant property: The number of steps that may be executed by the protocol, when started from a certain initial configuration, before it fulfills its task, is unbounded.

In this paper we propose an approach for analyzing asynchronous protocols which avoids the difficulty mentioned above. In this approach, we restrict the set of runs for which the protocol is required to behave correctly to a set of a simple structure, which we call "closed". A closed set of runs has the property that if a protocol is guaranteed to fulfill some task in each run in it, then it is guaranteed to fulfill that task within a fixed number of steps. We use this approach to provide alternative proofs for the impossibility of $t$-resilient consensus protocols in various models. One of these proofs generalizes the result of [6] in an interesting way.

## 1.1 Protocols and Runs

A *distributed system* consists of a set of $n$ ($n \geq 2$) asynchronous processors $\{p_1, \ldots, p_n\}$, modeled as (not necessarily finite) state machines, and of some means of communication among the processors (e.g., shared memory or message passing).

Each processor $p$ acts according to a deterministic transition function $t_p$. The transition function is described by the set of *atomic steps* which can be taken by the processor. An atomic step consists of a possible change of the processor's state, and of reading and/or writing from the communication means. A *protocol* for a given distributed system is a set of $n$ transition functions, one per processor.

A *configuration* of the system is a description of the system at some moment. It consists of the internal state of each processor and of the contents of the communication means. An *initial configuration* is one in which each processor is in an *initial state*, and the communication means contains some default value.

For each processor $p$ and for each configuration $c$, there is a (finite) set of atomic steps that can be taken by $p$ from the configuration $c$. A *run* of a protocol is an *infinite* sequence of atomic steps that can be taken in turn starting from some (initial) configuration $c$. Each atomic step is performed by one of the processors, and brings the system to a subsequent configuration. We say that a run $r$ is *applicable* to a configuration $c$ if it is a run that may start from the configuration $c$. If $r$ is applicable to $c$, then for every (finite) prefix $r'$ of $r$, the configuration resulted from applying $r'$ to $c$ is denoted by $\sigma(c, r')$.

## 1.2 Closed Sets of Admissible Runs

A distributed protocol is required to fulfill a certain task w.r.t. a specified set of runs, which we call the set of *admissible runs*. Thus, the correctness of a protocol depends not only on the task it should accomplish, but also on the set of admissible runs which are assumed. For example, there are protocols which are correct in a synchronous environment but not in an asynchronous one, and there are protocols which are correct when all processors are non-faulty but are incorrect when processors are subject to failures. In both these examples, protocols which are correct for a restricted set of admissible runs become incorrect when the set of admissible runs is extended.

Let $R$ be a set of runs, and $c$ be a given configuration. We denote by $R^c$ the set of all runs in $R$ which are applicable to $c$. $R^c$ defines an infinite directed tree, $T(R^c)$, in a natural way: the root of $T(R^c)$ is the empty run, and each vertex in it represents a finite prefix of a run in $R^c$; a vertex $u$ in $T(R^c)$ has a son $v$ iff $v$ represents a prefix of a run in $R^c$, which extends $u$ by one atomic step. When there is no ambiguity, we will identify vertices in $T(R^c)$ with the prefixes of runs they represent.

For an infinite tree $T$, $Paths(T)$ denotes the set of infinite directed paths in $T$. Note that for each set of runs $R$ and for each configuration $c$, $Paths(T(R^c))$ is a set of runs which are applicable to $c$, and $Paths(T(R^c)) \supseteq R^c$. However $Paths(T(R^c))$ may contain runs which are not in $R^c$. For instance, it is possible that for every $r \in R^c$, every processor takes an atomic step infinitely often in $r$, but $Paths(T(R^c))$ contains a run in which only one processor is activated forever.

A set $R$ of runs is *closed* iff for every possible configuration $c$, each path in $T(R^c)$ is a run in $R^c$, i.e.: $Paths(T(R^c)) = R^c$. Closed sets of runs appear to be much easier to analyze than other sets of runs, since they have the simple combinatorial structure possessed by the set of paths of an infinite tree of bounded degree. One specific useful property which is possessed by such sets, is the following: if it is given that each run in $R^c$ eventually satisfies certain property, then it is guaranteed that this property is achieved within a constant number of steps. This property is proved in the following lemma:

**Lemma 1.** *Let $R$ be a closed set of runs of some protocol $PR$. Assume that for some predicate Pred and for some configuration $c$, every run $r \in R^c$ has a prefix $r'$ which satisfies Pred. Then there is an absolute constant $M_c$, such that every run $r \in R^c$ has a prefix of length at most $M_c$ which satisfies Pred.*

*Proof.* Let $T = T(R^c) = (V, E)$. Define:

$$V' = \{v \in V \mid \text{each prefix } v' \text{ of } v \text{ does not satisfy} Pred\}$$

$$E' = \{e = (v, u) \in E \mid v, u \in V'\}$$

By the definition, $T' = (V', E')$ is a subgraph of $T$, and for each $v \in V'$ the directed path in $T$ from the root to $v$ is in $T'$. Hence $T'$ is a directed tree. If $|V'| < \infty$, then $M_c = 1 + \max\{depth(v)|v \in V'\}$ satisfies the requirement of the lemma. Otherwise, $T'$ is an infinite tree, the degree of its vertices is bounded, so by König's Infinity Lemma [4] there is an infinite directed path $r$ in $T'$. This means that $r$ is a run in $R^c$, all whose prefixes do not satisfy *Pred*, a contradiction.

Unfortunately, in many cases the set of admissible runs which is of interest is not closed. The most notable example is probably the sets of admissible runs for $t$-resilient protocols, which must guarantee correct behavior in all runs in which at most $t$ processors are subject to crash (fail-stop) failures. Admissible runs of such protocols are runs which are *fair* with respect to at least $n - t$ processors. The exact definition of "fair" depends on the specific model studied, but under all common definitions, the set of all $n - t$ *fair* runs of a given protocol is not closed for $0 \leq t \leq n - 2$.

In this paper we suggest a unified method for proving impossibility results concerning $t$-resilient protocols. In this method, we prove the impossibility result with respect to a proper subset of the set of all $n - t$ fair runs, which is closed, by using Lemma 1 above. The definition of this subset is based on a purely combinatorial construction, which is independent on the specific model studied. We demonstrate our technique by using it to prove impossibility of $t$-resilient consensus protocols in some variants of the shared memory model and of the message passing model. The results for the shared memory model are similar to results in [7], while one of the results in the message passing model is similar to a result of [5], and others are new extensions of the basic impossibilty result of [6]. In particular, we show that this result holds even if one assumes a global FIFO on the outgoing messages of each single processor, and that in one atomic step a processor may receive a message and send arbitrarily many messages. This should be contrasted with a result of [5], which shows that if there is a global FIFO on incoming messages of each processor then that impossibility result is not valid any more.

Note that impossibility results proved for restricted sets of $n - t$ fair runs as above are stronger than similar results proved for sets of **all** $n - t$ fair runs, since the protocols are required to behave correctly for smaller sets of admissible runs. For instance, our proofs of the results of [7, 5] mentioned above, show that there are no $t$-resilient protocols for the models studied there ($t$ is either 1 or 2, depending on the model), even if it is given that during any three consecutive steps of each processor, at least $n - t - 1$ other processors are activated.

## 1.3 Summary of Results

In the next section we define the consensus problem and present a general, model-independent, proof of our results. This proof assumes the existence of closed sets of runs which satisfy certain properties. In Section 3 we provide a combinatorial construction of closed *schedulers*, which are the main tool we use to construct the closed sets of runs needed for our proofs. Finally, in sections 4 and 5 (and in the Appendix) we use the closed schedulers to prove the desired impossibility results.

# 2   Consensus Protocols

A *consensus protocol* is a protocol in which each processor $p$ has a binary input register $in_p$ and an output register $out_p$. The initial content of the output register is $\perp$. A consensus protocol is correct w.r.t. a given set of admissible runs $R$, if in each run $r \in R$, some non-faulty processor decides on a binary value $v$, by writing it in the output register, such that

1) **consistency:** all the processors which decide, decide on the same value $v$.

2) **nontriviality:** $v$ is the input of at least one of the processors.

A $t$-resilient consensus protocol is a protocol which is correct w.r.t. the set of all $n - t$-fair runs (i.e, at most $t$ processors are faulty in them), which are applicable to some initial configuration.

Let $PR$ be a consensus protocol, $R^c$ be a set of runs of $PR$ applicable to an initial configuration $c$, and $T(R^c)$ be the tree associated with $R^c$ as described in Section 1.2. Each vertex $v \in T(R^c)$ represents a finite prefix $r'$ of some run $r$ in $R^c$.

Let $u$ be a vertex in $T(R^c)$, and let $D_u$ be the set of decision values of the runs in $R^c$ which are extensions of $u$. $u$ is *bivalent in* $T(R^c)$ if $\mid D_u \mid = 2$. $u$ is *univalent in* $T(R^c)$ if $\mid D_u \mid = 1$, and we say that $u$ is *0-valent in* $T(R^c)$ or *1-valent in* $T(R^c)$ according to the corresponding decision value. Note that if $PR$ is a $t$-resilient protocol and all the runs in $R^c$ are $n - t$-fair runs, then each vertex in $T(R^c)$ is either bivalent or univalent in $T(R^c)$. When the tree $T(R^c)$ is obvious from the context, we will not mention it in the terms univalent, bivalent and 0(1)-valent.

## 2.1   Proving Impossibility of Consensus by Using Closed Sets of Runs

In this subsection we present a model-independent impossibility proof of $t$-resilient consensus protocols, for $t \geq 1$, which is based on the existence of cof losed sets of $n - t$-fair runs, which satisfy certain properties. We start with some definitions.

Throughout the paper, $Q$ denotes a subset of $\{1, \ldots, n\}$, and for such a $Q$, $P_Q$ denotes the set of processors $\{p_i \mid i \in Q\}$. For sequences $x$ and $y$, $x \cdot y$ denotes the concatenation of $x$ and $y$.

**Definitions:** A $P_Q$-*run* is a run in which the set of non-faulty processors is included in $P_Q$. Runs $r_1$ and $r_2$ are $P_Q$-*equivalent* if for each $p \in P_Q$, $p$ makes the same sequence of atomic steps in $r_1$ and in $r_2$.

Let $T_1 = T(R^{c_1})$ and $T_2 = T(R^{c_2})$ be the trees of the sets of admissible runs applicable to configurations $c_1$ and $c_2$ resp. Let $v_1$ be a vertex in $T_1$ and let $v_2$ be a vertex in $T_2$. We say that $v_1$ and $v_2$ are $P_Q$-*similar* if there exist $P_Q$-runs $r_1$ and $r_2$ which are $P_Q$-equivalent, such that $(v_1 \cdot r_1)$ is in $Paths(T_1)$ and $(v_2 \cdot r_2)$ is in $Paths(T_2)$.

In our proof, we define for a given $t$-resilient consensus protocol $PR$ and for each initial configuration $c$, a subset of the set of $n - t$-fair runs of $PR$ starting from $c$, denoted as $R_{n,t}^c$, and we let $R_{n,t}$ be the union $\bigcup_c R_{n,t}^c$, taken over all initial configurations $c$. $R_{n,t}$ is a closed set of $n-t$-fair runs, and it satisfies the following properties:

*initial similarity:* Let $c_1$, $c_2$ be initial configurations, and let $Q \subseteq \{1,\ldots,n\}$, s.t. $|Q| \geq n-t$. If each processor $p \in P_Q$ has the same input in $c_1$ and in $c_2$, then the roots of $T(R^{c_1})$ and of $T(R^{c_2})$ are $P_Q$-similar.

*siblings similarity:* Let $c$ be an initial configuration, and let $u, v, w \in T(R^c_{n,t})$ s.t. $v$ and $w$ are sons of $u$. Then for some $Q \subseteq \{1,\ldots,n\}$, $|Q| \geq n-t$, there is a descendant $v'$ of $v$ and a descendant $w'$ of $w$ such that $v'$ and $w'$ are $P_Q$-similar.

**Theorem 2.** *For each $t \geq 1$, there is no $t$-resilient consensus protocol which is correct w.r.t. a closed set of $n-t$-fair runs $R_{n,t}$ which satisfies the initial similarity and siblings similarity properties.*

*Proof.* Assume by the way of contradiction, that $PR$ is a $t$-resilient consensus protocol which is correct w.r.t. a set of runs $R_{n,t}$ which satisfies the above properties, where $t \geq 1$.

We derive a contradiction in three steps:

**Step 1:** Proof of the existence of an initial configuration $c_0$, s.t. the root $T(R^{c_0}_{n,t})$ is bivalent.

Assume by the way of contradiction that for each initial configuration $c$, the root of $T(R^c_{n,t})$ is univalent. Let $c_0$ be the initial configuration in which the value of each input register $in_p$ is 0, and $c_1$ be the initial configuration in which the value of each input register $in_p$ is 1. By the nontriviality property for consensus protocol, the root of $T(R^{c_0}_{n,t})$ is 0-valent and the root of $T(R^{c_1}_{n,t})$ is 1-valent. Hence, there must be initial configurations $c_a$ and $c_b$ which differ only in the initial value $in_{p_i}$ of a single processor $p_i$, the root $v_a$ of $T(R^{c_a}_{n,t})$ is 0-valent and the root $v_b$ of $T(R^{c_b}_{n,t})$ is 1-valent. Let $Q = \{1,\ldots,i-1,i+1,\ldots,n\}$. Since $t \geq 1$ and $|Q| = n-1$, the *initial similarity* property implies that there are $P_Q$-runs $r_a \in R^{c_a}_{n,t}$ and $r_b \in R^{c_b}_{n,t}$, which are $P_Q$-equivalent. $r_a$ is an $n-t$-fair $P_Q$-run, and hence there must be $p \in P_Q$ s.t. $p$ eventually reaches a decision state in $r_a$. Since $v_a$ is 0-valent, $p$ must decide on 0 in $r_a$. $r_a$ and $r_b$ are $P_Q$-equivalent, so $p$ takes on $r_b$ the same steps as in $r_a$, and therefore $p$ decides on 0 also in $r_b$. This contradicts the 1-valency of $v_b$. Therefore, there exists an initial configuration $c_0$, s.t. the root of $T(R^{c_0}_{n,t})$ is bivalent.

**Step 2:** Proof of the existence of vertices $u, v, w \in T = T(R^{c_0}_{n,t})$, $v$ and $w$ are sons of $u$, s.t. $v$ is 0-valent and $w$ is 1 valent.

For $v \in T$, we define $Pred(v)$ to be *true* if $v$ is univalent and *false* if $v$ is bivalent. Since every run $r \in R^{c_0}_{n,t}$ is $n-t$-fair, every such run $r$ has a prefix $r'$ s.t. the vertex representing $r'$ in $T(R^{c_0}_{n,t})$ satisfies $Pred$. By Lemma 1, there is a constant $M_c$ s.t. every vertex of depth $\geq M_c$ in $T$ satisfies $Pred$. Assume that $M_c$ is as small as possible. Since by **Step 1** the root of $T(R^{c_0}_{n,t})$ is bivalent (i.e. does not satisfy $Pred$), $M_c \geq 1$ and hence there exists a bivalent vertex, $u$, of maximal possible depth. This implies that $u$ has one son $v$ which is 0-valent in $T$ and another son $w$ which is 1-valent in $T$.

**Step 3:** Let $v$ and $w$ be as in Step 2. By the *siblings similarity*, there is a vertex $v'$ which is a descendant of $v$, and a vertex $w'$ which is a descendant of $w$, s.t. for some $Q \subseteq \{1, \ldots, n\}$, $|Q| \geq n - t$, $v'$ and $w'$ are $P_Q$-similar. Then there are $P_Q$-runs $r_1$ and $r_2$ which are $P_Q$-equivalent, such that both $(v' \cdot r_1)$ and $(w' \cdot r_2)$ are in $Paths(T)$. Like in **Step 1**, since $v'$ is 0-valent, some processor $p \in P_Q$ decides on 0 in $r_1$. Since $p$ takes the same steps in both runs, $p$ decides on 0 also in $r_2$. But this is a contradiction, since $w'$ is 1-valent.

In order for the above proof to hold, we have to construct the closed sets of $n - t$-fair runs $R_{n,t}$, which satisfy the *initial similarity* and *siblings similarity* properties. This construction is carried out in two steps: First, we define and construct "closed schedulers", and prove that they satisfy certain properties. Then, for each specific model, we construct the corresponding sets of run $R_{n,t}$ by providing a mapping of schedulers to runs of $t$-resilient protocols in that model.

## 3  Closed Schedulers

Let $I$ be a (finite) set of integers. A *schedule* $s = (s_1, s_2, \cdots)$ over $I$, denoted *I-schedule*, is an infinite sequence of integers from $I$; $s^{(\ell)} = (s_1, \cdots, s_\ell)$ denotes the prefix of the first $\ell$ elements of $s$ ($s^{(0)} = \epsilon$). A schedule $s$ is *fair* for an integer $i$, if $i$ appears in it infinitely often. $s$ is fair for a subset $Q$ of $I$ if it is fair for every $i \in Q$. $s$ is *m-fair* for $1 \leq m \leq n$ if it is fair for a subset $Q$ where $|Q| \geq m$. Note that each schedule is 1-fair.

A *scheduler* $S$ over $I$ is a set of schedules as above. $S$ is *m-fair* if all the schedules in it are *m-fair*.

Each scheduler $S$ defines an infinite directed tree $T(S)$ in a natural way, as follows: The vertices of $T(S)$ are all the finite prefixes of schedules in $S$, and a vertex $u$ is the father of a vertex $v$ iff $v = u \cdot (i)$ for some $i$. The edge $(u, v)$ is marked with $i$. In this way, each schedule $s \in S$ is an infinite path in $T(S)$.

Let $Paths(T(S))$ be, as before, the set of infinite paths in $T(S)$. Note that $Paths(T(S))$ is a scheduler, and that for each scheduler $S$, $Paths(T(S)) \supseteq S$. A scheduler $S$ is *closed* if $Paths(T(S)) = S$, i.e. all the infinite paths in $T(S)$ are in $S$.

**Examples:**

- For each $n \in N$, the set $S_n$ of all 1-fair schedules over $\{1, \ldots, n\}$ (which is the set of all schedules over $\{1, \ldots, n\}$) is closed.
- For each $n \geq 2$, $0 \leq t \leq n-2$, let $S_{n,t}$ denote the set of all $n-t$-fair schedules over $\{1, \ldots, n\}$. $S_{n,t}$ is not closed: $\forall i \in N$ the schedule $(\underbrace{1, \ldots, 1}_{i \text{ times}}, 1, \ldots, n - t, 1, \ldots, n-t, \ldots)$ is $n-t$-fair, so the vertex $\underbrace{(1, \ldots, 1)}_{i \text{ times}}$ is in $T(S_{n,t})$. This implies that the schedule $(1, 1, 1, \ldots)$, which is not $n-t$-fair, is in $Paths(T(S_{n,t}))$. In fact, $T(S_{n,t}) = T(S_n)$ for all $n \geq 2$, $0 \leq t \leq n - 2$.

- Each finite scheduler (i.e. a finite set of schedules) is closed.
- Let $T$ be an infinite directed tree with no leaves whose vertices are finite sequences of integers from $\{1,\ldots,n\}$, and a vertex $u$ is the father of a vertex $v$ iff $v = u \cdot (i)$ for some $i$ (the edge $(u,v)$ is marked with $i$). Then the scheduler $S = Paths(T)$ is closed.

## 3.1 Construction of Closed and Fair Schedulers

In this subsection we define for each $n \geq 2, 0 \leq t \leq n-1$, a tree $T_{n,t}$ s.t. each infinite path in $T_{n,t}$ is $n-t$-fair. So the scheduler $S_{n,t} = Paths(T_{n,t})$ is $n-t$-fair and closed. In the next subsection we prove some combinatorial properties of $T_{n,t}$, which are used in the impossibility proofs based on our construction. For $t = n-1$, $T_{n,n-1} = T(S_n)$, where $S_n$ is the set of all $\{1,\ldots,n\}$-schedules. Below we present the construction of $T_{n,t}$ for $0 \leq t \leq n-2$.

Each vertex in $T_{n,t}$ will have either $t+1$ or $t+2$ sons. Informally, the sons of a vertex $u \in T_{n,t}$ are determined by the suffix of the last $n-t$ elements in (the sequence representing) $u$. In order to generalize the definition also for sequences of length $< n-t$, we associate with each finite sequence $s'$ a sequence of $n-t$ integers in $\{1,\ldots,n\}$, called $suf(s')$, which is defined by induction on the length of $s'$ as follows:

1. $suf(\epsilon) = (1,\ldots,n-t)$, where $\epsilon$ is the empty sequence.
2. For $s'$ of length $m > 0$, $s' = s'' \cdot (i)$ where $s''$ is of length $m-1$. Let $suf(s'') = (s_1,\ldots,s_{n-t})$. Then $suf(s') = (s_2,\ldots,s_{n-t},i)$.

Note that if the length of $s'$ is at least $n-t$, then $suf(s')$ is the suffix of length $n-t$ of $s'$. For a finite sequence $s'$, we denote by $SUF(s')$ the set of elements in $suf(s')$.

For $0 \leq t \leq n-2$, the tree $T_{n,t}$ is defined inductively as follows:

1. The empty sequence $\epsilon$ is the root of $T_{n,t}$.
2. Let $u$ be a vertex in $T_{n,t}$, and assume that $suf(u) = (s_1,\ldots,s_{n-t})$, where $s_i \neq s_j$ for $i \neq j$ (that is: all the elements in $suf(u)$ are distinct). A vertex $u$ with this property is said to be *normal*. Let $i_1,\ldots,i_t$ be the integers in $\{1,\ldots,n\} \setminus SUF(u)$. Then the sons of $u$ are $u \cdot (i_1),\ldots,u \cdot (i_t), u \cdot (s_1), u \cdot (s_2)$.
3. Let $u$ be a vertex in $T_{n,t}$, and assume that $suf(u) = (s_1,\ldots,s_{n-t-1},s_1)$, where $s_i \neq s_j$ for $i \neq j$ (that is: the first and last elements are equal and all the others are distinct). A vertex $u$ with this property is said to be *special*. Let $i_1,\ldots,i_{t+1}$ be the integers in $\{1,\ldots,n\} \setminus SUF(u)$. Then the sons of $u$ are $u \cdot (i_1),\ldots,u \cdot (i_{t+1})$.

For the above definition to be complete, we need to show that every vertex in $T_{n,t}$ must be either normal or special. This follows from Lemma 3 bellow.

**Lemma 3.** *Each normal vertex in $T_{n,t}$ has $t+2$ sons, exactly one of which is special and the others are normal, and each special vertex in $T_{n,t}$ has $t+1$ sons which are all normal.*

*Proof.* Follows immediately from the definition of $T_{n,t}$.

The definition of $T_{n,t}$ guarantees that for each schedule $s$ in $Paths(T_{n,t})$, in each subsequence of $n-t+1$ consecutive elements of $s$, at least $n-t$ elements are distinct. This implies that the closed scheduler $S_{n,t} = Paths(T_{n,t})$ is $n-t$-fair. **Example:** Let $n = 5, t = 2$. The vertex $u_1 = (1,2,3)$ is a normal vertex in $T_{5,2}$, and its sons are $(1,2,3,4), (1,2,3,5), (1,2,3,1)$ and $(1,2,3,2)$. The vertex $u_2 = (1,2,3,2)$ is a special vertex (the only special son of $u_1$) and its sons are $(1,2,3,2,1), (1,2,3,2,4), (1,2,3,2,5)$, which are all normal vertices.

## 3.2  Similarity Properties

In this subsection we prove that the trees $T_{n,t}$ defined above satisfy certain properties, which are needed to guarantee that the *initial similarity* and *siblings similarity* properties are satisfied by the sets of runs we construct in the various models.

**Definition:** For each $v \in T_{n,t}$, $T_{n,t}(v)$ is given by:

$$T_{n,t}(v) = \{u \mid v \cdot u \in T_{n,t}\}$$

i.e. $T_{n,t}(v)$ is the subtree of $T_{n,t}$ which consists of $v$ and all its descendants, when omitting the prefix $v$ from all the vertices. Note that for each $v \in T_{n,t}$, the scheduler $Paths(T_{n,t}(v))$ is $n-t$ fair and closed.

**Lemma 4.** *let $u$ be a vertex in $T_{n,t}$, and let $Q \subseteq \{1,\ldots,n\}$, be of cardinality $\geq n-t$. Then $Paths(T_{n,t}(u))$ contains a $Q$-schedule.*

*Proof.* Let $Q = \{i_1, \cdots, i_m\}$, and let $suf(u) = (s_1, \cdots, s_{n-t})$. Assume that the elements in $Q$ are ordered so that for each $k$, $1 \leq k < m$, if $i_k$ is in $suf(u)$, then for every $\ell$ s.t. $k < \ell \leq m$, $i_\ell$ also appears in $suf(u)$, and the last occurrence of $i_k$ in $suf(u)$ precedes the last occurrence of $i_\ell$ in $suf(u)$[1]. Since $m \geq n-t$, this implies that for $1 \leq k \leq m$, $i_k$ does not occur $(s_{k+1}, \cdots, s_{n-t})$. This easily implies that the periodical schedule $(i_1, \cdots, i_m, i_1, \cdots)$ is in $Paths(T_{n,t}(u))$.

**Definitions:** Vertices $u$ and $v$ in $T_{n,t}$ are *equivalent* iff $T_{n,t}(u) = T_{n,t}(v)$. $u$ and $v$ are *$Q$-similar*, $Q \subseteq \{1,\ldots,n\}, |Q| \geq n-t$, iff there exists a $Q$-schedule $s$ s.t. $s \in Paths(T_{n,t}(v)) \cap Paths(T_{n,t}(u))$.

The existence of pairs of vertices which are $Q$-similar for some $Q \subseteq \{1,\ldots,n\}$ is used in all our impossibility proofs.

**Lemma 5.** *For each $u, v \in T_{n,t}$:*

(a) *If $suf(u) = suf(v)$, then $u$ and $v$ are equivalent.*
(b) *Let $Q \subseteq \{1,\ldots,n\}, |Q| \geq n-t$. If there exists a sequence $s' \in Q^{n-t}$, s.t. both $u \cdot s'$ and $v \cdot s'$ are in $T_{n,t}$, then $u$ and $v$ are $Q$-similar.*

---

[1] Note that if $u$ is special, then one integer appears twice in $suf(u)$.

20

*Proof.*

(a) We have to show that for each schedule $s$, $s$ is in $T_{n,t}(u)$ iff it is in $t_{n,t}(v)$. Let $s = (s_1, s_2, \cdots)$, be given. An easy induction shows that for each $\ell \geq 0$, the prefix $(s_1, \cdots s_\ell)$ of $s$ is in $T_{n,t}(u)$ iff it is in $T_{n,t}(v)$. This proves (a).

(b) By Lemma 4, $Paths(T_{n,t}(u \cdot s'))$ contains a $Q$-schedule, say $s$. Hence $suf(u)$ contains the $Q$-schedule $s' \cdot s$. By (a) above and the fact that $suf(u \cdot s') = suf(v \cdot s') = s'$, $s' \cdot s$ is also in $Paths(T_{n,t}(v))$. This proves (b).

The next technical claim follows directly from the inductive definition of $T_{n,t}$, and its proof is left to the reader.

**Claim 3.1** *For each $n \geq 2, 0 \leq t \leq n - 2$, let $v_n$ be a normal vertex in $T_{n,t}$, $suf(v_n) = (s_1, \ldots, s_{n-t})$ and $v_s$ be a special vertex in $T_{n,t}$, $suf(v_s) = (t_1, \ldots, t_{n-t-1}, t_1)$.*

(a) *Let $s' = suf(v_n)$. Then, $v_n \cdot s'$ is a normal vertex in $T_{n,t}$.*

(b) *Let $s' = (s_1, \ldots, s_{n-t-2}, s_{n-t}, s_{n-t-1})$ (i.e. $s'$ is obtained by switching the last two elements in $suf(v_n)$). Then, $v_n \cdot s'$ is a normal vertex in $T_{n,t}$.*

(c) *Let $s' = (l, s_1, \ldots, s_{n-t-2}, s_{n-t})$ where $l \in \{1, \ldots, n\} \setminus SUF(v_n)$. Then, $v_n \cdot s'$ is a normal vertex in $T_{n,t}$.*

(d) *Let $s' = (l, t_2, \ldots, t_{n-t-1}, t_1)$ where $l \in \{1, \ldots, n\} \setminus SUF(v_s)$. Then, $v_s \cdot s'$ is a normal vertex in $T_{n,t}$.*

(e) *Let $v$ be a vertex in $T_{n,t}$ and $s'$ a sequence of length $n - t$ s.t. $v \cdot s'$ is a normal vertex in $T_{n,t}$. Let $s''$ be a sequence obtained by replacing elements in $s'$ by distinct integers from $\{1, \ldots, n\} \setminus \{SUF(v) \cup SUF(v \cdot s')\}$. Then, $v \cdot s''$ is normal vertex in $T_{n,t}$.*

**Lemma 6.** *Let $n \geq 2, 0 \leq t \leq n - 1$. Then for each $u \in T_{n,t}$, and for each $i, j$ s.t. both $u \cdot (i)$ and $u \cdot (j)$ are in $T_{n,t}$, it holds that both $u \cdot (i, j)$ and $u \cdot (j, i)$ are in $T_{n,t}$, and for each $Q \subseteq \{1, \ldots, n\}, |Q| \geq n - t$,*

1. *$u \cdot (i, j)$ and $u \cdot (j, i)$ are $Q$-similar.*
2. *If $t \geq 1$ and $i \notin Q$ then $u \cdot (i, j)$ and $u \cdot (j)$ are $Q$-similar.*
3. *If $t \geq 2$ and $i, j \notin Q$ then $u \cdot (i)$ and $u \cdot (j)$ are $Q$-similar.*

*Proof.* If $t = n - 1$ then $T_{n,t}$ is the complete $n$-ary tree, and the lemma holds trivially. Thus, we assume that $1 \leq t \leq n - 2$. Let $u$ be a vertex in $T_{n,t}$, $Q \subseteq \{1, \ldots, n\}, |Q| \geq n - t$. It is easy to see that if $u \cdot (i)$ and $u \cdot (j)$ are vertices in $T_{n,t}$, then $u_1 = u \cdot (i, j)$ and $u_2 = u \cdot (j, i)$ are normal vertices in $T_{n,t}$, where the only difference between $suf(u_1)$ and $suf(u_2)$ is the order of the last two elements. We now prove each of the three claims in the lemma.

1. Let $u_1 = u \cdot (i, j)$ and $u_2 = u \cdot (j, i)$. By lemma 5 (b) it suffices to show that there is a sequence $s' \in Q^{n-t}$, s.t. both $u_1 \cdot s'$ and $u_2 \cdot s'$ are in $T_{n,t}$. Assume first that $suf(u_1) \in Q^{n-t}$. In this case, we take $s' = suf(u_1)$. Then, by Claim 3.1 (a) $u_1 \cdot s'$ is a normal vertex in $T_{n,t}$, and by Claim 3.1 (b) $u_2 \cdot s'$ is a normal vertex in $T_{n,t}$.

If $suf(u_1) \notin Q^{n-t}$, we let $s'$ be the sequence obtained by replacing all the elements in $suf(u_1) \setminus Q$ by elements in $Q \setminus SUF(u_1)$ (this is possible since $|Q| \geq |SUF(u_1)|$). Since $SUF(u_1) = SUF(u_1 \cdot suf(u_1)) = SUF(u_2 \cdot suf(u_1))$, by Claim 3.1 (e), both $u_1 \cdot s'$ and $u_2 \cdot s'$ are normal vertices in $T_{n,t}$. Hence, by Lemma 5 (b), $u_1$ and $u_2$ are $Q$-similar.

2. Let $u_1 = u \cdot (j)$, $u_2 = u \cdot (i)$ and let $u_3 = u \cdot (i,j)$. As in 1. above, it suffices to show that there is a sequence $s' \in Q^{n-t}$, s.t. both $u_1 \cdot s'$ and $u_3 \cdot s'$ are in $T_{n,t}$. Let $suf(u_1) = (s_1, \cdots, s_{n-t-1}, j)$ and let $suf(u_2) = (s_1, \cdots, s_{n-t-1}, i)$. Assume first that $SUF(u_1) \setminus \{i\} \subseteq Q$. In constructing $s'$ we distinguish between two cases:

   Case 1: Both $u_1$ and $u_2$ are normal. In this case $i \notin SUF(u_1)$, and hence $SUF(u_1) \subseteq Q$. Let $s' = suf(u_1)$. Then $u_1 \cdot s'$ is in $T_{n,t}$ by Claim 3.1 (a), and $u_3 \cdot s'$ is in $T_{n,t}$ by Claim 3.1 (c).

   Case 2: Not case 1. Then $s_1 \in \{i,j\}$, and hence $|SUF(u_1) \bigcup SUF(u_2) \setminus \{i\}| < n - t \leq |Q|$. Since $i \notin Q$, there is an $\ell \in Q$, which is not in $SUF(u_1) \bigcup SUF(u_2)$. In this case we let $s' = (\ell, s_2, \cdots s_{n-t-1}, j)$. Then $u_3 \cdot s'$ is in $T_{n,t}$ by Claim 3.1 (c). If $s_1 = j$ then $u_1 \cdot s'$ is in $T_{n,t}$ by Claim 3.1 (d), else $u_1 \cdot s'$ is in $T_{n,t}$ by application of (a) and then (e) of Claim 3.1.

   Assume now that $SUF(u_1) \setminus \{i\} \not\subseteq Q$. We replace in each of the two cases above the sequence $s'$ by a sequence $s''$, which is obtained by replacing the elements in $s'$ which are not in $Q$ by distinct elements from $Q$ (again, this is possible since $|Q| \geq n - t$). By Lemma 3.1 (e) both $u_1 \cdot s''$ and $u_3 \cdot s''$ are normal vertices of $T_{n,t}$, and by Lemma 5 (b) they are $Q$-similar.

3. Let $u_1 = u \cdot (i)$ and $u_2 = u \cdot (j)$. Again, it suffices to show that there is a sequence $s' \in Q^{n-t}$, s.t. both $u_1 \cdot s'$ and $u_2 \cdot s'$ are in $T_{n,t}$. Let $suf(u_1) = (s_1, \cdots, s_{n-t-1}, i)$ and let $suf(u_2) = (s_1, \cdots, s_{n-t-1}, j)$. Assume first that $SUF(u_1) \setminus \{i,j\} \subseteq Q$. At least one out of $u_1$, $u_2$ is normal, so assume that $u_1$ is normal. We let $s' = (m, \cdots, s_{n-t-1}, \ell)$, where (i) $\ell \in Q \setminus SUF(u_1)$, and (ii) if $s_1 \neq j$ then $m = s_1$, else $m \neq \ell$, and $m \in Q \setminus SUF(u_1)$. Then by Claim 3.1 (e), both $u_1 \cdot s'$ and $u_2 \cdot s'$ are in $T_{n,t}$.

   Assume now that $SUF(u_1) \setminus \{i,j\} \not\subseteq Q$. As in the previous cases, we construct a sequence $s''$ by replacing the elements in $s'$ above which are not in $Q$ by distinct elements from $Q$. By Claim 3.1 (e) both $u_1 \cdot s''$ and $u_2 \cdot s''$ are normal vertices in $T_{n,t}$, and by Lemma 5 (b) they are $Q$-similar.

## 4 The Shared Memory Model

In this section we apply the proof technique of Section 2 to prove impossibility of $t$-resilient consensus protocols for various shared memory models. For this, we define a mapping $M_{sm}$ which, for each protocol $PR$, maps each pair $(c, s)$ of a configuration $c$ and a schedule $s$ to a run of $PR$ which is applicable to $c$. Then we use in our proof the sets of runs $R_{n,t}$ which is the union $\bigcup_c R^c_{n,t}$, taken over all initial configurations $c$, where

$$R^c_{n,t} = \{M_{sm}(c,s) \mid s \in \mathcal{S}_{n,t}\},$$

where $\mathcal{S}_{n,t}$ is the closed scheduler defined in Section 3. The impossibility proof is then completed by showing that $R_{n,t}$ is a closed set of $n - t$-fair runs which satisfies the *initial similarity* and *siblings similarity* properties.

## 4.1 The Model

In a shared memory system, processors communicate via a set of shared registers. We consider two kinds of protocols which differ in the atomicity of the shared registers. In a *read/write protocol* a processor may atomically read or atomically write a shared register. In a *read-modify-write protocol* a processor may atomically read a shared register, and depending on its value write a new value into it.

A *configuration* of the system consists of the internal states of the processors and the contents of the shared registers. An *initial configuration* is one in which each processor is in an initial state and all the shared registers have some default initial values.

An *atomic step* of a processor $p$ consists of an atomic operation to a shared register followed by an internal state transition. Given a configuration $c$, an atomic step is completely determined by specifying the active processor $p$.

A processor $p$ is *non-faulty* in a run if it takes infinitely many steps in it, and it is *faulty* otherwise. A run is $n - t$-*fair* if at most $t$ processors are faulty in it.

We start by defining a mapping $M_{sm}$, which for each protocol $PR$ in a shared memory model, maps schedules to runs of $PR$. Let $c$ be a configuration and $s = (s_1, s_2, \cdots)$ be a schedule. $s^{(\ell)} = (s_1, \cdots, s_\ell)$ denotes the prefix of length $\ell$ of $s$. The run $r = M_{sm}(c, s) = (a_1, a_2, \cdots)$ is defined by defining, for each $\ell \geq 0$, the prefix of $r$, $r^{(\ell)} = M_{sm}(c, s^{(\ell)})$, as follows:

- $r^{(0)} = M_{sm}(c, s^{(0)}) = M_{sm}(c, \epsilon) = \epsilon$.
- Let $M_{sm}(c, s^{(\ell)}) = r^{(\ell)} = (a_1, \cdots, a_\ell)$. Then $M_{sm}(c, s^{(\ell+1)}) = r^{(\ell+1)} = r^{(\ell)} \cdot (a_{\ell+1})$, where $a_{\ell+1}$ is the atomic step taken by processor $p_{s_{l+1}}$ from the configuration $\sigma(c, r^{(\ell)})$.

For each initial configuration $c$, $R_{n,t}^c = \{M_{sm}(c, s) \mid s \in \mathcal{S}_{n,t}\}$. The mapping $M_{sm}$ defines isomorphism from $T_{n,t}$ onto $T(R_{n,t}^c)$. We denote the image of a vertex $u \in T_{n,t}$ under this isomorphism by $u_c$. By the definition of the mapping $M_{sm}$ and the fact that $\mathcal{S}_{n,t}$ is an $n - t$-fair scheduler, the set $R_{n,t}$ is a closed set of $n - t$-fair runs. In order to prove that it satisfies also the *initial similarity* and *siblings similarity* properties, we need one more definition and lemma:

**Definition:** Configurations $c_1$ and $c_2$ are $P_Q$-*equivalent*, for $Q \subseteq \{1, \ldots, n\}$, if all the shared registers have the same values in $c_1$ and in $c_2$, and each processor $p \in P_Q$ is in the same internal state in $c_1$ and in $c_2$.

**Lemma 7.** *Let $c_1$ and $c_2$ be $P_Q$-equivalent configurations, and let $s$ be a $Q$-schedule. Then the runs $r_1 = M_{sm}(c_1, s)$ and $r_2 = M_{sm}(c_2, s)$ are $P_Q$-runs which are $P_Q$-equivalent.*

*Proof.* First, observe that if $c$ and $d$ are $P_Q$-equivalent configurations, then for every $i \in Q$, $M_{sm}(c, (i)) = M_{sm}(d, (i))$, and the configurations $\sigma(c, M_{sm}(c, (i)))$ and $\sigma(d, M_{sm}(d, (i)))$ are $P_Q$-equivalent.

For each integer $\ell$, let $r_1^{(\ell)} = M_{sm}(c_1, s^{(\ell)})$ and $r_2^{(\ell)} = M_{sm}(c_2, s^{(\ell)})$. Using the above observation, a straightforwards induction on $\ell$ shows that the configurations $\sigma(c_1, r_1^{(\ell)})$ and $\sigma(c_2, r_2^{(\ell)})$ are $P_Q$-equivalent. It follows that the runs $r_1$ and $r_2$ are $P_Q$-runs which are $P_Q$-equivalent (and, in fact, are identical).

The *initial similarity* property follows from Lemma 7, Lemma 4 and the definition of the mapping $M_{sm}$. The *siblings similarity* property will be proved for each specific model.

## 4.2 Impossibility of 1-Resilient Read/Write Consensus Protocols

Let $PR$ be a given protocol in the read/write model. We prove below that $PR$ is not a 1-resilient consensus protocol. By the said above, it suffices to prove that $R_{n,1}$ satisfies the *siblings similarity* property.

**Lemma 8.** *Let $u, v = u \cdot (i), w = u \cdot (j)$ be vertices in $T_{n,1}$, and let $u_c, v_c, w_c$ the corresponding vertices in $T(R_{n,1}(c))$. Then there is a descendant $v_c'$ of $v_c$ and a descendant $w_c'$ of $w_c$ such that $v_c'$ and $w_c'$ are $P_Q$-similar, for some $Q \subseteq \{1, \ldots, n\}, |Q| \geq n - 1$.*

*Proof.* By Lemma 7, it suffices to find a descendant $v'$ of $v$ and a descendant $w'$ of $w$ s.t. $v'$ and $w'$ are $Q$-similar and $\sigma(c, v_c')$ and $\sigma(c, w_c')$ are $P_Q$-equivalent.

Let $v_c = u_c \cdot (a)$ and $w_c = u_c \cdot (b)$, where $a$ is an atomic step taken by $p_i$, and $b$ is an atomic step taken by $p_j$. Let $reg_1$ be the register that $p_i$ accesses in $a$, and $reg_2$ be the register that $p_j$ accesses in $b$.

**Case 1:** One of the two steps $a, b$ is a read step.
Suppose w.l.o.g. that the step $a$ taken by $p_i$ is a read step. Let $Q = \{1, \ldots, n\} \setminus \{i\}$, $w' = w = u \cdot (j)$ and $v' = v \cdot (j)$. Then, $\sigma(c, w_c')$ and $\sigma(c, v_c')$ are $P_Q$-equivalent, and by Lemma 6 (2) $u \cdot (j), v \cdot (j)$ are $Q$-similar. Therefore $w_c'$ and $v_c'$ are $P_Q$-similar.

**Case 2:** Both steps $a, b$ are write steps, $reg_1 \neq reg_2$.
Let $w' = w \cdot (i)$, $v' = v \cdot (j)$, and let $Q = \{1, \ldots, n\}$. Then, $\sigma(c, w_c')$ and $\sigma(v_c')$ are $P_Q$-equivalent, and by Lemma 6 (1), $w \cdot (i)$ and $v \cdot (j)$ are $Q$-similar. Therefore $w_c'$ and $v_c'$ are $P_Q$-similar.

**Case 3:** Both steps $a, b$ are write steps, $reg_1 = reg_2$.
Let $w' = w = u \cdot (j)$, $v' = v \cdot (j)$, and let $Q = \{1, \ldots, n\} \setminus \{i\}$. Then, $\sigma(c, w_c')$ and $\sigma(c, v_c')$ are $P_Q$-equivalent, and like in Case 1, $w_c'$ and $v_c'$ are $P_Q$-similar.

Thus, we conclude the following:

**Theorem 9.** *[7] There is no 1-resilient read/write consensus protocol.*

### 4.3  Impossibility of 2-Resilient Read-modify-Write Consensus Protocols

Let $PR$ be a given protocol in the read-modify-write model. We prove below that $PR$ is not a 2-resilient consensus protocol. By the said above, it suffices to prove that $R_{n,2}$ satisfies the *siblings similarity* property.

**Lemma 10.** *Let $u, v = u \cdot (i), w = u \cdot (j)$ be vertices in $T_{n,2}$, and let $u_c, v_c, w_c$ the corresponding vertices in $T(R_{n,2}(c))$. Then there is a descendant $v'_c$ of $v_c$ and a descendant $w'_c$ of $w_c$ such that $v'_c$ and $w'_c$ are $P_Q$-similar, for some $Q \subseteq \{1, \ldots, n\}, |Q| \geq n - 2$.*

*Proof.* Let $u_c, v_c, w_c$ be the images of $u, v, w$ in $T(R^c_{n,2})$. Let $v_c = u_c \cdot (a)$ and $w_c = u_c \cdot (b)$, where $a$ is the step taken by $p_i$ and $b$ is the step taken by $p_j$. Let $reg_1$ be the register that $p_i$ accesses in $a$, and $reg_2$ be the register that $p_j$ accesses in $b$.

We have to show that $v_c$ and $w_c$ have descendants $v'_c$ and $w'_c$ which are $P_Q$-similar for $|Q| \geq n - 2$.

**Case 1:** $reg_1 \neq reg_2$.
  Let $w' = w \cdot (i)$ and $v' = v \cdot (j)$, and let $Q = \{1, \ldots, n\}$. Then $\sigma(c, w'_c)$ and $\sigma(c, v'_c)$ are $P_Q$-equivalent, and by Lemma 6 (1) $w'$ and $v'$ are $Q$-similar. Therefore $w'_c$ and $v'_c$ are $P_Q$-similar.

**Case 2:** $reg_1 = reg_2 = reg$, the value of $reg$ in $\sigma(c, u_c)$ is equal to its value in $\sigma(c, v_c)$.
  Let $w' = w$ and $v' = v \cdot (j)$, and let $Q = \{1, \ldots, n\} \setminus \{i\}$. Then $\sigma(c, w'_c)$ and $\sigma(c, v'_c)$ are $P_Q$-equivalent, and by Lemma 6 (2) $w', v'$ are $Q$-similar. Therefore $w'_c$ and $v'_c$ are $P_Q$-similar.

**Case 3:** $reg_1 = reg_2 = reg$, the value of $reg$ in $\sigma(c, u_c)$ is equal to its value in $\sigma(c, w_c)$.
  Similar to **Case 2**.

**Case 4:** $reg_1 = reg_2 = reg$, the value of $reg$ in $\sigma(c, u_c)$ is not equal to its value in $\sigma(c, v_c)$, and is not equal to its value in $\sigma(c, w_c)$.
  Let $Q = \{1, \ldots, n\} \setminus \{i, j\}$. Since $reg$ is a one bit register, its value in $\sigma(c, v_c)$ is equal to its value in $\sigma(c, w_c)$. Hence, $\sigma(c, v_c)$ and $\sigma(c, w_c)$ are $P_Q$-equivalent, and by Lemma 6 (3) $v$ and $w$ are $Q$-similar. Therefore $v_c$ and $w_c$ are $P_Q$-similar.

Lemma 10 implies the following:

**Theorem 11.** *[7] There is no 2-resilient read-modify-write consensus protocol, for $n \geq 3$ processors and one bit shared registers.*

## 5  The Message Passing Model

In the shared memory models studied in the previous section, in each given configuration, each processor could take a single atomic step. This is not the case in asynchronous message passing models, where the atomic step taken by a processor in a given configuration may depend also on the messages delivered to it. Thus, in order to make the mapping of schedules to runs well defined, one has to specify, for each configuration $c$ and each processor $p$, which messages which are destinated to $p$ in $c$ are delivered. By choosing appropriate policies for this specification, one imposes various restrictions on the resulted runs. These restrictions are translated to restrictions on the resulted closed sets of admissible runs, and thus to sharper impossibility results.

## 5.1 The Model

In message-passing systems, processors communicate by sending each other messages along communication links. Each communication link delivers messages from processor $p_i$ to processor $p_j$ ($1 \leq i, j \leq n$) in a FIFO order.

A *configuration* of the system consists of the internal states of the processors and the contents of the communication links. An *initial configuration* is a configuration in which every processor is in an *initial state*, and the communication links are empty, except for *wakeup* messages: for each processor $p$, the link from $p$ to itself contains a wakeup message.

A processor $p$ is *non-faulty* in a run if it takes infinitely many steps in this run, and all its messages to non-faulty processors are eventually delivered. A processor $p$ is *faulty* in a run if it takes only finitely many steps in this run, or if from some point on, no message of $p$ is ever delivered ([6], [2]). A run is $n-t$-fair if at most $t$ processors are faulty in it.

Next, we present two types of mappings of schedules to runs of message passing protocols: the first type is "processor oriented", which, similarly to the mapping we used in the shared memory model, maps each occurrence of an integer $i$ to an atomic step of processor $p_i$. The second type is "message oriented", which maps each occurrence of $i$ to an atomic step in which a message of $p_i$ is delivered. Mappings of the former type provide impossibility results similar to ones achieved in [5], while mapping of the latter type provide new impossibility results. In the Appendix we use a variant of message oriented mapping to strengthen one of our results.

## 5.2 Impossibility of Consensus via Processor Oriented Mappings

A *processor oriented mapping* is a mapping $M_{proc}$ which maps each pair of an initial configuration $c$ and a schedule $s = (s_1, s_2, \cdots)$ to a run $r = (a_1, a_2, \cdots)$, where $a_i$ is an atomic step of processor $p_{s_i}$. In the case when $a_i$ involves the receiving of message(s), $M_{proc}$ must specify which of the messages sent to $p_{s_i}$ but not yet received (if there are any) are delivered in $a_i$. By varying the rules specifying these messages, one obtains various extensions of the basic impossibility result of [6]. Two possible rules, which can be used to obtain impossibility results appearing in [5], are:

- Deliver to $p_{s_i}$ all the messages that were sent to it, but not yet received.

– Deliver to $p_{s_i}$ the first message that was sent to it, but not yet received.

When using processor oriented mappings, it is convenient to describe the content of the communication links as follows: Each processor $p$ has a message buffer of *incoming* messages, $buf\_in_p$, which contains all the messages sent to $p$, but not delivered yet. The specific order in which the messages are stored in $buf\_in_p$ depends on the model studied.

We now apply a processor oriented mapping for proving one of the impossibility results of [5]: We show that there is no 2-resilient consensus protocol in a model where: (a) an atomic step of a processor $p$ consists of receiving *all* the messages sent to $p$ but not yet received, and then sending at most one message, and (b) there is a global FIFO order on incoming messages, meaning that the messages delivered to each processor are ordered according to the time they were sent (i.e., that $buf\_in_p$ is a queue).

Formally, Let $c$ be an initial configuration and $s = (s_1, s_2, \cdots)$ be a schedule. The run $r = M_{proc}(c, s)$ is defined by defining, for each $\ell \geq 0$, the prefix $r^{(\ell)} = M_{proc}(c, s^{(\ell)})$, as follows:

– $M_{proc}(c, \epsilon) = r^{(0)} = \epsilon$.
– Let $M_{proc}(c, s^{(\ell)}) = r^{(\ell)} = (a_1, \cdots, a_\ell)$. Then $M_{proc}(c, s^{(\ell+1)}) = r^{(\ell+1)} = r^{(\ell)} \cdot (a_{\ell+1})$, where $a_{\ell+1}$ is the atomic step taken by processor $p_{s_{l+1}}$ from the configuration $\sigma(c, r^{(\ell)})$, in which it receives all the messages sent to it but not yet received (if there are any), ordered according to the time they were sent.

Let $PR$ be a protocol in the above model. The set $R_{n,2}$ of admissible runs of $PR$ which we assume in our proof is the union $\bigcup_c R_{n,2}^c$, taken over all initial configurations $c$, where:

$$R_{n,2}^c = \{M_{proc}(c, s) \mid s \in \mathcal{S}_{n,2}\}$$

$M_{proc}$ defines for each configuration $c$ an isomorphism from $T_{n,2}$ to $T(R_{n,2}^c)$. The image of a vertex $u \in T_{n,2}$ under this isomorphism is denoted by $u_c$.
$R_{n,2}$ is a closed set of $n-2$-fair runs by the definition of the mapping $M_{proc}$ and the fact that $\mathcal{S}_{n,2}$ is an $n-2$-fair scheduler.

In order to prove that $R_{n,2}$ satisfies also the *initial similarity* and *siblings similarity* properties we need one more definition and lemma.

**Definition:** Configurations $c_1$ and $c_2$ are $P_Q$-*equivalent*, for $Q \subseteq \{1, \ldots, n\}$, if for each processor $p \in P_Q$: $p$ is in the same internal state in $c_1$ and in $c_2$, and the contents of $buf\_in_p$ is the same in $c_1$ and in $c_2$.

**Lemma 12.** *Let $c_1$ and $c_2$ be $P_Q$-equivalent configurations, and let $s$ be a $Q$-schedule. Then the runs $r_1 = M_{proc}(c_1, s)$ and $r_2 = M_{proc}(c_2, s)$ are $P_Q$-runs which are $P_Q$-equivalent.*

*Proof.* Similar to the proof of Lemma 7.

$R_{n,2}$ satisfies the *initial similarity* property by lemmas 12 and 4, and by the fact that two initial configurations in which each processor $p \in P_Q$ has the same input are $P_Q$-equivalent. Next we prove that $R_{n,2}$ satisfies also the *siblings similarity* property.

**Lemma 13.** *Let $u, v = u \cdot (i)$ and $w = u \cdot (j)$ be vertices in $T_{n,2}$, and let $u_c, v_c, w_c$ be the corresponding vertices in $T(R_{n,2}^c)$. Then there is a descendant $v_c'$ of $v_c$ and a descendant $w_c'$ of $w_c$ such that $v_c'$ and $w_c'$ are $P_Q$-similar, for some $Q \subseteq \{1, \dots, n\}, |Q| \geq n - 2$.*

*Proof.* By Lemma 12, it suffices to find a descendant $v'$ of $v$ and a descendant $w'$ of $w$ s.t. $v'$ and $w'$ are $Q$-similar, and the configurations $\sigma(c, v_c')$ and $\sigma(c, w_c')$ are $P_Q$-equivalent.

Let $v_c = u_c \cdot (a)$ and $w_c = u_c \cdot (b)$, where $a$ and $b$ are atomic steps executed by $p_i$ and $p_j$ respectively. We consider two cases:

**Case 1:** Any message sent in $a$ or $b$ (if at all) is destinated to $p_i$ or to $p_j$. Let $v' = v$ and $w' = w$, and let $Q = \{1, \cdots, n\} \setminus \{i, j\}$. Then for every $k \in Q$, both $p_k$ and $buf\_in_{p_k}$ are in the same state in $\sigma(c, v_c')$ and in $\sigma(c, w_c')$, hence $\sigma(c, v_c')$ and $\sigma(c, w_c')$ are $P_Q$-equivalent. Also, by Lemma 6 (3) $v'$ and $w'$ are $Q$-similar. Therefore $v_c'$ and $w_c'$ are $P_Q$-similar.

**Case 2:** Not Case 1. Then w.l.o.g. $p_i$ sends a message to $p_k$ for $k \notin \{i, j\}$. Let $v' = v \cdot (j)$ and $w' = w$, and let $Q = \{1, \cdots, n\} \setminus \{i, k\}$. Then for every $\ell \in Q$, both $p_\ell$ and $buf\_in_{p_\ell}$ are in the same state in $\sigma(c, v_c')$ and $\sigma(c, w_c')$, hence $\sigma(c, v_c')$ and $\sigma(c, w_c')$ are $P_Q$-equivalent. Also, by Lemma 6 (2) $v'$ and $w'$ are $Q$-similar. Therefore $v_c'$ and $w_c'$ are $P_Q$-similar.

From Lemma 13 above we get the following:

**Theorem 14.** *[5] There is no 2-resilient consensus protocol for a message-passing model, in which there is a global FIFO order on incoming messages of each processor, and an atomic step consists of receiving all the messages sent to a processor and sending at most one message.*

### 5.3 Impossibility of Consensus via Message Oriented Mappings

In this subsection we present impossibility results based on *message oriented mappings* of schedules to runs. Informally, a message oriented mapping maps each occurrence of an integer $i$ to an atomic step in which an undelivered message of $p_i$ (if there is one) is received. To make the mapping well defined, we assume that all the outgoing messages of each processor are received in the order they are sent. Thus, the runs obtained by this mapping maintain a global FIFO order on the *outgoing* messages of each processor.

The content of the communication links is now specified as follows: Each processor $p$ has a message buffer of outgoing messages, $buf\_out_p$, which is a queue containing all the messages sent by $p$, but not delivered yet, ordered in a FIFO order. The wakeup message to $p$ is assumed to be the first message in $buf\_out_p$.

An atomic step of a processor $p$ consists of (a) receiving some message $m$ that was sent to $p$ but not received yet, and (b) sending messages to all the processors (including itself). Thus, in each given configuration, an atomic step can be specified by a pair $(p, m)$ of the active processor $p$ and the message $m$ it receives. In addition, an atomic step of a processor $p$ may also be a *null* step, which does not change the system configuration, and is denoted by $(p, \phi)$. Note that our definition of atomic step implies that each non-faulty processor sends infinitely many messages in a run.

We now define the mapping, called $M_{msg}$, of schedules to runs in this model. Given an initial configuration $c$ and a schedule $s = (s_1, s_2, \cdots)$, the run $r = M_{msg}(c, s)$ is defined by defining, for each $\ell \geq 0$, the prefix $r^{(\ell)} = M_{msg}(c, s^{(\ell)})$, as follows:

- $M_{msg}(c, \epsilon) = r^{(0)} = \epsilon$.
- Let $M_{msg}(c, s^{(\ell)}) = r^{(\ell)} = (a_1, \cdots, a_\ell)$. Then $M_{msg}(c, s^{(\ell+1)}) = r^{(\ell+1)} = r^{(\ell)} \cdot (a_{\ell+1})$, where $a_{\ell+1} = (q, m)$, where $m$ is the first undelivered message in $buf\_out_{p_{s_{l+1}}}$, and $q$ is the destination of $m$. If $buf\_out_{p_{s_{l+1}}}$ is empty in $\sigma(c, r^{(\ell)})$, then $a_{l+1} = (p_{s_{l+1}}, \phi)$, the null step taken by $p_{s_{l+1}}$.

Observe that the run $M_{msg}(c, s)$ defined above maintains global FIFO on outgoing messages, and that if $s$ is fair for $i$, then $p_i$ is non-faulty in $M_{msg}(c, s)$ (and hence if $s$ is $n - t$-fair, then $M_{msg}(c, s)$ is a $n - t$-fair run).

As in the previous cases, the set $R_{n,1}$ of admissible runs of $PR$ is the union $\bigcup_c R_{n,1}^c$, taken over all initial configurations $c$, where:

$$R_{n,1}^c = \{M_{msg}(c, s) \mid s \in \mathcal{S}_{n,1}\}$$

The rest of the proof is carried out in a way similar to the previous proofs:
**Definition:** Configurations $c_1$ and $c_2$ are $P_Q$-*equivalent*, for $Q \subseteq \{1, \ldots, n\}$, if for each processor $p \in P_Q$: $p$ is in the same internal state in $c_1$ and in $c_2$, and the contents of $buf\_out_p$ is the same in $c_1$ and in $c_2$.

**Lemma 15.** *Let $c_1$ and $c_2$ be $P_Q$-equivalent configurations, and let $s$ be a $Q$-schedule. Then the runs $r_1 = M_{msg}(c_1, s)$ and $r_2 = M_{msg}(c_2, s)$ are $P_Q$-runs which are $P_Q$-equivalent.*

*Proof.* Similar to that of Lemma 12

$R_{n,1}$ satisfies the *initial similarity* property by lemmas 15 and 4, and by the fact that two initial configurations in which each processor $p \in P_Q$ has the same input are $P_Q$-equivalent. Next we prove that $R_{n,1}$ satisfies also the *siblings similarity* property.

**Lemma 16.** *Let $u, v = u \cdot (i), w = u \cdot (j)$ be vertices in $T_{n,1}$, and let $u_c, v_c, w_c$ be the corresponding vertices in $T(R_{n,1}^c)$. Then there is a descendant $v'_c$ of $v_c$ and a descendant $w'_c$ of $w_c$ such that $v'_c$ and $w'_c$ are $P_Q$-similar, for some $Q \subseteq \{1, \ldots, n\}, |Q| \geq n - 1$.*

*Proof.* By Lemma 15, it suffices to find a descendant $v'$ of $v$ and a descendant $w'$ of $w$ s.t. $v'$ and $w'$ are $Q$-similar, and the configurations $\sigma(c, v'_c)$ and $\sigma(c, w'_c)$ are $P_Q$-equivalent.

Let $v_c = u_c \cdot ((p_{i'}, m_1))$ and $w_c = u_c \cdot ((p_{j'}, m_2))$.

**Case 1:** $i' \neq j'$, and both $m_1$, $m_2$ are not $\phi$. Let $v' = v \cdot (j)$ and $w' = w \cdot (i)$ (and hence $v'_c = u_c \cdot ((p_{i'}, m_1), (p_{j'}, m_2))$ and $w'_c = u_c \cdot ((p_{j'}, m_2), (p_{i'}, m_1))$) and let $Q = \{1, \ldots, n\}$. Then, $\sigma(c, w'_c)$ and $\sigma(c, v'_c)$ are $P_Q$-equivalent, and by Lemma 6 (1) $v'$ and $w'$ are $Q$-similar. Therefore $v'_c$ and $w'_c$ are $P_Q$-similar.

**Case 2:** $i' = j' = k$, and both $m_1$ and $m_2$ are not $\phi$. Let $v' = v \cdot (j)$ and $w' = w \cdot (i)$ (and hence $v'_c = u_c \cdot ((p_k, m_1), (p_k, m_2))$ and $w'_c = u_c \cdot ((p_k, m_2), (p_k, m_1))$) and let $Q = \{1, \ldots, n\} \setminus \{k\}$. Then, $\sigma(c, w'_c)$ and $\sigma(c, v'_c)$ are $P_Q$-equivalent, and by Lemma 6 (1) $v'$ and $w'$ are $Q$-similar. Therefore $v'_c$ and $w'_c$ are $P_Q$-similar.

**Case 3:** $m_1 = \phi$ or $m_2 = \phi$. Suppose w.l.o.g that $m_1 = \phi$. Let $v' = v \cdot (j)$, $w' = w$ (and hence $v'_c = u_c \cdot ((p_i, \phi), (p_{j'}, m_2))$ and $w'_c = u_c \cdot ((p_{j'}, m_2))$) and let $Q = \{1, \ldots, n\} \setminus \{i\}$. Then, $\sigma(c, w'_c)$ and $\sigma(c, v'_c)$ are $P_Q$-equivalent (actually, they are $\{p_1, \ldots, p_n\}$-equivalent), and by Lemma 6 (2) $v'$ and $w'$ are $Q$-similar. Therefore $v'_c$ and $w'_c$ are $P_Q$-similar.

From Lemma 16 above we get the following:

**Theorem 17.** *There is no 1-resilient consensus protocol for the message-passing model with the global FIFO property.*

A stronger version of Theorem 17 above is given in the Appendix.

# 6 Conclusion and Further Research

In this paper we introduced the concept of closed sets of runs, which are sets of runs that can be described as the paths of an infinite tree of bounded degree. Then we introduced the concept of closed schedulers, and presented a unified, model independent technique to construct closed sets of runs of $t$-resilient protocols by using closed schedulers.

The sets constructed by our technique preserve many of the properties possessed by the sets of *all* runs of $t$-resilient protocols, which makes these sets a convenient tool for proving properties of such protocols. To demonstrate this, we used these sets to provide unified proofs of the impossibility of $t$-resilient consensus protocols in few distinct models of distributed computing, and obtained some new impossibility results.

The full applicability of closed sets of runs, and in particular of the sets constructed by the closed schedulers $S_{n,t}$ introduced in this paper, is yet to be explored. It is anticipated that the simple combinatorial structure of these schedulers will make them a useful tool for studying further problems related to $t$-resilient protocols.

# References

1. H. Attiya, A. Bar-Noy, D. Dolev, D. Peleg, and R. Reischuk. Renaming in an asynchronous environment. *Journal of the ACM*, 37(3):524–548, 1990.
2. O. Biran, S. Moran, and S. Zaks. A combinatorial characterization of the distributed 1-solvable tasks. *Journal of Algorithm*, (11):420–440, 1990.
3. S. Chaudhuri. Agreement is harder than consensus: Set consensus problems in totally asynchronous systems. In *Proceedings of 9-th PODC Conference*, pages 311–324, 1990.
4. König. D. Theorie der endlichen und unendlichen graphen. Liepzig 1936. reprinted by Chelsea, 1950.
5. D. Dolev, C. Dwork, and L. Stockmeyer. On the minimal synchronism needed for distributed consensus. *Journal of the ACM*, 34(1):77–97, January 1987.
6. M. J. Fischer, N. A. Lynch, and M. S. Paterson. Impossibility of distributed consensus with one faulty process. *Journal of the ACM*, 32(2):374–382, April 1985.
7. M.C. Loui and H.H Abu-Amara. Memory requirements for agreement among unreliable asynchronous processes. *Advances in Computing Research*, 4:163–183, 1987.

# APPENDIX

## A   A Modified Message Oriented Mapping

The mapping $M_{msg}$ of Subsection 5.3 has the following disadvantage: it may provide runs in which out of the messages sent by a (faulty) processor in one atomic step, some messages are delivered and others are not. Here we modify that mapping to overcome this disadvantage. Thus, the resulted runs satisfy *atomicity of broadcast*, i.e.: for each atomic step of a processor $p$, either all the messages sent by $p$ in this step are delivered, or none of them is delivered.

**Definition:** A *package* $\mathcal{P}$ is a sequence of all the messages sent in one atomic step. A package $\mathcal{P}$ is *used* in a prefix $r'$ of a run $r$ if some but not all of the messages in $\mathcal{P}$ were delivered in $r'$.

Note that in any prefix of a run that maintains a global FIFO order on the outgoing messages of each processor, each message buffer $buf\_out_p$ contains at most one used package.

**Definition:** A run $r$ satisfies the *atomic broadcast property* if for each package $\mathcal{P}$ sent in $r$, either all the messages in $\mathcal{P}$ are delivered in $r$, or no message from $\mathcal{P}$ is delivered in $r$.

We now modify the mapping $M_{msg}$ to a new mapping, $\overline{M}_{msg}$, which maps a pair $(c, s)$ of an initial configuration $c$ and a schedule $s$ to a run with the atomic broadcast property. $\overline{M}_{msg}$ is constructed in two steps: first we map the schedule $s$ to a sequence called $\widehat{s}$, and then we apply a (variant of) message oriented mapping to $\widehat{s}$.

**Definition:** Let $s = (s_1, s_2, \cdots)$ be a schedule, and let $s_\ell = i$. Then $s_\ell$ is an *odd occurrence of $i$ in $s$* if $i$ appears an odd number of times in $s^{(\ell)} = (s_1, \cdots, s_\ell)$. Otherwise, $s_\ell$ is an *even occurrence of $i$ in $s$*.

Note that for each $i$, the occurrences of $i$ in $s$ are odd and even alternatingly. We say that $s_\ell$ is an *odd (even) element of $s$* if it is an odd (even) occurrence of some $i$ in $s$. $s_\ell$ is the $m-th$ *odd (even) element of $s$* if it is an odd (even) element of $s$, and $s^{(\ell)}$ contains $m$ odd (even) elements.

Given an initial configuration $c$ and a $\{1, \cdots, n\}$-schedule $s$, we describe below how the run $r = \overline{M}_{msg}(c, s)$ is constructed. Intuitively, $\overline{M}_{msg}$ acts on the odd elements of $s$ as the mapping $M_{msg}$ does, while the even elements of $s$ are used to guarantee that $r$ satisfies the atomic broadcast property.

As a first step in defining $\overline{M}_{msg}(c, s)$, we map $s$ to a sequence $\widehat{s} = (\widehat{s}_1, \widehat{s}_2, \cdots)$ as follows:

- if $s_\ell$ is an odd element of $s$, then $\widehat{s}_\ell = (s_\ell, odd)$; else:
- let $s_\ell$ be the $m-th$ even element of $s$. Then $\widehat{s}_\ell = (m - 1(\bmod n) + 1, even)$.

**Example:** Let $n = 3$ and $s = (2, 1, 2, 2, 1, 2, \cdots)$. Then $s_1, s_2$ and $s_4$ are odd elements of $s$ and $s_3, s_5$ and $s_6$ are even elements of $s$. Thus, $\widehat{s} = ((2, odd), (1, odd), (1, even), (2, odd), (2, even), (3, even), \cdots)$.

The property of $\widehat{s}$ needed for our construction is that for every $i \in \{1, \cdots, n\}$, $(i, even)$ occurs infinitely often in $\widehat{s}$, and $(i, odd)$ occurs infinitely often in $\widehat{s}$ iff $i$

occurs infinitely often in $s$. Informally, each occurrence of $(i, odd)$ in $\hat{s}$ is mapped to an *o-type step*, which delivers the first undelivered message in $buf\_out_{p_i}$. This guarantees that if $i$ occurs infinitely often in $s$ then $p_i$ is non-faulty in $\overline{M}_{msg}(c, s)$. An occurrence of $(i, even)$ is mapped to an *e-type step*, which delivers a message of $p_i$ *only if it is in a used package in* $buf\_out_{p_i}$. This guarantees that all the messages from a used package are eventually delivered in $\overline{M}_{msg}(c, s)$ (even if $p_i$ is faulty).

Formally, given an initial configuration $c$ and a schedule $s = (s_1, s_2, \cdots)$, the run $r = \overline{M}_{msg}(c, s)$ is defined by defining, for each $\ell \geq 0$, the prefix $r^{(\ell)} = \overline{M}_{msg}(c, s^{(\ell)})$, as follows:

- $\overline{M}_{msg}(c, \epsilon) = r^{(0)} = \epsilon$.
- Let $\overline{M}_{msg}(c, s^{(\ell)}) = r^{(\ell)} = (a_1, \cdots, a_\ell)$. Then $\overline{M}_{msg}(c, s^{(\ell+1)}) = r^{(\ell+1)} = r^{(\ell)} \cdot (a_{\ell+1})$, where $a_{\ell+1}$ is defined as follows:
  If $\hat{s}_{\ell+1} = (k, odd)$ for some $k$ then $a_{\ell+1}$ is an *o*-type step $(q, m)$, where $m$ is the first undelivered message in $buf\_out_{p_k}$ and $q$ is the destination of $m$; if $buf\_out_{p_k}$ is empty then $a_{\ell+1} = (p_k, \phi)$.
  Otherwise $\hat{s}_{\ell+1} = (k, even)$ for some $k$. In this case $a_{\ell+1}$ is an *e*-type step, defined as follows: If in the configuration $\sigma(c, r^{(\ell)})$, $buf\_out_{p_k}$ contains a used package $\mathcal{P}$, and there is no odd occurrence of $k$ after the last even element of $s^{(\ell)}$, then $a_{\ell+1} = (q, m)$, where $m$ is the first undelivered message in $\mathcal{P}$, and $q$ is the destination of $m$. Otherwise, $a_{\ell+1} = (p_k, \phi)$.

**Lemma 18.** *For each configuration $c$ and for each sequence $s$, $\overline{M}_{msg}(c, s)$ is a run which satisfies the atomic broadcast property.*

*Proof.* Let $r = \overline{M}_{msg}(c, s)$. To see that $r$ satisfies the atomic broadcast property, consider any processor $p_i$. If $i$ occurs infinitely often in $s$ then $(i, odd)$ occurs infinitely often in $\hat{s}$, and by the mapping $\overline{M}_{msg}$ *every* message sent by $p_i$ is eventually delivered. So assume that $i$ occurs only finitely many times in $s$.

If $i$ never occurs in $s$ then no message of $p_i$ is ever delivered and we are done. Otherwise, there is an $\hat{s}_\ell$ in $\hat{s}$ which is the last occurrence of $(i, odd)$ in $\hat{s}$. $\hat{s}_\ell$ is mapped by $\overline{M}_{msg}$ on an atomic step in which a message $m$ from some package $\mathcal{P}$ in $buf\_out_{p_i}$ is delivered. Since $\hat{s}_\ell$ is the last occurrence of $(i, odd)$ in $\hat{s}$, no messages of packages that were sent by $p_i$ after $\mathcal{P}$ are delivered. Thus, we only need to show that all the messages of $\mathcal{P}$ are eventually delivered. Assume that following $m$ there are $k \geq 0$ messages in $\mathcal{P}$. These messages are delivered in the atomic steps corresponding to at most $k + 1$ occurrences of elements of the form $(i, even)$ which follow $\hat{s}_\ell$ in $\hat{s}$.

In order for our proof to apply for the new mapping $\overline{M}_{msg}$, we need to strengthen the notions of similarity and equivalence as follows.

**Definition:** Let $Q \subseteq \{1, \ldots, n\}$. Vertices $u$ and $v$ in $T_{n,t}$ are *strongly Q-similar*, iff there exists a $Q$-schedule $s = (s_1, s_2, \cdots)$ s.t.

1. $u \cdot s$ and $v \cdot s$ are in $S_{n,t} = Paths(T_{n,t})$.
2. For each $s_\ell$ in $s$, $s_\ell$ is mapped to the same element in $\widehat{u \cdot s}$ and $\widehat{v \cdot s}$.

**Definition:** Configurations $c_1$ and $c_2$ are *strongly $P_Q$-equivalent*, for $Q \subseteq \{1, \ldots, n\}$, if $c_1$ and $c_2$ are $P_Q$-equivalent, and in addition, each message buffer $buf\_out_p$ contains a used package in $c_1$ iff it contains an identical used package in $c_2$.

Let $\overline{R}_{n,1}$ be the set of runs of $PR$ defined by the union $\bigcup_c \overline{R}^c_{n,1}$, taken over all initial configurations $c$, where:

$$\overline{R}^c_{n,1} = \{\overline{M}_{msg}(c, s) \mid s \in \mathcal{S}_{n,1}\}$$

$\overline{M}_{msg}$ defines for each configuration $c$ an isomorphism from $T_{n,1}$ to $T(\overline{R}^c_{n,1})$. The image of a vertex $u \in T_{n,1}$ under this isomorphism is denoted by $u_c$.

We need a stronger version of Lemma 15.

**Lemma 19.** *Let $u$ and $v$ be strongly $Q$-similar vertices in $T_{n,1}$. Let $c$ be an initial configuration and let $u_c = \overline{M}_{msg}(c, u)$ and $v_c = \overline{M}_{msg}(c, v)$. If $\sigma(c, u_c)$ and $\sigma(c, v_c)$ are strongly $P_Q$-equivalent configurations, then $u_c$ and $v_c$ are $P_Q$-similar.*

*Proof.* Similar to that of Lemma 15.

We also need the following modification of Lemma 6:

**Lemma 20.** *Let $n \geq 2, 0 \leq t \leq n - 1$. Then for each $u \in T_{n,t}$, and for each $i, j$ s.t. both $u \cdot (i)$ and $u \cdot (j)$ are in $T_{n,t}$, it holds that: For each $Q \subseteq \{1, \ldots, n\}, |Q| \geq n - t$,*

1. *$u \cdot (i, j)$ and $u \cdot (j, i)$ are strongly $Q$-similar.*
2. *If $t \geq 1$, $i \notin Q$, and $i$ is an odd element of $u \cdot (i)$, then $u \cdot (i, j)$ and $u \cdot (j)$ are strongly $Q$-similar.*

*Proof.* Similar to that of Lemma 6, using the observation that for each $k \in \{1, \cdots n\}$, $k$ occurs in $u \cdot (i, j)$ and in $u \cdot (j, i)$ the same number of times, and if $k \neq i$, then $k$ occurs in $u \cdot (i, j)$ and in $u \cdot (j)$ the same number of times.

We sketch below a proof of a stronger version of Lemma 16, which is needed for our generalization.

**Lemma 21.** *Let $u, v = u \cdot (i), w = u \cdot (j)$ be vertices in $T_{n,1}$, and let $u_c, v_c, w_c$ the corresponding vertices in $T(\overline{R}^c_{n,1})$. Then there is a descendant $v'_c$ of $v_c$ and a descendant $w'_c$ of $w_c$ such that $v'_c$ and $w'_c$ are $P_Q$-similar, for some $Q \subseteq \{1, \ldots, n\}, |Q| \geq n - 1$.*

*Proof.* If $i$ is an odd element of $v$ and $j$ is an odd element of $w$ then the proof of Lemma 16 applies, with minor modifications.

If $i$ is an even element of $v$ and $j$ is an even element of $w$ then, by the definition of $\overline{M}_{msg}$, $v' = u \cdot (i, j)$ and $w' = u \cdot (j, i)$ are mapped by $\overline{M}_{msg}$ to identical runs, and hence, by lemmas 19 and 20 (1), $v'_c$ and $w'_c$ are $P_Q$-similar for $Q = \{1, \cdots, n\}$.

The only case left to consider is when $i$ is an odd element of $v$ and $j$ is an even element of $w$ or vice versa. W.l.o.g. let $i$ be an odd element of $v$ and $j$

be an even element of $w$. Then the last element in $\hat{v}$ is $(i, odd)$ and the last element in $\hat{w}$ is $(k, even)$ for some $k \in \{1, \cdots, n\}$. Let $v_c = u_c \cdot ((p_{i'}, m_1))$ and let $w_c = u_c \cdot ((p_{k'}, m_2))$. As before, we let $v' = v \cdot (j)$ and $w' = w \cdot (i)$.

Assume first that $k \neq i$. Then $v'_c = v_c \cdot ((p_{k'}, m_2))$ and $w'_c = w_c \cdot ((p_{i'}, m_1))$. In the case that both $m_1$ and $m_2$ are not $\phi$, the proof is similar to cases 1 and 2 of Lemma 16. In the case that $m_1 = \phi$ the proof is similar to Case 3 of Lemma 16. So we are left with the case where $m_2 = \phi$ and $m_1 \neq \phi$. In this case both $v'_c$ and $w'_c$ are obtained by extending $u'_c$ by the same non-null step $(p_{i'}, m_1)$, and hence $\sigma(c, v'_c)$ and $\sigma(c, w'_c)$ are strongly $P_Q$-equivalent for $Q = \{1, \cdots, n\}$. Hence $v'_c$ and $w'_c$ are $P_Q$-similar for $Q = \{1, \cdots, n\}$.

Assume now that $k = i$. Then the definition of $\overline{M}_{msg}$ implies that $v'_c = v_c \cdot ((p_i, \phi))$. We consider two cases:
(a): $m_2 \neq \phi$. Then $m_1 = m_2$ is the first message in $buf\_out_{p_i}$, and the configurations $\sigma(c, v'_c)$ and $\sigma(c, w_c)$ are strongly $P_Q$-equivalent for $Q = \{1, \cdots, n\}$. By Lemma 20 (2) $v'$ and $w$ are strongly $Q$-similar for $Q = \{1, \cdots, n\} \setminus \{i\}$, and hence $v'_c$ and $w_c$ are $P_Q$-similar for $Q = \{1, \cdots, n\} \setminus \{i\}$.
(b): $m_2 = \phi$. Then $w'_c = w_c \cdot ((p_{i'}, m_1))$, and hence $\sigma(c, v'_c)$ and $\sigma(c, w'_c)$ are strongly $P_Q$-equivalent for $Q = \{1, \cdots, n\}$. This implies that $v'_c$ and $w'_c$ are $Q$-similar, for $Q = \{1, \cdots, n\}$.

From Lemma 21 above we get the following generalization of the main result in [6]:

**Theorem 22.** *There is no 1-resilient consensus protocol for the message-passing model in which there is a global FIFO order on the outgoing messages of each processor, and which satisfies the atomic broadcast property.*

This result should be contrasted with the fact that when one assumes a global FIFO order on the *incoming* messages and atomic broadcast, the consensus is solvable in the presence of arbitrarily many failures by the following simple protocol: each processor broadcasts its input to all the processors (including itself), and decides on the value of the first message it receives.

# Efficient Atomic Snapshots Using Lattice Agreement

## (Extended Abstract)

Hagit Attiya[1], Maurice Herlihy[2], Ophir Rachman[1]

[1] Department of Computer Science, the Technion.
[2] DEC Cambridge Research Laboratory.

**Abstract.** The *snapshot* object is an important tool for the construction of wait-free asynchronous algorithms. We relate the snapshot object to the *lattice agreement* decision problem. It is shown that any algorithm for solving lattice agreement can be used to implement the snapshot object. Several new lattice agreement algorithms are presented. The most efficient is a lattice agreement algorithm (and hence, an implementation of snapshot objects) using $O(\log^2 n)$ operations on 2-processor *Test&Set* registers, plus a linear number of operations on atomic single-writer multi-reader registers.

## 1 Introduction

The implementation of concurrent objects and the solution of decision problems are two major themes in the investigation of wait-free computation. There is a significant difference between these two themes. *Concurrent objects* are shared data structures which are accessed repeatedly and concurrently by processors, e.g., atomic read/write registers, snapshot objects and queues. In contrast, in a *decision problem*, processors start with inputs and have to halt with outputs that satisfy certain conditions, e.g., consensus and renaming. Long-lived concurrent objects are more useful than decision problems in practical applications of wait-free computing, e.g., in distributed operating systems. On the other hand, decision problems are intuitively simpler than concurrent objects, since each processor "enters the game" only once.

One of the basic concurrent objects is the *atomic snapshot* object. A snapshot object is a shared data structure partitioned into segments. Processors can either *update* an individual segment, or instantaneously *scan* all segments of the object. A snapshot object simplifies the design and verification of a number of important concurrent shared-memory algorithms, by reducing the possible interleaving of

Part of the work of the first author was performed while visiting DEC Cambridge Research Laboratory. The first and the third authors are partially supported by B. and G. Greenberg Research Fund (Ottawa) and by Technion V.P.R. funds. Contact author: Hagit Attiya, Department of Computer Science, Technion, Haifa 32000, Israel. Email: hagit@cs.technion.ac.il.

the execution. Atomic snapshot objects have been used for randomized consensus [5], approximate agreement [9], bounded timestamping [16], and the construction of wait-free concurrent objects [6].

In this paper, we consider a new decision problem, *lattice agreement*. In this problem, processors start with elements from some partially ordered lattice, and must (non-trivially) decide on new elements that are comparable in the lattice. Besides being interesting on its own right, lattice agreement is closely related to snapshot objects. Given a snapshot object it is straightforward to solve lattice agreement: Each processor updates the snapshot object with its input value; it then scans the snapshot memory and returns the join of all the inputs it reads.[3]

Our first major contribution is to show that the converse is also true. That is, given any solution to lattice agreement, it is possible to construct an implementation of a snapshot object. Furthermore, the transformation uses only a linear number of additional operations on atomic read/write registers. Thus, we show that the number of operations required to implement a snapshot object is equal to the number of operations required to solve lattice agreement (plus a linear number of atomic read/write operations). [4] This allows research to focus on the later problem, which is simpler, in our opinion.

Decision problems were previously used to prove impossibility results for long-lived objects [17], or to show lower bounds on the complexity of implementing long-lived objects [19, 11]. Also, solutions to a specific decision problem, *consensus*, can be used to implement any object [18]. Intuitively, this can be achieved because consensus is universal for the class of problems solvable in the asynchronous wait-free model of computation [12, 13, 17]. However, consensus is a very strong decision problem; in particular, it has only randomized solutions in this model. Thus, it is interesting to relate long-lived objects to weaker decision problems, i.e., those that can be solved deterministically or more efficiently than consensus. To the best of our knowledge, the transformation from lattice agreement to snapshots is the first time a decision problem, weaker than consensus, is shown to yield upper bounds for long-lived objects.

Our second major contribution is a linear algorithm for solving lattice agreement, and hence for implementing snapshot objects. This algorithm uses 2-processor *Test&Set* registers, as well as atomic single-writer multi-reader registers.

In the past, atomic snapshot algorithms have been proposed by Anderson [5] (bounded registers and exponential number of operations), Aspnes and Herlihy [6] (unbounded registers and $O(n^2)$ operations), and by Afek, Attiya, Dolev, Gafni, Merritt, and Shavit [1] (bounded registers and $O(n^2)$ operations). Kirousis, Spirakis, and Tsigas [21] give an $O(n)$ atomic snapshot algorithm for a *single* scanner, and Dwork, Herlihy, Plotkin, and Waarts [15] give an efficient

---

[3] This relationship was also noted by others [14].

[4] As presented in this abstract, the transformation from lattice agreement to long-lived snapshot object is highly expensive in memory requirements, and uses an unbounded number of memory blocks. In the full paper we show how these high memory costs can be drastically reduced.

non-linearizable snapshot scan. All these snapshot objects are constructed from atomic read/write registers only.

Our algorithm for lattice agreement is based on a crash-tolerant synchronous algorithm. This synchronous algorithm is presented in the message-passing model; in this model, it requires $\log n$ rounds. The algorithm does not fully exploit the synchronization power available in this model. We then show how this mild synchronization can be achieved by *one-time counting networks*. (A special case of *counting networks* introduced in [7].) Since there are wait-free asynchronous implementations of one-time counting networks (using 2-processor *Test&Set* registers), this yields an asynchronous algorithm for lattice agreement, and hence, for implementing snapshot objects.

The exact implementation of this general idea results in two asynchronous algorithms. The first algorithm that we introduce requires a linear number of operations. Unfortunately, it uses dynamic allocation of processors to registers. Namely, the identity of the processors that access certain registers in the shared memory, is determined dynamically during the algorithm's execution. The second algorithm is less efficient and requires $O(n \log^2 n)$ operations, but does not use dynamic allocation.

Both asynchronous algorithms use 2-processor *Test&Set* registers, as well as atomic read/write registers. In order to use read/write registers only, one can use randomization to implement a 2-processor register from atomic registers with constant expected overhead [23, 18]. Thus, the above algorithms can be viewed as randomized algorithms, using only read/write registers, and requiring linear or $O(n \log^2 n)$ expected number of operations. Note that these randomized algorithms never err, that is, when (and if) they halt, their output is always correct, (unlike the algorithms in [21], that may produce incorrect outputs). Chandra and Dwork [10] has independently obtained a similar result; their methods are completely different and are based on randomized consensus.

The rest of this paper is organized as follows. In Section 2, we define lattice agreement and the snapshot object. In Section 3, we present the transformation from a lattice agreement algorithm to a snapshot object. In Section 4, we describe the synchronous lattice agreement algorithm. In Section 5, based on this algorithm, we present the two asynchronous lattice agreement algorithms. We conclude and suggest directions for further research in Section 6.

## 2 Lattice agreement and Snapshot Objects

In this section we formally define lattice agreement and the snapshot object.

Fix a set $S$ with partial order $\leq$. For some subset $T \subseteq S$, $x \in S$ is an *upper bound* of $T$ if, for all $a \in T$, $a \leq x$. A *least upper bound* of $T$ is an upper bound $x$ of $T$, such that if $y$ is an upper bound of $T$, then $x \leq y$. The least upper bound of $T$ is denoted $join(T)$. The *lower bound* and the *greatest lower bound* are defined similarly. A *complete lattice* is a partially ordered set $S$ such that for every nonempty subset $T$ of $S$ the least upper bound and the greatest lower bound of $T$ exist.

Consider a system with $n$ processors, denoted $P_1, \ldots, P_n$. In the *lattice agreement* problem, each processor $P_i$ is assigned some input $x_i$, and must decide on some output $y_i$. Both input and output values are elements from a complete lattice with partial order $\leq$. An algorithm that solves lattice agreement must satisfy three conditions:

**Validity(a):** For all $i$, $x_i \leq y_i$.
**Validity(b):** For all $i$, $y_i \leq join(x_1, \ldots, x_n)$.
**Comparability:** For all $i$ and $j$, either $y_i \leq y_j$ or $y_j \leq y_i$.

An *atomic snapshot* object is partitioned into $n$ segments (where only processor $P_i$ may write to the $i$th segment). A snapshot object supports two operations, *scan* and *update(v)*. The *scan* operation allows a processor to obtain an instantaneous view of the segments, as if all $n$ segments are read in a single atomic step. A *scan* operation returns a vector *view*, where *view[i]* is a value of the $i$th segment. The *update(v)* operation allows a processor to write the value $v$ into its segment.

An implementation of the snapshot object should be *linearizable* [20]. That is, any execution of *scan* and *update* operations, should appear as if it was executed sequentially in some order that preserves the real time order of the operations. In more detail, define the partial order $\rightarrow$ on operations in some execution: $op_1 \rightarrow op_2$ if (and only if) the operation $op_1$ has terminated before the operation $op_2$ has started. The partial order $\rightarrow$ reflects the external real time order of non-overlapping operations in the execution. For the snapshot implementation to be correct, we require that there exists a total order $\Rightarrow$ of the *scan* and *update* operations, such that:

a. $\Rightarrow$ extends the real time order of operations as defined by the partial order $\rightarrow$; and

b. $\Rightarrow$ maintains the sequential semantics of the snapshot operations; i.e., if *view* is returned by some *scan* operation, then for every segment $i$, *view[i]* is the value written by the last update to the $i$th segment which precedes the scan operation in $\Rightarrow$.

In order to relate lattice agreement to the snapshot object, it is convenient to regard the views that are returned by *scan* operations as elements of a lattice. This is done by associating a *sequence number* with each segment, which is initially 0. The sequence number of a segment is incremented whenever the segment is updated. For clarity of presentation, we identify a value with the sequence number associated with it. For two views $view_1$ and $view_2$, $view_1 \leq view_2$ if and only if for all $i$, $view_1[i] \leq view_2[i]$. Intuitively, the partial order defined on views reflects the fact that one view is "later" than the other, that is, for all segments, it contains values that are more (or equally) updated.

## 3 From Lattice Agreement to Snapshot Objects

In this section, we show how an algorithm that solves lattice agreement can be used to implement a snapshot object.

To implement the snapshot object, we associate with each segment a read/write register that contains the latest value written to this segment. It is fairly straightforward to implement a snapshot object using lattice agreement if each processor executes at most one operation: In a scan operation, each processor reads all registers and performs lattice agreement using the vector obtained as input. It returns the value it outputs in the lattice agreement algorithm. Each updater writes its value to the register associate with its segment, and then follows the same algorithm as a scan operation. (A similar idea, for a specific lattice agreement algorithm, appears in [6].)

The delicate issue is how to generalize the above algorithm to the case where each processor may execute an arbitrary number of operations. The basic idea is to have an unbounded number of copies of lattice agreement. A processor wishing to execute an operation joins the highest active copy of the lattice agreement algorithm, and follows the simple algorithm presented above. If it has already executed this copy, it activates the next copy of lattice agreement.

The final difficulty is how to assure that operations using different copies of lattice agreement return comparable values. It can be shown that non-overlapping operations return comparable values. So, we only need to deal with overlapping operations. In this case, if after completing lattice agreement, a processor discovers that a higher copy of lattice agreement was activated, then it joins this copy. If, after completing the second copy of lattice agreement, the processor again discovers it was taken over, it borrows some output of another processor in this copy. We show that such a value exists, and that it is a valid value for this operation.

## 3.1 Detailed Description of the Transformation

In order to describe the transformation, assume we are given a *black-box* that solves lattice agreement. Assume we have an infinite number of copies of this black-box, denoted by $LA_1, LA_2, \ldots$ . The black-box $LA_i$ is called the lattice agreement of round $i$.

The transformation uses the following shared structures: $S_1, \ldots, S_n$ are the registers associated with the segments; $S_i$, associated with the $i$th segment, is written by $P_i$ and read by all processors. $R_1, \ldots, R_n$, is an additional set of registers, that is used by the processors to hold their current round number. In addition, for every round $r$, there is a set of registers, $V_{1,r}, \ldots, V_{n,r}$. These registers are used to hold the views that processors obtain in round $r$.

The precise code for the *scan* and *update* operations of processor $P_i$ is given in Figure 1.

In the *scan* operation, $P_i$ starts in some round (that appears maximal to $P_i$), and collects a local view by reading $S_1, \ldots, S_n$. $P_i$ then participates in the lattice agreement of its round, and as a result, obtains a new view. $P_i$ then checks whether other processors have started more advanced rounds of lattice agreement. If not, it returns the result of lattice agreement. Otherwise, $P_i$ collects a new view and starts lattice agreement again (in the round that now appears

```
operation scan()

1:    FIRST_TRY:
1.1:      round = max(max_{j=1..n}(R_j), round + 1)
1.2:      R_i = round
1.3:      collect = read S_1, ..., S_n
1.4:      view = execute LA_round with collect as input
1.5:      read R_1, ..., R_n
1.6:      if found some R_j > round
1.7:      then
1.8:          goto SECOND_TRY;
1.9:      else
1.10:         V_{i,round} = view
1.11:         return(V_{i,round})

2:    SECOND_TRY:
2.1:      round = max_{j=1..n}(R_j)
2.2:      R_i = round
2.3:      collect = read S_1, ..., S_n
2.4:      view = execute LA_round with collect as input
2.5:      read R_1, ..., R_n
2.6:      if found some R_j > round
2.7:      then
2.8:          V_{i,round} = some non empty V_{j,round}
2.9:          return(V_{i,round})
2.10:     else
2.11:         V_{i,round} = view
2.12:         return(V_{i,round})


operation update(value)
1:   S_i = (value, S_i.sequence_number + 1)
2:   scan()
```

**Fig. 1.** Using lattice agreement to implement a snapshot object

maximal to $P_i$). If after the second trial $P_i$ again finds processors in more advanced rounds of lattice agreement, $P_i$ returns a view of some processor from $P_i$'s last round. Otherwise, $P_i$ returns the result of the second lattice agreement algorithm.

In the *update* operation, $P_i$ updates its register with the new value (and increments the sequence number of its register), and then executes a *scan* operation. Notice that although the formal specifications require only *scan* operations to return a value, in our implementation both *scan* and *update* operations return some view. This is later used to linearize both the *scan* and the *update* operations.

## 3.2 Correctness and Complexity

To prove the correctness of the snapshot object, we explicitly construct a total order $\Rightarrow$ of the *scan* and *update* operations such that:

a. $\Rightarrow$ extends the real time order of operations as defined by the partial order $\rightarrow$; and

b. $\Rightarrow$ maintains the sequential semantics of the snapshot operations; i.e., if *view* is returned by some *scan* operation, then for every segment $i$, $view[i]$ is the value written by the last update to the $i$th segment which precedes the scan operation in $\Rightarrow$.

The views returned by operations are used in order to define $\Rightarrow$. We start with some properties of these views.

Notice that a processor can return a view in one of the following ways. First, it can return a *direct* view, that is, the output of lattice agreement (either in line 1.11, or in line 2.12). Alternatively, it can return an *indirect* view, that is, a view that was borrowed from some other processor (in line 2.9). We first show that a value returned by a *scan* operation, in some round, was returned directly at least once for this round.

**Lemma 1.** *Any processor that returns a view in round $r$, either returns a direct view, or returns an indirect view that is direct for some other processor in round $r$.*

**Lemma 2.** *Consider two operations by processors $P_i$ and $P_j$ that return $view_i$ and $view_j$, respectively. Then $view_i$ and $view_j$ are comparable.*

*Proof.* By Lemma 1, it suffices to prove the lemma for the case $view_i$ and $view_j$ were returned directly.

Let $P_i$ and $P_j$ be two processors (possibly the same one) that have directly returned $view_i$ and $view_j$, respectively. $P_i$ and $P_j$ may return their views either in the same round, or in different rounds.

First, assume $P_i$ and $P_j$ return $view_i$ and $view_j$ in the same round, say $r$. Since $view_i$ and $view_j$ are direct, they are outputs of the lattice agreement of round $r$. By the comparability property of lattice agreement, $view_i$ and $view_j$ are comparable.

Otherwise, assume that $P_i$ returns $view_i$ in round $r_i$ and $P_j$ returns $view_j$ in round $r_j > r_i$. Since $view_i$ is direct, it is $P_i$'s output from the lattice agreement of round $r_i$. Without loss of generality, assume $P_i$ returns $view_i$ in FIRST_TRY. Then, in line 1.5, $P_i$ finds no processor with round number greater than $r_i$. Therefore, $P_i$ obtains $view_i$ before $P_j$ writes $r_j$ into the register $R_j$. It follows that $P_i$ obtains $view_i$ before $P_j$ starts to read $S_1, ..., S_n$ in round $r_j$. Therefore, each entry in $view_i$ is smaller or equal to the corresponding entry in $P_j$'s input

for the lattice agreement of round $r_j$. By the validity(a) property of lattice-agreement, and since $P_j$ returns its view directly, it follows that $view_j \geq view_i$.
□

**Lemma 3.** *Consider two operations $op_i$ and $op_j$, by processors $P_i$ and $P_j$, that return $view_i$ and $view_j$, respectively. If $op_i \rightarrow op_j$, then, $view_i \leq view_j$.*

*Proof.* $P_j$ may return $view_j$ either directly or indirectly.

Assume that $P_j$ returns $view_j$ directly in some round $r_j$. By the validity(a) property of lattice agreement, each entry in $view_j$ is greater than or equal to the corresponding register value that $P_j$ reads in $r_j$. But, when $P_j$ starts reading the registers values, $op_i$ has already been completed. Therefore, each register value that $P_j$ reads has a value greater than or equal to the corresponding entry in $view_i$. It follows that $view_j \geq view_i$.

Otherwise, assume that $P_j$ returns $view_j$ indirectly. Let $r_i$ be the round at which $op_i$ was completed. Since $op_i \rightarrow op_j$, $P_j$ starts $op_j$ in round $r'_j \geq r_i$. Then, since $P_j$ returns $view_j$ indirectly, it fails to obtain a direct view in $r'_j$, enters SECOND_TRY in some round $r_j > r_i$, and fails to obtain a direct view in this round as well. Consequently, $P_j$ copies a view of some processor in $r_j$. By Lemma 1, this view is a direct view of some other processor in $r_j$, say $P_k$. However, $P_k$ starts reading $S_1, ..., S_n$ in $r_j$ only after $P_j$ starts $op_j$ (otherwise, $P_j$ would not have started $op_j$ in $r'_j < r_j$). Since $op_i \rightarrow op_j$, it follows that $P_k$ reads $S_1, ..., S_n$ only after $op_i$ ended. As in the first case, by the validity(a) property of lattice agreement, the view returned by $P_k$ is greater than or equal to $view_i$. Since $P_j$ returns the same view as $P_k$, it follows that $view_j \geq view_i$.
□

**Lemma 4.** *Let up be an update operation by $P_i$ that writes the value $v$, and returns $view_i$. Then, $view_i[i] \geq v$.*

*Proof.* $P_i$ may return $view_i$ either directly or indirectly.

Assume $P_i$ returns $view_i$ directly. Thus, $view_i$ is $P_i$'s output in some lattice agreement. However, $P_i$'s input to any lattice agreement that it executes in $up$ always has $v$ in its $i$th entry. By the validity(a) property of lattice agreement, $view_i[i] \geq v$.

Otherwise, assume $P_i$ obtains $view_i$ indirectly. Thus, it starts $up$ in some round $r'_i$, fails to obtain a direct view in this round, enters SECOND_TRY in some round $r_i > r'_i$, and fails to obtain a direct view in this round as well. Consequently, $P_i$ copies a view of some other processor who participated in the lattice agreement of round $r_i$. By Lemma 1, this view is a direct view of some other processor in round $r_i$, say $P_k$. However, $P_k$ reads $S_1, ..., S_n$ in round $r_i$ only after $P_i$ writes $v$ to $S_i$, (otherwise $P_i$ would not have entered $r'_i < r_i$ in FIRST_TRY). Since $P_k$ obtains its view directly in $r_i$, and by the validity(a) property of lattice agreement, the view of $P_k$ has a value greater than or equal to $v$ in its $i$-th entry. Since $P_i$ has the same view as $P_k$, it follows that $view_i[i] \geq v$.
□

In order to define the total order $\Rightarrow$ on all operations, we first order *scan* operations, and then insert the *update* operations. Consider any two *scan* operations $sc_1$ and $sc_2$. If the view returned by $sc_1$ (respectively, $sc_2$) is strictly smaller than the view returned by $sc_2$ (respectively, $sc_1$), then $sc_1 \Rightarrow sc_2$ (respectively, $sc_2 \Rightarrow sc_1$). Otherwise, if both operations return the same view, then we break symmetry first by the partial order $\rightarrow$, and if the operations are not ordered with respect to $\rightarrow$, then we break symmetry by the identity of the processors that execute the operations. Note that this is sufficient, since two operations by the same processor are ordered by $\rightarrow$.

Now, we insert the *update* operations between the ordered *scan* operations. Each *update* operation that wrote some value $v$ in register $S_i$, is inserted between the last *scan* operation that returns a view smaller than $v$ in its $i$th entry, and the first *scan* operation that returns a view greater than or equal to $v$ in its $i$th entry. Since *scan* operations are ordered by their views, each *update* operation fits exactly between two successive *scan* operations. Breaking symmetry between *update* operations that fit between the same two *scan* operations is done in the same manner as in the *scan* operations (that is, first by the partial order $\rightarrow$, and then by processor's identity).

We now prove that the total order $\Rightarrow$ has properties (a) and (b) that are mentioned at the beginning of this section (and also in Section 2).

The way *update* operations are inserted between the *scan* operations, and the way *scan* operations are ordered by their views, imply:

**Lemma 5.** *Let $sc$ be a scan operation that returns $view_{sc}$, and $up$ be an update operation by $P_i$ that writes the value $v$. Then, $view_{sc}[i] \geq v$ if and only if $up \Rightarrow sc$.*

Lemma 5 shows that the total order $\Rightarrow$ satisfies property (b). The following lemma shows that $\Rightarrow$ satisfies property (a) as well.

**Lemma 6.** *The total order $\Rightarrow$ extends the partial order $\rightarrow$.*

*Proof.* Consider four different cases, according to operation types.

*Case 1.* Let $sc$ be a *scan* operation that returns $view_{sc}$, and $up$ be an *update* operation by processor $P_i$ that writes the value $v$ and returns $view_{up}$. Assume that $sc \rightarrow up$.
Since $sc$ terminates before $up$ starts, it is clear that $view_{sc}[i] < v$. By the definition of $\Rightarrow$, $sc \Rightarrow up$.

*Case 2.* Let $up$ be an *update* operation by processor $P_i$ that writes the value $v$ and returns $view_{up}$, and $sc$ be a *scan* operation that returns $view_{sc}$. Assume that $up \rightarrow sc$.
By Lemma 4, $view_{up}[i] \geq v$. By Lemma 3, $view_{sc} \geq view_{up}$, and therefore, $view_{sc}[i] \geq v$. By the definition of $\Rightarrow$, $up$ is inserted before $sc$, which means that $up \Rightarrow sc$.

*Case 3.* Let $sc_i$ and $sc_j$ be two *scan* operations that return $view_i$ and $view_j$, respectively. Assume that $sc_i \rightarrow sc_j$.

By Lemma 3, $view_j \geq view_i$. Recall that *scan* operations are ordered in $\Rightarrow$ by the views they return. Since $\rightarrow$ is used to break symmetry between *scan* operations with equal views, it follows that $sc_i \Rightarrow sc_j$.

*Case 4.* Let $up_i$ and $up_j$ be two *update* operations by $P_i$ and $P_j$, which write $v_i$ and $v_j$, and return $view_i$ and $view_j$, respectively. Assume that $up_i \rightarrow up_j$. Assume, in the way of contradiction, that $up_j \Rightarrow up_i$. When constructing $\Rightarrow$, symmetry between *update* operations that fit between the same two *scan* operations is first broken by $\rightarrow$. Therefore, it is possible that $up_j \Rightarrow up_i$ only if there exists some *scan* operation $sc$, such that $up_j \Rightarrow sc \Rightarrow up_i$. Let $view_{sc}$ be the view returned by $sc$. The way updates are inserted in $\Rightarrow$ implies that $view_{sc}[j] \geq v_j$ and $view_{sc}[i] < v_i$. However, since $up_i$ terminates before $up_j$ starts, Lemma 4 implies that $view_i[j] < v_j$ and $view_i[i] \geq v_i$. Therefore, $view_{sc}$ and $view_i$ are incomparable, a contradiction to Lemma 2.

□

Lemma 5 and Lemma 6 imply the correctness of the snapshot object. The complexity of the transformation is obvious. Thus, we have the following:

**Theorem 7.** *Given a lattice agreement algorithm as a black-box, the above transformation yields an atomic snapshot object that requires, per an update or a scan operation, $O(1)$ executions of the lattice agreement black-box, plus $O(n)$ operations on atomic single-writer multi-reader registers.*

## 4 Synchronous Lattice Agreement

In this section, we describe a synchronous algorithm that solves the lattice agreement decision problem in the presence of crash failures. The ideas of this algorithm are used in the following section to implement an asynchronous wait-free lattice agreement algorithm.

Although the synchronous algorithm is the base for shared-memory asynchronous algorithms, it is best described using a message-passing model.[5] In this model, a processor may send messages to any group of processors in a single round, and the processors in that group are guaranteed to receive these messages before the next round. If a processor crashes in a certain round, then only some (possibly empty) subset of the messages it sent during that round arrives. Furthermore, this processor will not participate in any of the following rounds.

This synchronous message-passing model is used in [19, 11].

### 4.1 The algorithm

The synchronous lattice agreement algorithm is recursive, and employs a divide and conquer policy.

---

[5] The translation of this algorithm to a synchronous shared memory model is straightforward.

At the first recursion level, processors are divided into two groups, the *subordinated* processors, $P_1, ..., P_{\frac{n}{2}}$, and the *ordinated* processors, $P_{\frac{n}{2}+1}, ..., P_n$. Each subordinated processor sends its input to all ordinated processors. (This takes one round.) Now, the two groups recursively initiate two independent lattice agreement algorithms for $\frac{n}{2}$ processors. In the algorithm for the $\frac{n}{2}$ subordinated processors, the inputs of the processors are their original inputs. In the algorithm for the $\frac{n}{2}$ ordinated processors, the input of a processor is the join of its original input with inputs it received in messages from subordinated processors. (Recall that the join of a set of lattice elements is their least upper bound.)

At level $(\log n + 1)$, each processor is an independent group, and it simply decides on its current input as its final output.

**Theorem 8.** *The synchronous lattice agreement algorithm satisfies validity(a), validity(b), and comparability.*

*Proof.* The proof is by induction on the number of processors that participate in the algorithm. For the induction base, it is obvious that 1-processor algorithm satisfies the three conditions. For the induction step, assume that the two $\frac{n}{2}$-processor algorithms that are executed in the second recursion level by the ordinated and the subordinated groups satisfies the three conditions. We prove that the $n$-processor algorithm satisfies them as well:

*Validity(a)*: the input of any processor (subordinated or ordinated) for the $\frac{n}{2}$-processor algorithm dominates its original input. Therefore, since each $\frac{n}{2}$-processor algorithm satisfies validity(a), the output of any processor dominates its original input.

*Validity(b)*: the input of any processor (subordinated or ordinated) for the $\frac{n}{2}$-processor algorithm is a join of some original inputs. Therefore, since each $\frac{n}{2}$-processor algorithm satisfies validity(b), the output of any processor is the join of some original inputs.

*Comparability*: since each $\frac{n}{2}$-processor algorithm satisfies comparability, outputs of any two ordinated (or any two subordinated) processors are comparable. In order to prove comparability of all outputs, we prove that the final output of any ordinated processor, dominates the final outputs of all the subordinated processors.

Any subordinated processor starts the algorithm of its group using its original input. Thus, since this algorithm satisfies Validity(b), the final output of any subordinated processor is a join of some original inputs of subordinated processors. Moreover, by the construction of the algorithm, inputs of subordinated processors that fail during the first round, are transparent with respect to the algorithm of the subordinated group. Thus, the final output of a subordinated processor is only a join of some original inputs of subordinated processors that did not fail in the first round. On the other hand, any ordinated processor receives, in the first round, the original inputs of at least all the subordinated processors that did not fail in the first round. These inputs are joined to form the ordinated processor's input for the algorithm of its group. Since this algorithm satisfies Validity(a), the final output of the ordinated processor dominates the join of all the original inputs of subordinated processors that did not fail in the first round. Thus, the final output of the ordinated processor dominates any final output of a subordinated processor.

□

The number of levels is $\log n + 1$. Since each level takes exactly one communication round, the algorithm terminates after $\log n + 1$ rounds. The maximal number of messages sent by a single processor is $(n - 1)$.

# 5 Asynchronous Lattice Agreement

In this section we construct an asynchronous wait-free lattice agreement algorithm, that is based on the ideas of the synchronous algorithm presented in the previous section. The crux of the synchronous algorithm is creating two groups of processors, subordinated and ordinated. The algorithm guarantees that any ordinated processor "knows" the inputs of all the subordinated processors that proceed to the next level. Given this property, each group can recursively initiate a lattice agreement algorithm of its own.

Implementing this idea in a synchronous environment is quite simple. The division into groups is made *a priori*, and thus, each processor knows in advance to which groups it belongs at all levels. Implementing the same idea in an asynchronous environment is not as straightforward. What we need is a synchronization mechanism that (dynamically) classifies processors either as ordinated or as subordinated, and guarantees that ordinated processors can access the inputs of subordinated processors. We achieve this type of synchronization by employing known constructions of software networks called *counting networks* [7].

In general, a software network does not represent some physical connections between nodes, but rather a virtual network that determines execution routes for the various processors. In particular, counting networks, as presented in [7], are software networks originaly used to implement distributed counters in an asynchronous environment. A processor may "execute" the network, and as a result, the processor is provided with some integer number. These numbers induce a certain counting process in the system. For our purposes, we employ a simple instance of counting networks, called *one-time* counting networks. This type of counting networks allow each processor to execute the network only once. In the following section we give a brief description of one-time counting networks.

## 5.1 One-Time Counting Networks

A one-time counting network with fan-out $n$, is a software network with $n$ input wires, numbered $1, \ldots, n$, and $n$ output wires, numbered $1, \ldots, n$.[6] The network

---

[6] For the rest of the paper, we assume that $n$ is a power of 2. Otherwise, simple padding techniques can be used. The impossibility results of [2] on the construction of networks with arbitrary fan-out does not apply here, since we use our networks only once.

is constructed from 2-processor *Test&Set* registers as nodes, where each node has two input wires and two output wires.

As was mentioned, each processor may execute the network only once. An execution of the network by some processor, say $P_i$, proceeds as follows: $P_i$ enters the network on input wire $i$, and follows that wire until some node, (actually a 2-processor *Test&Set* register), is encountered. Then, $P_i$ tries to set the node. If $P_i$ succeeds in setting the node, it follows the first output wire of the node, and otherwise, it follows the second wire of the node. This is done whenever a node is encountered, and eventually, $P_i$ exits the network on one of the $n$ output wires. (We consider networks that are both finite and acyclic, and thus, it is guaranteed that $P_i$ will eventually exit the network.)

A one-time counting network must satisfy the following "counting" property: at most one processor exits the network on each output wire, and if a processor exits the network on output wire $j$, then at least $j-1$ processors have already entered the network, and will exit on wires $1, \ldots, j-1$. Exploiting this property, we use one-time counting networks in order to classify ordinated and subordinated processors. This is done in the following way: a processor writes its input into some shared register, and then executes the network. Processors that exit the network on wires $j > \frac{n}{2}$ are classified as ordinated, and the others are classified as subordinated. By the counting property of the network, this classification indeed guarantees that an ordinated processor can access the inputs of all the subordinated processors.

There are known constructions of general counting networks that can be used as one-time counting networks [7, 22]. However, as was proved in [7], any *sorting network* can be used as a one-time counting network. Thus, the best construction of a one-time counting network with fan-out $n$, is due to a sorting network construction by [3]. In the following sections we refer to several properties of this construction. These properties are listed below:

1. The counting property: at most one processor exits the network on each output wire, and when some processor exits the network on output wire $j$, all the $j-1$ processors that will exit on output wires $k < j$ have already entered the network.
2. $O(\log n)$ depth: between entering and exiting the network, a processor traverses $O(\log n)$ nodes.
3. Each node is accessed by at most two processors, however, the identity of the two processors that access a certain node is *a-priori* unknown, and is dependent on the execution.

## 5.2 Asynchronous Lattice Agreement: First Version

The properties of one-time counting networks enable us to transform the recursive synchronous lattice agreement algorithm of Section 4 into an asynchronous algorithm. As in the synchronous algorithm, $n$ processors start in level 1 as a single group of size $n$, and are recursively halved into ordinated and subordinated groups. After $(\log n + 1)$ levels, each processor is an individual group. For brevity, we name the groups that are created by the algorithm. The single group in level $\ell = 1$ is denoted $G$. Inductively, for any group $G_*$, the groups of subordinated and ordinated processors that are created from $G_*$, are denoted $G_{*s}$ and $G_{*o}$, respectively. Throughout the description of the algorithm, we use $|G_*|$ to denote the size of $G_*$. By the inductive construction of the groups, if $G_*$ is a group of level $\ell$, then $|G_*| = \frac{n}{2^{\ell-1}}$.

The algorithm makes use of the following shared data structures: For each level $\ell$, and for each group $G_*$ in this level, there is a set of $|G_*|$ single-writer multi-reader atomic registers, $R_1, ..., R_{|G_*|}$, which are called the registers of $G_*$. In addition, $G_*$ is associated with a one-time counting network with fan-out $|G_*|$, which is called the one-time counting network of $G_*$.

In order to describe the algorithm, assume that $P_i$, as a member of some group $G_*$ of level $\ell$, starts level $\ell$ with some input. The algorithm for $P_i$ at level $\ell$ is:

## Algorithm Asynch1:

1. $P_i$ writes its input into $R_i$ (of $G_*$).
2. $P_i$ executes the one-time counting network of $G_*$, and exits on some output wire $j$. If $1 \le j \le \frac{|G_*|}{2}$, then $P_i$ belongs in level $\ell+1$ to the subordinated group $G_{*s}$, and otherwise, $P_i$ belongs to the ordinated group $G_{*o}$.
3. Next, $P_i$ decides on its input for the recursive algorithm of its group in level $\ell+1$. If $P_i$ is in $G_{*s}$, then its input for the recursive algorithm is the same as its input in level $\ell$. If $P_i$ is in $G_{*o}$, then it reads the registers of $G_*$, and joins all inputs it reads to form its input for the recursive algorithm.
4. If $l = \log n + 1$, then $P_i$ returns its current input and terminates. Otherwise, $P_i$ changes its identity, and adopts a new name, $P_{(j \bmod \frac{|G_*|}{2})+1}$. This name is actually $P_i$'s index in its new group ($G_{*s}$ or $G_{*o}$), as it appears from the order in which the processors of this new group exit the one-time counting network of $G_*$. Now, $P_i$ uses its new name and starts the recursive algorithm within its group.

By the properties of one-time counting networks, and the construction of the algorithm, we have the following:

**Lemma 9.** *Let $G_*$ be a group of processors in some level $\ell$. Algorithm Asynch1 satisfies the following properties:*

    *a. The input of a processor in $G_{*o}$ (for the algorithm of level $\ell+1$) dominates all the inputs of processors in $G_{*s}$.*

    *b. The final output of any processor in $G_{*s}$ is a join of some inputs of processors in $G_{*s}$.*

Using Lemma 9, we can prove the following theorem along the lines of Theorem 8.

**Theorem 10.** *Algorithm Asynch1 solves lattice agreement.*

By straightforward calculations, we can prove the following:

**Lemma 11.** *In the algorithm Asynch1, each processor executes $O(\log^2 n)$ operations on 2-processor Test&Set registers, and $O(n)$ operations on single-writer multi-reader read/write registers.*

## 5.3 Asynchronous Lattice Agreement: Second Version

Unfortunately, in Algorithm Asynch1, processors are dynamically allocated to registers. That is, the identity of processors that access a certain register is not known *a priori*, and is determined dynamically during the execution. The dynamic allocation occurs in two places: First, it is *a priori* unknown which two processors will access a certain node (register) in the network. Second, in the algorithm itself, since processors dynamically obtain new identities during the algorithm, it is *a priori* unknown which processor will write to each single-writer read/write register in the registers of the various groups.

Algorithms that use dynamic allocation have several drawbacks. First, in order to implement such an algorithm, one must physically design the system in a way that enables each processor to access each of the shared registers. In addition, it is harder to reuse the shared data objects of the algorithm.[7]

In this section, we present a version of Algorithm Asynch1 that does not use dynamic allocation. This version is slightly less efficient than Algorithm Asynch1.

We first modify the construction of one-time counting networks, and then the algorithm itself.

In order to construct a one-time counting network with no dynamic allocation, we replace the nodes of the network with a more complex data structure. Each node is now a triangular "matrix" of $\binom{n}{2}$ 2-processor *Test&Set* registers, one for each pair of processors. In each node, each processor has access only to its extended row, which contains $n-1$ registers (one for each other processor).

An execution of the modified one-time counting network proceeds as before with the following modification: When a processor arrives at a node, it tries to set *all* registers in its extended row in the matrix of this node. Only if it succeeds in setting all of them, it follows the first output wire of that node. Otherwise, it follows the second output wire of that node.

By the properties of the one-time counting network, each node is accessed by at most two processors. Thus, it easy to see that the modified construction of one-time counting networks maintains their original properties. In addition, there is no dynamic allocation of processors to registers. Note that the complexity of the modified construction is worse. A processor that executes the modified one-time counting network with fan-out $n$ executes $O(n \log n)$ operations on 2-processor *Test&Set* registers.

The following asynchronous algorithm, Asynch2, shares the same recursive construction of algorithm Asynch1. However, in order to prevent dynamic allocation, it uses slightly different data structures. For each level $\ell$ there is a set

---

[7] This is very important if we want to guarantee that algorithms use only bounded shared memory; we return to this issue in Section 6.

of registers $R_{l,1}, ..., R_{l,n}$, which are the registers of level $\ell$. In addition, for each group $G_*$ there is a one-time counting network with fan-out $n$ (of the modified type), that is called the one-time counting network of $G_*$. Notice that, regardless of the size of $G_*$, a one-time counting network with fan-out $n$ is used.

To describe the algorithm, assume that $P_i$, as a member of some group $G_*$, starts level $\ell$ with some input. The algorithm for $P_i$ at level $\ell$ is:

**Algorithm Asynch2:**

1. $P_i$ writes its input, and its group name $G_*$, into $R_{l,i}$.
2. $P_i$ executes the one-time counting network of group $G_*$, and exits on some output wire $j$. If $1 \le j \le \frac{|G_*|}{2}$, then $P_i$ belongs to the subordinated group $G_{*s}$. Otherwise, $P_i$ belongs to the ordinated group $G_{*o}$.
3. Next, $P_i$ decides on its input for the recursive algorithm of its group. If $P_i$ is in $G_{*s}$, then its input for the recursive algorithm is the same as in the previous level. If $P_i$ is in $G_{*o}$, then it reads the registers of level $\ell$, and joins the inputs of registers that have $G_*$ as their group name, to form its input for the recursive algorithm.
4. $P_i$ executes the recursive algorithm within its group. If $l$ is the last level, $P_i$ returns its current input and terminates.

To prove correctness, we note that Algorithm Asynch2 satisfies the properties of Lemma 9. This implies the following:

**Lemma 12.** *The algorithm Asynch2 solves lattice agreement.*

**Lemma 13.** *In Algorithm Asynch2, each processor executes $O(n \log^2 n)$ operations on 2-processor Test&Set registers and $O(n \log n)$ operations on single-writer multi-reader read/write registers.*

*Proof.* The algorithm has $(\log n + 1)$ levels. In each level, a processor executes a one-time counting network with fan-out $n$ of the modified type. Each execution of such network, requires $O(n \log n)$ operations on 2-processor Test&Set registers. Thus, each processor executes $O(n \log^2 n)$ operations on 2-processor Test&Set registers. In addition, in each level a processor reads all $n$ registers of that level, and thus, each processor executes $O(n \log n)$ operations on single-writer multi-reader registers.
□

## 6 Discussion

We have proved that any algorithm solving lattice agreement can be used to implement a snapshot object. We presented a linear algorithm for solving lattice agreement, and hence for implementing snapshot objects. This algorithm uses 2-processor Test&Set registers.

This is a significant improvement in the number of operations required to implement a snapshot object, but it is achieved using a shared memory primitive which is stronger than read/write registers. Although *Test&Set* registers are stronger than read/write registers, they are not very powerful, as they can only be used to solve 2-processor consensus; they cannot be used to implement powerful objects such as *Compare&Swap* [17]. Moreover, our algorithms have low-contention since each register is accessed by at most two processors.

So far, all our snapshot algorithms use an unbounded amount of shared memory. This is due to the fact that the transformation from lattice agreement to snapshot objects relies on an unbounded number of rounds of lattice agreement. We believe that in most cases, for a specific lattice agreement algorithm, these unbounded rounds can be simulated by the bounded rounds construction of [8]. The main difficulty in applying this idea is how to reuse the shared data structures of the algorithm. In the full version of the paper, we show that when using algorithm Asynch2 as the lattice agreement algorithm, the transformation can be accomplished using only a bounded amount of shared memory.

The obvious question left open by our work is improving the bounds for implementing snapshot objects. The results presented here suggest that it might be helpful to concentrate on lattice agreement. If there is a non-linear lower bound, then our linear synchronous algorithm implies that it must exploit asynchrony, while our linear asynchronous algorithm using *Test&Set* registers implies that it must exploit the weakness of read/write registers.

We have shown a strong relation between snapshot objects and lattice agreement. It is interesting to show a similar relation between other decision problems and concurrent objects.

In our opinion, the $\log n$-rounds synchronous algorithm for lattice agreement is interesting on its own right. Lattice agreement joins other decision problems that can be solved faster than consensus: *renaming*, which can be solved within $O(\log n)$ rounds [19], and *k-set consensus* which can be solved within $O(\frac{n}{k})$ rounds [11]. This gives more evidence to the fine structure of the problems weaker than consensus in the synchronous model.

*Acknowledgements:* We thank Tal Rabin and Asaf Shirazi, for helpful comments on an earlier version of this paper.

# References

1. Y. Afek, H. Attiya, D. Dolev, E. Gafni, M. Merritt and N. Shavit, "Atomic Snapshots of Shared Memory," proceedings of *the 9th Annual ACM Symposium on Principles of Distributed Computing*, 1990, pp. 1–14.

2. E. Aharonson and H. Attiya, "Counting Network with Arbitrary Fan-Out," proceedings of *the 3rd Annual ACM-SIAM Symp. on Discrete Algorithms*, Orlando, Florida, January 1992, pp. 104–113.

3. M. Ajtai, J. Komlos and E. Szemeredi, "An $O(n \log n)$ sorting network," proceedings of *the 15th ACM Symposium on the Theory of Computing*, 1-9, 1983.

4. J. H. Anderson, "Composite Registers," proceedings of *the 9th Annual ACM Symposium on Principles of Distributed Computing*, 1990, pp. 15–29.

5. J. Aspnes, "Time- and Space-Efficient Randomized Consensus," proceedings of *the 9th Annual ACM Symposium on Principles of Distributed Computing*, 1990, pp. 325–331.

6. J. Aspnes and M. P. Herlihy, "Wait-Free Data Structures in the Asynchronous PRAM Model," proceedings of *the 2nd Annual Symposium on Parallel Algorithms and Architectures*, 1990, pp. 340–349.

7. J. Aspnes, M. P. Herlihy and N. Shavit, "Counting Networks and Multi-Processor Coordination," proceedings of *the 23rd annual Symposium on Theory of Computing*, 1991, pp. 348–358.

8. H. Attiya, D. Dolev and N. Shavit, "Bounded polynomial randomized consensus," proceedings of *the 8th Annual ACM Symposium on Principles of Distributed Computing*, 1989, pp. 281–293.

9. H. Attiya, N. A. Lynch and N. Shavit, "Are wait-free algorithms fast?" proceedings of *the 31st IEEE Symposium on on Foundations of Computer Science* 1990, pp. 55–64.

10. T. Chandra and C. Dwork, personal communication.

11. S. Chaudhuri, "Towards a Complexity Hierarchy of Wait-Free Concurrent Objects," proceeding of *the 3rd IEEE Symposium on Parallel and Distributed Processing*, 1991, pp. 730–737.

12. B. Chor and L. Moscovici, "Solvability in Asynchronous Environments," proceedings of *the 30th IEEE Symposium on on Foundations of Computer Science* 1989, pp. 422–427.

13. B. Chor and L. Nelson, proceedings of *the 10th ACM Symp. on Principles of Distributed Computing*, 1991, pp. 37–49.

14. C. Dwork, personal communication.

15. C. Dwork, M. P. Herlihy, S. A. Plotkin, and O. Waarts, "Time-Lapse Snapshots," proceedings of *Israel Symposium on the Theory of Computing and Systems*, 1992, to appear.

16. R. Gawlick, N. Lynch and N. Shavit, "Concurrent Timestamping Made Simple," proceedings of *Israel Symposium on the Theory of Computing and Systems*, 1992, to appear.

17. Herlihy, M. P. "Wait-free synchronization," *ACM Transactions on Programming Languages and Systems*, Vol. 13, No. 1 (Jan. 1991), pp. 124–149.

18. M. P. Herlihy, "Randomized Wait-Free Objects," proceedings of *the 10th ACM Symp. on Principles of Distributed Computing*, 1991, pp. 11–21.

19. M. Herlihy and M. Tuttle, "Wait-Free Computation in Message-Passing Systems," proceedings of *the 9th ACM Symp. on Principles of Distributed Computing*, 1990, pp. 347–362.

20. M. P. Herlihy and J. M. Wing, "Linearizability: A correctness condition for concurrent objects," *ACM Transactions on Programming Languages and Systems,* Vol. 12, No. 3 (July 1990), pp. 463–492.

21. L. M. Kirousis, P. Spirakis and Ph. Tsigas, "Reading Many Variables in One Atomic Operation: Solutions with Linear or Sublinear Complexity," proceedings of *the 5th International Workshop on Distributed Algorithms,* Delphi, Greece, October 1991 (S. Toueg, P. Spirakis and L. Kirousis, eds.), pp. 229–241, Lecture Notes in Computer Science #579, Springer-Verlag.

22. M. Klugerman and G. Plaxton, "Small-Depth Counting Networks," *Proceedings of the 24th ACM Symp. on Theory of Computing,* 1992, pp. 417–428.

23. J. Tromp and P. M. B. Vitanyi, "Randomized Wait-Free Test-and-Set," manuscript, November 1990.

# Choice Coordination with Multiple Alternatives (Preliminary Version)

David S. Greenberg[1], Gadi Taubenfeld[2], and Da-Wei Wang[3]

[1] Sandia National Labs, P.O. Box 5800, Albuquerque, NM 87185
[2] AT&T Bell Laboratories, 600 Mountain Avenue, Murray Hill, NJ 07974
[3] Yale University, New Haven, CT 06520

**Abstract.** The Choice Coordination Problem with $k$ alternatives ($k$-CCP) was introduced by Rabin in 1982 [Rab82]. The goal is to design a wait-free protocol for $n$ asynchronous processes which causes all correct processes to agree on one out of $k$ possible alternatives. The agreement on a single choice is complicated by the fact that there is no *a priori* agreement on names for the alternatives. Furthermore processes must state their choice and do all communication via registers associated with the alternatives. We exactly characterize when the $k$-CCP can be solved deterministiclly, prove upper and lower space bounds for deterministic solutions, and provide a randomized protocol which is significantly better than the deterministic lower bound.

## 1 Introduction

### 1.1 The Choice Coordination Problem

A central issue in distributed computing is how to coordinate the actions of asynchronous processes. Coordination becomes even more difficult if as many as $n-1$ of the $n$ processes can fail. The Choice Coordination Problem (CCP) [Rab82] highlights many of the difficulties inherent in such *wait-free* situations. Solutions to the CCP thus lend insight into how to coordinate asynchronous actions.

In the $k$-CCP, $n$ asynchronous processes must choose between $k$ alternatives. Each process has its own naming convention for the alternatives. A solution to the $k$-CCP is a protocol which guarantees that all correct processes terminate having chosen the same alternative. A slightly more concrete version of the $k$-CCP associates a shared register with each alternative. All inter-process communication must be accomplished by writing in these registers. However, the registers do not have global names; the first register examined and the subsequent order in which registers are scanned may be different for each process. A special symbol must be written in exactly one register and all correct processes must terminate pointing to this register. The efficiency of the protocol is defined by the number of different symbols which may be written in the registers.

It seemed intuitively obvious that adding more alternatives and hence more registers would just make the coordination more difficult. One of our results is that, surprisingly, having more alternatives can lead to requiring fewer symbols. Besides giving protocols which take advantage of additional registers we exactly characterize the values of $k$ and $n$ for which the $k$-CCP can be solved by $n$ deterministic processes, prove lower bounds on the number of symbols required by deterministic protocols, and provide randomized protocols which are significantly better than the deterministic lower bounds.

## 1.2  Computational Model

Our model of computation consists of a fully asynchronous collection of $n$ processes. It is assumed that each process has an identifier but the identifiers need not be unique. Processes may fail only by crashing; that is, they fail only by never entering the protocol or by leaving the protocol at some point and thereafter permanently refraining from writing the shared registers. We require that all protocols be wait-free. That is, they can tolerate up to $n-1$ process failures.

All inter-process communications are via finite sized shared registers which are initially in a known state. Access to the shared registers is via atomic "read-modify-write" instructions which, in a single indivisible step, read the value in a register and then write a new value that can depend on the value just read. In the $k$-CCP each of the $k$ alternatives has an associated register shared by all processes. The registers do not have global names; a single register may be considered the fifth register by one process and the eighth by another. Even the order of the names may be different. Thus one process may scan four alternatives in order 3, 2, 1, 4 while another scans 2, 4, 1, 3.

The lack of global names for the registers makes it is convenient to think of each process as being assigned an initial register and an ordering of the registers which determines how it scans the registers. An interesting special case is when all the orderings coincide. If all processes are assigned the same ordering (though potentially different initial registers) we say that the alternatives are arranged as a unidirectional ring. If all processes are assigned either one particular ordering or its inverse then the alternatives are said to be arranged as a bidirectional ring. Although in the bidirectional ring case the protocol can use the fact that all processes use a single ordering or its inverse there is no *a priori* agreement on which is the ordering and which the inverse.

Given the above definitions we now can formally define a solution to the $k$-CCP. A protocol is a solution to the general $k$-CCP if, for all possible orderings and initial registers assigned to the asynchronous processes, eventually the special symbol, $e$, is written in exactly one register and all correct processes terminate with a pointer to the register containing the $e$. A protocol is a solution to the unidirectional (bidirectional) $k$-CCP if the protocol solves the $k$-CCP when all processes are assigned the same ordering (or its inverse). Protocols requiring the least number of values in the shared registers are considered optimal. Other papers [BBD89] also measure internal memory size of the processes but we will not address this measure here.

56

## 1.3 Related Work

There are only two published papers about the $k$-CCP problem. Rabin's paper which introduced the problem [Rab82], and a paper by Bar-Noy, Ben-or and Dolev [BBD89]. Rabin is mainly interested in the case of $k = 2$ and $t = n - 1$. ($k$ is the number of alternatives and $t$ is the possible number of faulty processes.) He shows a deterministic protocol using $m = n + 2$ symbols (for each register) and a lower bound of $m \geq (n/8)^{1/3}$ for deterministic protocols. The upper bound can be modified to hold for any $k$. Also, as mentioned in [BBD89], the lower bound can be immediately extended to any $t$, obtaining $m = \Omega(t^{1/3})$. Rabin contrasts these deterministic results with a randomized protocol which, for $m$ symbols, terminates correctly with probability $1 - 1/2^{m/2}$.

Bar-noy, Ben-or and Dolev extend Rabin's analysis to arbitrary $t$, examine the local storage requirements, and study a semi-synchronous model. They present deterministic and randomized protocols which both use $O(t^2)$ symbols. The randomized solution, which is for identical processes, terminates with probability 1 and is always correctly. The deterministic solution requires $O(2^n \log t)$ bits of internal memory. Another deterministic solution which requires only $O(\log n)$ bits of internal memory but $O(t^2 \log n)$ symbols is given. For $k = 3$ they showed that $n/2 + 3$ symbols is sufficient for a deterministic wait-free solution, and that for every prime $k$ only $n/(k-1) + 3$ symbols are needed under the assumption that the registers are arranged as a unidirectional ring.

The $k$-CCP is related to the classic consensus problem[Fis83]. When all processes use the same set of names for the alternatives and the first register examined by a process in the $k$-CCP corresponds to the process' input in the consensus problem then a solution to the $k$-CCP is similar to a solution to consensus. However, in the consensus problem there is the additional requirement that the chosen alternative be the input of some process.

Impossibility results about the well-studied consensus problem therefore lend insight into the $k$-CCP. For example, Fischer, Lynch, and Paterson show that no consensus protocol can tolerate even a single crash failure in an asynchronous message-passing model [FLP85]. A similar result also holds for a shared memory model which supports only atomic read and write operations [LA87]. This last result can be used to show that: the $k$-CCP is not solvable in the presence of even a single crash failure if only atomic read and write operations are assumed. The Loui and Abu-Amara impossibility proof does not use the requirement that the chosen alternative be the input of some process but instead uses the weaker requirement that there are two runs in which different alternatives are chosen. Since it is easy to ensure that the $k$-CCP meets this weaker condition the impossibility for $k$-CCP follows.

## 1.4 Summary of Results

As mentioned, most of existing results examine only two alternatives (i.e., $k = 2$), and assume unique identifiers for deterministic protocols. We solve the problem for any number of alternatives, and also study the case where processes do not have unique identifiers. The two main questions that we try to answer are:

1. Assuming that there is no limitation on the size of each register, under what circumstances is the $k$-CCP solvable?
2. How many symbols for each of the $k$ registers are necessary and sufficient to solve the $k$-CCP, as a function of $k$ and $n$?

The answers to both these questions give a measure of the communication-space complexity of the problem and also provide a way of assessing the cost of achieving reliability. We give a brief overview of our results below.

SOLVABILITY CONDITIONS FOR THE $k$-CCP: Assuming that there is no limitation on the size of each register, we show that the $k$-CCP is solvable by a deterministic protocol if and only if the maximal number of processes having the same identifier is smaller than the least prime divisor of $k$. In proving this result, no assumption is made about the arrangement of the registers.

DETERMINISTIC SOLUTIONS – UPPER BOUND: When the registers are arranged on a ring we give a protocol which makes use of additional alternatives' registers to reduce the number of symbols required. For $n$ processes and $k$ alternatives (i.e., registers) our protocols use $O(n\,\eta(k)/k + \eta(k))$ symbols, where $\eta(k)$ is the number of prime factors of $k$ counting duplicates as separate. Furthermore, we give a simple protocol which for $k > n^2$ uses at most 6 symbols.

DETERMINISTIC SOLUTIONS – LOWER BOUND: When the registers are arranged in a ring we show that all correct protocols must use at least $\sqrt[3]{n/k^3}$ symbols. When no assumption is made about the arrangement of the registers, we tighten the bound to $m \geq \sqrt[3]{n/4k}$.

RANDOMIZED SOLUTIONS: We present a randomized protocol that solves the $k$-CCP, and terminates with probability greater than $1 - 2^{-(m - \log k - 2\log\log k - 3)/2}$, where $m$ is the number of symbols used by a protocol. Thus, if $k \leq 2^{100}$ a probability of success greater than $1 - 2^{-100}$ can be achieved for any number of processes using registers which are just 9 bits wide. In this protocol the processes are identical (i.e., have the same identifier) and no assumption is made about the arrangement of the registers.

## 2  Solvability Conditions for the $k$-CCP

A first question concerning the $k$-CCP is: Under what circumstances is the $k$-CCP solvable deterministically? In this section we show that the $k$-CCP is solvable if and only if the maximum number of processes having the same identifier is smaller than the least prime divisor of $k$. It is assumed that there is no limitation on the size of each register. In later sections the relation of register size to number of processes for which the $k$-CCP is solvable will be investigated.

More precisely, assume each process has an identifier but that the identifiers need not be unique. Let $\mathcal{N}$ be the maximum number of processes with the same identifier. Notice that when the processes are identical $\mathcal{N} = n$, and when they have unique identifiers $\mathcal{N} = 1$. Now recall that $k$ is the number of registers and define $\ell(k)$ to be the least divisor of $k$ which is greater than 1. The theorem below, gives a complete characterization for the solvable cases. (Notice that no assumption is made about the arrangement of the registers.)

**Theorem 1.** *For any k, n, and $\mathcal{N}$, there exists a deterministic protocol for n processes which solves the k-CCP if and only if $\mathcal{N} < \ell(k)$.*

*Proof.* We first assume that $\mathcal{N} \geq \ell(k)$, and prove that no solution exists. Pick a cyclic ordering of the k registers and divide it into $\ell(k)$ segments each containing exactly $k/\ell(k)$ registers. Pick $\ell(k)$ processes with the same identifier and assign one to the first register in each of the $\ell(k)$ segments. Now, schedule these and only these processes in a round robin fashion; each process, in turn, moves to the next register in the ordering and executes one read-modify-write operation. Because the processes are placed symmetrically, each operation of the first scheduled process is always followed by the *same* operation, on a different register, by each other process. Thus the original symmetry is restored after each round of the round robin. Therefore, if one process writes e into some register then at the end of the round each of these processes will write e in a different register.

Next, we assume that $\mathcal{N} < \ell(k)$, and show how to solve the k-CCP on a general graph. For simplicity we will start by assuming that $n = \mathcal{N}$, that is all processes have the same identifier. The general case of several different identifiers each associated with at most $\mathcal{N}$ processes is discussed at the end of the proof. The protocol for all processes having the same identifier is given in Figure 1.

In the protocol the constructs **lock** and **unlock** mark the beginning and end of atomic, exclusive access to the shared register at which pointer p is pointing. Each process can lock only one register at a time. The fact that the read-modify-write operation is wait-free and atomic is reflected by the assumption that a process does not fail between executing **lock** and the next **unlock**, and that any non-faulty process that reaches a **lock** instruction eventually executes it.

The goal of Procedure A is to break the symmetry of the processes. The full protocol logically divides the registers into n tracks and uses Procedure A repeatedly on different tracks in order to give each process a unique value. The unique values can then be used in a last track to identify a unique decision register.

In this abstract we only state without proof the main lemmas required by the proof of the theorem.

**Lemma 1.** *All processes scheduled k times in during a call to Procedure A terminate. Not all processes using Procedure A on the same track halt with the same value of c.*

An execution of Procedure A partitions the processes into groups depending on their final value of c. Although no process can know any other process' group number each can determine from the final configuration how many processes are in each possible group. The number of processes in group $i \geq 0$ (i.e., the number of processes where $c = i$) is simply the number of shared registers containing the value i minus the number of registers containing $i + 1$. Let $f(i)$ be the total number of processes in groups greater than i and $\lambda(i)$ be the number of processes in group i (let $f(-1) = n$).

---

**shared** $C$: ring of $k$ registers range over $n$-tuples of integers;;
**local** $S$: array $[1..k]$ of $n$-tuples of integers;
**local** $i$: integer $\{1...k\}$;                % **pointer into S**
**local** $c$: integer $\{0...k\}$;                % **counter**
**local** $t$: integer $\{1...n\}$;                % **track**
**local** $r$: integer $\{1...n\}$;                % **minimum rank**
**local** $p$: pointer which initially points to some arbitrary register of $C$;
$t := 1; r := 1;$
**Repeat**
    **Execute** Procedure A on track $t$ returning $c$ and $S$
    **if** $f(c) = 0$ **then** $t = t + 1$ **else** $t := t + f(c)$;
    $r := r + f(c)$;
**Until** $\lambda(c) = 1$
Write $r$ on track $n$ of any one register containing $\bot$ if any exists;
Write $0$ on track $n$ of all registers containing $\bot$ if any exists;
Write $e$ on the register containing the maximum value in track $n$
**end-protocol**

% **Using only track $t$ of $S$ divide processes into at least two groups**
% **Input: $S,p,t$, Output: $S,p,c$**
**Procedure A**
    $c := 0$;
    % **Write in $t$th track of as many registers as possible**
    **For** $i$ **from** 1 **to** $k$ **do**
        **lock**
            **if** $p\uparrow = \bot$ **then** $\{c:=c+1 ; p\uparrow := c\}$; % **change track $t$ of $p\uparrow$ only**
            $S[i] := p\uparrow$;
        **unlock**
        move $p$ to the next register;
    **end-for**
**end-procedure**

**Fig. 1.** Solution to the $k$-CCP when all processes have the same id.

Procedure A breaks some of the initial symmetry, producing at least two non-empty groups. The full protocol applies Procedure A recursively to each group of processes until each process is in a group of its own at which point it can be assigned a unique identifier.

If each instantiation of Procedure A used the same registers then they might interfere badly. It is not possible to agree *a priori* on a partition of the registers in order to avoid interference. Instead each register is logically divided into $n$ tracks; ie. the values in the registers can be thought of as $n$-tuples of track values. The full protocol arranges that all processes participating in a given instantiation of Procedure A use the unique track reserved for this instantiation. Since each instantiation uses its own track Lemma 1 will hold for all instantiations.

**Lemma 2.** *Each correct process eventually exits the main loop of the protocol in Figure 1 with a unique value of r.*

The proof of Theorem 1 follows easily from Lemma 2. The termination of the entire protocol is clear since the main loop terminates. The correctness follows from the fact that each process exits the main loop with a unique value of $r$ $(1 \leq r \leq n)$. In track $n$ each process then writes its value at most once and at least one process writes its value. Thus there must be a unique maximum value in track $n$ when it no longer contains any non-bottom symbols. Hence the value $e$ is written exactly one.

We started the proof by assuming that $n = \mathcal{N}$, that is all processes have the same identifier. When there are several identifier values, each assigned to fewer than $\ell(k)$ processes then separate tracks must be assigned *a priori* for each potential identifier value.

An immediate consequence of Theorem 1 is that for any $k$ and $n$, there exists a solution to the $k$-CCP, when the $n$ processes have unique identifiers; and when $k$ is even there is a solution only if the processes have unique identifiers.

A quick calculation shows that the protocol of Figure 1 requires a total of $(n+2)(k+1)^{n-1}$ symbols. There are several ways of saving symbols. Perhaps the easiest is to have processes not increment their counter above $k/2+1$ since this value must be unique. However the best solutions still use $(k/c)^n$ symbols for some constant $c$. When the registers are constrained to be visited as a unidirectional or bidirectional ring the number of symbols can be reduced to $\lceil (\#id \cdot \mathcal{N})/(\ell(k) - 1) \rceil + 3$, where $\#id$ is the number of different identifiers.

## 3 Upper Bounds

In this section we examine the $k$-CCP when each process has its own unique identifier and the alternatives are arranged as a unidirectional ring. We present a protocol which, for a fixed $n$, reduces the number of symbols required as $k$ increases. No more than $O((n \log k)/k + \log k)$ symbols are ever used by the protocol. When $k$ has few factors then even fewer symbols are needed. In addition, when $k > n^2$ at most 6 symbols are used.

We write $k$'s prime factorization as $k = \prod \rho_i^{e_i}$ (where $\forall i, \rho_i$ is prime and $\forall i \neq j, \rho_i \neq \rho_j$.) Let $\eta(k) = \sum_i e_i$; thus $\eta(k)$ is the number of prime factors of $k$, counting duplicates as separate. Note that if $k$ is a power of 2 then $\eta(k) = \log_2 k$, and that $\log_2 k$ is the maximum possible value of $\eta(k)$.

**Theorem 2.** *The $k$-CCP can be solved by $n$ processes having unique identifiers on a unidirectional ring using $m$ symbols if*

*1. $m \geq \lceil n/(k-1) \rceil + 3\eta(k) + \lceil 2n/(k-2) \rceil (\eta(k) - 1)$, or*
*2. $k > n^2$ and $m \geq 6$.*

In this abstract we give only a sketch of the proof of Part 1 of Theorem 2. The complete protocol on which the proof is based is given in Figure 2. The efficiency of the protocol could be increased in several ways which would, however, made the proof less transparent. For example, it is not necesary to check if $i \leq \eta(k)$ in the guard of the main **while** loop and a process can often skip ahead to a later phase once it has determined that it has fallen behind.

Let $S$ be the sequence $s_0, ..., s_{k-1}$. The $i$th rotation $(0 \leq i < k)$ of $S$ is the sequence $\mathrm{R}_i(S) = s_i, ..., s_k, s_1, ..., s_{i-1}$. A *lexicographically maximal rotation* (abbv. lmr) of $S$ is any rotation $\mathrm{R}_j(S)$ such that for all $0 \leq i < k$, $\mathrm{R}_j(S) \geq \mathrm{R}_i(S)$ according to the standard lexicographic order.

**Lemma 3.** *If a sequence of length $k$ has $L$ lmrs then $L$ divides $k$ and each symbol occurs a multiple of $L$ times.*

Recall that $\ell(k)$ is the least divisor of $k$ which is greater than 1 (when $k$ is prime $\ell(k) = k$). It follows from Lemma 3 that in a sequence of length $k$ where some symbol occurs fewer than $\ell(k)$ times, there is a unique lmr. Furthermore, in a sequence of length $k$ where some symbol occurs a number of times relatively prime to $k$, there is a unique lmr.

## Ideas Behind the Protocol

We are now ready for an intuitive description of the protocol. Initially the $k$ registers all contain the same known initial symbol and thus there are $k$ lmrs. The protocol proceeds in phases; each phase reduces the number of lmrs. Lemma 3 shows that the number of lmrs is always a divisor of $k$, thus the number of lmrs must actually decrease in each phase by a multiple of prime factors of $k$. Even if each phase divides the number of lmrs by only a single prime factor of $k$ then after $\eta(k)$ phases the number of lmrs would have to be reduced to one. Once a single lmr is achieved the processes choose the register at the start of the single lmr.

A different set of symbols is used in each phase. This allows processes which have been delayed to quickly determine the correct phase. In particular it prevents processes last scheduled in an earlier phase from interfering with a later phase. The protocol is nonetheless efficient because there are not many phases and relatively few symbols are used in each phase.

During each phase the processes must use these limited number of symbols to reduce the number of lmrs. In order to ensure that only a single lmr remains would require ensuring that some symbol occurs fewer than $\ell(k)$ times. Fortunately we need only to reduce the number of lmrs in each phase. In the first phase we only need to guarantee that some symbol occurs less than $k$ times. Consequently, the first phase uses only $\lceil n/(k-1) \rceil + 2$ symbols.

It might seem that as the number of lmrs decreases, more symbols will be needed to further reduce the number of lmrs. For example, if every symbol must occur less often than the number of lmrs and the number of lmrs is 2 then $n$ symbols are necessary. The protocol avoids this growth of number of symbols by taking advantage of symbol placement around the ring of registers.

**shared** $C$: ring of $k$ registers range over pairs of integers, initially all $= (1, -1)$;
**local** $S$: array $[1..k]$ of pairs of integers;
**local** $i, j, val, pos, lmrs, bl, index$: integer;
**local** $p$: pointer which initially points on some *arbitary* register of $C$;
**boolean** *writeactive*: flag specifying whether active symbol needs to be written;
**constant** $marker = \infty$; $mfill = -1$; $afill = 0$; $e = (\infty, \infty)$;

$i := 1$; $val := \lceil id_p/(k-1) \rceil$; $lmrs := k$; $writeactive := true$;
**while** $(lmrs \neq 1)$ and $(i \leq \eta(k))$ **do**
    % Ensure that an active symbol is written in this phase
    **lock if** *writeactive* and $(p\uparrow = (i, mfill))$ **then** $p\uparrow := (i, val)$ **unlock**;

    % Loop A: Ensure completion of active phase by writing fill symbols
    **for** $j$ from 1 to $k$ **do**
        **move** $p$ to the next register;
        **lock if** $p\uparrow = (i, mfill)$ **then** $p\uparrow := (i, afill)$ **unlock** ;
        $S[j] := p\uparrow$ **end-for**

    % If $S$ holds only phase $i$ symbols then
    % found an active configuration and must write a marker symbol
    **if** $\forall j, S[j] < (i+1, -1)$ **then**
        $index :=$ index in $S$ of the beginning of an lmr;
        **move** $p$ forward $index$ times;
        **lock if** $p\uparrow < (i+1, -1)$ **then** $p\uparrow := (i+1, marker)$ **unlock**;

    % Loop B: Ensure completion of marker phase by writing fill symbols
    **for** $j$ from 1 to $k$ **do**
        **move** $p$ to the next register;
        **lock if** $p\uparrow < (i+1, -1)$ **then** $p\uparrow := (i+1, mfill)$ **unlock**;
        $S[j] := p\uparrow$ **end-for**

    % $S$ holds a copy of $C$, possibly the phase $i+1$ marker configuration
    % Prepare to write active symbol in next phase if necessary
    $i := i + 1$; $writeactive := false$;
    **if** $\forall j, S[j] = (i, marker)$ or $S[j] = (i, mfill)$ **then**
        $lmrs :=$ the number lmrs of $S$;
        **if** $lmrs = 1$ **then** $pos := 0$;
        **else** $\{ bl := k/lmrs$; $pos := 1 + id_p \bmod (lmrs - 1)$;
            $val := \lceil id_p/((lmrs - 1)(bl - 1)) \rceil$; $writeactive := true \}$ ;
        $index :=$ index in $S$ of the beginning of an lmr;
        **move** $p$ forward $index + pos$ times;
**end-while**
**lock** $p\uparrow := e$ **unlock**.

This protocol has several non-optimal features which were included in order to simplify the proof.

**Fig. 2.** Solution to the $k$-CCP — program for process $p$ (with identifier $id_p$).

A sequence containing $L$ lmrs can be divided into $L$ equal blocks of $b = k/L$ registers such that the cyclic sequence beginning at the start of each block is an lmr. Instead of a phase ensuring that some symbol occurs fewer than $L$ times it ensures that not all blocks are the same. Since all blocks will not be the same, not all blocks can still begin lmrs and the number of lmrs is reduced.

One detail omitted in the previous paragraph is that we need to guarantee that lmrs begin only at registers which are the beginning of lmrs of the previous phase. Thus we add a special marking subphase at the beginning of each phase. The marking subphase marks, with the largest symbol possible for the phase, some of the registers at the beginnings of lmrs in the previous phase; thus only these marked registers can be at the start of lmrs in the new phase.

It is also possible to show that at most $log_{k/n}k$ symbols are needed, when $k > n$. In this case, in each phase the number of lmrs must decrease by a factor of $n/k$ and thus the number of phases is at most $log_{k/n}k$. In addition each phase requires at most one active symbol.

Part 2 of Theorem 2 depends on a very simple protocol. The remainder of this section contains a description of the protocol along with intuitive reasons why it works.

The six symbols are denoted $\perp, a, \mathtt{fill\text{-}a}, b, \mathtt{fill\text{-}b},$ and $e$. Initially all registers contain $\perp$. Each process then writes $a$ in its first register if the register still contains $\perp$ and writes $\mathtt{fill\text{-}a}$ in every other register which still contains $\perp$. Having done a Read-modify-write on each register once it now has a record of all registers in which $a$ will ever be written.

Since $k > n^2$ and at most $n$ registers contain an $a$ (each process writes $a$ at most once) there must be at least one register containing $a$ followed by $n$ registers containing $\mathtt{fill\text{-}a}$. Process $i$ moves to the $i$th register containing $\mathtt{fill\text{-}a}$ in such a gap and writes $b$ if the register still contains $\mathtt{fill\text{-}a}$. Thereafter it writes $\mathtt{fill\text{-}b}$ on every register still containing $\mathtt{fill\text{-}a}$. Now, having performed a Read-modify-write on each register twice the process has a record of the final contents of all the registers before $e$ is written.

There is a unique $b$ which is furthest from its preceeding $a$ (and hence an unique lmr). Since the identity of $b$ is determined by relative distance from its preceeding $a$ all processes agree on its identity despite there different names for the registers. Thus each can write $e$ in the register containing this special $b$.

# 4   A Lower Bound

In this section, we establish a lower bound on the number of symbols required to solve the $k$-CCP. Our bound generalizes Rabin's lower bound for $k = 2$ to apply to general $k$. We examine both the case where it is known that the registers are arranged as a ring and the case where nothing is known about the registers' arrangement.

**Theorem 3.** *Let $P$ be a protocol for $n$ processes that solves the $k$-CCP. Let $m$ be the number of symbols used by $P$. Then,*

1. *$m \geq \sqrt[3]{n/k^3}$, assuming the registers are arranged as a unidirectional ring;*
2. *$m \geq \sqrt[3]{n/(4k \log k)}$, when no assumption is made about the arrangement of the registers.*

The proof relies on two key properties of the protocols. The wait-free property ensures that any process run sufficiently long will eventually write a new symbol until it finally writes $e$. The "anonymity" of the registers ensures that if all registers contain the same symbol then a process will take the same steps regardless of its initial register and, in the general case, regardless of the order in which the registers are visited.

Informally, the proof employs an adversary which progressively extends a run to lead from one configuration in which all registers contain the same symbol to another such configuration. Each configuration uses a symbol not used in the previous configurations. Eventually a configuration is reached with two registers containing $e$. The wait-free property allows the adversary to find processes which, when added to the run, will write new symbols and the anonymity property allows it to force these processes to write the symbol in every register.

In order to extend the run to the next configuration the adversary needs many processes which have not yet been used in the run. Protocols using more symbols require the adversary to go through more intermediate configurations before reaching one containing two $e$'s. Thus if more symbols are used than more processes can be allowed to participate without including enough for the adversary to force the protocol to fail.

The details of the adversary, which is a modified version of the one used by Rabin[Rab82], are omitted from this abstract. In order to achieve bounds when $k > 2$ we needed new combinatorial lemmas which bound the cost to the adversary of forcing processes to write in particular registers.

## 5    Randomized Protocol

We have seen that for large values of $k$, compared to $n$, the number of symbols used by a deterministic protocol in the ring case can be kept relatively small. Our lower bounds show, however, that the number of symbols must grow as a function of $n$. It is natural to ask if the number of symbols can be reduced if a small probability of non-termination is allowed. In his seminal paper Rabin showed that randomization could reduce the number of symbols when $k = 2$. In this section we show that, for any value of $k$, randomization can reduce the number of symbols needed.

Our strategy for randomized protocols draws many ideas from our deterministic protocols. Randomization allows us to simultaneously reduce the number of symbols required, dispense with process identifiers, and succeed regardless of whether or not the registers are arranged in a ring. For example, if $k \leq 2^{100}$ then a probability of success greater than $1 - 2^{-100}$ can be achieved for any number of identical processes using registers which are just 9 bits wide.

**Theorem 4.** *For any $k, n$, and security parameter $q$, there exists a randomized protocol for $n$ processes using $m = 2q + \log\min\{k,n\} + 2\log\log\min\{k,n\} + 3$ symbols which solves the $k$-CCP for $n$ processes and terminates with probability greater than $1 - 2^{-q}$.*

The proof of Theorem 4 is based on the analysis of the protocol given in Figure 3. This protocol was designed to make the analysis of the worst case simple. There are many obvious optimizations which improve its behavior on fortuitous runs. Before analysing the protocol we give an informal description of it and an intuitive idea of why it works.

## The Protocol

The randomized protocol, like the deterministic one, works in phases. Each phase uses some new symbols in an attempt to reduce the number of registers which may end up containing $e$. If in a predetermined number of phases the number of *live* registers (ones in which $e$ may eventually be written) is reduced to one then the protocol succeeds. The use of more symbols per phase or more phases will increase the probability of success. Thus given a bound on allowable failure probability we can ask what is the smallest number of symbols which can attain this failure probability.

More specifically, in each phase each process picks a register which survived the previous phase (we call these registers *live*), writes in this register a random symbol from those symbols assigned this phase, and then attempts to write the *kill* symbol in all registers containing symbols from earlier phases. Intuitively, it has ensured that at least one register survives the phase and then tried to kill all other registers. As in the deterministic protocol we use a lock construct to denote the read-modify-write. Inside the lock the process may generate a random value. The choice being made inside the lock is meant to denote that we assume that the scheduling of the read-modify-write cannot depend on the choice of random value.

A phase completes when all registers contain symbols from the same phase or the kill symbol. All registers containing the maximum-value, least-frequently-occurring symbol are considered to have survived the phase. If only one register survives (recall that at least one must survive) then the protocol has completed successfully and this register is chosen. Otherwise, if more phases remain the next phase is begun. If this was the last phase then the protocol fails.

As in the deterministic protocols, care must be taken to make sure that all processes, no matter how long they are delayed, make consistent decisions. In particular any processes deciding to go to the next phase must agree on which registers survived the previous phase.

The simplest version of the protocol uses two symbols at each phase. By bounding the number of phases required to, with high probability, successively

**shared** $C$: ring of $k$ registers range over pairs of integers, initially $(0,0)$;
**local** $S$: array $[1..k]$ of pairs of integers;
**local** $i$: integer $\{1...k\}$;                    % pointer into S
**local** *phase*: integer;                           % # of phases
**local** *number*: array$[0..1]$ of $\{0...k\}$;     % number of live registers
**local** *live*: boolean;                            % value of the live register
**local** $p$: pointer which initially points on some *arbitary* register of $C$;
**constant** $H = q + \log \min\{k, n\} + \log \log \min\{k, n\}$; $kill = (-1, -1)$;
**function** RANDOM;                                  % Returns 0 Or 1 at random

$phase := 1$; $number[0] = k$; $live = 0$;
**while** $number[live] \neq 1$ **and** $phase \leq H$ **do**
   % Try to write new value on a live register
   **lock**
      **if** $p\uparrow = (phase - 1, live)$ **then** $p\uparrow := (phase, \text{RANDOM})$;
      $(phase, live) := p\uparrow$; % Note that both *phase* and *live* are set here.
   **unlock**
   $S[1] := (phase, live)$; move $p$ to the next register; $i := 2$;

   % Look for a post-phase configuration
   **while** $(p\uparrow \neq e)$ **and** $(i \neq 1)$ **do**
      **lock**
         **if** $p\uparrow < (phase, -1)$ **then** $p\uparrow := kill$
         **elseif** $p\uparrow \geq (phase + 1, 0)$ **then** $i := 1$;
         $(phase, live) := p\uparrow$;
      **unlock**
      $S[i] := (phase, live)$; move $p$ to the next register;
      **if** $i = k$ **then** $i := 1$ **else** $i := i + 1$;
   **end-while**

   % Compute the number and value of the live registers
   $number[0] = 0$; $number[1] = 0$;
   **for** $i = 1$ **to** $k$ **do**
      **if** $S[i] = (phase, 0)$ **then** $number[0] := number[0] + 1$
      **elseif** $S[i] = (phase, 1)$ **then** $number[1] := number[1] + 1$
   **end-for**
   **if** $number[1] \geq number[0]$ **then** $live = 1$ **else** $live = 0$;

   % Move to a register which contained live when $S$ was read
   **while** $S[i] \neq (phase, live)$ **do**
      move $p$ to the next register;
      **if** $i = k$ **then** $i := 1$ **else** $i := i + 1$;
   **end-while**
   $phase := phase + 1$;
**end-while**
**lock if** $number[live] = 1$ **then** $p\uparrow := e$ **unlock**.

**Fig. 3.** Randomized Solution to the $k$-CCP.

halve the number of surviving registers the upper bound on number of symbols required for the entire protocol given in Theorem 4 is achieved.

The protocol can be fine-tuned by varying the number of symbols used by each phase. For example, in the $k = 2$ case studied by Rabin, the protocol in which processes randomly choose, at each phase, between three symbols to write yields a probability of termination which is slightly greater then the probability in Rabin's protocol. If the registers are known to be arranged on a ring the ideas from Section 3 can increase the termination probability even more.

Using a recent result of Karp[K91] it is possible improve our analysis to show that fewer phases and thus fewer symbols achieves the same success probability. Karp's result on probabilistic recurrence equations shows that $q + \log \min\{k, n\}$ phases suffice.

# 6 Conclusions and Open Questions

We have examined the $k$-CCP under varying assumptions about the structure of the alternatives and about the relative values of the number of alternatives and the number of processes. Our results generalize and extend most of the previously known results to the case where more than two alternatives are available. A major surprise of these extensions is that when more alternatives (and hence more registers) are added the complexity of the problem does not necessarily increase. In fact, in certain cases more alternatives means that fewer symbols are used for each register.

Several variants of the $k$-CCP remain as interesting open questions. Our deterministic protocols are correct even if the initial states of the registers are not known. However, the size of the registers is no longer bounded; can this be improved? When the atomic operations are just reads and writes (rather than read-modify-write) then the presence of even a single crash failure implies that there is no solution to $k$-CCP. What is the effect of using an intermediate strength operations such as test-and-set?[1] It is not difficult to extend our wait-free protocols to create protocols which tolerate up to $t < n - 1$ failures with costs which decrease as $t$ decreases.

# Acknowledgements

The authors would like to thank Sandeep Bhatt, Mike Fischer, Michael Merritt, Nick Reingold, Jeff Westbrook, and Lenore Zuck for helpful discussions.

This work was supported in part by NSF/DARPA grant CCR-8908285, NSF grants CCR-8807426, CCR-8910289, and IRI-9015570, AFOSR grant 89-0382, ONR contract N00014-89-J-1980, DOE contract DE-AC04-76DP00789, a Hebrew Technical Institute scholarship, and an IBM Graduate Fellowship.

---

[1] In the test-and-set operation the read together with the write is atomic but the the value written cannot depend on the value read.

# References

[BBD89] A. Bar-Noy, M. Ben-Or, and D. Dolev. Choice coordination with limited failure. *Distributed Computing*, 3:61–72, 1989.

[Fis83] M. J. Fischer. The consensus problem in unreliable distributed systems (a brief survey). In M. Karpinsky, editor, *Foundations of Computation Theory*, pages 127–140. Lecture Notes in Computer Science, vol. 158, Springer-Verlag, 1983.

[FLP85] M. J. Fischer, N. A. Lynch, and M. S. Paterson. Impossibility of distributed consensus with one faulty process. *Journal of the ACM*, 32(2):374–382, April 1985.

[K91] R. M. Karp. Probabilistic Recurrence Relations. In *Proc. 23rd ACM Symp. on Theory of Computing*, pages 190–197, 1991.

[LA87] C. M. Loui and H. Abu-Amara. Memory requirements for agreement among unreliable asynchronous processes. *Advances in Computing Research*, 4:163–183, 1987.

[Rab82] M. O. Rabin. The choice coordination problem. *Acta Informatica*, 17:121–134, 1982.

# Some Results on the Impossibility, Universality, and Decidability of Consensus*

Prasad Jayanti and Sam Toueg

Department of Computer Science, Cornell University, Ithaca, New York 14853, USA

## 1  Introduction

### 1.1  Background

A *concurrent system* consists of processes communicating via shared objects. Examples of shared object types include data structures such as `register`, `queue`, and `tree`, and synchronization primitives such as `test&set`, and `compare&swap`. Even though different processes may concurrently access a shared object, the object must behave as if all these accesses occur in some sequential order. More precisely, the behavior of a shared object must be *linearizable* [9]. One way to ensure linearizability is to implement shared objects using critical sections [5]. This approach, however, is not fault-tolerant: The crash of a process while in the critical section of a shared object can permanently prevent the rest of the processes from accessing that object. This lack of fault-tolerance led to the concept of *wait-free implementations* of shared objects [11, 16, 7]. Informally, an implementation of a shared object is wait-free if every process can complete every operation on that object in a finite number of its own steps, regardless of the execution speeds of the remaining processes. Thus, a concurrent system in which all implementations of shared objects are wait-free is resilient to process crashes. Most implementations in the literature build complex registers from simpler ones [1, 2, 3, 10, 12, 14, 16, 15, 18, 19, 20, 21], while the others are related to consensus objects [13, 4].

The bigger picture emerged when Herlihy discovered a close connection between wait-free implementations and objects of a particular type called `consensus`[1]. In [7], he presented a "universal" construction that transforms the sequential implementation of an object into a wait-free concurrent implementation using only consensus objects and registers. He also showed that analysing primitives in terms of their ability to implement consensus objects helps order primitives

---

* Research supported by NSF grants CCR-8901780 and CCR-9102231, DARPA/NASA Ames grant NAG-2-593, grants from the IBM Endicott Programming Laboratory and Siemens Corp.

[1] A consensus object supports two operations, *propose 0* and *propose 1*, and satisfies the following two properties. An operation gets a response *v* only if there is some prior invocation of *propose v*. Further, the response is the same for all invocations of both operations.

according to their "strength". For instance, his results help conclude that compare&swap is a strictly stronger primitive than test&set. In summary, his research brought forth several interesting theoretical issues, and we study some of these in this paper.

## 1.2 Results

- We pose and answer the fundamental question: Given (the specification of) an object $\mathcal{O}$, and a set $\mathcal{S}$ of objects, does $\mathcal{O}$ have a wait-free implementation from objects in $\mathcal{S}$? We show that this question is undecidable.
- Herlihy showed that the problem of consensus is irreducible in the following sense: It is impossible to achieve consensus among $2n$ processes by combining protocols that solve consensus among $2m$ processes $(m < n)$ [9]. We strengthen this result: It is impossible to achieve consensus among $n$ processes by combining protocols that solve consensus among $m$ processes $(m < n)$.
- We study how initialization of shared objects affects their ability to solve consensus. In particular, although a queue or a stack can solve *name-consensus* between two processes, we prove that an *initially empty* queue or stack cannot. However, with a tiny extra resource such as a 1-bit safe register, an empty queue or stack suffices to solve consensus.
- We study (in a limited sense) the relative capabilities of queues and stacks. We show that the problems, consensus and *repeated name-consensus*, are solvable using a single queue, but not a single stack. Along the same lines, we show that a single queue can implement a 1-reader, 1-writer, multi-valued atomic register, but a single bounded stack cannot implement even a (1-reader, 1-writer) 3-valued regular register!
- Universal constructions to realize wait-free implementations of arbitrary objects from consensus objects and registers are due to Herlihy [8, 9], and Plotkin [18]. Of these, the construction in [9] is intuitive and simple. But it requires unbounded registers. In contrast, bounded registers suffice for Plotkin's construction, but the construction (we believe) is complicated to understand. We show that a small modification turns Herlihy's construction into a bounded construction, but preserves the original simplicity.

## 2  Preliminaries

A *concurrent system* consists of processes and (shared) objects. A process interacts with an object by invoking an operation, and receiving a corresponding response from the object. Processes may exhibit arbitrary variations in their execution speeds.

An object is specified by a *type*. An object type $T$ is defined by the set of operations supported by an object $\mathcal{O}$ of type $T$, and the *sequential specification* that specifies how $\mathcal{O}$ behaves when these operations are applied sequentially. For instance, the sequential specification of a stack specifies that a *pop* must return the latest item *pushed* into the stack object. In a concurrent system, operations from different processes may overlap on an object. The sequential specification is therefore not sufficient to understand the behavior of an object. *Linearizability* defined by Herlihy and Wing [10] is a widely accepted criterion for the correctness of a shared object. Informally, linearizability requires every operation execution to appear to take effect instantaneously at some point in time between its invocation and response.

Let $T$ be an object type and let $\mathcal{L} = (T_1, T_2, \ldots, T_n)$ be a list of object types. An *implementation* of $T$ from $\mathcal{L}$ is a function $\mathcal{I}$ such that given any distinct objects $O_1, O_2, \ldots, O_n$ of type $T_1, T_2, \ldots, T_n$, respectively, $\mathcal{O} = \mathcal{I}(O_1, O_2, \ldots, O_n)$ is an object of type $T$. We call $\mathcal{O}$ a *derived object (of $\mathcal{I}$)* and $o_i$'s the *base objects* of $\mathcal{O}$. Such an implementation provides a procedure $\mathtt{Apply}(p_i, op, \mathcal{O})$ (for each operation $op$ of $T$) that process $p_i$ must execute in order to invoke an operation $op$ on $\mathcal{O}$ and receive the corresponding response from $\mathcal{O}$. A *step* in $\mathtt{Apply}(p_i, op, \mathcal{O})$ corresponds to invoking an operation on a base object and receiving the corresponding response, or some local computation. The *implementation is wait-free* if $\mathtt{Apply}(p_i, op, \mathcal{O})$ returns a response in a finite number of steps, regardless of the execution speeds of the remaining processes. The implementation is *bounded wait-free* if the number of steps is not only finite, but also bounded.

## 3   Decidability

Given an object type $T$, and a list $\mathcal{L}$ of object types, can we determine whether $T$ has a wait-free implementation from $\mathcal{L}$? We show that even the restriction of this question corresponding to $\mathcal{L}$ containing only **register** is undecidable. The proof is by an easy reduction of the halting problem for Turing machines to the above problem.

Given a Turing machine $M$, let $T(M)$ represent an object type that supports a single operation $op$ and has the sequential specification given in Fig. 1.

**Claim 1.** *If a Turing machine $M$ does not halt on blank tape, $T(M)$ has a wait-free implementation from* **register***.*

*Proof.* If $M$ does not halt, an object $O$ of type $T(M)$ returns the response 0 to every invocation of $op$. So the trivial implementation which always returns 0 is correct and wait-free.    □

**Claim 2.** *If a Turing machine $M$ halts on blank tape, $T(M)$ has no wait-free implementation from* **register***.*

*Proof.* If $M$ halts, we show that an object $O$ of type $T(M)$ can be used to solve name-consensus[2] between two processes $P_0$ and $P_1$ as follows. A process

---

[2] The *name-consensus* problem requires processes to agree on the name of some process $P$ such that $P$ has taken at least one step of the protocol. Further, each process is required to reach its decision in a finite number of steps.

Object state

$flag$ : boolean initialized to $false$
$TM$ : configuration of the Turing machine,
        initialized to the initial configuration of $M$ (on a blank tape)

Apply($op$)
    if $TM$ is in halting state then
        if $flag$ then
            return(2)
        else
                $flag := true$
                return(1)
    else
        Advance $TM$ by a single move
        return(0)
end-Apply

Fig. 1. Sequential specification of $T(M)$

---

$P_i$ applies $op$ on $O$ repeatedly until it gets either a 1 or a 2 as response. Since $M$ halts, $P_i$ is guaranteed to get such a response in a finite number of steps. If $P_i$ gets 1, it decides itself and quits. If $P_i$ gets 2, it decides $P_{\bar{i}}$ and quits. It is easy to verify that this protocol correctly solves name-consensus between $P_0$ and $P_1$.

It is well known that no object that solves name-consensus has a wait-free implementation from registers[14, 4, 8]. Hence the claim.          □

**Theorem 3.** *It is undecidable whether a given object type has a wait-free implementation from* register.

# 4  Irreducibility of Consensus

The *consensus problem* among $N$ processes is defined as follows. Each process $P_i$ is given a binary input $v_i$ initially. The consensus problem requires each correct process to eventually reach the *same* (irrevocable) decision value $d$ ("agreement") such that $d \in \{v_1, v_2, \ldots, v_N\}$ ("validity"). Further each process is required to decide in a finite number of its own steps ("wait-freedom").

Herlihy showed that $m$-register assignment can solve the consensus among $2m - 2$ processes, but not among $2m - 1$ processes [9]. From this he concluded that *when n is odd*, it is impossible to achieve consensus among $n$ processes by combining consensus protocols for $m$ processes, $m < n$. In this section, we exhibit for *every* $n$ there is an object that can be used to solve consensus among $n$ processes, but not among $n + 1$ processes. This leads to a strictly stronger conclusion than Herlihy's as it removes the constraint "when $n$ is odd" from the above statement.

Consider the object type **n-bounded peek queue** that supports **enq** and **peek**, and has the following sequential specification: When **enq**(*item*) is invoked, if the queue has fewer than $n$ items in it, then *item* will be enqued, and the response "completed" is returned; otherwise, the queue enters into a faulty state and returns $\perp$. A queue that is in a faulty state remains faulty forever, and returns $\perp$ to every subsequent invocation of every operation. **peek** returns the state of the queue: $\perp$ if the queue is faulty, and the list of enqued items (in the correct order) otherwise.

**Claim 4.** *The consensus problem among $n$ processes has a solution using a single $n$-bounded peek queue $Q$.*

*Proof.* Initialize $Q$ to contain no elements. Each process $P_i$ inserts $v_i$, its input value, into $Q$ by executing **enq**($v_i, Q$). Then $P_i$ invokes **peek**($Q$), and decides on the value at the front of $Q$. $\quad\square$

**Claim 5.** *The consensus problem among $n + 1$ processes has no solution using any number of $n$-bounded peek queue objects and registers.*

*Proof.* For a contradiction, assume there is a protocol. The proof is by the standard bivalency argument [6]. A system state is *bivalent* if either decision value (0 or 1) is still possible. Let $P$ and $Q$ be two processes with inputs 0 and 1 respectively. Then the initial system state is bivalent: When $P$ runs by itself from the initial state, then due to wait-freedom, it eventually decides, and by validity, it decides 0; Similarly, $Q$ running by itself results in $Q$ deciding 1.

Starting from the above bivalent initial state, schedule processes in the system such that system state progresses from one bivalent state to another. This cannot be done ad infinidum as that would contradict the assumption that the protocol is wait-free. Thus there is a (reachable) bivalent system state $S$ such that whichever process $P_i$ $(1 \leq i \leq n + 1)$ takes a step $s_i$, the resulting system state $S_i$ is univalent. Since $S$ is bivalent, there must be two processes $P_j$ and $P_k$ such that $S_j$ is 0-valent and $S_k$ is 1-valent. Let $P_{i_1}, P_{i_2}, \ldots, P_{i_{n-1}}$ be the remaining $n - 1$ processes.

By standard arguments, we show that the enabled step $s_i$ of every process $P_i$ in system state $S$ is on the same shared object $O$, that $O$ is an $n$-bounded peek queue and not a register, and that every enabled step in $S$ is an **enq** on $O$ and not a **peek**.

Given the above, let $S'$ be the system state that results when processes are scheduled (starting from $S$) in the order given by $P_j, P_k, P_{i_1}, P_{i_2}, \ldots, P_{i_{n-1}}$. Also let $S''$ be the system state that results when processes are scheduled (starting from $S$) in the order given by $P_k, P_j, P_{i_1}, P_{i_2}, \ldots, P_{i_{n-1}}$. Clearly object $O$ is in a faulty state in both $S'$ and $S''$. Thus every process and object is in the same state in $S'$ and $S''$. Therefore no process can ever distinguish $S'$ from $S''$. Yet $S'$ is 0-valent, and $S''$ is 1-valent, which is impossible. $\quad\square$

The above claim holds even if the object type is strengthened to also support the deq operation with the obvious semantics.

# 5  Initialization and Consensus

In this section, we show that the solvability of consensus is sometimes sensitive to the initial state of the underlying shared objects.

Herlihy showed that a single queue or a stack suffices to solve the name-consensus problem among 2 processes [8]. We show that when the initial state of the queue or stack is restricted to be empty, neither can solve name-consensus. We also show that with a tiny additional resource of a single (1-reader, 1-writer) safe bit, an initially empty stack/queue solves name-consensus (between 2 processes). Finally we exhibit some objects whose ability to solve consensus does not depend on their initial state.

To show that a single initially empty queue does not suffice to solve the name-consensus problem among two processes, we need some definitions and a lemma. A sequence $S$ is a *+/- sequence* if each element in $S$ is either a "+" or a "-". $S$ is *positive* if in *every* prefix of $S$, there are strictly more "+"s than "-"s. If $e$, $e'$ are elements of $S$, we say $e$ *consumes* $e'$ if $e$ is a "-", $e'$ is a "+", and if $e$ is the $k^{th}$ "-" of $S$, then $e'$ is the $k^{th}$ "+" of $S$. Thus every "-" of $S$ consumes the earliest unconsumed "+" of $S$. We say $S$ is colored with (a color) $C$ if each element of $S$ is colored $C$.

Given two finite positive +/- sequences $R$ and $G$ colored red and green respectively, a *hiding sequence of $R$, $G$* is any interleaved sequence $S$ of $R$ and $G$ with the property that every "-" in $S$ consumes a "+" in $S$ of the same color.

**Lemma 6.** *Given two finite positive +/- sequences $R$ and $G$ colored red and green respectively, there is a hiding sequence of $R$ and $G$.*

*Proof.* By induction on $|G|$. The base case when $|G| = 0$ (*i.e.*, $G$ is an empty sequence) is obvious. Now we show the induction step. Write $R$ as $R_1 \circ R_2$, where $R_1$ is the prefix up to the $k^{th}$ "+" of $R$, $k$ being the number of "-"s in $R$. Similarly write $G$ as $G_1 \circ G_2$. From the definitions, it is obvious that $|R_1| < |R|$, $|G_1| < |G|$, and $R_1, G_1$ are positive +/- sequences. From the induction hypothesis, there is a hiding sequence $S_1$ of $R_1$ and $G_1$. Note that there will be exactly as many unconsumed "+"s in $S_1$ as there are "-"s in $R_2$ and $G_2$ put together. It should be obvious that $R_2$ and $G_2$ can be interleaved into $S_2$ such that an unconsumed "+" in $S_1$ is consumed by a "-" in $S_2$ of the same color. Thus $S_1 \circ S_2$ is a hiding sequence of $R$ and $G$. □

**Theorem 7.** *There is no protocol that solves name-consensus among two processes using a single initially empty queue.*

*Proof.* For a contradiction, assume there is such a protocol $\mathcal{P}$ for two processes $p$ and $q$. Let $S_p = s_1, s_2, \ldots, s_k$ be the sequence of all steps executed by $p$ when it runs all by itself from the initial system state. At the end of the run $S_p$, $p$

decides itself. Similarly, let $S_q = t_1, t_2, \ldots, t_l$ be the sequence of steps executed by $q$ before it decides itself when running all by itself from the initial system state. Clearly each step $s_i$ and $t_j$ is either an **enq** or a **deq**. Interpreting the **enq** as a "+", and the **deq** as a "-", let $S_p'$ be the *maximal* prefix of $S_p$ such that every **enq** in $S_p'$ is consumed by some **deq** in $S_p'$. Let $S_p = S_p' \circ S_p''$. Define $S_q'$ and $S_q''$ similarly. It is easy to see that $S_p''$ and $S_q''$ are both positive +/- sequences, and thus (by the previous lemma) have a hiding sequence $S''$. It is easy to verify that $S_p' \circ S_q' \circ S''$ is a valid run from the initial state in which $p$ decides $p$, and $q$ decides $q$. This contradicts that $\mathcal{P}$ is a name-consensus protocol.    □

The following theorem has a proof similar to that of Theorem 11, and is omitted.

**Theorem 8.** *There is no protocol that solves name-consensus among two processes using a single initially empty stack.*

**Theorem 9.** *Figure 2 gives a name-consensus protocol for processes $p$ and $q$ using only a single initially empty stack and a 1-bit (1-reader, 1-writer) safe register.*

---

$S$ : shared stack (initially empty)
$R$ : 1-bit safe register (initially contains 0)


Procedure **name-consensus**($p$)
```
1       push(S, "P won")
2       val := R
3       if (val = 1) then
4           if pop(S) = nil then
5                decide(p)
6           else decide(q)
7       else decide(p)
end-Procedure
```


Procedure **name-consensus**($q$)
```
8       R := 1
9       if (pop(S) = nil) then
10          decide(q)
11      else decide(p)
end-Procedure
```


**Fig. 2.** Name-consensus protocol from an empty stack and a 1-bit register

---

In fact, the protocol in Fig. 2 works correctly even for an empty queue: just change **push** to **enq** and **pop** to **deq**. Also instead of the register $R$, an empty stack $S'$ or an empty queue can be used: replace "val := $R$" (Line 2) by "val := pop($S'$)", and replace "R := 1" (Line 8) by "push($S'$,1)".

Finally we point out that there are objects whose ability to solve consensus does not depend on their initial state. For instance, **fetch&add** can solve consensus among 2 processes, and **read-modify-write**, **compare&swap** can solve consensus among $n$ processes, no matter how they are initialized. Of course, we require that the initial state be "common knowledge" to all processes.

# 6 Queue vs. Stack

In this section we present three problems, each of which can be solved using a single queue, but not a single stack.

## 6.1 Consensus

**Theorem 10.** *The protocol in Fig. 3 solves the consensus problem among 2 processes using a single queue.*

---

$Q$ : shared queue
Initialize $Q$ to contain two elements: *winner, loser*
/* *winner* is at the head of $Q$ */

Procedure consensus($P_i, v_i$) /* $v_i$ is the input value of $P_i$ */
    enq([$P_i, v_i$], $Q$)
    if deq($Q$) = *winner* then
        decide($v_i$)
    else
        Apply deq (once or twice) until [$P_{\bar{i}}, v_{\bar{i}}$] is returned
        decide($v_{\bar{i}}$)
end-Procedure

**Fig. 3.** Consensus protocol using a single queue

---

**Theorem 11.** *There is no protocol to solve 2 process consensus using a single stack, no matter what the initial state of the stack is.*

*Proof.* Suppose, for a contradiction, there is a protocol $\mathcal{P}$ for consensus among $p$ and $q$ using a single stack, initialized to a sequence $\alpha_{init} = a_1, a_2, \ldots, a_t$ of items (where $a_t$ is at the top of the stack).

Let $R_i$ be the sequence of steps of $p$ when $p$'s input value is $i$ ($i \in \{0, 1\}$) and $p$ runs all by itself (from the initial system state) to completion. Let $\alpha_i$ be the contents of the stack at the end of the run $R_i$ from the initial state. Let $\beta_i$ be the maximal common prefix of $\alpha_{init}$ and $\alpha_i$. Without loss of generality, let $\beta_0$ be the bigger of $\beta_0$ and $\beta_1$. From the above definitions, the following facts can be easily deduced:

1. Let $R_0'$ be the maximal prefix of $R_0$ such that the stack holds $\beta_0$ at the end of the run $R_0'$ of $p$. Thus $R_0 = R_0' \circ R_0''$ for some $R_0''$. It is easy to see that every prefix of $R_0''$ has at least as many *push* steps as *pop* steps.
2. $R_1$ can be split into $R_1'$ and $R_1''$ such that $R_1 = R_1' \circ R_1''$ and starting from the initial system state, at the end of the run $R_1'$ of $p$, the contents of the stack are $\beta_0$.

Now consider the following scenario.

**Scenario S1**

1. Process $p$'s input value is 0. And $p$ executes the steps in $R_0'$ and temporarily stops.
2. Process $q$'s input value is 1. And $q$ executes to termination, deciding some value $v_q$. (This termination of $q$'s execution is guaranteed by the wait-freedom of the protocol $\mathcal{P}$).
3. Process $p$ resumes and executes to termination, deciding $v_p$.

We claim that $v_p = 0$ in the above scenario. This is because when $p$ resumes in item 3, it executes steps in $R_0''$, and since every prefix of $R_0''$ has as many *push* steps as *pop* steps, process $p$ never realizes that $q$ took any steps at all. In other words, the run in S1 is indistinguishable to $p$ from the run $R_0$. Thus $p$ decides 0 in S1 as in $R_0$. Due to the agreement property of consensus, it follows that $v_q = v_p = 0$ in S1.

Now consider another possible scenario S2.

**Scenario S2** (starts from initial system state)

1. The input value of $p$ is 1, and $p$ executes the steps in $R_1'$ and temporarily halts.
2. Process $q$'s input value is also 1, and $q$ executes to completion, deciding some value, $v_q$.
3. $p$ resumes and completes its execution, deciding some value $v_p$

Note that Scenarios S1 and S2 are indistinguishable to $q$. Thus $q$ decides 0 in S2 as in S1. Note however that neither process proposed 0 in S2. This contradicts that $\mathcal{P}$ is a consensus protocol. $\quad\square$

## 6.2 Repeated Name-Consensus

In this problem, a process $p$ executes **name-consensus**$(p, i)$ to learn the outcome of the $i^{th}$ contest of the name-consensus. We require: (for all $p, q, i$), (1) **name-consensus**$(p, i)$ and **name-consensus**$(q, i)$ return the same value; (2)

name-consensus$(p, i)$ returns $q$ only if $q$ has already executed at least one step of name-consensus$(q, i)$; (3) Process $p$ invokes name-consensus$(p, i + 1)$ only after completing name-consensus$(p, i)$.

The (single) name-consensus protocol for two processes using a queue was given in [8]. The idea is to initialize the queue to two items, *winner* and *loser* (*winner* at the head). The process that deques *winner* is the winner of name-consensus. We adopt the same basic idea to solve repeated name-consensus.

Before performing the round $k$ of repeated name-consensus, a process inserts items that will be useful to perform round $k + 1$ later. However, if each process inserts items for round $k + 1$, the question arises as to which of them must actually be used. We made up a simple rule: For round $k + 1$, use the items inserted by the process that won round $k$. Thus items are of the form $[p, k]$ where $p$ is the name of the process that inserted the item in the queue, and $k$ is the round number of the consensus it is intended for. A process wins round $k$ only if it deques 2 (out of the 3) items with round number $k$ that were inserted by the winner of round $k - 1$.

A process maintains three persistent local variables: $round_p$ is $p$'s knowledge of the number of rounds the outcomes are already known for; $prev\text{-}winner_p$ is the name of the process winning $round_p$; $Seen_p$ is the set of all items $p$ has so far removed from the queue[3]. The algorithm appears in Fig. 4.

**Theorem 12.** *Figure 4 gives a repeated name-consensus protocol for processes $p$ and $q$ using a single queue.*

In contrast, we can show the following impossibility result for a stack. The proof is similar in spirit to the proof of Theorem 11, and is omitted.

**Theorem 13.** *There is no protocol that solves repeated name-consensus for two processes using a single stack.*

However we can show that using four stacks, repeated name-consensus for two processes can be solved.

## 6.3 Atomic Register

**Theorem 14.** *Figure 5 gives an implementation of a (1-reader, 1-writer) $N$-valued atomic register using a single queue $Q$. $Q$ will never contain more than two items, and each item is of size $N$.*

We state the following theorem omitting the proof.

**Theorem 15.** *The following are true:*

1. *A single bounded stack implements a (1-reader, 1-writer) $N$-valued safe register.*

---

[3] We don't need to maintain this set. We do so for ease of writing the algorithm.

$Q$ : shared queue (initialized to 3 identical items where each item is $[p, 1]$)
$round_p$, $prev\text{-}winner_p$, $Seen_p$: local persistent variables of $p$
(initialized to 0, $p$, $\emptyset$ respectively)
$round_q$, $prev\text{-}winner_q$, $Seen_q$: local persistent variables of $q$
(initialized to 0, $p$, $\emptyset$ respectively)

```
Procedure name-consensus(p, k)
    if k ≤ round_p then
        return(q)
        exit Procedure
    /* insert 3 identical items for potential use in round k + 1 */
    for i := 1 to 3 do
        enq([p, k + 1], Q)
    repeat
        v := deq(Q)
        Seen_p := Seen_p ∪ {v}
    until either (Seen_p has two copies of [prev-winner_p,k]) or (Seen_p has [*, l] and l > k)
    In the former case, do
        prev-winner_p := p
        round := k
        return(p)
        exit Procedure
    In the latter case, do
        prev-winner_p := q
        round_p := l - 1
        return(q)
        exit Procedure
end-Procedure
```

**Fig. 4.** Repeated name-consensus using a queue

2. *A single bounded stack implements a (1-reader, 1-writer) boolean atomic register.*

3. *A single stack cannot implement a 3-valued (1-reader, 1-writer) regular register if the number of items in the stack cannot grow unbounded.*

4. *If stack can have an unbounded number of items, then it can implement a (1-reader, 1-writer) N-valued atomic register.*

## 7 A Simple and Bounded Universal Construction

An object type $T$ is *universal* for a set $S$ of object types if every $T' \in S$ can be implemented from $(T, \text{register})$. Herlihy showed that **consensus** is universal for any object type that has a sequential specification [8, 9]. Herlihy's construction is intuitive, but requires unbounded registers. We make a simple modification

Q: shared queue
Initialize Q to contain an item $v$ where $v$ is initial value of register
*prev-read*: local persistent variable of the reader
*prev-written*: local persistent variable of the writer

| Read() | Write(v) |
|---|---|
| $v := \text{deq}(Q)$ | if $v \neq$ *prev-written* then |
| if $v = nil$ then | $\text{enq}(v, Q)$ |
| return(*prev-read*) | $w := \text{deq}(Q)$ |
| else *prev-read* $:= v$ | if $w = v$ then |
| return($v$) | $\text{enq}(v, Q)$ |

**Fig. 5.** Implementing an atomic register using a queue

to his construction to achieve the same result using only bounded registers. In the following, we assume that the reader knows Herlihy's construction, and its proof [9]. The discussion and the claims below also use the terminology in [9].

We first turn Herlihy's construction without memory management into an equivalent construction (without memory management). We then explain how the memory management works on top of this modified construction.

In Herlihy's construction, the field **seq** serves two purposes: First, in Statement 6 in [9], it helps all processes to determine the unique identity of the process that must be "helped" in a given slot of the list. This is crucial to achieving wait-freedom (rather than just "non-blocking"). Second, in Statement 3, it helps a process $P$ to move "close" to the head of the list after $P$ has announced its operation. This is crucial to achieving *bounded* wait-freedom (as opposed to finite wait-freedom). The first purpose is served just as well even if **seq** is bounded in the range $[0 \ldots n]$. The second purpose, however, will no longer be served since the correctness of Statement 3 depends on the monotonic rise of the sequence numbers. We fix this by adding an extra field, a boolean **flag**, to each cell. The idea is to maintain **flag** = *true* for the head of the list, and **flag** = *false* for the remaining cells, and thus locate the head of the list without depending on a total order on the sequence numbers.

Initially, the object is represented by a unique *anchor* cell with **seq** = 1, **flag** = *true*, a creation operation, and an initial state. All other cells hold **flag** = *false*. For all $P$, announce[$P$] and head[$P$] hold the pointer to the anchor cell.

The modified construction (without memory management) is shown in Fig. 6. Statement 3 of Herlihy's construction has been replaced with a new Statement 3. Statements 1e, 5a, and 13a have been added. The **seq** field is still assumed to be unbounded.

The following claim is identical to Lemma 1 in [9].

**Claim 16.** *The following assertion is invariant:* $|concur(P)| > n \Rightarrow$ announce[$P$] $\in$

UNIVERSAL (what: INVOC) returns (RESULT)
mine : *cell :=

```
1a          [seq : 0
1b           invoc : what
1c           new : creat(consensus object)
1d           after : creat(consensus object)
1e           before : null
1f *         flag : true]
```

2        ⟨ announce[P] := mine; start(P) := max(head); concur(P) := ∅ ⟩
3a *     repeat
             ptr := Find-Head()
         until (ptr ≠ null) ∨ (announce[P].seq ≠ 0)
3b       if (announce[P].seq= 0) then
             ⟨ head[P] := ptr; head := head ∪ {ptr}; ∀Q : concur(Q) := concur(Q) ∪ {ptr} ⟩
4        while (announce[P].seq= 0) do
5            c : *cell := head[P]
5a *         (c.before).flag := false
6            help : *cell := announce[c.seq modn + 1]
7            if help.seq= 0 then
                 prefer := help
             else prefer := announce[P]
8            d := decide(c.after,prefer)
9            decide(d.new, Apply(d.invoc,c.new.state))
10           d.before := c
11           d.seq := c.seq+1
12           ⟨ head[P] := d; head := head ∪ {d}; ∀Q : concur(Q) := concur(Q) ∪ {d} ⟩
13       head[P] := announce[P]
13a *    head[P].before.flag := false
14       return(announce[P].new.result)
```

**Fig. 6.** Modified universal construction

---

*head.*

When a process accesses a cell $d$ (*i.e.*, $d$ is the pointer to the cell) in the list, it sets ($d$.before.flag) to *false* (Statements 5a, 13a). Also notice that if a cell $c \notin head$, then either $c$.flag = *false* or (because of the order in which seq and flag are initialized) $c$.seq = 0. Putting these elements together, the following can be shown. Define a predicate $\mathcal{P}(c)$ on cell $c$ as: $\mathcal{P}(c) \equiv c$.flag $\wedge$ $c$.seq $\neq 0$.

**Claim 17.** *For every cell $c$ in the system, the invariant $\mathcal{I}(c)$ holds: $\mathcal{I}(c) \equiv (c = max(head) \wedge \mathcal{P}(c)) \vee (c = max(head)$.before$) \vee (c \in head \wedge \neg c$.flag$) \vee (c \notin head \wedge \neg\mathcal{P}(c))$.*
```

```
Procedure Find-Head()
    ptr := null
    for Q := 1 to n do
        temp := head[Q]
        if (temp.flag) then
            if (temp.seq ≠ 0) then
                ptr := temp
    end-for
    return(ptr)
end-procedure
```

**Fig. 7.** The Find-Head procedure

We use $M$ to denote a snapshot of the system[4]. We write $[\ ]_M$ to denote the value of the expression enclosed in the square brackets evaluated in the snapshot $M$. If $M$ and $M'$ are snapshots, $M' \geq M$ denotes that $M'$ is taken no earlier than $M$.

The following claims are phrased so that they will remain true even after the memory management details are imposed. The order in which seq and flag are initialized, and the order in which the conditions are evaluated in the procedure Find-Head() (Fig. 7) are crucial to the correctness of these claims.

Let $M, M'$ denote snapshots just before and after the execution of Find-Head() by process $P$. Let $m = [max(head)]_M$, $s = [max(head)]_M.seq$, and $m' = [max(head)]_{M'}$, $s' = [max(head)]_{M'}.seq$.

**Claim 18.** $s = s'$ implies Find-Head() returns $p$ such that $[p.seq]'_M = s + 1$ or $s$ or $s - 1$.

**Claim 19.** Suppose Find-Head() returns $p \neq null$. Then $[p.seq]'_M \geq s - 1$ or announce$[P].seq \neq 0$.

Following is an easy consequence of the above two claims.

**Claim 20.**

- The repeat ... until loop (Statement 3a) terminates in at most $n+1$ iterations.
- The following holds just before Statement 4: (start$(P).seq-1 \leq$ head$[P].seq \leq max(head).seq) \vee ($announce$[P].seq \neq 0)$.

The above claim is the analog of Lemma 4 in [9]. Using Claims 16 and 20, and proceeding exactly as in [9], we have

**Theorem 21.** The protocol in Fig. 6 is correct and bounded wait-free.

[4] Our construction does not take snapshots. We only use them for convenience in the proofs.

## 7.1 Memory Management

We adopt the same idea as in [9]. A process executing an operation traverses no more than $n + 2$ cells[5]. When a process is finished threading its cell, it releases each of the $n + 2$ preceding cells by setting a *release* bit: It sets the $i^{th}$ release bit in a cell that is $i$ hops away from itself. A cell may be claimed and reused by its owner process if all the $n + 2$ release bits of the cell are set. Just before reinitializing a reclaimed cell, the owner resets all the release bits.

In addition to the above, the following Statement (13b) needs to be added to the basic construction[6].

13b        announce[P] := *anchor*

While process $P$ is allocating a cell, there could be a maximum of $n - 1$ outstanding operations. Each cell corresponding to such an incomplete operation could prevent the reclamation of a maximum of $n + 2$ cells. In addition, there could be a maximum of $n + 2$ cells (each corresponding to a completed operation of $P$) locked up in the list, because there are not enough cells following them to have all their release bits set[7]. Thus the maximum number of cells that $P$ will be prevented from reclaiming is $n(n + 2)$. Thus if each process has a private pool of $n(n + 2) + 1 = (n + 1)^2$ cells, allocating a new cell for $P$'s operation will always be possible. Our requirement of $(n + 1)^2$ cells per process is $n$ more than the $(n^2 + n + 1)$ cells per process of [9]. However we can match that number with a slightly more complex algorithm for Find-Head() (not shown here).

Proceeding exactly as in [9], our construction with the above memory management, can be proved correct.

We have so far assumed that the field **seq** in a cell is an unbounded register. While it facilitates the proof, our construction does not make use of its unboundedness *anywhere*. Well, this was the whole purpose of our construction! So we make it a bounded variable in the range $[0 \ldots n]$, and change Statement 11 to "d.**seq** := c.**seq** $mod\, n + 1$". It is trivial to verify that this change does not alter correctness.

### Acknowledgement

We thank Tushar Deepak Chandra for his help with some results in Sect. 6.2 and 6.3.

## References

1. Bard Bloom. Constructing two writer atomic registers. In *The 6th Annual Symposium on Principles of Distributed Computing*, pages 249–259, 1987.

---

[5] As opposed to $n + 1$ in [9]. This difference is due to the difference between Lemma 4 of Herlihy's and Claim 20 of ours.

[6] Statement 13b or some alternative fix is needed for correctness even in Herlihy's construction, although this detail was not mentioned in [9].

[7] This point was overlooked in [9] in the counting.

2. J. Burns and G. Peterson. Constructing multi-reader atomic values from non-atomic values. In *The 6th Annual Symposium on Principles of Distributed Computing*, pages 222–231, 1987.

3. Soma Chaudhuri and Jennifer Welch. Bounds on the costs of register implementations. Technical report, University of North Carolina at Chapel Hill, Dept. of Computer Science, Univ. of North Carolina at Chapel Hill, Chapel Hill, NC 27599-3175, 1990.

4. B. Chor, A. Israeli, and M. Li. On processor coordination using asynchronous hardware. In *The 6th ACM Symposium on Principles of Distributed Computing*, pages 86–97, August 1987.

5. P.J. Courtois, F. Heymans, and D.L. Parnas. Concurrent control with readers and writers. *Communications of the ACM*, 14(10):667–668, 1971.

6. Michael Fischer, Nancy Lynch, and Michael Paterson. Impossibility of distributed consensus with one faulty process. *JACM*, 32(2):374–382, 1985.

7. M.P. Herlihy. Impossibility and universality results for wait-free synchroniz ation. In *The 7th ACM Symposium on Principles of Distributed Computi ng*, 1988.

8. M.P. Herlihy. Wait-free synchronization. *ACM TOPLAS*, 13(1):124–149, 1991.

9. M.P. Herlihy and J.M. Wing. Linearizability: A correctness condition for concurrent objects. *ACM TOPLAS*, 12(3):463–492, 1990.

10. Prasad Jayanti, Adarshpal Sethi, and Errol Lloyd. Minimal shared information for concurrent reading and writing. In *Workshop on Distributed Algorithms, Delphi, Greece*, October 1991. (Will appear in Lecture Notes in Computer Science, Springer-Verlag).

11. Leslie Lamport. Concurrent reading and writing. *Communications of the ACM*, 20(11):806–811, 1977.

12. Leslie Lamport. On interprocess communication, parts i and ii. *Distributed Computing*, 1:77–101, 1986.

13. M.C. Loui and Abu-Amara. Memory requirements for agreement among unreliable asynchronous processes. *Advances in computing research*, 4:163–183, 1987.

14. R. Newman-Wolf. A protocol for wait-free, atomic, multi-reader shared variables. In *The 6th Annual Symposium on Principles of Distributed Computing*, pages 232–248, 1987.

15. G. Peterson and J. Burns. Concurrent reading while writing ii: the multi-writer case. In *The 28th Annual Symposium on Foundations of Computer Science*, 1987.

16. Gary L. Peterson. Concurrent reading while writing. *ACM TOPLAS*, 5(1):56–65, 1983.

17. Serge Plotkin. Sticky bits and universality of consensus. In *The 8th ACM Symposium on Principles of Distributed Computing*, pages 159–175, August 1989.

18. R. Schaffer. On the correctness of atomic multi-writer registers. Technical report, TR No: MIT/LCS/TM-364, MIT Laboratory for Computer Science, 1988.

19. A. Singh, J. Anderson, and M. Gouda. The elusive atomic register, revisited. In *The 6th Annual Symposium on Principles of Distributed Computing*, pages 206–221, 1987.

20. K. Vidyasankar. An elegant 1-writer multireader multivalued atomic register. *IPL*, 30:221–223, 1989.

21. P. Vitanyi and B. Awerbuch. Atomic shared register access by asynchronous hardware. In *The 27th Annual Symposium on Foundations of Computer Science*, 1986.

# Wait-free Test-and-Set

## (Extended Abstract)

Yehuda Afek[1,4], Eli Gafni[2]*, John Tromp[3], and Paul M.B. Vitanyi[3,5]

[1] Computer Science Department, Tel-Aviv University, Ramat-Aviv 69978 Israel.
[2] Department of Computer Science, University of California, Los Angeles CA 90024.
[3] Centrum voor Wiskunde en Informatica, Kruislaan 413, 1098 SJ Amsterdam, The Netherlands.
[4] AT&T Bell Laboratories, 600 Mountain Avenue, Murray Hill, NJ 07974.
[5] Faculteit Wiskunde en Informatica, Universiteit van Amsterdam.

**Abstract.** This paper presents an economical, randomized, wait-free construction of an $n$-process *test-and-set* bit from read write registers. The test-and-set shared object has two atomic operations, **test&set**, which atomically reads the bit and sets its value to 1, and the **reset** operation that resets the bit to 0.

We identify two new complexity measures by which to evaluate wait-free algorithms: (a) The amount of randomness used, and (b) 'Parallel-Time'—the maximum sequential depth of an execution (i.e. longest chain of operations that must precede each other).

The previously best known algorithm for $n$-process test-and-set [Her91] takes an expected $\Omega(n^2)$ parallel time, and $\Omega(n^4)$ sequential time per operation, and $\Omega(n^2 \log n)$ space per processor. In contrast, our direct implementation improves this on all counts by using $O(\log n)$ coin flips, $O(\log n)$ parallel time, $O(n)$ sequential time, per operation, and $O(n)$ space per processor. Thus the question on the difference in the expected complexity of randomized constructions of concurrent objects from read/write registers is raised.

## 1 Introduction

A recent watershed paper by Herlihy [Her88] established the existence of a hierarchy of wait-free concurrent objects. The hierarchy classifies objects according to the number of processes among which these objects can solve the consensus problem. An object has a consensus number $k$ if $k$ is the maximum number of processors for which the object can be used to solve the consensus problem. Thus objects with higher consensus number cannot be deterministically implemented by employing objects with lower consensus numbers. Randomized implementations are required in order to implement higher objects in the hierarchy from lower ones. This gives rise to the intuitive feeling that as one goes up the hierarchy more randomness is needed.

* Supported by NSF Presidential Young Investigator Award under grant DCR84-51396 & matching funds from XEROX Co. under grant W881111.

The test-and-set consensus number is 2 while that of read/write atomic registers is 1. In this paper we propose an economical randomized implementation of $n$-processes test-and-set from read/write registers.

Each of the $n$ processors that share the test-and-set object accesses it through the operations test&set and reset. The *sequential* specification of the object assumes that the two operations operate on a binary register which is initialized to 0. The test&set operation is like a swap of the register with a local variable whose value is 1, i.e. it atomically reads the register, writes 1 into it, and returns the value read. A reset operation writes 0 to the register and, returns no value. The specification also imposes a well-formedness requirement on the processors behavior, a processor can perform a reset only if its most recent operation was a test&set returning 0 (i.e. a successful test&set). Concurrent test-and-set is linearizable if each operation appears to occur in an indivisible time instant inside the operation's interval, and with respect to these serial instances the object satisfies the sequential specification above [Lam86].

Aside from their consensus number concurrent objects may be characterized by the following parameters:

- **Single use vs. Multi use:** A single use concurrent object can be accessed at most one time by each processor. It is in general easier to construct single use objects than multi use ones.
- **The number of processors that can access the object.**

Note that 2-process binary consensus is equivalent to a single use 2-process test-and-set object. Furthermore, the consensus number of n-process test-and-set is 2, but the consensus number of n-process *ternary* test-and-set is already $\infty$ [LAA87, Her91] (ternary test-and-set is a variant of read-modify-write).

In the same paper, [Her88], Herlihy established the existence of universal objects, whose consensus number is $\infty$. That is, objects which are at the top of the hierarchy. The randomized implementation of these objects, especially repeated consensus, from read/write registers has been the subject of research for a few years now [Abr88, Plo88, ADS89, Asp90, SSW90, Her91].

Previous work to implement $n$-process wait-free test&set proceeded by implementing a universal wait-free concurrent object in terms of repeated randomized $n$-process 'sticky bits', and bounding space by garbage collection, [Plo88]. The previously best known algorithm [Her91] for $n$-process test-and-set goes by way of constructing a general read-modify-write object using repeated randomized $n$-process consensus and a space garbage collection subroutine as building blocks. It uses $\Omega(n^2)$ mutually independent coin flips, to implement the best algorithm for $n$-process consensus [Asp90, SSW90, Her91], and its time complexity is $\Omega(n^4)$, per operation, and $\Omega(n^2 \log n)$ space per processor.

In this paper we give a simple direct implementation of wait-free $n$-process test-and-set in terms of atomic read/write variables. It improves the best previous method on all counts by using $O(\log n)$ flips of pairwise independent coins, $O(n)$ sequential time, per operation, and $O(n)$ space per processor.

A feature of shared memory algorithms is the fact that from time to time a processor may perform a set of (many, e.g. $O(n)$) operations, whose order of execution is unimportant. This gives rise to the question about the time it takes to complete such a set of operations. We advocate the view that processors communicate with memory via an interface, be it a communication network or a bus. In either case, getting to the memory in the former, or getting control of the bus in the latter, is the dominant factor. Thus in both cases it can be argued that making $n$ simultaneous requests or a single one should not make much difference. In the case of communication networks the node issues $n$ simultaneous requests to the network (very much in the same way that we allow a processor in a network to simultaneously send messages to all of its neighbors). We thus define the *parallel time* complexity measure in which we charge each set of simultaneous concurrent operations 1 unit of time. Under the new measure, the time complexity of Herlihy's algorithm is $\Omega(n^2)$, while the parallel time complexity of our algorithm is $O(\log n)$.

Our construction proceeds in two steps: First we construct a single-use n-process test-and-set object from a 2-process test-and-set object. Second we transform the single-use test-and-set object into a multi-use (repeated) test-and-set object. Any single use 2-process test-and-set object can be used as the building block of the first step, thus one can use the 2-process test-and-set construction of Tromp and Vitányi [TV90], or any 2-process consensus protocol [Asp90, AH90, SSW90, BR91]. All of these constructions have a constant expected complexity $(n = 2)$.

Our protocols to extend test-and-set from 2-process single-use to $n$-process repeated are deterministic (the consensus number of $n$-process test-and-set is also 2 !). The randomness of the algorithm is only in the building block of a single-use 2-process test-and-set. Although it may take any 2-process test-and-set solution, it does not implement the $n$-process solution from the 2-process solution in the strict sense of the word (a la [Her88]). Rather, it is more like a compiler. All the formal proofs of correctness and of the complexity results are omitted from this extended abstract.

We view test-and-set as the wait-free equivalent of mutual exclusion. Capturing the test&set bit is analogous to getting the critical section (CS). However, in mutual exclusion, a processor that failed to get the CS is kept busy waiting until it enters the CS, while in test-and-set, a failed processor returns to the "remainder" section without going through the "Critical-Section". In test-and-set we should only be able to linearize its decision, that the "CS" is occupied, to be after we linearized another processor decision to enter the "CS" (which is in general not required from mutual exclusion protocols, where a processor may be denied entry at some point while at that point there is still no other processor that is about to enter the CS). The ease and simplicity of implementing test-and-set as opposed to consensus, stems from the fact that well punctuated rounds are now identified by the execution of the "CS" exit protocol (the reset operation). Thus, if the execution of the "CS" is slow, as long as the single processor executing it did not finish, this processor can still be accounted for rejecting other processors from entering the "CS". Therefore, we can rely on this single processor to do all the book-keeping so that we can precisely know what is obsolete and what is current data. This is not the case with consensus, fetch-and-add and other concurrent objects, where the moment any processor makes a decision, it can start a new round. Thus test-and-set is much more 'sequential' in this respect.

## 2 Informal Description of the $n$-Process Algorithm

We assume that the $n$ processors perform **test&set** and **reset** operations according to the following generic template:

> **Forever do**
> $remainder_1 - section$
> **if** test&set $= 0$ **then**
> $zero - section$
> reset
> **fi**
> **od**

Conceptually any run of the $n$-process solution will be divided into rounds. A round is the interval between the termination of two consecutive reset operations. (The first round starts in the beginning of the run and ends in the first reset operation.) The test-and-set semantics together with the assumption that processors follow the above template guarantee that no two such operations are concurrent.

In each round a single-use $n$-process test-and-set protocol is executed. That is, an algorithm which is correct for an execution in which no processor will execute reset. The single-use algorithm is then composed into a multi-use algorithm (the desired solution).

We assume that in the single-use algorithm all variables are atomic single-writer-multi-reader registers.

### 2.1 Single-use $n$-process test-and-set

In this section we construct an $n$-process single-use test-and-set from similar 2-process building blocks. The basic idea is rather simple: have the $n$ processors contest each other in a tennis like (binary tree) tournament [PF77]. Only one processor can win the tournament, and it is the winner in the single-use test-and-set, while all other processors lose. In each level of the tournament we match the winners of the previous level in pairs (according to a fixed binary tree) that compete each other using a 2-process test-and-set. A processor loses (returning 1) as soon as it loses in a match. The problem with this solution is that one processor could lose, while the eventual winner has not yet started to play. This kind of a scenario violates the serializability condition of $n$-process test-and-set. To overcome this problem each processor that loses will prevent any processor that has not yet started, from winning (see Figures 2.1 and 2.1).

The following facts hold for the single use Test&set:

---

**Code for processor $i$ single-use $n$-process test-and-set**

```
function SINGLE-USE-TEST&SET
      for j=1 to n do if r[j].D = 1 then return(1) and exit fl od
      if tournament= 1 then                    %See next figure for the tournament.
            r[i].D := 1                         %Close the door.
            return(1)
      else
            return(0)
      fl
end-function SINGLE-USE-TEST&SET
```

**Fig. 1.** Single use $n$-process test-and-set.

If processor $i$ had lost, then any processor arriving after $i$ had lost should also lose. This is implemented by an array, called "door", of atomic single-writer/multi-reader bits. That is, every processor has a 1-bit field in its own variable, together comprising an $n$-bit vector $D$. The door is open for a processor if all the $r[k].D$ bits are found $= 0$, $1 \leq k \leq n$. It is otherwise closed. Processor $i$ closes the door by by setting $r[i].D$ to 1. Initially all the registers are set to 0.

---

1. In a bounded expected number of steps a processor returns either 0 or 1. Sketch: 2-process T&S involves a constant expected number of steps. Therefore the work at each floor is bounded and since the number of floors is bounded, the total number of steps is bounded.
2. Exactly one of all the test&set operations in a single use returns 0, and it starts before any other terminates. Sketch: by induction on the floor numbers of the tournament. Also the winner necessarily found the door open, which losers close before they terminate.

## 2.2 The multi-use test-and-set algorithm

For ease of exposition we present the multi-use algorithm using unbounded *round_numbers*. In the sequel we show that the system of round_numbers we use is required to satisfy the requirements of a *sequential* time stamp system, thus, replacing the unbounded numbers with bounded ones is conceptually straight forward using [LTV89, IL87].

Each processor has its own variable which it alone can write and all others can read. This variable is divided into a number of fields (so far we have seen *field-1*: the single-use 2-process variables, *field-2*: the D bit of the door, and *field-3*: the floor variable for the single-use n-process tournament). We add another field now, called round_number, which will determine whether the other fields are considered up to date, or out of date, in which case certain default values are assumed instead.

The code of the multi-use shell appears in Figure 3. The reset operation by processor $p$ consists of atomically setting all the single-use test-and-set fields of $p$ to their initial values and increasing $p$'s round number by 1 (this is the only way by which round numbers are increased). Each test-and-set copies the

---

**Code of the tournament for processor** $i$

**function** TOURNAMENT
    **for** j=1 **to** log $n$ **do**
        **if** 2-process-test&set($Sb[i,j]$)=1        %Each read in the 2-process-test&set
        **then** return(1) **and exit fi**           %is performed as explained below.
    **od**
    return(0)
**end function** TOURNAMENT


**function** READ(X) when called from within 2-process-test&set($Sb[i,j]$)
    **for each** $p$ **in** $Sb[i,j]$ **do**
        $rp := r[p]$
        **if** $rp.floor > j$ **then** return(1) **and exit the protocol fi**
        **if** $rp.floor = j$ **then** return(rp.X) **and exit the** READ **fi**
    **od**
    return($x$)                %x is X's initial value in the 2-process-test&set
**end function** READ(X)


**Fig. 2.** The tournament function.

The implementation of the tournament follows the ideas of Peterson and Fischer [PF77] (who constructed n-processes mutual exclusion from 2-process mutual exclusion). We assume that in the 2-process single-use test-and-set each processor has one register that it writes and the other processor reads. The tournament consists of log $n$ *floors*, corresponding to the levels of a binary tree tournament, whose leaves are the processors. Each internal node in the tree corresponds to a 2-process test-and-set fight between winning processors from each subtree of that node. A processor that test&set 0 in a 2-process test-and-set is considered to win the fight. Processors go up the floors, to the corresponding node in the binary tree. To this end, we add a *floor* field to the 2 process test-and-set register of each processor, indicating its progress up the floors of the tournament. Processor $i$ that gets to the $j$'th floor looks for the group of processors that belong to the subtree sibling to the subtree it came from. This group is called $Sb[i,j]$ and assuming that processor ids are $0, 1, 2, \ldots, n-1$,

$$Sb[i,j] = \{a[i,j], a[i,j]+1, \ldots, a[i,j]+2^{j-1}-1\}.$$

where $a[i,j] = 2^{j+1} \left\lfloor \frac{i}{2^j} \right\rfloor - 2^{j-1} \left( \left\lfloor \frac{i}{2^{j-1}} \right\rfloor - 1 \right)$. Now we use the invariant that only one processor from that group may change its 2-process test&set variables at this level. Whenever, in the 2-process algorithm it reads a variable X of the other processor, it will now read the variable X of all processors in the sibling subtree, $Sb[i,j]$. There are three cases according to which the processor interprets the value of X. *Case 1:* If one of $Sb[i,j]$ has a higher floor number, then the processor has lost the fight (returns 1 and exits). *Case 2:* If none of $Sb[i,j]$ has floor number equal to that of $i$, processor $i$ assumes the default initial value for X. *Case 3:* There is only one processor, $k$, in $Sb[i,j]$ with equal floor number (the winner of the sibling subtree), then processor $i$ reads the value of X of processor $k$. A processor that arrives at the highest floor has won the tournament.

---

**Code for processor $i$:**

```
function TEST-AND-SET
    read all r[j] registers
    max := max_j {r[j].round_number}
    if (participated_i = max)
        then return(1) and exit                    %Already lost in this round
        else atomically{ r[i] := [2-process-variables: initial values,
                         D: 0,                      %set all i's single-use fields
                         floor: 0,                  %to their initial values
                         round_number: max]}
             participated_i := max
             return(SINGLE-USE-TEST&SET)   %Each read of a shared variable in the
                                           single-use is done via the extended-read of Figure 4
    fi
end-function TEST-AND-SET

function RESET
        atomically{ r[i] := [2-process-variables: initial values,
                     D: 0,                          %set all i's single-use fields
                     floor: 0,                      %to their initial values
                     round_number: participated_i + 1]}
end-function RESET
```

---

**Fig. 3.** Implementing multi-use test-and-set from single-use.

---

**Code for extended-read of variable $X$ of $j$ (with initial value $x$) by processor $i$:**

```
extended-read(X, j):
    m := read(r[j])
    if r[j].round_number = r[i].round_number then
            return(m.2-process-variables.X) fi
    if r[j].round_number < r[i].round_number then
            return(x) fi                           {* x is the initial value of X *}
    if r[j].round_number > r[i].round_number then
            return 1 and exit the algorithm fi
```

---

**Fig. 4.** Extended read.

round number it participates in into a local variable 'participated', so it can later check for a new round. To start the algorithm a processor checks for the maximum round number of all other processors. If it has already participated in this round it returns 1. Otherwise it writes the new round number, and sets all its single-use variables to their initial values in one atomic write. When executing the single-use algorithm, any value which is read together with a round number which is less than its own, is interpreted to have the initial default value of the single-use algorithm. A processor executing the single-use algorithm, that reads a variable with a round number larger than its own, returns 1 for its test&set and exits.

For the code of how to interpret a read in the single-use algorithm see Figure 4.

To dispense with the unbounded round numbers we employ standard techniques like the scheme of [LTV89], or the Sequential Time Stamps System (STSS) [IL87]. The extra cost of such schemes is not more than $O(n)$ sequential time, and $O(1)$ parallel time.

The use of the sequential time stamp system (STSS) involves placing tokens on a graph of a complete tournament in which for any $n - 1$ nodes there is a node that majorizes them. Each processor is assigned one such token whose location in the tournament corresponds to a time-stamp given by the STSS to that processor. The property of the STSS is that it gives a total order on token positions if the actions of advancing tokens are done sequentially. Usually, as the case is here, when a token is advanced it is advanced to a position in which it dominates, at the time of the advancement, all other token positions in the tournament.

The use of STSS in our algorithm is complicated because processors can either do advances in the STSS (sequentially, by the resetter) or adapt the time-stamp of the processor that dominates all others (when taking the maximum and putting it into their own round_number). This new operation of equating the time-stamp to that of the maximum time-stamp has two sources of complications: (1) This operation may take place concurrently with other such operations, and concurrently with a sequence of token advancement operations, and (2) the equating operation is not atomic, first the processor reads all other time-stamps, and then in a later operation it writes the value it decided to equate to. That is, concurrently with the sequential advancement of tokens in the tournament, some processors might move their tokens to location which they have observed another token in. In the following we extend the standard STSS to accommodate the new equate operation.

The specification of the *advance*, and time-stamp *comparison* operations in the extended STSS are the same as in the original STSS. The serial specification of the additional *equate* operation is that it acquires a time-stamp equal to the maximum time-stamp in the system. The *equate* and *advance* operations are implemented as follows: To equate the most dominant time-stamp a processor goes through two cycles of reading and writing. In the first cycle it reads the sequence-numbers of all the processors and selects the most dominant one if there is such a time-stamp, then it writes it as its tentative time-stamp. In the second cycle it again reads the sequence-numbers of all the processors and double check that the register it copied from, is still holding the same sequence-number and it is still the most dominant. If it is, then the equating processor updates its time-stamp to be valid (not tentative). If in the first cycle a processor finds out that its own valid time-stamp is the maximum one, then it does not change its time-stamp and does not go through the second cycle, it may assume its own time-stamp to be valid. In case the processor did not see a majorizing time-stamp in the first cycle, it failed to equate and returns without changing its time-stamp, in this case it may return 1 and exit the test-and-set operation. To *advance* the maximum time-stamp (i.e., to acquire a new time-stamp) (performed by the resetter), a processor reads twice all the time-stamps (valid and tentative ones) and selects a new time-stamp that dominates all of the ones it read, according to the algorithm of [IL87]. When a processor reads a variable in the extended read of the test-and-set operation, it compares its valid time-stamp only with other valid time-stamps. One time-stamp is larger than the other if and only if it majorizes it in the time-stamp tournament graph. A processor with a tentative time-stamp is regarded to have a lower time-stamp.

## 3  Complexity Analysis

We now analyze the time complexity of the algorithm. Each 2 process test-and-set takes constant expected time. The outer algorithm requires once (at the beginning) that a processor will read all the time-stamps. This takes $O(n)$ sequential time and $O(1)$ parallel time. Similarly, in the single use algorithm reading the state of the door requires $O(n)$ sequential time and $O(1)$ parallel time. Finally, each level in the tournament requires $O(2^{level})$ sequential time and $O(1)$ parallel time and there are $\log n$ levels. Thus the sequential time adds up to $O(n)$ and the parallel time adds up to $O(\log n)$. Similar calculation shows that each test&set requires $O(\log n)$ coin flips.

## 4  Conclusion

This paper has presented: (1) A direct implementation of randomized wait-free test-and-set instead of an implementation in terms of repeated $n$ process randomized consensus; (2) A deterministic implementation of wait-free $n$-process test-and set from wait-free 2-process test-and-set; (3) Introduced and argued the notion of randomness and parallel time as new cost measures in wait-free algorithms; and finally (4) Improved the complexity of existing constructions for test-and-set [Her88, Plo88] in terms of the new resources, random bits, and parallel time, as well as in terms of the standard complexity measures of sequential time and space.

Aside from the above, the paper raises the question of the randomized computational complexity (sequential time, parallel time, space, and number of coins) of implementing concurrent objects with consensus number $k$ from concurrent objects with consensus number smaller than $k$.

**Acknowledgments:** We thank Michael Merritt and Michael Saks for helpful comments on earlier drafts.

# References

[Abr88]  K. Abrahamson. On achieving consensus using a shared memory. In *Proc. of the 7th ACM Symp. on Principles of Distributed Computing*, pages 291–302, 1988.

[ADS89]  Hagit Attiya, Danny Dolev, and Nir Shavit. Bounded polynomial randomized consensus. Extended Abstract, January 1989.

[AH90]  J. Aspnes and M. Herlihy. Fast randomized consensus using shared memory. *Journal of Algorithms*, pages 281–294, September 1990.

[Asp90]  J. Aspnes. Time and space efficient randomized consensus. In *Proc. of the Ninth ACM Symp. on Principles of Distributed Computing*, pages 325–331, August 1990.

[BR91]  G. Bracha and O. Rachman. Randomized consensus in expected $o(n^2 log n)$ operations. In *Proceedings of the 4th International Workshop on Distributed Algorithms*, October 1991.

[Her88]  M. P. Herlihy. Impossibility and universality results for wait-free synchronization. In *Proc. of the Seventh ACM Symp. on Principles of Distributed Computing*, pages 291–302, 1988.

[Her91]  M. P. Herlihy. Randomized wait-free concurrent objects. In *Proc. of the Tenth ACM Symp. on Principles of Distributed Computing*, pages 11–22, 1991.

[IL87]  A. Israeli and M. Li. Bounded time stamps. In *Proc. of the 28th IEEE Annual Symp. on Foundation of Computer Science*, pages 362–371, October 1987.

[LAA87]  M. C. Loui and H. H. Abu-Amara. Memory requirements for agreement among unreliable asynchronous processes. *Advances in Computing Research, JAI Press*, 4:163–183, 1987.

[Lam86]  L. Lamport. On interprocess communication, parts i and ii. *Distributed Computing*, 1:77–101, 1986.

[LTV89]  M. Li, J. Tromp, and P. M. B. Vitányi. How to construct concurrent wait-free variables. Technical Report CS-8916, CWI, Amsterdam, April 1989. See also: pp. 488–505 in: *Proc. International Colloquium on Automata, Languages, and Programming*, Lecture Notes in Computer Science, Vol. 372, Springer Verlag, 1989.

[PF77]  G. L. Peterson and M. J. Fischer. Economical solutions for the critical section problem in a distributed system. In *Proc. 9th ACM Symp. on Theory of Computing*, pages 91–97, 1977.

[Plo88]  S. A. Plotkin. *Chapter 4: Sticky Bits and Universality of Consensus*. PhD thesis, M.I.T., August 1988.

[SSW90]  M. Saks, N. Shavit, and H. Woll. Optimal time randomized consensus – making resilient algorithms fast in practice. In *Proc. of SODA 90*, December 1990.

[TV90]  J. Tromp and P. M. B. Vitányi. Randomized wait-free test-and-set. Manuscript, November 1990.

# A Concurrent Time-Stamp Scheme which is Linear in Time and Space

Amos Israeli[1*] and Meir Pinhasov[2]

[1] Dept. of Electrical Engineering, Technion, Israel
[2] Dept. of Computer Science, Technion, Israel

**Abstract.** A *concurrent time-stamp scheme* is an abstraction which enables the representation of temporal relationship among the objects of a distributed system. In this abstraction the system objects are labeled by a process called *labeling*. Using these labels a *scanning* process can return a set of labeled objects ordered temporally. In this paper we present a time-stamp system with *linear* time and space complexity. To achieve this complexity we introduce two way communication between labelers and scanners.

## 1 Introduction

A *Time-stamp scheme* is an abstraction which enables the representation of temporal relations among system objects. This is done by labeling the system's objects using labels called *time-stamps*. A time-stamp scheme consists of a set of *labels*, a *labeling* protocol and a *scanning* protocol. The labeling protocol uses labels of existing objects to choose new labels for newly created objects, the scanning protocol scans the labels of existing objects and returns a set of the labeled objects ordered temporally. In a distributed system each of these protocols might be executed by many processes. A process executing the labeling (scanning) protocol is called *labeler* (*scanner*). In some systems a process may function sometimes as a labeler and sometimes as a scanner but for the sake of simplicity we choose to separate these activities.

If many labelers and scanners can run concurrently and if the labeling and scanning protocols are *wait-free*, as defined by [9], then the time-stamp scheme is called *concurrent*. The most common concurrent time-stamp scheme is the *natural* time-stamp scheme which uses the natural numbers as labels. The labeling protocol consists of reading the labels of all existing objects and taking the maximum label plus 1 as the label for the new object. When several copies of the labeling protocol are executed concurrently the chosen labels may not be distinct. To break these ties the name of the process which executes the labeling protocol is added to the chosen label. The scanning protocol in the natural time-stamp scheme is simply to read all labels of existing objects and order them in the natural order. Ties are resolved by using the process' names in lexicographic

* Partially supported by Technion VPR Funds - Japan TS Research Fund and B. & G. Greenberg Research Fund (Ottawa).

order. This time-stamp scheme is used in a slew of distributed algorithms such as [2, 6, 8, 14].

In many theoretical applications one seeks for bounded protocols, protocols which use communication of bounded size. In this case the natural time-stamp scheme is not useful any more. A *bounded time-stamp scheme* is a time-stamp scheme with a finite set of labels. Such a scheme should reflect the temporal order among all existing objects, therefore the number of objects which may exist concurrently is bounded too. This number is the *order* of the time-stamp scheme. In a distributed system, that uses single-writer atomic registers as its communication primitive, both objects and labels are stored in atomic registers. The complexity of an implementation of a bounded concurrent time-stamp scheme in such a system is measured by two criteria. The space criterion is the maximal size of an atomic register owned by some process and used to control the scheme's operation. This measure is called *label size*. The time criterion is the number of atomic read and write operations to shared registers for executing each of the labeling and the scanning protocols. This measure is called *execution time*.

The definition of a time-stamp scheme as a separate abstraction was first suggested by Israeli and Li in [7]. There they give the basic definitions for time-stamp schemes and suggest the use of the nodes of a precedence graph as the label set. Using the precedence graph method they present lower and upper bounds for bounded time-stamp schemes. First they derive an $\Omega(w)$ lower bound on the label size for a time-stamp scheme of order $w$. Then they present a *sequential*[3] time-stamp scheme of order $w$ whose label-size is $O(w)$. For this purpose they suggest the method of digraph multiplication. Israeli and Li also present a concurrent wait-free labeling protocol for a system of processes which communicate through the use of atomic single-writer-multi-reader registers. This protocol captures only some of the temporal relations in the system.

Following [7], Dolev and Shavit in [3] give the precise definition for concurrent time-stamp scheme, as used in this paper, and present a bounded concurrent time-stamp scheme. The label set for this time-stamp scheme consists of the nodes of a precedence graph which is obtained by an operation which is a slight modification of digraph multiplication. Let $w$ and $r$ stand for the number of labelers and scanners, respectively, in the system. In the scheme of [3] the processes communicate by using single-writer-$n$-reader atomic registers, where $n = w + r$ is the total number of system's processes, the label size in this scheme is $O(w)$. Each execution of the labeling protocol takes $O(w)$ operations and each execution of the scanning protocol takes $O(w^2 \log w)$. A nice property of their protocol is that communication is one-sided. Scanners do not write, they only read values written by the labelers.

In this work we present a new time-stamp scheme whose execution time is *linear* in $n$, the total number of processes in the system. The label-size of the scheme is $O(r \cdot n)$ if single-writer-$n$-reader registers are used for communication

---

[3] In a sequential time-stamp scheme it is assumed that both the labeling and the scanning protocols are executed atomically

However, we show that if one assumes that single-writer-$n$-reader registers are built from single-writer-single-reader registers then the space complexity of our scheme is (asymptotically) the same as the space complexity of a scheme that uses single-writer-$n$-reader registers of linear size (and there is no additional time complexity). To get this improved time complexity we introduce two-way communication between scanners and labelers. The time complexity of the new implementation is smaller than the time complexity of the [3] implementation as long as $w \geq O(\sqrt{\frac{n}{\log n}})$ .

To prove the correctness of the new implementation we use the *interleaving* model. In this model it is assumed that every system execution is equivalent to some serial system execution. A protocol is considered correct with respect to some set of specifications if every serial execution of the protocol satisfies these specifications. This extended abstract contains a full description of the time-stamp scheme and some important theorems which should serve as guidelines for the correctness proof. A full correctness proof appears in [12] and will be given in the full paper which is under preparation.

Independently and slightly later than our result, a linear-time concurrent bounded time-stamp scheme was presented by Dwork and Waarts in [4]. This result based on a completely different approach yields an *amortized* linear time using single-writer-$n$-reader atomic registers of size $O(n \log n)$. Recently, a new technique developed by Dwork, Herlihy, Plotkin and Waarts in [5], enables them to modify the scheme of [3] to be linear in both time and label size. However, since this modification uses the Traceable Use abstraction of [4] its time complexity is amortized.

The rest of this paper is organized as follows: Section 2 contains a formal definition of a time-stamp scheme, Section 3 contains a description of a new time-stamp scheme which we call the *basic-scheme*. In Section 4 we present the linear time-stamp scheme, which is based on the basic scheme, and analyze its complexity. Concluding remarks are brought in Section 5.

## 2 Definitions

The system consists of $n$ processes of two kinds – labelers and scanners. A process, $i$, whether it is a labeler or a scanner, owns an atomic *single-writer-multi-reader* register, $r_i$, written only by $i$ and read by all other processes in the system. A register, $r_i$, is logically partitioned into several fields. The partition of a register owned by a scanner may be different from the partition of a register owned by a labeler. However, an *active label* field, $\ell_i$ exists in the register of every process, $i$.

The only *atomic* operations in the system are: A read operation from some register, and a write operation to some register. The execution of an atomic operation is called *atomic action*. A *protocol* is an operation composed of a finite number of atomic operations executed one after the other. The execution of a protocol is called *action*. A non-atomic action *begins* by executing its first atomic action, it *ends* by executing its last atomic action.

The scheme consists of two protocols – a *labeling* protocol, executed by labelers, and a *scanning* protocol, executed by scanners. Therefore, an execution of a labeler, $x$, is a sequence: $L_x^{[1]}$, $L_x^{[2]}$, ... of labeling actions, and an execution of a scanner, $p$, is a sequence: $S_p^{[1]}$, $S_p^{[2]}$, ... of scanning actions (the processes do not necessarily know the superscripts, they are only used for notation). A labeling action, $L_x^{[a]}$, accepts an *object* (denoted $v_x^{[a]}$) to be written to $x$'s register. It reads the active label fields of all the processes in the system, and based on the this information a label, $\ell_x^{[a]}$, is associated with the given object. Then, both the object and the label are written to $x$'s register by a single atomic write action. The labels written by labeling actions help to establish a total order on the labeling actions, which is consistent with their temporal order. A scanning action, $S_p^{[d]}$, returns an ordered set, $\bar{v}$ of *labeled-objects* (i.e. (object,label) pairs), one per each labeler in the system. Intuitively, the order on the elements of $\bar{v}$ should reflect the temporal order of the labeling actions that wrote these elements. If the executions of all the processes in the system satisfy the following properties, equivalent to those given by Dolev and Shavit in [3], then the scheme is a *concurrent-time-stamp-scheme*.

**P1** *ordering*: There exists an irreflexive total order, $\Rightarrow$, on the set of all labeling actions, such that:

   **a.** *precedence*: For any pair of labeling actions, $L_x^{[a]}$ and $L_y^{[b]}$ (where possibly $x = y$), if $L_x^{[a]}$ ends before $L_y^{[b]}$ begins, then $L_x^{[a]} \Rightarrow L_y^{[b]}$.

   **b.** *consistency*: For any scanning action, $S_p^{[d]}$, returning the ordered set $\bar{v}$, $(v_x^{[a]}, \ell_x^{[a]})$ is before $(v_y^{[b]}, \ell_y^{[b]})$ in $\bar{v}$, if and only if $L_x^{[a]} \Rightarrow L_y^{[b]}$.

**P2** *regularity*: For any pair $(v_x^{[a]}, \ell_x^{[a]})$ in the ordered set $\bar{v}$ returned by $S_p^{[d]}$, $L_x^{[a]}$ begins before $S_p^{[d]}$ ends, and no labeling action of $x$, later than $L_x^{[a]}$, ends before $S_p^{[d]}$ begins.

**P3** *monotonicity*: For any pair of scanning actions, $S_p^{[d]}$ and $S_q^{[e]}$, returning the ordered sets $\bar{v}$ and $\bar{u}$ respectively. If $S_p^{[d]}$ ends before $S_q^{[e]}$ begins, $(v_x^{[a]}, \ell_x^{[a]}) \in \bar{v}$ and $(v_x^{[b]}, \ell_x^{[b]}) \in \bar{u}$, then it can not be that $b < a$.

Note that scanners do not necessarily know the order in terms of $\Rightarrow$ between every pair of labeled objects they read. Yet they should be able to choose from all the labeled objects they read a set of $w$ labeled objects (one for each labeler) on which they do know the order $\Rightarrow$.

## 3 The Basic Time-Stamp Scheme

### 3.1 The Set of Labels

As in [7, 3] the labels are the nodes of a bounded *precedence-graph*. A precedence-graph is a partial *tournament*, used to establish an irreflexive and anti-symmetric relation on the set of labels. In order to define the precedence-graph we use the $\alpha$-*composition operator* defined by [3]. Let $G$ and $H$ be two tournaments, and let $\alpha$ be a subset of the nodes of $G$, The $\alpha$-composition of $G$ and $H$, $G \circ_\alpha H$, is the tournament received by the following operation:

> Replace every node $v \in \alpha$ by a copy of $H$, denoted $H_v$ (if $v \notin \alpha$ then $H_v = \{v\}$). If there is a directed edge from $v$ to $u$ in $G$, then there is a directed edge from every node of $H_v$ to every node of $H_u$ in $G \circ_\alpha H$.

Let $D \geq 3$ be a constant integer called the *graph-constant*. Based on this graph-constant, define $T^2$ to be the following tournament over the nodes $\{1 \ldots 2D + 3\}$: Nodes $3 \ldots 2D + 3$ form a directed cycle such that for every $i$, $3 < i \leq 2D + 3$, there is an edge directed from $i$ to $i - 1$, and there is an edge directed from 3 to $2D + 3$. From every node in this cycle there is a directed edge to nodes $\{1, 2\}$, and there is a directed edge from 2 to 1. Define the tournament $T^k$ inductively as follows: Let $T^1$ be a single node, and for every $k > 1$, $T^k = T^2 \circ_\alpha T^{k-1}$, where $\alpha$ is the set of all the nodes of a $T^2$-subgraph except from node 2.

In both time-stamp schemes, introduced in this paper, we use the tournament $T^n$ as the set of labels (remember that $n$ is the total number of processes in the system). Every node of $T^n$ represents a possible label. A label is therefore a string, $\ell_i[n..1]$, over the alphabet $\{1 \ldots 2D + 3\}$. The prefix, $\ell_i[n..k]$, of a label specifies the $T^k$-subgraph in which the node corresponding to this label resides. Since all labels come from the same $T^n$ graph, $\ell_i[n] = 1$, for all the labels. A *supernode*, $i$, of a $T^k$-subgraph is the $T^{k-1}$-subgraph that replaces node $i$ of $T^2$, in the construction of this $T^k$-subgraph (it is a simple node if $i = 2$). Any $T^k$-subgraph has a $C^k$-cycle, which is the cycle composed of supernodes $\{3 \ldots 2D + 3\}$ of that $T^k$-subgraph. In the sequel we use the term *component* in order to refer to either a $T^k$-subgraph or a $C^k$-cycle. The only difference between the family of precedence-graphs we and the precedence-graph of [3] is the larger size of the $C^k$-cycles in our precedence graphs. This difference however, is vital for the correctness of the schemes we introduce.

Since our precedence-graph is not a *complete tournament* we cannot use the simple dominance relation which was used in [7, 3]. Instead we generalize it to be the following irreflexive anti-symmetric *dominance* relation on the set of labels. A label $\ell_i$ *dominates* a label $\ell_j$, (denoted $\ell_j \prec \ell_i$), if there exists a directed path in $T^n$, of length greater than 0 but less than or equal to D, from the $\ell_i$ to $\ell_j$. The dominance relation can be also be applied to components, using the following generalization: A component $\alpha$ dominates a component $\beta$ if there exists a proper directed path in $T^n$, of length less than or equal to D, from every node of $\alpha$ to every node of $\beta$.

## 3.2 The Basic Labeling Protocol

The basic labeling protocol and the labeling function introduced in this subsection are slightly modified variants of the labeling protocol and labeling function given in [3].

The basic labeling protocol (see Fig. 1) performed by process $i$, reads the contents of all the registers in the system in arbitrary order, this sequence of $n$

read operations is denoted *collect*. The set of the labels, $\bar{\ell}$, read from the active label fields by the collect operation is then sent to a *labeling function*, $\mathcal{L}$. Based on this information the function computes a label, $\ell'_i$, that dominates all the labels in $\bar{\ell}$. This label and the value sent to the labeling protocol are then written in $r_i$ by one atomic write operation, such that $\ell'_i$ is written to the active label field. Note that throughout this paper we use the "$\leftarrow$" operator to indicate an atomic read/write of data from/to shared register, while the ":=" operator indicates an assignment from one *internal* memory location to another, and therefore is not included in time coplexity calculations.

**procedure** labeling($i, obj$)
   **begin**
      $\bar{\ell} \leftarrow collect$;
      $r_i \leftarrow (obj, \mathcal{L}(\bar{\ell}, i))$;
   **end** ;

Fig. 1. The Basic Labeling Protocol (for labeler $i$)

The labeling function, $\mathcal{L}$, that appears in Fig. 2, accepts two arguments. The first one – $\ell$ is a set of $n$ labels, one per each process, and the second one is the *id* of the process executing the function. The function returns a label, which is the new label for the process called it. The notation used in the code is as follows: The "." is the concatenation operator between strings. $\ell_i$ is the label from $\ell$ read for process $i$ itself. The function "num_labels" accepts a subgraph and returns the number of labels from $\ell$ that are in the given subgraph. The function "Max_label" accepts a set of labels, $\hat{\ell}$, and returns a label from this set, $\ell_x$, that is least dominated by other labels in $\hat{\ell}$. The function "dom" accepts an integer from $\{1 \ldots 2D + 3\}$ and returns its *immediate dominator*, which is $i + 1$ for every $i \in \{1 \ldots 2D + 2\}$, and 3 for $2D + 3$.

The labeling function, $\mathcal{L}$, begins by calculating a "maximal" label, in terms of "$\prec$", $\ell_{max}$. The natural way to do this would have been to choose the label, from the set $\ell$, that dominates all the other labels in $\ell$. Unfortunately, this is not always possible, since some of the labels in $\ell$, may form a cycle of dominance. Therefore, $\ell_{max}$, is chosen to be a label from $\ell$ that dominates at least as many labels of $\ell$ as any other label in $\ell$. Once $\ell_{max}$ is calculated, the labeling function chooses a new label, $\ell'_i$, that is either equal to $\ell_{max}$ or dominates it, to substitute $\ell_i$. This choosing process is guided by two principles: (A) $\ell'_i$ should be as "close" as possible to $\ell_{max}$ (i.e. the minimal $T^k$-subgraph that contains both $\ell'_i$ and $\ell_{max}$ should be as small as possible). (B) For every moment in time $t$, and for every $C^k$-cycle, $\gamma$, there should not be more than $k$ labels in $\gamma$. Therefore, as long as the second principle is not violated, the labeling function follows the first principle by performing the recursive call at line 4, which assures that $\ell'_i$ will be in yet a smaller $T^k$-subgraph of $\ell_{max}$.[4] In lines 1,2 the recursion is stopped since

---

[4] $\ell_{max}$ is in exactly one $T^k$-subgraph of any order, hence this statement is meaningful.

```
function L(ℓ, i);
    function L^k(G);
        begin
        1:      if k = 1 then return(G);
        2:      if ℓ_max[n..k − 1] = G.2 then return(G.3.1^{k−2});
        3:      if k > 2 then
                    if (ℓ_i[n..k − 1] ≠ ℓ_max[n..k − 1]) and
                       ℓ_max[k − 2] ≠ 1
                    then return(G.dom(ℓ_max[k − 1]).1^{k−2});
        4:      if (num_labels(ℓ_max[n..k − 1]) < k − 1) or
                   {(num_labels(ℓ_max[n..k − 1]) = k − 1) and
                    ℓ_max[n..k − 1] = ℓ_i[n..k − 1] }
                then return(L^{k−1}(G.ℓ_max[k − 1]))
        5:      else return(G.dom(ℓ_max[k − 1]).1^{k−2});
        end
    begin
        ℓ_max := Max_label(ℓ);
        return(L^n(1))
    end ;
```

**Fig. 2.** The Labeling Function

it is not possible to get any "closer" to $\ell_{max}$. In lines 3,5 the recursion is stopped since any further recursive call could cause a violation of the second principle.

### 3.3 Properties of the Basic labeling

In this subsection we assume that every process $x$ in the system executes a sequence of basic labeling actions denoted $\Lambda_x^{[1]}$, $\Lambda_x^{[2]}$, etc. The following definition helps us to capture the behavior of labels, written by the basic labeling actions, during such an execution:

**Definition 1.** A label $\ell_y^{[b]}$ influences a component $\alpha$, if either $\ell_y^{[b]}$ is in $\alpha$, or, $\ell_y^{[b]}$ dominates $\alpha$ and there exists $b' < b$ such that $\ell_y^{[b']}$ is in $\alpha$ and for every $b''$, $b' < b'' < b$, $\ell_y^{[b'']}$ is either in $\alpha$, or dominates $\alpha$.

**Theorem 2.** *At any time $t$, the following are true:*

**IH1** *If a $T^k$-subgraph, $\alpha$, is influenced by less than $k$ active labels, then all the active labels that are in $\alpha$, are located in supernode 1 of $\alpha$.*

**IH2** *If a $C^k$-cycle, $\gamma$, is influenced by less than $k$ active labels, then all the active labels that are in $\gamma$, are located in supernode 3 of $\gamma$.*

**IH3** *There are active labels in at most two adjacent supernodes of every $C^k$-cycle.*

Define $\prec$ to be the following extension of the dominance relation: $\ell_y^{[b]} \prec \ell_x^{[a]}$ if either $\ell_y^{[b]} \prec \ell_x^{[a]}$, or, $\ell_y^{[b]} = \ell_x^{[a]}$ and $y < x$. The $\prec$ relation uses the processes *ids* to break symmetry between labels owned by distinct processes. It is important to note that **IH3** implies that all active labels at any time $t$ are totally ordered by the $\prec$ relation. Let $t$ be a moment in time. Denote by $\mathcal{B}_t^0$ the set of active labels at time $t$. For every integer $m$, denote $\mathcal{B}_t^m$ to be $\mathcal{B}_t^{m-1} \cup \left\{ \ell_x^{[a]} \; : \; \ell_x^{[a-1]} \in \mathcal{B}_t^{m-1} \right\}$. That is, if $\ell_x^{[a]} \in \mathcal{B}_t^m$ then either $\ell_x^{[a]}$ is the active label of $x$ at time $t$, or, $\ell_x^{[a]}$ is written by one of the first $m$ basic labeling actions of $x$ that end after $t$. The changes in time made to the active label of a certain process can be viewed at as a "movement" of this process. From **IH3** and from the labeling function, it can be shown that by completing a single basic labeling action a process can "move" at most 2 edges on the graph (the "movement" is always against the edge direction). Therefore, the assertion made on the labels in $\mathcal{B}_t^0$ can be generalized for $m$'s that are small relative to the graph-constant, $D$. This generalization appears in the following lemma.

**Lemma 3.** *Let $t$ be a moment in time and let $m$ be some integer. If $m \le \frac{D-1}{2}$ then every subset of $\mathcal{B}_t^m$, that contains labels of distinct processes, is totally ordered by the $\prec$ relation.*

We now define a total order ,$\Rightarrow$, on all basic labeling actions executed during some system execution, as it was defined in [3]:

**Definition 4.** A basic labeling action, $\Lambda_y^{[b]}$, is *observed* by another basic labeling action, $\Lambda_x^{[a]}$, if either $\ell_y^{[b]}$ is read during $\Lambda_x^{[a]}$, or there exists some basic labeling action $\Lambda_z^{[c]}$, such that $\ell_z^{[c]}$ is read during $\Lambda_x^{[a]}$ and $\Lambda_y^{[b]}$ is observed by $\Lambda_z^{[c]}$.

**Definition 5.** Let $\Lambda_x^{[a]}$ and $\Lambda_y^{[b]}$ be basic labeling actions. $\Lambda_y^{[b]} \Rightarrow \Lambda_x^{[a]}$ if either $\Lambda_y^{[b]} \xrightarrow{obs} \Lambda_x^{[a]}$, or, $\Lambda_y^{[b]} \xleftrightarrow{obs} \Lambda_x^{[a]}$ and $\ell_y^{[b]} \prec \ell_x^{[a]}$.

**Theorem 6.** *The relation $\Rightarrow$ is an irreflexive total order on the set of all labeling actions.*

Let $t$ be some moment in time. As explained above, if $m \le \frac{D-1}{2}$, then no process succeeds to complete a whole cycle (actually not even half of a cycle) of the precedence graph within $m$ basic labeling actions. This implies that the total order induced on the labels in $\mathcal{B}_t^m$ is consistent with the order $\Rightarrow$ on the basic labeling actions that wrote these labels. This claim is formalized by the following lemma:

**Lemma 7.** *Let $t$ be a moment in time. Let $\ell_x^{[a]}$ and $\ell_y^{[b]}$, $y \ne x$, be labels from $\mathcal{B}_t^m$ where $m \le \frac{D-1}{2}$. If $\ell_y^{[b]} \prec \ell_x^{[a]}$ then $\Lambda_y^{[b]} \Rightarrow \Lambda_x^{[a]}$.*

### 3.4 The Basic Scanning Protocol

In this subsection we describe the basic scanning protocol which appears in Fig. 3. In spite of its simplicity this scanning protocol is more efficient than the scanning protocol of [3], unless $w \gg r$. The set of labels of the scheme for $n = w + r$ processes is the set of nodes of $T^n$, with the graph constant $D = 3$. The labeling protocol of this scheme is the basic labeling protocol. The scanning protocol is described below. Unlike the scanning protocol of [3], this scanning protocol is not a *read only* protocol. We found that allowing the scanning protocol to write into shared registers, reduces the number of atomic operations needed for a scanning.

Remember that the purpose of the scanning protocol is to find $w$ labeled-values, one per each labeler, such that the order in terms of $\Rightarrow$ among the (basic) labeling actions that wrote them can be determined by the scanner. In the sequel we, for sake of simplicity we refer to a labeled-value only by its label.

The scanning protocol works in phases. In each phase it extracts a *non-empty* set of labels that belong to distinct labelers for which no label was found in the previous phases. All labels extracted in a certain phase are "older" in terms of $\Rightarrow$ than all the labels returned in later phases.

```
procedure scanning(j);
    begin
    1:       final := φ
             rem := Labelers;
    2:       old ← collect;
             while (rem ≠ φ) do
                     begin
    3:                       ℓ_j ← L(old, j);
    4:                       new ← collect;
    5:                       dominated := dominated_set(new, rem, ℓ_j);
    6:                       if dominated = φ then dominated := arb(old, rem);
    7:                       arrange(dominated, final);
                             rem := rem \ {j/ℓ_j^[c] ∈ dominated};
                             old := new
                     end ;
    8:       ℓ_j ← L(old, j);
             return(final)
    end ;
```

Fig. 3. The Basic Scanning Protocol (for scanner $j$)

In each phase the labels of all processes are read and the active label of the scanner is moved to "cover" all the read labels (these actions in lines 2 and 3, amount to performing a basic labeling action). Then the labels of labelers for which no label was found so far are read once again (line 4). Let $\hat{\ell}$ be the set of labels read in the second sequence of reads. There are two possible cases concerning the labels in $\hat{\ell}$. The first case is that some of the labels in $\hat{\ell}$ are found still covered by the scanner's active label. In this case we prove that all the covered labels in $\hat{\ell}$ are in $\mathcal{B}_t^1$, where $t$ is the moment immediately after the scanner's active label was written. This according to lemmas 3 and 7, implies that the order in terms of $\Rightarrow$ among the labeling actions that wrote the covered labels can be deduced from the order induced on these labels by the $\prec$ relation. The second case is that all the labels in $\hat{\ell}$ dominate the scanner's active label. In this case we deduce that *all* the labelers for which no label was found yet, made at least one move since their label was read in the first sequence of reads. Therefore, the scanner can arbitrarily pick any label read in the first sequence of reads (that belongs to a labeler for which no label was found yet). In this case the scanner cannot return more than one label in this phase since there is no way for the scanner to determine the relations (in terms of $\Rightarrow$) among the labeling actions that wrote the labels collected in the first sequence of reads.

This technique yields (in the worst case) a $w$-phase scanning protocol. Since every phase consists of $O(n)$ atomic operations, the overall time complexity is $O(w \cdot n)$.

## 4  The Linear Time-Stamp Scheme

In this section we introduce, for the first time, a bounded concurrent time-stamp scheme whose scanning protocol has *linear* time complexity in the number of processes. The labeling protocol of this *linear scheme* is based on the basic labeling protocol, and its time complexity remains $O(n)$. The shared memory requirements of the linear scheme are as follows: every labeler owns an atomic 1-W-$n$-R register of $O(n \cdot r)$ bits, and every scanner owns an atomic 1-W-$n$-R register of $O(n)$ bits. Thus, the length of 1-W-$n$-R registers, used by labelers in the linear scheme, is greater than the length of 1-W-$n$-R registers, used by labelers in the basic scheme. However, in subsection 4.4, we show that if the communication registers in the system are assumed to be 1-W-1-R atomic registers, (rather than 1-W-$n$-R atomic registers), then the total length of primitive registers owned by every labeler in the linear scheme is (asymptotically) the same as in basic scheme.

The task of the scanning protocol is to find $w$ labels, one per each labeler, such that the order in terms of $\Rightarrow$ among the labeling actions that wrote thee labels can be determined by the scanner. By lemmas 3 and 7, it follows that the scanners' task can be reduced to:

**Task A:** The scanning protocol should find a set $S$ of $w$ labels, one for each labeler, such that there exists a moment, $t$, during the scanning action, and there is a constant $m$, for which: $S \subseteq \mathcal{B}_t^m$.

A protocol that accomplishes this task, can be converted to a scanning protocol simply by returning the labels of $S$ ordered by the $\prec$ relation. The graph-constant $D$ in for a scheme composed of such a protocol should be chosen to satisfy: $m \leq \frac{D-1}{2}$.

Actually, every phase of the basic scanning protocol attempts to accomplish task **A**. All the labels returned by a single phase are from $\mathcal{B}_t^1$, where $t$ is the moment right after the scanner's write action executed in this phase. Unfortunately, it is not guaranteed that a single phase succeeds to accomplish task **A**, since we saw that in the worst case the set of labels found in a single phase may contain a single label (instead of $w$). The main obstacle in accomplishing task A in a single phase, is that no matter how large $m$ is, there may still exist a labeler that completes more than $m$ basic labeling actions after moment $t$, and before its register is read by the second sequence of reads of this phase.

One possible way to accomplish task A is as follows: A labeler $x$ that finds out that it had completed $m$ basic labeling actions after a specific moment $t$ during the scanning action $S_p^{[e]}$, and before its label is read by $S_p^{[e]}$, suspends any further labeling actions until its label is read by $S_p^{[e]}$. This assures that the label read by $S_p^{[e]}$ for every labeler is in $\mathcal{B}_t^m$. However, this solution leads to a non wait-free labeling protocol, and therefore cannot be a part of a concurrent time-stamp scheme. The waiting of labelers in the scenario described above can avoided if the each labeler that wishes to proceed executing additional labeling actions keeps a *historic* label of itself for the stalled scanner. This way the stalled scanner is provided a label from $\mathcal{B}_t^m$, even though the labeler's active label when its register is read by the scanner is a much later one.

In our specific implementation of the above solution $t$ is the moment right after the write action performed during a scanning action, and $m = 2$. The latter implies the graph constant $D$ should be greater than or equal to 5, so that $m \le \frac{D-1}{2}$.

### 4.1 Register Structure

In order to implement the above ideas, labelers and scanners should write additional information to their shared registers. The exact partition of labelers' and scanners' registers are depicted in Fig. 4. Both labelers and scanners still have an active label field denoted $\ell$. In the scanners' registers this field is accompanied by an alternating $tog$ bit. This bit assures that no two consecutive active labels of a certain scanner are equal.

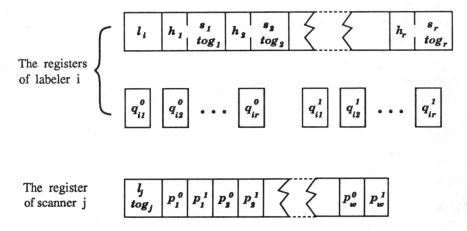

The registers of labeler $i$

The register of scanner $j$

Fig. 4. Register Structure

The $h_j$ fields in the register of labeler $i$ are used to store a historic labels of $i$ for every scanner $j$. The $s_j$ fields, on the other hand, are used to notify scanner $j$ of the latest label (and its *tog* bit) of $j$ that was read by labeler $i$. We later explain why these fields are needed.

Finally, the shared 1-W-1-R atomic bits $q_{ij}^b$, $b \in \{0,1\}$ of the labelers, and the $p_i^b$ fields of the scanners' registers are used for the *Hand-shake bits* mechanism of [1]. This mechanism allows a labeler $i$ to detect whether any write action was made by a scanner between every two consecutive collect actions.

## 4.2 The Labeling Protocol

The labeling protocol of the linear scheme is presented in Fig. 5. The protocol is based on the basic labeling protocol (lines 5,6 and 10 constitute a basic labeling action). Since every labeling action contains exactly one basic labeling action, we refer to the basic labeling action enclosed in $L_x^{[a]}$ as $\Lambda_x^{[a]}$. Another important activity of the protocol is to keep a historic label of itself for every scanner. The historic label stored by labeler $i$ for scanner $j$ is updated by labeling action $L_x^{[a]}$ iff the scanner $j$ made a write action after its label was read by $\Lambda_x^{[a-1]}$ and before its label is read by $\Lambda_x^{[a]}$ (line 8). The write actions of every scanners are monitored using the *Hand-shake bits* mechanism (lines 3 and 7). The labeler also "echoes" the label (and *tog* bit) read for every scanner (line 9). This information is written to the $s_j$ fields. The use of this information by the scanners is elaborated in the following subsection.

```
procedure labeling(i, obj) ;
    begin
    1:      b := ¬b ;
    2:      tmp ← collect ;
    3:      foreach scanner j do q_ij^b ← p_i^b(tmp_j) ;
    4:      old := new ;
    5:      new ← collect ;
    6:      ℓ_i := L(labels(new), i) ;
            foreach scanner j do begin
    7:          if {p_i^¬b(old_j) = p_i^¬b(new_j) = q_ij^¬b  and  tog(old_j) = tog(new_j)}
                then /* Do nothing! */
    8:          else hist_j := ℓ_i ;
    9:          slab_j := ⟨ℓ(new_j), tog(new_j)⟩ ;
            end ;
    10:     r_i ← ⟨obj, ℓ_i, hist, slab⟩ ;
    end ;
```

**Fig. 5.** The Linear Labeling Protocol (for labeler $i$)

## 4.3   The Scanning Protocol

The scanning protocol, presented in Fig. 6 is similar to a single step of the basic scanning protocol given above, except it always finds $w$ labels. In lines 3-5 of the protocol a basic labeling action is performed. Then the all the registers of labelers are read once again (line 6). In this *second collect* an active label and a historic label is read for every labeler. To accomplish **task A**, the scanning protocol should be able to choose correctly between the active and historic labels of every labeler. Note that the scanner cannot always choose the historic label, since this historic label could have been kept for an earlier scanning action after which the scanner has started an additional scanning action. In this case the historic label stored for this scanner is too old and therefore irrelevant. For this purpose the labeler echoes the most recent label it read for every scanner in $s_j$ fields. The scanner compares the label in $s_j$ field to its active label. If these labels are not-equal then the historic label is not chosen (lines 7-9).

```
function scanning(j) ;
   begin
   1:      foreach labeler i do begin
               fᵢ⁰ ← ¬qᵢⱼ⁰ ;
               fᵢ¹ ← ¬qᵢⱼ¹ ;
           end ;
   2:      toggleⱼ := ¬toggleⱼ ;
   3:      first ← collect ;
   4:      ℓⱼ := L(labels(first), j) ;
   5:      rⱼ ← ⟨ℓⱼ, toggleⱼ, f̂⁰, f̂¹⟩ ;
   6:      second ← collect ;
           foreach labeler i do
   7:          if {ℓⱼ ≺ ℓ(secondᵢ) and  sⱼ(secondᵢ) = ⟨ℓⱼ, toggleⱼ⟩}
   8:          then gᵢ := hⱼ(secondᵢ) ;
   9:          else gᵢ := ℓ(secondᵢ) ;
   10:     return(arrange(ĝ)) ;
   end ;
```

**Fig. 6.** The Linear Scanning Protocol (for scanner $j$)

**Theorem 8.** *Let $S_p^{[e]}$ be a scanning action, and let $t$ be the moment right after the write action made during $S_p^{[e]}$. All the labels returned by $S_p^{[e]}$ belong to $B_t^2$.*

This theorem together with lemmas 3 and 7 implies the correctness of the scanning protocol.

## 4.4  Space Complexity

The labelers' 1-W-$n$-R atomic registers are of length $O(n \cdot r)$ (since every historic label field is of $O(n)$ bits). However the fields $h_j$ and $s_j$ of labeler $i$ is read only by scanner $j$. Thus the total length of all the information stored by labeler $i$ for scanner $j$ is of length $O(n)$. This observation motivates the following definition: Let $v_i$, be $n$ values to be distributed to processes $P_i$ $1 \le i \le n$, where $v_i$ is given to $P_i$. The *atomic distribution* operation is the operation in which the values $v_i$ are distributed atomically, i.e. as if all values are distributed in the same time. A trivial implementation of atomic distribution is to use a an atomic 1-W-$n$-R register in which process $P$ writes the $v_i$-s. This yields a space complexity of $\sum |v_i|$ where $|v_i|$ denotes the length of $v_i$. If communication in the system is handled by 1-W-1-R registers, (rather than by 1-W-$n$-R registers) then atomic distribution can be done in space complexity $\max |v_i|$. As a result the linear scheme can be implemented in *linear* space complexity. The more efficient implementation of atomic distribution is done by assuming that initially communication is done using an implementation of a 1-W-$n$-R atomic register by atomic 1-W-1-R registers. In addition we assume that the implementing protocols do not depend on the values written in the register, e.g. the implementation of [11]. To implement atomic distribution we modify the write protocol in the implementation as follows:

> Instead of writing the same value, $v$, to the $n$ 1-W-1-R registers owned by the writer (of the 1-W-1-R register), a different value $v_i$ is written to every register read by reader $i$.

This change of the writer's protocol, allows the labeler, when writing to its 1-W-$n$-R register, to "write" distinct values for distinct scanners, without harming the atomicity of this write. The total amount of 1-W-1-R registers needed to implement this is the same as the amount of 1-W-1-R registers needed to implement a 1-W-$n$-R register of length $O(n)$.

## 5  Concluding Remarks

We presented a new bounded time-stamp scheme whose time and space complexity is linear in $n$, the total number of processes in the system. Our, previous and recent results concerning time-stamp schemes are summed up in Table 1, columns appear in chronological order. Future work should try to reduce the complexity to depend only on the number of labelers in the system as well as to try to improve the complexity of schemes in which communication is only one-sided. Another interesting direction is to explore the possibility of implementing bounded schemes directly from 1-W-1-R atomic registers.

**Table 1.** Efficiency comparison among time-stamps schemes

| | [3] | basic scheme | linear scheme | [4] | [5] |
|---|---|---|---|---|---|
| labeling time | $O(w)$ | $O(n)$ | $O(n)$ | $O(n)$ | $O(n)$ |
| scanning time | $O(w^2 \log w)$ | $O(w \cdot n)$ | $O(n)$ | $O(n)$ | $O(n)$ |
| register length | $O(w)$ | $O(n)$ | $O(r \cdot n)$ $(O(n))^*$ | $O(n \log n)$ | $O(n)$ |
| scanners write | | √ | √ | √ | √ |

# References

1. Afek Y., Attiya H., Dolev D., Gafni E., Merritt M., Shavit N.: Atomic snapshots of shared memory. Proc. 9th ACM Symp. on Principles of Distributed Computation (1990) pp. 1-13.
2. Chor B., Israeli A., Li M.: On processor coordination using asynchronous hardware. Proc. 6th ACM Symp. on Principles of Distributed Computation (1987) pp. 86-97.
3. Dolev D., Shavit N.: Bounded concurrent time-stamp systems are constructible! Proc. 21st Annual ACM Symp. on Theory of Computing (1989) pp. 454-466.
4. Dwork C., Waarts O.: Simple efficient bounded concurrent timestamping or Bounded concurrent timestamp systems are comprehensible! Proc. 24th Annual ACM Symp. on Theory of Computing (1992) pp. 655-666.
5. Dwork C., Herlihy M., Plotkin S.A., Waarts O.: Time-lapse snapshots. Proc. of the Israeli Symposium on the Theory of Computing and Systems (1992) pp. 154-170.
6. Herlihy M.P.: Waitfree implementations of concurrent objects. Proc. 7th ACM Symp. on Principles of Distributed Computation (1988) pp. 276-290.
7. Israeli A., Li M.: Bounded time-stamps. Proceedings of the 28th Annual Symposium on Foundations of Computer Science (1987) pp. 371-382.
8. Lamport L.: A new solution of Dijkstra's concurrent programming problem. CACM 17, 8 (1974) pp.453-455.
9. Lamport L.: The mutual exclusion problem. J. ACM 33, 2 (1986) pp.313-348.
10. Lamport L.: On interprocess communication. Distributed Computing 1, 2 (1986) pp. 77-101.
11. Li M., Tromp J., Vitanyi P.M.B.: How to share concurrent wait-free variables. preprint.
12. Pinhasov M.: A Linear-time bounded concurrent time-stamp scheme. M.Sc. thesis, Dept. of Computer Science, Technion, Haifa, Israel, (1991). (in Hebrew)
13. Singh A.K., Anderson J.H., Gouda M.G.: The elusive atomic register revisited. Proc. 6th ACM Symp. on Principles of Distributed Computation (1987) pp. 206-221.
14. Vitanyi P., Awerbuch B.: Atomic shared register access by asynchronous hardware. Proceedings of the 27th Annual Symposium on Foundations of Computer Science (1986) pp.233-243.

---

\* This complexity analysis is explained in subsection 4.4

# Tentative and Definite Distributed Computations: An Optimistic Approach to Network Synchronization

J. Garofalakis[1], S. Rajsbaum[2] ,P. Spirakis[1] and B. Tampakas[1]

[1] Computer Technology Institute and
Computer Science and Engineering Department
Patras University - Greece
[2] Instituto de Matemáticas
U.N.A.M. - Mexico

**Abstract.** We present here a general and efficient strategy for simulating a synchronous network by a network of limited asynchrony. Our proposed synchronizer is *optimistic* in the sense that it uses very efficient but *tentative protocols* to simulate a contiguous block of synchronous steps. However, since a tentative execution does not guarantee correct simulation, we *audit* the computation at selected points. The audits are used to check whether the computation of the block can be *certified* to be correct. We show that a wide class of networks of limited asynchrony admits practical tentative protocols which are highly likely to produce a correct simulation of one step with very small overhead. For those networks, the synchronizer exhibits a trade-off between its communication and time complexities which is below the lower bounds for deterministic synchronizers. On one extreme the amortized complexity of our synchronizer is $O(1)$ messages and $O(\log n)$ time (expected) per "step" of the simulated synchronous protocol. On the other extreme the communication complexity is $O(e/\Delta^2)$ and the time complexity is $O(log\Delta)$, for networks with $e$ edges and maximum degree $\Delta$.

# 1  Introduction.

## 1.1  The Need for Synchronizers.

Consider a network of $n$ processors and maximum degree $\Delta$. The processors communicate by sending messages along $e$ communication channels (edges). Assume that a program has been written for a *synchronous* network operation: On a global start-up signal, all processors start computing simultaneously. On every beat of the global clock each processor, according to its program, performs one computational step and sends messages to some of its neighbours. The transmission delay in the communication channels guarantees here that all messages arrive at their destinations in time to be used in the next computational step. We do not care about the exact nature and purpose of the program and we assume that processors and channels are reliable.

If one wants to run the same program on an *asynchronous network* of the same topology, where no global start-up signal exists and where transmission delays are unpredictable, then certain measures have to be taken to keep the computation correct. The use of *synchronizers* was suggested by Awerbuch [A,85] in order to simulate synchronous networks by asynchronous ones.

## 1.2 Complexity Measures.

The *communication complexity* of a synchronous algorithm $\pi$, $C(\pi)$, is the worst-case number of messages sent during the run of the algorithm. The *time complexity* of a synchronous algorithm $\pi$, $T(\pi)$, is the number of beats generated during the run of the algorithm. In our paper, for an asynchronous algorithm, the communication complexity is the worst case (among all possible starting time paterns) *expected* number of messages sent during a run, and the time complexity is the expected time of execution of a run. The expectation is taken with respect to a class of distributions of the transmission delays.

We are interested in studying what are the complexities of executing a synchronous program $\pi$ on an asynchronous network of limited asynchrony. Namely, the complexities of a synchronizer $S$ in our paper, are as follows: The time complexity is the worst case (among all synchronous programs $\pi$) expected duration of the execution of a (synchronous) step of $\pi$ by the synchronizer $S$. The message complexity of $S$ is the expected message overhead per step added by the synchronizer.

## 1.3 Previous Work.

For networks of unlimited asynchrony, Awerbuch presented synchronizers whose communication - time tradeoff is proved to be within a constant factor of the lower bound. The problem of designing efficient synchronizers has been studied in the past ([AP,90], [PU,89]). Even and Rajsbaum examined the performance of synchronizer - controlled networks which have a global clock but no global start-up signal and whose transmission delays are either negligible ([ER,88]) or fixed ([ER,90]). The results were generalized to other protocols by Malka and Rajsbaum. The performance of the synchronizer of [ER,88] and [ER,90] under random transmission delays and processing times was analyzed in [RS,90]. It was shown that any synchronizer has time delay (average) per step of $\Omega(\log \Delta)$.

Most of the above techniques provide *per-step synchronization*: the execution of the next "synchronous" step (of the original ideal synchronous program) begins only after the current "synchronous" step *is guaranteed* to have finished correctly. In such synchronizers, a communication (number of messages per "synchronous step" simulation) penalty of at least $\Theta(n)$ is paid where $n$ is the number of network nodes.

An exception to the above is the synchronizer alpha of [A,85]. In that synchronizer the network essentially runs free, locally delaying the computation only as long "as necessary". In particular, each processor waits for messages to arrive from all its neighbours before it performs the next computation step (It is assumed that every message is followed by an "end - of - message" marker, even if the message is empty). A similar mechanism was used by Chandy and Lamport ([CL,85]) and the whole approach is also encountered in models of marked graphs (see e.g. [CHEP,71]).

## 1.4   Our Results.

To avoid the possibly long waits introduced by the simple synchronizer presented above, we propose that each processor waits only for a certain amount $W$ of steps, hoping that all messages from neighbours will indeed arrive with high likelihood. This *optimistic* approach provides *tentative* executions which do not guarantee the corectness of the computation. Thus, we use a *definite* synchronization scheme, only at certain selected points, to *audit* the network's computations. The definite protocol checks whether the whole sequence of many tentative simulated steps can be *certified* to be correct. If not, the network's computation is *rolled back* to the previous audit point, and we restart the computation from there. A similar scheme was also employed in [KPRS,91] to provide robust parallel computations on faulty PRAMs (Parallel Random Access Machines, see [Wy,81]). Our work shows how to apply such ideas to get efficient synchronizers. For a wide class of networks we show our optimistic synchronizer to get an amortized mean delay of $O(\beta \log m)$ per "synchronous" step and an amortized mean number of messages of $O(e/m^{\beta})$ per "synchronous" step, for a parameter $m$, $\Delta \leq m \leq n$, and a constant $\beta > 2$ thus having a performance which is better than the performance of all previously proposed synchronizers. Moreover, by chosing $m = \Delta$, for networks with $e = O(\Delta^{\beta})$, we obtain a synchronizer with constant overhead in communication and time. Also by choosing $m = n$ we obtain a synchronizer with constant message complexity.

We assume (as in [ER,90]) that our networks have individual site clocks which run *at the same rate* but are *not* necessarily synchronized. Our networks have transmission delays that are random variables "with memory" (less variable than the exponential). Note that the assumptions about the distribution of the transmission delays affect *only the performance* of our synchronizer. Its correctness is guaranteed independently of those assumptions.

## 2   The Optimistic Synchronizer.

In the sequel, $m$ is the protocol's parameter, and $\alpha$, $\beta$, $\theta$ are constants that will be determined later. When we say $x$ time units, we assume that they are measured according to the processors' clocks (anyone of them, since they all run at the same rate). The synchronizer is similar to the synchronizer of [ER,88], [ER,90]; it has two operating modes. In the *steady state mode* a processor executes a step of the synchronous algorithm by performing the following *phase*.

**begin**
- wait $W = (\alpha + \beta) \log m$ time units;

- read messages that arrived and originated from neighbours within the previous phase;
- compute, as the simulated synchronous algorithm requires;
- send messages to neighbours for the next phase, as the simulated algorithm requires;

**end**

The phase is a *tentative* synchronization method. Note that in each phase, each node just waits $W$ time units and does not use any other messages than messages of the algorithm to be simulated received so far. The messages have to be *tagged* by *phase number*. If a message of an older phase arrives (late) at a node, then the node just sets an ERROR flag locally.

While a processor is in steady state mode it repeats the phase. After repeating the phase $k = m^\theta$ times, the processor enters the *audit mode*, which has the goal of backtracking the computation in case an error has occured in any of the phases since the last audit mode, namely, during the current *round*.

**Audit test:** When a processor enters the audit mode, it first finds out if it has executed any phase incorrectly during the current round. This test can be performed as follows. If ERROR is set, then some step has been performed incorrectly. Thus the processor starts the **Restarting** procedure described below. If ERROR is not set, a mistake could have been performed only in case a late message has not yet been received. To check this, each processor sends an END-ROUND message to every neighbour, and waits for an END-ROUND message from every neighbour. The message sent from $u$ to $v$ includes the number of times $u$ sent a message to $v$ during the current round. When $v$ has received an END-ROUND message from every neighbour it knows if it has received all the messages of the current round. If any of the messages did not arrive on time, $v$ sets its ERROR flag, and waits for any messages that have not arrived yet. This concludes the Audit Test.

**Restarting:** Once the auditing test is completed, a processor reenters steady state mode by invoking the following distributed restart algorithm (similar to the initialization mechanism of [ER,88], [ER,90]). Two cases are possible.

(i) The ERROR flag is not set. The processor sends s START-ROUND message to every neighbour and waits for a START-ROUND message from every neighbour. Then the processor enters steady state mode. This interchange of START-ROUND messages guarantees that neighboring processors enter steady state mode more or less at the same time. If instead of receiving a START-ROUND from a neighbour, the processor receives a RETRACT message, then it sends a RETRACT message to every neighbour, rolls back the computation to the previous round, unsets the ERROR and begins the Restart. Thus the RETRACT messages propagate in the network via flood.

(ii) The ERROR flag is set. The processor sends a RETRACT message to every neighbour, rolls back the computation to the previous round, unsets the ERROR and begins the Restart. Thus the RETRACT messages propagate in the network via flood.

Note that if at least one processor sets it flag to error, then every processor in the network rolls back the computation to the begining of the round. This can be improved by appending to the RETRACT messages a counter with the distance from the originator of the RETRACT: If a processor receives a message with counter $i$, it sends the messages with counter $i+1$, and rolls back $i$ phases. Hence a RETRACT propagates only a distance of $k$. Correctness: if $p$ has to execute phase $i$ again, then a neighbour has to execute $i+1$ again. We do not consider further the improvement of the protocol in this version of the paper.

Observe that the difference between the times on which two neighbours reenter steady state mode is bounded by the message delay of a START-ROUND message.

# 3  Correctness and Complexity of the Optimistic Synchronizer.

## 3.1  Outline.

From the synchronizer's protocol it is clear that a round which has been incorrectly performed (because some message arrived too late) will be rolled back by every processor. If the window $W$ is big enough, then no too many errors will occur, and a round will be eventually *commited* when the computations of all nodes during the round were correctly done. Thus our synchronizer is correct (it never commits erroneous computations).

Intuitively, if at the beginning of each phase of a node the node and its neighbours are "approximately synchronized" then they will remain so, at the end of the phase (with high probability, depending on a succesful selection of $W$). The audit test (and the initialization phase) serve two purposes: To make all nodes "approximately synchronized" and to preserve the correctness of the computation (by a *definite* protocol).

## 3.2  Complexity Analysis.

For the performance analysis we use the fact that the delays are random variables with memory, of mean at most $1/\lambda$ ($\lambda$ a parameter). Intuitively, a random variable is with memory if it is "new better than used" in expectation. Many natural distributions belong to this class, such as normal, uniform, and exponential. As we shall now see, the exponential is the one that produces the worst performance of the synchronizer. Therefore, the complexity analysis will be done assuming that the delays are exponentially distributed with mean $1/\lambda$.

**Definition** (See also [Ro,83]):
A random variable $x$ is called a random variable *with memory* if

$$\forall a \geq 0 \quad E(x-a/x>a) \leq E(x)$$

(where $E(x)$ is the expected value of $x$).

**Definition**:
A random variable $x$ is called *less variable* than a random variable $y$ if, for all increasing convex functions $h$,

$$E(h(x)) \leq E(h(y)).$$

We denote this by $x \leq_v y$.

**Fact 1** [Ro,83]:
Let $x$ be a random variable with memory and $y$ be an exponential random variable of same mean. Then $x \leq_v y$.

**Fact 2** [Ro,83]:
If $x_1, x_2, \ldots, x_n$ are independent random variables and $y_1, y_2, \ldots, y_n$ are independent random variables and $x_i \leq_v y_i$ then $g(x_1, x_2, \ldots, x_n) \leq_v g(y_1, y_2, \ldots, y_n)$ for any increasing convex function $g$ which is convex in each of its arguments.

**Theorem 1**
The probability of an error during a phase of a node is maximized when the message delays are *exponential random variables*, among all possible delay distributions with memory.

**Proof sketch**
An error happens when the maximum of the message delays from the neighbours (*plus* the *max* "slack" in initial neighbour synchronization) exceeds $W$. Since the *max* function (and the *plus*) are convex, by Facts 1 and 2, all moments are maximized when the delays are exponential random variables.

$\square$

**Corollary 1**
The exponential delays of messages provide the worst case performance of the optimistic synchronizer, among all possible distributions of delays (of the same mean) which are random variables with memory.

**Theorem 2**
For each $\beta > 2$ and $\alpha > 0$ there is a $\gamma > 0$ such that the following holds: Assume that all the neighbours of a node $v$, and $v$ itself, finish phase $i$ within a time interval of $\alpha \cdot \log m$ (where $\alpha$ is a positive constant). Then, all the messages that are sent to $v$ at the end of phase $i$ will be received within the window $W = (\alpha + \beta) \log m$ of phase $i + 1$ of $v$, with probability $\geq 1 - m^{-\beta}$, provided that $W$ is at least $\gamma \cdot \log m$.

**Proof**
Let $t_0$ be the instant at which the last phase $i$ of $v$'s neighbours finishes. In the worst case all neighbours finish at $t_0$ their phase $i$ (else they finish earlier).

Let $D_1, D_2, \ldots, D_{m'}$ be the message delays of the messages that were sent to $v$ at the end of phase $i$.

Let $D = max\{D_1, D_2, \ldots, D_{m'}\}$.

Clearly $m'$ is at most equal to the number of $v$'s neighbours, and hence $m' \leq \Delta$.

$$Prob\{D \leq x\} = Prob\{\forall D_i, \; D_i \leq x\} = \prod_{i=1}^{m'} Prob\{D_i \leq x\}$$

because of independence. Since in the worst case all $D_i$'s are exponential, the above probability (of small delay) is minimized when all $D_i$'s are exponential. Thus, $Prob\{D \leq x\} \geq (1 - e^{-\lambda \cdot x})^m$
(where $\lambda$ is the rate of the exponential).

If we want $Prob\{D \leq x\}$ to be $\geq 1 - m^{-\beta}$ then it is enough to have

$$(1 - e^{-\lambda x})^{m'} \geq 1 - m^{-\beta} \Rightarrow \; e^{-\lambda x} \leq 1 - (1 - m^{-\beta})^{\frac{1}{m'}} \Rightarrow \; x \geq \frac{1}{\lambda} \ln\left(\frac{1}{1 - (1 - m^{-\beta})^{\frac{1}{m'}}}\right)$$

But

$$\left(1 - \frac{1}{m^\beta}\right)^{\frac{1}{m'}} \geq 1 - \frac{1}{mm'^\beta} \geq 1 - \frac{1}{m^{\beta+1}}$$

(since $m' \leq m$). Thus

$$1 - \left(1 - \frac{1}{m^\beta}\right)^{\frac{1}{m'}} \leq \frac{1}{m^{\beta+1}} \Rightarrow \; x \geq \frac{\beta+1}{\lambda} \log m$$

Thus, if we pick a $\gamma \geq \alpha + (\beta + 1)/\lambda$ then all the messages from the various phases $i$ of $v$'s neighbours will indeed arrive at $v$ during the window $W = (\alpha + (\beta + 1)/\lambda) \log m$ of $v$'s phase $i + 1$, with probability $\geq 1 - m^{-\beta}$.

$\square$

## Corollary 2
$\exists \; \beta_0 > 0 : \forall \beta > \beta_0$, if all phases $i$ finish correctly within an interval of $O(\log m)$ time then all phases $i+1$ will finish correctly within an interval of $O(\log m)$ time with probability at least $1 - m^{-\beta}$.
(Proof ommited).

In the sequel, let $k = m^\theta$, $\theta > 0$.

## Theorem 3
For each $\beta_1 > 3$ and $\alpha_1 > 0$, $\exists \gamma > 0$ : If a round of the network starts in such a way that all starting moments of neighbour nodes are in an interval of size $\alpha_1 \cdot \log m$ ($\alpha_1 > 0$ a constant) then all nodes will finish the round *correctly* with probability at least $1 - m^{-\beta_1}$, provided $W = \gamma \cdot \log m$.

## Proof
Let $\beta = \beta_1 + \theta$. Choose $\gamma \geq \alpha_1 + (\beta + 1)/\lambda$.
Let $E_j$ be the event "phase $j$ of the round finishes correctly provided that all

nodes start it within an interval of $\alpha_1 \cdot \log m$ ".
Then, if $E = \bigcap_{j=1}^{k} E_j$ , we wish to find the $Prob\{E\}$. But

$$Prob\{\bar{E}\} = Prob\{\bigvee_{j=1}^{k} \bar{E_j}\} \leq \sum_{j=1}^{k} Prob\{\bar{E_j}\} \leq k \cdot m^{-\beta} = m^{-(\beta-\theta)} = m^{-\beta_1}$$

Thus, $Prob\{E\} \geq 1 - m^{-\beta_1}$ .

□

## Theorem 4
For each $\alpha > 0$ $\exists \beta > 0$ : Each round of our synchronizer starts in such a way that all starting moments of neighbour nodes are within an interval of size $\alpha \cdot \log m$ ($\alpha > 0$ is an appropriate constant) with probability at least $1 - m^{-\beta}$ .

## Proof
The starting time of the last of any set of neighbours to start is at most the maximum of $m$ exponential independent random variables of mean $d = 1/\lambda$ . The probability that this maximum can exceed $\alpha \cdot \log m$ is at most $m^{-\beta}$ for some $\beta$ depending on $\alpha$. (Proof as in Theorem 2).

□

Theorems 3 and 4 show that:

## Corollary 3
Each round terminates *correctly* with probability at least $1 - m^{-\beta}$ and $\beta$ can be controlled by adjusting the window size $W$.

From Corollary 3 and from the fact that the mean value of a geometric random variable $Y$ of density $Prob\{Y = i\} = (1-p)^{i-1}p$ is bounded above by $1/p$, we get that:

## Corollary 4
The mean number of unsuccesful repetitions of a round before *commit*, is bounded above by 2.

## Proof
Since a round fails with probability $\leq n^{-\beta}$ just put $p = 1 - m^{-\beta}$.

□

Thus we get our main result:

## Theorem 5
*The amortized (over a round) expected number of synchronizer messages (per synchronous step of the simulated algorithm) is $O(\frac{e}{m^\beta})$. The amortized (over a round) expected delay of the synchronizer (per "synchronous" step of the simulated algorithm) is $O(\beta \log m)$, for a constant $\beta$ and $\Delta \leq m \leq n$.*

## Proof
Select a $\theta > 0$ $(k = m^\theta)$ , for $\theta = \beta - \beta'$ and $\beta' > 3$. The number (expected)

of messages of the synchronizer per round is at most $2e$ ($e$ = number of network edges), $e$ for RETRACT messages and $e$ for START-ROUND messages by Corollary 4 and by the fact that no messages of the synchronizer are used in phases. Thus the amortized number is $2e/k = O(\frac{e}{m^\theta})$, for the constant $\theta$.

The total delay per round is two times at most $\alpha \cdot k \cdot \log m$ (for the phases of the round, where $\alpha$ is as in Theorem 4) with probability at least $1 - m^{-\beta}$, plus the delay of the commit protocol. The mean delay of the commit protocol is $O(1/\lambda)$. Thus the total delay is (expected) $O(k \log m)$ and the amortized value is $O(\log m)$.

□

Note that the estimates of Theorem 5 can be shown to hold with high probability (proof in the full paper), since by a theorem of [Ro,83] if $\{X_i\}$ is a sequence of independent exponential random variables of mean $\lambda^{-1}$ then for every positive $k'$ and $c > 4 \log 2$, $Prob\{\sum_{i=1}^{k'} X_i \geq ck\lambda^{-1}\} \leq exp(-ck/4)$.

## 4   An Adaptive Extension of the Protocol.

Our optimistic synchronizer presented so far has to know an appropriate window size $W$ in order to work efficiently, since the multiplication constant of $W$ depends on the mean message delay. The mean message delay can be estimated (and adjusted when the protocol starts doing a lot of restarted rounds) by the following simple protocol:

### Mean delay estimation protocol for node $v$.

1. For each neighbour $w$ of $v$, $v$ sends a "count delay" message, and stores the sending time $t(v, w)$. If $v$ receives such a message, it sends it back to its originator as soon as it receives it.
2. When $v$ receives the count delay message back, it notes the receipt time (according to $v$'s clock) $t'(v, w)$. Let $d(v, w) = t'(v, w) - t(v, w)$.
3. The above is repeated $g$ times. Let $d_i(v, w)$ the estimate of each time. Then

$$\tilde{d} = \frac{d_1(v, w) + d_2(v, w) + \cdots + d_g(v, w)}{2g}$$

### Lemma 1
If we choose a $g \geq 1/\varepsilon$ then with probability at least $1 - \varepsilon$, $|\tilde{d} - d| \leq 2$ where $d$ is the mean message delay.
(Proof in full paper).

With the delay estimation protocol our synchronizer can be applied to networks where mean message delays vary with time, and where message delay distributions are not the same in each neighbour (then one has to use the *largest* estimated mean delay in the formula for $W$). (Details in full paper).

# 5 Future Work.

We are currently extending our optimistic synchronizer to work for networks whose node clocks are not accurate but can be synchronized by another protocol.

**Acknowledgments:** P. Spirakis wishes to thank Z. Kedem and K. Palem for insightful comments on rollback techniques. The authors wish to thank the referees of WDAG for their useful remarks.

# References

[A,85]     Awerbuch B., *"Complexity of Network Synchronization"*, JACM, Vol. 32, No 4, Oct. 1985.

[AP,90]    Awerbuch B., Peleg D., *"Network Synchronization with Polylogarithmic Overhead"*, Proc. IEEE FOCS, 1990.

[CHEP,71]  C Commoner F., Holt W., Even S., Pnueli A., *"Marked Directed Graphs"*, JCSS, Vol. 5, No 5, 1971.

[CL,85]    Chandy K.M., Lamport L., *"Distributed Snapshots: Determining Global States of Distributed Systems"*, ACM Trans. on Computer Systems, Vol. 3, No 1, 1985.

[ER,88]    Even E., Rajsbaum S., *"Lack of Global Clock Does Not Slow Down the Computation in Distributed Networks"*, TR #522, Dep. of Comp. Sc., Haifa, Israel, Oct. 1988. The first part of this paper will appear with the title *"Unison in Distributed Networks"* in Sequenses, Combinatorica, Compression, Security and Transmission, R.M. Capocelli (ed.), Springer-Verlag.

[ER,90]    Even E., Rajsbaum S., *"The use of a Synchronizer Yields Maximum Rate in Distributed Networks"*, Proc. 22nd ACM STOC, 1990.

[KPRS,91]  Kedem Z., Palem K., Raghunathan A., Spirakis P., *"Combining Tentative and Definite Executions for Very Fast Dependable Parallel Computing"*, Proc. ACM STOC 1991.

[PU,89]    Peleg D., Ullman J., *"An Optimal Synchronizer for the Hypercube"*, SIAM J.Computing, Vol. 18, No 4, Aug. 1989, pp 740-747.

[Ro,83]    Ross S.M., *"Stochastic Processes"*, Wiley, 1983.

[RS,90]    Rajsbaum S., Sidi M., *"On the Average Performance of Synchronized Programs in Distributed Networks"*, Proc. WDAG 1990.

[Wy,81]    J. C. Wyllie, *"The Complexity of Parallel Computations"*, PhD dissertation, Comp. Sc. Department, Cornell University, Ithaca, New York, 1981.

# Semisynchrony and Real Time

## Extended abstract

Stephen Ponzio[1] and Ray Strong[2]

[1] MIT Laboratory for Computer Science, 545 Technology Sq., Cambridge, MA 02139,
ponzio@theory.lcs.mit.edu
[2] IBM Almaden Research Center, 650 Harry Rd., San Jose, CA 95120-6099
strong@almaden.ibm.com

**Abstract.** This paper represents the confluence of several streams of research on the real time complexity of distributed algorithms. The primary focus of our study is on two models and two problems: the timed automata model of Attiya and Lynch and the ("latency") model of approximately synchronized clocks studied by Strong et. al., and the problems of consensus and atomic broadcast. We compare these models and problems, producing new results and significant improvements of previously known bounds. In particular, we are able to significantly improve the upper bound of Strong, Dolev, and Cristian on latency for Byzantine failures, giving an algorithm that is much simpler with vastly easier analysis. For this problem, we also improve the best known lower bound on latency. We also provide certain reductions between problems and models and provide preliminary answers to some new questions in the timed automata model.

## 1    Introduction

In the interest of obtaining more accurate and useful time bounds for distributed algorithms, there recently has been much attention devoted to deriving time bounds that explicitly account for the degrees of asynchrony that exist in distributed systems. Several different models of semisynchrony have been used, capturing different concerns about issues of real time. Similar but different problems have been studied in these models, yielding quantitative results that are seemingly related. This paper attempts to present a unified view of these research efforts, summarizing the concerns addressed by each. We compare solutions to the general problem of simulating round-based synchronous algorithms and focus on specific solutions to consensus-type problems, which, as the fundamental distributed problems requiring some synchrony, are the natural candidates for the initial stages of this research. By comparing the concerns and approaches in both studies, we have sometimes been able to achieve significant and surprising improvements over existing results. Although we have found that most techniques do not carry over from one setting to the other, understanding the disparity has led to a greater appreciation of what aspects of these two problems are important to different measures of real-time performance. In addition, our study has revealed some very natural unanwered questions regarding these problems as well as the area of clock synchronization.

For this extended abstract we consider two models of timing in distributed message-passing systems[3]; briefly (see Section 2 for complete definitions), these are

1. The TA ("Timed Automata") model: A basic model of semisynchrony, formalized and studied by Attiya and Lynch ([AL89, ADLS90, P91]). Studies in this model focus on the effect of the maximum possible ratio of processor rates, denoted $C$. Message delay time is denoted $d$.

2. The AC ("Approximately synchronized Clocks") model: A model in which processors are assumed to have approximately synchronized clocks. Studied by Strong, Dolev, and Cristian ([CASD86, SDC90, GSTC90]). Work in this model have focused on the effect of the maximum difference $e$ between clocks ("skew" or "precision"). The maximum possible ratio of clock rates is denoted $A$ and the message delay is denoted $d_{AC}$.

In each of the models, it is easy to simulate arbitrary synchronous round-based algorithms by allowing the maximum possible time for each round. However such straightforward simulations are generally inefficient. The motivating question is

**Can one do better than directly simulating round-based algorithms?**

Natural vehicles to explore time complexities are the fundamental fault-tolerant problems of consensus and atomic broadcast. We distinguish atomic broadcast from consensus in two ways: consensus is *"multi-source"* and *one-time only*—each processor gets exactly one input value and the output is a single value; atomic broadcast is *"single-source"* and *dynamic*—each processor may get input values repeatedly and the output is a sequence of these values, which must be identical for each processor. The consensus problem has been studied in the TA model ([ADLS90, P91]) and the atomic broadcast problem has been studied in the AC model ([CASD86, SDC90, GSTC90, BGT90]).

## 1.1 Our results

We apply algorithmic techniques used for consensus (with Byzantine failures) in the TA model to obtain a greatly improved algorithm for atomic broadcast (with Byzantine failures) in the AC model. The best previous algorithm ([SDC90]) for atomic broadcast in the presence of Byzantine failures had "latency"[4] $2e + 3(2 + A + A^2 + \cdots + A^f)d_{AC}$, where $f$ is the number of Byzantine processor failures to be tolerated. We adapt an algorithm from [P91] to obtain a vastly simpler algorithm with much simpler analysis and an improved latency of $2e + ((1 + 2A)f + 1)d_{AC}$.

---

[3] In the full paper, we also include comparisons with the related model studied by Herzberg and Kutten ([HK89]).

[4] A measure of time complexity defined in Section 2.4.

We also prove that, even for more benign failures (such as authenticated Byzantine or clock failures with send and receive omissions), a lower bound for latency is $2e + (f + 1)d_{AC}$. This improves on the previously best known lower bounds of $2e + 2d_{AC}$ ([SDC90]) and $e + (f + 1)d_{AC}$ ([CASD86]).

Although there is a vast literature on the problem of atomic broadcast (e.g., [CM84, BJ87, MMA90, MMA91, ADKM92]), we know of no work that focuses on the real time complexity of this problem when processors are not fully synchronous. Surprisingly, there is no simple algorithm for solving atomic broadcast in the TA model (even inefficiently). We consider implementing synchronized clocks in the TA model as one way of solving the atomic broadcast problem. Unfortunately, many important clock synchronization algorithms such as [ST87], [DHSS89] and [LL88] were designed only for systems with extremely small drift ($C \approx 1 + \epsilon$); it is not clear whether these algorithms can be extended to work for the case we are interested in, when $C$ is large. [5] We also adapt a lower bound proof of [ST87] to show that $A \geq C$ for any clocks implemented in TA.

Finally, we derive several simple reductions between the problems and models. They relate latency of atomic broadcast with the real time required to achieve consensus. We first show that if there is an atomic broadcast protocol with latency $L$, then there is a consensus protocol for the AC model that requires at most real time $R \approx (L + 2e)/\sqrt{A}$. We also show that if there is a consensus protocol that requires at most real time $R$, then there is an atomic broadcast protocol with latency $L \approx \sqrt{A}R + d_{AC} + e$.

# 2 Models, problems, and discussion

Consensus-type problems are the most natural candidate to study in a semisynchronous model: their time complexity is well understood in the case of synchronous round-based computation; they are well known to be impossible for completely asynchronous systems, and the necessary degrees of synchrony have been thoroughly studied ([DDS87]). However, the different models of semisynchrony have inspired the study of different versions of the consensus problem. We begin by describing the two models in more detail. In both models, processors are completely connected by reliable message links and all parameters are known to the processors. We consider the standard failure modes; unless otherwise stated, "omission" failures refers "send-omission" failures only.

## 2.1 Model TA: A basic model of semisynchrony

A basic model of semisynchrony is developed in the work of Attiya and Lynch ([AL89]), based on the timed automaton model ([MMT90]). Conceptually, the model is very simple: successive steps of a nonfaulty process are separated by at least time $c_1$ and at most $c_2$ and all messages sent are delivered within time $d$.

---

[5] The question of whether $e$ and $A$ can be simultaneously minimized—$e \approx d$ and $A = C$—is a long-standing open question in the area of clock synchronization.

Although these constants are common knowledge among the processors, a processor cannot directly determine the exact time between any two particular steps. A "step" of a process consists of performing some local computation and sending messages to other processors. Messages may be delivered to a processor between two of its steps. Processors are assumed to obey the timing constraints if they suffer omission failures but not if they suffer Byzantine failures. (An interesting but unstudied alternative model of failure is "timing" failures, where processors act correctly except that they may violate the step-time constraint. The most efficient algorithm known for this class of failures is the algorithm for Byzantine failures.)

In this model, the ratio $c_2/c_1$ is used as a measure of the timing uncertainty and denoted simply $C = c_2/c_1$. This parameter measures the rate of drift between processors. Processor steps are typically much faster than message transmission, so we usually consider $c_2 \ll d$ and make approximations appropriately. An essential factor in the running time of a round-based simulation is the time required to timeout the message of another processor. We therefore first outline why a timeout may take up to time $Cd + d$ in this model. Suppose processors implement fault-detection by continuously sending "I'm alive" messages to each other, so that $d$ is approximately an upper bound on the time between the delivery of any two successive messages. If $q$ fails to send a message to $p$ at time $t$, $p$ will begin to notice an absence of messages at time $t + d$. Processor $p$ concludes that $q$ has failed when it is sure that time $d$ has elapsed since the last message received. It can only conclude that time $d$ has elapsed by waiting for $d/c_1$ steps, which may take up to time $t + d + c_2(d/c_1) = t + d + Cd$. Thus we see that although it takes only time $d$ to receive a message, it may take up to time $Cd + d$ to *detect the absence* of a message.

Any round-based algorithm may then be simulated despite stopping or omission failures by continuously performing this timeout protocol between every pair of processors. Each processor simulates round $i$ by waiting until for each processor $q$, $p$ has either received a round $i - 1$ message from $q$ or has detected the failure of $q$. Each round then takes approximately time $Cd + d$ to simulate. The goal of the work of [ADLS90, P91] is to quantify the effect of semisynchrony on the real-time complexity of distributed computing problems: given a system with parameters $c_1, c_2, d$, what are tight upper and lower bounds on the *real time* required for these problems?

## 2.2   Model AC: Approximately synchronized clocks

A higher-level model of semisynchrony in the spirit of the work on clock synchronization has been studied by Dolev, Strong, and Cristian ([SDC90]). Each processor has a clock that stays within a linear envelope of real time: there exist positive constants $a_1 \leq 1 \leq a_2$ and $a_3$ such that for each clock of a correct processor and for all real times $t_1 < t_2$,

$$a_1(t_2 - t_1) - a_3 \leq Clock(t_2) - Clock(t_1) \leq a_2(t_2 - t_1) + a_3.$$

Clocks of correct processors never differ by more than $e$. This is a discretized version of the standard model of clocks that has been used throughout the literature on clock synchronization (e.g., [DHSS89, DHS86, LM85]). Processors are interrupt-driven: they may be caused to take a step either by the arrival of a message or by its clock reaching a prespecified time. As in the TA model, a processor may send messages to several other processors during one step. Also, processors are assumed to obey the timing constraints if they suffer omission failures but not if they suffer Byzantine failures.

In the AC model, the maximum delay of any message is defined in terms of clock time: the interval between the sending and delivery of any message measures at most $d_{AC}$ on the *clock* of *any* correct processor. We use the subscript $AC$ to distinguish this term from $d$, defined in the TA model, which we retain to denote maximum *real time* between sending and delivery. To put the drift assumption into a more usable form, we first note that if an interval is timed to be of length $t$ on the clock of a correct processor, then it measures at most $(a_2/a_1)t + 2a_3 \approx At$ on the clock of any other correct processor (take $t_2 - t_1 = t/a_1$ in the above definition). As with the TA model, we will generally assume that the granularity of the clocks is much less than message delay—$a_3 \ll d_{AC}$—and make appropriate approximations. We denote $A = a_2/a_1$ and call this quantity the *relative accuracy*[6].

How can synchronous round-based algorithms be simulated in this model? Because clocks are available, timing out other processors is a simple matter: if $p$ is supposed to send a message to $q$ at time $t$ on its clock, then $q$ knows that the message should be sent no later than time $t + e$ on its own clock and therefore should be received no later than time $t + e + d_{AC}$ on its clock. To simulate a round-based algorithm starting at clock time $t$, each processor waits until time $t + i(d_{AC} + e)$ on its clock to receive round $i$ messages and then sends its round $i + 1$ message.

## 2.3 Consensus

This version was studied in [ADLS90, P91]. It is the standard classical binary consensus problem: each processor has a one-bit input and all correct processors must agree on a one-bit output which is equal to the input if all inputs are equal.

Because each processor is supposed to receive an input for the problem, it makes the most sense to assume that these inputs arrive within some known time interval. (In the synchronous round-based model, processors are assumed to begin executing the algorithm at the same time.) We therefore introduce a parameter $x$ to denote the length of the interval of real time in which all processors receive their inputs. We measure running time as the difference between the real time at which the last correct processor decides on a value and the real time at which the first correct processor gets its input. Note that this definition applies to all failure models. (The algorithms from [ADLS90] and [P91] work for $x > 0$ with little or no modifications.)

---

[6] This ratio is equivalent to "$(1+\rho)^2$" in [ST87, LL88, DHSS89] and "$1+\rho$" in [SDC90].

125

## 2.4 Atomic broadcast

This version was studied in [CASD86, SDC90, GSTC90]. It is a dynamic problem in the sense that inputs arrive repeatedly and asynchronously. At any time, a processor may receive a binary input which must be broadcast to all other processors. Processors must output a sequence of values such that (1) all correct processors output the same sequence of values, and (2) the input sequence of each correct processor appears as a distinct subsequence of this sequence. Note that this definition allows for the possibility that processors may agree on a value different from the sender's input even if the sender suffers only stopping or omission failure. When a processor (irreversibly) adds a message to its list, it is said to *deliver* the message.

A natural definition of real-time complexity for this problem is to measure the difference between the time that a processor gets an input and the time the last correct processor delivers the message. This definition is workable for omission failures, but it is not meaningful if a Byzantine processor delays acting on its input and then correctly executes the broadcast algorithm on that input; in this case the time cannot be bounded.

In [CASD86], this difficulty is resolved for the AC model by defining a time complexity measure called the *latency*. This measurement requires as part of the *problem statement* that when a processor initiates a message, it should attach its local time to the message.

**Definition 1.** The *latency* of an algorithm for atomic broadcast is the maximum difference (over all executions, processors, and messages) between the *local clock time* that a correct processor delivers the message and the *timestamp* on that message.

Thus the algorithms developed for atomic broadcast in the AC model are concerned not with minimizing the elapsed real time, but with minimizing the age of any message (as defined by its timestamp) that must be accepted by a processor, relative to its current clock time. Although this measure may seem unnatural at first, it does have the advantage of being directly observable by processors. Note that for stopping or omission failures, the latency is equal to $e$ plus the maximum time that can elapse on a processor's clock between the real time of the input and the real time that the processor delivers the corresponding message. Of course, this is not true for Byzantine failures, as clocks of faulty processors need not be within $e$ of each other.

## 2.5 Previous work

Work on consensus in the TA model has focused on the extent to which the drift, or timing uncertainty, $C$, affects the real-time complexity. A straightforward rounds simulation (for omission failures) requires time approximately $Cd$ per round. Interesting new algorithms were developed with running times of $2fd+Cd$ for stopping failures ([ADLS90]) and $4(f+1)d + Cd$ for omission failures and $(2f+1)Cd + fd$ for Byzantine failures ([P91]).

Work on atomic broadcast in the AC model, however, has focused on the extent to which the clock skew $e$ affects the running time; the effect of drift ($A$) has not been a primary concern of this research. A straightforward rounds simulation may require clock time $d_{AC} + e$ per round. It is easy to show that this is not optimal for stopping and omission failures; a simple message-diffusion algorithm gives a total latency of $(f + 1)d_{AC} + e$ ([CASD86]). However, a great deal of effort was needed to achieve a latency of $3(2 + \sum_{i=0}^{f} A^i)d_{AC} + 2e$ for Byzantine failures ([SDC90]).

From looking at the results above, it is tempting to infer some kind of relationship between the additive factor of $Cd$ which the TA bounds minimize and the additive factor of $e$ which the AC bounds minimize. However, we shall see that no such relationship exists.

# 3 Improved latency bounds for atomic broadcast

## 3.1 Round simulations

We first consider the general problem of simulating synchronous rounds. For simplicity, we will assume that all processors begin a TA rounds simulation at the same real time and an AC rounds simulation at the same clock time. We saw in Section 2 that rounds may be simulated in the AC model at a cost of $d_{AC} + e$ elapsed clock time per round (for all failure models) and in the TA model at a cost of $Cd + d$ real time per round (for stopping or omission failures) or $(2C + 1)d$ per round (for Byzantine failures). In neither model does the respective round simulation yield an efficient algorithm for consensus or atomic broadcast (except for the Byzantine consensus algorithm in the TA model, which is not known to be suboptimal—i.e., it is not known whether $O(fd) + Cd$ is sufficient or if $\Omega(fCd)$ is required).

We consider adapting rounds-simulation algorithms of the TA model to work in the AC model. The algorithms for the TA model use the bounds on step time exclusively for deriving upper bounds on elapsed time—for instance, counting enough steps to ensure that time $d$ has passed after sending a message in order to be sure that it has been delivered. These algorithms can thus be used in the AC model with little change by instead using the clocks to give such guarantees—for example, if a processor waits for time $d_{AC}$ on its clock after sending a message, it ensures that the message must be delivered because at most time $d_{AC}$ can elapse on *any* correct clock while the message is in transit. Thus the clocks are used as "timers" to measure the length of intervals, and their synchronization–that they are within $e$ of each other—is ignored.

The rounds simulation for omission failures in the TA model described in Section 2.1 uses real time $(C+1)d$ per round. To analyze the adapted algorithm in the AC model, we must ask how much any clock may advance during a "round". As with the analysis in the TA model, the worst case is when a single processor fails just before sending its round message; this causes the other processors to wait for $d/c_1$ steps, or $Cd$ time, before concluding that a failure has occurred. In the AC model, this failure leads to a worst-case latency if a processor with a fast clock quickly concludes that a failure has occurred while another processor with a slow clock takes longer to reach that conclusion; on the slower clock, time $d_{AC}$ elapses while on the faster clock, time $A \cdot d_{AC}$ elapses. By a similar argument as in Section 2.1, we see that some clock may advance $(A+1)d_{AC}$ each round. We note that the worst-case execution in the TA bound is with all processors going fast, whereas in the AC bound, it is with one clock going slow and another going fast.

Thus the adapted simulation is successful in avoiding an additive $e$ with each round, improving in that respect on the first simulation described for the AC model. It suffers, however, from the $A + 1$ factor of $d_{AC}$. Suppose we use this round simulation to run a standard atomic broadcast algorithm for omission failures (assuming a common clock start time). Simulating $f + 1$ rounds gives a total latency of about $(f+1)(A+1)d_{AC} + e$, as a faster clock may have started out $e$ ahead of that of the processor receiving (and timestamping) the input. This fails to improve the latency of the simple message-diffusion algorithm of [CASD86].

Indeed, even if we translate the efficient consensus algorithm of [ADLS90], the resulting latency is $2fd_{AC}+Ad_{AC}+e$, which is also worse than [CASD86]. We remark that the algorithm of [ADLS90] can be viewed as an optimized simulation of a synchronous early-stopping consensus algorithm with a special property regarding the circumstances under which a processors must advance to successive rounds (see [P91]). This suggests that it may be possible to identify a class of efficiently simulatable synchronous algorithms whose simulations need incur neither the $e$ per round nor the $A + 1$ factor of $d_{AC}$.

The algorithm for consensus with Byzantine failures in the TA model [P91] works by simulating synchronous rounds efficiently (relative to naive strategies). In Section 3.2 below, we show that this simulation, which uses time $(2C+1)d$ per round, may be adapted to the AC model so that any clock advances at most $(2A+1)d_{AC}$ per round. However, because the clocks of Byzantine processors may differ from correct clocks by more than $e$, the total latency for simulating $f + 1$ rounds turns out to be $(f+1)(2A+1)d_{AC} + 2e$ (instead of plus $1e$). Surprisingly, this is far better than the latency bound of [SDC90] (modulo the synchronized start assumption).

We see that except for this assumption the adaptation of the TA rounds-simulation improves the atomic broadcast latency bound for Byzantine failures but not for stopping or omission failures. We can now see that the differing factor of $e$ for omission and Byzantine failures (1 and 2, respectively) is precisely due to the difference on the clocks at the beginning of the algorithm.

## 3.2 The algorithm

The following algorithm simulates synchronous rounds despite Byzantine failures, under the assumption that it is common knowledge that the input message should be timestamped $T$. The algorithm uses the synchronized clocks to wait for round one messages (this is where the additive $2e$ is incurred) and then relies only on the rates of the clocks for the rest of the algorithm. All times are measured on local clocks.

---

1a.     **Wait** until time $T + d_{AC} + e$ **or** until $f + 1$ round 2 messages received
1b.     **Send** round 2 message

2a.     **Wait** until $2f + 1$ round 2 messages received
2b.     **Wait** for time $2d_{AC}$ **or** until $f + 1$ round 3 messages received
2c.     **Send** round 3 message

$$\vdots$$

$(i - 1)$a. **Wait** until $2f + 1$ round $i - 1$ messages received
$(i - 1)$b. **Wait** for time $2d_{AC}$ **or** until $f + 1$ round $i$ messages received
$(i - 1)$c. **Send** round $i$ message

$$\vdots$$

$r$a.     **Wait** until $2f + 1$ round $r$ messages received          ;the last round
$r$b.     **Wait** for time $2d_{AC}$
        **END**

---

**Theorem 2. (Correctness)** *For $n \geq 3f + 1$, the above simulation ensures that each correct processor receives round $i - 1$ messages from all correct processors before sending its round $i$ message.*

*Proof.* First note that because $n \geq 3f + 1$, processors will eventually advance to all rounds of the simulation. It is clear that a processor does not send its round 2 message before receiving a round 1 message from all correct processors: consider the first correct processor to send a round 2 message. It cannot receive $f + 1$ round 2 messages before it sends, so it must wait until $T + d_{AC} + e$ on its clock before sending. Clearly, all round 1 messages of correct processors are delivered by this time. All other correct processors send their round 2 messages later.

In subsequent rounds, when the first correct processor $p$ sends its round $i$ message, the round $i - 1$ messages of all correct processors have been delivered: Because $p$ is the first correct processor to send its round $i$ message at $(i - 1)$c, it could not have received $f + 1$ round $i$ messages before then and therefore must have waited for a period of $2d_{AC}$ on its clock after it received $2f + 1$ round $i - 1$ messages. After $p$ has waited $d_{AC}$, all correct processors have received at least $f + 1$ of those messages and therefore, by the code, they must have sent round $i - 1$ messages (they must already be at least to $(i - 2)$b, since they have each sent a round $i - 2$ message to $p$ by the induction hypothesis and then advanced to $(i - 2)$a, and subsequently received at least $2f + 1$ round $i - 2$ messages from each other). These round $i - 1$ messages are received by all processors within another time $d_{AC}$ on $p$'s clock, which is when $p$ sends its round $i$ message.   $\square$

To tolerate Byzantine failures with authentication and $n \geq 2f + 1$, simply change "**Wait** until $2f + 1$ round $i - 1$ messages received" to "**Relay** $f + 1$ round

$i - 1$ messages." Thus a processor $p$ executing this statement ensures that all other correct processors will send their $i - 1$ messages within $2d_{AC}$ because the signed relayed messages satisfy $(i - 2)$b.

**Theorem 3. (Latency)** *The latency for simulating a synchronous algorithm of $f + 1$ rounds in the presence of Byzantine failures is $((1 + 2A)f + 1)d_{AC} + 2e$.*

*Proof.* For a given execution define
- $C_p(t)$ = the value of processor $p$'s clock at real time $t$,
- $t_i$ = the latest real time at which a correct processor sends a round $i$ message,
- $t_i^{del}$ = the latest real time at which the round $i$ message of any correct processor is delivered.

So we have $C_p(t_2) \leq T + d_{AC} + 2e$ for all correct $p$, since every correct processor sends a round 2 message by time $T + d_{AC} + e$ on its clock, at which time the clock of any other correct processor reads at most $(T + d_{AC} + e) + e$.

By induction on the round number $i \geq 2$, we show $C_p(t_{i+1}) - C_p(t_i) \leq d_{AC} + 2d_{AC}A$: First note that $C_p(t_i^{del}) - C_p(t_i) \leq d_{AC}$ for all correct $p$, by the definition of $d_{AC}$. Now consider the last correct processor $q$ to send a round $i + 1$ message (at time $t_{i+1}$). It receives a round $i$ message from each correct processor by real time $t_i^{del}$ and sends its round $i + 1$ message no more than $2d_{AC}$ on its clock thereafter, so we have $C_q(t_{i+1}) - C_q(t_i^{del}) \leq 2d_{AC}$. As we showed in Section 2.2, this implies that $C_p(t_{i+1}) - C_p(t_i^{del}) \leq A(2d_{AC})$ for all correct $p$.

Summing over rounds 2 through $f + 2$ (the processors END at "$t_{f+2}$"), we have $C_p(t_{f+2}) - C_p(t_2) \leq f(1 + 2A)d_{AC}$ for all correct processors $p$.

Because a processor knows the initial message was scheduled to be sent at time $T$, it need not deliver a message with timestamp older than $T$, and the latency of the algorithm is

$$C_p(t_{f+2}) - T \leq C_p(t_{f+2}) - (C_p(t_2) - d_{AC} - 2e) \leq (1 + 2A)fd_{AC} + d_{AC} + 2e$$

□

**Removing the synchronized start assumption.** A simple but message- and computation-inefficient way to remove the assumption that processors know the starting time is for the processors to execute the broadcasts as if an input were known to be received every $\epsilon$ time on their clocks, using "dummy" messages if they have received no input. When a processor gets an input, it sends the initial message with the beginning of the next scheduled execution of the simulation. The total latency is then $\epsilon + ((1 + 2A)f + 1)d_{AC} + 2e$, for any $\epsilon$.

A less wasteful way to remove this assumption is to use a clever protocol developed in [BGT90] to synchronize the starting round of an agreement algorithm.[7] This protocol adds $3(e+d)$ to the latency. When a processor receives an input $m$ at local time $t$, it broadcasts a message "start: $t$" announcing that an execution of the broadcast algorithm will begin at clock time $t + 3(d_{AC} + e)$. At that time, the processors will execute $n$ atomic broadcast algorithms in parallel

---

[7] One could use the "firing squad" algorithms for this purpose, but they require $f + 3$ rounds, whereas this technique requires only an additional three.

as each processor broadcasts a vote (the original processor broadcasts $m$ along with its vote). That is, the broadcast algorithms are executed by each processor as if it knew that every processor were scheduled to receive an input (which is actually its vote) at clock time $t + 3(d_{AC} + e)$. The vector of votes produced by the broadcasts determines whether $m$ is delivered by the processors. Any processor that receives a "start: $t$" message by $t + d_{AC} + e$ on its clock and relays the message to everyone and participates in the broadcasts with a vote of YES. Any processor that receives a (possibly relayed) "start: $t$" message by time $t + 2(d_{AC} + e)$ on its clock (but not by $t + d_{AC} + e$) relays the message to everyone and participates in the broacasts with a vote of NO. In either case, if the broadcasts produce a vector of votes with at least $f + 1$ YES's, then these processors deliver $m$ iff they would deliver $m$ according to the atomic broadcast algorithm corresponding to the originator. However, a processor that does not receive a relayed message by time $t + 2(d_{AC} + e)$ participates in the broacasts (to the best of its ability—depending upon when it first hears about the broadcasts) but does *not* deliver $m$ as a result of the broadcasts. The claim is that despite the fact that the original atomic broadcast algorithm is guaranteed to work only if all correct processors participate, with the addition of this protocol a correct processor delivers $m$ if and only if all correct processors deliver $m$.

**Claim 1** *For any atomic broadcast algorithm that is correct when the clock time of input is common knowledge, the protocol above ensures that even without this common knowledge a correct processor delivers $m$ if and only if all correct processors deliver $m$.*

*Proof.* Suppose a correct processor $p$ delivers $m$. Then $p$ must have received a "start: $t$" message by time $t + 2(d_{AC} + e)$ on its clock and therefore all processors received a "start: $t$" message by time $t + 3(d_{AC} + e)$ on their clocks. Thus, all correct processors participated in the entire broadcasts and the same vector of votes is therefore produced at each processor. In particular, all correct processors agree on whether or not $m$ was received. Now, for $p$ to deliver $m$, at least $f+1$ of those votes must be YES, so some correct processor received a "start: $t$" message by time $t + d_{AC} + e$ on its clock. It follows that each processor receives a "start: $t$" message by time $t + 2(d_{AC} + e)$ on its clock and therefore delivers $m$ as a result of seeing $f + 1$ YES's. □

### 3.3 Optimal precision

In this section, we prove a lower bound on the latency of the atomic broadcast problem of $(f + 1)d_{AC} + 2e$ if processors fail by omitting messages and having clocks that differ from correct clocks by more than $e$. By improving over the previously best known lower bounds of $2e + 2d_{AC}$ ([SDC90]) and $e + (f+1)d_{AC}$ ([CASD86]), we obtain the first lower bound that is tight (with the Byzantine upper bound) both precisely in the factor of $e$ and to within a "constant" factor in its coefficient of $d_{AC}$. The "constant" factor is in fact equal to about twice the drift rate $A$; it remains a major open question in this area to obtain lower bounds that depend substantially on the drift ($A$ or $C$).

**Theorem 4.** *Any algorithm for atomic broadcast in the AC model tolerating send and receive omission failures and clock failures has latency at least $(f + 1)d_{AC} + 2e$.*

*Proof.* Let $Q = \{2, \ldots, n - f\}$ and $R = \{n - f + 1, \ldots, n\}$ be subsets of the processors. For the purposes of the proof, the rate of clocks and all absolute readings are unimportant. We will assume throughout the proof all clocks run at the rate of real time, with 1's clock displaying real time exactly, $Q$'s clocks reading $e$ greater than real time, and $R$'s clocks reading $2e$ greater than real time. Processor 1 receives an input message $x$ at real time 0. All times and intervals in the proof refer to real time unless otherwise specified. We use $d = d_{AC}$.

Let $E_0$ be an execution in which (1) for all $k$, any message sent in the interval $[(k - 1)d, kd)$ is delivered at time $kd$, and (2) processor 1 acts as if it has done everything correctly, but it omits $x$ to $R$. By delivering messages only at multiples of $d$, we can identify each interval $[(k - 1)d, kd)$ with a "round" in the natural way. Although processor 1 is clearly faulty in $E_0$ from the point of view $R$, to $Q$ it is equally possible that all processors in $R$ (which number $f$) received $x$ but are claiming otherwise. Note that $Q$ may also be able to discern that either 1 or $R$ must be faulty by discovering that their clocks differ by more than $e$. Now, if 1 sends follows the algorithm with respect to $Q$, then processors in $Q$ must deliver it, despite what 1 says to $R$. To ensure agreement, correct processors in $R$ must deliver $x$ if those in $Q$ deliver it. Thus, in $E_0$, all correct processors deliver $x$.

We can now mimic the argument of the synchronous lower bound ([DS83, DM86, M85, CD86]) of creating a chain of executions $E_0, \ldots, E''$ such that in $E''$ no input is received by processor 1. Each pair of successive executions is indistinguishable to some correct processor in $R$ before time $T + (f + 1)d + 2e$ on its clock. All correct processors must deliver $x$ in $E_0$ but not in $E''$, so some pair of executions must be distinguishable to all correct processors by time $T$ plus the latency on their clocks. Thus, the latency must be at least $(f+1)d+2e$.

Each successive pair of executions differ only in the existence of a single message. Clearly, if a message $m$ is sent in the interval $[(f - 1)d, fd)$, then only the recipient can tell by time $fd$ if $m$ has been sent or not. Since subsequent messages sent by the recipient are not delivered until time $(f + 1)d$, processors in $R$ cannot tell before time $(f + 1)d + 2e$ on their clocks if $m$ has been sent or not. Thus, only one processor in $R$ (if it is the recipient of $m$) can distinguish before local time $(f + 1)d + 2e$ between two executions that differ only in whether or not $m$ is sent in the interval $[(f - 1)d, fd)$.

Starting with execution $E_0$, for any processor $p$ we may construct a sequence of executions $E_0, \ldots, E'$ such that $p$ sends no messages at all in the interval $[(f - 1)d, fd)$ of $E'$ and each pair of successive executions is indistinguishable to some correct processor in $R$. This is done by removing one at a time each message sent by $p$ in the interval. Another execution created by removing a message sent by $p'$ to $p$ in the interval $[(f - 2)d, (f - 1)d)$ is then clearly indistinguishable from $E'$ to all processors but $p$ (since $p$ sends no messages in $E'$ after time $(f-1)d$). Now, by adding back one at a time the messages sent by $p$ in the interval $[(f-1)d, fd)$, we can continue the sequence to arrive at an execution that differs from $E_0$ only in the message from $p'$ to $p$. In this manner, we can remove any messages of up to $f-1$ processors in addition to processor 1. This is easily proved formally with a (standard) recursive proof (see [DS83, CD86, M85, DM86]). We finally arrive at an execution $E''$ in which processor 1 omits $m$ to all processors, completing the proof.

The key fact is that this sequence of executions leading to $E''$ has the property that each consecutive pair is *indistinguishable to some correct processor in R*. This is because the recursion requires that for each execution, at most $i$ processors fail in the first $i$ rounds. Since processors in $R$ don't receive $m$ directly from 1 by time $d$, there is no need to remove any messages sent by processors in $R$ before time $2d$; therefore at most $f-2$ processors in $R$ are faulty in any pair of successive executions. At most one processor can distinguish between any pair of successive executions, leaving us at least one in $R$ that cannot. □

### 3.4 Real-time bounds for atomic broadcast

In addressing the atomic broadcast problem in the TA model, we encounter two problems. The first is that new techniques are needed to establish a common ordering of messages—atomic broadcast algorithms for the AC model establish this ordering by delivering messages in timestamped order, making critical use of the synchronized clocks. The second problem, discussed in Section 2.4, is with defining the running time for Byzantine failures. In this section, we avoid Byzantine failures altogether and take solve the ordering problem by simply implementing synchronized clocks in the TA model.

The extensive literature on clock synchronization has thoroughly studied almost exactly this problem of implementing clocks—given "hardware" clocks that drift from real time at some rate bounded by a constant, implement logical "software" clocks that drift from real time as little as possible and are also within some constant ("skew") of each other. Unfortunately, to the best of our knowledge, all clock synchronization algorithms (e.g., [ST87], [DHSS89], [LL88]) were designed only for assume extremely small rates of drift in the "hardware" clocks ($C \approx 1 + \epsilon$).

We can implement a "hardware clock" as a counter that increments by $\sqrt{c_1 c_2}$ at each step. An interval with $k$ steps is measured to be of length $\ell = k\sqrt{c_1 c_2}$ on the hardware clock but its real time may be as little as $kc_1 = \ell/\sqrt{C}$ or as great as $kc_2 = \sqrt{C}\ell$. Thus we essentially get a drift of $\sqrt{C}$ relative to real time; the relative accuracy is $C$. The clock synchronization algorithm of Srikanth and Toueg ([ST87]) preserves this drift in the logical clocks and gives a worst-case skew of $\sqrt{C}(2C+1)d$ (c.f. their expression for $D_{\max}$ on p. 631, with their $(1+\rho)$ equal to $\sqrt{C}$ and their $d_{\min} = 2t_{\text{del}}$ equal to our $2d$).

Using the synchronized clocks, we can run the message diffusion algorithm ([CASD86]) with latency $L = (f + 1)d_{AC} + e$. Because an interval of $t$ units of real time may be measured as $\sqrt{C}t$ on a fast clock, we conclude that the delay $d$ of any message measures at most $\sqrt{C}d$ on the clock of any correct processor; this is "$d_{AC}$". Because any clock reads at least $T - e$ when the input is received at time $t$, the maximum elapsed clock time from $t$ to the last delivery

is $L + e$. The maximum elapsed real time is at most a factor of $\sqrt{C}$ greater:
$$\sqrt{C}\left[(f+1)\sqrt{C}d + 2\left(\sqrt{C}(2C+1)d\right)\right] = (f+1)Cd + 2C(2C+1)d.$$ This gives

**Theorem 5.** *For sufficiently small values of $C$, there is an algorithm for atomic broadcast tolerating omission failures with real time complexity at most $(f + 1)Cd + 2C(2C + 1)d$.*

It is not obvious how to achieve such a running time without explicitly implementing clocks. Algorithms are known to solve atomic broadcast without clocks; it would be interesting to investigate their real time complexities.

As might be expected, the relative accuracy of $C$ achieved above is optimal; it is not difficult to adapt a lower bound of Srikanth and Toueg ([ST87]) to show

**Theorem 6.** *For any logical clocks implemented in the TA model, the relative accuracy $A$ must be at least $C$.*

This theorem shows that blind syntactic translation of maximum elapsed clock time to maximum elapsed real time will always incur a factor of $C$. Clocks measure message delay to be at most $a_2 d + a_3 = d_{AC}$ and if elapsed clock is expressed as $g(n, f, e, A)d_{AC}$ for some function $g$ then an upper bound on the elapsed real time is $\approx \frac{1}{a_1} g(n, f, e, A)a_2 d = Ag(n, f, e, A) \geq Cg(n, f, e, A)$. However, it may be that the elapsed real time can be better bounded by more carefully examining the possible executions of an algorithm.

### 3.5 Reductions

In this section, we work exclusively within the AC model, converting back and forth between real time bounds for consensus and latency bounds for atomic broadcast.

**Theorem 7.** *If there is an atomic broadcast protocol with latency $L$, then for each $x \geq 0$ there is a consensus protocol for the AC model with start interval length $x$ and real time from start to finish bounded above by $\approx x + (L + 2(e + x_{AC}))/a_1$, where $x_{AC} \approx a_2 x$.*

Of course, the idea is to have each processor use the atomic broadcast algorithm to send its value to all other processors. Note that a trivial algorithm of merely adopting the first message delivered is incorrect by our definition of atomic broadcast: if the sender is faulty, the atomic broadcast algorithm may cause processors to deliver a value different from the sender's input, possibly violating the validity condition of consensus. For $n \geq 3f + 1$, it is sufficient for processors to wait for the first $2f + 1$ messages delivered and decide on the majority of those; this gives a real time of $(L+e)/a_1$. Our theorem is interesting for $f < n \leq 3f$. The problem is how to ensure that all processors resolve the vector of delivered messages in the same way. In particular, we need to ensure that if a faulty processor starts its broadcast too late, then all correct processors either include that value in their vector or not. To solve this problem, we use a technique developed in studies of the AC model, of reducing the vector of delivered messages to a subset that are "believable" in the sense that for each one, there are enough other messages with timestamps inside a small enough interval.

Finally, we have the following simple theorem which we state without proof.

**Theorem 8.** *If there is a consensus protocol in AC with $x \geq (e + a_3)/a_1$ and with real time from start to finish bounded above by $R$, then there is an atomic broadcast protocol in AC with latency bounded above by $L \approx a_2 R + e + d_{AC}$.*

# 4  Directions for further research

- Is there an algorithm for multi-source consensus with Byzantine failures in the TA model, assuming synchronized start, that runs in time $o(fCd)$? $O(fd)$? Same question but for 'timing" failures (see Section 2.1)?
- What are good bounds for the real time complexity of atomic broadcast in the TA model?
- How well can clocks be synchronized for very inaccurate "hardware" clocks $(C > 3/2)$?
- Can the algorithm for atomic broadcast in the AC model presented in section 3 be generalized for authenticated Byzantine failures with $n \leq 2f$ to give an algorithm running in time with $\approx \frac{2n}{n-f}$ as the coefficient of $e$? (See [SDC90].)

# 5  Acknowledgments

We thank Faith Fich for her comments.

# References

[ADKM92] Y. Amir, D. Dolev, S. Kramer and D. Malki. Total ordering of messages in broadcast domains. Manuscript.

[ADLS90] H. Attiya, C. Dwork, N. Lynch, and L. Stockmeyer. Bounds on the time to reach agreement in the presence of timing uncertainty. MIT/LCS/TM–435, November 1990. Also: STOC 1991.

[AL89] H. Attiya and N. A. Lynch. Time bounds for real-time process control in the presence of timing uncertainty. *Proc. 10th IEEE Real-Time Systems Symposium*, 1989, pp. 268–284. Also: MIT/LCS/TM–403, July 1989.

[BJ87] K. Birman and T. Joseph. Reliable communication in the presence of failures. *ACM TOCS*, Vol. 5, No. 1 (February 1987), pp. 47–76.

[BGT90] N. Budhiraja, A. Gopal and S. Toueg. Early-stopping distributed bidding with applications. *Proc. 4th Int'l. WDAG* 1990.

[CASD86] F. Cristian, H. Aghili, R. Strong and D. Dolev. Atomic broadcast: from simple message diffusion to Byzantine agreement. *Proc. 15th Int. Conf. on Fault Tolerant Computing*, 1985, pp. 1–7. Also: IBM Research Report RJ5244, revised October 1989.

[CM84] J. M. Chang and N. Maxemchuck. Reliable broadcast protocols. *ACM TOCS*, Vol. 2, No. 3 (August 1984), pp. 251–273.

[CD86] B. A. Coan and C. Dwork. Simultaneity is harder than agreement. *Information and Computation* Vol. 91, No. 2, 1991.

[DDS87]    D. Dolev, C. Dwork and L. Stockmeyer. On the minimal synchronism needed for distributed consensus. *JACM*, Vol. 34, No. 1 (1987), pp. 77–97.

[DHS86]    D. Dolev, J. Y. Halpern and R. Strong. On the possibility and impossibility of achieving clock synchronization. *JCSS*, Vol. 32, No. 2, 1986, pp. 230–250.

[DHSS89]   D. Dolev, J. Halpern, R. Stong and B. Simons. Dynamic fault-tolerant clock synchronization. IBM Research Report RJ 6722, March 1989. Also: Fault-tolerant clock synchronization. *Proc. 3rd ACM PODC* 1984, pp. 89–102.

[DS83]     D. Dolev and H. R. Strong. Authenticated algorithms for Byzantine agreement. *SIAM J. Computing*, Vol. 12, No. 3 (November 1983), pp. 656–666.

[DLS88]    C. Dwork, N. Lynch, and L. Stockmeyer. Consensus in the presence of partial synchrony. *JACM*, Vol. 35 (1988), pp. 288–323.

[DM86]     C. Dwork and Y. Moses. Knowledge and common knowledge in Byzantine environments I: crash failures. *Information and Computation*, Vol. 88, No. 2 (1990), pp. 156–186.

[DS91]     C. Dwork and L. Stockmeyer. Bounds on the time to reach agreement as a function of message delay. IBM Research Report RJ8181, June 1991.

[FL82]     M. Fischer and N. Lynch. A lower bound for the time to assure interactive consistency. *IPL*, Vol. 14, No. 4 (June 1982), pp. 183–186.

[FLP85]    M. Fischer, N. Lynch and M. Paterson. Impossibility of distributed consensus with one faulty process. *JACM*, Vol. 32, No. 2 (1985), pp. 374–382.

[GSTC90]   A. Gopal, R. Strong, S. Toueg and F. Cristian. Early-delivery atomic broadcast. *Proc. 9th ACM PODC*, 1990, pp. 297–309.

[HK89]     A. Herzberg and S. Kutten. Efficient Detection of Message Forwarding Faults. *Proc. 8th ACM PODC*, 1989, pp. 339–353.

[LM85]     L. Lamport and P. M. Melliar-Smith. Synchronizing clocks in the presence of faults. *JACM*, Vol. 32, No. 1 (January 1985), pp. 52–78.

[LSP82]    L. Lamport, R. Shostak and M. Pease. The Byzantine generals problem. *ACM TOPLAS*, Vol. 4, No. 3 (1982), pp. 382–401.

[LL84]     J. Lundelius and N. Lynch. An upper and lower bound for clock synchronization. *Information and Control*, Vol. 62, Nos. 2/3 (1984), pp. 190–204.

[LL88]     J. L. Welch and N. Lynch. A new fault-tolerant algorithm for clock synchronization. *Information and Computation*, Vol. 77, No. 1, (1988), pp. 1–36.

[MMA90]    P. M. Melliar-Smith, L. Moser and V. Agrawala. Broadcast protocols for distributed systems. *IEEE Trans. on Parallel and Dist. Systems*, Vol. 1, No. 1 (January 1990), pp. 17–25.

[MMA91]    L. Moser, P. M. Melliar-Smith and V. Agrawala. Asynchronous fault-tolerant total ordering algorithms. Manuscript.

[M85]      M. Merritt. Notes on the Dolev-Strong lower bound for Byzantine agreement. Unpublished manuscript, 1985.

[MMT90]    M. Merritt, F. Modugno and M. Tuttle. Time constrained automata. Unpublished manuscript, August 1990.

[P91]      S. Ponzio. Consensus in the presence of timing uncertainty: omission and Byzantine failures. *Proc. 10th ACM PODC*, 1991, pp. 125–138. Also: MIT SM Thesis, June 1991. MIT/LCS/TR–518, October 1991.

[ST87]     T. K. Srikanth and S. Toueg. Optimal clock synchronization. *JACM*, Vol. 34, No. 3, July 1987, pp. 626–645.

[SDC90]    R. Strong, D. Dolev and F. Cristian. New latency bounds for atomic broadcast. *Proc. 11th IEEE Real-Time Systems Symposium*, 1990.

# Optimal Time Byzantine Agreement for $t < n/8$ with Linear Messages

Arkady Zamsky, Amos Israeli and Shlomit S. Pinter

Dept. of Electrical Engineering, Technion, Israel

**Abstract.** The **Byzantine Agreement** problem provides an abstract setting in which methods for tolerating faults in distributed systems may be explored and perhaps influence practical designs. A *Byzantine Agreement* protocol is a distributed protocol in which one distinguished processor called the *source* broadcasts some initial value to all other processors. The protocol is designed to tolerate up to $t$ faulty processors. The receiving processors should agree on some common output value. In case the source is correct the output value should be equal to the source's initial value. The quality of a Byzantine agreement protocol is measured by the following parameters: the ratio between the total number of processors $n$ and the number of faulty processors $t$, the number of rounds of message exchange needed to reach an agreement, and the communication complexity, given by the size $m$ of the maximal message. This paper presents a Byzantine Agreement protocol with $n = 8 \cdot t + 1$, *optimal* number of rounds (namely $min\{f + 2, t + 1\}$ where $f$ is number of actual faults), and messages of *linear* size (namely $m \leq n + O(\log n)$ ). This is the first protocol that reaches Byzantine Agreement in optimal time, tolerates $t = O(n)$ faults and uses messages of linear size. All previous protocols that stop in optimal time and tolerate $t = O(n)$ faults require messages of size at least $O(n^2)$. The new protocol uses a novel technique called *Reconstructed Traversal* which is based on the *Reconstruction Principle* and on the *Coordinated Traversal* protocol.

## 1   Introduction and Problem Statement

The *Byzantine Agreement* problem [12] provides an abstract setting in which methods for tolerating faults may be explored and perhaps influence practical designs. A *Byzantine Agreement* protocol is a distributed protocol in which one distinguished processor called the *source* broadcasts some initial value to all other processors. The broadcast value $v$ is drawn from a finite *domain $W$*. For simplicity we assume that $W = \{0, 1\}$ where 0 is called the *default* value. The protocol is designed to tolerate up to $t$ faulty processors. The receiving processors should agree on some common output value. In case the source is correct the output value should be equal to the source's initial value. We say that the system reaches *Byzantine Agreement* (BA) if the following two conditions hold:

- (i) **Validity:** If the source is correct then the decision value is the value broadcast by the source.
- (ii) **Agreement:** All correct processors decide on the same value.

We consider a synchronous distributed system consisting a finite collection of $n \geq 2$ processors, each pair of which is connected by a two-way reliable communication link. We assume that processor names are unique, globally known and totally ordered. Computation in the system proceeds in a sequence of *rounds*; during each round every (correct) processor sends messages, receives messages and performs local computations according to the protocol. Round $i$ takes place between time $i - 1$ and $i$. We assume that a message sent at the beginning of some communication round is received in the same round.

We assume the *Byzantine* model of faults in which a faulty processor may crash, omit messages or send contradicting messages to different processors. Let $t$ be the maximal number of faults that the protocol can tolerate. The practicality of agreement protocols depends on their computational complexity. For BA protocols the relevant parameters are *fault tolerance* or *resilience* — namely the ratio of $t$ and $n$, the *time* needed to complete the protocol — namely the number of rounds required and *message traffic* generated. For the latter we measure the total number of bits sent by one processor to another during each round of the protocol (denoted by $m$). Let $f$, $f \leq t$ be the number of actual faults in some run of a BA protocol. The known lower bounds for the aforementioned parameters are $n = 3t + 1$ [12], $min\{f + 2, t + 1\}$ rounds [8] and $m = 1$ respectively.

Table 1 compares the parameters of existing deterministic protocols which stop after at most $t + 1$ rounds. By the lower bound of [8] a protocol that stops within $min\{f + 2, t + 1\}$ rounds is **optimal** in **time**.

**Table 1.** Byzantine Agreement in at most $t + 1$ rounds.

| Protocol | $n$ | time | $m$ |
|---|---|---|---|
| Lamport *at el* [12] | $3t + 1$ | $t + 1$ | $O(t^t)$ |
| Bar-Noy and Dolev [1] | $\Omega(t^2)$ | $t + 1$ | 1 |
| Waarts [13] | $3t + 1$ | $min\{f + 3, t + 1\}$ | $O(f! \cdot n^2)$ |
| Moses and Waarts [11] | $8t + 1$ | Optimal | $O(n^2)$ |
| Berman, Garay and Perry [5] | $4t + 1$ | Optimal | $O(n^3 \cdot f^2)$ |
| Berman and Garay ([4]): ESDM | $3t + 1$ | $min\{f + 3, t + 1\}$ | $O(1.5^f \cdot n)$ |
| Berman and Garay ([4]): CVDM | $(3 + \epsilon) \cdot t$ | $min\{f + 3, t + 1\}$ | $O(t^5 \cdot 2^{4/\epsilon})$ |
| Zamsky [14] | $4t + 1$ | Optimal | $O(f^3 \cdot n)$ |
| | $6t + 1$ | Optimal | $O(f^2 \cdot n)$ |
| | $3t + 1$ | Optimal | $O(min\{2^{t/6} \cdot f^4 \cdot n, 2^{f/2} \cdot n\})$ |
| this paper | $8t + 1$ | Optimal | $O(n)$ |

There is a huge number of papers which discuss Byzantine Agreement. The most relevant papers are those of [11], [5], [4] and [14]. In [11] Mozes and Waarts introduced the *early prediction* and the *Coordinated-Traversal* technique and derived the first BA protocol that runs in optimal time, tolerates a linear number of faults and uses polynomial message size. The results of [11] were improved by Berman, Garay and Perry in [5], using the new technique of *Cloture Vote*. Following that, Berman and Garay, in [3], Combined *Cloture Vote* with another technique called *Dynamic Fault Masking* to obtain the CVDM protocol. Finally, in [14], the new *reconstruction* principle was introduced and combined with *Cloture Vote* of [5], to achieve yet another improvement. Independently, the idea of *reconstruction* (in a more complex form) was presented in [3].

Sometimes it is important to measure the total number of bits sent by all correct processors during execution of the protocol. For this measure the lower bound is $\Omega(n^2)$ bits [7]. Because *Byzantine Failures* are relatively rare we are interested in algorithms which are as efficient as possible if our network is *failure-free*. In [10] it is proved that the total message traffic in the *failure-free* case in any BA protocol is at least $\Omega(n \cdot t)$.

In this paper we combine some of the techniques used in [14] with a modified version of the *Coordinated-Traversal* technique to obtain a novel technique called *Reconstructing Traversal*. The new protocol, which is called LS8, is *round-optimal* and tolerates up to $t < n/8$ faults by using messages of *linear* size ($m \leq n + O(\log n)$ ). Our protocol is much simpler then the original *Coordinated Traversal* of [11].

The remainder of this paper is organized as follows. Some important definition are presented in Section 2. In Section 3 we describe the "classic" full information protocol FIP of [12]. In Section 4 we present the **Prediction, Reconstruction** and **Fault-Masking** techniques and combine them into FIP to obtain the *Optimal-Early-Stopping Fault Masking protocol for* $t < n/4$ (called ESFM4). Both FIP and ESFM4 require exponential communication. Protocol ESFM4 is used as an intuitive basis for LS8: *Linear-Size messages protocol for* $t < n/8$ presented in Section 5. Concluding remarks and open problems are brought in Section 6.

## 2   Definitions

Names of processors are denoted by small letters (e.g. $p$, $q$). Sequences of processor names beginning with $s$ (*source*) and without repetitions are denoted by small greek letters. For a sequence of processors $\alpha$ processor $last(\alpha)$ denotes the processor whose name appears in the last place of $\alpha$. $\alpha q$ denotes the sequence obtained by concatenation of $q$ to the sequence $\alpha$.

Generally, all the protocols described below consists of two parts: *Information Exchange* and *Decision*. During *Information Exchange* each processor constructs an *Information Gathering* tree denoted by IG. Every node of IG is labeled by some sequence $\alpha$, where the *root* node is always labeled by $s$ and if $j$ is not in $\alpha$ then $\alpha$ is the father of the node labeled $\alpha j$. Therefore, node $\alpha$ has exactly $n - |\alpha|$ sons. To every node $\alpha$ a processor may associate a value $v$ drawn from the domain $W$. Subscript $p$ denotes local variables and values in processor $p$. Processor $p$ is *correct* if it follows the protocol; otherwise it is *faulty*. We say that node $\alpha$ is correct if $last(\alpha)$ is correct.

At the beginning of the protocol all IG trees of correct processors are empty. At the *Init* round the *source* processor (assuming it is correct) broadcasts its value to all the processors in the network (including itself). Every processor stores the received value at the root of its IG tree. If, for some processor $p$, no value arrives then *default* value (i.e. 0) is stored in $s_p$. All subsequent rounds consist of three basic steps: sending messages to all other processors, collecting some of the incoming messages, performing local computation in which the IG tree is updated and generating next round messages (depending on the local state and the round currently executed). The *Decision* is reached in one of two ways: *Resolving* by applying the recursive procedure *resolve* on IG generated during the $t + 1$ communication rounds and *Early Decision* (will be discussed in Section 4).

# 3    Full Information Protocol (FIP)

The following basic protocol with its lemmas are the one presented in [2]. In this section we assume that $t < n/3$. For every correct processor after $i$, $1 \leq i \leq t+1$, rounds the IG *tree* is a balanced tree of height $i$, where *every* node $\alpha$ has some value from domain $W$. The protocol is outlined below:

1. **Information Exchange:** After the *Init* round and in each subsequent round every correct processor sends to all other processors tree values of all *new leaves* (at the second round it means the root value), collects the incoming messages and builds the next level of its tree. The value of node $\alpha q$ is the value of node $\alpha$ reported by processor $q$ in round $|\alpha| + 1$; (if such a value is not reported by $q$ then node $\alpha q$ gets value 0). This process is repeated for $t + 1$ rounds.
2. **Decision:** At the end of round $t + 1$ every processor applies the recursive function *resolve* to its tree. This function reassigns values to nodes, where leaves values remains unchanged and the rest of the values are computed from the leaves by recursive *Majority Voting*. Let $\alpha$ be some internal node. If there exists some value $v$ supported by more than half of $\alpha$ sons then $resolve(\alpha) := v$, otherwise $resolve(\alpha) := 0$. Finally processor $p$ *decides* on $resolve(s_p)$.

We denote the initial value of node $\alpha$ by $tree(\alpha)$. The final value of $\alpha$ is computed by the *resolve* function and is called the *resolve* value of $\alpha$. We say that node $\alpha$ is *common* in run $\sigma$ of the protocol if all correct processors in $\sigma$ calculate the same $resolve(\alpha)$; if on every *path* from the root to some leaf there exists at least one common node, we say that there exists a *common frontier*. Let $T$ be an IG tree. Denote by $path(\alpha)$ the set of nodes in $T$ whose labels are prefixes of $\alpha$. Denote by $subtree(\alpha)$ the subtree of $T$ rooted by $\alpha$ and excluding $\alpha$.

**Lemma 1.** *If* $last(\alpha)$ *is correct then* $\alpha$ *is common and* $tree(\alpha) = resolve(\alpha)$.

*Proof.* Since $t < n/3$, for every node $\alpha$, the majority of $\alpha$'s sons are correct. Since $last(\alpha)$ is correct, the protocol implies that the tree value of the majority of $\alpha$'s sons is equal to the tree value of $\alpha$. According to the definition of the *resolve* function, we can prove, using simple down-counting induction on $|\alpha|$, starting from $|\alpha| = t + 1$, that $resolve(\alpha) = tree(\alpha)$. By the protocol, the tree values of $\alpha$ in the IG trees of all correct processors are equal. □

**Lemma 2.** *In every run of the* FIP *protocol there exists a common frontier.*

*Proof.* Consider the IG tree of an arbitrary correct processor after the $t+1$ round is completed. This is a balanced tree of height $t + 1$. Since there are at most $t$ faulty processors, each path has at least one correct node. By Lemma 1 this node is common, hence each path has at least one common node. □

**Theorem 3.** *The* FIP *protocol reaches* Byzantine Agreement *for $t < n/3$.*

*Proof.* If $s$ is correct then Lemma 1 implies that for every correct processor $p$, $resolve(s_p) = tree(s_p)$, hence the protocol satisfies **validity**. To prove **agreement**, it can be shown that if there exists a common frontier then the *root* node is also common, hence the lemma follows from Lemma 2. □

## 4 Prediction Reconstruction and Fault-Masking

In this section we assume that $t < n/4$ and present the **prediction, reconstruction** and **fault-masking** techniques which are integrated into the FIP protocol to obtain an early stopping protocol called ESFM4. This is an intermediate protocol which will be modified once again in the next section to get the linear protocol.

**Reconstruction:** If at round $|\alpha| + 1$ processor $p$ does not receive the value of node $\alpha q$ (from processor $q$), then $tree(\alpha q_p) := tree(\alpha_p)$. It is easy to see that in this case $q$ is faulty, since a faulty processor can send arbitrary values, the protocol tolerates these values as well and its correctness is preserved.

**Prediction:** The following two prediction rules detect a situation in which the *resolve* value $v$ of some node $\alpha$ can be evaluated before the end of round $t + 1$. In this case we say that node $\alpha$ is *closed* with $v$, and denote it by $close(\alpha) = v$.

**rule 1:** If the tree value of more than $\frac{n-|\alpha|}{2} + (t - |\alpha|)$ of $\alpha$'s sons is $v$ then $close(\alpha) := v$.

**rule 2:** If more than (at least) $\frac{n-|\alpha|}{2}$ of $\alpha$'s sons are closed with 1 (with 0, respectively) then $close(\alpha) := 1$ ($close(\alpha) := 0$ respectively)

If $path(\alpha)$ has a closed node then it is *closed*, otherwise $path(\alpha)$ is open. For the time being we assume that the *close* values are not used and the protocol is executed without any changes. At the end of every communication round each processor applies rules 1 and 2 to close as many as possible nodes which are not on a subtree of a closed node. We now prove that the prediction rules indeed predict the resolve values of closed nodes:

**Lemma 4. a.** *If $p$ and $last(\alpha)$ are correct processors then $p$ closes $path(\alpha_p)$ no later than round $|\alpha|+1$.*
**b.** *If $p$ and $last(\alpha)$ are correct processors and $path(\alpha_p)$ is open before round $|\alpha|+1$ then in round $|\alpha|+1$ node $\alpha_p$ is closed with $tree(\alpha_p)$.*

*Proof.* If $last(\alpha)$ and $p$ are correct, then the *tree* values of all correct sons of $\alpha_p$ are equal to $tree(\alpha_p)$. The proof proceeds by induction on $|\alpha|$. If $|\alpha|=1$ (i.e. the root is correct) then every correct processor closes the root of its tree at the end of the second round using rule 1. Suppose that the lemma holds for all nodes of $\beta$ s.t. $|\beta| < k$ and let $\alpha$ be an arbitrary node s.t. $|\alpha| = k$. If $p$ is correct and if at the end of round $k+1$ $path(\alpha_p)$ is open, then by the induction hypothesis all first $|\alpha|-1$ processors in $\alpha$ are faulty. Let $v = tree(\alpha_p)$. By rule 1, $\alpha_p$ is closed with $v$ at the end of round $|\alpha|+1$. □

**Corollary 5.** *If in run $\sigma$ node $\alpha$ is closed by some correct processor then all $|\alpha|-1$ first processor in $\alpha$ are faulty.*

If node $\alpha_p$ is closed in round $r$ then we say that the *depth* of $\alpha$'s prediction in $IG_p$ (denoted by $d(\alpha)_p$) is $r - |\alpha|$.

**Lemma 6.** *If some correct processor $p$ closes node $\alpha$ with value $v$ then $v = resolve(\alpha_p)$.*

*Proof.* The proof is done by induction on the depth. Suppose that the lemma holds for all predictions of depth$< k$.

**Base-case:** $d(\alpha)_p = 1$. In this case $\alpha_p$ is closed by rule 1. If $last(\alpha)$ is correct then Lemma 1 implies that $resolve(\alpha_p) = tree(\alpha_p)$ and Lemma 4 (b) implies that $close(\alpha_p) = tree(\alpha_p)$. Hence if $last(\alpha)$ is correct then $close(\alpha_p) = v = resolve(\alpha_p)$. If $last(\alpha)$ is faulty then Corollary 5 implies that all processors in $\alpha$ are faulty. Therefore at most $t - |\alpha|$ of $\alpha$'s sons might be faulty. Since $close(\alpha_p) = v$ and since $\alpha_p$ is closed by rule 1 it holds that $v$ is the tree value of more then $\frac{n-|\alpha|}{2} + (t - |\alpha|)$ sons of $\alpha_p$. In this case the majority of $\alpha_p$ sons are correct nodes with tree value $v$ and Lemma 1 implies that $v$ is the resolve value for the majority of $\alpha$'s sons, hence the resolve value of $\alpha$ is also $v$.

**Induction step:** Every prediction of depth greater than one is done by applying rule 2, therefore it is based on predictions of smaller depth. Let $\alpha j_p$ be one of the closed sons of $\alpha_p$. Then $d(\alpha j)_p < k$ and by induction hypothesis $close(\alpha j_p) = resolve(\alpha j_p)$. If $close(\alpha_p) = 1$ then, by rule 2, the majority of $\alpha_p$'s sons are closed with 1, therefore 1 is the *resolve* value for the majority of $\alpha_p$'s sons. Hence $resolve(\alpha_p) = 1$. The proof for $close(\alpha_p) = 0$ is similar. □

**Lemma 7.** *If node $\alpha$ is closed by some correct processor $p$ then $\alpha$ is common.*

*Proof.* If $last(\alpha)$ is correct then Lemma 1 implies that $\alpha$ is common. If $last(\alpha)$ is faulty then Corollary 5 implies that all processors of $\alpha$ are faulty. In this case the proof is done by induction on $d(\alpha)_p$ as follows:

**Base-case:** $d(\alpha)_p = 1$. In this case $\alpha_p$ is closed by rule 1. If $close(\alpha_p) = v$ it can be shown that the *majority* of $\alpha_p$'s sons are correct nodes with tree value $v$. Let $q$ be another correct processor. Since for every correct $\beta$ $tree(\beta_p) = tree(\beta_q)$ the majority of $\alpha_q$ sons are correct nodes with tree value $v$. Since Lemma 1 implies that for every correct $\beta$ $resolve(\beta_q) = tree(\beta_q)$ we get $resolve(\alpha_q) = v$. Hence node $\alpha$ is common.

**Induction step:** every prediction of depth greater then one is based on predictions of smaller depth. The complete proof is done in a way similar to the induction step of Lemma 6. $\qquad\square$

**Lemma 8.** *Let $\alpha$ be a node closed by some correct processor $p$ in round $r$. Under this conditions, for every correct processor $q$, $\mathrm{path}(\alpha_q)$ is closed no later than the end of round $r + 1$.*

*Proof.* For correct $last(\alpha)$ the proof follows immediately from Lemma 4(a). If $last(\alpha)$ is faulty the proof is by induction on $d(\alpha)_p$ as follows:

**Base-case:** $d(\alpha)_p = 1$ (i.e. $r = |\alpha| + 1$). Corollary 5 implies that all processors in $\alpha$ are faulty. In this case, if $close(\alpha_p) = v$ then for every correct $q$ node $\alpha_q$ has more then $\frac{n-|\alpha|}{2}$ correct sons with tree value $v$. If $path(\alpha_q)$ is open at the end of round $r$ then Lemma 4 implies that until the end of round $r + 1$ all correct sons of $\alpha_q$ are closed hence the lemma follows from prediction rule 2.

**Induction step:** Suppose that the lemma holds for all predictions of depth $< k$ and let $\alpha_p$ be a node closed with value $v$ in round $r$ s.t. $r - |\alpha| = k$. Let $q$ be a correct processor and suppose (by contradiction) that at the end of round $r + 1$ $path(\alpha)_q$ is open. Let $\alpha j_p$ be a closed son $\alpha_p$. Then $\alpha j_p$ is closed in depth no greater than $k - 1$ and by induction hypothesis at the end of round $r + 1$ node $\alpha j_q$ is also closed. Lemma 7 implies that node $\alpha j$ is common and Lemma 6 implies that for every node $\beta$ in IG tree of correct processor $close(\beta) = resolve(\beta)$. Therefore $close(\alpha j_p) = close(\alpha j_q)$. In particular, if at the end of round $r$ $close(\alpha j_p) = v$ then at the end of round $r + 1$ $close(\alpha j_q) = v$. Hence by prediction rule 2 at the end of round $r + 1$ node $\alpha_q$ also closed with $v$. Contradiction. $\qquad\square$

We now amend the FIP protocol as follows: at the end of every communication round each processor applies reconstruction to get the values of missing nodes. Following reconstruction the processor applies prediction to close as many nodes as possible. Communication rounds are performed as before and at the end of round $t + 1$, closed nodes are treated like leaves. The amended protocol is called FIP(RP), for FIP with reconstruction and predictions. It is obvious that all the properties proved for FIP hold for FIP(RP) as well.

A BA protocol is *early stopping* if its time-complexity can be improved when the *actual* number of faulty processors is smaller then $t$. In the sequel we outline some further modification to protocol FIP(RP) that yield an early stopping protocol called ES4. If node $\alpha_p$ is closed in round $r$ then starting from round $r + 2$, no processor uses the transmitted values of leaves in $subtree(\alpha)$ to determine its decision value. For this reason it is enough that $p$ transmits the values of $\alpha$'s descendants only in round $r + 1$. In case $p$ does not transmit any values of $\alpha$'s descendants in round $r + 1$, every correct processor for which $path(\alpha)$ is open at the end of round $r$, *reconstructs* these values. Let $\beta$, $|\beta| = r$, be a correct descendent of $\alpha$. It may be shown that for every correct $q$, $tree(\beta_q) = tree(\alpha_q)$. In the next lemma we prove that protocols FIP(RP) and ES4 are equivalent.

**Lemma 9.** *Let $\sigma'$ be a run of* FIP(RP)*, and let $\sigma$ be the run accepted by replacing* FIP(RP) *by* ES4*: supposed that the set of values broadcast by the sender at the* Init *round and the set of all faulty processors and all their messages in $\sigma$ and $\sigma'$ are equal. If $p$ is a correct processor in $\sigma'$ (and therefore in $\sigma$) then the following claims are true:*

1. *If at the end of round $r$ of $\sigma'$ path$(\alpha)_p$ remains open then the same is true for $\sigma$.*
2. *If in round $r$ of $\sigma'$ processor $p$ closes node $\alpha$ with $v$ then the same is true for $\sigma$.*
3. *If at the end of round $r$ of run $\sigma'$ path$(\alpha_p)$ is open and if tree$(\alpha_p) = v$ then the same is true for run $\sigma$.*
4. *If at the end of round $t + 1$ of $\sigma'$ path$(\alpha_p)$ is open and resolved$(\alpha_p) = v$ then the same is true for run $\sigma$.*

*Proof.* The proof of the claims is by induction on the round number $r$ and (within round $r$) by induction on $r - |\alpha|$. $\qquad\qquad\qquad\qquad\qquad\qquad$ $\square$

It is not hard to prove that Lemma 4 and Lemma 8 hold for ES4. The next theorem is an immediate consequence of Lemma 9.

**Theorem 10.** *The* ES4 *protocol reaches* Byzantine Agreement *for $t < n/4$.*

The following three lemmas are called CDR for Contradiction Detection Rules, FDR for Fault Detection Rules and FMR for Fault Masking Rule. Note that masking techniques were used also in [2], [6].

**Lemma 11.** (CDR) *Let $\sigma$ be a run of* ES4 *and let $p$ be a correct processor in $\sigma$ s.t. path$(\alpha_p)$ is not closed before the end of round $|\alpha| + 1$. Let $\alpha q_p$ be one of $\alpha_p$'s sons and suppose that tree$(\alpha_p) \neq$ tree$(\alpha q_p)$. Then at least one out of last$(\alpha)$ and $q$ is faulty.*

*Proof.* By the protocol $tree(\alpha q_p)$ is a value of node $\alpha$ reported to $p$ by processor $q$. Lemma 8 implies that if $q$ is correct then $path(\alpha_q)$ is not closed before round $|\alpha|$. Hence if both $q$ and $last(\alpha)$ are correct then $tree(\alpha_q)$ is the value of $\alpha$'s father reported to $q$ by processor $last(\alpha)$. In this case $tree(\alpha_p) = tree(\alpha_q)$, therefore $tree(\alpha_p) = tree(\alpha q_p)$, contradiction. $\qquad\qquad\qquad\qquad\qquad\qquad\qquad$ $\square$

We say that processor $p$ *detects a contradiction* between processors $q$ and $q'$ if $p$ can claim that at least one of them is faulty. This definition is used in the next lemma whose proof is immediate from Lemma 11 and the model assumptions.

144

**Lemma 12.** (FDR) *Let $\sigma$ be a run of* ES4 *and let $p$ be a correct processor in $\sigma$. If $p$ detects that some processor $q$ contradicts at least $t+1$ other processors then $p$ can claim that $q$ is faulty.*

The next lemma was proved by [2]:

**Lemma 13.** (FMR) *Let $\sigma$ be a run of some synchronous agreement protocol and suppose that at the end of round $r$ processor $p$ can claim that another processor, $q$, is faulty. Then processor $p$ may pretend that starting at round $r+1$ all values reported to it by $q$ are 0, without jeopardizing the correctness of the protocol.*

We modify ES4 as follows: in every communication round after collecting the incoming information and building the next level of the IG tree (and before applying *prediction*) the processors apply CDR, FDR and FMR. For this purpose each processor maintains *contradiction-list* which is a list of processor pairs and *faulty-list* which is the list of processors. Both are initiated to empty lists and updated at the end of each communication round. The new protocol is called *Early Stopping* protocol with *Fault Masking* for $t < n/4$ and denoted by ESFM4. It is obvious that Lemma 4 and Lemma 8 also hold for ESFM4.

**Theorem 14.** *The* ESFM4 *protocol achieves* Byzantine Agreement *for $t < n/4$.*

For correct $p$ in run $\sigma$ of ESFM4 node $\alpha_p$ is *corrupted* if $path(\alpha_p)$ is open at the end of round $|\alpha| + 1$. Obviously if $\alpha_p$ is corrupted then all processors in $\alpha$ are faulty.

**Lemma 15.** *Let $\sigma$ be a run of* ESFM4 *in which node $\alpha_p$ is corrupted. Then $p$ detects (using* FDR*) that $last(\alpha)$ is faulty not later than the end of round $|\alpha|+1$.*

*Proof.* The proof is done by induction on $|\alpha|$.

**Base-case:** $|\alpha| = 1$ (i.e. $\alpha = s$). If $s_p$ is open at the end of the second round then rule 1 implies that the number of $s_p$'s sons whose tree value is $tree(s_p)$ is not greater than $\frac{n-1}{2} + (t-1)$. Since $n > 4 \cdot t$ we get that processor $p$ recognizes more then $t$ contradictions with processor $s$ and therefore detects that $s$ is faulty.

**Induction step:** Suppose that the lemma holds for all $\beta$ s.t. $|\beta| < k$ and let $|\alpha| = k$. Since Lemma 4 (a) holds for ESFM4 we get that all the processors of $\alpha$ are faulty and by induction hypothesis at the end of round $|\alpha|$ all of them (except, possibly, $last(\alpha)$ ) are detected by $p$ as faulty. Since $\alpha_p$ is open at the end of round $|\alpha| + 1$ then from prediction rule 1 follows that for at least $\frac{n-|\alpha|}{2} - (t - |\alpha|)$ of $\alpha_p$'s sons the tree values are differ from $tree(\alpha_p)$. Therefore at the end of round $|\alpha| + 1$ processor $p$ recognizes at least $\frac{n-|\alpha|}{2} - t + 2 \cdot |\alpha| - 1)$ contradictions to $last(\alpha)$. Hence FDR rule implies that until the end of round $|\alpha| + 1$ $p$ detects that $last(\alpha)$ is faulty. $\square$

Let $\sigma$ be a run of ESFM4 s.t. for every correct $q$, node $\alpha_q$ is corrupted; then we say that processor $last(\alpha)$ is a *delay-causer* of round $|\alpha|$.

**Lemma 16.** *Let $\sigma$ be a run of ESFM4 s.t. processor $q$ is one of the delay-causers of round $r$. Let $\beta$ be a node s.t. $last(\beta) = q$ and $|\beta| > r$. Then for every correct $p$ path($\beta_p$) is closed not later than the end of round $|\beta| + 1$.*

*Proof.* By Lemma 15 at the end of round $r+1$ all of the correct processors detect that $q$ is faulty. Hence FMR implies that the tree values of all the correct sons of $\beta_p$ are 0. Since Lemma 4 (a) holds for ESFM4, from Corollary 5 we get that all the processors of $\beta$ are faulty, hence the lemma follows by prediction rule 1. □

**Lemma 17.** *Let $\sigma$ be a run of ESFM4 and $f$ be the number of actual faults in $\sigma$. Then all of the correct processors in $\sigma$ stop within $\min \{ f+2, t+1 \}$ rounds.*

*Proof.* The proof follows from the observation that on every path of length $f+1$ there exists at least one correct node. Let $p$ be an arbitrary correct processor. Then at the end of round $f+2$ every path from $s_p$ to some leaf in $IG_p$ is closed. In such a case it is not hard to show that node $s_p$ is also closed, hence $p$ halts within at most $min\{f+2, t+1\}$ rounds. □

## 5 Protocol for $t < n/8$ with Linear-Size messages

### 5.1 The Algorithm

In ES4 every faulty processor could be a *delay-causer* in every communication round. By using **fault-masking** we restrict the power of each faulty processor to be a *delay-causer* for just one round. Even under these conditions every faulty processor can corrupt an exponential number of nodes: it is not hard to see that in the worst case the total number of bits that is sent by a correct processor to each of the other processors in a single communication round of ESFM4 with $f$ actual faults is $O(3^{f/3} \cdot n)$.

In this section we introduce a novel technique called **reconstructed traversal** to get a protocol that tolerates up to $n/8$ faults using messages of *linear size*. The new protocol is denoted by LS8 for *linear-Size messages* protocol for $t < n/8$. In LS8 a faulty processor can corrupt at most one node. Denote by $q_i(\alpha)$ the processor whose name appears in the $i$'th place (from left) of $\alpha$ (therefore $q_1(\alpha) = s$). Define the following order between *sequences* of processor names: $\alpha \succ \beta$ if $|\alpha| > |\beta|$ or $\exists k\, \forall i < k : q_i(\alpha) = q_i(\beta)$ and $q_k(\alpha)$ is greater than $q_k(\beta)$ according to the global order of processor names. We define $\alpha \succeq \beta$ if $\alpha \succ \beta$ or $\alpha = \beta$.

**Reconstructed traversal** is based on the following claim:

**Claim 18.** *Let $\sigma$ be a run of ESFM4 with $t < n/6$, and let $p$ and $last(\alpha)$ be correct processors s.t. path($\alpha_p$) is not closed before the end of round $|\alpha|$. Choose $S$ to be some arbitrary set of $n-t$ sons of $\alpha_p$. Then node $\alpha_p$ can be closed using only the tree values of nodes in $S$.*

*Proof.* Lemma 4 (a) implies that all processors in $\alpha$ except $last(\alpha)$ are faulty, hence at least $n - (t - |\alpha| + 1)$ of $\alpha_p$'s sons are correct. Since $last(\alpha)$ is correct, the tree values of all correct sons of $\alpha_p$ are equal to $tree(\alpha_p)$. Hence $tree(\alpha_p)$ is the tree value of at least $n - 2 \cdot t + |\alpha| - 1$ of $\alpha_p$'s sons chosen from the set $\mathcal{S}$. Since $|\alpha| \geq 1$ and since $n > 6 \cdot t$ we get that there exist more than $\frac{n-|\alpha|}{2} + (t - |\alpha|)$ nodes $\beta$ s.t. $\beta \in \mathcal{S}$ and $tree(\beta) = tree(\alpha)$. Thus the claim follows by prediction rule 1. $\square$

The first two rounds of LS8 are exactly like those of ESFM4. Starting from round 3 every processor that does not stop during the first two rounds performs a procedure called **reconstructed traversal** (described below) for at most $t - 2$ extra rounds. If some correct processor $p$ does not halt within $t + 1$ rounds then it applies *resolve* to $\mathrm{IG}_p$.

LS8 (at processor $p$):
1. first two rounds: like in ESFM4;
2. for $3 \leq r \leq t + 1$ perform **reconstructed traversal**;
3. apply *resolve* to $\mathrm{IG}_p$.

At any round of the **reconstructed traversal**, every correct processor $p$ corresponds to some node $\alpha$ that is called the *current* node of $p$ and denoted by $current(p)$; at the beginning of the traversal $current(p) := s$. Let $p$ be a correct processor and assume that at some round $current(p) = \alpha$. In this case $\alpha_p$ is *new* if the tree values of $\alpha_p$ sons were not broadcast by $p$. We say that node $\beta_p$ is *almost full* if at least $n - |\beta| - t$ sons of $\beta_p$ have some tree values, and node $\beta_p$ is *full* if all of its sons have tree values. As we shell see, when $current(p) = \alpha_p$, each $\beta_p$ s.t. $|\beta| \leq |\alpha|$ is full or closed.

In LS8 every processor $p$ maintains $\mathrm{IG}_p$, *faulty-list$_p$* and *contradiction-list$_p$* which are used in ESFM4 and three additional data structures: *reported-list$_p$*, *current-list$_p$* and *halted-list$_p$*. In *reported-list*, $p$ stores all the incoming messages, *halted-list$_p$* is a list of processors that $p$ claims as being halted (i.e. they stopped assuming they are correct). For every processor $q$ s.t. $q \notin (halted\text{-}list_p \cup faulty\text{-}list_p)$, processor $p$ chooses some node $\beta$, in *current-list$_p$*, to be the current node of $q$ with respect to $p$ (i.e. $current(q)_p = \beta$). All the above structures are initiated to empty. We say that processor $q$ is at least as *fast* as $p$ if $current(q)_p \succeq current(p)$ or if $q \in (halted\text{-}list_p \cup faulty\text{-}list_p)$.

Each *round* of the **reconstructed traversal** at $p$ consists of three parts: (i) if $\alpha_p$ is new then $p$ broadcasts the tree values of every son of $\alpha_p$; (ii) $p$ collects all the incoming messages and updates the appropriate data structures; (iii) at the end of the round $p$ counts the number of processors that are at least as *fast* as $p$; in case that there are at least $n - t$ such processors $p$ performs the **traverse** procedure.

**reconstructed traversal:**
1. If $\alpha = current(p)$ is *new* then broadcast the tree values of every son of $\alpha_p$, otherwise broadcast special *beep* signal;

2. Receive the incoming messages from all processors (including yourself);
3. **update** *current-list$_p$* and *halted-list$_p$*;
4. If at least $n - t$ processors are at least as *fast* as $p$ then **traverse**.

**update** (*halted-list$_p$*): At each communication round every correct non-halted processor broadcasts some message to all the processors. Therefore, if during round $r$ processor $p$ does not receive any message from processor $q$ and $q \notin$ *faulty-list$_p$* then $p$ adds $q$ to *halted-list*, and claims that $q$ is halted.

**update** (*current-list$_p$*): If in round $r$ processor $p$ receives from processor $q$ a message containing values of $\beta_q$'s sons and if $q \notin$ (*faulty-list$_p$* $\cup$ *halted-list$_p$*) then $current(q)_p := \beta$.

Processor $p$ performs **traverse** when it recognizes $n - t$ processors that are at least as *fast* as $p$. The procedure consists of four parts; (i) updating the subtree rooted at $\alpha_p$ (i.e. **update-tree** at $\alpha_p$); (ii) looking for the smallest $\beta_p$ s.t. $|\beta| = |\alpha|$, $\beta \succ \alpha$, and $Path(\beta_p)$ is open; if such $\beta_p$ does not exist then $p$ applies the prediction rules to IG$_p$; (iii) changing the current node to be the smallest open node $\beta_p$ s.t. $\beta_p \succ \alpha_p$; (iv) updating *subtree*($\beta_p$).

Let consider the procedure **update-tree** of **traverse**. From the description above we can see that for each node $\alpha_p$ which is $current(p)$ at some stage of the run $\sigma$, **update-tree** at $\alpha_p$ is performed exactly twice: when $\alpha_p$ becomes new $current(p)$ and when $p$ leaves $\alpha_p$. In both cases in **update-tree** processor $p$ generates tree values to some of $\alpha_p$'s *grandchildren* and performs **fault-detection** and **fault-masking**. In the second case ($p$ leaves $\alpha_p$) every node $\alpha j_p$ becomes almost full and $p$ tries to close it. If $p$ cannot close some node $\alpha j_p$ it generates a tree value 0 to every $\alpha j q_p$ that has no tree value.

**traverse:**
    1. **update-tree** at $\alpha_p$;
    2. If there is no $\beta_p$ s.t. $\beta \succ \alpha$, $|\beta| = |\alpha|$ and $path(\beta_p)$ is open
        then begin
                2.1 Apply prediction rules to IG$_p$;
                2.2 If $\exists v$, $v \in \{0, 1\}$, s.t. $close(s_p) = v$ then HALT;
                      (* $v$ is the decision value *)
                2.3 Remove all descendants of closed nodes;
        end;
    3. new $current(p):=$ the smallest open $\beta_p$ s.t. $\beta \succ \alpha$;
    4. **update-tree** at $\beta_p$. (* the new $current(p)$ *)

**update-tree** at $\alpha_p$:
    1. For every $\alpha j_p$, son of $\alpha_p$, and for every $q$ not in $\alpha j$ do
        begin
                If the value $v$ of $tree(\alpha j)$ was reported by $q$
                      then $tree(\alpha j q_p) := v$;
                If $q \in$ *faulty-list$_p$* then $tree(\alpha j q_p) := 0$;
                Otherwise if $current(q)_p \succeq \alpha$ or if $q \in$ *halted-list$_p$* then

$$tree(\alpha j q_p) := tree(\alpha j_p);$$

end;

2. For every $\alpha j_p$ son of $\alpha$ apply CDR and FDR;
3. For every $q$ detected as faulty at step 2 do
    for every $\beta \succ \alpha$ s.t. $q \notin \beta$ and $path(\beta_p)$ is open do $tree(\beta q_p) := 0$;
4. If $\alpha_p$ is not *new* and at least $n - t$ processors are at least as *fast* as $p$
    then begin
        Apply prediction rule 1 to each node $\alpha j_p$;
        If node $\alpha j_p$ remains open then
            for every $q$ s.t. $q$ not in $\alpha j$ and $\alpha j q_p \notin \mathrm{IG}_p$ do
                $tree(\alpha j q_p) := 0$;
        Apply prediction rules 1 and 2 to $subtree(\alpha_p)$;
    end;
5. Remove all the descendants of closed nodes from $subtree(\alpha_p)$.

Now we can show why a processor performs **update-tree** twice. Denote the *father* node of $\alpha$ by $f(\alpha)$. Suppose that $p$ traverses node $\alpha_p$ before some correct $j$ broadcast $tree(\alpha_j)$. Consider the situation when $p$ leaves $f(\alpha)_p$. In this case node $\alpha$ is full but not closed and $tree(\alpha_j) = 0$. Since at that time there are at least $n - t$ processors that are at least as *fast* as $p$ then there are at least $n - 2 \cdot t$ correct processors that traversed $f(\alpha)$ or halted. When processor $j$ reaches $f(\alpha)$ it performs **update-tree** during which it recognizes that $last(\alpha)$ is faulty. Hence if $j$ broadcast $tree(\alpha_j)$ the broadcast value is 0.

## 5.2 Correctness Proof and Complexity

Let $\sigma$ be a run of LS8 and let $p$ be a correct processor in $\sigma$. $Per(r)_p$ is the set of communication rounds during which the $r$th level of $\mathrm{IG}_p$ is built (i.e. $level_p = r$). By $T(p,r)$ we denote the $\mathrm{IG}_p$ tree at the end of $Per(r)_p$. For every correct processor $p$ we define $level_p = |\alpha| + 2$ were $\alpha$ is $current(p)$. To make our proof simpler we start with a modified protocol, denoted by LS8'. In LS8' each correct processor $p$ that does not halt in **traverse** builds tree of height $t + 1$ (and then applies *resolve*). Later we shell see that in LS8' processors halt within at most $t + 2$ rounds. Afterwards we prove that LS8 indeed reaches BA for $t < n/8$ using optimal time and messages of linear size. We assume that all the structures of LS8 are defined for LS8'.

**Lemma 19.** *Let $\sigma$ be a run of LS8' and let $p$ be an arbitrary correct processor. Then the following claims hold:*

a. *If $|\alpha| < r$ and $last(\alpha)$ is correct then $path(\alpha_p)$ is closed in $T(p,r)$;*
b. *If $j$ is correct and $path(\alpha_j)$ is closed in $T(j, r - 1)$ then $path(\alpha_p)$ is closed in $T(p, r)$;*
c. *Let $j$ be a correct processor and suppose that in $T(j, r - 1)$ $close(\alpha_j) = v$ when $path(\alpha_p)$ in $T(p, r - 1)$ is open. Then somewhere in $Per(r)_p$ node $\alpha_p$ is closed with $v$;*

149

**d.** *Let $\alpha_p$ be a node in $T(p, r-1)$ s.t. $tree(\alpha_p) = v$, $last(\alpha)$ is correct and $path(\alpha_p)$ is open. Under these conditions, somewhere in $Per(r)_p$, p performs $close(\alpha_p) := v$;*

**e.** *At least until the end of $Per(r)_p$ of $\sigma$, processor p does not find any contradiction between any two correct processors.*

*Proof.* The proof of this lemma is done by induction on $r$.

**Base-case:** $r = 2$. First two rounds of LS8' are equivalent to the first two rounds of ESFM4 for which the claims hold.

**Induction Step:** Suppose that the lemma holds for all $r < k$ and prove it for $r = k$. Let $\alpha_p$ be a node in $T(p, k-1)$ s.t. $|\alpha| = k-2$ and $path(\alpha_p)$ is open. In this case in $Per(k)_p$ processor p broadcasts the values of $\alpha_p$'s sons. Induction hypothesis (b) implies that for each correct $j$ $path(\alpha_j)$ in $T(j, k-2)$ is open, hence $j$ broadcasts $tree(\alpha_j)$ during $Per(k-1)_j$. Induction hypothesis (a) implies that all processors in $\alpha$ are faulty. First we have to show that for each correct $j$ the broadcast value of $tree(\alpha_j)$ is equal to $tree(\alpha_j_p)$ broadcast by p. It is easy to see that somewhere before p reaches $\alpha_p$ $current(p) = f(\alpha)$. Consider two cases. If processor $j$ reaches $f(\alpha)$ before p leaves $f(\alpha)$ then by the protocol $tree(\alpha_j_p) = tree(\alpha_j)$. Otherwise when p leaves $f(\alpha_p)$ $tree(\alpha_j_p)$ is set to 0. At this time node $\alpha_p$ is almost full but not closed. When $j$ reaches $f(\alpha)$ it performs **update-tree** at $f(\alpha_j)$. Hence it gives $tree$ values for at least $n - 2 \cdot t$ sons of $\alpha_j$ and then performs **fault-detection**. Since $n > 8 \cdot t$ and since every correct processor reports on $tree(\alpha)$ we can show that in this case $j$ detects that $last(\alpha)$ is faulty, $tree(\alpha_j)$ is set to 0 and this is the broadcast value of $tree(\alpha_j)$. Therefore at least until the end of $Per(k)_p$ processor p does not find any contradiction between any two of correct processors, hence we fulfill condition (e). In this condition for every correct $j$ node $\alpha_j_p$ is closed during $Per(r)_p$ s.t. $close(\alpha_j_p) := tree(\alpha_j_p)$. Hence (a) and (d) are satisfied. The proof of (b) and (c) is done in similar way to that of Lemma 8. □

**Theorem 20.** LS8' *reaches Byzantine Agreement for $t < n/8$.*

*Proof.* If $s$ is correct then Lemma 19 (a&d) implies that at the end of the second round for every correct p $close(s_p) = tree(s_p)$ where $tree(s_p)$ is the value broadcast by $s$. Hence we get the **validity** property.

To prove **agreement** let $\sigma$ be a run of LS8'. Consider two cases.

**a.** If for some correct p node $s_p$ is closed before the end of $Per(t)_p$ then Lemma 19 (b&c) implies that for every correct $q$, the root $s_q$ is closed not later than the end of $Per(t+1)_q$ and $close(s_q) = close(s_p)$.

**b.** Suppose that no correct processor closes the root before the end of $Per(t+1)$. Let p and q be two arbitrary correct processors and let $\alpha$ be a node s.t. $|\alpha| < t+1$ and $path(\alpha_p)$ and $path(\alpha_q)$ are open in $T(p,t)$ and in $T(q,t)$ respectively. Let $\alpha$ be a node s.t. $path(\alpha)$ is open in $T(p,t)$ and in $T(q,t)$. Then the *final* value of $\alpha_p$ (i.e. $resolve(\alpha_p)$ or $close(\alpha_p)$) is equal to the final ($resolve$ or $close$) value of $\alpha_q$. Consider first the case of $|\alpha| = t$. If $last(\alpha)$

is correct then Lemma 19 (a&d) implies that in $t + 1$th period both $p$ and $q$ closes node $\alpha$ and $close(\alpha_p) = close(\alpha_q)$. If $last(\alpha)$ is faulty Lemma 19 (a) implies that $t$ first processors in $\alpha$ are faulty. Hence all the sons of $\alpha_p$ and $\alpha_q$ are correct, therefore their tree values in $\text{IG}_p$ and $\text{IG}_q$ are equal and obviously the final values of $\alpha$ are also equal. By down-counting induction on $|\alpha|$ we can prove that the *final* value of $s_p$ is equal to the final (*resolved* or *closed*) value of $s_q$. Hence we get the **agreement**. $\qquad\square$

Let $\sigma$ be a run of LS8' and let $\alpha$ be the smallest node s.t. at round $r$ of $\sigma$ $current(p) = \alpha$ for some correct $p$. Then we denote $m^r = \alpha$. By $\mathcal{M}_\sigma$ we denote the set of all such nodes, and by $\mathcal{C}_\sigma$ the set of all nodes that during the run $\sigma$ were *current* for the correct processors.

**Lemma 21.** *For every run $\sigma$ of LS8' $m^r \succ m^{r-1}$.*

*Proof.* If all the processors with current on $m^{r-1}$ halt before round $r$ the lemma holds. Otherwise let $p$ be a correct processor s.t. in round $r - 1$ $current(p) = m^{r-1}$. In the end of round $r - 1$ $p$ recognizes at least $n - t$ processors are at least as *fast* as him, and therefore $p$ performs **traverse**. Hence if $p$ does not halt before round $r$ then it begins round $r$ with $current(p) \succ m^{r-1}$. $\qquad\square$

**Lemma 22.** *Let $\sigma$ be a run of LS8', $p$ correct in $\sigma$ and $\alpha \in \mathcal{C}_\sigma$. Then $p$ detects that $last(\alpha)$ is faulty not later then the round in which $p$ finishes **update-tree** at $f(\alpha)_p$.*

*Proof.* If $\alpha \in \mathcal{C}_\sigma$ then for some correct $j$ $path(\alpha_j)$ is not closed at $T(j, |\alpha|)$. In this case Lemma 19 (b) implies that $path(\alpha_p)$ is open in $T(p, |\alpha| - 1)$, hence at some point $correct(p) = f(\alpha)_p$. Processor $p$ does not leave $f(\alpha)$ without performing **update-tree** at $f(\alpha)_p$. Since $n > 8 \cdot t$ and since $j$ does not succeed to close $\alpha_j$ immediately after $\alpha_j$ becomes full, it is not hard to see that when $\alpha_p$ becomes almost full in $\text{IG}_p$ processor $p$ detects that $last(\alpha)$ is faulty. $\qquad\square$

**Lemma 23.** *Let $\sigma$ be a run of LS8'. Then the following holds:*

**a.** *If $\beta \succ \alpha$ s.t. $\alpha \in \mathcal{C}_\sigma$ and $last(\beta) = last(\alpha)$ then for every correct $p$ $path(\beta_p)$ is closed not later than the round in which $p$ is first visiting a node that is greater than $f(\beta)$. In the case that $f(\beta)$ becomes $p$'s current node, $\beta_p$ is closed with 0.*

**b.** *For every $\alpha, \beta \in \mathcal{C}_\sigma$ $last(\alpha) \neq last(\beta)$.*

*Proof.* Lemma 22 implies that each correct processor that reports $tree(\beta)$ reports for it a value of 0. On the other hand tree values of $\beta_p$'s sons that are accepted by reconstruction are also 0. Since $n > 8 \cdot t$, the above implies that if $path(\beta_p)$ is open when $p$ reaches $\beta$ then when node $\beta_p$ becomes almost full $close(\beta_p)$ is set to 0. Lemma 23 (b) is an easy corollary from part (a). $\qquad\square$

**Lemma 24.** *In each run of LS8' every correct processor halt within at most $f + 2$ rounds.*

*Proof.* Let $\sigma$ be a run of LS8' with $f$ actual faults. In this case Lemma 23 (b) implies that $|\mathcal{M}_\sigma| \leq f$. Hence Lemma 21 implies that the number of **reconstructed traversal** rounds performed by some arbitrary correct processor in $\sigma$ is at most $f$. Therefore the total number of the communication rounds in $\sigma$ is at most $f + 2$. $\qquad\square$

**Lemma 25.** *Let $\sigma'$ be a run of LS8' and $\sigma$ be a run accepted from $\sigma'$ by the replacement of LS8' with LS8. Then the replacement does not affect the set of decisions taken by correct processors.*

*Proof.* Let $f$ be the total number of actual faults in $\sigma'$. If $f < t$ then Lemma 24 implies that in $\sigma'$ all correct processors halt within at most $t + 1$ rounds, hence $\sigma'$ is completely equivalent to $\sigma$. Let $f = t$ and let $p$ be an arbitrary correct processor that does not halt at the end of round $t+1$ of $\sigma'$. In this case $|\mathcal{M}_{\sigma'}| = t$ and Lemma 21 implies that $current(p) = m^t$ at the end of round $t + 1$ of $\sigma'$. Denote by $\beta_p$ a son of $m_p^t$. Lemma 23 implies that for each son $\beta_p$, $last(\beta_p)$ is correct or was found faulty by all correct processors. Suppose $tree(\beta_p) = v$, then in round $t + 2$ of $\sigma'$ $p$ closes $\beta_p$ with value $v$; thus, in this case it is easy to see that the result remains unchanged if $p$ uses $resolve(\beta_p) = v$ at the end of round $t + 1$. $\qquad\square$

The theorem below is an easy corollary from lemmas 25 and 24.

**Theorem 26.** LS8 *reaches Byzantine Agreement for $t < n/8$ using at most $min\{f + 2, t + 1\}$ communication rounds.*

**Lemma 27.** *The size of a message in LS8 is at most $n + O(\log n)$.*

*Proof.* Let $\sigma$ be a run of LS8 and $p$ be an arbitrary correct processor s.t. in round $r$ $current(p) = \alpha$. If $\alpha_p$ is not *new* then $p$ broadcasts a special *beep* signal: for this case the lemma is obvious. Otherwise in round $r$ of $\sigma$ processor $p$ has to broadcast

of all sons of $\alpha_p$. If $\alpha$ is identified then every message is of size $n - |\alpha|$ bits: the values of $\alpha_p$ sons appear in the above defined order of nodes. If $\alpha \neq s$ then Lemma 19 (b) implies that $\alpha_p$ is the son of some node $\beta_p$ s.t. $current(p) = \beta$ at some previous round. Therefore to determine $\alpha$ it is enough to determine $last(\alpha)$ and the round number in which the sons of $f(\alpha)$ were reported by $p$. Since both could be determined by $\log n$ bits the lemma follows. $\qquad\square$

# 6   Conclusion and Open Questions

We strongly believe that LS8 can be modified to tolerate up to $n/6$ faults in optimal time with messages of linear size. A related open problem is the question whether our technique of **reconstructed traversal** can be combined with *Cloture Vote* of [5] to obtain new improved protocols for tolerating more than $n/6$ faults.

# References

1. Bar-Noy, A., Dolev, D.: Families of Consensus Algorithms. Proc. Aegean Workshop on Computing **3** (1988) 380–390
2. Bar-Noy, A., Dolev, D., Dwork, C., Strong, H.R.: Shifting Gears to Expedite Byzantine Agreement. Proc. Annual ACM Symposium on Principles of Distributed Computing **6** (1987) 42–51
3. Berman, P., Garay, J.: Optimal Early Stopping in Distributed Consensus. IBM Research Report RC 16746 (1990)
4. Berman, .P, Garay, J.: Distributed Consensus with $n = 3 \cdot (t + \epsilon)$ Processors. Proc. International Workshop on Distributed Algorithms, LNCS, Springer-Verlag **5** (1991)
5. Berman, P., Garay, J., Perry, K.J.: Towards Optimal Distributed Consensus. Proc. Symposium on Foundation of Computer Science **30** (1989) 410–415
6. Coan, B.: Efficient Agreement using Fault Diagnosis. Proc. Allerton Conference on Communication, Control and Computing **26** (1988) 663–672
7. Dolev, D., Reischuk, R.: Bounds of Information Exchange for Byzantine Agreement. JACM **32** 1985 191–204
8. Dolev, D., Reischuk, R., Strong, H.R.: Early Stopping in Byzantine Agreement. JACM **37** (1990) 720–741
9. Fisher, M., Lynch, N.: A Lower Bound for the Time to Assure Interactive Consistency. Information Processing Letters **14:4** (1982) 183–186
10. Hadzilacos, V., Halpern, J.: Message-Optimal Protocols for Byzantine Agreement. Proc. Annual ACM Symposium on Principles of Distributed Computing **10** (1991) 309–324
11. Moses, Y., Waarts, O.: Coordinated Traversal: $t+1$-Round Byzantine Agreement in Polinomial Time. Proc. Symposium on Foundation of Computer Science **29** (1988) 246–255
12. Pease, M., Shostak, R., Lamport, L.: Reaching Agreement in the Presence of Faults. JACM **27:2** (1980) 228–234
13. Waarts, O.: Coordinated Traversal: Byzantine Agreement in Polynomial Time. M.Sc. Thesis, Weizmann Institute of Science, Rehovot, Israel (1988)
14. Zamsky, A.: New Algorithms for Agreement Problem in Synchronous Distributed Networks. M.Sc. Thesis, (in Hebrew), Technion, Haifa, Israel (1992)

# A Continuum of Failure Models for Distributed Computing

Juan A. Garay[1,2] and Kenneth J. Perry[2]

[1] Department of Applied Mathematics and Computer Science,
The Weizmann Institute of Science,
Rehovot, 76100 Israel
[2] I.B.M. T.J. Watson Research Center, P.O. Box 704,
Yorktown Heights, New York 10598

**Abstract.** A range of models of distributed computing is presented in which processors may fail either by crashing or by exhibiting arbitrary (Byzantine) behavior. In these models, the total number of faulty processors is bounded from above by a constant $t$ subject to the proviso that no more than $b \leq t$ of these processors are Byzantine. At the two extremes of the range (i.e., $b = 0$ or $b = t$) we get models that are equivalent to the traditional models of either pure crash failures or pure Byzantine failures. For $0 < b < t$, the models that we introduce accommodate "real-world" experience that shows that the overwhelming majority of failures are crashes but occasionally some number of less-restrictive failures occur.
We examine the Reliable Broadcast and Consensus problems within this new family of models and prove lower bounds on the relationship required between the number of processors, $t$, and $b$. We also present protocols to solve these problems, which match the lower bounds. In presenting the protocols, we emphasize new algorithmic techniques that are fruitful to use in the new models but which have limited value in either of the pure models.

## 1  Introduction

Suppose that we are to design a distributed computing system tolerant of up to $t$ processor failures. Key problems in such systems are achieving consensus and performing reliable broadcast. If the failures are mild, i.e., solely processor crashes, then known results [7] indicate that the total number of processors required to solve these problems merely has to exceed $t$. But if failures are severe, i.e., arbitrary "Byzantine" behavior, then the lower bounds [8] indicate that more than $3t$ processors are required.

Experience demonstrates that processor hardware failures are predominantly, but not exclusively, crashes. Moreover, software subsystems on the same processor may function or crash independently on one another, thereby producing an overall processor behavior more malevolent than a simple crash, e..g., some services may continue to function – albeit with incorrect clocks – in spite of a crashed time-server. Thus, our dilemma is either to assume the best (that *only* crashes will occur), use low redundancy, and possibly suffer occasional catastrophic results, or to assume the worst (i.e., all failures are Byzantine) and pay a high cost in processors in order to tolerate rare events.

In this paper, we propose a range of failure models that allows a mix of crash and Byzantine failures. At extremes of the range, the model turns into either the pure crash fault or pure Byzantine models. Within this range, we examine two problems that lie at the core of distributed computing: performing reliable broadcast and achieving consensus.

## 1.1 Comparison with Previous Results

The Agreement problems (i.e., Byzantine Generals and Consensus) [8, 10] introduced a model in which the behavior of a faulty processor could be "Byzantine" (i.e., not restricted in any way), even to the extent of giving the impression that faulty processors were colluding to foil agreement. In this pure Byzantine model, it was shown that the Agreement problems admitted solutions if and only if $n$, the total number of processors, exceeded three times $t$, the upper bound on number of faulty processors. A less restricted model in which processors fail only by halting (i.e., crash failures) has also been used to study these problems and several protocols requiring only $n > t$ have been found [7].

It has been recognized that processors fail in ways that are less restrictive than crashing and more restrictive than acting arbitrarily. A "send omission" model in which processors can fail either by halting or failing to send some messages was proposed by Hadzilacos [5] as a model of intermediate power. This model was subsequently made even less restrictive by permitting faulty processors the additional power of arbitrarily failing to receive messages [11]. In both these models, Agreement protocols were presented that only required $n > t$. However, the failure types admitted in these weaker models of failure are still considered "benign" in the sense that any message sent by a processor is correct relative to the protocol and the processors state. In contrast, the messages sent by a faulty processor in the Byzantine model is in no way constrained.

More recent work has provided mechanisms that restrict the behavior of faulty processors in the Byzantine model [13, 9, 1]. Still, these mechanisms require $n > 3t$ and lower bounds have been established [1] that show that such mechanisms multiply the running time of algorithms designed for the weaker models.

## 1.2 Our Results

One contribution of this paper is the introduction of a new family of models of failure in distributed computing. The new models permit some processors to behave in an unrestricted Byzantine manner but do not require the high processor redundancy of the pure Byzantine model. In contrast to all the previous models, the new models that are introduced in this paper are the only non-authenticated ones to admit solutions to the Agreement Problems for $n \leq 3t$ processors in the presence of even one Byzantine failure.

A second contribution is the introduction of several algorithmic techniques for coping with a mixture of crash and Byzantine failures. These simple techniques are particularly interesting since they are of limited value at best in either the pure crash or pure Byzantine failure model.

A further contribution is to establish the relationship necessary between the number of processors, total faults, and Byzantine faults if these problems are to be solvable in the new model. Protocols that achieve these bounds are presented. We also give a lower bound on the time required to solve these problems. "Early-stopping" variants of these protocols are also presented. (Early stopping is a technique introduced by [4] as a means of circumventing the lower bound on running time.)

Our protocols are interesting because they show how a solution to a weakened version of the Consensus problem (*Frangible* Consensus) can be used to create a solution to the stronger version of the Consensus and Byzantine Generals Problems.

## 1.3 Difficulties of the Models

A trivial way of addressing the problem of mixed failures is to assume that *all* faulty processors may behave in a Byzantine manner, but some faulty processors "choose" to only exhibit benign faults. However, doing so rules out the possibility of low redundancy since the lower bound on Byzantine faults would apply. In contrast, we demonstrate a lower bound on mixed failures that admits the possibility of using fewer processors.

Another interesting aspect of the lower bound that we establish is that it admits the possibility of solutions to the Agreement problems even if the *majority* of processors are faulty. Note that in the pure Byzantine model, non-faulty processors outnumber faulty processors by a factor of more than two. By demonstrating protocols meeting the lower bounds, we show this not to be an obstacle.

## 2 A New Family of Failure Models

We are given $n$ processors numbered 0 through $n - 1$ that may communicate only by exchanging messages. For simplicity, this extended abstract assumes the synchronous round-based message-passing model.

The Flexible Failure model is a family FF of models indexed by the triple $(n, t, b)$ where $n > t \geq b$. In model $FF(n, t, b)$, there are a total of $n$ processors, any of which may fail either by crashing or by acting arbitrarily (Byzantine), but in any event the total number of failed processors is no more than $t$, and of these $t$ processors, no more than $b$ may be Byzantine. Model $FF(n, t, 0)$ corresponds to the traditional crash failure model while $FF(n, t, t)$ corresponds to the traditional Byzantine failure model.

In the Consensus Problem, each processor begins with an initial binary value and the non-faulty processors are required to compute a final binary value subject to an *Agreement* condition:

- *Agreement*: The final values of non-faulty processors are equal.

and a *Validity* condition. The usual Validity Condition:

- *Strong Validity*: If the initial value of at least $n - t$ non-faulty processors is equal to $v$, then the final value is $v$.

gives rise to the "strong" Consensus Problem. That is, no matter what failures occur, if all non-faulty processors have the same initial value, then that value is the final value. The Weak Consensus Problem [6] uses the weaker condition:

- *Weak Validity*: If the initial value of at least $n$ non-faulty processors (i.e., no failures occur) is equal to $v$, then the final value is $v$.

Weak Validity restricts the final value only in the case of failure-free executions. We define the *Frangible Consensus Problem* to use a Validity condition lying between the other two:

- *Frangible Validity*: If the initial value of at least $n - b$ non-faulty processors is equal to $v$, then the final value is $v$.

The motivation behind Frangible Validity is that if the non-Byzantine processors, including the ones that subsequently fail by crashing, begin with the same initial value, then that value must be the final value as well.

## 3  Lower Bounds

In this section we examine lower bounds in the new failure models. We establish a necessary relationship among $n, t$ and $b$ if the Agreement Problems are to be solvable. A (trivial) lower bound on the time to reach agreement is also stated.

**Theorem 1** *Consensus is achievable in the model* $\mathrm{FF}(n, t, b)$ *only if* $n > t + 2 \cdot b$.

    **Proof** [Sketch] To the contrary, suppose Consensus were achievable with $n \leq t + 2 \cdot b$. Then consider the following failure scenario: Of the $t$ faulty processors, some number $c$ are initially crashed (and therefore do not participate in the protocol) and the remaining $b = t - c$ faulty processors fail in a Byzantine manner. Any Consensus protocol for the participating processors must be a protocol that achieves consensus among $n' = n - c$ processors while being resilient to $b$ Byzantine failures. By the results of Lamport, Shostak, and Pease [8] a Consensus protocol that tolerates this number of Byzantine failures is possible if and only if $n' > 3 \cdot b$. But this condition implies that $n > t + 2 \cdot b$, contradicting the assumption on $b$. ∎

    The lower bound on time required to achieve Consensus in the new model follows from the lower bound in the crash model [5] and is stated without proof.

**Theorem 2** *A protocol to achieve Consensus in the model* $\mathrm{FF}(n, t, b)$ *requires at least* $(t + 1)$ *rounds of communication in some runs.*

Finally, a lower bound on network connectivity is established.

**Theorem 3** *Consensus is achievable in the model* $FF(n, t, b)$ *only if the connectivity of the network exceeds* $(t + b)$.

**Proof** [Sketch] To the contrary, suppose Consensus were achievable with a network having connectivity $k \leq (t + b)$. Then consider the following failure scenario: Of the $t$ faulty processors, some number $c$ are initially crashed (and therefore do not participate in the protocol) and the remaining $b = t - c$ faulty processors fail in a Byzantine manner. Any Consensus protocol for the participating processors on the surviving network must be be resilient to $b$ Byzantine failures. By the results of Dolev [3] a Consensus protocol that tolerates this number of Byzantine failures is possible if and only if the surviving network has connectivity exceeding $(2 \cdot b)$-connected. But this condition implies that the connectivity of the original network was more than $c + 2 \cdot b = t + b$. contradicting the assumption on $b$. ∎

## 4  New Algorithmic Techniques

We have solved several problems within the new models, among them, the Byzantine Generals, Consensus, and Clock Synchronization problems. Our solutions meet the lower bound on number of processors. In this abstract, rather than emphasizing the individual protocols, we choose to focus on the new techniques that are useful within this model, and illustrate their use in a Consensus protocol.

Many "obvious" techniques fail to work as expected in the Flexible Failure models. For example, one might be tempted to take a Consensus protocol for the Byzantine model and convert it into a protocol for the Flexible Failure model by selectively replacing the quantity $t$ by the quantity $b$. This can fail because it may totally ignore the crash failures. Even worse, it may result in the crashed processors exhibiting near-Byzantine failure. This is because many Byzantine protocols implicitly use a "default" value in place of the value not sent by a silent processor. For example, suppose that 0 were the default value and processor $p$ crashed after having sent 1 to a single non-faulty processor. Then all other non-faulty processors interpret $p$'s silence as being equivalent to having sent 0, thereby causing $p$ to appear Byzantine.

Even when the "obvious" techniques work, they often succeed only for a suboptimal number of processors. For example, we have formulated time-efficient protocols this way but only for $n > 2t + b$ processors. In the full paper, we shall more fully illustrate the use and limitations of some obvious techniques.

### 4.1  Veto

The "veto" is the first new technique that we introduce. A "veto" occurs when a minority of processors expresses a preference for some value other than the one indicated by the majority of processors. For example, in order for a non-faulty processor $p$ to accept value $v$ from processor $q$, we can require not only that there be a sufficient number $T$ (usually equal to $n - t$) of witnesses to $q$ having sent $v$ but *also* no more than $b$ witnesses to any other value. Thus, a quorum of at least $b + 1$ processors can "veto" $v$. This is in contrast to several existing protocols, e.g., [9, 13, 12], that only require a minimum number of positive witnesses.

In order to prevent Byzantine processors from vetoing the actions of non-faulty processors, it is necessary that a veto quorum include at least one non-Byzantine processor. But, if we tried to implement the veto in the pure Byzantine model with the most common value of $T$, i.e., $n - t$, we would discover that the existence of $T$ positive witnesses necessarily precludes the existence of a veto quorum. Thus, the veto is redundant in the pure models. Only in the Flexible Failure models, e.g., $FF(n, t, b)$ where $t > b > 0$, is it possible to simultaneously have both $n - t$ positive witnesses and a veto quorum of size at least $b + 1$.

Use of the veto technique is illustrated in the MakeUnique protocol of Figure 1 which implements a form of Crusader Agreement [3]. Each processor simultaneously executes MakeUnique, supplying its current value of the binary-valued variable $V$. MakeUnique utilizes the veto technique to ensure that all processors that accept a value accept the same value, but some processors may not accept any value (indicated by "accepting" the value 2). In the sequel, the value of a variable local to processor $i$ will be denoted by a subscript, e.g., $V_i$ denotes the value of processor $i$'s $V$ variable.

**Lemma 1** *If $p, q$ are non-faulty processors such that, in MakeUnique, $p$ assigns $v \neq 2$ to $V_p$ and $q$ assigns $w \neq 2$ to $V_q$, then $v = w$.*

**Proof** [Sketch] Since of the at least $n - t$ non-faulty processors, there is some value that is sent in MakeUnique by the majority of them and $\lceil (n - t)/2 \rceil > b$. Thus, if the majority sent $v$, no non-faulty processor could set $V$ to $\bar{v}$ at the end of Universal Exchange 1. ∎

```
MakeUnique(V):
     send(V) to all processors;
     C[0] := number of 0's received;
     C[1] := number of 1's received;
     if      C[0] ≥ n − t ∧ C[1] ≤ b then V := 0
     elseif  C[1] ≥ n − t ∧ C[0] ≤ b then V := 1
     else    V := 2
     fi;
```

**Fig. 1.** MakeUniqueProtocol for processor $0 \leq i < n$.

## 4.2 Double Echo

Many existing protocols [9, 13] utilize a "broadcast-accept" sub-protocol for "broadcasting" a value. These sub-protocols involve having a "broadcaster" first send its value to all processors who in turn act as witnesses to this fact by "echoing" the value to all processors. Only if a processor receives a certain number of echoes does it "accept" a value from the broadcaster. This number serves to limit the abilities of a faulty broadcaster.

We introduce a variation of "broadcast-accept" protocols in which each processor receiving a value from the "broadcaster" *immediately* sends two consecutive identical echoes. Although the second echo does not appear at first to convey any information, it does in fact serve an important purpose: receipt of the second echo from a non-Byzantine processor $q$ proves that $q$ did not crash before sending the first echo to all processors. We demonstrate the value of this information through the Unicast protocol of Figure 2 and its proof.

Unicast is similar in purpose to MakeUnique in that each processor executes MakeUnique, supplying its current value of variable $V$. At the end of Unicast each processor "accepts" some value from every other processor, and the array $D$ is set to indicate how many of each value is accepted, e.g., $D[v]$ is the number of $v$'s accepted. It is stronger than MakeUnique in that it also guarantees that if non-faulty processor $p$ accepts value $v \neq 2$ from processor $j$, any other non-faulty processor $q$ either also accepts $v$ from $j$ or accepts 2 from $j$. Thus, a Byzantine processor is prevented from having 0 accepted by one non-faulty processor while 1 is accepted by some other non-faulty processor. This property will be vital in allowing us to implement "early stopping" in a subsequent section.

The power of the double echo technique is made clear by the following lemma.

**Lemma 2** *If $p,q$ are non-faulty processors such that, in Unicast, $p$ accept's $\langle v,j \rangle, v \neq 2$ and $q$ accept's $\langle w,j \rangle, w \neq 2$, then $v = w$. Moreover, a value sent by a non-faulty processor is accepted by all non-Byzantine processors.*

**Proof** [Sketch] For the sake of contradiction, suppose $p$ accepted $\langle v,j \rangle, v \neq 2$ and $q$ accepted $\langle w,j \rangle, v \neq 2$ such that $w \neq v$. Then there were at least $n-t$ processors that sent $\langle v,j,1 \rangle$ and $\langle v,j,2 \rangle$ to $p$. But $q$ must have received $n-t-b > b$ of these $\langle v,j,1 \rangle$'s since there are no more than $b$ Byzantine failures. Thus, $q$ could not accept $w$ unless $v = w$.

That the value $v$ sent by a non-faulty processor $j$ is accepted can be seen by simple inspection of the code. There are guaranteed to be at least $n-t$ double echoes of $\langle v,j \rangle$ since all non-faulty processors receive $v$ from $j$ and the only echoes with contrary values can come from the at most $b$ Byzantine processors. ∎

## 5 A Protocol for Frangible Consensus

We illustrate the use of the new algorithmic techniques via a Consensus protocol. A protocol that solves the Frangible Consensus problem for $FF(n,t,b)$ where $n > t+2 \cdot b$ is shown in Figure 3. It follows the Phase King paradigm of [2] in which

```
Unicast(V,D):
    send(V) to all processors ;

    for j := 0 to n - 1 do
        if receive w from processor j then
            send(⟨w, j, 1⟩) to all processors ;
            send(⟨w, j, 2⟩) to all processors
        fi;

        for l := 0 to 2 do
            E[l, j] := number of ⟨l, j, 1⟩'s received;
            F[l, j] := number of processors from which both ⟨l, j, 1⟩ and ⟨l, j, 2⟩ was received;
        od;

        if      F[0, j] ≥ n - t ∧ E[1, j] ≤ b ∧ E[2, j] ≤ b then accept(⟨0, j⟩)
        elseif  F[1, j] ≥ n - t ∧ E[0, j] ≤ b ∧ E[2, j] ≤ b then accept(⟨1, j⟩)
        elseif  F[2, j] ≥ n - t ∧ E[0, j] ≤ b ∧ E[1, j] ≤ b then accept(⟨2, j⟩)
        fi;
    od;

    D[0] := number of 0's accepted;
    D[1] := number of 1's accepted;
    D[2] := number of 2's accepted;
```

**Fig. 2.** Unicast Protocol for processor $0 \leq i < n$.

the computation proceeds in phases, each of which has a processor designated as "phase king." Each phase $K$ consists of 3 rounds of communication. During the first two rounds of a phase, all processors communicate with one another; in the final round only processor $K$ (the king) sends messages.

In the final statement of the figure, there is the notation DecidedAction. This notation is merely a place-hold for either of two statements: skip or halt.

We now sketch a proof of correctness of the protocol. In the sequel, assume that the DecidedAction is skip. As a preliminary step, we show that if all non-Byzantine processors begin a phase with the same value of $V$, then all non-faulty processors end the phase with $V$ unchanged.

**Lemma 3 (Persistence)** *If there is a $v$ such that for each non-Byzantine processor $p$, $V_p = v$ at the beginning of a phase, then at the end of the phase $V_q = v$ for each non-faulty processor $q$.*

**Proof** [Sketch] Observe that during Universal Exchange 1, each of the at least $n-t$ non-faulty processors send $v$ and only the Byzantine processors send a value other than $v$. By inspection of the code of MakeUnique, at the end of Universal Exchange 1, $V = v$ for each non-faulty processor. Similarly by inspection of the

```
V := "initial value";
for K := 1 to t + 1 do
    /* Universal Exchange 1 */
        MakeUnique(V) ;

    /* Universal Exchange 2 */
        Unicast(V, D);

            if      D[0] > b then V := 0
            elseif  D[1] > b then V := 1
            fi;

    /* King's Broadcast */
        if i = K then send(V) to all processors fi;
        W := value received from processor K;
        if      (V = 2 ∨ D[V] ≤ b ∨ D[2] > b) then V := min(1, W) ;
        elseif  (V ≠ 2 ∧ D[V] ≥ n − b ∧ D[2] ≤ b) then DecidedAction;
        fi
od;
"final value" := V
```

**Fig. 3.** (Early-stopping) Frangible Consensus Protocol for processor $0 \le i < n$.

code of Unicast, at the end of Universal Exchange 2, $D[\bar{v}] \le b$, $D[2] \le b$ and $D[v] \ge n - t > b$ for each non-faulty processor. Thus $V_q = v$ for each non-faulty processor $q$ at the end of Universal Exchange 2 and all non-faulty processors ignore the Phase King's broadcast. ∎

We now show that the *Agreement* property is established.

**Lemma 4 (Agreement)** *At the end of phase $t+1$ for any non-faulty processors $p$ and $q$, $V_p = V_q$.*

**Proof** [Sketch] Let $g \le t + 1$ be the non-faulty processor with the lowest number. At the end of phase $g$, there are two possibilities:

1. All non-faulty processors replace $V$ with the value received from processor $g$. By assumption $g$ is non-faulty so all non-faulty processors assign the same value to $V$.

2. For some non-faulty processor $p$, at the end of Universal Exchange 2 of phase $g$, $V_p \ne 2$, $D[V_p]_p > b$, $D[2]_p \le b$ and thus $p$ ignores the King's Broadcast. First observe that, by Lemma 1, at the end of Universal Exchange 1 if processors $p$ and $q$ are non-faulty and $V_p = v \ne 2$ and $V_q = v' \ne 2$ then $v = v'$. So in Universal Exchange 2, any two non-faulty processors that send values less than 2 must send the same value. Because $D[V_p]_p > b$, this value must be equal to $V_p$.

In Universal Exchange 2, the majority of non-faulty processors either sends $V_p$ or 2. But by assumption $D[2]_p \leq b$ so the majority of non-faulty processors did not send 2 in Universal Exchange 2. Therefore every non-faulty processor $q$ has $D[V_p]_q \geq \lceil (n-t)/2 \rceil > b$ and $V_q = V_p$ at the end of Universal Exchange 2. In particular, processor $g$, the King of phase $g$ has $V_g = V_p$ at the end of Universal Exchange 2.

Therefore, any non-faulty processor that does not ignore the King's Broadcast of phase $g$ ends the phase with the same value of $V$ as any non-faulty processor that does ignore the phase's King.

By Lemma 3, no non-faulty processor changes its value of $V$ subsequent to phase $g$. ∎

Note that the above proof does not use any of the special properties of the Unicast protocol and would, in fact, remain true even if Unicast was replaced by "send($V$) to all processors" and where every message received was accepted. Doing so would save 2 rounds per phase. We have chosen to express the algorithm in the manner we have so that "early-stopping" may be easily added, as discussed in a subsequent section.

**Theorem 4 (Correctness)** *The protocol of Figure 3 solves the Frangible Consensus problem for $n > t + 2 \cdot b$.*

**Proof** The Agreement property follows from Lemma 4 and Frangible Validity follows from Lemma 3. ∎

# 6 Protocols for the Strong Agreement Problems

We now demonstrate how a protocol for Frangible Consensus can be used to derive protocols for the Agreement problems with the *Strong Validity* condition. This shows that the "strong" variants of the Agreement problems are solvable in our new models.

In the Byzantine Generals Problem [8], a distinguished processor (called the General) needs to broadcast a value subject to *Agreement* and *Strong Validity* conditions similar to those described for the Consensus Problem in Section 2. That is, all non-faulty processors must agree on the value broadcast by the General and, if the General is non-faulty, the agreed-upon value is the one chosen by the General.

Given a protocol that solves the Frangible Consensus Problem in FF($n, t, b$), a protocol that solves the Byzantine Generals Problem in FF($n, t, b$) is obtained as follows:

1. In round 1, the General sends the value it wishes to broadcast to all processors including itself.
2. The processors subsequently execute the Frangible Consensus Protocol using the value received from the General in round 1 (or 0 if no value was received) as the initial value.

If the General is non-faulty, all non-Byzantine processors execute the Frangible Consensus protocol with the same initial value and, by the correctness of the Frangible Consensus protocol, that is the value computed as the final value. Thus, the above protocol satisfies both the Agreement and Strong Validity conditions.

Given a protocol that solves the Byzantine Generals Problem in $FF(n, t, b)$,, a protocol that solves the Consensus Problem with the *Strong Validity* condition in $FF(n, t, b)$ is obtained as follows:

1. Each processor acts as the General in a separate instance of the Byzantine Generals Protocol. Thus, each processor obtains an identical vector of $n$ values.
2. The final value is the majority value in the vector.

Thus, the existence of a protocol for Frangible Consensus in the new model implies that the Agreement problems with the *Strong Validity* condition are solvable in the new model that is introduced in this paper.

# 7 Protocols with Reduced Running Time

When `DecidedAction` is a `skip` statement, the protocol of Figure 3 always takes exactly $(t + 1)$ phases to complete even if no processors fail during its execution. Protocols that terminate in fewer phases when the number of processors that fail during its execution is less than $t$ are called "early-stopping." By having an early-stopping protocol that runs in time proportional to the number of failures that actually occur during its execution, we pay only for the degree of fault tolerance actually needed. Figure 3 can be turned into an early-stopping protocol for the Frangible Consensus problem by defining the `DecidedAction` action to be `halt`.

We now turn to the correctness of the early-stopping protocol for Frangible Consensus. Because some non-faulty processors halt before others, we adopt the convention that if processor $p$ receives no value from processor $q$ in any round, $p$ assumes that $q$ sent a value equal to $V_p$ at the start of the phase.

The correctness of the early-stopping algorithm is now sketched. Because the proof is similar to that of the non-early-stopping protocol, most details are omitted from this extended abstract.

**Theorem 5** *The protocol of Figure 3 solves the Frangible Consensus problem for $n > t + 2 \cdot b$ and always terminates by phase $t + 1$. Moreover, let $f$ be the number of processors that actually fail. If $f \leq b$ then the protocol terminates in at most $f + 2$ phases.*

**Proof** [Sketch] The following facts are easy to establish:

1. If $n - b$ non-faulty processors begin a phase with the same value of $V$, they all halt at the end of the phase with $V$ unchanged.
   The proof is similar to that of Lemma 3.

2. If the King of phase $K$ is non-faulty all non-faulty processors will end phase $K$ with the same value of $V$.

   The proof is similar to that of Lemma 4. By fact 1, all non-faulty processors will halt by phase $K + 1$ provided that no more than $b$ processors fail.

3. If the King of phase $K$ is faulty and the first non-faulty processor $p$ halts in phase $K$, then all non-faulty processors end phase $K$ with the same value of $V$.

   By inspection of the code's stopping condition, $p$ halts only if at the end of phase $K$, $V_p \neq 2, D[V_p]_p \geq n - b$ and $D[2]_p \leq b$. Since at most $t$ processors are faulty, this implies that for all non-faulty $q$, at the end of phase $K$, $D[V_p]_q \geq n - b - t > b$. Moreover, since the values are sent by Unicast, by Lemma 2, $D[2]_q \leq b$. By inspection of the code, this implies that all non-faulty $q$ ignore the King's Broadcast of phase $K$ and have $V_q = V_p$ at the end of phase $K$.

   By fact 1, all non-faulty processors will halt by phase $K + 1$ provided that no more than $b$ processors fail.

Taken together, the above facts imply that if no more than $f \leq b$ failures occur, all non-faulty processors reach agreement and halt by phase $f + 2$. ∎

## 8  Discussion

We have presented a new model of failure for distributed computing and demonstrated protocols that solve the Agreement Problems in that model. The attractiveness of the model is that it allows some processors to fail in an unrestricted manner while not incurring the high redundancy required in a model of pure Byzantine failures. Since experience shows that failures worse than processor crashes do occur, the new model is closer to reality than either the pure crash or pure Byzantine models.

The new failure models introduced in this paper necessitate types of reasoning different from that commonly employed in either the pure crash or pure Byzantine models of failure. For example, the technique of forcing a processor to repeat an action in the presence of witnesses contributes little in either of the pure models but proves useful in the new model, as illustrated by the Unicast protocol of Figure 2 and its proof.

This extended abstract focussed on introducing a new model and showing that important problems could be solved within it. Thus, our protocols emphasized simplicity over efficiency. Our protocol without early-stopping requires $3(t+1)$ rounds (when Unicast is replaced by a simple send($V$) to all processors) and single-bit messages; we also presented a simple extension that was able to stop early under certain conditions. In the full paper we address the issues of efficiency and early-stopping in greater generality.

# References

1. R. Bazzi and G. Neiger. Optimally simulating crash failures. In *Proceedings of the Fifth International Workshop on Distributed Algorithms*. Springer-Verlag, 1991.
2. P. Berman, J.A. Garay, and K.J. Perry. Towards optimal distributed consensus. In *Proceedings of the Thirtieth Annual Symposium on Foundations of Computer Science*, pages 410–415. IEEE Computer Society Press, 1989.
3. D. Dolev. The byzantine generals strike again. *Journal of Algorithms*, 3(1):14–30, 1982.
4. D. Dolev, R. Reischuk, and H.R. Strong. Early stopping in byzantine agreement. *Journal of the ACM*, 37(4):720–741, 1990.
5. V. Hadzilacos. Issues of fault tolerance in concurrent computations. *Ph.D. Dissertation, Harvard University*, 1984.
6. L. Lamport. The weak byzantine generals problem. *Journal of the ACM*, 30(3):668–676, 1983.
7. L. Lamport and M. Fischer. Byzantine generals and transaction commit protocols. Technical Report Opus 62, SRI, 1982.
8. L. Lamport, R.E. Shostak, and M. Pease. The byzantine generals problem. *ACM Transactions on Programming Languages and Systems*, 4(3):382–401, 1982.
9. G. Neiger and S. Toueg. Automatically increasing the fault-tolerance of distributed algorithms. *Journal of Algorithms*, 11(3):374–419, 1990.
10. M. Pease, R.E. Shostak, and L. Lamport. Reaching agreement in the presence of faults. *Journal of the ACM*, 27(2):228–234, 1980.
11. K.J. Perry and S. Toueg. Distributed agreement in the presence of processor and communication faults. *IEEE Transactions on Software Engineering*, 12(3):477–482, 1986.
12. K.J. Perry S. Toueg and T.K. Srikanth. Fast distributed agreement. *SIAM Journal of Computing*, 16(3):445–457, 1987.
13. T.K. Srikanth and S. Toueg. Simulating authenticated broadcasts to derive simple fault-tolerant algorithms. *Distributed Computing*, 2(2):80–94, 1987.

# Simulating Crash Failures
# with
# Many Faulty Processors*
# (Extended Abstract)

Rida Bazzi** and Gil Neiger

College of Computing, Georgia Institute of Technology, Atlanta, Georgia 30332–0280
U.S.A.

**Abstract.** The difficulty of designing fault-tolerant distributed algorithms increases with the severity of failures that an algorithm must tolerate. This paper considers methods that *automatically* translate algorithms tolerant of simple *crash failures* into ones tolerant of more severe *omission failures*. These translations simplify the design task by allowing algorithm designers to assume that processors fail only by stopping. Earlier results had suggested that these translations must, in general, have limited *fault-tolerance*: that crash failures could not be simulated unless a majority of processors remained correct throughout any execution. We show that this limitation does not apply when considering a broad range of distributed computing problems that includes most classical problems in the field. We do this by exhibiting a hierarchy of translations, each with different fault-tolerance and complexity; for *any* number of possible failures, we give an appropriate translation. Each of these translations is shown to be optimal with respect to the joint measures of fault-tolerance and round-complexity (the round-complexity of a translation is the number of communication rounds that the translation uses to simulate one round of the original algorithm). That is, the hierarchy of translations is matched by a corresponding hierarchy of impossibility results. Furthermore, this hierarchy has more structure than that seen for other failure models, indicating that the relationship between crash and omission failures is more complex than had been previously thought.

## 1 Introduction

Distributed computer systems give algorithm designers the ability to write fault-tolerant applications in which correctly functioning processors can complete a computation despite the failure of others. It has been well-established that the complexity of writing such applications depends upon the type of faulty behavior that processors may exhibit. While simple stopping failures are relatively

---

* Partial support for this work was provided by the National Science Foundation under grants CCR-8909663 and CCR-9106627.
** This author was supported in part by a scholarship from the Hariri Foundation.

easy to tolerate, intermittent omission failures are more difficult to identify and compensate for. Consider the following:

- If processors may omit to send messages and later function correctly, then the correct processors may have more difficulty agreeing on the identity and timing of failures than they would if only stopping failures occurred.
- If processors may also omit to receive messages, the situation is even more complex. Faulty processors may be sending incomplete information; furthermore, it becomes difficult to tell whether it is the sender or the receiver of an omitted message that is at fault.

To assist the designers of fault-tolerant applications, researchers have developed *translations* that automatically increase the fault-tolerance of distributed algorithms [2,4,6,11,16]. Such translations automatically convert algorithms tolerant of relatively benign types of failure into ones that tolerate more severe faulty behavior. These simplify the design task: the algorithm can be written with the assumption that faulty behavior is benign; the translated algorithm can then be run correctly in a system with more severe failures. In addition, these translations can provide insight into the relative impact of different models of faulty behavior on the ability to provide fault-tolerant applications. Such insights can be gained by examining the properties of the translations.

Work in this area has concentrated on the following failure models: *crash failures*, under which processors fail by stopping prematurely [6]; *omission failures*, under which processors may stop intermittently fail to send or receive messages [13]; and *arbitrary failures*, under which faulty processors may take any action whatsoever [10] (such failures are also called *malicious* or *Byzantine*). The first two types are considered relatively benign, because processors never perform incorrect actions; they only omit to perform some correct actions.

Many researchers have developed translations for failures within this hierarchy. Coan considered systems with *asynchronous* message-passing and developed a "compiler" that converts algorithms that tolerate crash failures into ones that tolerate arbitrary failures [4]. Other researchers have considered systems with *synchronous* message-passing. Hadzilacos developed a technique to translate agreement algorithms tolerant of crash failures into ones that tolerate omission-to-send failures [6]; it was later shown that his translation was not general in that it could not be applied to all algorithms [9].[1] Srikanth and Toueg showed how algorithms written for systems in which message authentication was used to mitigate arbitrary failures could be run in systems without this authentication [16]. Neiger and Toueg developed a family of translations; some translate from crash to omission failures, while others translates from omission failures to arbitrary failures [11]. In an earlier paper [2], we gave a series of direct translations from crash to arbitrary failures and showed that each was optimal with respect to the combined measures of fault-tolerance and round-complexity (see below).

---

[1] All other translations described in this paper *are* general.

Most translations require simulating one round of communication of the original algorithm by some fixed number of rounds in the new algorithm. This number is the translation's *round-complexity*. Some translations are correct only if no more than a certain fraction of processors may fail. Typically, the *fault-tolerance* of an algorithm or of a translation is measured by comparing $n$ (the total number of processors in the system) to $t$ (the number of failures tolerated). If the requirements of a particular translation between two types of failures are *necessary*, then this indicates that there is a certain "separation" between these two types failures. For example, Neiger and Toueg showed that any translation from crash to omission failures requires that a majority of processors remain correct ($n > 2t$); this indicated a fundamental difference between these two systems that has since been studied elsewhere [3,12].

This paper explores translations from crash to omission failures in synchronous systems and circumvents the fault-tolerance requirement of Neiger and Toueg by refining the class of problems to which these translations apply. Specifically, the proof that $n > 2t$ is required for such translations appealed to a problem for which the states of faulty processors was important; such problems cannot typically be solved in systems with general omission failures if $n \leq 2t$ [3,12]. However, the solutions to many problems considered for distributed fault-tolerance do not depend on the states (or actions) of the faulty processors. The results of this paper apply to this broad class of problems.

This paper presents a hierarchy of translations, only the first of which requires $n > 2t$. These vary with respect to their fault-tolerance and round-complexity, showing a tight trade-off between the two measures. Each is optimal in the sense that it uses the minimum number of rounds necessary for a given fault-tolerance. Thus, we provide not only a series of translations but also a series of matching impossibility results. Specifically, we give a function $z$ of $n$ and $t$ and show that, if up to $t$ of the $n$ processors in the system may fail, then there is a translation from crash to omission failures that requires $z(n,t)+1$ rounds to simulate one round and that there is no translation that requires only $z(n,t)$ rounds. The function is $z(n,t) = \lfloor t/(n-t) \rfloor + \lceil t/(n-t) \rceil$. In the cases where $n > 2t$, this gives a translation with exactly the round-complexity of that of Neiger and Toueg: two rounds. This hierarchy of translations is more complex than the one previously discovered between crash and arbitrary failures [2]. In that case, there were three possible translations. The hierarchy presented here is unbounded. Thus, our results greatly improve the understanding of the relationship between crash and omission failures and may lead to the development of improved fault-tolerant algorithms for the two systems.

## 2 Definitions, Assumptions, and Notation

This paper considers distributed systems in which computation proceeds in synchronous *rounds*. This section defines a formal model of such a system. This model is an adaptation of that used by Neiger and Toueg [11].

## 2.1 Distributed Systems

A *distributed system* is a set of processors $\mathcal{P} = \{p_1, \ldots, p_n\}$ ($n$ is the number of processors in the system) joined by bidirectional communication links. Each processor has a local state, but the processors share no memory; processors communicate only by passing messages along the communication links. For the sake of simplicity, the results in this paper assume that processors are fully connected.[2]

Processors communicate with each other in synchronous *rounds*. In each round, a processor first sends messages, then receives messages, and finally changes its state. Let $\mathcal{M}$ be the set of messages that may be sent in the system, let $\perp \notin \mathcal{M}$ be a value that indicates "no message," and let $\mathcal{M}' = \mathcal{M} \cup \{\perp\}$.[3]

## 2.2 Protocols

Processors run a *protocol* $\Pi$, which specifies the messages to be sent and the states through which to pass. A protocol consists of two functions, a *message function* and a *state-transition function*. The message function is $\mu_\pi : \mathbf{Z} \times \mathcal{P} \times \mathcal{Q} \mapsto \mathcal{M}$ (where $\mathbf{Z}$ is the set of positive integers). If processor $p$ begins round $i$ in state $s$ then $\Pi$ specifies that it send $\mu_\pi(i, p, s)$ to all processors in that round. The state-transition function is $\delta_\pi : \mathbf{Z} \times \mathcal{P} \times (\mathcal{M}')^n \mapsto \mathcal{Q}$. If processor $p$ receives in round $i$ the messages $m_1, \ldots, m_n$ ($m_j$ from processor $p_j$), then $\Pi$ specifies that it change its state to $\delta_\pi(i, p, m_1, \ldots, m_n)$ at the end of round $i$. Figure 1 illustrates the execution of a protocol $\Pi$.

*state* = initial state;

**for** $i = 1$ **to** $\infty$ **do**
    *message* = $\mu_\pi(i, p, state)$;
    send *message* to all processors;
    **foreach** $q \in \mathcal{P}$
        **if** received some $m$ from $q$ **then**
            $msgs[q] = m$
        **else**
            $msgs[q] = \perp$;
    *state* = $\delta_\pi(i, p, msgs)$

**Fig. 1.** Execution of protocol $\Pi$ by processor $p$

---

[2] Work by Dolev and by Hadzilacos suggests that they may be extended to network topologies in which there is less (but sufficient) connectivity [5,8].

[3] If a processor sends no message in a round, we say that it "sends" $\perp$, although no message is actually sent.

Note that the following assumptions are made about protocols:

- they are "loquacious"; all processors send some message in every round;
- they require each processor to broadcast the same message to all (in any given round);
- their state transition functions depend solely on the messages that a processor has just received and *not* its current state; and
- they never have processors "halt."

These assumptions are made only to simplify the exposition and do not restrict the applicability of the results.

## 2.3 Histories and Problem Specifications

*Histories* are defined to describe the executions of a distributed system. Each history includes the following:

- the protocol being run by the processors,[4]
- the states through which the processors pass,
- the messages that the processors send, and
- the messages that the processors receive.

Let $Q(i,p)$ be the state in which processor $p$ begins round $i$. Let $S(i,p,q)$ be the message that $p$ sends to $q$ in round $i$ or $\perp$ if $p$ sends no message to $q$. Let $R(i,p,q)$ be the message that $p$ receives from $q$ in round $i$ or $\perp$ if $p$ does not receive a message from $q$.[5] $H = \langle \Pi, Q, S, R \rangle$ is a *history of protocol $\Pi$*.

A *system* is identified with the set of all histories (of all protocols) in that system. Thus, a system can be specified by a set of histories. A system can also be defined by giving the properties that its histories must satisfy. If $S$ is a system and $H = \langle \Pi, Q, S, R \rangle \in S$, then $H$ is a *history of $\Pi$ running in $S$*.

Protocols are run to solve particular problems. Formally, such problems can be specified by predicates on histories. Such a predicate, called a *specification*, distinguishes histories that solve the problem from those that do not. For example, the serializability problem in distributed databases can be specified by a predicate $\Sigma$ that is satisfied exactly by those histories of the database in which transactions are serializable. Protocol $\Pi$ *solves problem with specification $\Sigma$* (or *solves $\Sigma$*) *in system $S$* if all executions of $\Pi$ in $S$ satisfy $\Sigma$.

The solutions to many problems are not concerned with the behavior of the faulty processors. For example, the *Byzantine Generals* problem requires only that all *correct* processors reach agreement [10]. The specification of such a problem is *failure-insensitive*. Formally, a specification $\Sigma$ is failure-insensitive if the following is true: if some history $H_1$ satisfies $\Sigma$ and $H_2$ differs from $H_1$ only with respect to the behavior (state and message histories) of the faulty processors

---

[4] Given any history $H$ we want to be able to identify incorrect behavior in $H$; this requires that $H$ include the protocol $\Pi$ that processors should be following.

[5] Because of failures, the states and messages specified by $\Pi$ may be different from those indicated by $Q$ and $S$, and $R(i,p,q)$ need not equal $S(i,q,p)$; see Section 3.

(e.g., the correct processors still reach the same decision), then $H_2$ also satisfies $\Sigma$. Many problem considered in fault-tolerant distributed computing have failure-insensitive specifications. Neiger and Tuttle [12] give a careful analysis of the distinction between these problems and those that *are* sensitive to the behavior of faulty processors.

# 3 Correctness and Failures

Individual processors may exhibit *failures*, thereby deviating from *correctness*. They may do so by failing to send or receive messages correctly or by otherwise not following their protocol. This section informally defines crash and omission failures. Neiger and Toueg [11] provide formal definitions for a range of failures.

## 3.1 Correctness

Protocol $\Pi$ defines the actions that a correct processor takes when executing it. Consider a history $H = \langle \Pi, Q, S, R \rangle$. Processor $p$ *sends correctly in round $i$ of* $H$ if

$$\forall q \in \mathcal{P}[s(i,p,q) = \mu_\pi(i,p,Q(i,p))].$$

Processor $p$ *receives correctly in round $i$ of* $H$ if

$$\forall q \in \mathcal{P}[R(i,p,q) = s(i,q,p)].$$

Processor $p$ *makes a correct state transition in round $i$ of* $H$ if

$$Q(i+1,p) = \delta_\pi(i,p,R(i,p)).$$

Processor $p$ is *correct* in a history if it sends and receives correctly, and makes correct state transitions throughout that history. Let

$$Correct(H) = \{p \in \mathcal{P} \mid p \text{ is correct in } H\}.$$

If a processor is not correct, it is *faulty*.

## 3.2 Crash Failures

A *crash failure* is the most benign type of failure that this paper considers [6]. A processor commits a *crash failure* by prematurely halting in some round. Formally, $p$ commits a crash failure in round $i_c$ of $H = \langle \Pi, Q, S, R \rangle$ if $i_c \in \mathbf{Z}$ is the first round in which $p$ is not correct and

- either $p$ crashes during sending:
  - it sends to each processor $q$ either what the protocol specifies, or nothing at all:

$$\forall q \in \mathcal{P}[s(i_c,p,q) = \mu_\pi(i_c,p,Q(i_c,p)) \vee s(i_c,p,q) = \bot]; \text{ and}$$

- it receives no messages in round $i_c$:

$$\forall q \in \mathcal{P}[\mathrm{R}(i_c,p,q) = \perp];$$

- or $p$ crashes after sending:
  - it sends correctly in round $i_c$:

$$\forall q \in \mathcal{P}[\mathrm{S}(i_c,p,q) = \mu_\pi(i_c,p,\mathrm{Q}(i_c,p))]; \text{ and}$$

  - it receives from each processor $q$ either what $q$ sent or nothing at all:

$$\forall q \in \mathcal{P}[\mathrm{R}(i_c,p,q) = \mathrm{S}(i_c,q,p) \vee \mathrm{R}(i_c,p,q) = \perp].$$

In either case, $p$ takes no action after the crash:

- it sends and receives no messages: $\forall i > i_c \, \forall q \in \mathcal{P}[\mathrm{S}(i,p,q) = \mathrm{R}(i,p,q) = \perp]$, and
- it makes no state transitions: $\forall i > i_c[\mathrm{Q}(i,p) = \mathrm{Q}(i_c,p)]$.

The system $C(n,t)$ corresponds to the set of histories in which $t$ processors are subject only to crash failures and all other processors are correct. That is, $\mathsf{H} \in C(n,t)$ if and only if $\mathcal{P}$ can be partitioned into sets $C$ and $F$ such that $C = Correct(\mathsf{H})$, $|F| \leq t$, and

$$\forall p \in F \, \exists i_p \in \mathbf{Z}[p \text{ commits a crash failure in round } i_p \text{ of } \mathsf{H}].$$

## 3.3 Omission Failures

A more complex type of failure, called an *omission failure*, occurs if a processor intermittently fails to send and receive messages [13]. Such failures have also been called general omission failures. Processor $p$ may commit such failures in history $\mathsf{H} = \langle \Pi, \mathrm{Q}, \mathrm{S}, \mathrm{R} \rangle$ if it always makes correct state transitions, always sends to each processor what its protocol specifies or nothing at all, and always receives what was sent to it or nothing at all:

- $\forall i \in \mathbf{Z} \, \forall q \in \mathcal{P}[\mathrm{S}(i,p,q) = \mu_\pi(i,p,\mathrm{Q}(i,p)) \vee \mathrm{S}(i,p,q) = \perp]$; and
- $\forall i \in \mathbf{Z} \, \forall q \in \mathcal{P}[\mathrm{R}(i,p,q) = \mathrm{S}(i,q,p) \vee \mathrm{R}(i,p,q) = \perp]$.

Let $O(n,t)$ be the set of histories in which all processors are correct except for $t$, which are subject to omission failures. (Note that omission failures a strictly more severe than crash failures; a processor effectively crashes if it omits to send and receive all messages from some point onward.)

## 4 Translations between Systems with Failures

This section formally defines the concept of a translation from $C(n,t)$ to $O(n,t)$. The definition of translation used here is an adaptation of a more general definition used in other papers [2,11].

A *translation* is a function $T$ that converts protocol $\Pi_c$, designed to run correctly in $C(n,t)$, into a protocol $\Pi_o = T(\Pi_c)$ that runs correctly in $O(n,t)$. One round of $\Pi_c$ may be simulated by more than one round in $\Pi_o$. One can think of $\Pi_o$ as protocol $\Pi_c$ running with an additional underlying layer of software that "hides" more severe failures from $\Pi_c$. The simulating rounds of $\Pi_o$ are part of this underlying software. $\Pi_o = T(\Pi_c)$ may use a sequence of rounds of communication to simulate each round of $\Pi_c$; this sequence is called a *phase*. If each round of $\Pi_c$ is simulated by $z$ rounds in $T(\Pi_c)$, then $T$ has a *round-complexity* of $z$.

The state s of a processor executing a translated protocol $\Pi_o = T(\Pi_c)$ has two components, $s = \langle ss, cs \rangle$, called the *simulated state* and the *control state*, respectively. The simulated state ss corresponds to the state of a processor running $\Pi_c$. If a processor running $\Pi_o$ is in state $s = \langle ss, cs \rangle$, then let $S(s)$ denote the simulated state ss. $\Pi_o$ updates the simulated state only at the end of the $z$ rounds that make up a phase. For the translation we define, it will be clear what part of a processor's state is the simulated state.

Translation function $T$ *translates from* $C(n,t)$ *to* $O(n,t)$ *in* $z$ *rounds* (or *is a* $z$-*round translation from* $C(n,t)$ *to* $O(n,t)$) if there is a corresponding *history simulation function* $\mathcal{H}$ with the following property: given any protocol $\Pi_c$ and any history $H_o$ of $\Pi_o = T(\Pi_c)$ running in $O(n,t)$, $\mathcal{H}$ maps $H_o$ into a corresponding simulated history $H_c = \mathcal{H}(H_o)$ of $\Pi_c$ running in $C(n,t)$, where $z$ rounds in $H_o$ simulate each round of $H_c$. Formally, $\mathcal{H}$ is such that for any protocol $\Pi_c$ and any history $H_o = \langle \Pi_o, Q_o, S_o, R_o \rangle$ of $\Pi_o = T(\Pi_c)$ running in $O(n,t)$, the following hold:

(a) $H_c = \mathcal{H}(H_o) = \langle \Pi_c, Q_c, S_c, R_c \rangle$ is a history of $\Pi_c$ running in $C(n,t)$,
(b) $Correct(H_o) \subseteq Correct(H_c)$, and
(c) $\forall i \in \mathbf{Z} \, \forall p \in Correct(H_o)[S(Q_o(z \cdot (i-1)+1, p)) = Q_c(i, p)]$.

Condition (b) states that the translation preserves the correctness of processors. That is, any processor correct in $H_o$ is also correct in the simulated history $H_c$. However, processors faulty in $H_o$ may be correct in $H_c$. In fact, most translation techniques can mask minor failures, typically by using redundant communication. Condition (c) states that the states of *correct* processors at the beginning of round $i$ of $H_c$ are correctly simulated at the beginning of corresponding phase of $H_o$.

Arguments given by Neiger and Toueg can be used to show that any problem (with a failure-insensitive specification) solved by $\Pi_c$ is "effectively solved" by $\Pi_o$ [11]. Since protocols are easier to design for systems with crash failures, translations simplify the task of designing fault-tolerant protocols. The designer can first derive (and prove correct) a protocol $\Pi_c$ that tolerates only crash failures, a relatively simple task. Applying $T$ to $\Pi_c$ automatically results in a protocol $\Pi_o = T(\Pi_c)$ that effectively solves any problem solved by $\Pi_c$ and which tolerates more severe failures.

## 5 A Hierarchy of Translations

This section shows a hierarchy of translations from crash to omission failures. It exhibits a canonical translation, which translates from $C(n,t)$ to $O(n,t)$ in $z$ rounds, where $z = \lfloor t/(n-t) \rfloor + \lceil t/(n-t) \rceil + 1$. Note that the larger the ratio $t/(n-t)$ (i.e., the more failures), the higher the round-complexity. Section 6 will show that each of these translations is optimal with respect to the combined measures of fault-tolerance and round-complexity.

The translation is given in Fig. 2. In each phase, each processor maintains in *msgs* the array of messages for that phase of which it is aware; initially, it is aware only of its own message. During the $z$ rounds of a phase, processors exchange these arrays and other information; they use these arrays to decide which messages to simulate the receipt of at the end of a phase (see below for more details). The redundant communication given is needed to mask the more severe omission failures and make them appear to be only crash failures.

Consider a message to be sent by processor $p$ to processor $q$ in round $i$. In a system with omission failures, if $q$ does not receive this message in round $i$, then either $p$ omitted to send or $q$ omitted to receive. To make omission failures appear as crash failures, the faulty processor must appear to crash by the end of round $i$. The translation enforces the following informal properties:

1. [FAULTY-RECIPIENT] If $q$ does not receive $p$'s message in round $i$ and $p$ is a correct processor, then no correct processor will receive a message from $q$ after round $i$.
2. [FAULTY-SENDER] If $q$ does not receive $p$'s message in round $i$ and $q$ is correct, then no correct processor will receive a message from $p$ after round $i$.

In either case, the faulty processor appears to crash in round $i$ because no correct processor will receive from it after that round.

Each processor keeps track of the set of processors it considers to be faulty in the variable *faulty*. As Lemma 1 will show, all processors in the *faulty* set of a correct processor are indeed faulty. A processor includes its set *faulty* with every message that it sends; it disregards messages received directly from processors in *faulty* and does not send messages to those processors. However, a processor may *simulate* (at the end of a phase) the receipt of messages from processors in *faulty* if these messages are relayed to it by other processors.

Each processor $p$ maintains its set *faulty* as follows. It adds to it any other processor from which it fails to receive a message. In addition, it maintains for each processor $q$ a set *accuse*[$q$]. This contains the set of other processors that "accuse" $q$ of being faulty. If this set gets sufficiently large, then $p$ adds $q$ to *faulty*. Also, $p$ will add $q$ to *faulty* if it believes that $q$ is "accusing" too many other processors. Specifically if the union of the set $p$ believes to be faulty, the set $q$ claims is faulty, and the set accusing $q$ of being faulty has size greater than $t$, then $p$ and $q$ cannot both be correct and $p$ places $q$ in its set *faulty*. Note that, if $q$ is in $p$'s *faulty* set at the end of some round $i$, then $p$ will be in $q$'s *faulty* set by the middle of round $i + 1$; this is because a processor refuses to send to members of its *faulty* set.

/* $\Pi_o$ is tolerant of omission failures */

$state =$ initial state;
$faulty = \emptyset$;
**foreach** $q \in \mathcal{P}$
$\quad accuse[q] = \emptyset$;

**for** $i = 1$ **to** $\infty$ **do**
$\quad$ **foreach** $q \in \mathcal{P} - \{p\}$ /* begin phase $i$ */
$\quad\quad msgs[q] = \bot$;
$\quad msgs[p] = \mu_\pi(i, p, state)$;

$\quad$ **for** $j = 1$ **to** $z$ **do**
$\quad\quad$ **send** $[msgs, faulty]$ to $\mathcal{P} - faulty$; /* begin round $j$ */
$\quad\quad$ **receive** $[msgs_q, faulty_q]$ **from** each $q \in \mathcal{P}$;

$\quad\quad$ **foreach** $q \in \mathcal{P}$
$\quad\quad\quad$ **if** did not receive from $q$ **then**
$\quad\quad\quad\quad$ Add $q$ to $faulty$;
/* middle of round $j$ */
$\quad\quad$ **foreach** $q \in \mathcal{P} - faulty$
$\quad\quad\quad accuse[q] = accuse[q] \cup \{r \in \mathcal{P} - faulty \mid q \in faulty_r\}$;
$\quad\quad\quad$ **if** $(|accuse[q] \cup faulty_q \cup faulty| > t)$ **then**
$\quad\quad\quad\quad$ Add $q$ to $faulty$;

$\quad\quad$ **foreach** $q \in \mathcal{P} - faulty$ and $r \in \mathcal{P}$ /* get relayed messages */
$\quad\quad\quad$ **if** $msgs[r] = \bot$ and $msgs_q[r] \neq \bot$ **then**
$\quad\quad\quad\quad msgs[r] = msgs_q[r]$;

$\quad state = \delta_\pi(i, p, msgs)$

**Fig. 2.** Protocol $\Pi_o = \mathcal{T}(\Pi_c)$ as executed by processor $p$

At the beginning of each phase, a processor's array $msgs$ is initially all $\bot$ (except for its own entry). Whenever it receives such an array from a processor not in its set $faulty$, its combines the two arrays, removing $\bot$ entries when possible. At the end of round $z$, it simulates the receipt of messages in the array at that time.

The rest of this section is organized as follows. We first prove some important properties about any execution of translated protocol. We then argue that the translation is correct because it satisfies the two conditions given above. We begin by showing that no correct processor ever considers another correct processor faulty.

**Lemma 1.** *No correct processor ever belongs to the faulty set of another correct processor.*

*Proof.* The proof is by induction on the number of rounds executed. The base case is trivial because all processors have empty *faulty* sets initially. Now assume that the lemma holds through round $i$. Suppose that some correct processor $p$ adds another processor $q$ to its faulty set in round $i + 1$. This can happen for one of two reasons:

- $p$ does not receive a message from $q$. In this case, $q$ must have omitted to send a message and is thus faulty.
- $p$ found $|accuse[q] \cup faulty_q \cup faulty| > t$. Since there are only $t$ faulty processors and, by induction, all elements of $p$'s set *faulty* are faulty, there must be at least one correct processor $r \in accuse[q] \cup faulty_q$. If $r \in accuse[q]$, then $q$ was in $r$'s *faulty* at the end of round $i$, so $q$ is faulty by induction. If $r \in faulty_q$, then $r$ was in $q$'s *faulty* at the end of round $i$ and, again, $q$ is faulty.

In all cases, $q$ is faulty, so the lemma holds. □

The following lemma shows that the translation does not inhibit normal communication between correct processors.

**Lemma 2.** *If a correct processor $p$ sends $m$ at the beginning of a phase, every correct processor $q$ simulates the receipt of $m$ at the end of that phase.*

*Proof.* In the first round of the phase, $p$ sends an array *msgs* to $q$ with $msgs[p] = m$. Since both $p$ and $q$ are correct, $q$ receives this array. By Lemma 1, $p$ cannot be in $q$'s set *faulty*. Thus, $q$ sets $msgs[p] = m$ at the end of this round and thus simulates the receipt of $m$ from $p$ at the end of the phase. □

The following lemma is the core of the correctness of proof of the translation. It shows that, if there are failures sufficient to prevent two processors from communicating in a given phase, then the *faulty* sets of all processors will cause a "partition" to occur in the next phase. One of the two processors is faulty and will be separated from the correct processors; to them, it will appear to crash. This is sufficient to simulate crash failures.

**Lemma 3 (Partition Lemma).** *For any two processors $p$ and $q$, if $q$ does not simulate the receipt of $p$'s message at the end phase $i$, then there is a partition of $\mathcal{P}$ into two sets $C$ and $F$ such that*

- *all correct processors are in $C$,*
- *$p$ and $q$ are not both in $C$,*
- *every $r \in C$ has $F \subseteq faulty$ by the end of the first round of phase $i + 1$, and*
- *every $s \in F$ has $C \subseteq faulty$ by the end of the first round of phase $i + 1$.*

*Proof.* For the remainder of this proof, round numbers will be measured from the beginning of phase $i$; thus, when we talk about a round $k$ we mean the $k$th round of phase $i$. Thus, "the first round of phase $i + 1$" is numbered $z + 1$. Let $M_j$ be the set of processors that have $msgs[p] \neq \perp$ at the end of round $j$; conventionally define $M_{-1} = \emptyset$ and $M_0 = \{p\}$. Let $N_j = \mathcal{P} - M_j$. Note that, for all $j \geq 0$, each processor in $N_j$ has $M_{j-1} \subseteq faulty$ at the end of round $j$ (if it received a message from a processor in $M_{j-1}$ in round $j$, then it would have $msgs[p] \neq \perp$ and be in $M_j$ and not in $N_j$). Consequently, each processor in $M_{j-1}$ has $N_j \subseteq faulty$ by the middle of round $j + 1$ (recall that processors refuse to send to processors in their *faulty* set). For all $j$ ($1 \leq j \leq z$), let $L_j = M_j - M_{j-2}$. Informally, $L_j$ is the set of processors that learn of $p$'s message for the first time in round $j$ or round $j - 1$. We consider the following two cases:

- $|L_j| \geq n - t$ for all $j$, $1 \leq j \leq z$. Recall that $z = \lfloor t/(n - t) \rfloor + \lceil t/(n - t) \rceil + 1$. If $t$ is a multiple of $n - t$, then $z = 2t/(n - t) + 1$ is odd, and we have

$$
\begin{aligned}
|M_z| &= |L_1| + |L_3| + \cdots + |L_{z-2}| + |L_z| \\
&\geq ((z + 1)/2)(n - t) \qquad \text{(all $L_i$'s have size at least $n - t$)} \\
&= (t/(n - t) + 1)(n - t) \\
&= n.
\end{aligned}
$$

  This means that all processors, and in particular $q$, belong to $M_z$; this contradicts the assumptions of the lemma.
  If $t$ is not a multiple of $n - t$, $z = 2 \lfloor t/(n - t) \rfloor + 2$ is even, and we have

$$
\begin{aligned}
|M_{z-1}| &= |L_1| + |L_3| + \cdots + |L_{z-1}| \\
&\geq (z/2)(n - t) \\
&= (\lfloor t/(n - t) \rfloor + 1)(n - t) \\
&= \lfloor n/(n - t) \rfloor (n - t) \\
&> t \qquad \qquad (\lfloor (a + b)/a \rfloor \cdot a > b \text{ if } a > 0).
\end{aligned}
$$

  Since $q$ does not simulate the receipt of $p$'s message at the end of first phase, it should not receive any messages from any processor in $M_{z-1}$ in round $z$. Thus, $q$ will add more than $t$ processors to its *faulty* set at the end of phase $i$. Thus, by Lemma 1, $q$ is faulty. At the end of the first round of phase $i + 1$, each processor will either receive nothing from $q$ or will receive $faulty_q$, which contains more than $t$ elements. In either case, $q$ will be added to the processor's *faulty* set. Also, $q$ will add every other processor $r$ to its *faulty* set by round $z$ because it will find $|accuse[r] \cup faulty_r \cup faulty| \geq |faulty| > t$. Thus, the desired partition can be $\langle C, F \rangle = \langle \mathcal{P} - \{q\}, \{q\} \rangle$.
- $|L_j| < n - t$ for some $j$, $1 \leq j \leq z$. Recall that, at the end of round $j - 1$, every processor in $N_{j-1}$ has $M_{j-2} \subseteq faulty$. Similarly, all processors in $N_j$ have $M_{j-1} \subseteq faulty$ at the end of round $j$. Thus, at the end of round $j + 1$, each processor $\hat{p} \in N_{j-1}$ will have every processor $\bar{p} \in N_j$ either in its *faulty* set (if $\hat{p}$ receives no message from $\bar{p}$ in round $j + 1$) or in the set $accuse[r]$ for every processor $r \in M_{j-1}$ (if it does). This means that, at that time, processors in $N_{j-1}$ will have $|accuse[r] \cup faulty_r \cup faulty| \geq |accuse[r] \cup$

$faulty| \geq |N_j \cup M_{j-2}| = |\mathcal{P} - L_j| > n - (n - t) = t$ for every processor $r \in M_{j-1}$. Thus, all processors in $N_{j-1}$ will have $M_{j-1} \subseteq faulty$ by the end of round $j + 1$. Now consider a processor $r \in M_{j-1}$. As noted earlier, it has $N_j \subseteq faulty$ by the middle of round $j + 1$. Consider now some processor $s \in M_j - M_{j-1} \subseteq N_{j-1}$. Because it is in $N_{j-1}$, $s$ will have $M_{j-2} \subseteq faulty$ by the end of round $j - 1$. Thus, in round $j + 1$, $r$ finds $|accuse[s] \cup faulty_s \cup faulty| \geq |faulty_s \cup faulty| \geq |M_{j-2} \cup N_j| > t$ (as above) and thus adds $s$ to $faulty$ by that time. This means that, by the end of round $j+1$, all processors in $M_{j-1}$ have $N_j \cup (M_j - M_{j-1}) = N_{j-1} \subseteq faulty$. By Lemma 1, all correct processors are either in $M_{j-1}$ or $N_{j-1}$. Let $C$ be the one of them containing the correct processors and let $F$ be the other (its complement). Then $\langle C, F \rangle$ is desired partition.

The desired partition exists in either case, completing the proof. ☐

The two desired properties are corollaries to the Partition Lemma:

**Corollary 4 (Faulty-Recipient).** *If $q$ does not receive $p$'s message in round $i$ and $p$ is a correct processor, then no correct processor will receive a message from $q$ after round $i$.*

*Proof.* Suppose that $q$ does not receive $p$'s message in round $i$ and that $p$ is a correct processor. By the Partition Lemma, there is a partition of $\mathcal{P}$ into $\langle C, F \rangle$ such that $p \in C$, $q \in F$, all the correct processors are in $C$, and each processor in $C$ has $F \subseteq faulty$ by the end of the first round of phase $i + 1$. This means that, in phase $i + 1$ and thereafter, all correct processors will refuse messages from $q$ and from any processor that might relay a message from $q$. ☐

**Corollary 5 (Faulty-Sender).** *If $q$ does not receive $p$'s message in round $i$ and $q$ is correct, then no correct processor will receive a message from $p$ after round $i$.*

*Proof.* Similar to the proof of Corollary 4. ☐

Lemma 2 shows that the translation always allows correct processors to communicate with each other. Corollaries 4 and 5 show that any sufficiently severe failure manifests itself as a crash failure. Together, these allow us to conclude that the translation is correct:

**Theorem 6.** *Translation $T$ translates from $C(n,t)$ to $O(n,t)$ in $z$ rounds, where $z = \lfloor t/(n - t) \rfloor + \lceil t/(n - t) \rceil + 1$.*

The formal proof of Theorem 6 requires the construction of the history simulation function $\mathcal{H}$ and a proof of its correctness; given the Partition Lemma, this is straightforward and omitted. One note, however, is warranted. This regards how these translations circumvent the impossibility results of Neiger and Toueg [11]. Their definition required that the history simulation function $\mathcal{H}$ correctly simulate the states of *all* processors. We require only that the state of *correct* processors be correctly simulated. In our construction of $\mathcal{H}$, the states of correct processors in simulated history $H_c$ (see Section 4) will be simply the contents of the variable *state* from Fig. 2 (Neiger and Toueg would require this of all processors). The states of the faulty processors will be functionally determined by the states of and messages received by the correct processors.

## 6 Impossibility Results

This section shows that the translations given in Sect. 5 are optimal with respect to the combined measures of fault-tolerance and round-complexity. It proves that there can be no translation from $C(n,t)$ to $O(n,t)$ with fewer rounds. Specifically, there can be no $z$-round translation from $C(n,t)$ to $O(n,t)$ if $z = \lfloor t/(n-t)\rfloor + \lceil t/(n-t)\rceil$.

The proof considers the executions of a simple protocol $\Pi_c$ and shows that it cannot be translated in the specified number of rounds. The protocol operates as follows. Let $Q = M = \{0, 1, f\}$. In the first round, $p_1$ (the broadcaster) sends its initial state to all processors. At the end of that round, every processor that receives a message from $p_1$ sets its state to the value received. All other processors set their states to $f$. In each of the following rounds, each processor sends its state to all others. If a processor receives $f$ from any processor, it sets its own state to $f$; otherwise, it does not change its state. Formally, the protocol is specified as follows:

$$\mu_c(i,p,s) = \begin{cases} s & \begin{cases} \text{if } i = 1 \text{ and } p = p_1 \text{ or} \\ \text{if } i > 1 \end{cases} \\ f & \text{otherwise} \end{cases}$$

$$\delta_c(i,p,r) = \begin{cases} r[p_1] & \text{if } i = 1 \text{ and } r[p_1] \neq \perp \\ f & \begin{cases} \text{if } i = 1 \text{ and } r[p_1] = \perp \text{ or} \\ \text{if } i > 1 \text{ and } r[p] = f \text{ for some p} \end{cases} \\ r[p] & \text{otherwise.} \end{cases}$$

$\Pi_c$ is a simple protocol in which processors relay information about the broadcaster's initial state or its failure, a structure that is not uncommon in distributed protocols. The fact that it cannot be translated in a certain number of rounds suggests that the same must be true for other distributed protocols with a similar message structure.

Any history $H_c = \langle \Pi_c, Q_c, S_c, R_c \rangle$ of $\Pi_c$ in a system with *crash* failures must satisfy the following constraints:

1. If $p \in Correct(H_c)$ and $Q(j,p) = f$ for some $j > 1$, then $Q(k,q) = f$ for all $k > j$ and $q \in Correct(H_c)$.
2. If $p_1 \in Correct(H_c)$ and $Q(1,p_1) \neq f$, then $Q(j,p) \neq f$ for all $j > 1$ and $p \in Correct(H_c)$.
3. For all $q \in P$ and $j > 1$, $Q(j,q) = f$ or $Q(j,q) = Q(1,p_1)$.

The idea behind the impossibility results is to prove that the above constraints cannot all be satisfied by the simulated states of a translated protocol if the translation used has round-complexity $z = \lfloor t/(n-t) \rfloor + \lceil t/(n-t) \rceil$. (Obviously, translations with lower round-complexity will also fail.)

Assume for a contradiction that there is a $z$-round translation $\mathcal{T}$ from $C(n,t)$ to $O(n,t)$. We will describe an execution of $\Pi_o = \mathcal{T}(\Pi_c)$ and show that it cannot simulate a history of $\Pi_c$ that meets all three of the above constraints. This will contradict the existence of the translation.

Let $k = \lfloor t/(n-t) \rfloor$. Note that $z = 2k + b$, where $b$ is $0$ if $t$ is a multiple of $n-t$ and is $1$ otherwise. Define the sets $L_0, L_1, \ldots, L_{z+1}$ as follows:

$$L_0 = \{p_1\},$$
$$L_1 = \{p_2, \ldots, p_{n-t}\},$$
$$\vdots$$
$$L_{2i} = \{p_{i(n-t)+1}\},$$
$$L_{2i+1} = \{p_{i(n-t)+2}, \ldots, p_{(i+1)(n-t)}\},$$
$$\vdots$$
$$L_{2k} = \{p_{k(n-t)+1}\}, \text{ and}$$
$$L_{2k+1} = \{p_{k(n-t)+2}, \ldots, p_{(k+1)(n-t)}\};$$

if $b = 1$, we define $L_{2k+2} = \{p_{(k+1)(n-t)+1}, \ldots, p_n\}$. It is easy to see that none of the defined sets is empty. (Remember that $k = \lfloor t/(n-t) \rfloor$, so $k+1 = \lfloor n/(n-t) \rfloor$ and $n \leq (k+1)(n-t)$; this is a strict inequality if $b = 1$.) Furthermore, the last set is always $L_{z+1}$, regardless of the value of $b$. Note that $L_i \cap L_j = \emptyset$ if $i \neq j$ and $|L_i \cup L_{i+1}| \geq n - t$ for all $i$, $0 \leq i \leq z$.

Consider the following run of $\Pi_o$, the translated protocol. No communication takes place between processors in $L_i$ and those in $L_j$, $j > i+1$ in any round $i+1$ or afterward. (Note that this implies that processors outside $L_0 \cup L_1$ never receive any message from $p_1$.) All processors behave correctly otherwise. Although we have not identified the faulty processors, it should be clear that this can be a run in system $O(n,t)$. For example, $L_0 \cup L_1$ might be the set of correct processors because it contains $n-t$ processors and there is no communication failure among its members. All missing messages can be accounted for by assuming that the remaining processors are faulty and fail either to send or to receive (or both). In fact, any set $L_i \cup L_{i+1}$, $0 \leq i \leq z$, could be correct for the same reason. Thus, what we have described is actually a set of histories, all of which are indistinguishable to the processors in the system. It is the processors' inability to determine the identity of the correct processors that leads to the impossibility result.

It is clear that processors in $L_i$ first learn of $p_1$'s initial state at the end of round $i$. In particular, processors in $L_{z+1}$ do not know $p_1$'s initial state until the end of round $z + 1$ (the first round of the second phase) and thus do not know $p_1$'s initial state at the end of the first phase. This fact will be critical to the proof because it will contradict the following lemma:

181

**Lemma 7.** *At the end of every phase of the history described above, each processor's state is equal to $p_1$'s initial state.*

*Proof.* Let $s$ be $p_1$'s initial state. We will prove by induction on $i$ $(0 \leq i \leq z+1)$ that the state of each processor in $L_i$ is equal to $s$ at the end of every phase.

For the basis step, the only processor in $L_0$ is $p_1$. By the third constraint, its state must always be either $s$ or $f$. Because $p_1$ can never tell that it is faulty (it might be that $L_0 \cup L_1$ is the set of correct processors), it can never set its state to $f$ or else the second constraint might be violated. Thus, its state is always $s$.

For the induction step, assume that each processor in $L_i$, $0 \leq i < z+1$, has its state equal to $s$ at the end of every phase. By the third constraint, all processors in $L_{i+1}$ must always set their states to either $s$ or $f$. Suppose for a contradiction that some processor in $L_{i+1}$ sets its state to $f$ at the end of some phase $j$. Because it is possible that the processors in $L_i \cup L_{i+1}$ are all correct, the processors in $L_i$ must set their states to $f$ at the end of phase $j+1$ or else the first constraint might be violated. But this contradicts the inductive hypothesis. Thus, the state of each processor in $L_{i+1}$ must be $s$ at the end of every phase. □

Lemma 7 implies that all processors in $L_{z+1}$ must set their states to $p_1$'s initial state at the end of the first phase. But, as noted above, these processors do not learn of $p_1$'s initial state until the second phase. Thus, they must set their state in the absence of this information. Assume without loss of generality that $\Pi_o$ specifies that they set their states to 0. Then the third constraint is violated in histories in which $p_1$'s initial state is 1. Thus, the existence of the translation $\mathcal{T}$ is contradicted, giving us the following theorem:

**Theorem 8.** *There can be no $z$-round translation from $C(n,t)$ to $O(n,t)$ if $z \leq \lfloor t/(n-t) \rfloor + \lceil t/(n-t) \rceil$.*

Theorem 8 implies that the translations given in Section 5 are all optimal with respect to round-complexity for a given $n$ and $t$. That section shows the existence of a translation requiring $\lfloor t/(n-t) \rfloor + \lceil t/(n-t) \rceil + 1$ rounds, while Theorem 8 shows that $\lfloor t/(n-t) \rfloor + \lceil t/(n-t) \rceil$ rounds is inadequate.

# 7 Conclusions

This paper presented a complete characterization of translations from systems with crash failures to those with omission failures. As with all translations between systems with failures, these translations simplify the task of designing fault-tolerant protocols. Using these translations, the designer can work with the assumption that only crash failures can occur and then convert the protocol automatically to tolerate the more severe omission failures.

These translations circumvent an earlier impossibility result of Neiger and Toueg [11], which held that no such translation was possible if $n \leq 2t$ (i.e., if as many as half the processors may fail). Their proof was based on a problem whose specification depends on the actions made faulty processors. A primary contribution is that, when considering problems whose specifications are independent of these actions, the impossibility result does not hold. For cases in which $n \leq 2t$, we exhibit a hierarchy of translations; the number of rounds used in each translation depends on the particular values of $n$ and $t$. In general, the larger that $t$ is relative to $n$, the more rounds that are needed to perform the translation.

The round-complexities of these translations are all optimal. Thus, our results give a precise characterization of the relationship between crash and omission failures. The hierarchy given here is quite different from the one given earlier for translations from crash to arbitrary failures [2]. In that case, the translations were all quite different from each other. The translations given here are uniform in that they have the same structure, varying only in their round complexity. When translating to arbitrary failures, three translations covered the entire hierarchy. The hierarchy presented here is unbounded (it contains $t$ levels for any fixed $t$). Table 1 summarizes this hierarchy of translations. The first column gives progressively weaker conditions on $n$ and $t$; the second gives a number of rounds that is adequate to perform the desired translation (fewer rounds may be necessary if a stronger condition holds). In the weakest case, $n = t + 2$, $t + 1$ rounds are required. Note that $t + 1$ rounds are always sufficient, because *fail-stop* failures [15] can always be simulated in $t+1$ rounds, and they are a more restrictive type of failure than crash failures.

| Condition | Rounds |
|:---------:|:------:|
| $n > 2t$ | 2 |
| $n \geq 2t$ | 3 |
| $n > 3t/2$ | 4 |
| $n \geq 3t/2$ | 5 |
| $n > 4t/3$ | 6 |
| $n \geq 4t/3$ | 7 |
| $\vdots$ | $\vdots$ |
| $n \geq t + 2$ | $t + 1$ |

**Table 1.** Summary of translations

All the translations are efficient in that they generate protocols that do not require substantially more local computation than the original protocols. In all cases, if the largest message sent in original protocol is of size $b$, then the largest message sent in the translated protocol has size $O((b + 1)n)$.

Translations such as those presented in this paper have been developed for completely asynchronous systems [4] as well as the completely synchronous systems considered here. Other researchers have studied problems in which there exists timing uncertainty that is bounded. Attiya et al. consider the consensus problem in such systems with crash failures [1]. Ponzio extends this work to systems with omission and arbitrary failures [14]. It seems likely that translations applicable to such systems would simplify the latter and may lead to improved algorithms. In fact, the prominence of the term $t/(n-t)$ in Ponzio's work (as well as in our own) suggests that an adaptation of our translations may generalize his work. In addition, an adaptation of our previous work with arbitrary failures [2] may result in new, more efficient algorithms for consensus in partially synchronous systems with arbitrary failures.

Our work defines the correctness of a translation based on the behavior (states and messages) of processors in a system. Alternatively, one could make a specification based on the system's input-output behavior. It is not hard to extend the model we consider to add input and output events. Correctness based on input-output behavior would have to take into account the timing changes that result from one round being simulated by several. In addition, one could consider translations that do not require every round to be simulated by a fixed number of rounds. These topics may be considered in future work.

# References

1. Hagit Attiya, Cynthia Dwork, Nancy Lynch, and Larry Stockmeyer. Bounds on the time to reach agreement in the presence of timing uncertainty. In *Proceedings of the Twenty-Third ACM Symposium on Theory of Computing*, pages 359–369, May 1991.
2. Rida Bazzi and Gil Neiger. Optimally providing fault-tolerance in a Byzantine environment. In S. Toueg, P. G. Spirakis, and L. Kirousis, editors, *Proceedings of the Fifth International Workshop on Distributed Algorithms*, volume 579 of *Lecture Notes on Computer Science*, pages 108–128. Springer-Verlag, October 1991.
3. Rida Bazzi and Gil Neiger. The complexity and impossibility of achieving fault-tolerant coordination. In *Proceedings of the Eleventh ACM Symposium on Principles of Distributed Computing*, August 1992. To appear.
4. Brian A. Coan. A compiler that increases the fault-tolerance of asynchronous protocols. *IEEE Transactions on Computers*, 37(12):1541–1553, December 1988.
5. Danny Dolev. The Byzantine generals strike again. *Journal of Algorithms*, 3(1):14–30, 1982.
6. Vassos Hadzilacos. Byzantine agreement under restricted types of failures (not telling the truth is different from telling lies). Technical Report 18-83, Department of Computer Science, Harvard University, 1983. A revised version appears in Hadzilacos's Ph.D. dissertation [7].
7. Vassos Hadzilacos. *Issues of Fault Tolerance in Concurrent Computations*. Ph.D. dissertation, Harvard University, June 1984. Technical Report 11-84, Department of Computer Science.
8. Vassos Hadzilacos. Connectivity requirements for Byzantine agreement under restricted types of failures. *Distributed Computing*, 2(2):95–103, 1987.
9. Joseph Y. Halpern and H. Raymond Strong, March 1986. Personal communication.

10. Leslie Lamport, Robert Shostak, and Marshall Pease. The Byzantine generals problem. *ACM Transactions on Programming Languages and Systems*, 4(3):382–401, July 1982.

11. Gil Neiger and Sam Toueg. Automatically increasing the fault-tolerance of distributed algorithms. *Journal of Algorithms*, 11(3):374–419, September 1990.

12. Gil Neiger and Mark R. Tuttle. Common knowledge and consistent simultaneous coordination. In J. van Leeuwen and N. Santoro, editors, *Proceedings of the Fourth International Workshop on Distributed Algorithms*, volume 486 of *Lecture Notes on Computer Science*, pages 334–352. Springer-Verlag, September 1990. To appear in *Distributed Computing*.

13. Kenneth J. Perry and Sam Toueg. Distributed agreement in the presence of processor and communication faults. *IEEE Transactions on Software Engineering*, 12(3):477–482, March 1986.

14. Stephen Ponzio. Consensus in the presence of timing uncertainty: Omission and Byzantine faults. In *Proceedings of the Tenth ACM Symposium on Principles of Distributed Computing*, pages 125–138, August 1991.

15. Richard D. Schlichting and Fred B. Schneider. Fail-stop processors: an approach to designing fault-tolerant computing systems. *ACM Transactions on Computer Systems*, 1(3):222–238, August 1983.

16. T. K. Srikanth and Sam Toueg. Simulating authenticated broadcasts to derive simple fault-tolerant algorithms. *Distributed Computing*, 2(2):80–94, 1987.

# An Efficient Topology Update Protocol for Dynamic Networks

Baruch Awerbuch * and Yishay Mansour **

**Abstract.** Topology update is a major component in routing protocols operating in existing communication networks. This paper presents a new efficient topology update protocol that works in dynamic networks that may never stabilize. Our protocol does not use unbounded counters and has $O(m)$ amortized message complexity per topological change, where $m$ is the number of edges. The protocol is very simple and is based on a "hop counter" technique. Our protocol uses a novel technique that combines a dynamic protocol (that works under the assumption that the network never stabilizes) and an eventually stable protocol (that works under the assumption that the network stabilizes).

## 1 Introduction

Maintaining an accurate view of the network topology is one of the basic tasks in communication networks. The topology information is used to perform efficient routing (e.g. using shortest paths) as well as other tasks (e.g. checking connectivity between nodes).

The topology update problem was introduced by Vishkin [Vis83], who suggested a solution that uses unbounded counters and $O(m)$ messages per topological change. A more efficient solution, that also uses unbounded counters, has been suggested in [AE83]. If only a finite number of topological changes occur in the network, the problem of topology update can be solved with bounded counters, as shown in [SG89], but there is no simple transformation of this algorithm to solve the topology update problem for the case that the network does not stabilize.

In this work we are interested in dynamic networks that are continuously changing. Since the network is continuously changing we cannot expect the entire topology information to stabilize, and the estimates about the status of the links cannot be completely accurate. However, it is reasonable to require that, for each link whose status eventually stabilizes (in the sense that it changes only finite number of times), nodes eventually learn the final status of the link, i.e. eventually their estimates become accurate. (This requirement can be applied

* Department of Mathematics and Laboratory for Computer Science, MIT, Cambridge, MA 02139 (baruch@theory.lcs.mit.edu.arpa). Supported by Air Force contract TNDGAFOSR-86-0078, ARO contract DAAL03-86-K-0171 and NSF contract CCR8611442.
** IBM - T. J. Watson Research Center, P. O. Box 704, Yorktown Heights, NY 10598. Part of the work was done while the author was at LCS,MIT, Cambridge, MA 02139.

only to nodes that are not "permanently disconnected" from both endpoints of that link.)

One way to solve the topology update problem is to use existing solutions for the end to end problem. Afek and Gafni [AG88] gave the first bounded solution to the end-to-end problem in dynamic networks. The first polynomial solution was given in [AMS89], which was later improve in [AGR] and [AG91]. Still the best complexity of solving the end-to-end problem requires $O(mn)$ messages per data item that is sent, where $m$ is the number of edges and $n$ is the number of nodes. For the topology update problem we need to have each node communicate to each other node the status of all its link. This implies that using the best known end-to-end protocol to solve the topology update problem requires $O(mn^2)$ per topological change. In this work we present a much more efficient solution that requires only $O(m)$ messages per topological change, and is also considerably simpler.

A weaker model is one with dynamic networks that eventually stabilize. The main difference is that the algorithm guarantees to output a correct value *only* if the network is stable. Infact, the topology update algorithms in this model (e.g. [SG89]) do not solve topology update problem in a dynamic network that does not stabilize. A general technique of transforming an arbitrary static protocol into a dynamic protocol, in a network that eventually stabilizes, was given in [AAG87]. The technique of [AAG87] restarts the computation each time a topological change occurs. Since the computation is restarted each time a topological change occurs, it would not stabilize if there is an infinite number of topological changes.

The problem of topology update in a network that eventually stabilizes was studied in [ACK90], where a topology update algorithm that has $O(n)$ amortize message complexity per topological change is given. However the algorithm requires that the network would eventually stabilizes, otherwise the information about the stable links does not stabilize.

Our main contribution is a new simple topology update protocol, which does not use unbounded counters. Our protocol uses a well-known method in which packets "age" as they travel through the network by using a "hop counter". The "hop counter" method is very widely used in practice, due to it simplicity and efficiency (see [Tan81]). It is worth mentioning that the correctness and the complexity of the protocol depends on the implementation of this method, different implementations of the "hop counter" method lead to protocols which are either extremely inefficient (e.g. require exponential communication overhead), or, at least theoretically, incorrect.

Our protocol operates in a realistic network model, which takes into consideration the buffer limitations of lower-level data link protocols. This implies that only a constant number of messages are in transit on a link at a given time. Thus, the implementation of the protocol requires bounded buffer space in the lower-level data-link protocols. This consideration, although crucial in practice, has not received the proper attention in the previous theoretical literature.

We introduce a general technique that enables to control communication complexity of protocols, in particular of topology update protocol, in dynamic networks that never stabilize. The idea behind the technique is to "tie" sending messages to topological changes. Roughly speaking, in order to send a message over a given link, a node must "learn" that a new topological change occurred. This strategy guarantees that at most $O(m)$ messages are sent per each topological change, which implies a linear communication complexity. Observe that we take advantage of frequent topological changes in order to send more messages, "amortizing" those messages on the topological changes. Thus, number of messages sent per topological change remains fix. A clear disadvantage in what we described so far is that the protocol operates properly if the sequence of topological changes is infinite. When the number of topological changes is finite, the protocol may operate incorrectly, and terminate prematurely with an incorrect output. To address this problem we run in parallel an additional algorithm, which takes care of the case that the number of topological changes is finite. This algorithm is based on a simple topology update protocol, for a static network, that is complied for dynamic network that eventually stabilize, using [AAG87]. The last stage is to combine the outputs of the two protocols into one output. This is a very delicate stage and at the end of the paper we show how a different way of combining the outputs may yield a completely different behavior of the protocol.

Recently, Afek, Gafni and Rosen [AGR] used our technique of coupling a dynamic protocol with a static protocol to present a general methodology in which the worst case performance is dominated by the dynamic algorithm while the best case is controlled by the static algorithm.

We define the analog of the notion of "time complexity" for dynamic networks that do not stabilize as the *convergence time*. This measure captures how much time passes since a link is stable until all the nodes have it's correct status. It turns out that there is trade-off between the convergence time and the amortized message complexity, therefore it makes sense to evaluate protocols based on both complexity measures. The definition of convergence time is general and can be applied to any other problem[3].

The convergence time has two parameters. One is the message delay over an operational link. The second is the time for a link that it takes a non-operational link to become operational (if it does become operational). The convergence time is written as $a\pi + b\rho$, where $\pi$ is the message delay and $\rho$ is the link recovery delay. We make no assumptions about the relationship between $\rho$ and $\pi$, and they are used only for the analysis of the time complexity of the protocol.

Our topology update algorithm has amortized message complexity $O(m)$ and convergence time of $O(n^2\pi + n\rho)$, where $n$ is the number of nodes in the network and $m$ the number of edges in the network.

The paper is organized in the following way. In Section 2, we state briefly the model of a dynamic network and some related models. In Section 3, we state the topology update problem. In Section 4, we state the complexity measures. The topology update protocol is given in Section 5, its correctness proof is given

---

[3] A related complexity measure for time was introduced in [HK89].

in Section 6, and Section 7 contains the complexity analysis. We conclude, in Section 8, with a discussion on the convergence time measure.

## 2  Models of Networks

The following are three well-known theoretical models for networks:

- **Static networks**- Every message that is sent is eventually delivered.
- **Fail-Stop networks**- The sequence of messages that are delivered, over a specific link, is a prefix of the sequence of messages that were sent on the link.
- **Dynamic networks**- Each node has, for each of its links, a status variable which is either DOWN or UP. The node can send a message on a link only if the link's status is UP. The fact that a link status is UP does not imply that a message sent on that link is eventually delivered. A dynamic network is *eventually stable* if there exists a time after which no link changes its status.

*Comment:* The data link layer, ensures that if a node on one side of the link has the link's status as $UP$ then, from some time and on, the node on the other side has the link's status $UP$ as well. This means that if $status_v(v, u) = UP$ from some time and on, then eventually $status_u(u, v) = UP$.

The data link layer in a communication network has only a fixed number of buffers, therefore only a fixed number of messages can be in transit over a link. The network models above do not ensure that the number of messages in transit over a link is bounded. We define the *non-pumping restriction* that ensures that only a constant number of messages are sent simultaneously over the same link.

*Non-pumping restriction-* For every message that is received an acknowledgment is sent. The link is said to be *busy* from the time a message is transmitted until an acknowledgment for it is received. No message is sent while the link is busy.

Note that the non-pumping restriction implies that at any time there are at most two messages in transit over a link.

A link in a fail-stop network is *connected* if every message that is sent on that link is eventually received, otherwise the link is *disconnected*. A link in a dynamic network is *connected* if for every time $t$, there exists a time $\hat{t}$, $\hat{t} > t$, such that at time $\hat{t}$ the link is UP and if infinitely many messages are sent then eventually a message is received, otherwise the link is *disconnected*. A fail-stop network is *equivalent* to a dynamic network if every link has the same status (connected or disconnected) in both networks. The following theorem ensures that a protocol for a non-pumping fail-stop network can be transformed to a protocol for a non-pumping dynamic network.

**Theorem 1.** *A non-pumping fail-stop network, with space complexity $S$, can be simulated by an equivalent non-pumping dynamic network, with space complexity $O(S)$.*

*Proof.* A non-pumping fail-stop network has four abstract actions: send/receive message and send/receive acknowledgement. The simulation is based on the "alternating bit" data link protocol (see [Tan81]).

The information is transmitted as though the link never fails (i.e. the protocol is never informed that the link is down). Since the protocol requires only a constant space, the space complexity is $O(S)$. The transmitting station has a variable $b_s$ and the receiving station has a variable $b_r$. Initially, $b_s = b_r = 0$.

The simulation in the transmitting station is the following. For each send message action, $m$, the message is stored in $m_s$ and a packet with $< b_s, m_s >$ is sent. When an acknowledgement $b$ is received, and $b = b_s$, then $b_s = 1 - b_s$, $m_s$ is emptied and the acknowledgment is forwarded (the link is not busy). When the link changes from DOWN to UP, if $m_s$ is not empty, then a packet $< b_s, m_s >$ is sent. See Figures 1 and 2 for details. The simulation in the receiving station is the following. For each receive packet action, $< b, m >$, an acknowledgement $b$ is sent and if $b = b_r$ then the message $m$ is received. The correctness of the simulation is similar to that of the alternating bit data link protocol (see [Tan81]).

```
For send_message(m)
    m_s = m
    send_packet(< b_s, m_s >)
For receive_packet(acknowledgement < b >)
    If b = b_s then b_s = 1 - b_s
    m_s = ∅
    Invoke the FAIL-STOP PROTOCOL with receive_acknowledgment
When the link changes from DOWN to UP
    If m_s ≠ ∅ then receive_packet(< b_s, m_s >)
```

**Fig. 1.** Sender protocol

```
For receive_packet(< b, m >)
    send_packet(acknowledgement < b >)
    If b = b_r then
            Invoke the FAIL-STOP PROTOCOL with send_message(m)
            b = 1 - b
```

**Fig. 2.** Receiver protocol

Since the fail-stop protocol is non-pumping, a *send_message(m)* action can occur only when $m_s$ is empty (since otherwise the link is *busy*). We focus on links that are connected since a disconnected link is allowed not to deliver any packet, making the simulation trivial. For a connected link, every packet that is sent is either delivered or the link changes its status to DOWN. (If the link is DOWN and does not change to UP then the link is disconnected.) Furthermore, every connected link that at time $t$ is DOWN will eventually be UP. In the simulation the transmitter retransmits the message every time the link changes from DOWN to UP until eventually the message is acknowledged. Therefore, every message, sent on a connected link, is eventually forwarded to the fail-stop protocol. Since the simulation requires only two more variables per station, the space complexity is $O(S)$. $\square$

# 3 The Topology Update Problem

## 3.1 Eventual connectivity and stability

Each node $v \in V$ has a variable *status*$(v, u)$, for each of its links $(v, u) \in E$. The value of this variable, denoted by *status*$_v(v, u)$, is either UP or DOWN, according to the status of the link $(v, u)$.

- **Eventually stable link**- A link $(u, v)$ is an *eventually stable*, if there exists a time $t$ , such that for any time $\hat{t}$, $\hat{t} > t$, both the values *status*$_u(u, v)$ and *status*$_v(v, u)$ do not change. (I.e. from some time on, either the link is constantly UP or the link is constantly DOWN). Note that in this case *status*$_u(u, v)$ and *status*$_v(v, u)$ are equal.
- **Eventually connected link**- A link $e = (u, v)$ is *eventually connected*, if for any time $t$, there exists a time $\hat{t}$, $\hat{t} > t$, such that at time $\hat{t}$ the status of $e$ is UP (on both sides), and if infinitely many messages are sent on $e$, starting at $\hat{t}$, eventually a message is received.
- **Eventually connected path**- A path that is composed from eventually connected edges.
- **Eventually connected sub-network** - A maximal set of nodes that any two of them have an eventually connected path to between them.

## 3.2 The specification for the topology update and data update

The topology update protocol has in each node $v \in V$ a variable *status*$(u, w)$, for every link $(u, w) \in E$. The value of *status*$(u, w)$, denoted by *status*$_v(u, w)$, is either UP or DOWN. Intuitively, *status*$_v(u, w)$ reflects the estimation of $v$ about the status of link $(u, w)$. The topology update protocol "succeeds" if for every stable link $e = (u, w)$, there exists a time $T_e$, such that at any time $t$, $t > T_e$, *status*$_v(u, w) =$ *status*$_u(u, w)$, for every node $v$ that is in the eventually connected sub-network of $u$. (In other words, if $(u, w)$ is an eventually stable link, then every node in the eventually connected sub-network of $u$ will eventually have the "stable" status of the link $(u, w)$.)

A data update problem has a single *source* with a data variable. The value of the data variable may change over time. The data variable is stable, at time $t$, if for any time $\hat{t}$, $\hat{t} > t$, its value does not change. The aim of the data update protocol is to enable each node to learn the value of the data variable. The specification of the data update problem, which resembles the specification of the topology update problem, is as follows.

1. There is one source with a variable *RealData*.
2. Every node $v$ has a variable *data*, whose value is denoted by $data_v$.
3. If at time $T_0$ the variable *RealData* is stable, there exists a time $T_1 > T_0$, such that at each node $v$, which is in the eventually connected sub-network of the source, the value of $data_v$ equals value of *RealData* at time $T_1$ and $data_v$ does not change at any time $t > T_1$.

It is clear that the topology update problem can be reduced to $2m$ data update problems. For each edge $(u, v) \in E$, $u$ would be the source for the status of $(u, v)$ and the the source for the status of $(v, u)$. Note that if $(u, v)$ is eventually stable, then the two statuses are eventually equal.

## 4  Complexity Measures

The dynamic network model that we consider an infinite number of topological changes may occur. Clearly, the more topological changes happen, the more messages that the protocol will send, therefore we would like to relate the two. The *amortized message complexity* is the number of messages sent per topological change. However, we show that this criteria, by it self, is not sufficient to capture the "true" complexity.

In a dynamic network that does not stabilize the communication paths may be disconnected for arbitrary long periods of time. For this reason it is impossible to define for such networks the time complexity in terms identical to that of stable networks or dynamic networks that eventually stabilize. We introduce the notion of *convergence time*, which is the equivalent of time complexity in static networks. We show a trade-off between convergence time and the amortized message complexity (see Section 7.1).

The convergence time in a dynamic network has two components. One component is a bound on the propagation delays over a link, associated with the physical delay in the transmission media. The second component is a bound on the recovery delay of a link, i.e. time between the failure and subsequent recovery of a link. This component is associated with the time required to reinitialize the transmission media and establish communication between two nodes. The two components are orthogonal one to the other and a simple way to express such a time system is by a linear combination of the form $a\pi + b\rho$, where $\pi$ is the maximal propagation delay and $\rho$ is the maximal recovery delay.

*Comment:* Analogously to the definition of time complexity in static asynchronous networks, the values of $\pi$ and $\rho$ are used exclusively for the purpose of the analysis of the convergence time of the protocol, but not for proving its correctness. Intuitively, they are evaluated in terms of some symbolic global clock; nodes do not have access to that global clock and do not know those values, and the protocol should work for any values of $\pi$ and $\rho$.

We define a partial ordering among all linear combinations of $\pi$ and $\rho$ as follows: $a_1\pi + b_1\rho$ is greater than $a_2\pi + b_2\rho$ iff $a_1 > a_2$ and $b_1 > b_2$. Formally, each event has a label $a\pi + b\rho$ that is subject to the constraints below:

- **Message delay:** For every message that is sent at time labeled $t$, and is eventually received at time labeled $\tau$ holds, $t < \tau < t + \pi$.
- **Link Failure:** For each link that fails at time labeled $t$ and recovers at time labeled $\tau$, holds $t < \tau < t + \rho$.
- **Initial time:** Each change in the value of *RealData* in the source node is labeled by $a\pi + b\rho$, such that $a \leq 0$ and $b \leq 0$. (We are interested to measure the time only after the data stabilizes.)
- **Causality:** Any two events $x, y$ at the same node, such that $x$ causally precedes $y$, the labeling of $x$ is strictly less than the labeling of $y$, according to the partial order defined above.

The *convergence event* at node $v$ is define as the update of *data* at node $v$ such that from that time and on, $data_v = RealData$. The *convergence time* of a data update protocol is define as the maximum labeling of the convergence event at $v$, over all $v$ which are eventually connected to the source.

## 5 Topology Update Protocol

We describe a protocol for the data update problem, which is equivalent to the topology update problem. The code of the data update protocol is described for a non-pumping fail-stop network, but in fact it is running in a dynamic non-pumping network. Theorem 1 guarantees that the protocol can be transformed to a protocol for a non-pumping dynamic networks with the same space complexity.

The data update protocol we describe satisfy the non-pumping restriction. In order to simplify the protocol each node $v$ has a variable $CanSend_v[u]$, for each $(v, u) \in E$. The value of $CanSend_v[u]$ is TRUE if the link $(v, u)$ is not busy. Node $v$ can send a message to $u$ only if $CanSend_v[u]$ is TRUE.

Our protocol is composed from two protocols that run concurrently. The first protocol, *the eventually stable protocol*, performs the computation based on the assumption that the network is eventually stable. The second protocol, *the dynamic protocol*, performs the computation based on the assumption that the network never stabilizes (i.e. the network is not eventually stable).

### 5.1 The Interface with the lower layer

We would like to write the protocol for the non-pumping FAIL-STOP model. However we would like to analyze the complexity with respect to the number of topological changes. For this reason we introduce an interface with a lower layer, that informs our protocol about topological changes. The work of [AAG87] is one implementation of such a lower level.

The interface between our protocol and the lower level is the following. A node can be in one of two states, *working* or *aborting*. The lower level guarantees the following properties:

**Property I:** At each node, every change from *working* to *aborting* can be mapped to a unique topological change in the network.

**Property II:** The period of time in which $State = aborting$ is finite and its length is bounded by $\Lambda$.

**Property III:** Each node, whose eventually connected sub-network includes links that are not eventually stable, changes from $State = working$ to $State = aborting$ (and vis versa) an infinite number of times.

The work of [AAG87] implements such a lower level and guarantees that $\Lambda = O(n\pi)$.

## 5.2 The Eventually Stable Protocol

The eventually stable protocol is composed from a static protocol that constructs a spanning tree, then broadcasts on the tree the value of the data with a hop counter. (The hop counter is incremented by each node that forwards the message.) The static protocol is compiled through [AAG87] to run in dynamic networks that eventually stabilize.

## 5.3 The Dynamic Protocol

The dynamic protocol assumes a knowledge of $n$, the number of nodes, or at least an upper bound on the number of nodes. It also assumes that the source is continuously generating messages. Each message is composed from the data value and a hop counter. A node that receives a message, increases the hop counter by one, if the hop counter is not $n$ it forwards the message to all its neighbors. The source initializes the hop counter to 0 in the messages it generates. The hop counter ensures that each message is forwarded only a finite number of times. Recall, from the specification of the data update problem, that each node $v$ has a variable $data_v$. The value of $data_v$, in our protocol, is the last data value that $v$ received.

The source generates a new message if at least one topological change occurred since the previous message it generated. To control the message complexity of the dynamic protocol, each node forwards a message only if a least one topological change occurs since the previous message it sent. A node is informed about such a topological change, when the eventually stable protocol enters state *aborting*. The protocol, as described above, requires an infinite number of buffers to store the messages that a node has to forward. To reduce the number of buffers, messages that are in the queue of the same outgoing link are coalesced. Two messages, with an identical data value are coalesced to one message and the hop counter is the minimum of the two hop counters. Two messages, with different data values, are replaced by the message that was received later. This enable the protocol to use only one buffer per edge.

The algorithm in each node is the following. Each node has one buffer for the data value and each link has a buffer that holds a hop counter. When a message arrives, if its value is different then the current data value in the node, we replace the data value to the new data value and put its hop counter (incremented by one) in all the link buffers. If the message that is received has the same data value as the node's data value, then each link buffer is updated to the minimum between its current value and the message's hop counter value (incremented by one). When a message is sent (i.e. the node enters state *aborting*) the hop counter on the link is set to $\emptyset$. The code of the data update protocol is presented in Figures 3 and 4.

**Remark:** It seems essential to have a hop counter on every edge rather than one hop counter for the entire node. The reader can verify that keeping one hop counter per node, either the minimum or maximum of the node's buffers, yields an incorrect protocol. It seems that the main problem, in such a protocol, is that edges that are not eventually connected have an undesirable effect on eventually connected edges.

### 5.4 Combining the protocols

Each node $v$ has a value $d$, which is the last value that it received in either the dynamic protocol or the eventually stable protocol. For each link we have a hop counter which is the minimum between the one in the dynamic protocol and the eventually static protocol. In what follows we elaborate more on this construction.

The eventual stable protocol builds a tree, and broadcasts on it the value of *RealData* from the source. This is done, as in the dynamic protocol, with a hop counter that is incremented by every node that forwards it on the tree. In each node, those messages, are treated as messages in the dynamic protocol. (More precisely, the node checks if the data value equals its data value, if not, it replaces its data value by the new data value, and updates buffers of the links with the new hop counter. Otherwise it only updates the link's buffers to the minimum between the new and old hop counter.) Therefore at any point in time, each node $v$ has one value $data_v$ which it "believes" to be the value of *RealData*.

Note that once the eventually stable protocol terminates, all the nodes in the tree have their data value set to *RealData*. This is since the last message overrides any previous data value.

## 6 The Correctness of the Protocol

In this section we prove the correctness of the protocol. The proof is split to two cases, one when the data value stabilizes and the other when it does not. If the data value never stabilizes, then the protocol is correct by definition (since no claim is made in this case). For this reason in the rest of this section we assume that from sometime on the data value stabilizes. The intuition for the correctness proof is the following. Either the network is eventually stable or infinitely many topological changes occur. If a finite number of topological changes occur the network eventually stabilizes, and the eventually stable protocol succeeds to broadcast the correct output. If infinitely many topological changes occur, then the source generates infinitely many messages in the dynamic protocol. Since the data stabilizes, only a finite number of the messages have an incorrect value. The following claims are essential for the correctness of the protocol.

1. Eventually, no message with an incorrect data value is sent.
2. Messages with a correct data value reach all the nodes in the eventually connected sub-network.

Let $T_{fin}$ be a time such that no stable edge changes its status after $T_{fin}$. Such a time exists by the definition of stable edges. Assume that at time $T_{stable}$, $T_{stable} > T_{fin}$, the value of the data at the source is stable and equals $X_{stable}$. Let $V_{conn}$ be the eventually connected sub-network that includes the source, and $E_{conn}$ the set of edges in this sub-network.

We say that the eventually connected sub-network of the source is eventually stable if all the edges in $E_{conn}$ are eventually stable. Note that if it is not eventually stable, then there exists at least one edge in $E_{conn}$ that changes its status an infinite number of times.

The following notations are used in the proofs:

$NODES(D, t)$ The set of nodes $v$, such that $v$ has an eventually connected path to the source (i.e. $v \in V_{conn}$), and at time $t$ have $data_v = D$.

$MESSAGE(D, t)$ The set of messages that are in transit at time $t$ (i.e. where sent before time $t$ and received after time $t$), and were sent on an edge $e \in E_{conn}$ with data value $D$.

$BUFFER(D, t)$ The set of buffers, $\text{buffer}_v[u]$, such that $v \in NODES(D, t)$ and $(v, u)$ is an eventually connected edge.

$MIN\text{-}HOPS(D, t)$ A function that computes the minimum of the hop counters in the messages of $MESSAGE(D, t)$ and in the buffers of $BUFFER(D, t)$ (an empty buffer is considered to have hop counter $n + 1$).

The following lemma shows that the hop counter of obsolete data value has to increase, and thus eventually disappear from the network.

**Lemma 2.** *Assume that the eventually connected sub-network of the source is not eventually stable. Let $D$ be a data value, such that $D \neq X_{stable}$, and $t$ be a time, such that $t > T_{stable}$. If $MIN\text{-}HOPS(D, t) \leq n$ then there exists a time $\hat{t}$, $\hat{t} > t$, such that $MIN\text{-}HOPS(D, \hat{t}) > MIN\text{-}HOPS(D, t)$.*

*Proof.* Let $M = MIN\text{-}HOPS(D, t)$. A buffer changes its hop counter if either a message with a new value is received, or, a message with the same value and a smaller hop counter is received.

In both cases the buffer is updated to the message's hop counter plus one. All the messages in $MESSAGE(D,t)$ have hop counter at least $M$. This implies that no message in $MESSAGE(D,t)$ can decrease the hop counter of a buffer to a value less than $M+1$. Therefore, at any time $t_1$, $t_1 > t$, any buffer in $BUFFER(D,t_1)$ has hop counter at least $M$ and any message in $MESSAGE(D,t_1)$ has hop counter at least $M$, since the source did not generated new messages with data value $D$ between $t$ and $t_1$. This implies that the value of $MIN\text{-}HOPS(D,t_1)$ is at least $M$.

For every $\text{buffer}_v[u]$, such that $\text{buffer}_v[u] \in BUFFER(D,t)$, there is a time $t_v$, $t_v > t$, such that $CanSend_v[u]$ is TRUE (since the link $(v,u)$ is eventually connected). Since the network is not eventually stable, by Property III, there exists a time $\hat{t}_v$, $\hat{t}_v > t_v$, such that $v$ enters state *aborting* at time $\hat{t}_v$. The dynamic protocol of node $v$, at time $\hat{t}_v$, sends a message to $u$ and empties the buffer.

Let $t_2$ be the maximum $\hat{t}_v$, where $v \in NODES(D,t)$. At time $t_2$, all the nodes in $NODES(D,t)$ performed a SendMessage of each buffer in $BUFFER(D,t)$ at least once. Therefore, from time $t$ to time $t_2$, every buffer in $BUFFER(D,t)$ changed its value to $\emptyset$ at least once. Since all the messages in $MESSAGE(D,t)$ have hop counter at least $M$, the buffers in $BUFFER(D,t_2)$ have a hop counter of at least $M+1$.(Recall that an empty buffer is considered as hop counter $n+1$.) At any time $\hat{t}_2$, $\hat{t}_2 > t_2$, the number of hop counters in each of the buffers of $BUFFER(D,\hat{t}_2)$ is $M+1$.

The messages in $MESSAGE(D,t_2)$ are sent on edges in $E_{conn}$, which are eventually connected edges. The fail-stop model guarantees that such messages are delivered eventually. Therefore, there exists a time $t_3 \geq t_2$ such that all the messages $MESSAGE(D,t_2)$ are received. Since at time $t_2$ the minimum hops of $BUFFER(D,t_2)$ is $M+1$, any message sent between $t_2$ and $t_3$ has a hop counter of at least $M+1$. At $t_3$ the hop counter in each of the messages of $MESSAGE(D,t_3)$ is $M+1$. □

The next lemma states that eventually no message with incorrect data is in transit over a link in $E_{conn}$. Therefore, no message with incorrect data can be delivered after that time.

**Lemma 3.** *Assume that the eventually connected sub-network of the source is not eventually stable. Let $T_{stable}$ be a time such that at any time $t$, $t > T_{stable}$, $RealData = X_{stable}$. There exists a time $T_1$, $T_1 > T_{stable}$, such that at any time $t_2$, $t_2 > T_1$, $MESSAGE(D,t_2) = \emptyset$, for any $D \neq X_{stable}$*

*Proof.* Let $\tau_i$ be a time such that for any time $t$, $t > \tau_i$, $MIN\text{-}HOPS(D,t) \geq i$. We need to show that $\tau_i$ exists, for $0 \leq i \leq n+1$. Clearly, we can set $\tau_0 = T_{stable}$, hence, $\tau_0$ exists. Lemma 2 guarantees that if $\tau_i$ exists, and $i \leq n$, then $\tau_{i+1}$ exists.

Therefore, there is a time $T_1$, such that for each data value $D$, $D \neq X_{stable}$, $MIN\text{-}HOPS(D,t_1) = n+1$. Clearly, if $MIN\text{-}HOPS(D,T_1) = n+1$, then no messages with data value $D$ is sent. □

Let $T_\alpha$ be the time after which no message with value different from $X_{stable}$ is received. Lemma 3 guarantees that such a time exists. We still need to show that messages with data value $X_{stable}$ eventually reach each node $v \in V_{conn}$.

What we show is that the hop counter in a node $w$ will at some time reflect the distance from the source to $w$ in $E_{conn}$. Note that we do not assume that the tree used in the eventually stable protocol is a BFS tree. This property is guarantee by the behavior of the messages sent in the dynamic protocol. (Note that the eventually stable protocol cannot invalidate this, since we are always updating the hop counter to the minimum between the previous one and the new one.)

**Lemma 4.** *Assume that the eventually connected sub-network of the source is not eventually stable. If at time $t$, $t > T_\alpha$, at node $u$, $data_u = X_{stable}$, $\mathtt{buffer}_u[v] = k$ and $(u, v)$ is an eventually connected edge in the sub-network of the source, then there exists a time $\hat{t}$, $\hat{t} > t$ such that $data_v = X_{stable}$ and $\mathtt{buffer}_v[w] \leq k + 1$, for all $(v, w) \in E$.*

*Proof.* Since $(u, v)$ is an eventually connected edge, there exists a time $t_1 > t$ such that $CanSend_u[v]$ is TRUE. Since an infinite number of topological changes occur in the sub-network of the source, by Property III, there exists a time $t_2$, $t_2 > t_1$, such that node $u$ enters state *aborting*. At time $t_2$ the dynamic protocol sends a message on link $(u, v)$. Since all the messages after $T_\alpha$ have value $X_{stable}$, and the hop counter can only decrease while the data value does not change, the hop counter of $\mathtt{buffer}_u[v]$ is at most $k$ at $t_2$.

Since the link is an eventually connected edge, and the fail-stop property of the data link guarantees that this message will be delivered. Therefore there exists a time $t_3$, $t_3 > t_2$, such that the message reaches $v$. The protocol at $v$ updates each of the buffers to the minimum between $k + 1$ and the previous value of the buffer and sets $data_v$ to $X_{stable}$. □

We allow the hop counter to grow till $n$, therefore the message with the correct data value will eventually reach all the nodes in $V_{conn}$. The following lemma formalizes this.

**Lemma 5.** *Assume that the eventually connected sub-network of the source is not eventually stable. There exists a time $t > T_\alpha$ such that every node $v$, $v$ in the sub-network of the source, has $data_v = X_{stable}$.*

*Proof.* The proof is by induction on the distance between node $v$ and the source. The base of the induction is trivial. The step of the induction is Lemma 4. □

So far we have shown that if there is an infinite number of topological changes, then each node in the eventually connected component of the source has the correct value. A much simpler case is when only a finite number of topological changes occur in the eventually connected sub-network of the source.

**Lemma 6.** *Assume that the eventually connected sub-network of the source is eventually stable at time $T$. There exists a time $t > T$ such that every node $v \in V_{conn}$ has $data_v = X_{stable}$.*

*Proof.* Consider the last message that the eventually stable protocol broadcasts. First its data value is $X_{stable}$. We need to show that the last message received by each node $v \in V_{conn}$, is the one from the eventually stable protocol. (This would imply that the last message contains the correct value.)

On each particular link the messages are delivered in FIFO order. This implies that a message a node sent during an aborting state, or before it, arrive before any message sent during the following working state. Therefore the last message that each node would receive would come from the eventually stable protocol and would have the value $X_{stable}$. □

We can now state the correctness theorem.

**Theorem 7.** *The data update protocol satisfies the data update specification.*

*Proof.* If the network is eventually stable then, the eventually stable protocol terminates with the data value in each node set to the correct value, by Lemma 6. If the network does not stabilized Lemma 5 ensure that the dynamic protocol succeeds. □

# 7 The Complexity of the protocol

In this section we discuss the time and message complexity of the topology update protocol. The communication complexity is measured by amortized message complexity. The time complexity uses the convergence time, as defined in Section 4.

## 7.1 Amortized Message Complexity

**Theorem 8.** *The amortized message complexity of the protocol is $O(m)$.*

*Proof.* The amortized message complexity of the eventually stable protocol is $O(m)$. In the dynamic protocol a node send a message only when it enters state *aborting*. By Property I this change in state can be mapped to a unique topological change. This implies that the the amortized message complexity of the dynamic protocol is $O(m)$. □

## 7.2 Time Complexity

We start by analyzing the case that the eventually stable protocol succeeds in broadcasting the correct value.

**Lemma 9.** *If the sub-network eventually connected to the source is eventually stable then every node $v$ in that sub-network receives the correct value of the data after at most $O(\Lambda + n\pi)$ time units of time since last topological change in that sub-network.*

*Proof.* The eventually stable protocol requires time $\Lambda$ to move from the state *aborting* to *working*. Building a tree and broadcasting on can be done in $O(n\pi)$ (see [Awe87]. □

The other case is that the eventually stable protocol does not succeed. In this case we have a bound on the time between two events that a node enters state *aborting*.

**Lemma 10.** *If the eventually stable protocol does not succeed then, for every node $v$ that has an eventually connected path to the source, at most $O(\Lambda+n\pi+\rho)$ time units pass between two consecutive times $v$ enters state* aborting.

*Proof.* Assume that a node enters state *aborting* at time $t$. By Property II, at time $\hat{t}$, $\hat{t} = t + \Lambda + O(n\pi)$ the eventually stable protocol terminates. Since the eventually stable protocol did not succeeds, node $v$ entered state *aborting* before $\hat{t}$. Since $v$ entered state *aborting*, a new topological change has occurred, this adds to the time at most $\rho$. Hence, the difference between two consecutive times $v$ enters state *aborting* is bounded by $O(\Lambda + n\pi + \rho)$. □

Recall the definitions of $T_{stable}$, $X_{stable}$ and $T_\alpha$ from Section 6. At time $T_{stable}$ the value at the source is $X_{stable}$, and never changes after this time. $T_\alpha$ is the time after which no message with value different from $X_{stable}$ is received.

**Lemma 11.** *Assume the sub-network eventually connected to the source is not eventually stable. The number of time units between $T_{stable}$ and $T_\alpha$ is at most $O(n\Lambda + n^2\pi + n\rho)$.*

*Proof.* Let $D$ be a data value, such that $D \neq X_{stable}$. Let $\tau_i$ be a time such that for any time $t$, $t > \tau_i$, $MIN\text{-}HOPS(D,t) \geq i$. In the proof of Lemma 3 we show that, for $0 \leq i \leq n+1$, $\tau_i$ exists and $\tau_0 = T_{stable}$. Lemma 2 requires, in the worst case, that every node sends one message in the dynamic protocol. Therefore, by Lemma 10, the value of $\tau_{i+1} - \tau_i$ is at most $O(\Lambda + n\pi + \rho)$. Hence, $\tau_{n+1} - \tau_0$ is at most $O(n\Lambda + n^2\pi + n\rho)$ and the total time is $O(n\Lambda + n^2\pi + n\rho)$. □

**Lemma 12.** *Assume the sub-network eventually connected to the source is not eventually stable. Let $v$ be a node in the eventually connected sub-network of the source. At any time $t$, $t > T_\alpha + O(n^2\pi + n\rho + n\Lambda)$, $data_v = X_{stable}$.*

*Proof.* Each application of Lemma 4 requires that a node sends a message on an eventually connected link. In order for a node to forward a message on a link it has to enter a *aborting* state. By Lemma 10, at most $O(\Lambda + n\pi + \rho)$ time units are required until $v$ enters an $State = aborting$, and is able to broadcast on an eventually connected link. Therefore, after $O(k(n\pi + \rho + \Lambda))$ time units all the nodes at distance $k$ from the source have already updated their value. Since the distance between a node and the source is at most $n$ the Theorem follows. □

This establishes the following theorem about the convergence time of each node.

**Theorem 13.** *The convergence time of a node $v$ is at most $O(n^2\pi + n\rho + n\Lambda)$.*

*Proof.* If the network never stabilizes then the theorem follows from Lemma 11 and Lemma 12. Let $T_\beta = T_\alpha + O(n\Lambda + n^2\pi + n\rho)$. If the network stabilizes at time $t$, $t > T_\beta$, the dynamic algorithm already succeeded, and the theorem follows. If the network stabilizes at $t$, $t \leq T_\beta$, then, by Lemma 9, at $t + O(n\pi)$ the eventually stable protocol succeeds. $\qquad\square$

The construction of [AAG87] show that $\Lambda = O(n\pi)$, therefore,

**Corollary 14.** *The convergence time of a node $v$ is at most $O(n^2\pi + n\rho)$.*

## 8  Discussion on convergence time

The following is an interesting variation of the topology protocol. Each node $v$ has two values: $d_1$, the last value that $v$ received during a eventually stable protocol, and $d_2$, the last value that it received during the dynamic protocol. If the value of $d_1$, from the eventually stable protocol, was received during the current *working* state, then $data_v$ equals $d_1$ else it equals to $d_2$. This modified protocol can be proven, in a very similar to the correctness proof of our protocol, to solve the topology update problem. Namely, either there are a finite number of changes in the network (then $d_1 = data_v$ and $data_v$ does not change) or an infinite number of changes (then, eventually, $d_2$ has the correct value). This modification also preserves the $O(m)$ amortized message complexity.

There is a subtle drawback to this protocol. If there are only a finite number of topological changes, then it can be the case that at some node $v$, $d_1 \neq d_2$. If an additional topological change occurs at $v$, then the value of $data_v$ changes to $d_2$. If the number of changes is less than $n$, the time until the value in $v$ is correct and does change any more can not be bounded (although it is finite). The convergence time of the new protocol captures this phenomena. The convergence time is greater than $k\pi + m\rho$, for **any** $k$ and $m < n$. (Since at any time $k\pi + m\rho$ the value of $d_2$ may be incorrect.) In the original protocol the convergence time is bounded by $n\pi + m\rho$, also for $m < n$. This shows the that of the definition for convergence time enables to capture notions that the previous complexity measures could not express.

In some cases we can trade the convergence time and the amortized message complexity. Consider the dynamic protocol. The amortized message complexity of the dynamic protocol can be reduced to $O(m/k)$, if each node forwards a message only after $k$ times the node entered an *aborting* state. In this case the convergence time would increase by a factor of $k$.

## References

[AAG87] Yehuda Afek, Baruch Awerbuch, and Eli Gafni. Applying static network protocols to dynamic networks. In $28^{th}$ *Annual Symposium on Foundations of Computer Science.* IEEE, October 1987.

[ACK90] B. Awerbuch, I. Cidon, and S. Kutten. Optimal maintenance of replicated information. In *Proceedings of the 31st Annual IEEE Symposium on Foundations of Computer Science (FOCS), St. Louis, Missouri*, pages 492–502, 1990.

[AE83] Baruch Awerbuch and Shimon Even. A formal approach to a communication-network protocol; broadcast as a case study. Technical Report TR-459, Electrical Engineering Department, Technion-I.I.T., Haifa, December 1983.

[AG88] Yehuda Afek and Eli Gafni. End-to-end communication in unreliable networks. In *Proceedings of the $7^{th}$ Annual ACM Symposium on Principles of Distributed Computing, Toronto, Ontario, Canada*, pages 131–148. ACM SIGACT and SIGOPS, ACM, 1988.

[AG91] Yehuda Afek and Eli Gafni. Bootstrap network resynchronization. In *Proceedings of the $11^{th}$ Annual ACM Symposium on Principles of Distributed Computing*, pages 295–308, August 1991.

[AGR] Yehuda Afek, Eli Gafni, and Adi Rosen. The slide mechanism with applications in dynamic networks. to appear in PODC 1992.

[AMS89] B. Awerbuch, Y. Mansour, and N. Shavit. Polynomial end-to-end communication. In *$30^{th}$ Annual Symposium on Foundations of Computer Science*, pages 358–363, 1989.

[Awe87] Baruch Awerbuch. Optimal distributed algorithms for minimum weight spanning tree, counting, leader election and related problems. In *Proceedings of the $19^{th}$ Annual ACM Symposium on Theory of Computing*, pages 230–240. ACM, May 1987.

[HK89] Amir Herzberg and Shay Kutten. Efficient detection of message forwarding faults. In *Proceedings of the $8^{th}$ Annual ACM Symposium on Principles of Distributed Computing, Edmonton, Alberta, Canada*, pages 339–353, 1989.

[SG89] John M. Spinelli and Robert G. Gallager. Broadcasting topology information in computer networks. *IEEE Trans. Comm.*, May 1989. to appear.

[Tan81] A. Tannenbaum. *Computer Networks*. Prentice Hall, 1981.

[Vis83] U. Vishkin. A distributed orientation algorithm. *IEEE Trans. Info. Theory*, June 1983.

```
RealData                          /* The real data value at the source*/
Neighbors                         /* The set of neighbors of the source */
CanSend = Array [ Neighbors ] of Boolean /*TRUE -> can send a message to u */
When entering state aborting
      FOR u ∈ Neighbors DO
      IF CanSend[u] THEN SendMessage ({RealData,0}) to u
```

**Fig. 3.** The algorithm for the source in the dynamic protocol

```
data                              /* The data value as v knows it*/
Neighbors                         /* The set of neighbors of a node */
CanSend = Array [Neighbors] of Boolean /*TRUE -> can send a message to u */
buffers = Array [Neighbors] of hops      /*The hops number that will be sent on that link*/

When entering state aborting
      FOR u ∈ Neighbors DO
            IFbuffer[u] ≠ ∅ AND CanSend[u] THEN
            SendMessage ({data,buffer[u]}) to u
            buffer[u] := ∅
            END

For a ReceiveMessage({NewDataValue , hops}) from u
      IF NewDataValue ≠ data THEN
         data := NewDataValue
         FOR u ∈ Neighbors DO buffer[u] := NEXT(hops) END
      ELSE
         FOR u ∈ Neighbors DO buffer[u] := MIN-BUF(NEXT(hops),buffer[u]) END

Function MIN-BUF (x,y)
         IF y = ∅ THEN Return x
               ELSE Return MIN(x,y)

Function NEXT (x)
         IF x = n THEN Return ∅
               ELSE Return x+1
```

**Fig. 4.** The algorithm for node $v$, that is not the source, in the in the dynamic protocol.

# Memory Adaptive Self-Stabilizing Protocols [*] (Extended Abstract )

Efthymios Anagnostou    makis@csri.toronto.edu
Ran El-Yaniv    ran@theory.toronto.edu
Vassos Hadzilacos    vassos@db.toronto.edu

Department of Computer Science
University of Toronto
Toronto M5S 1A4, Canada

**Abstract.** We present a token-based diffusion scheme that forms the basis of efficient self-stabilizing protocols for a variety of problems including unique naming, network topology, token management. For the model where processors' initial knowledge about the network is restricted only to their neighbours, we introduce the concept of *memory adaptive* protocols. In these, once the system stabilizes, the size of the memory used by each processor is a function of the *actual* network size — even though the system may have been started in a state where each processor "thinks" that it is embedded in a network much larger (or smaller) than the actual one. For this model, we develop memory adaptive self-stabilizing protocols for the problems mentioned above that stabilize in time $O(n \log \log n)$, where $n$ is the number of processors. For the model where processors also know an upper bound $D$ on the diameter of the network and an upper bound on $n$, we develop bounded-memory self-stabilizing protocols for the same problems that stabilize in $O(\min\{D, n\})$ time. All our protocols are based on a token diffusion scheme, and are uniform, in the sense that processors with the same number of neighbours execute the same program.

## 1 Introduction

A protocol is *self-stabilizing* for property $P$ if it will eventually satisfy $P$, even when the processors participating in the protocol start their computation from an arbitrary state. This means that the correctness of the protocol (described by property $P$) does not depend on the initial values of variables or program counters. Self-stabilization is an attractive form of fault-tolerance because it provides a distributed system with the means to tolerate *transient* errors, the type of errors that corrupt volatile memory of the system momentarily but do not change the programs themselves. System configuration changes (addition of new processors, removal of communication edges, etc.) can be viewed as transient "errors" and thus self-stabilizing protocols are very well-suited for dynamic networks.

---

[*] Research supported by the Natural Sciences and Engineering Research Council of Canada.

Self-stabilizing protocols were introduced in [Dij74]. Recently there has been a great deal of interest in the subject (for example, [BGW89], [BP89], [AG90], [AKY90], [DIM90], [DIM91], [IJ90], [KP90], [AV91], [APV91] and more). Many self-stabilizing protocols assume the existence of a distinguished processor, or the existence of distinct IDs for the processors. This may be undesirable, especially in the case of dynamic networks where we would like processors to join the system or drop out of it without requiring special intervention for the system to adapt to the new configuration. Thus, in this abstract we focus on *uniform* protocols, i.e., those where all processors run the same "code", parameterized only by the number of their neighbours in the network. As was already shown by Dijkstra in his seminal paper on the subject, for many important problems in distributed computing there are no uniform *deterministic* self-stabilizing protocols, except in special cases (cf. [BP89]). Consequently, we are forced to resort to randomized protocols.

In this abstract we describe a simple self-stabilizing "diffusion protocol with echo" which, roughly speaking, allows a processor to disseminate some piece of information to all processors and receive some feedback from them. Using this diffusion mechanism we can develop protocols for a variety of problems, including: (1) The *Unique Naming* (UN) problem where each processor must select an ID different from all other processors'. (2) The *Ranking* problem, a special case of UN where the unique names of the processors must be the integers $1, 2, \ldots n$, where $n$ is the number of processors in the system. (3) The *Topology* problem, where each processor must compute the network in which it is embedded. (4) The *Token Management* problem, where a unique token circulates through the system in a fair way and can be seized by any processor that wishes to capture it. (5) The *Spanning Tree* problem, where each processor must select a subset of its adjacent edges so that the set of all edges selected forms a spanning tree of the network. (6) The *Leader Election* problem, in which exactly one processor (the "leader") enters a distinguished state.

In this abstract we concentrate on UN. The diffusion mechanism can be used to derive efficient self-stabilizing protocols for all the other problems, as well as problems not enumerated in the above list. Space restrictions do not permit us to describe these protocols in this abstract.

To state the properties of our UN protocols and compare our results to related work we classify system models according to two criteria: the knowledge that processors have about the system, and their use of memory. Regarding the knowledge of processors we distinguish two models:

$\mathcal{M}_\emptyset$: Processors have no global information about the system; each only knows its neighbours.

$\mathcal{M}_{D,N}$: In addition to their neighbours, processors know an upper bound $D$ on the diameter $d$ of the network, and an upper bound $N$ on the number $n$ of processors in the network.

Regarding the use of memory, we distinguish three models:

1. Bounded protocols: The amount of memory used by the protocol is bounded.

2. Adaptive protocols: The amount of memory used by the protocol after stabilization is a function of the actual network.
3. Unbounded protocols: The amount of memory used by the protocol is unbounded.

A desirable solution for a problem would be a bounded protocol that works in the $\mathcal{M}_\emptyset$ model. For many interesting problems, however, such solutions do not exist. For instance, in any protocol that solves the UN problem, each processor must have at least $\log n$ bits (to store its name), and thus no bounded protocol can exist if the processor knows nothing about the number of processors in the system. (A bound on memory would imply an upper bound on the number of processors!) Similar comments apply to several other problems, such as Ranking and Topology.

This realization has led us to define *memory adaptive* protocols which, in a sense, are the best thing one can hope for in the $\mathcal{M}_\emptyset$ model. In a memory adaptive protocol, each processor has access to an unbounded amount of memory. However, after the system stabilizes, the amount of memory used is bounded from above by a function of the *actual* network. For instance, consider a self-stabilizing UN protocol for the $\mathcal{M}_\emptyset$ model and suppose that the protocol is started at a state in which the processors think that they are embedded in a huge network (and thus their initial names are very long). If the protocol is memory adaptive, not only must processors make sure that their names are distinct, but they must also reduce their initially long names to ones whose size is a function of the actual number of processors.[2] In other words, we view the nodes of the network as processors that dynamically request memory from their "environment" when the need arises and release memory back to their environment when they no longer need it.

In this paper we present a memory adaptive protocol for UN. To our knowledge, the definition of memory adaptive protocols and the existence of self-stabilizing protocols with this property for the $\mathcal{M}_\emptyset$ model are original contributions. All other self-stabilizing protocols for the $\mathcal{M}_\emptyset$ model with which we are familiar are not memory adaptive; the amount of memory used eventually stops growing but depends on the initial state in which the protocol started (and hence can be arbitrarily large, even if the network is small). Our memory adaptive protocol stabilizes in $O(n \log \log n)$ time. Its space complexity (i.e., the amount of memory used per processor after stabilization) is $O(n^2 \log n)$ bits.

Another property of the memory adaptive protocol is that it uses a modest amount of *intermediate space*, by which we mean the amount of space used until stabilization, including the space of the initial state. In our protocol this intermediate space is expected to be at most the maximum of the space in the

---

[2] The memory adaptive UN problem has some similarities to the "renaming problem" studied in [ABD$^+$87] and [BD89], but the two problems are incomparable: In the renaming problem *a fraction* of the processors may be *permanently* faulty, while in our case *all* processors are subject to *a transient* failure. In addition, in the renaming problem processors have some knowledge about the network (they know $n$ and the maximum number of faulty processors $t$).

initial state (for which there is no *a priori* bound) and twice the space used after stabilization (which, as we have stated, is bounded by $O(n^2 \log n)$). A final feature of the protocol is that we can decrease the stabilization time from $O(n \log \log n)$ to essentially any superlinear function of $n$ (for example, $n \log^* n$), at the expense of increasing the intermediate space, but with no increase in the space after stabilization.

In addition to memory adaptive protocols for the $\mathcal{M}_\emptyset$ model, we also present a bounded UN protocol for the $\mathcal{M}_{D,N}$ model. This protocol stabilizes in $O(\min\{D, n\})$ expected time. By comparison, the fastest UN self-stabilizing protocol for the $\mathcal{M}_{D,N}$ model previously known stabilizes in $O(n)$ expected time (cf. [DIM91]).

To summarize, the main contributions of this paper are:

- A simple self-stabilizing diffusion mechanism that can be used to derive self-stabilizing protocols for a variety of problems.
- A memory adaptive UN protocol for the $\mathcal{M}_\emptyset$ model that stabilizes in $O(n \log \log n)$ expected time (to be more precise, in $O(n(1 + \log \log n - \log \log(\Delta + 1)))$) where $\Delta$ is the maximum degree in the network), based on the diffusion mechanism.
- A UN protocol for the $\mathcal{M}_{D,N}$ model that stabilizes in $O(\min\{D, n\})$ expected time, also based on the diffusion mechanism.

## 1.1 Comparison to Related Work

Among the many recent papers on self-stabilizing protocols, the most relevant to our work are [AKY90], [AV91], and [DIM91].

Awerbuch and Varghese [AV91] present a general transformation that can turn a given protocol for a problem $P$ to a *self-stabilizing* protocol for $P$, provided that $P$ and the given protocol satisfy certain properties. In particular, $P$ must be what the authors call a "non-interactive" problem, i.e., a problem that can be described as a relation between inputs and outputs. Of the problems listed earlier, Token Management is not in this category.[3] In addition, the given protocol must be deterministic, thus precluding the use of the transformation to obtain uniform solutions for problems known not to be solvable by uniform deterministic protocols. Finally, the transformation requires a time bound for the given protocol, which renders it inapplicable in model $\mathcal{M}_\emptyset$: Any information about the time complexity of a protocol for a non-trivial task would imply some information about the network (e.g., a bound on its size, or the length of its diameter), which violates the assumptions of model $\mathcal{M}_\emptyset$. Thus, our techniques can be used to solve problems that are beyond the power of Awerbuch and Varghese's transformation.

---

[3] Although the transformation of [AV91] does not directly yield a solution to the TM problem, it can be used in combination with other methods to obtain such a solution. In particular, one can combine the leader election protocol of [AV91] with a leader-based TM protocol, such as is described in [DIM90], to obtain an $O(D)$ TM protocol.

In [AKY90] and [DIM91] the authors focus on self-stabilizing protocols for the closely related Spanning Tree and Leader Election problems. The protocols in [AKY90] require processors to have unique names[4] and stabilize in $O(n^2)$ expected time in the $\mathcal{M}_\emptyset$ model and in $O(D^2)$ expected time in the $\mathcal{M}_{D,N}$ model. The protocols in [DIM91] do not assume unique names and stabilize in $O(d)$ expected time in the $\mathcal{M}_{D,N}$ model and in $O(d \log n)$ expected time in the $\mathcal{M}_\emptyset$ model. In this paper it is also shown how to transform a Spanning Tree protocol to a Ranking (and hence UN) protocol, but the transformation incurs a penalty of $O(n)$ for the stabilization time. In both papers, the protocols are bounded in the $\mathcal{M}_{D,N}$ model, but unbounded (*not* memory adaptive) in the $\mathcal{M}_\emptyset$ model.

Our protocols in the $\mathcal{M}_{D,N}$ model and for all the problems listed at the beginning of the introduction stabilize in $O(\min\{D, n\})$ time. Thus, our protocols for UN and Ranking stabilize faster than the Ranking protocol in [DIM91]. This comparison also holds for the Topology problem.[5] On the other hand, if $D$ is not an accurate bound for the actual diameter $d$ the protocols of [DIM91] for Spanning Tree and Leader Election stabilize faster than ours.

In terms of space, our protocols for the $\mathcal{M}_\emptyset$ model are memory adaptive, while those of the other two papers are unbounded. However, for the $\mathcal{M}_{D,N}$ model our protocols are not as good as those in [AKY90] and [DIM91], as they require more memory and considerably longer messages.

The rest of this extended abstract is organized as follows: In Section 2 we describe the important aspects of the model of computation we use. Section 3 contains the self-stabilizing diffusion mechanism. In Section 4 we give the memory adaptive protocol for the $\mathcal{M}_\emptyset$ model, while the next Section sketches its correctness proof. Finally, in Section 6 we outline the protocol for the $\mathcal{M}_{D,N}$ model, give our conclusions and list some open questions.

## 2 Model of Computation

Without loss of generality we adopt the popular *link-register* model introduced in [DIM90]. At the end of this section we show that our protocols also work in the message-passing model. A *communication network* is an undirected graph whose nodes correspond to processors and whose edges indicate which pairs of processors can communicate directly. Two adjacent processors $u$ and $v$ communicate by means of a pair of unidirectional links. Each link is modeled as a register that can only be written by one of the neighbours and read by the other. $R_{u \to v}$ is the register written by $u$ and read by $v$. We say that a processor *owns* the

---

[4] We have been informed, however, that this assumption can be removed (private communication, August 1991).

[5] Although Topology is not explicitly treated in [DIM91], it is not difficult to see that given a protocol for Ranking one can solve Topology with no increase to the (asymptotic) stabilization time. Thus, the $O(n)$ Ranking protocol of [DIM91] gives rise to a $O(n)$ protocol for Topology.

registers into which it can write. We can assume w.l.o.g. that these registers are atomic (see [Lam86a], [Lam86b]).

Each register $R_{u \to v}$ owned by $u$ has a unique *port number*, denoted $P_u(v)$. This is used by $u$ to distinguish $R_{u \to v}$ from all the other registers it owns. We assume that $v$ knows $P_u(v)$, since we can require $u$ to write that number into a component of $R_{u \to v}$ every time that it writes into that register.

Each processor $u$ follows an *algorithm* which can be thought of as an automaton having a set of states, and whose individual steps allow $u$ to read a neighbour's register, write a register it owns, or change its own state. The effect of a read step by processor $u$ is to modify $u$'s local state (we can think of this as copying the value read into a local variable of $u$). The value written by a write step of $u$ is determined by $u$'s local state. A step that just changes $u$'s state models local computation by $u$. The new state of $u$ depends on the old state and, possibly, on random choices (when $u$ follows a randomized algorithm).

We assume that the computation of each processor $u$ proceeds in *cycles*, each of which consists of a sequence of steps in which $u$ accomplishes all of the following in the specified order: $u$ reads the values of all registers owned by its neighbours; it changes its own state; and it writes into the registers it owns. We do *not* assume that the write steps of a cycle write the same value into all of $u$'s registers.

A *protocol* is a collection of algorithms (i.e., automata), one for each processor in the network. A *global state* of a protocol is a function mapping each processor $u$ to a state of $u$, and each register to a value of that register. An *execution* of a protocol starting from a global state $S$ is an infinite sequence of alternating global states and processor steps, beginning with state $S$, so that the application of each step to the preceding global state results in the following global state. Since we want to model asynchronous systems, we do not impose any restriction on how steps of different processors are interleaved in an execution, aside from requiring that each processor takes infinitely many steps. A protocol is *self-stabilizing* with respect to property $P$ if every execution has a suffix which contains only states that satisfy $P$. We say that an execution *stabilizes* as soon as it has reached a state so that $P$ holds in that and all subsequent states.

Following [AFL83], we define a *round* of an execution to be a minimal subsequence of contiguous steps in which each processor has completed at least one *cycle*.[6] The main measure of time efficiency for a self-stabilizing protocol is the time required for stabilization. More formally, the *stabilization time* for a deterministic (resp. randomized) protocol is the maximum (resp. maximum expected) number of rounds until an execution stabilizes starting from any initial state. The space complexity of the protocol can be expressed as the number of bits required to store the state of each processor. The communication complexity is measured in terms of the number of bits of the registers. A protocol is *uniform*

---

[6] We should point out that sometimes a round is defined to be a minimal subsequence of steps in which every processor has taken at least one *step*, rather than a cycle. We find it more convenient to define it using cycles. In all the comparisons we made in Section 1.1 the results were normalized in accordance with our definition.

if all processors with the same degree (number of neighbours) have the same algorithm. Note that in our model we do not assume that processors have unique names. In this paper we restrict our attention to uniform protocols and drop the adjective "uniform" from now on. On the basis of the definitions given in this section it is straightforward to formalize the notions of bounded, memory adaptive, and unbounded protocols, and of the $\mathcal{M}_\emptyset$ and $\mathcal{M}_{D,N}$ models discussed in the introduction. These are omitted from the extended abstract.

Even though our results are for the shared memory model, they can be easily extended to the message-passing model using the self-stabilizing alternating bit protocol of Afek and Brown [AB89]. In particular, we can substitute each unidirectional link register by a copy of the randomized self-stabilizing alternating bit protocol. In the message passing model each message of our protocol has size $O(n^2 \log n)$ bits in the $\mathcal{M}_\emptyset$ model, and $O(n \log N)$ bits in the $\mathcal{M}_{D,N}$ model. Furthermore, if we make the common assumption of unit (or any bounded) capacity channels ([APV91]) then the stabilization time of our protocols remains the same as well.

# 3  Self-Stabilizing Diffusion with Echo

In this section we describe a useful primitive which is the basis of our other protocols, namely the *self-stabilizing diffusion with echo*. Informally, a diffusion primitive enables a processor to disseminate a piece of information to all other processors. In addition, the echo mechanism allows the processors to respond to the information they received by sending some feedback to the initiator of the diffusion. Diffusion protocols have been used extensively in distributed computing (cf. [DS79], [Awe88], [AS88], [AG90], [APV91] etc.).

We concentrate here on the $\mathcal{M}_\emptyset$ model and at the end of the section we show how to do diffusion on $\mathcal{M}_{D,N}$. Roughly speaking, to diffuse a piece of information, processor $u$ creates a *token* containing that information and some additional control information. It then sends copies of that token to its neighbours (by writing into its registers), which send further copies to their neighbours and so on, until copies of the token have been received by all processors, whereupon the token copies are returned retracing their path in reverse, with the feedback information attached. When the initiator of the diffusion receives all token copies it knows that the diffusion has been completed and has feedback from the processors.

We refer to the copy of a token possessed by a processor as a *token tuple*. A token tuple has the form $\langle name, dir, path, info \rangle$. Field *name* contains a "name" for the token. For example, in the application of diffusion to the UN protocol, this field contains the ID of the processor that created the token and a random bit. Field *dir* is a bit that indicates whether the token tuple is traveling forward ($F$) or backward ($B$). Field *path* is a list of the port numbers through which the token tuple has passed; it is used so that the token tuple can retrace its route on the way back. Field *info* contains the information that the initiator $u$ of the diffusion wants to disperse, and can also be used for any feedback information that processors wish to give to $u$. Since this field is application-specific we do not discuss it further in this section, and treat token tuples as triples $\langle name, dir, path \rangle$.

The basic data structure used by each processor $u$ in this protocol is a *consistency table*, denoted $Tab_u$.[7] In this table, $u$ keeps information about all the token tuples that have passed through it and which it has not returned yet. The table indicates to $u$ which token tuples it must give to which of its neighbours, and which token tuples it expects back from which of its neighbours.

Consider now a processor $v$ that receives a token tuple $t$ with name $\nu$ and $dir = F$ from neighbour $w$. If $v$ does not contain a token tuple with name $\nu$, $v$ *accepts* $t$; otherwise $v$ *rejects* $t$. Processor $v$ informs $w$ of the fate of $t$ (acceptance or rejection) by writing this information (among other things) in $R_{v \to w}$. If $v$ rejects $t$ it does not take any further action in response to the receipt of that token tuple from $w$. If, on the other hand, $v$ accepts $t$ then $v$ appends the port number $P_v(w)$ through which $v$ received $t$ to the path field, resulting in token tuple $t'$. Processor $v$ inserts $t'$ into $Tab_v$ and sends $t'$ to all its neighbours.

The token tuple $t'$ remains in $Tab_v$ until it is time for $v$ to return it to $w$. This occurs as soon as $v$ receives back all the copies of token tuple $t'$ that it sent to its neighbours and *were accepted* by them.[8] In particular, if $v$ finds out that all token tuples $t'$ that it sent were rejected, then it is time to return $t'$ to the processor from which $v$ received $t'$. To return $t'$, $v$ removes from $Tab_v$ $t'$, changes the direction bit to $B$, removes the last port number from the path field of $t'$ (this is $w$'s port number at $v$) and sends the resulting token tuple through that port to $w$.

When processor $u$ that initiated the diffusion of a token $t$ with name $\nu$ receives back all token tuples it sent to its neighbours that were accepted, the diffusion of that token is completed. Processor $u$ then creates another token and initiates another diffusion in the same way.

To define the self-stabilizing properties of our diffusion protocol we must introduce some terminology. Consider a global state $S$, in which the table of some processor $u$ contains the token tuple $t = \langle \nu, d, p_1 p_2 \ldots p_k \rangle$, where $k \geq 1$. Let $v$ be the process to which $u$ is connected via its port $p_k$; if $u$ does not have a port with number $p_k$, $v$ is undefined. We say that $t$ is a *dangling* token tuple in global state $S$ iff:

- $v$ is undefined; or
- $v$ is defined and the table of $v$ either does not contain the token tuple $t' = \langle \nu, F, p_1 p_2 \ldots p_{k-1} \rangle$; or it contains $t'$, but $t'$ is (recursively) dangling.

A global state $S$ is *legal* iff it satisfies the following three invariants:
I1: No table in $S$ contains two token tuples with the same name.

---

[7] The use of such tables for self-stabilizing protocols originated in [AE91]. Similar data structures were used in [SG89] for topology update and in [AKP91] for routing protocols. However, both these applications did not involve self-stabilization.

[8] Recall that the neighbours write in their registers whether they accepted a token tuple $t$ or not, so $v$ can know which of the token tuples it sent were accepted.

I2: For each processor $u$, the table of $u$ in $S$ contains exactly one token tuple with *path* component equal to the empty sequence. (That is, for each $u$, there is a unique token initiated by $u$.)

I3: There is no dangling token tuple in $S$.

We wish our diffusion protocol to be self-stabilizing with respect to legality. It is easy to see that, if we start our protocol in a legal state, then no illegal state will ever be entered. However, since it is possible for the protocol to be started in an arbitrary state, some actions must be taken by the processors to eliminate violations of these three invariants.

It is straightforward to eliminate violations of invariants I1 and I2, since these can be locally checked by each processor. In particular, a processor can eliminate violations of I1 by removing from its table all token tuples with the same name except one. Also, it can eliminate a violation of I2 by removing all token tuples that have an empty *path* component except one, and initiating a diffusion if it happens to have no token tuple with an empty *path* component.

Eliminating violations of I3 requires more work, since these cannot necessarily be detected locally by any one processor. To eliminate dangling tuples each processor $u$ does the following: It discards from $Tab_u$ any tuples with meaningless data. Also if $u$ receives back from a neighbour a token tuple $t$ that it is not expecting (according to the information in $Tab_u$), then $u$ ignores $t$. Finally, if $Tab_u$ indicates that $u$ is expecting a token tuple from a neighbour $v$ but $v$'s register ($R_{v \to u}$) indicates that $v$ knows nothing about this tuple (and thus will never return it to $u$), then $u$ assumes that is has received the token from $v$. These "house-cleaning" activities guarantee the following: (1) No processor waits for tokens that will not be returned to it, thereby avoiding indefinite waiting. (2) Every dangling token tuple will be eliminated from the system very soon, since such a tuple can move forward for at most $n$ rounds, and will then return back and be eliminated in at most $n$ additional rounds. It is important to notice here that inconsistent token tuple elimination is done only one way, backwards. This way we avoid endless cycles of eliminating token tuples while their "front" keeps visiting the same parts of the network and their "tale" is eliminated. This would be the case if we were applying two way elimination.

The following claim states the self-stabilizing property of the diffusion protocol and its stabilization time:

**Claim 1** *Within at most $2n$ rounds after the diffusion protocol starts, the global state will be legal and will remain legal thereafter.*

In addition, the diffusion protocol satisfies the following liveness properties:

**Claim 2** *Each diffusion terminates within at most $2n$ rounds after its initiation.*

**Claim 3** *Consider the execution of the diffusion protocol after stabilization has been reached. If the diffusion of a token $t$ with name $\nu$ by some processor does not overlap in time with the diffusion of a token with the same name $\nu$ by a different processor, then the table of each processor will contain a token tuple with name $\nu$ at some time during the diffusion of $t$.*

**Diffusion in $\mathcal{M}_{D,N}$**

We can use a similar protocol for diffusion in the $\mathcal{M}_{D,N}$ model. However, the additional knowledge in this model (the bounds $D$ and $N$) can be exploited to achieve better protocols. There are two major differences.

First, since processors know the bound $D$ on the diameter, they can use $D$ to determine when to stop the diffusion of a token tuple and send it back. This is done instead of diffusing each token tuple "as far as it will go", i.e., until it reaches a processor all of whose neighbours have already received a token tuple with the same name, as is done in the $\mathcal{M}_\emptyset$ model. In addition, invariant I1 is implemented by applying the *shortest path* resolution rule: If $u$ receives a token tuple with the same name as a token tuple already recorded in the table, but the new token tuple came from a strictly shorter route (as can be determined by comparing the lengths of the *path* fields of the two tuples) then the old tuple is deleted and the new one kept; otherwise the new tuple is discarded. In addition to enforcing I1, this rule also guarantees that every node receives each token tuple through one of the shortest paths between it and the processor that initiated the token. Consequently, each processor is guaranteed to receive a token tuple within $D$ rounds after its diffusion was initiated. These modifications cause each diffusion to take time of order $O(\min\{D, n\})$ rounds, rather than $O(n)$ rounds.

The second difference is that since processors know the bound $N$ on the number of processors, they can bound the size of their consistency tables. $Tab_u$ has space for $N$ token tuples, one for each processor. Note that when the system reaches a good global state (within $2 \cdot \min\{D, n\}$ rounds), each table will contain no more than $n$ token tuples. If $u$ receives a token tuple $t$ with a different name than all the token tuples in $Tab_u$, but $Tab_u$ is full, then $u$ ignores $t$. This can only happen in the first $2 \cdot \min\{D, n\}$ rounds of the system, i.e. until it enters a legal state.

## 4   A Memory Adaptive UN Protocol for the $\mathcal{M}_\emptyset$ Model

In this section we describe a memory adaptive self-stabilizing UN protocol for the minimum information model $\mathcal{M}_\emptyset$, where processors do not have any bound on the number of processors $n$, or the diameter of the network $d$. After stabilization, the memory consumed by each processor is $O(n^2 \log n)$ bits, even if initially the processors have large estimates for the network (and therefore large IDs). The stabilization time of our protocol is $O(n \log \log n)$ expected rounds. In fact, we can replace $n \log \log n$ by any superlinear function, for example $n \log^* n$ or even $n\alpha(n)$, where $\alpha(n)$ is the inverse of Ackermann's function. Such a speed-up, however, is attained at the expense of an increase in intermediate space, i.e., the amount of space used until stabilization and memory adaptation occurs.

In the memory adaptive protocol each processor $u$ is in one of three phases:

**Phase 1:** $u$ diffuses a token containing its present ID and collects the IDs of all other processors (these are provided as the "echo" to the diffusion), and waits for all others to do so.

**Phase 2:** $u$ computes its rank (i.e., the number of IDs less than or equal to its own) and sets its ID to its rank.

**Phase 3:** $u$ diffuses continuously a token with its ID, collects all the IDs and checks that the set of IDs covers exactly the range $\{1, 2, \ldots n_u\}$, where $n_u$ is the number of different IDs from phase 1. After stabilization every processor remains forever in phase 3.

The *name* field of the token diffused by $u$ in both phases 1 and 3 contains the triple $(id_u, isRank_u, b_u)$ where $id_u$ is the current ID of processor $u$, $isRank_u$ is a bit with value 1 if $u$ is in phase 3 (in which case $id_u$ is actually the rank of $u$) and value 0 otherwise, and $b_u$ is a bit randomly chosen by $u$ at the beginning of each diffusion. The *info* field of each token tuple contains the triple $(diffusion1Done, rankingDone, IDList)$, where:

– $diffusion1Done$ is a bit set to true at the beginning of each diffusion and set to false if the token tuple visits a processor that has not yet completed its first diffusion of phase 1.

– $rankingDone$ is a bit set to true at the beginning of each diffusion and set to false if the token tuple visits a processor that has not completed its phase 2.

– $IDList$ contains the list of different IDs of the processors visited by the token tuple. It is set to the ID of the processor initiating the diffusion at the beginning of each diffusion; each processor visited by the token tuple attaches its ID to the list before forwarding it to its neighbours.

Processor $u$ maintains its current estimate of the network size $n_u$. This is always set to a value greater than the number of $u$'s neighbours. If at some point $u$ determines that there is "something wrong" (e.g., some processors have the same ID — we shall be more precise shortly), then it initiates a *Reset*. Reset is a primitive ([Fin79], [APV91]) that can be roughly defined as follows (a formal definition is given in the full paper): If any processor invokes Reset then eventually all processors will adjust their state (in some specific manner, depending on the application), and will restart their computation from the adjusted state, with the requirement that no processor restarts its computation until all have adjusted their state. In our case, when processor $u$ adjusts its state on Reset, it must set its estimate $n_u$ of the network size to $n_{max}^2$, where $n_{max}$ is the maximum estimate of all processors. $n_{max}$ becomes available to the processors via the Reset primitive. We discuss how to implement Reset at the end of this section.

The main reason for initiating a Reset is the discovery that there are multiple processors with the same ID. The detection of conflicting IDs is accomplished via the use of the random bit $b_u$. If two processors have the same name then in constant expected number of diffusions their tokens will have different random bits. When a processor $u$ receives a token tuple whose name contains the same ID but a different random bit as some other token tuple contained in $Tab_u$ then $u$ discovers the existence of processors with the same ID and enters the state *conflict*. When $u$ finds itself in state *conflict* at the end of a diffusion, it initiates a Reset. We can now describe in more detail the algorithm followed by each processor $u$.

In phase 1, $u$ begins by setting its ID, $id_u$, to an element chosen randomly from the set $\{1, 2, \ldots, n_u^2\}$. It then repeatedly diffuses a token tuple with the *name* and *info* fields as described above. At the end of each diffusion if $u$ finds itself in state *conflict* (i.e., has detected that there are two processors with the same ID as its own), it initiates a Reset. The diffusions of phase 1 are repeated until all token tuples returned at the end of a diffusion have the *diffusion1Done* component of the *info* field set to true. This marks the end of phase 1.

Given the properties of diffusion and the way the *diffusion1Done* component of the *info* field is manipulated, no processor completes phase 1 until all of them have done at least one diffusion. This is important because when processors determine their rank in the next phase, they must all do so on the basis of the same list of existing IDs (*IDLists*).

In phase 2, $u$ determines its rank, i.e., the number of different processor IDs less than or equal to its own. Processor $u$ obtains a list of the different IDs in the echo of the first diffusion of phase 1 (cf. field *IDList* in the *info* field). It is important to use the *IDList* of the *first* diffusion, because in this way all processors compute their ranks on the basis of the same list of IDs.[9] Processor $u$ then sets $id_u$ to its rank, sets its estimate $n_u$ to the number of elements in *IDList*, and proceeds to phase 3. Notice that memory adaptation occurs in this phase.

In phase 3, $u$ repeatedly diffuses a token tuple just as in phase 1 (except that the $isRank_u$ bit is now 1). At the end of each diffusion, if $u$ finds itself in state *conflict*, it initiates a Reset. In addition, $u$ checks if all token tuples returned from the diffusion have the *rankingDone* bit of the *info* field set to true. If so, then it knows that all processors have completed phase 2, and therefore the set of IDs in the *IDList* of the returned token tuples must be precisely the set $\{1, 2, \ldots, n_u\}$. If not, $u$ initiates a Reset. The reason for this check is that the adversary may start the system in a state where each processor thinks that has unique IDs which are not ranks. In this case there will never be a name conflict but, if this check is not performed, the system will never adapt and the protocol will not be memory-adaptive.

---

[9] The purpose of the first diffusion in phase 1 is to collect the list of IDs. All subsequent diffusions in that phase serve merely as a "synchronization barrier" to ensure that all processors have completed their first diffusion before proceeding to phase 2. Strictly speaking these diffusions do not need to carry around the *IDList* in the *info* fields. In fact, each processor can base its ranking on the *IDList* of any one of the phase 1 diffusions except the last one. (Since the last diffusion of phase 1 by one processor may overlap diffusions of other processors that are already in phase 2, the *IDList* collected in that diffusion may contain IDs that are ranks - as opposed to the original IDs of phase 1 - and can not be used to correctly calculate the processor's rank.) For specificity, we assume that each processor uses the *IDList* of its first diffusion of phase 1.

**Implementation of the Reset**

We now briefly discuss the Reset primitive. Reset primitives have been used extensively in network protocols (cf. [Fin79], [Awe88], [APV91] etc.). The usual implementation of Reset (cf. [APV91]) begins with the diffusion of a token with name "reset" (thus, all processors that initiate a Reset diffuse the same token). Each processor $u$ keeps track of the processor $v$ from which $u$ received the first reset token tuple; $v$ is $u$'s *parent*. When the diffusion is completed, the initiator of the Reset sends a message to its children to signal that they can adjust their state and restart "normal" computation. We say that a processor is in the *reset phase* in the period between the receipt of a reset token tuple and the subsequent receipt of the message signaling to restart its computation.

Unfortunately, this simple implementation is not adequate for our purposes since, when processors restart, they must know the maximum estimate $n_{max}$ of all processors for the size of the network. We accomplish this by modifying the previous implementation in the following manner: The "reset token" diffused by processor $u$ uses $n_u$ as its name. Now, consider a processor $v$ that receives a reset token tuple with name $n_u$.

- If $v$ is not in the reset phase and $n_u \geq n_v$ then $v$ sets $n_v := n_u$ and relays the reset token tuple; if $n_u < n_v$ then $v$ initiates its own Reset with $n_v$ as its reset token name.
- If $v$ is in the reset phase when it receives the reset token tuple and $n_u > n_v$ then $v$ sets $n_v := n_u$, relays the new reset token tuple to its neighbours as described before, and *changes its parent to $u$*; otherwise $v$ ignores the new reset token tuple.

By using these rules, the reset token (or tokens) with the maximum name (i.e., estimate) "dominates" all others and its tuples visit all processors. In this way, all processors become aware of the maximum estimate, which is what we wanted. When a processor $u$ finishes the Reset it squares its estimate ($n_u := n_u^2$) and starts in phase 1.


# 5   Sketch of Correctness Proof

One of the difficulties in proving that the protocol eventually stabilizes is that if it is started at a bad global state, "small" regions of the network may incorrectly determine that they constitute the entire network and perform memory adaptation (i.e., execute phase 2 of the protocol) prematurely. This seems like a dangerous situation because it could potentially cause processors to oscillate between a memory adaptation period, followed by a period of Resets to increase the estimate when it is discovered that the memory adaptation was done prematurely. If such oscillatory behavior is likely, stabilization may be prevented. Fortunately, the probability of this occuring repeatedly vanishes. Call a memory adaptation *global*, if it involves all processors in the network. Before we give the main lemma we need the following preliminary claims.

**Claim 4** *Each reset lasts at most $2d + n$ rounds.*

**Claim 5** *If two nodes $u$ and $v$ have the same ID then within at most $O(n)$ expected number of rounds some node of the network will order reset.*

**Claim 6** *After a reset the system within $4n$ rounds will either do global memory adaptation or it will do another reset.*

Note that $4n$ is the maximum number of rounds needed for the completion of phases 1 and 2.

**Lemma 1.** *If $n$ processors choose random IDs from the set $\{1, 2, \ldots N^2\}$ where $N \geq n$, then with probability greater than some constant all IDs will be unique.*

**Proof:** By elementary probability, the probability that all processors choose distinct IDs is

$$p = \frac{N^2 - 1}{N^2} \frac{N^2 - 2}{N^2} \frac{N^2 - 3}{N^2} \cdots \frac{N^2 - n + 1}{N^2} \geq \left(\frac{N^2 - N + 1}{N^2}\right)^{N-1}.$$

Therefore $p \geq ((N^2 - N)/N^2)^N \geq (1 - 1/N)^N \to e^{-1}$ as $N \to \infty$. In the worst case where $N = 2$, $p \geq \frac{1}{4}$. $\square$

**Lemma 2.** *If after a Reset there exist $n' < n$ different IDs in the network then a Reset will be performed before global memory adaptation with probability $\geq 1 - 2^{n' - n}$.*

**Proof:** (sketch) Partition the set of processors into equivalence classes, where two processors are in the same class iff they have the same ID. Let $S_1, S_2, \ldots, S_{n'}$ be the equivalence classes. The probability that all processors in $S_i$ choose the same random bit for their diffusion is $2^{1 - |S_i|}$. Thus, the probability that name conflict among the processors in $S_i$ is *not* detected by the end of phase 2 is $\leq 2^{1 - |S_i|}$. Therefore, the probability that name conflict among processors in *all* equivalence classes is not detected by the end of phase 2 is $\leq \Pi_{i=1}^{n'} 2^{1 - |S_i|} = 2^{n' - n}$.

Consequently, the probability that name conflict *is* detected (and hence Reset is initiated) by the end of phase 2 (and hence before memory adaptation) is $\geq 1 - 2^{n' - n}$. $\square$

Say that a global state is *legal* if all processors have distinct IDs. Informally speaking, if processors have small estimates for the size of the network then the global state is bad: The processors will choose their IDs from small domains and many will pick the same ID and so with high probability the global state will be illegal. The previous lemma then implies that the probability of staying in a bad state forever is small: If the state is "very" illegal; i.e., there are few distinct IDs relative to the size of the network ($n' \ll n$), then Reset will occur with high probability, and this will improve the state, since processors will increase their estimates. If, on the other hand, the state is "almost" legal, i.e., there are lots of distinct IDs relative to the size of the network ($n' \approx n$), then global memory adaptation has a better chance of occurring before a Reset, and such premature memory adaptation will cause the global state to regress. However, precisely because there are lots of distinct IDs, the resulting global state, although worse, will still remain close to being legal. This, intuitively, is the reason why oscillations of the type described above are avoided.

**Lemma 3.** *Let $\Delta$ be the maximum degree of the network. Starting from any state, the probability that the system will stabilize in $O\big(n(1 + \log\log n - \log\log(\Delta + 1))\big)$ rounds is greater than a constant that does not depend on the system.*

**Proof:** (sketch) We can assume that the maximum estimate is at least $\Delta + 1$ because otherwise after one reset it will be so. Consider the following experiment: resets occur in a row without total memory adaptation until each processor has a unique name. When the estimate of each processor exceeds $n$ then with high probability the processors will choose distinct IDs (lemma 1). The maximum number of consecutive resets required for the estimate of each node to exceed $n$ is bounded by $r = \log\log n - \log\log(\Delta + 1)$ because the estimate is squared each time.

We distinguish between two stages in the experiment. Stage 1, lasts as long as the maximum estimate for the size of the network is $\leq t = n^{1/2} - n^{1/3}$. Stage 2 starts after the estimate becomes larger than $t$ and ends when the processors choose unique IDs. In stage 1, after each reset the number of different names $n'$ can not be larger than $t^2$. By Lemma 2, the probability of a reset before global memory adaptation in this stage is at least $p = 1 - 2^{-n^{5/6}}$.

The probability that enough resets without total memory adaptation occur in a row until the system goes to stage 2 is at least $p^r$ which after some manipulation can be shown to tend to $e^{-r2^{-n^{5/6}}}$, which converges to 1 as $n \to \infty$. By Claims 4, 5 and 6 we conclude that this period lasts at most $O(n \cdot (1 + r))$ rounds. So we proved that with probability that tends to 1 the system will reach stage 2 in at most $O(n \cdot (1 + r))$ rounds. After reaching stage 2, if the processors have unique IDs then we are done. Otherwise by Lemma 2 with probability at least $1 - 2^{-1}$ a reset will be ordered within $4n$ number of rounds and the processors will have an estimate of the graph of order $\Omega(n)$. By Lemma 1 this implies that with probability greater than some constant all processors have distinct IDs. Hence with probability greater than some constant that does not depend on the network the system will reach a legal state after at most $O(n \cdot (1 + r))$ rounds. $\square$

The following theorem summarizes our main result and its proof follows from the previous lemma.

**Theorem 4.** *The expected number of rounds until the system stabilizes is $O\big(n(1 + \log\log n - \log\log(\Delta + 1))\big)$. After stabilization each processor uses at most $O(n^2 \log n)$ bits. The intermediate space used by each processor until stabilization is expected to be the maximum of the initial space and twice the space* *used after stabilization.*[10]

# 6 Conclusions

We presented a general token-based diffusion protocol that yields interesting self-stabilizing protocols for many problems. We considered two models: the model where each processor knows nothing about the network ($\mathcal{M}_\emptyset$), and the model where the processors have some bounds on the diameter and the size of the network ($\mathcal{M}_{D,N}$). However, our results can be used in other "intermediate" models as well such as the model $\mathcal{M}_N$, where processors know $N \geq n$ but do not know $D \geq d$. In this extended abstract we presented only the protocols for the Unique Naming problem but similar protocols work for a large variety of other problems including interactive tasks such as Token Management. For the $\mathcal{M}_\emptyset$ model we presented the first memory adaptive protocol. This protocol stabilizes within $O(n \log \log n)$ expected number of rounds and after stabilization it uses space of $O(n^2 \log n)$ bits, where $n$ is the actual size of the network.

A similar but simpler protocol works for the $\mathcal{M}_{D,N}$ model. The main differences are:

- Since a bound $D$ is known each diffusion, including the "resets", take time $O(\min\{n, D\})$.
- Since $N$ is a known bound on $n$, after each conflict all the processors choose new names from the set $\{1, 2, \ldots, N^2\}$, and hence after each reset there is a constant probability that all the names will be unique.

The complete description is postponed for the full version where we prove the following.

**Theorem 5.** *The above protocol for UN in $\mathcal{M}_{D,N}$ stabilizes within $O(\min\{n, D\})$ expected number of rounds.*

Some problems that remain open deserve further consideration. The first and most tantalizing is whether there exists a protocol for the model $\mathcal{M}_N$ (a bound on $n$ is known) or even the $\mathcal{M}_{D,N}$ model with *minimum* stabilization time of order $d$, where $d$ is the unknown actual diameter of the network. Another problem is that, although our protocols are fast, their message complexity is high ($O(n \log N)$ bits). Can this be reduced while keeping the protocols fast? Is it possible to develop memory adaptive protocols by using simpler techniques than the ones used in this paper?

---

[10] If processors increase their estimate by setting it to $2^{n_{max}}$ (instead of $n_{max}^2$) after each Reset, the double logarithms in the time bound become iterated logarithms, but the expected intermediate space complexity becomes the maximum of the initial space and $n$ times the space after stabilization.

# Acknowledgments

We are grateful to Jan Pachl for helpful discussions. We also wish to thank Boaz Pat-Shamir and the anonymous referees for their comments.

# References

[AB89]      Y. Afek and G.M. Brown. Self-Stabilization of the Alternating-Bit Protocol. *IEEE Proc. on Reliable Distr. Systems*, pages 80–83, 1989.

[ABD⁺87]   H. Attiya, A. Bar-Noy, D. Dolev, D. Koller, D. Peleg, and R. Reischuk. Achievable cases in an asynchronous environment. In *FOCS*, pages 337–346, 1987.

[AE91]      E. Anagnostou and R. El-Yaniv. More on the Power of Random Walks: Uniform, Bounded Self-Stabilizing Protocols. In *Distributed Algorithms, 5th IWDAG*, pages 31–51, Delphi, Greece, October, 1991. Lecture Notes in Computer Science, 579 Springer-Verlag.

[AFL83]     E. Arjomandi, M. Fisher, and N. Lynch. Efficiency of Synchronous Versus Asynchronous Distributed Systems. *Journal of the ACM*, 30 (3):449–456, 1983.

[AG90]      A. Arora and M. Gouda. Distributed Reset (Extended Abstract). In *Tenth Conference on FSTCS*, pages 316–329, Bangalore, India, 1990.

[AKP91]     B. Awerbuch, S. Kutten, and D. Peleg. Efficient Deadlock-Free Routing. In *10th PODC*, pages 177–188, 1991.

[AKY90]     Y. Afek, S. Kutten, and M. Yung. Memory-Efficient Self Stabilizing Protocols for General Networks. In *4th IWDAG*, pages 15–28, Bari, Italy, September, 1990.

[APV91]     B. Awerbuch, B. Patt-Shamir, and G. Varghese. Self-Stabilization by Local Checking and Correction. In *32nd FOCS*, October, 1991.

[AS88]      B. Awerbuch and M. Sipser. Dynamic Networks are as fast as static networks. In *29th FOCS*, pages 206–219, 1988.

[AV91]      B. Awerbuch and G. Varghese. Distributed Program Checking: a Paradigm for Building Self-Stabilizing Distributed Protocols. In *32nd FOCS*, October, 1991.

[Awe88]     B. Awerbuch. On the effects of feedback in dynamic network protocols. In *29th FOCS*, pages 231–245, 1988.

[BD89]      A. Bar-Noy and D. Dolev. Shared-Memory vs. Message-Passing in an Asynchronous Distributed Environment. In *Proc. of the 8th ACM Symposium on Principles of Distributed Computing*, pages 307–318, 1989.

[BGW89]     G. Brown, M. Gouda, and C. Wu. Token Systems that Self-Stabilize. *IEEE Transactions on Computers*, 38, 6:845–852, 1989.

[BP89]      L. E. Burns and J. Pachl. Uniform Self-Stabilizing Rings. *ACM Transactions on Programming Languages and Systems*, 11, 2:330–344, 1989.

[Dij74]     E. W. Dijkstra. Self-stabilizing systems in spite of distributed control. *Comm. of the ACM*, 17(11):643–644, 1974.

[DIM90]     S. Dolev, A Israeli, and S. Moran. Self Stabilization of Dynamic Systems Assuming Only Read/Write Atomicity. In *Proc. of the 9th ACM Symposium on Principles of Distributed Computing*, pages 103–117, Quebec City, Canada, 1990.

[DIM91]   S. Dolev, A. Israeli, and S. Moran.   Uniform Dynamic Self-Stabilizing Leader Election. In *5th IWDAG*, Delphi, Greece, October, 1991.

[DS79]    E. W. Dijkstra and C. S. Scholten. Termination detection for diffusing computations. *IPL*, 11(1):1–4, 1979.

[Fin79]   S. G. Finn. Resynch Procedures and a Fail-Safe Network Protocol. *IEEE Transactions on Communications*, 27(6):840–845, 1979.

[IJ90]    A. Israeli and M. Jalfon. Token Management Schemes and Random Walks Yield Self Stabilizing Mutual Exclusion. In *Proc. of the 9th ACM Symposium on Principles of Distributed Computing*, pages 119–131, 1990.

[KP90]    S. Katz and K. J. Perry. Self-stabiling Extensions for Message-passing Systems. In *Proc. of the 9th ACM Symp. on Principles of Distr. Computing*, pages 91–101, Quebec City, Canada, 1990.

[Lam86a]  L. Lamport. On interprocess communication. Part I: Basic Formalism. *Distributed Computing*, 1:77–85, 1986.

[Lam86b]  L. Lamport. On interprocess communication. Part II: Algorithms. *Distributed Computing*, 1:86–101, 1986.

[SG89]    J. M. Spinelli and R. G. Gallager.   Broadcasting topology information in computer networks.   *IEEE Transactions on Communications*, COM-37(5):468–474, 1989.

# Optimal Early Stopping in Distributed Consensus

(Extended Abstract)

Piotr Berman[1] Juan A. Garay[2,3] Kenneth J. Perry[3]

[1] Department of Computer Science
The Pennsylvania State University
University Park, PA 16802, USA
[2] Dept. of Applied Math and Computer Science
The Weizmann Institute of Science
Rehovot, 76100 Israel
[3] IBM T.J. Watson Research Center
P.O. Box 704
Yorktown Heights, NY 10598, USA

**Abstract.** The *Distributed Consensus* problem involves $n$ processors each of which holds an initial binary value. At most $t$ processors may be faulty and ignore any protocol (even behaving maliciously), yet it is required that the non-faulty processors eventually agree on a value that was initially held by one of them. This paper presents consensus protocols that tolerate arbitrary faults, are *early-stopping* (i.e., run for a number of rounds proportional to the number of faults $f$ that actually occur during their execution), and are optimal in various measures.

Our first contribution is an early-stopping consensus protocol that is simultaneously optimal in round complexity (i.e., $min(t+1, f+2)$ rounds) and number of processors (i.e., $n > 3t$). This settles a long-standing open question [DRS, 1982]. These bounds were not known to be attainable even with the use of authentication. Since consensus is not attainable with $n \leq 3t$ we provide a definitive answer to the problem of early-stopping consensus. Previous protocols for this problem that achieved round optimality required $n = \Omega(t^2)$ [C, DRS], $n > 6t$ [MW] and $n > 4t$ [BGP]. Instrumental in achieving this result is the new *safe message reconstruction* technique, which we expect to be of broader applicability. The previous protocol is round- and processor-optimal, but not efficient. Our second contribution is a pair of optimal early-stopping consensus protocols that use messages of *constant* size. No previously existing early-stopping protocol, whether exactly or only asymptotically optimal in some measures, has used messages of constant size. The only other existing early-stopping protocol with constant-sized messages requires $n = \Omega(t^2)$ [C].

Finally, we indicate how to extend one of the previous protocols to be optimal in total bit (and message) complexity and number of processors. This is the first protocol that is both optimal in these measures and early-stopping.

# 1 Introduction and Problem Statement

There are many situations in the management of distributed systems with one common characteristic: a collection of processors must coordinate a decision. This problem becomes non-trivial when some of the processors are faulty and cannot be relied upon to faithfully obey a protocol. It is reasonable to at least demand that, regardless of the behavior of the faulty processors, correct processors can reach an agreement consistent with the initial value of a correct processor. The *Distributed Consensus* problem (and its twin, *Byzantine Agreement*) [LSP] provides an abstract setting in which methods for tolerating faults may be explored and perhaps influence practical designs. The problem can be formally stated as follows.

We are given a set of processors $P$ of which some unknown subset $T$, $\#T \leq t$, are *faulty* and may exhibit arbitrary (*Byzantine*) behavior. Processors from $P-T$ are called *correct*. Every processor is given an initial value, 0 or 1. After the execution of the protocol, the final values of the correct processors have to satisfy the following two conditions, regardless of the behavior of the faulty processors:

- *Agreement*: they are all equal.
- *Validity*: they are all equal to the initial value, if the latter is unique.

We use the standard model of a synchronous network of processors numbered from 1 to $n$. The computation performed by the network evolves as a series of *rounds*, during which the processors send messages, receive them and perform local computations according to the protocol.

There already exist many protocols for this problem because there are several quality parameters that can be optimized: the total number of processors $n$ (as a function of $t$), the number of rounds of communication $r$, and the communication complexity given by, e.g., the maximal message size $m$. Typically, some parameters are optimized to the detriment of the others, but there is no proof that all parameters cannot be made optimal simultaneously.

A lower bound of $t + 1$ rounds of communication has been established for this problem even if no failures actually occur [DS]. Thus, overcoming potential faults is expensive, even though, in practice, they are rarely observed. This has led others to explore ways in which the price of fault tolerance may be reduced. Hadzilacos and Halpern [HH] have recently concentrated on runs that are failure-free; they present protocols with optimal number of messages for these runs. Dolev, Reischuk, and Strong [DRS] are concerned with protocols that take a number of rounds proportional to $f$, the number of failures that actually occur, rather than $t$, the worst-case number of failures. By permitting processors to stop at different times (instead of simultaneously) they show that *early-stopping* protocols are possible and demonstrate a lower bound of $min(f+2, t+1)$ rounds. Randomization is another way of circumventing the $t + 1$ lower bound on round complexity. In this setting, protocols that run for an expected constant number of rounds are possible. Feldman and Micali [FM], in particular, have a randomized consensus protocol that achieves optimal number of processors and polynomial message size.

The contributions of this paper are deterministic early-stopping consensus protocols that are optimal in various measures. Our first contribution is the first consensus protocol to simultaneously achieve optimal early stopping (i.e., $r = min(t+1, f+2)$) and optimal number of processors (i.e., $n > 3t$ [LSP]). This settles a question posed by Dolev *et al.* in 1982 [DRS]. These (non-authenticated) bounds were not known to be attainable even when the faulty processors are restricted not to corrupt a given authentication scheme.[4] Previous protocols with optimal early stopping were sub-optimal in processors, namely, they required $n = O(t^2)$ [C, DRS], $n > 6t$ [MW] and $n > 4t$ [BGP]. Instrumental in achieving this result is the new *safe message reconstruction* technique, which we expect to be of broader applicability.

Our protocol is optimal in number of processors and number of rounds, but not in message size. Our second contribution is a pair of early-stopping consensus protocols that use messages of *constant* size. One of our protocols uses single-bit messages, is optimal in the number of processors, and asymptotically optimal in the number of rounds. No other early-stopping protocol [BGP, DRS, TPS, W], whether exactly or only asymptotically optimal in some measures, has used messages of constant size. To the best of our knowledge, the only other existing early-stopping protocol with constant-sized messages is also sub-optimal in processors, i.e., it requires $n = O(t^2)$ [C].

Finally, we present an early-stopping consensus protocol that is asymptotically optimal in the total number of bits transfered ($O(nt)$ [DR]) and the number of processors. This is the first protocol that is both optimal in these measures and early-stopping. A consensus protocol with optimal bit complexity is, *a fortiori*, optimal with respect to message complexity. Hadzilacos and Halpern have recently achieved consensus with (exact) message optimality, but only in the case of runs that are *failure-free* [HH]. The rationale is that since failures are hopefully rare, optimality in the usual case is to be emphasized. However, in case (even few) failures do occur, their solution requires either a large round overhead (if asymptotical message optimality is to be maintained), or a loss of $\Omega(n)$ in message complexity (if early termination is important). The consensus protocol we present here achieves message optimality in all runs, at the expense of a reasonably small constant and is early-stopping.

The remainder of the paper is organized as follows. In Section 2 we present the early-stopping consensus protocol that is optimal in both the number of processors and the number of rounds. In Section 3 we present the protocols that use messages of constant size, while in Section 4 we indicate how optimal bit (and message) complexity can be achieved, without sacrificing the early stopping property. Sections 3 and 4 use completely different techniques from those of Section 2, thus admitting independent readings.

---

[4] For the more restricted failure classes (crash, omission), the round and the corresponding processor lower bounds ($n > t + 1$) are known to be simultaneously attainable ([LF], [PT], respectively).

# 2 Early Stopping in the Minimum Number of Rounds

The early-stopping consensus protocol of this section is presented as the result of a sequence of transformations to the *Exponential Information Gathering (EIG)* protocol (a refinement of the original agreement protocol of Lamport *et al.* [LSP] due to Bar-Noy *et al.* [BDDS]). First we introduce the notion of *safe decisions* and the rules to obtain them. These rules by themselves allow us to re-derive a protocol first presented by Waarts [W] which omits certain messages of *EIG* and reduces the number of rounds to $min(t + 1, f + 3)$. Then we introduce the notion of *safe message reconstruction*, and show that a correct processor may stop sending messages after it decides because other correct processors can safely infer the omitted messages. The subtle part is that although the outcome of safe message reconstruction does not necessarily agree with the suppressed messages, it nevertheless leads to the same final decision. The safe decision rules and safe message reconstruction technique, when combined with the *EIG* protocol, allow us to prove our first result: an early-stopping consensus protocol that is optimal in both the number of processors and the number of rounds, i.e., $r = min(t + 1, f + 2)$.

In this section we assume that $n = 2p + t - 1$, where $p > t$ (equivalently, $n > 3t$ and $n - t$ is odd). We use $|\sigma|$ to denote the length of string $\sigma$.

## 2.1 EIG Overview

We first present a short synopsis of protocol $EIG$. Processors build trees of the following form: the set of nodes consists of sequences from $P^*$ without repetitions, and of length at most $t + 1$; the root is $\lambda$ (the empty sequence); the children of $\sigma$, $EXT(\sigma)$, are nodes of the form $\sigma j$. In each tree, a node $\sigma$ has a *value* denoted $Val(\sigma)$. Each correct processor initializes a one-node tree consisting of $\lambda$ and sets $Val(\lambda)$ to its initial value. Then, for rounds $0, 1, \cdots, t$ correct processor $i$ applies the following two primitives to all leaves of its tree:

- Send($\sigma$): send $Val(\sigma)$ to all processors (provided $i$ does not appear in $\sigma$).
- Receive($\sigma, j$): upon receiving $v$ when $j$ executes Send($\sigma$), create node $\sigma j$ and set $Val(\sigma j) = v$.

Once the tree is constructed, the processors use the rules given below to compute predicates $Dec(\sigma, v)$ and $PDec(\sigma, v)$ for each node $\sigma$ and $v \in \{0,1\}$ (we read $Dec(\sigma, v)$ ($PDec(\sigma, v)$) as "value $v$ is the decision (a partial decision) for $\sigma$"):

$$PDec(\sigma, v) \equiv \begin{cases} Val(\sigma) = v & \text{if } \sigma \text{ is a leaf,} \\ \#\{\tau \in EXT(\sigma) : Dec(\tau, v)\} \geq p & \text{otherwise;} \end{cases}$$

$$Dec(\sigma, v) \equiv PDec(\sigma, v) \land \neg PDec(\sigma, \overline{v}).$$

The final value for the consensus problem is 1 iff $Dec(\lambda, 1)$. Note that $Dec(\sigma, v)$ implies $\neg Dec(\sigma, \overline{v})$, although it is possible that $\neg Dec(\sigma, 0) \land \neg Dec(\sigma, 1)$ holds.

**Definition 1.** A predicate $\pi$ at node $\sigma$ is *common* iff $\pi$ is true at $\sigma$ in the tree of every correct processor. A node $\sigma$ is common iff either $\neg Dec(\sigma, 0) \wedge \neg Dec(\sigma, 1)$ is common, or for some $v$, $Dec(\sigma, v)$ is common.

The following two lemmas express the correctness of $EIG$ in terms useful for our further discussion. Lemma 2 implies the Validity condition, while Lemma 3 implies Agreement.

**Lemma 2.** *Assume that either*

- $\sigma = \lambda$ *and the initial value of every correct processor is* $v$, *or*
- $\sigma = \tau i$, *in* $i$'s *tree* $Val(\tau) = v$ *and* $i$ *executes* $Send(\tau)$ *correctly.*

*Then* $Dec(\sigma, v)$ *is common.*

The proof follows directly from the definition by induction on $|\sigma|$; the base case is $|\sigma| = t$ and the induction parameter is decreasing.

**Lemma 3.** *The root of the EIG tree,* $\lambda$, *is common.*

*Proof.* (Sketch) By an induction similar to the one in the previous lemma, we prove that if a common node exists on every path from $\sigma$ to a leaf, then $\sigma$ is common. Note that every leaf has an ancestor of the form $\sigma i$, where $i$ is correct and, as a consequence of Lemma 2, node $\sigma i$ is common. □

## 2.2 Safe Rules for Early Stopping

In the protocols presented later in this section the values of predicates are actually computed differently and *not always consistently* with $EIG$. The following definition and lemmas provide justification for such deviations. Ideally, every processor would reach the same decision as in $EIG$ for every node. However, we will show that it suffices to reach *safe* decisions for a well-defined class of nodes.

**Definition 4.** A predicate $\pi$ is *safe* if either

- $\pi$ is common, or
- $\pi$ refers to a node $\sigma \notin T^*(P - T)^*$, or
- $\pi$ is of the form $Dec(\sigma j, v)$ and the predicates $PDec(\sigma, v)$ and $PDec(\sigma j, v)$ are both common.

Note that the agreement value is 1 iff $Dec(\lambda, 1)$ is safe (i.e., iff $Dec(\lambda, 1)$ is common).

We now present a set of *Early Stopping Rules* that enable a processor to determine when "partial-decision" and "decision" predicates are safe. These rules can be used in a number of ways:

- In $EIG$, the rules are only used to determine what to decide, i.e., which "decision" predicate is safe for the root.

- In *Early-Stopping EIG* (the protocol of Theorem 8) rules 1-7 are additionally used to prevent the building of the entire tree, so that a process can stop early. That is, when "decision" predicates for a node are safe there is no need to continue determining the nodes descendants.
- Our contribution is to use *knowledge* about "decision" and "partial-decision" predicates in order to reason about what the descendants of a node *should be* without actually having to receive messages relating to them. We call this technique *safe message reconstruction*, and describe it in subsection 2.3. We call the resulting protocol *Safe EIG*.

The first set of rules is applied by each processor in order to calculate when "partial-decision" predicates are safe.

1. If in the tree of a correct processor $\sigma$ is created in round $t$ and $Val(\sigma) = v$, then $PDec(\sigma, v)$ and $\neg PDec(\sigma, \overline{v})$ are safe.
2. If in the tree of a correct processor $\#\{\tau \in EXT(\sigma) : Val(\tau) = v\} \geq p + t - |\sigma|$, then $PDec(\sigma, v)$ is safe.
3. If in the tree of a correct processor $\#\{\tau \in EXT(\sigma) : Val(\tau) = v\} \geq p + 2 \cdot (t - |\sigma|)$, then $PDec(\sigma, v)$ and $\neg PDec(\sigma, \overline{v})$ are safe.
4. If $\#\{\tau \in EXT(\sigma) : Dec(\tau, v) \text{ is safe }\} \geq p$, then $PDec(\sigma, v)$ is safe.
5. If $\#\{\tau \in EXT(\sigma) : PDec(\tau, \overline{v}) \text{ is safe }\} \geq p + t - |\sigma|$, then $\neg PDec(\sigma, v)$ is safe.

The next set of rules allows a processor to calculate when "decision" predicates are safe, given safe "partial-decision" predicates.

6. If $PDec(\sigma, v)$ and $\neg PDec(\sigma, \overline{v})$ are safe, then $Dec(\sigma, v)$ is safe.
7. If $PDec(\sigma, v)$ and $PDec(\sigma, \overline{v})$ are safe, then $\neg Dec(\sigma, v)$ and $\neg Dec(\sigma, \overline{v})$ are safe.
8. If $PDec(\sigma, v)$ and $PDec(\sigma j, v)$ are safe, then $Dec(\sigma j, v)$ is safe.

When a "decision" predicate is determined to be true for a node $\sigma$ of processor $i$'s tree, we say that $i$ *decides* on $\sigma$. We say that $i$ *decides promptly* on $\sigma$ whenever it is able to decide through the application of rules (3) and (6).

The proof that the rules are sound is omitted from the abstract but follows from an easy induction and the following case analysis: If $\sigma \notin T^*(P - T)^*$ the claim is vacuous—any predicate is safe; if $\sigma \in T^*(P - T)^+$ then we can apply Lemma 2; lastly, if $\sigma \in T^*$, then at most $t - |\sigma|$ elements of $EXT(\sigma)$ store values received from faulty processors.

The following example illustrates how rules and decisions work.

*Example 1.* We illustrate how "prompt decisions" are reached; processors reach "decisions" in a similar manner. Assume $t = 2$ (hence $p = 3$) and $n = 7$. Figure 1 shows processor 2's tree after the second round (recall that since $r = t + 1$, the depth of the final *EIG* tree in this case equals 3). In the example, processor $4 \in P - T$ and $6, 7 \in T$. Given that 5 of the children of node 4 store the same value (0), and $p + 2 \cdot (t - |\sigma|) = 5$, for $|\sigma| = |4| = 1$, rule 3 "fires." This in turn makes rule 6 to fire, allowing processor 2 to decide promptly that 0 is a safe value for node 4. We remark that, despite processor 2 already having decided on node 4, traditional thinking still requires the processor to continue to report values (in this case, regarding node 4's children), since those values might be needed by other correct processors in order to reach their own decisions. In subsection 2.3 we show how this can be avoided.

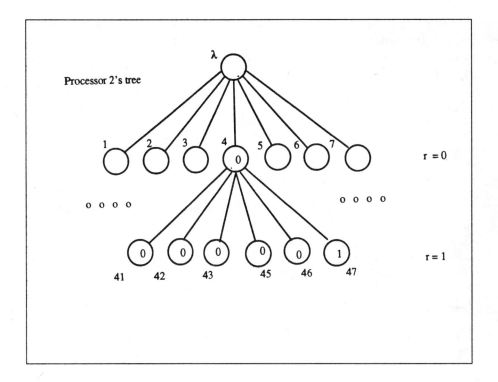

**Fig. 1.** How early stopping rules and decisions work.

When discussing the conclusions that may be derived from the above Early Stopping Rules, we use notation from the theory of knowledge in distributed systems [HM]. We read $K_i^r \phi$ as "after receiving round $r$'s messages processor $i$ knows fact $\phi$." We will also use the "everybody knows" operator $E^r \phi \equiv \bigwedge_{i \in P-T} K_i^r \phi$. We will drop $i$ and $r$ when obvious from the context. It is assumed that the Early Stopping Rules are applied by all the correct processors, and that all their knowledge is the one that may be derived by applying these rules. We also assume that processors do not forget, i.e. $K_i^r \phi$ implies $K_i^{r+1} \phi$. A statement of the form $\neg K_i^r \phi$ means that $i$ cannot deduce $\phi$ by round $r$ by applying the rules.

We begin by stating some properties about the level of knowledge concerning safe predicates. The next two lemmas, whose proofs are omitted from the abstract, are analagous to Lemmas 2 and 3 and show that the Early Stopping Rules are sufficient to infer the consensus value.

**Lemma 5.** *Assume that processor $i$ in round $r$ executes $Send(\sigma)$ correctly, and in its tree $Val(\sigma) = v$. Then $E^{r+2}[Dec(\sigma i, v)$ is safe].*

**Lemma 6.** *Assume that after round $r$ processor $i$ has decided on an ancestor of every leaf node. Then $i$ can also decide on $\lambda$.*

Let $f$ denote the number of processors that actually fail and let the initial round of the protocol be numbered 0. Now we can show that by round $f + 1$ all correct processors decide on $\lambda$. This happens because every leaf has an ancestor in $T^*(P - T)$. If a node of this form is created before round $f$, then all correct processors decide on it before round $f + 2$; if it is created at round $f$, then all of its children are created by correct processors and consequently all correct processors decide on it promptly in round $f + 1$.

**Lemma 7.** *Let $i \in P - T$ and $\sigma \in T^*(P - T)^*$. Then $K_i^r[Dec(\sigma, v)$ is safe] implies $E^{r+2}[Dec(\sigma, v)$ is safe]. Moreover, if $i$ decides promptly on $\sigma$ in round $r$, then $E^{r+1}[Dec(\sigma, v)$ is safe].*

The above lemma shows that processors not only can decide early, but that they may stop sending messages early. This justifies *Early-Stopping EIG*, a modified *EIG* protocol that enables early stopping by omitting the sending of messages as follows: a processor does not execute $Send(\sigma\tau)$, for any $\tau$, if it has decided on $\sigma$ before the previous round, or if it has decided promptly on $\sigma$ in the previous round. "Decided" here means according to Early Stopping Rules (1-7). This allows us to prove the following theorem, originally due to Waarts [W]:

**Theorem 8.** Early-Stopping EIG *solves the Distributed Consensus problem using $n > 3t$ processors and $min(t + 1, f + 3)$ communication rounds.*

## 2.3 Optimal Early Stopping

Using a different formalism and only Early Stopping Rules (1-7), we have thus far described and proved correct a version of $EIG$ that stops in $min(t+1, f+3)$. Now the task is to show that starting from round $f + 2$ the correct processors may stop sending messages, so that only rounds 0 to $f + 1$ are needed. Achieving this with the optimal number of processors settles a long-standing open question [DRS].

As shown above, processors decide on $\lambda$ by round $f + 1$ at the latest; however this is not yet a sufficient reason to stop sending messages. Existing early-stopping protocols operate on the principle that if a correct processor knows that no other correct processor will read its message, it does not send it. In other words, a processor does not send any messages if it knows that all correct processors know the consensus value. However, it can be shown that when $n < 4t$ this level of knowledge cannot be assured by round $f + 1$.

One can offer a different principle: a processor need not send a message if other processors can infer it from its silence. For example, if processor $i$ does not send anything in round 1, it means that $i$ decided on $\lambda$ promptly; this may happen only if all messages $i$ received in round 0 were the same. In general, such a complete reconstruction is not possible if the silence always immediately follows the round in which $i$ decided on $\lambda$. However, we will show that while an *accurate* reconstruction is not possible, a *safe* reconstruction is.

Given some rules for message reconstruction, silence is equivalent to sending a message which is an alteration of a message in the $EIG$ protocol. Such an alteration may *affect* some nodes in the sense that some correct processors may infer different predicates concerning these nodes. We say that an alteration of a message is *safe* if $\lambda$ is not affected. When a processor $i$ decides not to send some values and another processor $j$ computes the safe alterations of these values, we say that $j$ *safely reconstructs* these values.

We will use a very simple principle for not sending messages: processor $i$ does not execute Send($\sigma\tau$) iff it already decided on $\sigma$. Other processors can proceed in three stages: reconstructing $\sigma$, reconstructing $i$'s decision on $\sigma$, and reconstructing $i$'s messages on the descendants of $\sigma$.

The reconstruction of $\sigma$ is easy: first, all descendants of $\sigma$ are omitted from the message; second, either $\sigma = \lambda$, or $\sigma$ has a sibling with a descendant for which $i$ did execute a Send (this is true because when a processor decides on all the children of a node, then it also decides on the node itself).

The reconstruction of decisions uses the following definitions. Let us fix one correct processor, say $j$, and let $U$ be the set of nodes for which processor $i$ executed Send before round $r$.

**Definition 9.** For every $\tau \in U$
$$CDec(i, \tau, v) \equiv \neg K_j^{r-1}[\neg K_i^{r-1}[Dec(\tau, v) \text{ is safe}]];$$
$$CPDec(i, \tau, v) \equiv \neg K_j^{r-1}[\neg K_i^{r-1}[PDec(\tau, v) \text{ is safe}]].$$

In other words, $CDec(i, \tau, v)$ (resp., $CPDec(i, \tau, v)$) means that the assertion "$Dec(\tau, v)$ (resp., $PDec(\tau, v)$) may be inferred by $i$ before round $r$" is consistent with the messages received by $j$ before round $r$.

**Lemma 10.** $CDec(i, \tau, v)$ *implies* $\neg CPDec(i, \tau, \overline{v})$ *for every* $\tau \in U$, $v = 0, 1$.

The proof of this lemma follows by induction on the depth of the subtree of $U$ rooted by $\tau$. The basis is proved by the analysis of prompt decisions, the inductive case by the analysis of the remaining safe rules. Rule (8) is needed in one of the cases.

The general principle for reconstructing a message is also simple: the reconstructed values will "maximally help" to reach the same decision on $\sigma$ as $i$ did. If $i$ is faulty, then the reconstruction does not matter since a faulty processor is allowed to send anything. If $i$ is correct, then the affected nodes must be proper descendants of $\sigma$, which makes the reconstruction safe. The implementation of this principle is described in the following lemma.

**Lemma 11.** *Processor $j$ can safely reconstruct the values of Send's that $i$ did not execute in round $r$.*

*Proof.* (Sketch) First, $j$ finds those $\sigma$'s which had to be decided on by $i$. Then for each such $\sigma$, processor $j$ finds which of the following three cases holds: $CDec(i, \sigma, 0)$, $CDec(i, \sigma, 1)$ or $CPDec(i, \sigma, 0) \wedge CPDec(i, \sigma, 1)$; by Lemma 10 these cases are mutually exclusive. The safe reconstruction is as follows: in the first case, messages on all descendants of $\sigma$ are reconstructed to 0; the second case is analogous. In the third case we can show that a reconstruction is safe if it gives $v$ to a node of the form $\sigma k \tau$ whenever $CDec(i, \sigma k, v)$ is true. The reconstruction of the messages for the descendants of any $\sigma$ not covered by this rule is irrelevant. □

The following example illustrates the technique.

*Example 2.* Assume the same scenario as in Example 1 ($t = 2$, $p = 3$, $n = 7$). Figure 2(a) shows processor 2's tree after the third (and last) round, during which no messages from processor 5 are received regarding node 4's children. We note again that we can assume that processor 5 is non-faulty. Processor 2 is able to establish $CDec(5, 4, 0)$ by reasoning as follows. There are two cases:

1. $4 \in P - T$. Since the number of "reported" 0's for node 4 is four, processor 5 must have decided promptly on 0, since it is not possible for processor 5's tree to have five 1's reported for 4.
2. $4 \in T$. Since $t \leq 2$, there remains at most one other faulty processor, which means there can be at most one different value in the children of node 4 in processor 5's tree. This in turn implies that 5 must have received at least five 0's to be able to decide promptly.

Processor 2 then proceeds (Lemma 11) to reconstruct missing messages from processor 5 on all descendants of node 4 to 0 (see Figure 2(b)). We note that in the process some values of nodes might be affected (e.g., nodes 465 and 475 in Figure 2(b)), but this deviation won't propagate above the node under consideration (node 4 in the example).

For space considerations, the previous example illustrated the simplest case of message reconstruction originating from a prompt decision (processor 5's). We remark that the other cases—non prompt decision, "neutral" decision—are more involved, but the case analyses in the reconstruction of messages and decisions are similar and mostly reduce. We leave the details for the full version of the paper.

This justifies the protocol we call *Safe EIG*, similar to *EIG* except for the following:

- A processor executes Send($\sigma \tau$), for any $\tau$, iff it has not decided on $\sigma$ ("decided" here means derivable from Early Stopping Rules (1-8)), and
- missing messages that are needed are reconstructed according to the safe reconstruction technique of Lemma 11.

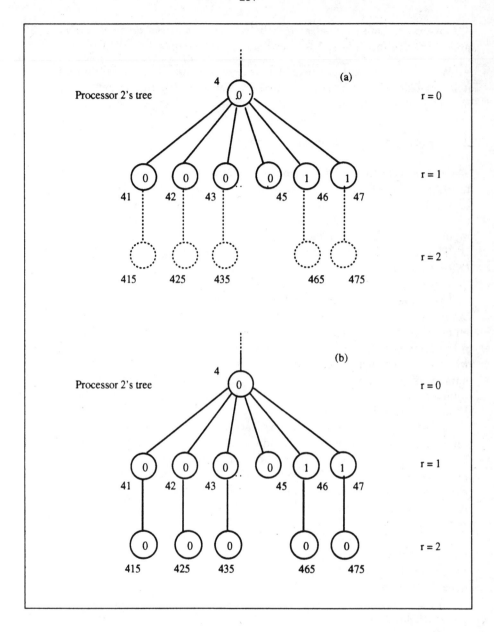

**Fig. 2.** Safe message reconstruction.

**Theorem 12.** Safe EIG *solves the Distributed Consensus problem using* $n > 3t$ *processors and* $min(t + 1, f + 2)$ *communication rounds.*

While the consensus protocol of Theorem 12 is processor- and round-optimal, it is not efficient—its maximum message size is $O(t!)$. In the next section we present protocols that are early-stopping and use messages of constant size.

## 3 Early Stopping with Constant Message Size

The protocols of this section are based on the *Phase Queen* and *Phase King* protocols of [BG1, BGP]. We first show how to transform them into early-stopping protocols—without jeopardizing their simplicity, and then demonstrate several techniques to further reduce the round and bit (and message) complexity while maintaining the early-stopping property.

The first early-stopping consensus protocol—*Early-Stopping Phase Queen* (*ESPQ* for short)—requires $n > 4t$ and is shown in Figure 3. It executes at most $t + 1$ phases each consisting of two communication rounds: the universal exchange and the broadcast of the "phase queen"; each phase has a distinct queen. (In this section the semantics of Send($U$) is to send (the contents of) $U$ to all processors—including the sending processor.) We assume that each processor $p$ has local variables $V$ (the subject of the consensus problem), $P$ (indicating whether or not there is a "strong preference" for $V$) and $S$ (which counts the number of processors with strong preferences), and integer array $C[0..1]$ (the counts of 0's and 1's received). In the universal exchange each processor changes $V$ to what it perceives as the majority value and sets $P$ to true if $V$ is strongly favored. During the queen's broadcast each processor sends the value determined to be the majority along with an indication of the strength of its preference for this value. After counting the number of processors with strong preferences, a processor replaces its own $V$ with the queen's value if there are too few processors with a strong preference; should it find many processors with a strong preference, it halts. Because some correct processors may halt before others, a convention is adopted to account for messages that are not received during a phase: if no message is received from $p$ during the universal exchange, the receiving processor assumes that the missing value is equal to the value of its own $V$ of the previous phase and that the silent processor indicates a strong preference during the queen's broadcast.

For ease of presentation the queen's broadcast uses two-bit messages. The remark below shows how to reduce this broadcast to one bit and thus make *ESPQ* a single-bit protocol.

**Theorem 13.** Early-Stopping Phase Queen *solves the Distributed Consensus problem using* $min(2(f + 2), 2(t + 1))$ *exchange rounds and one-bit messages, where $f$ is the number of processors that fail during its execution, provided $n >$ $4t$.*

*Proof.* As a preliminary step, we show the following property of protocol *ESPQ* (Fig. 3).

```
        for k := 1 to t + 1 do begin
                        (* universal exchange *)
            send(V);
            for j := 0 to 1 do
                        C[j] := the number of received j's;
            V := C[1] > 2t;
            P := C[V] ≥ n − t;
                        (* queen's broadcast *)
            send(⟨V, P⟩);
            S := the number of received ⟨v, 1⟩'s, for any v;
            if S ≤ t then
                        V := v, where ⟨v, w⟩ is the message
                        received from k
            elseif S > 2t then
                        halt;
        end;
```

**Fig. 3.** Protocol *Early-Stopping Phase Queen*, code for processor $p$.

*Persistence*: If for all $p \in P - T$, $V_p = v$ is true at the start of a phase, every processor decides on $v$ and halts at the end of the phase.

To see this, observe that the universal exchange results in every correct processor $p$ having $C[v]_p \geq n - t > 2t$, $C[\bar{v}]_p \leq t$, and $P$ being true. Therefore it computes $V_p = v$ with a strong preference. During the queen's broadcast, it detects that at least $n - t$ processors have strong preferences so it ignores the queen's broadcast and halts.

Now we can address the correctness of the protocol.

*Agreement*: Since the number of phases $(t + 1)$ exceeds the number of faulty processors $(t)$, there is some first phase $g$ with a correct queen. One of the following cases holds at the end of phase $g$:

1. $S \leq t$ for each $p \in P - T$. Then every correct processor assigns $V_g$ to $V$ during the queen's broadcast of phase $g$, where $\langle V_g, w \rangle$ is the message sent by $g$.

2. $S > t$ for some $p \in P - T$. Then $P$ is true for at least one correct processor $p'$ so at the end of the universal exchange, $V_{p'} = v$ and $C[v]_{p'} > n - t$. Among the $n - t$ processors from which $p'$ received value $v$, at most $t$ are faulty so at least $n - 2t$ are correct. Thus, *every* correct processor received $v$ at least $n - 2t > 2t$ times, and $\bar{v}$ at most $2t$ times. As a consequence, at the end of the universal exchange $V_q = v$ for every $q \in P - T$, including queen $g$; therefore the queen's broadcast must result in $V_q = v$ for all $q \in P - T$.

*Persistence* assures that no correct processor changes its value subsequent to phase $g$.

*Validity*: Follows trivially from *Persistence*.

As for the running time, *Agreement* shows that, if the queen of phase $k$ is correct, then for all $p \in P - T$, $V_p = v$ for some $v$. By *Persistence*, all processors that have not already halted will halt by the end of phase $k + 1$. If $k$ is the phase with the first correct queen, the number of faulty processors $f$ is at least $k - 1$ (because all prior queens were faulty). Thus $k + 1 \leq f + 2$. □

**Remark:** If a correct processor $p$ asserts that it has a strong preference during the queen's broadcast of a phase, then $C[v]_p \geq n - t$ at the end of the phase's universal exchange, for some $v$. Since at most $t$ of the processors in this count are faulty, $C[v]_q \geq 2t$ for for all $q \in P - T$ so $V_q = v$. Therefore, a correct processor with a strong preference need not send the value that it prefers during the queen's broadcast; it may be deduced by the receiving process as being equal to its own $V$. We can change the code so that a queen sends its own $V$ during the queen's broadcast if and only if it does not have a strong preference for $V$, and let all other processors interpret a missing message from the queen in this light. Therefore, *ESPQ* may use single-bit messages.

*ESPQ* is asymptotically optimal with respect to rounds and number of processors but is exactly optimal in message size. The second protocol—*Early-Stopping Phase King (ESPK)*—sacrifices exact optimality in message size (it uses two-bit messages) in order to achieve exact optimality in the number of processors, i.e., $n > 3t$. The protocol is shown in Figure 4.

```
for k := 1 to t + 1 do begin
                 (* universal exchange 1 *)
        send(V);
        for j := 0 to 1 do
                 C[j] := the number of received j's;
                 (* universal exchange 2 *)
        for j := 0 to 1 do
                 send(C[j] ≥ n − t)
                 D[j] := the number of received 1's;
        V := D[1] > t;
        P := D[V] ≥ n − t;
                 (* king's broadcast *)
        send(⟨V, P⟩);
        S := the number of received ⟨v, 1⟩'s, for any v;
        if S ≤ t then
                 V := v, where ⟨v, w⟩ is the message
                 received from k
        elseif S > 2t then
                 halt;
    end;
```

**Fig. 4.** Protocol *Early Stopping Phase King*, code for processor $p$.

*ESPK* is like *ESPQ* with an additional universal exchange. The additional exchange can be either one round using two-bit messages, or two rounds using single-bit messages. After this exchange, we can show that there is at most one $v$ for which $D[v]_p > t$ for any processor $p$. Therefore, a processor can compute a new value for $V$ using fewer processors ($t$ versus $2t$) than in *ESPQ*.

**Theorem 14.** Early-Stopping Phase King *solves the Distributed Consensus problem using* $min(3(f + 2), 3(t + 1))$ *exchange rounds and two-bit messages, or* $min(4(f+2), 4(t+1))$ *exchange rounds using single-bit messages, where f is the number of processors that fail during its execution, provided* $n > 3t$.

The proof is very similar to that of *ESPQ* (Theorem 13) and is omitted from the abstract.

## 3.1  Reducing the Number of Rounds

While the two early-stopping consensus protocols presented above have optimal message size, their round complexity is at least twice optimal. Using the committee technique of [BG1], we show in the full paper that the number of rounds may be reduced to $min(f(1 + 1/d) + 5, t(1 + 1/d))$ for every constant $d$ while maintaining the same number of processors and constant message size.

Briefly, the technique involves replacing the queen (king) processor of each phase with a *committee* of processors. Intra-committee the processors run any round-optimal early-stopping distributed consensus protocol. Any processor not in the committee of a phase merely listens and uses as the queen's (king's) message any value decided on by at least $t$ processors in the committee. By partitioning the processors into $R$ disjoint committees, the protocol can be run for at most $R$ phases (versus $t + 1$). Because of the intra-committee early-stopping, some processors may advance to the next phase before others; the full paper shows that this loss of total synchrony can be overcome without penalty in the round complexity.

If the intra-committee protocol of phase $m$ can tolerate $t_m - 1$ faulty processors, then a *bad committee* (one in which more than $t_m - 1$ processors are faulty) runs for at most $t_m$ rounds whereas a *good comittee* (one with $f_m < t_m$ faulty processors) runs for $min(f_m + 2, t_m + 1)$ rounds. Thus, the total number of rounds in a run in which the first good committee doesn't occur until phase $F$ is:

$$\underbrace{\sum_{m=1}^{F-1} 1 + t_m}_{\text{phases with bad committees}} + \underbrace{1 + (f_F + 2)}_{\text{phase with first good committee}} + \underbrace{2}_{\text{final phase}} \approx f(1 + 1/d) + 5$$

where $f = \sum_{m=1}^{F-1} t_m + f_m$.

# 4 Early Stopping with Optimal Bit and Message Complexity

In the full paper we show that the committee technique of the previous section may be applied in the extreme (as indicated in [BGP]) to obtain an early-stopping protocol with exact processor optimality, near round optimality, and asymptotically optimal bit (and message) complexity ($O(nt)$). The technique splits the processors into two committees, each acting the role of king in one of two phases of the *Early-Stopping Phase King* protocol. Intra-committee, the processors reach consensus by recursively applying the technique until the committee size becomes too small, in which case they use the *ESDM* protocol of [BG2]. We note that a straightforward application of the technique of [BGP] does not suffice: extra measures must be taken to prevent even a single faulty processor from delaying termination for a number of rounds equal to the depth of the recursion. Note that our protocol achieves message optimality in *all* runs (at the expense of a reasonably small constant), unlike the protocol of Hadzilacos and Halpern [HH] which only achieves exact message optimality for *failure-free* runs.

## Acknowledgements

The authors would like to thank Gil Neiger for his help in tracking down the message size of existing early-stopping consensus protocols, and Yoram Moses for commenting on an early draft of the manuscript and improving the presentation.

## References

[BDDS]  A. Bar-Noy, D. Dolev, C. Dwork and H.R. Strong, "Shifting gears: changing algorithms on the fly to expedite Byzantine Agreement," *Proc. 6th PODC*, pp. 42-51, August 1987.

[BG1]   P. Berman and J.A. Garay, "Asymptotically Optimal Distributed Consensus," *Proc. ICALP 89*, LNCS Vol. 372, pp. 80-94, July 1989.

[BG2]   P. Berman and J.A. Garay, "Distributed Consensus with $n = (3 + \varepsilon)t$ Processors," *Proc. 5th International Workshop on Dist. Algorithms*, LNCS, Springer-Verlag, October 1991.

[BGP]   P. Berman, J.A. Garay and K.J. Perry, "Towards Optimal Distributed Consensus," *Proc. 30th FOCS*, pp. 410-415, October/November 1989.

[C]     B. Coan, "Efficient agreement using fault diagnosis," *Proc. 26th Allerton Conf. on Comm., Control and Computing*, pp. 663-672, 1988.

[DR]    D. Dolev and R. Reischuk, "Bounds of Information Exchange for Byzantine Agreement," *JACM*, Vol. 32, No. 1, pp. 191-204, 1985.

[DRS]   D. Dolev, R. Reischuk and H.R. Strong, "Eventual is Earlier than Immediate," in *Proc. 23rd STOC*, 1982. Revised version appears in "Early Stopping in Byzantine Agreement," *JACM*, Vol. 37, No. 4 (1990), pp. 720-741.

[DS]    D. Dolev and H.R. Strong, "Authenticated Algorithms for Byzantine Agreement," in *SIAM Journal of Computing*, Vol. 12, pp. 656-666, 1983.

[FM]    P. Feldman and S. Micali, "Optimal Algorithms for Byzantine Agreement",
        *Proc. 20th STOC*, pp. 148-161, May 1988.
[HH]    V. Hadzilacos and J. Halpern, "Message-Optimal Protocols for Byzantine
        Agreement," *Proc. 10th PODC*, pp. 309-324, August 1991.
[HM]    J. Halpern and Y. Moses, "Knowledge and common knowledge in a distributed
        environment," *JACM*, Vol. 37, No. 3 (1990), pp. 549-587.
[LF]    L. Lamport and M. Fischer, *Byzantine Generals and Transaction Commit
        Protocols,* Opus 62, SRI International, April 1982.
[LSP]   L. Lamport, R.E. Shostak and M. Pease, "The Byzantine Generals Problem,"
        *ACM ToPLaS*, Vol. 4, No. 3, pp. 382-401, July 1982.
[MW]    Y. Moses and O. Waarts, "Coordinated Traversal: $(t+1)$-Round Byzantine
        Agreement in Polynomial Time," *Proc. 29th FOCS*, pp. 246-255, October
        1988.
[PT]    K.J. Perry and S. Toueg, "Distributed agreement in the presence of processor
        and communication faults," *IEEE Trans. on Software Engineering*, Vol. 12,
        No. 3, pp. 477-482, March 1986.
[TPS]   S. Toueg, K.J. Perry and T.K. Srikanth, "Fast Distributed Agreement," *SIAM
        Journal of Computing*, Vol. 16, No. 3, pp. 445-457, June 1987.
[W]     O. Waarts, "Coordinated Traversal: Byzantine Agreement in polynomial
        time," M.Sc. Thesis, Weizmann Institute of Science, Rehovot, Israel, August
        1988.

# Traffic-Light Scheduling on the Grid
## (Extended Abstract)

Guy Kortsarz *         David Peleg* †

### Abstract

This paper studies the problem of route scheduling under the telephone model of communication networks. Previous work in this model considered mostly the "broadcast" and "gossip" communication primitives. The approach studied here is that of devising simple, distributed universal schedules, that are efficient for wide families of routing instances, rather than attempting to solve individual instances separately. The paper concentrates on "traffic-light" type schedules for route scheduling on the two-dimensional grid.

In order to study the problem of scheduling given route instances, routes are classified according to the number of directions they use, and tight bounds are given on the time required for scheduling route instances in each class. For routes of length $d$ or less, using only one direction, scheduling is shown to require $d + O(1)$ time. For simple routes using only two or three directions, scheduling is shown to require $2d + 3$ and $2d + 4$ time, respectively. Finally, for arbitrary simple routes scheduling is shown to require $2d + \Theta(\sqrt{d})$ time.

## 1  Introduction

The study of useful communication primitives and their efficient implementation is at the heart of current research in the area of communication networks. This paper concerns the common *telephone* communication model (cf. [HHL88]). In this model, messages are exchanged during calls placed over edges of the network. A *round* is composed of a collection of calls carried out simultaneously. Each round is assumed to require one unit of time, so round $t$ begins at time $t - 1$ and ends at time $t$. A vertex may participate in at most one call during a given round, however there is no bound on the amount of information that can be exchanged during a given call.

Much of the previous work on communication in the telephone model has concentrated on the two important primitives of *broadcasting* and *gossiping*. A *broadcasting* problem refers to the process of message dissemination whereby a distinguished vertex originates a message that has to be made known to all other processors. A *gossiping* problem refers to the process of performing many broadcasts in parallel, with *each*

---

*Department of Applied Mathematics and Computer Science, The Weizmann Institute, Rehovot 76100, Israel.

†Supported in part by a Walter and Elise Haas Career Development Award and by a grant from the Israeli Basic Research Foundation.

vertex in the network originating one message. These problems have received considerable attention in the literature; for a comprehensive survey see [HHL88]. In this paper we study the somewhat more generalized *routing* problem, in which each node is allowed to send messages to arbitrary sets of destinations. More specifically, *routing* refers to the process where a number of sender-receiver pairs of vertices are given, and each sender originates a message to be sent to the receiver.

One may distinguish between two versions of the problem. In the more general version, referred to as the *telephone routing problem* (or TR), the algorithm is required to determine both the *routes* along which the messages are to be sent, and the *activation schedules* of the edges, so as to minimize the overall execution time. This problem is studied, for instance, in [LR91, Kor90] on the grid network.

In this paper we concentrate on a more limited version of the problem, named the *telephone route scheduling problem* (or TRS). In this version, the routes are *given* as part of the input, and it remains only to determine the activation schedules of the edges. We assume that all messages are distinct, but a vertex is allowed to participate in a given instance as a receiver or as a server more than once. For example, a vertex $v$ may send several (different) messages to the same vertex $w$. We again stress the fact that at each round, any vertex $v$ may exchange information with only one other vertex $w$, however in such a round it is allowed to deliver a large amount of information (corresponding to different messages of different input routes, that have reached $v$ earlier) along the corresponding edge $(v, w)$.

Another distinction of our approach concerns the *nature* of the solutions sought for the problem. Given any particular collection of routing requests, it is possible to look for a set of routes and a schedule that are *optimal* (or near optimal) for that particular instance. This corresponds to the kind of questions studied in several papers dealing with the broadcast and gossip problems. However, this approach typically leads to hard problems. In particular it is shown in [Kor90] that optimizing TR and TRS is NP-hard for general graphs. Restricted graph classes have been given complex centralized solutions [FP80, SCH81]. We therefore concentrate on the alternative approach (considered also in [LR91]) of designing simple, distributed schedules that are *universal* for wide families of routing requests. This naturally leads to the idea of "traffic-light" type schedules, based on *periodic* activation of edges.

Distributed traffic-light solutions are, in particular, suitable for what we call *continuous* routing problems. In the TRS problem, there is a distinguished starting point in time, upon which the input is presented to the processors and all the vertices start sending their messages. In contrast, a continuous TRS problem (denoted CTRS) is a version of the problem in which there is no such starting point. Rather, the system operates continuously, and at any given moment, any vertex may initiate a message to any other vertex on some specific path. The solution to such a problem is an algorithm that minimizes the time duration since a message is introduced into the system, until it is delivered at its destination. The solutions given in this paper for the TRS problem are especially oriented for continuous problems.

Let us now briefly describe the results presented in this paper. We focus our attention on the problem of scheduling given route instances on the grid. It turns out that in order to analyze the resulting complexities, it is convenient to classify the routes according to the number of *directions* they use. Using this classification, it is possible to establish tight bounds on the time required for scheduling route instances in each class.

In Section 3 we deal with the case where the input routes are one-directional. We give a (surprisingly nontrivial) single schedule $S_2$ that completes the routing on any such problem instance $A$, in no more than $d(A) + O(1)$ time units, where $d(A)$ is the maximal length of an input route in the input. The arrival times of the messages under schedule $S_2$ are distance dependent. (By *distance-dependent* we mean that each input message in $A$ that is to be sent from $v$ to $w$, reaches $w$ in time no larger than the distance from $v$ to $w$, plus $O(1)$.) An application of this schedule to the classical broadcasting and gossiping problems, discussed in [Kor90], establishes that it is possible to achieve broadcast and gossip on the grid with distance-dependent, $O(1)$ deviation from the optimum time, using *shortest paths* between every sender-receiver pair.

In Section 4 we introduce the traffic-light schedule $S_3$ and use it to deal with the problem of scheduling 2− and 3− directional routes on the grid. We show that when the input routes each use only 2 (resp. 3) directions, the scheduling requires $2 \cdot d(A)+3$ (resp. $2 \cdot d(A)+4$) time units, by giving matching upper and lower bounds.

Finally, in Section 5 we deal with the TRS problem on the grid where the input routes are arbitrary (4− directional) simple paths. In Subsection 5.1 we analyze the performance of the $S_3$ traffic-light schedule on such routes. We show that $S_3$ completes the routing in any such problem $A$ in no more than $2 \cdot d(A)+2\sqrt{2} \cdot \sqrt{d(A)}+2$ time units. This bound is complemented in Subsection 5.2, where we construct a problem $A$ for which the time needed to complete the routing is at least $2 \cdot d(A) + 2 \cdot \sqrt{d(A) + 1} - 1$. For lack of space, most proofs are defered to the full paper [KP92].

# 2 Preliminaries

## 2.1 The model

The communication network is modeled by a connected graph $G = (V, E)$ consisting of a set $V$ of $n$ vertices, $V = \{v_1, .., v_n\}$ representing the processors, and a set $E$ of $m$ edges, $E = \{e_1, ..., e_m\}$ representing the communication lines between the processors.

In this paper we focus on the (rectangular) $m \times n$ *grid* graph $Gr_{m,n} = (V, E)$. We think of the grid as embedded in the plane so that vertex $(1, n)$ is at the top, rightmost corner. Given a route (i.e., an oriented path) $\rho = (e_1, e_2, \ldots, e_{|\rho|})$ on the grid, we associate with each move $e$ in $\rho$ a *direction*, $dir(e) \in \{$"$l$", "$r$", "$u$", "$d$"$\}$, in the obvious way. We may also refer to a move $e = (i, j + 1) \to (i, j)$ on the route (i.e., such that $dir(e) = $ "$l$") as an "$l$" *move*, and say that the route is moving in the left direction, and similarly for the other directions. We denote a path $\rho$ by $\rho = (e_1, e_2, \ldots, e_{|\rho|})$ where $e_i$ are the path edges. The prefix containing the first $i$ edges of the route is denoted by $\rho(i) = (e_1, ..., e_i)$, for all $1 \leq i \leq |\rho|$. An edge $e$ on the route is regarded as a *directed* edge, i.e., an edge with the orientation imposed by the route. We shall refer to the edge $e_i$ as the $i$'th *move* on the route.

Given a graph $G = (V, E)$, two edges $e_1, e_2 \in E$ are called *adjacent* if they share a vertex. A subset of edges $E' \subseteq E$ is *independent* iff its edges are pairwise nonadjacent.

At a given round, if a call is placed over an edge $e$ we say that the edge $e$ is *active* in this round, else we say that the edge is *idle*. Note that by the definition of the telephone model, at each round $t$, the set of active edges must be independent. A *schedule* on a graph $G = (V, E)$ is an infinite sequence $(E_i)_{i \geq 1}$ such that for each $i$, $E_i \subset E$ and $E_i$ is independent. Intuitively, a schedule determines the set $E_i$ of active edges on the $i$'th round. A schedule induces for every edge $e$ a (possibly infinite) tuple $\mathcal{A}(e) = (t_e^1, t_e^2, \ldots)$, consisting of the rounds in which the edge $e$ is active in the schedule. Thus the collection $\{\mathcal{A}(e) \mid e \in E\}$ completely characterizes the schedule.

In order to simplify the process of designing and analyzing our schedules, it is some times convenient to view every edge $e$ as two directed edges $\overleftarrow{e}$ and $\overrightarrow{e}$ in opposite directions, and treat these edges separately. In particular, $\overleftarrow{e}$ and $\overrightarrow{e}$ may be given separate sets $\mathcal{A}(\overleftarrow{e})$ and $\mathcal{A}(\overrightarrow{e})$ of active rounds (these sets may of course intersect). Note that such a *directed schedule* must still obey the rules of the model. It can be thought of as obtained by starting with a regular bidirectional schedule (in which, whenever an edge $e$ is active, it can be used in both directions), and restricting it by forbidding the use of some edges $e$ in one of the directions at some of their active rounds. While such restrictions yield no actual gains for us (and in fact, can only degrade the performance of the resulting algorithm), they serve to simplify the analysis in some cases. When dealing with a directed schedule, we denote the directed graph obtained from $G$ by splitting the edges as described by $\hat{G}$.

## 2.2  The TRS problem

Posed formally, a TRS problem is defined as follows. The input consists of a set of $k$ routes, $\{\rho_1, \ldots, \rho_k\}$. For every $\rho_i$, its start vertex $v_i$ originates a message $M_i$, to be sent to its end vertex $w_i$. Each $v_i$ is called a *sender* and each $w_i$ is called a *receiver*. Any vertex $v$ may appear more than once as a server and as a receiver. The goal is for each message $M_i$ to be sent to $w_i$ along $\rho_i$, where the communication pattern obeys the requirements of the telephone model. A solution for an instance of the TRS problem consists of a schedule, that is, the solution must determine the (independent) set of edges $E_t$ to be active at round $t$, for every $t \geq 1$. Such a schedule completely specifies the progress of messages for the TRS instance, that is, for every path, the vertex currently holding the message forwards it to the next vertex in the path, in the next time that the corresponding edge is active. Given an instance $A$ of the TRS problem, we denote $d(A) = \max_i\{|\rho_i|\}$. Denote the time needed to complete the routing in $A$ by $T(A)$. Given a nonnegative integer $d$, denote the family of TRS problems instances $A$ such that $d(A) \leq d$ by $TRS_d$. We measure the efficiency of an algorithm $P$ for the set $TRS_d$ by the number of time units, $T(P, d)$, required to complete the routing in the *worst case*, using the algorithm. We denote by $TRS(i\text{-}DIR)$, $i \in \{1, 2, 3, 4\}$, the TRS problem on the grid $Gr_{m,n}$ where the input routes are $i$-directional (that is, the routes use only $i$ of the four possible forwarding directions on the grid.)

## 2.3  Traffic-light Schedules

In order to cope with the TRS problem, a possible approach is to ignore the particular inputs, and try to give a single *universal schedule* that deals simultaneously with a large set of problem instances. This motivates the following definitions.

A *traffic-light* schedule for a family $S$ of TRS instances on a *fixed* graph $G$ is a *fixed* schedule (i.e., a schedule that does not depend on the particular instance) such that for every edge $e$, if $\mathcal{A}(e) \neq \emptyset$ then it is *periodical*.

A fixed schedule for a family $S$ of TRS instances said to be a *directed traffic-light schedule* if it is a traffic-light schedule defined on $\hat{G}$ the directed version of $G$, that is both $\mathcal{A}(\overleftarrow{e})$ and $\mathcal{A}(\overrightarrow{e})$ are either empty or periodical.

# 3  Scheduling 1-directional paths on the grid

In this section we study scheduling of one-directional routes. Every vertex is allowed to send a message only to vertices in the same row or column, along this row (column). The "Manhattan-type" schedule used in [LR91, Kor90] can, in principle, be used here. However, in every row or column, this schedule allows delay-free message propagation only in one direction (by providing a "green-wave" in that direction). Thus if an input route requires the message to be sent in the direction opposite to the "green-wave", it leads to a $3d + O(1)$ scheduling time since the message is delayed for two rounds between any two consecutive steps. In this section we present a solution for this problem that achieves $d + O(1)$ scheduling time, which is optimal up to an additive constant. Intuitively, we achieve this by making sure that each row and column in the grid provides a "green wave" in *both* directions simultaneously. This seemingly simple requirement turns out to be surprisingly nontrivial to obtain.

The input of an instance in $TRS(1\text{-}DIR)$ contains four kinds of sender-receiver routes: $(i, j)$ sends a message to $(i, k)$ along the $i$'th row using only "l" moves if $j > k$, and only "r" moves if $k > j$. Likewise, $(i, j)$ sends a message to $(k, j)$ along the $j$'th column using only "d" moves if $k > i$ and only "u" moves if $i > k$. Since the schedule is directed we look at each edge $e = ((i, j), (i, j + 1))$ as two directed edges $e_l = \langle (i, j + 1), (i, j) \rangle$ and $e_r = \langle (i, j), (i, j + 1) \rangle$ in the two directions, and similarly for a vertical edge.

**Definition 3.1** A directed traffic-light schedule for the $m \times n$ grid $Gr_{m,n}$ is *directed rightward-wave* on the $i$'th row, if for every edge $e$ on row $i$, $\mathcal{A}(\overrightarrow{e}) \neq \emptyset$ and moreover, for each round $t \geq 1$ and $1 \leq j \leq n - 1$, if the edge $\langle (i, j - 1), (i, j) \rangle$ is active on round $t$, then the edge $\langle (i, j + k - 1), (i, j + k) \rangle$ is active on round $t + k$, for all $1 \leq k \leq n - j$. The definition for the up, down and left directions is similar.

**Definition 3.2** A traffic-light schedule for a given grid $Gr_{m,n}$ is called *bi-wave* if it is *rightward-directed wave* and *leftward-directed wave* on each row, as well as *upward-directed wave* and *downward-directed wave* on each column.

We now describe a directed bi-wave traffic-light schedule for the grid $Gr_{m,n}$. Such a schedule will allow each message to wait only $O(1)$ time units before departing, and never stop again. This of course leads to distance-dependent $O(1)$ delay of each message. Intuitively, we want to take advantage of the wave property of the schedule by making the message join a wave in the appropriate direction and "ride" it all the way to the destination, progressing by one row or column at each step. All a message has to do is to wait for the wave to reach its source and then start marching with it. The active times for any possible edge is described in the following schedule. For any

| 12 | 11 | 10 | 9 | 8 | 7 | 6 | 5 | 4 | 3 | 2 | 1 | i mod 24 |
|----|----|----|---|---|----|---|---|---|----|---|---|----------|
| 1 | 2 | 2 | 11 | 12 | 21 | 7 | 8 | 8 | 17 | 3 | 4 | "d" |
| 15 | 0 | 0 | 1 | 10 | 11 | 21 | 6 | 6 | 7 | 17 | 2 | "u" |

| 24 | 23 | 22 | 21 | 20 | 19 | 18 | 17 | 16 | 15 | 14 | 13 | i mod 24 |
|----|----|----|----|----|----|----|----|----|----|----|----|----------|
| 4 | 14 | 14 | 23 | 9 | 10 | 10 | 19 | 5 | 6 | 6 | 15 | "d" |
| 2 | 12 | 12 | 13 | 23 | 8 | 8 | 9 | 19 | 4 | 4 | 5 | "u" |

Figure 1: Definition of $d_d(i)$ and $d_u(i)$ for all $i$.

column index $i$ we define two numbers $d_u(i)$ and $d_d(i)$ depending only upon $i$ mod 24 (see Figure 1). The initial delay of a "vertical" message depends on its row, its column, and on $d_d(i)$ ($d_u(i)$) if the message heads downward (upward).

**Algorithm 3.3** *Directed bi-wave traffic-light schedule $S_2$*

1. Let $e$ be an horizontal edge $e = ((i,j),(i,j+1))$.

$$\mathcal{A}(e_r) = \{t > 0 : t \equiv (j - k) \bmod 12\}$$

$$\mathcal{A}(e_l) = \{t > 0 : t \equiv (q - j) \bmod 8\}$$

where $k = \begin{cases} 0; & \lfloor (i-1)/6 \rfloor \text{ is even;} \\ 6; & \text{otherwise;} \end{cases}$ and $q = \begin{cases} 2; & \lfloor (i-1)/4 \rfloor \text{ is even;} \\ 6; & \text{otherwise;} \end{cases}$

2. Let $e$ be a vertical edge $e = ((i,j),(i+1,j))$.

$$\mathcal{A}(e_d) = \{t > 0 : t \equiv (d_d(j) + i) \bmod 24\}$$

$$\mathcal{A}(e_u) = \{t > 0 : t \equiv (d_u(j) + (6 - i)) \bmod 24\}$$

The rather complicated proof that this schedule obeys the rules of the telephone model is omitted. (It appears in [Kor90].)

We note again that since the schedule is $bi - wave$, if $v$ sends a message to $w$ along a $1-$directional route, it arrives in $dist(v,w) + O(1)$ time units (where $dist(v,w)$ is the distance of $v$ and $w$ in the grid); the message may initially be delayed for up to 23 rounds, and is no longer delayed afterward.

**Theorem 3.4** *For every problem instance $A \in TRS(1\text{-}DIR)$, schedule $S_2$ guarantees that $T(A) = d(A) + O(1)$.* ∎

The schedule $S_2$ has an important application to the problem of broadcasting and gossiping in the grid. Using this schedule it is possible to perform gossip in such a way that the message sent from $v$ to $w$, will be transmitted along a shortest path, and will arrive after no more than $dist(v, w) + 35$ time units [Kor90]. This property was not enjoyed by the previous solutions [FP80, LR91].

**Theorem 3.5** *It is possible to perform broadcast and gossip on the grid along shortest paths, with only $O(1)$ distance-dependent delay.* ∎

# 4    Scheduling shortest paths and 3-directional paths on the grid

This section considers the problems $TRS(2\text{-}DIR)$ and $TRS(3\text{-}DIR)$, namely, route scheduling on the grid $Gr_{m,n}$, in the special case where the input routes are shortest paths or 3−directional paths. In Section 4.1 we present the "traffic-light" schedule $S_3$, achieving an upper bound on the schedule time for this class of instances. In Section 4.2 we study some properties of TRS on trees, which are then used in Section 4.3 to construct a matching lower bound.

## 4.1    The upper bound

The solution for $TRS(2 - DIR)$ and $TRS(3 - DIR)$ is based on a new schedule, $S_3$, which we shall call the *cyclic* schedule. The schedule $S_3$ relies on a partition of the grid to $3 \times 3$ blocks. Each edge is active once every four rounds. In Figure 2 we give the schedule of the first five rows and columns. The number beside each edge denotes the times when the edge is active (modulo 4). A clockwise (counterclockwise) turn in a route is, e.g., two consecutive moves of the form "r" and "d" ("l" and "d").

We refer to a clockwise turn that uses the directions "r" and "d", as a "rd" turn, and analogously for the other types. Given a route $\rho$ on the grid, let $\omega(\rho)$ denote the difference between the number of clockwise turns in $\rho$ and the number of counterclockwise turns in $\rho$. The following fact can be observed directly from the definition of schedule $S_3$.

**Fact 4.1** *Given a route $\rho$, the number of time units it takes to traverse $\rho$ using the cyclic traffic-light schedule $S_3$ is at most $2 \cdot |\rho| + \omega(\rho) + 2$.* ∎

The analysis of $\omega(\rho)$ is based on looking at the sequence of "significant" points along the run. These points are the ones in which $\omega(\rho)$ increases by one, and never falls below the current value afterwards. Bounding the number of such "significant" points in time immediately gives an upper bound on $\omega(\rho)$. Formally, we introduce the following definition.

**Definition 4.2** The "tuple of significant turns" of a route $\rho$ is the tuple of integers $S(\rho) = (t_1, ..., t_k)$ with the following properties. (Recall that $\rho(i)$ denotes the $i$-prefix of $\rho$).

1. $1 \leq t_1 \leq ... \leq t_k \leq |\rho|$.

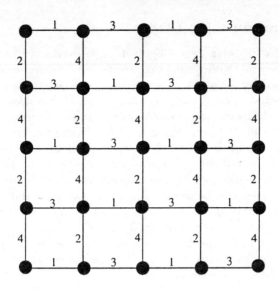

Figure 2: Active times for edges in the cyclic traffic-light schedule $S_3$.

2. $\omega(\rho(t_i)) = i$, for $1 \leq i \leq k$.

3. For every $1 \leq i \leq k$ and $t_i \leq t \leq |\rho|$, $\omega(\rho(t)) \geq i$.

4. For every $1 \leq i \leq k$, $t_i$ is the least integer satisfying properties 2 and 3.

The tuple $S(\rho)$ of significant turns is said to be of size $|S(\rho)| = k$. In case such a tuple does not exist (e.g., when $\omega(\rho) \leq 0$), $S(\rho)$ is empty and $|S(\rho)| = 0$.

**Fact 4.3** *For every route $\rho$, $\omega(\rho) \leq |S(\rho)|$.* ∎

**Lemma 4.4** *Given an $i$-directional route $\rho$ on a grid, for $i \leq 3$, $\rho$'s tuple of significant turn satisfies $|S(\rho)| \leq i - 1$.* ∎

Combining Fact 4.3, Lemma 4.4, and Fact 4.1 we get the desired result.

**Theorem 4.5** *Assume that the network uses the cyclic $S_3$ traffic-light schedule and that a vertex $v$ sends a message to a vertex $w$ along a route $\rho$, and $|\rho| = d$. If $\rho$ is a shortest path then the message arrives to $w$ within no more than $2 \cdot d + 3$ time units, and if $\rho$ is three directional then the message arrives within no more than $2 \cdot d + 4$ time units.* ∎

## 4.2   Telephone routing on trees

Our main goal in the following two subsections is to construct two instances of the
TRS problem on the grid, with routes that are 2— and 3-directional, for which the
upper bounds of Theorem 4.5 are the best possible. The construction is presented on
two steps. First we study some basic properties of the TRS problem on trees. Then,
in Subsection 4.3 we define the notion of a simple path embedding of a tree in a graph
and use such an embedding to build the desired problem instances.

Throughout the rest of this section, $T = (V_1, E_1)$ denotes a rooted tree with root
$r$. We associate with $T$ a TRS problem instance denoted $A_T$ in the following way. For
each leaf $l$ in $T$ create a message $M_l$. The message has to be delivered from $l$ to the
root $r$ along the (unique) path between them in the tree. Note that the time needed
for completing the schedule in this instance equals the broadcast time from $r$ in the
tree $T$ (see [SCH81]). In order to construct a TRS problem on a tree $T$ that is hard to
schedule, we need to enforce some degree constraints on the tree vertices. Specifically,
we need a tree with "many" vertices of "high" degree on every leaf-to-root path. For
this purpose we introduce the following definition.

**Definition 4.6** *Property $p(k, \mathcal{K})$*
Given an integer $k$, and a set of $m$ ordered pairs of integers $\mathcal{K} = \{(s_i, k_i) : 1 \leq i \leq m\}$
such that $1 \leq k < k_i$ for every $i$, the tree satisfies property $p(k, \mathcal{K})$ if the following
holds.

1. For every vertex $v$ in $T$, the number of children of $v$ in the tree is either $k$ or $k_i$
   for some $i$.

2. Every path from a leaf $l \in V_1$ to the root $r$ contains at least $s_i$ vertices with
   $k_i$ children, for every pair $(s_i, k_i)$ in the set $\mathcal{K}$. It is required that the sets of
   such vertices corresponding to $k_i$ and $k_j$, $k_i \neq k_j$, are disjoint (that is, the path
   contains at least $s_1$ vertices of degree $k_1$, and at least $s_2$ *different* vertices of
   degree $k_2$, etc.)

**Lemma 4.7** *Suppose $T = (V_1, E_1)$ is a full tree of height $n$ (i.e., all leaves are at depth
precisely $n$), and furthermore, it satisfies property $p(k, \mathcal{K})$ for $\mathcal{K} = \{(s_i, k_i) : 1 \leq i \leq
m\}$. Then $T(A_T) \geq n \cdot k + \sum_i s_i \cdot (k_i - k)$.* ∎

Applying Lemma 4.7 to the trees $Sp_j$ and $D3_j$ of Figures 3,4 we get that $T(A_{Sp_j}) \geq
2 \cdot j + 3$ and $T(A_{D3_j}) \geq 2 \cdot j + 4$.

## 4.3   The lower bound

**Definition 4.8** A function $F : V_1 \mapsto V$ is a *simple path embedding* of the tree $T =
(V_1, E_1)$ in the graph $G = (V, E)$ if the following conditions hold.

1. $(F(v_1), F(v_2)) \in E$ for every $v_1, v_2 \in V_1$ such that $(v_1, v_2) \in E_1$.

2. $F(v_1) \neq F(v_2)$ for every $v_1, v_2 \in V_1$ that are on the same path from a leaf to the
   root, or share the same parent.

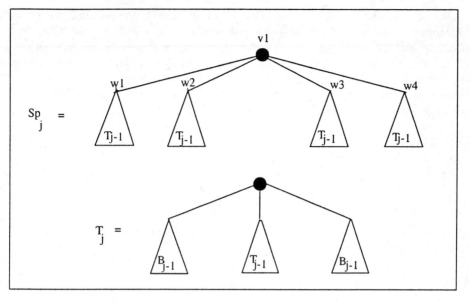

Figure 3: The trees $T_j$ and $Sp_j$, $j \geq 1$. The tree $T_0$ is a single vertex. $B_j$ is the full binary tree of height $j$.

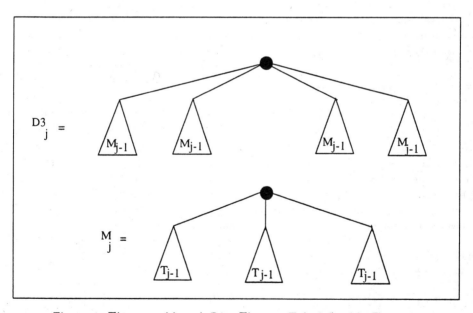

Figure 4: The trees $M_j$ and $D3_j$. The tree $T_j$ is defined in Figure 3

Note that in the above definition, each path from a leaf to the root in $T$ corresponds to a simple path on $G$. Given a simple path embedding of $T$ in a graph $G = (V, E)$, associate with $G$ a TRS problem instance by assigning a message $M_l'$ to each vertex $F(l) = l' \in V$ such that $l$ is a leaf in $T$, and requiring that $M_l$ is to be sent from $l'$ to $F(r)$ in $G$, along the path that corresponds to the path connecting $l$ and $r$ in $T$. Denote the associated problem instance by $A_{T,G}$. The following fact easily follows by induction on the height of $T$.

**Fact 4.9** $T(A_{T,G}) \geq T(A_T)$. ∎

By constructing a simple path embedding of $Sp_j$ in the grid, where the paths corresponding to root-to-leaves paths are shortest paths, we are able to show that $T(A_{SP_j, Gr_{m,n}}) \geq 2 \cdot j + 3$. Thus we can deduce.

**Theorem 4.10** *For sufficiently large $m$ and $n$, the cyclic traffic-light schedule $S_3$ is optimal for $TRS(2\text{-}DIR)$ in the worst case.* ∎

Using similar methods, we get.

**Theorem 4.11** *For sufficiently large $m$ and $n$, the cyclic traffic-light schedule $S_3$ is optimal for $TRS(3\text{-}DIR)$ in the worst case.* ∎

# 5   Scheduling arbitrary simple paths on the grid

In this section we deal with arbitrary (4-directional) simple paths on the grid. We first give an upper bound by analyzing the performance of the cyclic traffic-light schedule $S_3$, and then give a near-matching lower bound.

## 5.1   The upper bound

In this subsection we analyze the performance of the cyclic traffic-light schedule $S_3$ on TRS problems where the input routes are arbitrary simple paths. Fact 4.1 suggests that it is needed to bound $\omega(\rho)$ for a given route $\rho$. As some experimentation hints, $\omega(\rho)$ achieves its maximum value (asymptotically) on a route $\rho$ of carasol shape. In order to prove this formally, we show how starting with an arbitrary route $\rho$, one can perform a series of transformations on the route, each leaving $\omega(\rho)$ unchanged, but bringing $\rho$ to a "simpler" form which in a sense is closer to being a carasol. For this purpose we give some preliminary lemmas and definitions.

**Definition 5.1** Given a simple path $\rho$ on a grid, a "North U-turn" N-U-T$(i; j, \ldots, m)$, where $j+1 \leq m$, is a subpath $p = (e_1, e_2, \ldots, e_{m-j+2})$ of $\rho$ with the following properties:

1. Edge $e_1 = ((i+1, j), (i, j))$.

2. For all $2 \leq l \leq m - j + 1$, edge $e_l = ((i, j+l-2), (i, j+l-1))$

3. Edge $e_{m-j+2} = ((i, m), (i+1, m))$

The *length* of $p$, denoted $l(p)$, is $m - j$. "East", "South" and "West" U-turns are defined in an analogous fashion and denoted by E-U-T, S-U-T and W-U-T, respectively.

**Definition 5.2** Let $p = $ N-U-T$(i_1; j_1, \ldots, m_1)$ and $q = $ N-U-T$(i_2; j_2, \ldots, m_2)$. Then $q$ is the *parent* of $p$ (and $p$ is a *child* of $q$) iff they lie on adjacent rows, and that $p$'s row segment is fully contained in $p$'s, (or more formally: $i_1 = i_2 + 1$, $j_2 + 1 \leq j_1$, and $m_1 + 1 \leq m_2$) The parenthood relation for S-U-T, W-U-T and E-U-T is defined in an analogous fashion.

A U-turn is *external* if it has no parent. The *ancestor* (respectively *descendant*) relation is the transitive closure of the parent (resp. child) relation. The U-Turn $p = $ N-U-T$(i; j, \ldots, m)$ contains the start (resp., end) point of the route if the route starts (resp., ends) at vertex $(i + 1, s)$ for some $j \leq s \leq m$.

We need the following simple facts.

**Fact 5.3** *If $p$ is a parent of $q$ then $l(p) \geq l(q) + 2$.* ∎

**Fact 5.4** *Let $\rho$ be a path on the grid. Then the parent of each nonexternal U-turn is unique.* ∎

**Definition 5.5** A simple path $\rho$ in the grid is *canonical* if every U-turn that *does not contain the start or end points* has (at least) one child.

We now define an algorithm for modifying a given simple path $\rho$ on the grid into a canonical path. For that purpose we define a transformation $\Phi$ on U-turns. We state the definition for North U-Turns; analogous transformations apply to the other directions.

**Definition 5.6** Let $p = $ N-U-T$(i; j, \ldots, m)$, where $p$ doesn't contain the start or end points, and the path $\rho$ does not lie on the vertices

$$(i + 1, j + 1), (i + 1, j + 2), \ldots, (i + 1, m - 1).$$

Then the transformation $\Phi$ applied to $p$ in $\rho$ replaces the subpath $p$ by the subpath

$$(i + 1, j), (i + 1, j + 1), \ldots, (i + 1, m).$$

The resulting path is denoted $\Phi(p, \rho)$. Note that this path $\Phi(p, \rho)$ is kept simple.

**Lemma 5.7** *Given a route $\rho$, the transformation $\omega$ preserves $\omega(\Phi(p, \rho)) = \omega(\rho)$.* ∎

**Fact 5.8** *An application of the transformation $\Phi$ to $\rho$ decreases its length by 2.* ∎

We now present the modification algorithm. The algorithm takes as input a route $\rho$ and makes several applications of $\Phi$ to it.

**Algorithm 5.9** *Route canonization algorithm*

1. $\rho' \leftarrow \rho$

2. **While** there exists a U-turn $p$ on $\rho'$ to which transformation $\Phi$ can be applied **do** $\rho' \leftarrow \Phi(p, \rho')$.

3. Return($\rho'$).

**Lemma 5.10**

1. *Applying the canonization algorithm 5.9 to a path $\rho$ leaves $\omega(\rho)$ unchanged.*

2. *The output $\rho'$ of Alg. 5.9 is canonical.* ∎

**Lemma 5.11** *Given a canonical route $\rho$ having three (different) U-turn's of the same type, p,q and r, one of these U-turns is a descendant of one of the other two.* ∎

**Lemma 5.12** *Assume that $\rho$ is a canonical path on the grid. Then*

1. *$\rho$ contains at most two external N-U-T's.*

2. *If $\rho$ contains two external N-U-T's, then every N-U-T of $\rho$ has at most one child.*

3. *If $\rho$ contains only one external N-U-T then there is at most one N-U-T having two children, while all the other N-U-T's have at most one child.*

4. *A similar claim applies to E-U-T's, W-U-T's and S-U-T's.* ∎

Finally, we derive our main claim.

**Lemma 5.13** *For each route $\rho$ such that $|\rho| = d$, $\omega(\rho) \le 2 \cdot \sqrt{2} \cdot \sqrt{d}$.* ∎

By Fact 4.1 we now have

**Corollary 5.14** *Assume that the grid network employs the cyclic schedule $S_3$. Let $v$ and $w$ be a pair of vertices on a grid. Suppose that $v$ sends a message to $w$ along an arbitrary simple path $\rho$. Then the message arrives after no more than $2 \cdot |\rho| + 2 \cdot \sqrt{2} \cdot \sqrt{|\rho|} + 2$ time units.* ∎

We comment that for every constant $c < 2 \cdot \sqrt{2}$, there exists a route $\rho$ between two vertices $v$ and $w$ such that the cyclic traffic-light schedule $S_3$ completes the routing along the path in more than $2 \cdot |\rho| + c \cdot \sqrt{|\rho|}$ time units. This fact can be observed by inspecting the route in Figure 5.

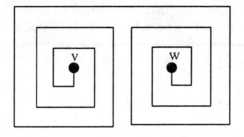

Figure 5: A route on which $\omega$ is maximal.

## 5.2 The lower bound

The purpose of this subsection is to construct an example of a TRS problem involving simple paths on the grid, for which the best possible schedule time approaches the upper bound presented in the previous subsection. For this purpose we introduce the definition of a *bounding frame* of a simple path on a grid.

**Definition 5.15** The *frame* $f(\rho)$ of a simple path $\rho$ on a grid is defined as the least rectangle containing the path. The length and height of the frame are the length and height of the rectangle.

Let $d$ be a positive integer. We want to construct a tree of height $d$ and embed it in the grid, in such a way that the TRS instance resulting from all leaf-to-root paths in the tree is "hard" to schedule. We choose a grid $Gr_{m,n}$ with sufficiently large $m$ and $n$, and a vertex $v$ in the grid such that the following construction is possible. Let us define a sequence of $d$ sets $S_i$, $1 \le i \le d$, of paths all starting at $v$. We define the paths in $S_i$ inductively with the paths in $S_{i+1}$ being the paths of $S_i$, each extended in several ways by additional edges. All the paths in $S_i$ have length $i$. We also maintain the following *out-propagation* property: *For every path $\rho$ in $S_i$, the end vertex $w$ of $\rho$ is on $f(\rho)$.*

**Algorithm 5.16** *Embedded tree construction*

1. $S_0 \leftarrow \emptyset$.

2. Stage 1: Create $S_1$ by adding to $S_0$ the four edges connecting $v$ to its four neighbors in the grid (the edges are regarded as paths of length one).

3. Stage $i + 1$: Assume that the sets $S_k$, for $1 \le k \le i < d$, are already defined. For every path $\rho = (e_1, \ldots, e_i)$ in $S_i$ perform the following. Let $w = (w_1, w_2)$ denote the end vertex of the path $\rho$. Extend this path to a number of new paths, by connecting $w$ to some of its neighbors, and add the augmented paths to $S_{i+1}$.

In doing so, it must be verified that the resulting paths remain simple. Thus add to $S_{i+1}$ the path obtained by extending $\rho$ by connecting $w$ to his left neighbor iff $\rho$ does not contain a point $(w_1, w_3)$ for some integer $w_3 < w_2$. I.e., extend $\rho$ leftward iff there is no vertex in $\rho$ at the same row and to the left of $w$. A similar action is performed for all the other directions.

If the above method can be used in order to connect $w$ to $l$ of its neighbors for some $0 \leq l \leq 3$, we say that $\rho$ can be extended in $l$ ways.

**Lemma 5.17** *Let* $w = (i_1, j_1)$ *be the end vertex of a route* $\rho \in S_k$. *Then*

*1. $w$ is on the border of $f(\rho)$, and*

*2. $\rho$ can be extended in at least two ways.* ∎

In the above construction it is possible to associate with $S_d$ a tree $F_d$ in the following way. Define a vertex $v_1$ to be associated with $v$. Assume now that for a given path $\rho$ in $S_i$ we extend the end vertex $w$ of $\rho$ in $2 \leq k \leq 4$ different ways. Then add to the tree $k$ new (distinct) vertices and connect them to the vertex in the tree, associated with $w$. Clearly this is a simple path embedding of $F_d$ in the grid.

**Lemma 5.18** *The tree $F_d$ satisfies property $p(k, \mathcal{K})$ with $k = 2$ and $\mathcal{K} = \{(2 \cdot \sqrt{d+1} - 3, 3), (1, 4)\}$.* ∎

By Lemma 4.7 and Fact 4.9 we have

**Corollary 5.19** $T(A_{F_d, G_{m,n}}) \geq 2 \cdot d + 2 \cdot \sqrt{d+1} - 1.$ ∎

We can summarize Corollary 5.19 and Corollary 5.14 in the following theorem.

**Theorem 5.20** *Routing an instance of $T R S_d(4\text{-}D I R)$ may require $2 \cdot d + O(\sqrt{d})$ rounds in the worst case.* ∎

# References

[FP80] A.M. Farley and A. Proskurowski. Gossiping in grid graphs. *Journal of Combinatorics information and system science*, 15:161–162, 1980.

[HHL88] S. Hedetniemi, S. Hedetniemi, and A. Liestman. A survey of gossiping and broadcasting in communication networks. *Networks*, 18:319–349, 1988.

[Kor90] G. Kortsarz. Telephone routing. M.Sc. Thesis, 1990.

[KP92] G. Kortsarz and D. Peleg. Traffic-light scheduling on the grid. *Discrete Applied Mathematics*, 1992. To appear.

[LR91] A.L. Liestman and D. Richards. Network communication in edge-colored graphs. Unpublished Manuscript, 1991.

[SCH81] P.J. Slater, E.J. Cockayne, and T. Hedetniemi. Information dissemination in trees. *SIAM J. on Comput.*, 10, 1981.

# DISTRIBUTED COMPUTING ON ANONYMOUS HYPERCUBES WITH FAULTY COMPONENTS*
## (Extended Abstract)

Evangelos Kranakis
(kranakis@scs.carleton.ca)
Nicola Santoro
(santoro@scs.carleton.ca)

School of Computer Science
Carleton University
K1S 5B6 Ottawa, Ontario, Canada

**Abstract.** We give efficient algorithms for distributed computation on anonymous, labeled, asynchronous hypercubes with possible faulty components (i.e. processors and links). The processors are deterministic and execute identical protocols given identical data. Initially, they know only the size of the network (in this instance, a power of 2) and that they are inter-connected in a hypercube network. Faults may occur only before the start of the computation (and that despite this the hypercube remains a connected network). However the processors do not know where these faults are located. As a measure of complexity we use the total number of bits transmitted during the execution of the algorithm and we concentrate on giving algorithms that will minimize this number of bits. The main result of this paper is an algorithm for computing boolean functions on anonymous hypercubes with at most $\gamma$ faulty components, $\gamma \geq 1$, with bit complexity $O(N \delta_n(\gamma)^2 \lambda^2 \log \log N)$, where $\gamma$ is the number of faulty components, of which $\lambda$ is the number of faulty links, and $\delta_n(\gamma)$ is the diameter of the hypercube.

**1980 Mathematics Subject Classification:** 68Q99
**CR Categories:** C.2.1
**Key Words and Phrases:** Anonymous labeled hypercube, boolean function, diameter, faulty component, group of automorphisms.

---

* Research supported in part by National Science and Engineering Research Council grants.

# 1 Introduction

In this paper we consider algorithms which are appropriate for distributed computation on anonymous, labeled, asynchronous, $n$-dimensional hypercubes $Q_n$ with faulty components (i.e. processors and links). The processors occupy the nodes of a hypercube and want to compute a given boolean function $f$ on $\leq N = 2^n$ variables. Initially each non-faulty processor $p$ has an input bit $b_p$. When the computation terminates all processors must output the same value $f(< b_p : p \text{ non-faulty} >).$[2]

The problem arising is to determine the bit complexity (i.e. total number of bits transmitted) of computing boolean functions on faulty hypercubes. In the present paper we give efficient algorithms for computing boolean functions on such networks.

## 1.1 Assumptions and Related Literature

The network we consider is the anonymous, asynchronous hypercube with possible faulty components. The number of faulty components may be arbitrary as long as the hypercube remains connected. If a processor is faulty then all the links adjacent to it are also interpreted as faulty. Faults may occur only before the start of the computation. We assume that the network links are FIFO, and that the processors have a sense of direction. By this we mean that the hypercube is canonically labeled (the label of link $xy$ is $i$ if and only if $x, y$ differ at exactly the $i$th bit) and that these labels are known to the processors concerned. In addition we assume that the following assumptions hold:

- the processors know the network topology (in this instance hypercube), and the size of the network, but they do not necessarily know where the faulty links may be,
- the processors are anonymous (i.e., they do not know either the identities of themselves or of the other processors), they are deterministic (i.e. they all run deterministic algorithms), and they all run the same algorithm given the same data.

The assumptions listed above are meant to take "maximum" advantage of network distributivity. For a discussion regarding the necessity of some of the above assumptions see [2]. Routing algorithms on hypercubes have been studied in [6]. Faulty hypercube networks have been examined in several papers under the much stronger assumption of synchronous and/or non-identical processors. In such networks it is possible to apply reconfiguring techniques [7] (nodes of an $n-1$-dimensional hypercube are mapped into non-faulty nodes of an $n$-dimensional hypercube with $O(1)$ dilation) or even non-faulty subcube techniques [5] (for a

---

[2] Our notation $b_p$ for the bit associated with processor $p$ does not mean that we assign names to processors. In addition the input $< b_p : p \in \text{non-faulty} >$ represents the assignment of bits to all the non-faulty processors of the network, and it will be computed by all the processors via an "input collection" algorithm.

given $k$ determine an $n - k$-dimensional subcube with no faulty links). However such techniques are not applicable in our case since they require the existence of processor identities.

## 1.2   Notation

We denote by $\lambda$ (resp. $\pi$) the number of faulty links (resp. processors) and let $\gamma = \lambda + \pi$ be the number of faulty components. Let $Q_n$ denote the $n$-dimensional hypercube on $N = 2^n$ nodes; $xy$ is a link of $Q_n$, where $x = x_1 \cdots x_n$ and $y = y_1 \cdots y_n$, if $x_i \neq y_i$ for a unique $i$; in addition, $i$ is called the label of $xy$ and we write $\ell(xy) = i$. Let $Q_n[l_1, \ldots, l_\lambda]$ denote the hypercube $Q_n$ with the links $l_1, \ldots, l_\lambda$ faulty. In general, the hypercube always remains a connected graph if the number $\lambda$ of faulty links is $< \log N$. However it is possible that the hypercube remains connected even if $\lambda \geq \log N$.

We define $\delta_n(\lambda)$ as the maximal possible diameter of a connected hypercube with at most $\lambda$ faulty links, i.e. $\delta_n(\lambda) := \max\{diam(Q_n[l_1, \ldots, l_\rho]) : \rho \leq \lambda$ and $Q_n[l_1, \ldots, l_\rho]$ is connected$\}$. We define similarly $\delta_n(\gamma)$ for the more general case of hypercubes with at most $\gamma$ faulty components. If a processor is faulty then we assume that all links adjacent to it are also faulty. This means that a hypercube has $\log N$ faulty links per faulty processor, which gives $\leq \pi \log N$ faulty links associated with these $\pi$ faulty processors.

## 1.3   Results of the paper

Previous results on computing boolean functions on anonymous, labeled networks can be summarized as follows.

| Network | Bit Complexity | Paper |
|---|---|---|
| Rings | $O(N^2)$ | [3] |
| $n$-Tori, $n$ constant | $O(N^{1+1/n})$ | [4] |
| Hypercubes: $\gamma = 0$ | $O(N \log^4 N)$ | [8] |
| Hypercubes: $\gamma \geq 1$ | $O(N \lambda^2 \delta_n(\gamma)^2 \log \log N)$ | This paper |

The result of [3] is valid both for oriented as well as unoriented rings. The result of [4] is valid for $n$-dimensional tori where $n$ is a constant (independent of the number of nodes). Moreover the constant implicit in the bit complexity bound $O(N^{1+1/n})$ depends on $n$ without the algorithm of [4] giving any indication of its size. Hence this result cannot apply to the hypercube which has variable dimension $n$. Bit complexity bounds for non-faulty hypercubes are given in [8].

In this paper we give an algorithm for computing boolean functions on anonymous hypercubes having bit complexity $O(N \lambda^2 \delta_n(\gamma)^2 \log \log N)$. Here $N$ is the number of nodes, $n = \log N$. Since a connected, $n$-dimensional hypercube with polylogarithmic number of faulty components has diameter $O(\log N)$ (see [1]) we have an $O(N polylog(N))$ bit complexity for $n$-dimensional hypercubes with $1 \leq \gamma = polylog(N)$ faulty components.

Notice the different estimates on the bit complexity implied by the algorithm for hypercubes with exactly one faulty link versus hypercubes with exactly one faulty processor; in the former case the bit complexity is $O(N \log^2 N \log \log N)$ while in the latter $O(N \log^4 N \log \log N)$. At first glance it may also come as a surprise that the bit complexity in a faulty hypercube can be lower than the bit complexity in a non-faulty hypercube (e.g. this can be the case when there are no faulty processors and $\lambda < \log N / \sqrt{\log \log N}$). This however can be explained by the fact that in hypercubes with faulty links we can take advantage of asymmetries in the network topology in order to design algorithms with improved bit complexity. Thus our main algorithm takes advantage of "symmetry breaking" by distinguishing faulty links from non-faulty links.

## 2 Hypercubes with Non-faulty Processors

In this section we give algorithms for computing boolean functions on a hypercube which does not have any faulty processors, i.e. $\pi = 0$. We indicate later how to extend our results to hypercubes with arbitrary faulty components. Our main theorem is the following.

**Theorem 1.** *In a hypercube with at most $\lambda$ faulty links, $\lambda \geq 1$, every computable boolean function can be computed in $O(N\lambda^2 \delta_n(\lambda)^2 \log \log N)$ bits.*

PROOF (outline) The proof of the theorem is outlined in subsections 2.1, 2.2. Before giving a detailed account of the algorithm we present a summary of the main steps of our construction. Let $f$ be a given boolean function. Each processor $p$ is given an input bit $b_p$ and the boolean function $f$. Let $Input = < b_p : p \in Q_n >$. Under the assumptions of subsection 1.1 each processor $p$ concerned executes the following algorithm: (1) determines whether or not the hypercube has a faulty link, (2) uses a "path-generation" algorithm in order to determine the location of the faulty links relative to itself, (3) uses an input collection mechanism in order to determine the entire input configuration $Input_p$, where $Input_p$ denotes $p$'s view of $Input$, (4) determines whether or not the given function is computable on the given input (this step is actually performed only locally and hence does not contribute to the overall bit complexity) by checking an invariance condition on the given function $f$, (5) if $f$ is computable then processor $p$ outputs $f(Input_p)$. In the sequel we describe the algorithm in several steps following the above summary.

### 2.1 Determining if there are any faulty links

The first step in our algorithm is to determine whether or not the hypercube has any faulty links. This follows from the following lemma.

**Lemma 2.** *There is an algorithm with bit complexity $O(N \log^2 N)$ which detects whether or not the hypercube has any faulty links.*

PROOF. Let $\mathbf{0} = $ "I have no faulty links" and let $\mathbf{1} = $ "I have a faulty link". Each processor initializes the variable *value*. To determine whether there is a faulty link the processors execute an algorithm for computing the boolean function $\text{OR}_N$ by using the boolean constants $\mathbf{0}, \mathbf{1}$ previously defined. If the output is $\mathbf{1}$ then there is a faulty link else there is no faulty link. The algorithm they execute is as follows:

**Faultylink**
**Algorithm for processor $p$:**
**Initialize:** $value_p$ ;
**for** $i := 1, \ldots, \log N$ **do**
    **send** $value_p$ to all neighbors of $p$;
    **receive** $value_q$ from all neighbors $q$ of $p$;
    **compute** $value_p := \text{OR}(\{value_q : q \text{ is neighbor of } p\}) \vee value_p$;
**od**;
**output** $value_p$.

There are $\log N$ iterations of the **for** loop and in each iteration $\leq \log N$ bits are transmitted by each processor. Hence the bit complexity of the algorithm is $O(N \cdot \log^2 N)$. It remains to prove the correctness of the algorithm. We show that if there is a faulty component then every processor of the hypercube is at distance $\leq 1 + \log N$ from a faulty link. Indeed, let $x$ be an arbitrary node. We want to show that $x$ is at distance $\leq 1 + \log N$ from a faulty link. Indeed, let $y$ be any node which is adjacent to a faulty link. There is a path $x_0 = x, x_1, \ldots, x_d = y$ of length $d \leq \log N$ connecting $x$ to $y$ in the faulty hypercube. Since $y$ is adjacent to a faulty link it is clear that $x$ is at distance $\leq 1 + \log N$ from a faulty link. Hence the lemma is proved. ∎

If it turns out there is no faulty link then (assuming that the given boolean function is computable in the network) they execute the algorithm of [8] which has bit complexity $O(N \log^4 N)$. Else they proceed to the next phase of our algorithm.

## 2.2 Path generation and input collection

The algorithm to be presented in this subsection requires the existence of processors which are adjacent to faulty links. Therefore this phase is executed only if it turns out from the execution of the algorithm in subsection 2.1 that $\lambda \geq 1$. Let $f$ be a boolean function known to all processors of the (faulty) hypercube. We present the algorithm in three steps. The processors execute the following algorithm.
**Main Algorithm ($\lambda \geq 1$):**
1. PATH-GENERATION: The processors adjacent to faulty links become leaders and compute the configuration of the hypercube as follows. Let $M$ be the set of faulty links. Let $L$ be a processor adjacent to a faulty link. For each $x \in Q_n$ there are many paths connecting $L$ to $x$. However $L$ can choose a set of paths (in a canonical way) $\{p(L, x) : x \in Q_n\}$ such that $p(L, x)$ connects $L$ to $x$, has length $\leq \delta_n(\lambda)$ and avoids the missing link(s). Each processor adjacent to a faulty link generates a set of paths, one path for each processor of the hypercube.

In generating paths the processor takes into account its current knowledge of the position of the set of faulty links (which is only a subset of the set of all faulty links). Each such path is transmitted to its destination node along the sequence of links determined by this path. If during transmission of this path a faulty link is encountered then the corresponding processor adjacent to this faulty link sends back (along this same path but in the reverse direction) to the originating processor a complete list of its missing links. Based on this information each processor adjacent to a link in $M$ updates its current list of faulty links and generates a new set of paths which avoid the previously encountered faulty links. Now iteration of this procedure continues as long as new faulty links are found.[3] After execution of this algorithm all processors receive a complete path from each processor adjacent to a link in $M$.

Since each iteration of this algorithm generates a new collection of paths by "eliminating" newly encountered faulty links and since there are at most $\lambda$ faulty links it is clear that after at most $\lambda$ iterations all processors will receive paths from all processors adjacent to processors with faulty links. The bit complexity of this algorithm depends on the length of the paths which are created during the execution of the $\lambda$ iterations of this algorithm (in this instance the paths have maximal possible length $\delta_n(\lambda)$) and can be computed as before. There are $\leq 2\lambda$ processors adjacent to the $\lambda$ faulty links. Paths can be coded with $\delta_n(\lambda) \log \log N$ bits. Each path is transmitted at a distance $\leq \delta_n(\lambda)$. Each iteration of the algorithm involves $\leq 2\lambda$ processors adjacent to a faulty link in $M$. Hence each iteration of the algorithm involves the transmission of at most $O(N\lambda\delta_n(\lambda)^2 \log \log N)$ bits. Since the number of iterations is $\leq \lambda$ the actual bit complexity of this step will be $O(N\lambda^2\delta_n(\lambda)^2 \log \log N)$ bits.

2. INPUT-COLLECTION: For each $x$, and $L \in M$, processor $x$ sends its input bit $b_x$ together with its identity $p(L, x)$ to $L$ in the reverse direction along path $p(L, x)$ ($p(L, x)$ is the path computed in step 1). Now $L$ has a view of the entire input configuration of the hypercube, say $I_L$, and can compute $f(I_L)$. The bit complexity of this step is $O(N\lambda\delta_n(\lambda) \log \log N)$.

3. Let $F$ be the set of processors which are adjacent to faulty links. By executing the above algorithm each processor $L \in F$ computes its "view" $I_L$ of the given input configuration. In particular, each $L \in F$ will know the view $I_{L'}$ of all processors $L' \in F$. Hence all processors $L \in F$ may execute the invariance test

$$f(I_L) = f(I_{L'}), \text{ for all } L, L' \in F. \tag{1}$$

If (1) is true each processor $L \in F$ computes $f(I_L)$ and transmits it to all processors of the hypercube along the paths previously specified. Finally, $f(I_L)$ is the output bit of each processor of the hypercube. If on the other hand (1) is false then the processors $L \in F$ will transmit to all processors of the hypercube that $f$ is not computable on the given input. Clearly, test (1) is local to the

---

[3] Notice that nowhere in this algorithm do the processors need to know an upper bound on the number of faulty links. The iterated procedure terminates execution when no new faulty links are found.

processors and does not contribute to the overall bit complexity of the algorithm. The bit complexity of this step is $O(N\lambda\delta_n(\lambda)\log\log N)$.

Notice that nowhere in this algorithm did we have to assume that the processors have identities. All identities used there were generated by the algorithm. In addition the processors execute identical algorithms given identical input data. This completes our outline of the proof of Theorem 1. ∎

Theorem 1 raises the problem of studying $\delta_n(\lambda)$ as a function of $\lambda$. Results of B. Aiello and T. Leighton in [1] show that an $n$-dimensional hypercube with $n^{O(1)}$ worst-case faults can simulate the fault-free $n$-dimensional hypercube $Q_n$ with only constant slowdown. In particular, this implies that $\delta_n(\lambda) = O(n)$, for $\lambda = n^{O(1)}$. As a consequence we obtain the following result for hypercubes with polylogarithmic number of faulty links.

**Theorem 3.** *The bit complexity of computing boolean functions on a hypercube with polylogarithmic number of faulty links (i.e. $\lambda = (\log N)^{O(1)}$) is*

$$\begin{cases} O(N\log^4 N) & \text{if } \lambda \leq \log N/\sqrt{\log\log N} \\ O(N\lambda^2\log^2 N\log\log N) & \text{if } \lambda \geq \log N/\sqrt{\log\log N}. \end{cases}$$

PROOF. If $\lambda = 0$ then by [8] the bit complexity of computing $f$ is $O(N\log^4 N)$. If $\lambda \geq 1$ then applying Theorem 1 we see that the bit complexity of computing $f$ is $O(N\lambda^2\delta_n(\lambda)^2\log\log N)$. Since the number of faulty links is $n^{O(1)}$ we have that $\delta_n(\lambda) = O(n)$. Hence the combined bit complexity is

$$O(N\log^2 N\max\{\log^2 N, \lambda^2\log\log N\}). \tag{2}$$

It follows from formula (2) that the bit complexity of computing boolean functions on a hypercube with $\lambda = (\log N)^{O(1)}$ faulty links is as in the statement of the theorem. ∎

Thus we see that $\log N/\sqrt{\log\log N}$ is the threshold number of faulty links for which the bit complexity of computing boolean functions on an $N$ node hypercube exceeds the bit complexity in a non-faulty hypercube.

## 3 Determining the Computability of $f$

Condition (1) tests the computability of the boolean function $f$ on the given input. However, in the case where the set $F$ of nodes which are adjacent to the set of faulty links $\{l_1, \ldots, l_\lambda\}$ is transitive (i.e. for any two processors $L, L' \in F$ there exists an automorphism $\phi \in Aut(Q_n[l_1, \ldots, l_\lambda])$ such that $\phi(L) = L'$) we can in fact test whether the given function $f$ is computable on all inputs. This is done by checking whether or not the given boolean function $f$ is invariant under all automorphisms of the network. Indeed, assume the function $f$ is computable on the hypercube $Q_n[l_1, \ldots, l_\lambda]$. Let $I$ be an input configuration and let $\phi$ be an automorphism of $Q_n[l_1, \ldots, l_\lambda]$. Let $p$ be a node and $q$ its image under $\phi$, i.e. $q = \phi(p)$. But is is clear that $f(I) = f(I^\phi)$ since $p, q$ execute the same algorithm given identical input views. Conversely, assume that $f$ is invariant under all automorphisms of the above faulty hypercube. The previous input collection algorithm shows that for any processors $L, L' \in F$ the views $I_L, I_{L'}$ generated by the algorithm are identical up to automorphism. Notice that the condition on the transitivity of the set $F$ is always satisfied when $\lambda = 1$. Hence we have the following theorem.

**Theorem 4.** *Assume that the set of processors adjacent to the faulty links of the connected hypercube $Q_n[l_1, \ldots, l_\lambda]$ is transitive. Then a boolean function $f$ is computable in $Q_n[l_1, \ldots, l_\lambda]$ if and only if it is invariant under all the automorphisms in $Aut(Q_n[l_1, \ldots, l_\lambda])$. Moreover the bit complexity of computing all such boolean functions is $O(N\lambda^2 \delta_n(\lambda)^2 \log \log N)$.* ∎

To check efficiently the invariance of a boolean function under all automorphisms of the network the processors execute locally the algorithm specified in Lemmas 5, 6. This requires computing the group of automorphisms of the corresponding hypercube. Consider the *bit-complement* automorphisms that complement the bits of certain sets of components components, i.e. for any set $S \subseteq \{1, \ldots, n\}$ let $\phi_S(x_1, \ldots, x_n) = (y_1, \ldots, y_n)$, where $y_i = x_i + 1$, if $i \in S$, and $y_i = x_i$ otherwise (here addition is modulo 2). Let $F_n$ denote the group of bit-complement automorphisms of $Q_n$. Let $Aut(Q_n[l_1, \ldots, l_\lambda])$ be the set of automorphisms of $Q_n[l_1, \ldots, l_\lambda]$ that preserve the labels of its links.

**Lemma 5.** *Let $l_1, \ldots, l_\lambda$ be arbitrary links of the hypercube $Q_n$. If the network $Q_n[l_1, \ldots, l_\lambda]$ is connected then $Aut(Q_n[l_1, \ldots, l_\lambda])$ is a vector subspace of $Aut(Q_n)$ of dimension $O(\log \lambda)$ which has at most $2\lambda^2$ elements. Moreover these elements can be computed in time $O(\min\{\lambda^3, \lambda 2^n\})$.*

PROOF. First we show that $Aut(Q_n[l_1, \ldots, l_\lambda]) \leq Aut(Q_n)$. As in [8] we can show that all the automorphisms of $Q_n[l_1, \ldots, l_\lambda]$ must be of the form $\phi_S$, for some $S \subseteq \{1, 2, \ldots, n\}$. Indeed, let $\phi$ be an arbitrary automorphism and let $x, y$ be arbitrary nodes in $Q_n[l_1, \ldots, l_\lambda]$. We claim that $\phi(x) + \phi(y) = x + y$ (here addition is componentwise modulo 2). To see this take a path, say $x_0 := x, x_1, \ldots, x_k := y$, joinning $x$ to $y$. Since by definition $\phi$ preserves labels we must have that $\phi(x_i) + \phi(x_{i+1}) = x_i + x_{i+1}$, for all $i < k$. Hence the claim follows by adding these inequalities modulo 2. Now if $\phi(0^n) = (p_1, \ldots, p_n)$ then it is clear that $\phi = \phi_S$, where $S = \{1 \leq i \leq n : p_i \neq 0\}$.

Next we give an algorithm for computing the elements of the automorphism group $Aut(Q_n[l_1, \ldots, l_\lambda])$. Put $L = \{l_1, \ldots, l_\lambda\}$. The automorphisms of the faulty hypercube $Q_n[l_1, \ldots, l_\lambda])$ act naturally on the set of links $L$ in the following way: if $l = xy$ then $\phi(l) = \phi(x)\phi(y)$. For this action it is easy to see that for all $l, l' \in L$ there exist at most two automorphisms, say $\phi_{l,l'}, \psi_{l,l'}$, which map $l$ into $l'$. This implies that $|Aut(Q_n[l_1, \ldots, l_\lambda])| \leq 2\lambda^2$. Since the automorphisms of $Q_n[l_1, \ldots, l_\lambda]$ are precisely the automorphisms of $Q_n$ which leave the set $L$ invariant we are lead to the following algorithm whose output $S$ is the set of automorphisms of $Q_n[l_1, \ldots, l_\lambda]$.

**Algorithm for computing the automorphism group**

```
begin S := ∅;
for l, l' = l₁, ..., lλ do
    compute φₗ,ₗ' , ψₗ,ₗ' ;
    if φₗ,ₗ'(L) ⊆ L then S := S ∪ {φₗ,ₗ'};
    if ψₗ,ₗ'(L) ⊆ L then S := S ∪ {ψₗ,ₗ'};
    fi;
    od;
output S.
```

The output $S$ of the above algorithm is the desired group of automorphisms of $Q_n[l_1, \ldots, l_\lambda]$ since $Aut(Q_n[l_1, \ldots, l_\lambda]) = \{\phi \in Aut(Q_n) : \phi(L) \subseteq L\}$. ∎

**Lemma 6.** *There is an algorithm computing the group $Aut(Q_n[l_1, \ldots, l_\lambda])$ in $O(N\lambda^2\delta_n(\lambda)^2 \log\log N)$ bits.*

PROOF (outline) Using the first part of the algorithm of subsection 2.2 the processors adjacent to faulty links can compute the missing links of the entire hypercube. At the end of this algorithm "only" the processors adjacent to faulty links can compute the automorphism group of $Q_n[l_1, \ldots, l_\lambda]$ using the algorithm of Lemma 5. These processors now compute a basis of the automorphism group consisting of $O(\log \lambda)$ automorphisms and transmit this to the rest of the processors. This proves the lemma. ∎

We also mention an interesting observation concerning the size of the automorphism group of the faulty hypercube.

**Theorem 7.** *If for some $i$ the number of faulty links labeled $i$ is odd then*

$$|Aut(Q_n[l_1, \ldots, l_\lambda])| \le 2.$$

PROOF. Let $G = Aut(Q_n[l_1, \ldots, l_\lambda])$ and assume that $G$ is not the identity group. For $1 \le i \le n$ define

$$L = \{l_1, \ldots, l_\lambda\}$$
$$L_i = \{l \in L : \text{label of } l \text{ is } i\}.$$

For each $i$ every automorphism in $G$ permutes $L_i$. Now we can show that for all $l \in L$, $|G_l| \le 2$, where $G_l$ is the group of automorphisms fixing $l$. Indeed, if $\phi \ne id$ and $\phi(l) = l$ then $\phi = \phi_{\{i\}}$ where $i$ is the label of link $l$. In fact, if the label of $l$ is $i$ then

$$G_l = \begin{cases} < id > & \text{if } \phi_{\{i\}} \notin G \\ < \phi_{\{i\}} > & \text{if } \phi_{\{i\}} \in G \end{cases}$$

If $l^G$ denotes the orbit of $l$ in $G$ then it follows from the identity $|G_l| \cdot |l^G| = |G|$ (see Wielandt [9]) that

$$|l^G| = \begin{cases} |G| & \text{if } \phi_{\{i\}} \notin G \\ |G|/2 & \text{if } \phi_{\{i\}} \in G \end{cases}$$

It follows that

$$|L_i| = (\# \text{ of orbits of } G \text{ acting on } L_i) \cdot \begin{cases} |G| & \text{if } \phi_{\{i\}} \notin G \\ |G|/2 & \text{if } \phi_{\{i\}} \in G \end{cases}$$

which completes the proof of the theorem. ∎

Notice that $\phi_{\{i\}}$ is the only automorphisms in $G$ that has "fix-points" when acting on $L_i$. In particular, if for all $S$ with $\phi_S \in G$ we have that $|S| \geq 2$ then for all $i$ $|L_i|$ is even.

# 4 Hypercubes with Faulty Components

So far we have considered the case of hypercubes having only faulty links. However, it is straightforward how to adapt the Path-generation and Input-collection algorithms presented in section 2 to the case of hypercubes whose faulty components may be links and/or nodes. If a node is faulty then all its adjacent links are interpreted as faulty. The Path-generation algorithm is initiated by non-faulty processors which are adjacent to faulty links (there are $\leq 2\lambda$ such processors) and the iterated procedure is repeated $\leq \lambda$ times. Thus we can prove the following theorem.

**Theorem 8.** *In a hypercube with $\gamma$ faulty components exactly $\lambda$ of which are faulty links, $\lambda \geq 1$, the bit complexity of computing boolean functions is*

$$O(N\delta_n(\gamma)^2 \lambda^2 \log\log N). \quad \blacksquare$$

# 5 Conclusion

We have presented algorithms for distributed computation on anonymous asynchronous hypercubes with faulty components. Our algorithms rely on the possibility of distinguishing faulty links from non-faulty ones and are based on broadcasting and path generation. The hypercubes may be faulty but the faults may occur only before the start of the computation. An interesting problem would be to design more "adaptive" algorithms that allow for faults to occur at different parts of the computation.

# Acknowledgements

Many thanks to Danny Krizanc and Hisao Tamaki for useful advice and the referees for useful comments.

# References

1. B. Aiello and T. Leighton, "Coding Theory, Hypercube Embedding and Fault Tolerance", Proceedings of 2nd Annual ACM Symposium on Parallel Algorithms and Architectures, 1991, 125 - 136.
2. D. Angluin, "Local and Global Properties in Networks of Processors", 12th Annual ACM Symposium on Theory of Computing, 1980, 82 - 93.
3. H. Attiya and M. Snir and M. Warmuth, "Computing on an Anonymous Ring", Journal of the ACM, 35 (4), 1988. Short version has appeared in proceedings of the 4th Annual ACM Symposium on Principles of Distributed Computation, 1985, 845 - 875.
4. P. W. Beame and H. L. Bodlaender, "Distributed Computing on Transitive Networks: The Torus", 6th Annual Symposium on Theoretical Aspects of Computer Science, STACS, 1989, B. Monien and R. Cori, editors, Springer Verlag Lecture Notes in Computer Science. 294-303.
5. B. Becker and H.-U. Simon, "How Robust is the $n$-Cube?", Proceedings of IEEE 27th Annual Symposium on Foundations of Computer Science, 1986, 283 - 291.
6. M-S. Chen and K. G. Shin, "Adaptive Fault-Tolerant Routing in Hypercube Multicomputers", IEEE Transactions on Computers, 39 (12), December 1990, 1406 - 1416.
7. J. Hastad and T. Leighton and M. Newmann, "Reconfiguring a Hypercube in the Presence of Faults", Proceedings of the 19th Annual ACM Symposium on Theory of Computing, 1987, 274 - 284.
8. E. Kranakis and D. Krizanc, "Distributed Computing on Anonymous Hypercube Networks", Proceedings of the 3rd IEEE Symposium on Parallel and Distributed Processing, Dallas, Dec. 2-5, 1991, 722 - 729.
9. H. Wielandt, "Finite Permutation Groups", Academic Press, 1964.

# Message Terminate Algorithms for Anonymous Rings of Unknown Size

Israel Cidon and Yuval Shavitt

Electrical Engineering Dept.
Technion - Israel Institute of Technology
Haifa 32000, ISRAEL

**Abstract.** We consider a ring of unknown number of anonymous processors. We restrict ourselves to algorithms that are message terminate, i.e. the algorithm terminates when no more messages are present in the system but the processors may lack the ability to detect this situation. The work addresses algorithms (both deterministic and probabilistic) that always terminate with the correct result. We show the following:

- A deterministic algorithm for orientation that requires a symmetry breaking marking on the links and uses $O(n \log^2 n)$ bits for communication and $O(n)$ time. A Las-Vegas version of this algorithm that uses probability to break symmetry has the same average communication and time cost.
- A deterministic algorithm for pattern searching that uses $O(n \cdot |S|)$ communication bits for a pattern of length $|S|$. Computing AND and OR are simple cases of that algorithm.
- A probabilistic algorithm for dividing an even ring to pairs that uses $O(n \log n)$ communication bits and time.
- The impossibility of computing a class of functions called *nonsymmetric* that includes: leader election, XOR and finding the ring size. The same technique can be applied to prove the impossibility of dividing an odd ring to a maximal number of pairs.

## 1  Introduction

Ring networks have traditionally been used as a simple framework for evaluating distributed computation and communication systems. The ring topology can be used to demonstrate the implication of symmetry on the performance and feasibility of certain distributed tasks.

In this work we consider a ring of unknown number of indistinguishable processor that communicate through messages sent over bidirectional links (*anonymous ring*). We use an asynchronous model in which message transfer time is arbitrary long but finite. Algorithms for such asynchronous systems are generally message driven in the sense that a processor acts (changes its state, sends messages, performs computation etc.) only upon the reception of a message and idles afterwards until a new message is received. We focus on algorithms that are *message terminate* (MT), i.e., the algorithm terminates when no more messages are present in the system (in buffers or in transit at the transmission lines) and no processor is at a state it can initiate a message. The processors may lack the ability to recognize such termination and it might be detected only by an outside observer. The stronger property of *processor termination* (PT) cannot be achieved for most non-trivial problems in anonymous ring of unknown size. In [4] Attiya, Snir and Warmuth prove that no (deterministic) processor terminate algorithm exists even for "simple" functions such as OR and AND. In fact their proof can be easily extended for probabilistic PT algorithms as well.

Most of the algorithmic work in the area of anonymous networks has concentrated on models where some knowledge on the size of the network is known in advance (See [3], for lower bounds see [1, 10]). In the absence of knowledge it was shown in [9] that functions such as finding the size of the ring or leader election can be computed by a probabilistic message terminate algorithm with some (arbitrarily small) error probability. The communication and time costs of these algorithms grow (to infinity) as the error probability reaches zero. These results were extended in [12] for general topology networks.

In this paper we focus on message terminate algorithms for anonymous rings of unknown size that terminates correctly for any size $n$, deterministicly or with probability 1. On the other hand the average communication and time complexities are always bounded. To the best of our knowledge this is the first time that such algorithms are given for non-trivial problems. However, most problems can not be solved this way. We prove impossibility results for a large class of problems (non-symmetric). It is interesting to note that when the size of the ring is known, some of the problems that are solved efficiently under our framework (such as orientation) are as difficult as some problems that are impossible to solve in our model (such as XOR, see [4]).

We present a deterministic orientation algorithm for a ring of unknown size that uses marking on the links (similar to [7]) to break symmetry and has a communication complexity of $O(n \log^2 n)$ bits and message complexity of $O(n \log n)$. IN [11] Pachl shows a matching lower bound for rings of unknown size with distinct identities. We also present a deterministic algorithm that generalize pattern searching. Simple examples of that algorithm are computing AND and OR. With some modifications the algorithm can also search for nonsymmetric regular expressions, such as $\alpha\beta^*\gamma$.

Then, we turn to probabilistic algorithms. In [8, 9] Itai and Rodeh present a message terminate probabilistic algorithm that calculates the ring size in $O(rn^3)$ messages of $O(\log n)$ bits, and an error probability of $O(2^{-nr/2})$. Note, that if the error probability is taken to zero (or $r$ is taken to infinity) the message and time cost approach infinity for any $n$. This is a typical case for a Monte-Carlo algorithm. In the Monte-Carlo type algorithm, probability is used to break symmetry and termination is assured, but since symmetric tosses have positive probability, algorithms in this model may terminate with an error.

We are interested in algorithms that terminate correctly with probability 1 and maintain a bounded average communication and time costs (Las-Vegas). We present a Las-Vegas version of the orientation algorithm mentioned above. Instead of using links' markings to break symmetry, the algorithm uses coin tossing and keeps the (average) bit complexity of $O(n \log^2 n)$. Another Las-Vegas algorithm presented here is for dividing an even size ring to neighboring pairs (maximum matching).

We also present an impossibility result for a class of tasks, *nonsymmetric* problems, that cannot be solved under this framework. Two of the problems in this class where shown to be unsolvable in the past: finding the ring size by Itai and Rodeh in [8] and solitude detection (leader election) by Abrahamson et al. in [2]. Other examples for nonsymmetric problems are XOR and dividing an odd size ring to a maximum number of pairs (maximum matching).

## 2 Deterministic Algorithms

### 2.1 Orientation

Consider a ring of unknown number of indistinguishable processors. Each processor (node) has a local notion of a left or right link which is termed the *orientation* or *notion of direction* of the node. Two neighboring nodes have the same orientation or same notion of direction if the link connecting them is considered to be right at one of them and left at the other. Throughout the paper the left or right link of a processor, means left or right according to the processor local notion of direction. The left or right side of a group of nodes with the same orientation means according to their common notion of direction.

In the course of the algorithm each node $i$ is always a member of a *segment* of consecutive nodes with the same orientation and keeps a local variable called $length_i$ that specifies its relative position (left to right) in the segment. The leftmost node in the sequence (the tail) has $length = 1$, its right neighbor has $length = 2$, etc. Therefore, a segment is a sequence of adjacent nodes with the same orientation that satisfy: 1) Only the leftmost node (the tail) has $length = 1$. 2) if $length_i \neq 1$ then $length_i = length_{left(i)} + 1$. 3) for the right most node (the head): $length_{right(i)} \neq length_i + 1$ OR $orientation_{right(i)} \neq orientation_i$

The *size* of a segment is defined as the $length$ of its head. We define a *shrinking segment* to be a segment whose head node has changed orientation, i.e. has left the segment.

**General Description.** When a node wakes up it determines an arbitrary orientation, forms a single node segment by setting $length=1$, and sends the message RIGHT(1) on its right link. Upon the reception of a RIGHT($k$) message from the left neighbor, the node does nothing except for recording the value $k+1$ in the variable $l\_from\_left$. Consequently, if all nodes initially decide on the same orientation, each node should receive a RIGHT(1) message on its left link and the algorithm terminates. However, if a node (which is in general the head of a segment) receives a RIGHT message on its right link, it knows that the node on its right has a conflicting orientation, and one of them must flip its orientation. The node that lost the conflict reverses its orientation and joins the new segment by setting its variable $length$ to be one higher than that of the winning node.

After joining the new segment, the loser becomes the spearhead of the segment and sends a RIGHT message with the new segment size to its right (its former left). In general, the winner is the node heading the longer segment. In case of a tie, a symmetry breaking marking for each link dictates the winner. One exception for this procedure is when the node has *length=1*. As was previously described a node with *length=1* that receives a RIGHT($k$) message on its left link, saves the length ($k+1$) of the segment on its left in the variable *l_from_left*. In this case (only), if a segment from its right will try to capture it, the node might join the segment on its left first (and will become its head). The decision which segment to join depends on the length of the two conflicting segments.[1] The algorithm eventually stops when all RIGHT messages arrive on left links.

**Formal Description.** Each node uses the following variables:
**length** – a node's position in a segment (from the left).
**l_from_left** – for a node with *length=1*, its possible position from the left in the segment on its left, if it would join it.
**state** – the state of the node, asleep or awaken.
Messages that are sent by the algorithm:
**WAKE_UP** – an initialization message received from a higher level.
**RIGHT(l)** – a message sent by a node over its right link, that contains its position in its segment (from left).

The algorithm is given in figure 1.

**Correctness Proof.** We start with a correctness proof to show that the algorithm always terminates with a complete orientation of the ring. Then we turn to analyze the message and time complexities of the algorithm.

**Lemma 1** *A segment can add a node (grow) or loose a node (shrink) only from its right side.*

See [5] for the proof.

**Lemma 2** *All awaken nodes in the ring belong to a segment.*

See [5] for the proof.

**Lemma 3** *A shrinking segment never grows, all its nodes eventually join the segment on its right except for the left most node that might join the segment on its left.*

---

[1] This can be viewed as if the node queues the message from the left until it was captured by the segment from the right and then changes orientation and reacted to the message from its new right that causes it to change orientation again. In this scenario one extra message is sent. We shall term this version "the basic algorithm" and use it in some of the following proofs.

Initially all nodes have *state* = *asleep*.

for WAKE_UP
⟨W.0⟩   set *state* ← *awaken*;   *l_from_left* ← −1
⟨W.1⟩   set *length* ← 1
⟨W.2⟩   Send RIGHT(*length*) on right link
for RIGHT(*l*)
⟨R.0⟩   if *state* = *awaken* then
⟨R.1⟩      if received on right link then
⟨R.2⟩         if (*l* > *length*) OR (*l* = *length* AND NOT SYM_BREAK(right link)) then
⟨R.3⟩            if ( (*length* = 1) AND (*l_from_left* > *l* OR
                                (*l_from_left* = *l* AND SYM_BREAK(right link)) ) ) then
                  /* join the long segment at your left */
⟨R.4⟩               *length* ← *l_from_left*
⟨R.5⟩               Send RIGHT(*length*) on right link
⟨R.6⟩            end
⟨R.7⟩            else /* the battle is lost - join the segment at your right */
⟨R.8⟩               change orientation
⟨R.9⟩               *length* ← *l* + 1
⟨R.10⟩              Send RIGHT(*length*) on right link
⟨R.11⟩           end
⟨R.12⟩      else /* message received on left link */
⟨R.13⟩         *l_from_left* ← *l* + 1
⟨R.14⟩   else /* node is asleep */
⟨R.15⟩      set link on which the message received to be the left one
⟨R.16⟩      *length* ← *l* + 1
⟨R.17⟩      Send RIGHT(*length*)
⟨R.18⟩   end

**Fig. 1.** Orientation Algorithm – Formal Description

Proof:

Let $i$ be the right most node of the shrinking segment before it joins another segment, and let $j$ be the right most node after $i$ has left the segment. Denote by $l_{i\ received}$ the value received by $i$ from right that caused $i$ to leave its segment. From line ⟨R.2⟩ it must hold for $i$ that at the reception time $l_{i\ received} \geq length_i$. Since $i$ changes orientation it must send the message RIGHT($l_{i\ received} + 1$) on its new right link, namely to $j$. At the reception of the message from $i$ at $j$ holds, $length_j = length_i - 1 < length_i \leq l_{i\ received} < l_{i\ received} + 1 = l_{j\ received}$, we get $length_j < l_{j\ received}$ and thus the condition in ⟨R.2⟩ will be satisfied leading to the execution of lines ⟨R.8⟩ - ⟨R.10⟩ (*length* ≠ 1) and $j$ must change its orientation too.

For the left most node in the shrinking segment condition ⟨R.3⟩ is either false which results exactly as before, or true in that case it will join the segment on its left.                                                                          □

**Theorem 1** *The algorithm terminates within finite number of messages.*

Proof:

Every node, upon waking up, sends exactly one message ($\langle W.2 \rangle$ and $\langle R.17 \rangle$) and joins a segment. A node that receives a message also sends only one when it joins a new segment (lines $\langle R.5 \rangle$ and $\langle R.10 \rangle$). By lemma 3 a segment that looses a node cannot grow any more, and since segments cannot grow longer than n, the process of segment growing is finite, and therefore also the number of messages sent by the algorithm. □

**Theorem 2** *When the algorithm terminates, all nodes are awaken and have the same orientation.*

Proof:

We shall first prove for the case where all nodes are awakened.

Assume the contrary, i.e. there are at least two nodes with different orientation, and no more messages are received after time $t_0$. Clearly, there must be also two neighbors each to the right of the other. By lemma 2, there must exist two adjacent segments with different orientation that each one of them is to the right of the other. The two heads of those segments must have exchange RIGHT messages, and since one of them must have lost the conflict it must have changed its orientation.

This proves the theorem when all nodes are awaken. We now show that all nodes eventually are awaken. Assume the contrary, i.e. a WAKE_UP message was delivered to some node and there is at least one node that sleeps after the algorithm has terminated. Since a WAKE_UP message was delivered then there is at least one segment in the network.

By the same reasoning as above it is clear that there are no adjacent segment one to the right of the other. Therefore there must be at least one sleeping node at the right of some segment. A sleeping node that is on the right side of a segment must receive a RIGHT message and wakes up which contradicts the assumption that some nodes sleeps forever. □

**Message Complexity.**

**Lemma 4** *[6]*

*Let $F(n)$ be a discrete function with the following recursive definition:*

$$F(1) = 1$$
$$F(n) = \max_{1 \le i < n} \{F(i) + F(n-i) + \min\{i, n-i\}\} = \max_{1 \le i \le n/2} \{F(i) + F(n-i) + i\}$$

*then for $n \ge 1$*
$$F(n) = \begin{cases} 2F(\frac{n}{2}) + \frac{n}{2} & \text{for even } n \\ F(\frac{n-1}{2}) + F(\frac{n+1}{2}) + \frac{n-1}{2} & \text{for odd } n \end{cases}$$

**Lemma 5** *For all natural $m$, $F(n) = n(1 + \frac{1}{2}\log_2 n)$ where $n = 2^m$.*

Proof:

By lemma 4: $F(n) = 2F(\frac{n}{2}) + \frac{n}{2} = 2[2F(\frac{n}{4}) + \frac{n}{4}] + \frac{n}{2}$.

Applying the recursion $m = log_2 n$ times results in: $F(n) = 2^m(F(1) + \frac{1}{2} m) = n(1 + \frac{1}{2} log_2 n)$. $\square$

**Lemma 6** $F(n) \le n(1 + \frac{1}{2} log_2 n)$ *for all* $n > 2$.

Proof:

We prove by induction on $n$.

$F(1) \le 1 \cdot (1 + \frac{1}{2} log_2 1) = 1$ and $F(2) = 2 \cdot (1 + \frac{1}{2} log_2 2) = 3$.

We assume that the hypothesis holds for all values less than $n$, and prove for $n$.

In the case that $n$ is even, then by lemma 4 and by the induction hypothesis:
$F(n) = 2F(\frac{n}{2}) + \frac{n}{2} \le 2[\frac{n}{2}(1 + \frac{1}{2} log_2 \frac{n}{2})] + \frac{n}{2} = n(1 + \frac{1}{2} log_2 \frac{n}{2}) + \frac{n}{2} = n(1 + \frac{1}{2} log_2 n)$

The case for odd $n$ is similar and can be found in [5]. $\square$

**Corollary 1** $F(n) = n(1 + \frac{1}{2} log_2 n)$ *only if* $n = 2^m$ *and* $m$ *is natural.*

**Lemma 7** $F(n)$, *as defined in lemma 4, is the maximal number of messages that can be sent for increasing the size of a segment to* $n$.

Proof:

Let $G(n)$ be the number of messages needed to be sent to form a segment of size $n$. Clearly $G(1) = 1$, since segments of size 1 are only formed when a node wakes up and sends a single message.

A segment of size $n$, $n > 1$ can be formed in one of the three following ways.

A segment of size $n - 1$ sends a RIGHT message that wakes up a node which is *asleep*, That node sends one message as it join the segment. The maximal number of messages sent in this scenario is $G(n - 1) + 1$.

A segment of size $i$ and a segment of size $n - i$ exchanging RIGHT messages and the bigger one capture the other. The maximal number of messages sent in this scenario is $G(i) + G(n - i) + \min\{i, n - i\}$. This is true since each processor in the defeated segment changes orientation and sends a single message (lines $\langle R.8 \rangle$ - $\langle R.10 \rangle$). Note that if a segment of size $n + 1 - i$ captures a segment of size $i$ except for its leftmost node (which joins its left side segment instead), the number of messages for forming a segment of size $n$ takes only $G(n + 1 - i) + G(i) + i - 1$. however, this situation should be viewed as if the segment grow to length $n + 1$ and shrink back, and indeed the segment will eventually be captured by the bigger one from the left.

A segment of size $n - 1$ is growing when the tail of the segment to its right (that has the same orientation) decides to join him (instead of joining the winning segment on the right). The cost of this scenario is $G(n - 1) + G(1) + 1$

We can bound $G(n)$ by the maximum of the above results:

$G(1) = 1$

$G(n) \le \max\{[G(n - 1) + 1], \max_{1 \le i < n} \{G(i) + G(n - i) + \min\{i, n - i\}, [G(1) + G(n - 1) + 1]\}$

which yields:

$$G(n) \leq \max_{1 \leq i < n} \{G(i) + G(n-i) + \min\{i, n-i\}\}$$

Therefore, $G(n) \leq F(n)$ □

**Theorem 3** *The algorithm for a ring of size $n$ terminates after no more than $n(1 + \frac{1}{2}\log_2 n)$ messages are sent.*

Proof:
  By the definition of $F$, for all integers $j \leq n$, $k \leq j$ and all $i_k > 0$ such that $i_1 + i_2 + \cdots + i_j \leq n$, it is clear that $F(n) \leq F(i_1) + F(i_2) + \cdots + F(i_j)$. By lemma 2 and theorem 2 all the nodes belong to segments and are awakened. By the observations above the algorithm stops after no more than $F(n) = n(1 + \frac{1}{2}\log_2 n)$ messages are sent. □

**Time Complexity.** For the purpose of time complexity analysis we consider a model in which a message is delivered after at most one time unit. In the basic algorithm, each node sends a message when it wakes up. If two nodes send messages to each other on the same link more messages are sent. We shall call such a situation a *conflict*. It is important to notice that a conflict can be created only when a node wakes up. After a conflict is created, one of the nodes changes its orientation and sends a message on its other link. This can lead to a conflict on that link and we shall say that the conflict *moves* one hop. Otherwise, we say that the conflict disappeared or resolved.

**Lemma 8** *In the basic orientation algorithm, delaying an incoming message, cannot cause a message to be sent earlier from this node.*

See [5] for the proof.

**Lemma 9** *If all nodes are awakened together, after $k$ time units there are no conflicts between segments that are both of size less than $k$.*

Proof:
  We assume in this proof that messages always travel exactly one time unit since by lemma 8 it is the worst case. The proof by induction on $k$ is immediate. □

**Corollary 2** *If all nodes are awakened together, the algorithm terminates after no more than $n$ time units.*

  A simple addition to the algorithm enable termination for a ring of size $n$ after no more than $\lceil \frac{3n}{2} \rceil$ time units. Every node that receives a message for the first time (wakes up) sends immediately a wake-up message on the other link (on both links). It is clear that after $\lceil \frac{n}{2} \rceil$ time units all the processors are awakened, and the extra cost is only $2n$ messages. By lemma 9 the algorithm terminates after $\lceil \frac{3n}{2} \rceil$ time units. Our conjecture is that the algorithm has linear time complexity even without this addition.

## 2.2 Pattern Searching

Consider the case of a ring of unknown number of indistinguishable processors each of which has a local variable $v_i$ ($i$ is only used for this discussion and is not known to the processors) of some alphabet. We are interested in detecting a pattern (a word) $S$ that is defined on the $v_i$s. We only consider algorithms that terminate after all nodes have the correct result. Termination is achieved when communication ceases (message termination).

An intuitive algorithm for the search will be as follows.

Upon wake-up or upon receiving the first message, set status to *not_found*, and if your local variable $v_i$ is equal to the first letter in the searched word $S$, send $FOUND(1)$ to both your neighbors. Upon receipt of a $FOUND(j)$ message ($j < |S|$), if $v_i$ is equal to the $j + 1$-th letter of $S$, send $FOUND(j + 1)$ on the other link. If $j = |S| - 1$ and your letter matches the last one of the searched word, set status to *found* and send $FOUND(|S|)$ on both links. Upon receipt of $FOUND(|S|)$ when your status is *not_found*, forward it to the other link and set your status to *found*. Upon all other cases, no message or status change is triggered.

To show that the algorithm (message) terminates after a finite number of messages are sent, consider the following.

Every node can initiate at most two $FOUND(1)$ messages. In addition every node can send at most one $FOUND(j)$ message for $1 < j < |S|$ and at most two $FOUND(|S|)$ messages. We can get, thus, an $O(n \cdot |S|)$ higher bound on the number of messages that the algorithm will send for a ring of size $n$.

Correctness can be easily proved.

Computing the functions OR or AND are simple cases of this algorithm as the OR function is basically a search for the pattern '1', and the AND function a search for the pattern '0'.

The algorithm can be generalized to search for hierarchically ordered patterns. An example for this is a search for winning poker sequences in a ring where each processor holds a card. We would like first to search for a royal flush, or if non found to search for a sequence of four identical cards, and if non found a full-house sequence etc. The change in the algorithm is mainly to add to the $FOUND$ message another parameter that holds the searched pattern i.d. A search starts simultaneously for all patterns, but when a pattern is found no more messages about patterns that are lower in the search hierarchy are forwarded. The complexity of this algorithm is only $h$ times the complexity of the simple algorithm described before, where $h$ is the hierarchy depth.

Search Algorithm for patterns of the form $\alpha\beta^*\gamma$ ($\alpha \neq \beta^*$) are also possible.

## 3 Probabilistic Algorithms

### 3.1 Orientation

The orientation algorithm presented before, uses a deterministic function to break symmetry among adjacent nodes. Consequently, it requires some predefined consistent input for each pair of neighboring nodes. This action can be replaced by probabilistic means that eliminate the need for such input values. Upon a need to break symmetry among neighbors, each node will toss a fair coin and send the result to the competing node. If they both get the same result, another round of coin tossing is performed, until exactly one of the nodes gets '1'. The expected number of rounds for such a process is $\sum_{i=1}^{\infty} i \cdot \left(\frac{1}{2}\right)^i = 2$, but theoretically the process can be arbitrary long. Since the number of messages for each coin tossing round is constant, the expected complexity for the probabilistic orientation algorithm stays $O(n \cdot \log n)$. Just like its deterministic counterpart the probabilistic algorithm is partially correct. It message terminates with probability 1 and has bounded expected time and message (or bit) complexities. Therefore, it conducts a message terminate Las-Vegas type algorithm.

## 3.2 Dividing an Even Size Ring to Pairs

We assume a bidirectional ring with unknown but even number of anonymous processors. We give a maximum matching algorithm for the ring, i.e. after the algorithm (message) terminates, every node of the ring is a member of exactly one group of two adjacent nodes.

**Algorithm Description** The algorithm works in phases: In each phase a node sends and receives a single message over both links. (We delay messages which arrive out of phase until next phase starts, there can be at most one such outstanding messages per node). Nodes are either *single* or *married*. Only *single* nodes initiate the communication of the next phase. Two messages are used: *invite* and *reject*. At the beginning of a phase (or upon wake-up) a *single* node selects randomly one of its links, marks it as *candidate*, sends an *invite* message over that link and sends a *reject* message over the other link. If it receives an *invite* message over the *candidate* link, it marks it as a *spouse* and becomes *married*. Otherwise, it waits until it has received a message over both links and starts a new phase. A *married* node only forwards the messages it gets to the opposite direction. In the case that both messages of the same phase are *invite* the *married* node should swap its *spouse*, i.e. it removes the *spouse* marking from one of the links and marks the other as *spouse*. The changing of the *spouse* marking breaks the matches of all the couples between two single nodes and re-divide these nodes and the two single nodes to neighboring couples. If all nodes are *married* after any phase completes, the algorithm terminates as no processor initiates a new phase.

**Complexity** At each phase a single node will become married with probability 1/2. Therefore, On the average half of the single nodes become married after each phase, so the average number of phases is logarithmic. Each phase requires exactly one message over any link in each direction, which gives us a total of $O(n \cdot \log n)$ messages. Since we have only two messages types (*invite* and *reject*), the bit complexity is also $O(n \cdot \log n)$.

# 4 Impossibility Results

Let $f : \Sigma^* \to T$ be a function computed on anonymous rings defined over some alphabet $\Sigma$. $f$ is *symmetric* if for every string $s \in \Sigma^*$ and for every natural $k$, $f(s) = f(s^k)$. Otherwise $f$ is *nonsymmetric*.

In [8] Itai and Rodeh prove the impossibility of calculating the ring size when the processors are anonymous, and the algorithm is partially correct. In the sequel we shall extend this proof in two directions. First we prove that the ring size cannot be calculated by algorithms that have bounded bit complexity and are partially correct with probability 1, where in [8] algorithms that might end with an error with probability 0 were not considered. Second we generalize this to all *nonsymmetric* functions.

Examples for *nonsymmetric* functions are leader election, XOR and computing the ring's size. For XOR $f(s) \neq f(s^k)$ whenever $s$ contains an odd number of 1s and $k$ is even. For computing the ring size $f(s)$ never equals $f(s^k)$ if $k > 1$. For leader election there is no meaning for the input and the function return value should be a bit that tells each processor whether it is the leader, it is clear that the vector $f(s^k)$ never equals the concatenation of the $k$ vectors of $f(s)$.

The proof is constructed for a synchronous algorithm and thus holds for asynchronous algorithms as well. We first examine a ring of $n$ processors $(p_1, p_2, \ldots, p_n)$ with inputs $s = (s_1, s_2, \ldots, s_n)$. (The processors are anonymous and the markings are only for our convenience.) We select an execution $\mathcal{R}$ of the algorithm on that ring that has a positive probability to terminate after a finite number of bits were sent, and yields $\mathbf{f}(s) = (f_1(s), f_2(s), \ldots, f_n(s))$ as output vector. We prove that execution with positive probability must exist. Then we look at a system of $k$ such rings with the same inputs and prove that the probability for $\mathcal{R}$ to be executed simultaneously on all the rings is still positive. In the final step, we form a single ring of size $kn$, by cutting all the rings at the same place, and reconnecting them to a ring of $kn$ processors. Since the processors are anonymous there is no way for a processor to tell if it is in the system of $k$ rings that each one of them has $\mathcal{R}$ executed at, or whether it is in a ring of $kn$ nodes that has $k$ 'copies' of $\mathcal{R}$ executed at its $k$ sections. The probability of getting $\mathbf{f}^k(s) = (\mathbf{f}(s), \mathbf{f}(s), \ldots, \mathbf{f}(s))$ in the concatenated ring is thus positive, too, and since $\mathbf{f}^k(s) \neq \mathbf{f}(s^k)$ we conclude our claim.

**Theorem 4** *There is no algorithm for computing a nonsymmetric function in a ring of unknown number of anonymous processors that is partially correct with probability 1 and its average bit complexity is bounded.*

Proof:

Let $\mathcal{A}$ be such an algorithm for computing the function $f$ in a ring of unknown number of anonymous processors, and let $E$ be the average number of bits sent by the algorithm. We examine a ring with $n$ processors $(p_1, p_2, \ldots, p_n)$ with inputs $s = (s_1, s_2, \ldots, s_n)$ Let $\mathbf{f}(s) = (f_1(s), f_2(s), \ldots, f_n(s))$ be the output vector where $f_i(s)$ is the output value that processor $p_i$ holds when the algorithm (message) terminates for inputs $s$. Select $s$ and $k$ s.t. $\mathbf{f}^k(s) \neq \mathbf{f}(s^k)$. We select an execution $\mathcal{R}$ of positive probability that terminates after a finite number of bits were sent, and yields $\mathbf{f}(s) = (f_1(s),\ f_2(s),\ \ldots,\ f_n(s))$ as output vector. We shall show that such $\mathcal{R}$ with probability greater then zero exists. By definition $E = \sum_{i=1}^{\infty} ip(i)$, where $p(i)$ is the probability that $\mathcal{A}$ terminates after $i$ bits were sent.

$$E \geq \sum_{i=2E+1}^{\infty} ip(i) \geq 2E \sum_{i=2E+1}^{\infty} p(i) \tag{1}$$

We get from eq. 1 that $\sum_{i=2E+1}^{\infty} p(i) \leq \frac{1}{2}$, and thus $\sum_{i=1}^{2E} p(i) \geq \frac{1}{2}$. We can deduce that at least one execution that uses less than $2E$ bits, has a positive probability $\varepsilon$.

Examine a system of $k$ rings each of $n$ nodes and input vector $s$. All the rings are stochasticly independent. Since the probability space of this system is the Cartesian product of $k$ identical probability spaces of the ring discussed before, the probability for $\mathcal{R}$ to be executed simultaneously on all the rings is $\varepsilon^k$.

Now let cut all the above rings in the same place, say between processor $p_i$ and processor $p_{i+1}$. Then, all the strips are connected to a ring of $kn$ processors such that every processor $p_i$ is connected to $p_{i+1}$: $(p_{i+1}^1,\ \ldots,\ p_n^1,\ p_1^1,\ \ldots,\ p_i^1, p_{i+1}^2,\ \ldots,\ p_i^2, p_{i+1}^3,\ \cdots, p_i^k)$. Since the processors are anonymous there is no way for a processor to tell if it is in the system of $k$ rings that each one of them has $\mathcal{R}$ executed at, or whether it is in a ring of $kn$ nodes that has $k$ 'copies' of $\mathcal{R}$ executed at its $k$ sections. The probability space of the concatenated ring and the $k$ ring system is identical. All the events in the probability space that cause simultaneous execution in the $k$ ring system cause also simultaneous execution of $k$ copies of $\mathcal{R}$ at the concatenated ring and yields $\mathbf{f}^k(s) = (\mathbf{f}(s),\ \mathbf{f}(s),\ \ldots,\ \mathbf{f}(s))$ as output. So the probability to get $\mathbf{f}^k(s)$ as output in the concatenated ring is at least $\varepsilon^k$. $\qquad\qquad\square$

A direct corollary of this theorem is that deterministic algorithms for non-symmetric functions do not exist.

The rationale for our restriction to algorithms with bounded average bit complexity can be demonstrated by the following simple algorithm. Each node select a real number in the range $(0..1)$. Since the probability for two nodes to choose the same real number is zero the ring's nodes own a unique identities with probability 1, a model that was studied in depth in the literature. Leader election can be easily performed with $O(n \log n)$ messages but here each one of them carry an infinite number of bits.

## 5  Concluding Remarks

We present here for the first time algorithms for anonymous rings of unknown size that always (or with probability 1) converge to the the right answer and have bounded (average) communication and time costs. All of our deterministic algorithms: orientation and general pattern searching which include computing OR and AND, have the same complexities as the corresponding algorithms in models where the ring size is known. Our probabilistic algorithm for dividing an even size ring to pairs can be generalized to dividing a ring of size $km$ to $m$ groups of $k$ neighboring nodes.

Our impossibility result shows that in general such an algorithm does not exist for arbitrary functions since most functions are non-symmetric. Some problems are more difficult to be presented in terms of functions. However the impossibility result still holds for such problems if they have a non-symmetric behavior. Such examples are: dividing a ring of size $n \neq km$ to a maximal number of groups of $k$ neighboring nodes; evaluating the size of the longest sequence of consecutive '1', where in the case that all inputs are '1' this translates into finding the ring size (which was also proved in [8]).

# References

1. K. Abrahamson, A. Adler, L. Higham, and D. Kirkpatrick. Randomized function evaluation on a ring. In J. van Leeuwen, editor, *Proceedings, 2nd International Workshop on Distributed Algorithms*, pages 324–331, July 1987. Lecture Notes in Computer Science, Vol. 312.
2. K. Abrahamson, A. Adler, L. Higham, and D. Kirkpatrick. Optimal algorithms for probabilistic solitude detection on anonymous rings. Technical report TR 90-3, University of British Columbia, 1990.
3. H. Attiya and M. Snir. Better computing on the anonymous ring. *Journal of Algorithms*, 12(2):204–238, June 1991.
4. H. Attiya, M. Snir, and M. K. Warmuth. Computing on the anonymous ring. *Journal of the ACM*, 35(4):845–875, 1988.
5. I. Cidon and Y. Shavitt. Message terminate algorithms for rings of unknown size. EE Pub. 793, Technion - Israel Institute of Technology, Dept. of Electrical Engineering, Haifa 32000, ISRAEL, August 1991.
6. D. H. Greene and D. E. Knuth. *Mathematics for the Analysis of Algorithms*. Birkhauser, second edition, 1982.
7. A. Israeli and M. Jalfon. Uniform self stabilizing ring orientation. *Information and Computation*, 1991. to be published.
8. A. Itai and M. Rodeh. Symmetry breaking in distributed networks. In *Proceedings of the 22nd annual IEEE symp. of fundations of computer science (FOCS)*, pages 150–158, 1981.
9. A. Itai and M. Rodeh. Symmetry breaking in distributed networks. *Information and Computation*, 88(1), September 1990.
10. S. Moran and M. K. Warmuth. Gap theorms for distributed computation. In *Proceedings of the Fifth Annual ACM Symposium on Principles of Distributed Computing (PODC)*, pages 141–150, 1986.
11. J. K. Pachl. A lower bound for probabilistic distributed algorithms. *Journal of Algorithms*, 8:53–65, 1987.
12. B. Schieber and M. Snir. Calling names on nameless networks. In *Proceedings of the Eighth Annual ACM Symposium on Principles of Distributed Computing (PODC)*, pages 319–328, 1989.

# Distributed Resource Allocation Algorithms

## (Extended Abstract)

Judit Bar-Ilan [*]        David Peleg [†]

## 1 Introduction

One of the major constraints of a multi-processing system is that a resource can usually be used by only one process at a time. This constraint introduces the problem of scheduling jobs with conflicting resource requirements in a distributed system. The problem (sometimes known as the *dining/drinking philosophers* problem) has received considerable attention in the last two decades (see [Dij71, RL81, Lyn81, CM84, SP88, AS90]).

In this paper we consider designing algorithms with low response time for resource allocation. The general framework we consider is a point-to-point message passing network of processors. Our main focus is on classifying the possible models according to several parameters, and looking for solutions that are appropriate (and efficient) in each of these submodels.

### 1.1 The Problem

A distributed system is a collection of processors connected through communication channels. We denote the underlying communication graph by $\mathcal{G}$. It is assumed that the processors in the system occasionally create jobs that need to be executed by the system. In order to execute its task, each job needs certain resources. If two jobs need the same resource they cannot be executed concurrently. Therefore it is necessary to find an efficient way to schedule the execution of these jobs so as to minimize the response time. In this model, the problem of resource allocation is sometimes referred to as the *dining/drinking philosophers* problem.

The conflicts caused by simultaneous demands are represented formally via a structure called the *conflict graph*, $\mathcal{C}$. The nodes of the graph are jobs, and there is an edge between two nodes if the corresponding jobs need a common resource. The graph is dynamic: once a job is created we add a node to the graph, and once it terminates its execution, the corresponding node is deleted from the graph.

---

[*]The Open University of Israel, Tel-Aviv 61392, Israel. This work was carried out while the author was with the Department of Applied Mathematics and Computer Science, The Weizmann Institute of Science.

[†]Department of Applied Mathematics and Computer Science, The Weizmann Institute, Rehovot 76100, Israel. Supported in part by a Walter and Elise Haas Career Development Award and by a grant from the Basic Research Foundation.

We make the following assumptions on the problem, following [AS90]. We assume that each job has a unique ID. In most of our algorithms we allow only one job per processor at a time, in which case the job ID can simply be the processor's ID. We assume that at any moment, there exist at most $\delta_j$ jobs conflicting with job $j$. We denote by $\delta$ the maximum number of conflicting jobs with any job $j$, which is also the maximum degree in the dynamic graph $\mathcal{C}$. We denote by $\mu$ the maximum execution time of any job, and by $\mu_j$ the maximum execution time of any neighbor of $j$ (including $j$ itself) at any time in the conflict graph, $\mathcal{C}$. By $\nu$ we denote the maximum time required for a message sent from one processor to the other to be prepared, transmitted and received. The *response time* for job $j$ is the total time elapsing from the creation of the job to the time it begins its execution.

The execution of the jobs is governed by an algorithm called the *scheduler*. Our aim is to devise algorithms for the distributed scheduler with low response time. When a new job is created, a *schedule(j)* message is sent to the scheduler. It contains the unique ID of the job, and a set *compete(j)*, which is a list of the ID's of the existing jobs that conflict with $j$ (that is, the neighbors of $j$ in $\mathcal{C}$). (In [AS90] it is only required that if $j$ and $k$ conflict, and the time periods of their existence in the system overlaps, then either $k \in compete(j)$ or $j \in compete(k)$. Several of our algorithms work under this weaker assumption as well.) When a job leaves execution it sends a *done(j)* message to the scheduler. We assume that no job terminates before the end of its execution and no job is executed forever.

The scheduler informs a job $j$ to start its execution by sending it an *execute(j)* message. The scheduler sends exactly one *execute(j)* message for each job $j$ (guaranteeing a liveness property for the system), and if jobs $j$ and $k$ conflict then either the *done(j)* message precedes the *execute(k)* message or the *done(k)* message precedes the *execute(j)* message (thus guaranteeing a safety property). With these notations we can rephrase the definition of *response time* as the time from the moment the *schedule(j)* message was sent by the originator of job $j$ to the moment the *execute(j)* message was received by the job. We say that a job is *active* between the time it sends the *schedule* message and the time it receives the *execute* message.

## 1.2 Model Classification

Our results are presented in this abstract under the assumption that we work in a synchronous environment with a complete communication graph $\mathcal{G}$. Communication is synchronous if all the processors work at the same rate and a message sent from processor $p$ connected to processor $q$ at time $t$ arrives at time $t+1$.

We classify the model according to two independent parameters. Our first parameter concerns the local computational requirements allowed for the resource allocation algorithm at hand. An algorithm is *bounded* if the amount of local computation it requires at a processor attempting to execute job $j$ in a single step is bounded by $O(\delta_j)$ (intuitively allowing it to exchange one round of communication with its competitors). We say that the model is bounded if it allows only bounded algorithms. Otherwise (if arbitrary computations are allowed in a single step) the model is said to be unbounded. Our second parameter concerns the question whether the execution time of a job is known at the time it is created.

This classification gives rise to four different models, which can be described formally by associating with each model two attributes, corresponding to the above parameters. The first attribute is $U$ when the model is computationally unbounded, and $B$ otherwise. The second attribute gets the value $K$ if the length of the job execution is known at the time the job is created, and $F$ otherwise.

In this paper we are concerned with the response time of jobs, as defined above, with different algorithms under these four models. Bounds on the time are expressed in terms of the maximum time needed for a message to be prepared, sent and received, $\nu$, and in terms of the maximum time needed for the execution of a job, $\mu$. (In the restricted model of synchronous communication over a complete network, $\nu$ can be set to 1.) We say that $B \geq U$ and $F \geq K$, where $\geq$ stands for "stronger", since any algorithm that works in a stronger model trivially works in the respective weaker model with the same time bound.

## 1.3   Results

In the following sections we suggest a number of different algorithms for the scheduler, and assess their appropriateness to the different models under consideration. In particular, we improve on the best known deterministic algorithm ([AS90]). In the $(B, F)$ model, the algorithm of [AS90] achieves a response time of $O(\delta_j \mu + \delta_j^2 \nu \log Z)$, where the ID's of the jobs are in the range $\{1, 2, \ldots, Z\}$. A randomized algorithm with response time $O(\delta_j \mu + \delta_j^2 \nu)$ is also presented in [AS90]. Here we present algorithms that achieve $O(\delta_j \mu + \delta_j \nu \log Z)$ in the deterministic case and $O(\delta_j \mu + \delta_j \nu)$ in the randomized case. Our results are summarized in Table 1. Notice that the response time of any algorithm cannot be better that $\Omega(\delta_j \mu_j + \nu)$.

Our algorithms can also be extended to the asynchronous model with an arbitrary communication graph $\mathcal{G}$. In particular, the central algorithm of Section 2 and the interval algorithm of Section 4 apply to the more general model without change. Our other algorithms can be adapted to the asynchronous, arbitrary topology model by an appropriate use of an $\alpha$ or $\beta$ synchronizer (see [Awe85]). The transformation to an asynchronous mode of communication (while maintaining the assumption of a complete communication network) entails no changes in asymptotic complexity. (Since the problem concerns a distributed operating system designed to work continuously and process an infinite stream of incoming jobs, we ignore the issue of set-up costs in this abstract.)

When generalizing our setting to that of an arbitrary communication network, it is necessary to discuss another significant issue, namely, the relationship between the topology of the conflict graph $\mathcal{C}$ and that of the underlying communication network $\mathcal{G}$. In particular, it is necessary to specify whether $\mathcal{C}$ is assumed to be a *subgraph* of the graph $\mathcal{G}$ (namely, every two competing processors must be neighbors in the network), and furthermore, whether it is assumed that a job may require resources located only at the nodes adjacent to its originating node.

It seems that in many natural situations, both assumptions cannot be made. That is, processors may require resources located at distant sites, and may compete over these resources with other distant processors. This implies that the diameter of the network $\mathcal{G}$ is an inherent lower bound on the problem, since some sort of communication between processes and resources, as well as among the competing processes

| Model | Complexity | Algorithm |
|-------|-----------|-----------|
| $(U, K)$ | $O(\delta_j \mu_j + \nu)$ | central |
|          | $O(\delta_j \mu_j + \nu)$ | interval |
| $(U, F)$ | $O(\delta_j \mu_j + \nu)$ | central |
| $(B, K)$ | $O(\delta_j \mu + \delta_j \nu)$ | randomized |
|          | $O(\delta_j \mu_j + \nu)$ | randomized interval |
|          | $O(\delta_j \mu + \delta_j \nu)$ | randomized synchronized queue |
|          | $O(\delta_j \mu + \delta_j \nu \log Z)$ | synchronized queue |
| $(B, F)$ | $O(\delta_j \mu + \delta_j \nu)$ | randomized |
|          | $O(\delta_j \mu + \delta_j \nu)$ | randomized synchronized queue |
|          | $O(\delta_j \mu + \delta_j \nu \log Z)$ | synchronized queue |

Figure 1: Time complexity in different models

themselves, is essential. Indeed, our synchronizer-based solutions introduce this factor into the complexity. Specifically, the complexity of all of our solutions remains as stated in this abstract, but for setting the parameter $\nu$ (measuring the maximum time needed for message transmission in the network) to be the network's diameter.

If we do make the assumptions restricting resource requests and conflict edges to neighboring nodes in $\mathcal{G}$, then some of our solutions, combined with an $\alpha$ synchronizer, still work properly, with only $O(1)$ factor increase in response time (again, ignoring set-up time for the synchronizer). Specifically, the randomized algorithm of Section 3 still meets the bound of $O(\delta_j(\mu + \nu))$ on the expected response time. Recently, an asynchronous randomized algorithm using no synchronizer, with $O(\delta(\mu + \nu) \log n)$ expected response time, was presented in [ACS92] for this model (with the subgraph assumption).

# 2 Centralized and Global Algorithms

## 2.1 The Central Algorithm

The *central* algorithm is based on using a central processor $r$ in the network. This processor is notified of every change in the system. When a new job is created, it registers with $r$ and waits to be executed until it receives an *execute*$(j)$ message from processor $r$. Processor $r$ gives each new job $j$ a number, called the *queue-number* and denoted $p(j)$. The central processor has complete information of the system, including the communication graph $\mathcal{G}$, the dynamic conflict graph $\mathcal{C}$, the current queue-number of each job, and the list of currently executing jobs.

The center implements the scheduler in a straightforward way. The initial queue-number of the job decreases until it reaches 0. Then the *execute*$(j)$ message is sent to $j$. Once $j$ completes execution, it sends the *done*$(j)$ message to $r$.

Since the algorithm is centralized, concurrent arrivals can be treated sequentially by $r$. We assume *compete*$(j)$ contains the list of *all* the currently existing conflicting jobs. The queue-number chosen for $j$ is the minimal unoccupied position by the

```
For each k ∈ compete(j) do:
    Mark p(k) and p(k) − 1.
    Set g(j) := min{unmarked number}.
```

Figure 2: Queue numbering

**On** receiving a *schedule(j)* message **do:**

1. Set $p(j) := g(j)$

2. For each $k \in compete(j)$ do:

   (a) If $p(k) < p(j)$ and $\not\exists l \in compete(j)$ s.t $p(k) < p(l) < p(j)$
       then add the edge $(k, j)$ to $\mathcal{C}'$

   (b) If $\exists l$ s.t. $p(k) < p(j) < p(l)$ and there is an edge $(k, l)$ in $\mathcal{C}'$
       then delete $(k, l)$ and add $(j, l)$ to $\mathcal{C}'$

**On** receiving a *done(j)* message **do:**

1. Delete $j$ and all the edges pointing to it from $\mathcal{C}'$.

2. For $q := 1$ to the maximum queue-number in the graph do:
   If ($\forall i$ s.t. $(i, k)$ is an edge in $\mathcal{C}'$, $p(i) < p(k) - 1$) then $p(k) := q - 1$

3. Send an *execute(k)* message to each $k$ with $p(k) = 0$.

Figure 3: The central algorithm: protocol for the central processor

jobs conflicting with $j$ (see Figure 2). Following [AS90] progress is guaranteed by disqualifying also the positions preceding the actual queue-number of these jobs. As explained later this ensures that the jobs are not stuck forever in their position. Notice that $p(j) \leq 2\delta_j$.

The central processor $r$ stores a dynamic graph $\mathcal{C}'$, which is a directed version of the conflict graph. After assigning the initial queue-number to $j$, $r$ adds it to the conflict graph. Specifically, it adds an edge $\langle k, j \rangle$ for every $k$ that conflicts with $j$ such that $p(k) < p(j)$ and there is no job $l$ that conflicts $j$ with $p(k) < p(l) < p(j)$. When the edge $\langle k, j \rangle$ is added, every edge $\langle k, l \rangle$ (for $l > j$) is deleted and instead an edge $\langle j, l \rangle$ is added to $\mathcal{C}'$. When $r$ receives a *done(j)* message, it updates the queue-numbers. In particular, it decreases $p(k)$ by one iff $p(i) \leq p(k) - 2$ for every $i$ such that $\langle i, k \rangle$ is an edge in $\mathcal{C}'$. If $p(k) = 0$ then $r$ sends $k$ an *execute(k)* message. The algorithm is given in Figure 3. It calls function $g$ defined in Figure 2.

Let us now explain the role of leaving an empty space in front of every occupied slot $p(k)$ in the queue. If $k$ conflicts with more than one other job, say with $i$ and $j$, then both jobs must have a queue-number strictly less than $p(k) - 1$ in order to decrease $p(k)$ by one. Assume $p(i) = p(k) - 2$, but $p(j) = p(k) - 1$. In this case we cannot decrease $p(k)$. Now suppose a new job $l$, conflicting with $i$ and $k$, enters the system. Had we not disqualified the position before $p(k)$ (see Figure 2) we could have assigned $p(k) - 1$ to the new job $l$. Now even if $p(j)$ is decreased, $p(k)$ will not be decreased, because the previous queue-number is occupied by $l$. In the meantime a job conflicting with $j$ and $k$ could occupy $p(k) - 1$, and so on, and the job $k$ could be stuck forever with $p(k) - 1$. It is easy to see that this is not the case when the position before the current queue-number of a conflicting job cannot be assigned to a new job entering the system. No job can suddenly "jump" immediately in front of any existing job $k$, since if $i$ and $k$ are conflicting and are already assigned queue-numbers, and if $p(i) < p(k)$, this inequality continues to hold until $i$ enters execution. Notice that with this queue-numbering, every $\mu + \nu$ time units $p(j)$ decreases by 1 and $j$ advances towards execution. Formal analysis is deferred to the full paper.

## 2.2 Model Classification

In the $(U, F)$ model, the central processor $r$ can assign a queue-number to all the new jobs and update all the existing ones in a single time unit. Every job interacts with the center exactly three times, namely, when it is created, when it gets the *execute* message and when it sends the *done* message to the center. Therefore, in this model the response time will be $O(\delta_j \mu + \delta_j \nu)$.

Let us examine the local computation of $r$. Assume each processor handles a single job at a time, and there are $n$ processors. Then $r$ must give a queue-number to each job, and since job entries are dealt with sequentially, this part can take $O(\delta_j n)$. Updating with the proper data structure will take $O(\delta n)$. Notice that the fixed vector or linked list data structures are inappropriate. In the full paper we shall discuss efficient implementations of the appropriate data structure.

The main disadvantage of the central algorithm is that $r$ is a bottleneck to the performance of the entire system. We may consider a global variant of this algorithm, in which every processor has a copy of $r$'s program. When a new job enters, it broadcasts its entrance. Every processor updates the conflict graph, concurrent entries are dealt with sequentially according to the ID's (to ensure that all the processors choose the same queue-number for the given job). When a job's queue-number reaches 0, the processor to which it belongs, starts to execute it. Before the job terminates, it broadcasts a *done* message to the network. This solution is more expensive in terms of communication complexity, since messages have to be broadcast, but there is no single processor that acts as a bottleneck.

## 3 Randomized Scheduling

The central algorithm achieves an almost optimal response time of $O(\delta_j \mu + \nu)$, but assumes the unbounded local computation model. The algorithm described next works in the bounded local computation model quite efficiently, but needs randomization and the almost optimal response time is only expected.

- Election subphase:

  1. Set $coin(j)$ to 1 with probability $\frac{1}{\delta_j}$ and to 0 otherwise.

  2. Send $(coin(j), \delta_j)$ to $\forall k \in compete(j)$.

  3. If $\exists k \in compete(j)$ s.t $(coin(k) = 1)$ and $(\delta_k \geq \delta_j)$ then $coin(j) = 0$.

- Execution subphase:

  1. If $coin(j) = 1$ then enter execution.

Figure 4: The randomized algorithm: protocol for an active $j$

## 3.1 The Randomized Algorithm

The randomized algorithm proceeds in phases, with each phase composed of two subphases, the execution subphase and the election subphase. In the election subphase, each active job flips a random coin with probability $\frac{1}{\delta_j+1}$ for turning 1. The job elects itself for execution in the execution subphase iff its coin turned 1 and there is no conflicting job $i$ with $\delta_i \geq \delta_j$ that also flipped 1. (Notice, that $i$ had smaller chance of flipping 1, which is why collisions should be resolved in its favor.) The procedure appears in Figure 4.

Note that the phases are essential, otherwise it is possible that a job waits forever: each time it flips 1, some of its neighbors in the conflict graph are being executed and it cannot start its execution. In the synchronous case, the phases can be imposed simply by fixing their length (with the execution subphase requiring $\mu$ time units). For the asynchronous case, the phases can be imposed by using a synchronization step between the execution subphase and the election subphase of the next phase. This synchronization step can be implemented as follows. Each resource indicates the end of its execution subphase by an "end phase" signal. These signals are collected from all resources via a "convergecast" process over a spanning tree of the network $\mathcal{G}$. The root of the tree then broadcast a "start phase" signal throughout the network.

## 3.2 Analysis and Model Classification

Next we bound the expected response time. Let us denote by $E_0$ the event that $j$ has drawn 1, and no neighbor of $j$ with degree higher than $\delta_j$ elected itself. The expected number of phases $j$ has to wait before entering execution is bounded by $4(\delta_j + 1)\mu$, since

$$
\begin{aligned}
\Pr\{E_0\} &= \frac{1}{\delta_j + 1} \prod_{k \in \Gamma(j), \delta_k \geq \delta_j} \left(1 - \frac{1}{\delta_k + 1}\right) \\
&\geq \frac{1}{\delta_j + 1}\left(1 - \frac{1}{\delta_j + 1}\right)^{\delta_j} = \frac{1}{4(\delta_j + 1)} .
\end{aligned}
$$

This algorithm works in the $(B, F)$ model with expected response time $O(\delta_j \mu + \delta_j \nu)$. Using the Chernoff bound, it follows that a response time of $O(\delta \log \frac{1}{p})$ rounds can be

> **On** arrival of a new job **do:**
>
> 1. Let the current time be $t_0$.
>
> 2. Mark the time interval $[t_0, t_0 + \nu]$.
>
> 3. For each $k \in compete(j)$ mark $T_k$.
>
> 4. $T_j := \min\{$unmarked time interval $T \mid |T| > j$'s execution time$\}$.
>
> 5. Send $j$ a message containing $t_{start}{}^{(j)}$.

Figure 5: The interval algorithm: protocol for the central processor

garanteed with probability at least $1 - p$, for $0 < p < 1$.

# 4  Interval Scheduling

All the algorithms discussed previously work in models where the execution time of a job was not necessarily known at the time of the jobs creation. Now we consider models where the execution time is known at the time of the jobs creation.

## 4.1  The Interval Algorithm

Our first algorithm in this model is the *interval* algorithm. This is a centralized algorithm where the center $r$ makes use of the execution time of the jobs. Here, instead of assigning a queue-number to each new job, the center assigns a time interval sufficient for the execution of the job. We denote by $T_j = [t_{start}^{(j)}, t_{end}^{(j)}]$ the time interval in which the job $j$ is executed (we assume the existence of a global clock, and denote the current time by $t_0$.

The center takes care of the jobs sequentially. When a new job arrives, the center assigns it the first sufficiently long time interval, $T$, in such a way that if $j$ and $k$ conflict, then $T_j \cap T_k = \emptyset$. After assigning $j$ a time interval, the center sends it a message containing $t_{start}^{(j)}$ - this is the *execute(j)* message of the general model. The algorithm is depicted in Figure 5.

## 4.2  Analysis and Model Classification

When the execution time is known at the time of the creation of the job the response time is a function of $\mu_j$ (the maximum execution time of $j$ and the jobs conflicting with it) instead of $\mu$ (the maximum execution time of a job in the system). It is easy to create scenarios where there can be a great difference between the two parameters.

Next we analyze the response time of the algorithm. The maximum length of time intervals occupied by conflicting jobs is $\delta_j \mu_j$, and the maximum length of free intervals in the initial interval not long enough for $j$ is also $\delta_j \mu_j$. Therefore $j$'s execution will commence after at most $2\delta_j \mu_j + \nu$ time units from the moment the center assigned it a time interval (as $\nu$ time units are needed for the message containing the starting time of the job to arrive). This algorithm works in the $(U, K)$-model with response time $O(\delta_j \mu_j + \nu)$. The time required to assign a job a time interval is extensive (i.e., polynomial in the number of jobs), hence the restriction to the unbounded local computation model.

# 5 Randomized Interval Scheduling

As noted earlier, the interval algorithm needs extensive local computation. Our next algorithm works in the bounded local computation model, when execution times are known. We also assume either the existence of a global clock, or at least that pulses are of identical duration (in real time), so jobs lengths can be specified in terms of number of pulses. (Applying this algorithm in the asynchronous case is possible, but requires some complications in the algorithm, which are deferred to the full paper.)

## 5.1 The Randomized Interval Algorithm

When a new job $j$ enters the system at time $t$, it sets $t_0 = t + 3\nu$ and subdivides the time interval $[t_0, t_0 + 4\delta_j \mu_j]$ into $4\delta_j$ subintervals of length $\mu_j$. The job randomly chooses one of the subintervals, and sends its choice to every other job in its *compete* set. If it hears no objections after $2\nu$ time units, it chooses this subinterval as the interval in which it executes. At time $t_0$ it starts execution. If any competing job objects, then $j$ abandons this subinterval, and starts the whole process again (updating $t_0$). In each attempt, $j$'s choice of the subinterval is random and independent of the previous choices.

During the period the job is active, it might receive messages from conflicting jobs. If job $k$ tries to choose a time interval that intersects the interval $j$ chose (or is currently trying to choose), then $j$ sends an objection to $k$. The algorithm is given in Figure 6.

## 5.2 Analysis and Model Classification

Let us first analyze the algorithm. Every time $j$ tries to choose a subinterval, there are at most $\delta_j$ jobs conflicting with $j$. Each such job occupies (or tries to occupy) an interval of length at most $\mu_j$. Each such occupied interval can intersect with at most two subintervals of $j$. Hence $j$'s interval contains at least $2\delta_j$ subintervals whose selection by $j$ will raise no objections. Therefore with probability $1/2$, job $j$ will succeed at the first trial. Thus the expected number of trials is 2. The expected response time in the $(B, K)$-model will be $O(\delta_j \mu_j + \nu)$.

# 6 The Awerbuch-Saks Algorithm Revisited

The goal of this section is to explain the main difficulties that lead to the complexity of $O(\delta_j \mu + \delta_j^2 \nu)$ of the randomized algorithm of [AS90], and show how a simple modification of their randomized algorithm yields the improved complexity of $O(\delta_j \mu + \delta_j \nu)$. Then we present a deterministic algorithm with a similar improvement in the complexity.

---

- Entering phase:

  1. Set $t_0 :=$ current time $+ 3\nu$; set $T_j := 0$.

  2. Divide the interval $[t_0, t_0 + 4\delta_j \mu_j]$ into $4\delta_j$ nonintersecting consecutive subintervals of length $\mu_j$:    $s_i = [t_0 + (i-1)\mu_j, t_0 + i\mu_j]$

  3. Choose randomly and uniformly $i \in [1, \ldots, 4\delta_j]$.

  4. Set $T_{temp}(j) := s_i$.

  5. Send a message to each $k \in compete(j)$ requesting to occupy $T_{temp}(j)$.

  6. If all responses are "OK" then set $T_j := s_i$
       and at time $t_0 + (i-1)\mu_j$ enter execution.
     Else goto 1

- Responses:
    **On** receiving a message from $k$ trying to occupy $T_{temp}(k)$ **do:**
    If $T_{temp}(j) \cap T_{temp}(k) \neq \emptyset$ then send an objection to $k$.
    Else send "OK".

---

Figure 6: The randomized interval algorithm: protocol for $j$

## 6.1   The Randomized Synchronized Queue Algorithm

Let us start by presenting a randomized algorithm, which is a variant of [AS90]. The main differences between the original algorithm and ours are in the entry-protocol and in our assumption that the system is synchronized: we assume that every $\nu$ time units each job gets a *pulse*, allowing it to send the next batch of new messages. Jobs can send messages only on pulses. This is easily achieved in a synchronous system by a clock, but can also be achieved in an asynchronous system using a synchronizer as discussed earlier.

First, let us give an outline of our algorithm. Each new job $j$, entering the system chooses a queue-number, $q$, in such a way that no two conflicting jobs have the same queue-number. After entering the queue, the job decreases its number by one, each time it is certain that no other conflicting job has that number. It notifies all the other conflicting jobs of its new queue-number. Once a job has number 0, it enters execution. When leaving execution, it sends a *done* message to all the jobs in its *compete* set and exits the system. The set of conflicting jobs is constantly updated. Each job decreases its queue-number in a deterministic fashion. We prove that every $\mu + \nu$ time a job decreases its queue-number by one. Therefore, the time the job spends in the queue is $O(q(\mu + \nu))$, thus it is important to pick a small initial queue-number. We give an algorithm that picks an initial queue number, $q$, such that $q = O(\delta_j)$.

In this algorithm, the process of picking the initial queue-number uses randomization. A new job randomly chooses a number $q$ in the range $[0, 6\delta_j]$ and sends this number to all the jobs in its *compete*-set. If this $q$ is the current queue-number of a job, or one less than the queue-number or one more, then it objects to this choice, and the new job has to try again. It chooses $q$ only if no existing conflicting job objects to this choice. It also takes into account the choices of the other new conflicting jobs that try to enter. It is easy to see that each trial has probability of success of at least 1/2. The choice is such, that both each previously existing job that a new job entered in front of it, and each new job can decrease its queue number by at least one without being delayed by another job. In such a way we leave enough time for the jobs to recover from the "shock" of a new entry.

The randomized synchronized queue protocol has two interleaving parts, the entry protocol and the queue protocol. They are given in Figures 7 and 8.

We made one major and two minor changes in the [AS90] algorithm. The major change is that a new job chooses a position, such that not only that position, but also the position below it is unoccupied. A position, as in [AS90], is occupied if a job has that number or it is one below a currently existing queue-number. The first minor change is that in the [AS90] randomized entry-protocol, a new job first collects information on the queue-numbers of the existing conflicting jobs, and chooses randomly one of the unoccupied places (where it considers the place directly in front of an existing job also occupied). It turns out that the information collection phase is unnecessary. The second change is that in the queue protocol, each job advances its position when no conflicting job is directly ahead of it, while in [AS90], each time a job asks for permission to decrease its queue-number.

In order to explain our solution, it is instrumental to first understand the source of the difficulty in the current algorithm of [AS90]. In order for the algorithm to be as efficient as possible, it is desired that each task advances its position in the queue once every $\mu + \nu$ time inits. In order for that to happen, it is required that the flow of information on task termination in the system is fully pipelined. The problem occurs when new tasks enter the queue in front of old ones, and form long, and as of yet unpipelined, queues. To demonstrate this point, consider a job $j$ currently in position $k$ in the queue, and suppose that new tasks $j_1, j_2, \ldots, j_{k-2}$ now enter the queue, and form a chain by taking the numbers $1, 2, \ldots, k-2$ respectively, all at the same time. Task $j$ is now allowed to advance its number to $k-1$, but then it must wait for $j_{k-2}$ to proceed. This may require $\mu + (k-2)\nu$ time units. Just then another new queue may form in the same fashion to postpone $j$'s progress to $k-3$, and so on, and the total delay can clearly accumulate to $O(\delta\mu + \delta^2\nu)$ time.

Our correction is therefore geared at preventing such delays from happening. It can be illustrated by the following analogy. Consider the line of cars formed in front of a red traffic-light. Once the light changes to green, the cars start moving one by one. However, each car in the line is delayed until the car right in front of it has started moving. Suppose, now, that when forming the line, each car leaves a space of one car length between itself and the car preceding it in the line. Then (assuming synchronicity) immediately when the light changes to green, all cars can start moving at once. The cost is limited to doubling the length of the line.

Our solution is thus to require each task taking a number $k$ in the queue to ensure that not only does it not disturb tasks following it, but it also has some space in front of it. Namely, it has to ensure that both $k-1$ and $k+1$ are free of competing tasks. This guarantees that a newly formed queue will enable each task to proceed for a while until the queue "crowds". For instance, in the example above, the new tasks $j_1, j_2, \ldots, j_{k-2}$ may take the numbers $2, 4, \ldots, 2(k-2)$ respectively.

---

**On** job $j$ entering the system:

1. Set $X \leftarrow compete(j)$, $D \leftarrow \emptyset$, $U \leftarrow \emptyset$.

2. Randomly select $q \in [0, 6\delta_j]$. Let $temp\_p := q$.

3. Send a message $(request, j, q)$ to every $k \in X$, and collect responses:
   On receiving $(agree, j', q', decided)$ from $j'$: set $D \leftarrow D \cup \{j'\}$.
   On receiving $(agree, j', temp(q'), attempting)$ from $j'$: set $U \leftarrow U \cup \{j'\}$.
   On receiving $done(j')$ from $j'$: set $X \leftarrow X \setminus \{j'\}$.
   On receiving $(object, j')$ from $j'$ do:
       set $X \leftarrow X \cup U \cup D$, $D \leftarrow \emptyset$, $U \leftarrow \emptyset$.
       send $(abandon, j, q)$ to every job in $X$.
       goto 1

4. After collecting answers from every job in $X$ (all responses are $agree$) do:

   (a) Send $(chosen, j, q)$ to every $k \in X$.

   (b) Set $p(j) \leftarrow q$.

   (c) Partition $D$ into $before(j)$ and $after(j)$: for every response $(agree, j', q', decided)$, if $q' < q$ then set $j' \in before(j)$ and if $q' > q$ then set $j' \in after(j)$.

   (d) Switch to the 'Queue Protocol'.

**On** job $j$ with $(p(j) = q)$ or $(temp\_p = q$ and no objections received so far) receiving a $(request, k, q')$ message:

1. Add $k$ to $U$.

2. If $\{q' - 1, q'\} \cap \{q - 1, q\} = \emptyset$ then do:
       if decided on $q$ then send $(agree, j, q, decided)$ to $k$,
       else send $(agree, j, q, attempting)$.
   Else send $(object, j)$.

**On** job $j$ receiving a $(chosen, k, q')$ message:
Transfer $k$ into $D$ (if $j$ is still in the trial phase) or to $after(j)$ or $before(j)$ according to $k$'s chosen number.

Figure 7: The entry protocol in the randomized synchronized queue algorithm

---

(* $X$ is partitioned into $before(j)$ and $after(j)$ *)

- If $j$ knows that $\forall k \in before(j) \setminus \{l : l$ sent out its $(agree)$ message when its queue-number is already $p(j)\} \cup \{l : l \in U$ s.t when $l$ sends its $(chosen)$ message it will join $before(j)\}$, $p(k) \neq p(j)$.

  1. Set $p(j) \leftarrow p(j) - 1$;
     Send $(decreased, j, p(j) - 1)$ to every $k \in after(j) \cup U$.

  2. If $p(j) = 0$ then start execution;
     when leaving execution send $(done, j)$ to every $k \in after(j) \cup U$.

  3. When receiving a message $(done, k)$, remove $k$ from $(before, j)$.

  4. Goto • (with updated sets $before(j)$ and $after(j)$.

---

Figure 8: The queue protocol in the randomized synchronized queue algorithm

Note that this "spaced" queue may "crowd" in a while, when $\mu > \nu$. In particular, by the time $j_i$ has advanced $i$ times, from number $2i$ to $i$, the queue in front of it has crowded completely, assuming $\mu$ is large enough. However, by that time, $i\nu$ time units have elapsed from the time $j_i$ has entered the queue, and this turns out to be precisely the time required in order for the queue to regain the "pipelining" property, i.e., by now, the queue segment ahead of $j_i$ is fully pipelined.

## 6.2 Analysis and Model Classification

Let us now analyze the randomized synchronized queue algorithm.

**Claim 6.1** *In each trial job $j$ has probability at least 1/2 in succeeding to choose an initial queue-number.*

**Proof:** Job $j$ chooses randomly from $6\delta_j$ positions. For at most $3\delta_j$ choices $j$ may hear objections (specifically if it tries to occupy a position in front of, behind or at the current place of a job). Therefore each attempt has probability at least 1/2 of succeeding. ∎

**Claim 6.2** *The entry phase takes expected $O(\nu)$ time.*

Assume that $\lceil \frac{\mu}{\nu} \rceil = l$.

**Lemma 6.3** *Let $p_i(j)$ be $j$'s queue-number at pulse number $i$. Then for every $j$ and for every pulse $i$,*

$$p_{i+l+1}(j) \leq p_i(j) - 1.$$

**Proof:** The proof of the lemma is by induction on the queue-number. The induction claim is as follows:

$$A_q : \quad \forall i \forall j \; p_i(j) \leq q \Rightarrow p_{i+l+1}(j) \leq q - 1$$

We assume that $i$ is the first pulse in which $j$'s queue-number is $q + 1$, that is, at pulse $i - 1$ its queue-number was still $q + 2$ or $j$ has sent the $(chosen, j, q + 1)$ message at pulse $i$.

If $q = 1$ at pulse $i$, then at pulse $i + l$ all jobs preceding $j$ in the queue will leave execution, and at pulse $(i + l) + 1$, job $j$ will be notified, decrease its queue-number and start execution.

Next we assume that $A_q$ is true, and prove $A_{q+1}$:

First we take care of the case where job $j$ already sent its $(chosen)$ message before or at pulse $i - 1$. Because of synchronicity, if at time $i$ the job $j$ has queue-number $q + 1$, then there is no job (other than possibly $j$) that conflicts with $j$ and was present in the system (i.e., already chose queue-numbers) at pulse $i - 1$, with queue-number $q + 1$ after pulse $i - 1$. That is, there is no job that decreased its queue-number from $q + 1$ to $q$ after pulse $i - 1$ and before pulse $i$ and its message got through to $j$ before the beginning of pulse $i$. (This is why we need the pulses for our algorithm to work).

There are four kinds of jobs.

1. Jobs that were in the system at pulse $i - 1$, with queue-number different from $q$. These jobs do not delay $j$ in the current phase.

2. Jobs $j'$ that were in the system at time $i - 1$ with queue-number $q$. By applying the induction assumption to them, we get that $p_{i-1+l+1}(j') \leq q - 1$, therefore at pulse $(i - 1 + l + 1) + 1 = i + l + 1$ their message arrives at $j$ and they do not delay $j$ anymore.

3. Jobs to whom $j$ sent the $(agree)$ message at or after pulse $i$. In our algorithm, $j$ does not wait for these jobs. This does not lead to collisions, since when $j$ granted them permission to choose their queue-number, $j$ made sure it has space to move forward. By the time $j$ sent out the $(agree)$ message, its queue-number was already $q + 1$. Therefore, if $j$ granted permission to these jobs, then $q$ is not occupied by them in either case, and therefore they cannot delay $j$ in this phase. (If $j'$ sends its $(request)$ message at pulse $m$, it gets the $(agree)$ messages at pulse $m + 1$, and sends out the $(chosen)$ message at pulse $m + 2$.)

4. Jobs that sent their $(chosen)$ message at pulse $i$. These might occupy position $q$, since when $j$ sent its $(agree)$ message, it was still in position $q + 2$. Since each such job has an unoccupied position in front of it, it will decrease its number by pulse $i + 1$, and will not delay $j$ after pulse $i + 2$.

In order to cover all the possibilities, we have to consider the case where $j$ also sent its $(chosen)$ message at pulse $i$. In this case, there is an unoccupied position in front of it, therefore $j$ will decrease its number by pulse $i + 1$.

This proves the induction claim and completes the proof of the lemma. ∎

**Corollary 6.4** *The above algorithm has expected response time $O(\delta_j(\mu + \nu))$.*

**Proof:** The initial position a job $j$ chooses is $\leq 6\delta_j$. If it entered the system at pulse $i$, then at pulse $i + 6\delta_j(l + 1)$ the job will enter execution. Since the pulses are $O(\nu)$ time apart, and $\lceil \frac{\mu}{\nu} \rceil = l$, the expected response time is $O(\delta_j(\mu + \nu))$. (The response time is expected because of the entry phase; the queue phase is deterministic.) ∎

This algorithm works in the $(B, F)$ model.

## 6.3 The Deterministic Synchronized Queue Algorithm

The deterministic synchronized queue algorithm follows the algorithm presented in [AS90]. We improve that algorithm by changing the protocol for decreasing the slot numbers in each level by the queue protocol of our randomized algorithm. (Recall that in the randomized algorithm only the entry protocol is randomized, the queue protocol is deterministic.) This change in the algorithm improves its complexity to $O(\delta_j \mu_j + \delta_j \nu \log Z)$, where $Z$ is the highest ID of any job in the system. The algorithm works in the $(B, F)$ model. Details of the algorithm and its correctness proof are omitted from this abstract.

# References

[Awe85]  B. Awerbuch. Complexity of network synchronization. *Journal of the ACM*, 32:804–823, 1985.

[ACS92]  B. Awerbuch, L. Cowen and M. Smith. Self-stabilizing symmetry breaking in poly-logarithmic time. Unpublished manuscript, 1992.

[AS90]  B. Awerbuch and M. Saks. A dining philosophers algorithm with polynomial response time. In *FOCS*, pages 65–74. IEEE, 1990.

[CM84]  K. Chandy and J. Misra. The dining philosophers problem. In *TOPLAS*, pages 632–646. ACM, 1984.

[Dij71]  E. W. Dijkstra. Hierarchical ordering of sequential processes. *ACTA Informatica*, pages 115–138, 1971.

[Lam78]  L. Lamport. Time, clocks and the ordering of events in a distributed system. *Communications of the ACM*, 21:558–565, 1978.

[Lyn81]  N. Lynch. Upper bounds for static resource allocation in a distributed system. *J. of Computation and System Sciences*, 23:254–278, 1981.

[RL81]  M. O. Rabin and D. Lehmann. On the advantages of free choice: a symmetric and fully distributed solution to the dining philosophers problem. In *8th POPL*, pages 133–138, 1981.

[SP88]  E. Styer and G. Peterson. Improved algorithms for distributed resource allocation. In *7th PODC*, pages 105–116. ACM, 1988.

# Membership Algorithms for Multicast Communication Groups

Yair Amir, Danny Dolev\*, Shlomo Kramer, Dalia Malki

The Hebrew University of Jerusalem, Israel

**Abstract.** We introduce a membership protocol that maintains the set of currently connected machines in an asynchronous and dynamic environment. The protocol handles both failures and joining of machines. It operates within a multicast communication sub-system.

It is well known that solving the membership problem in an asynchronous environment when faults may be present is impossible. In order to circumvent this difficulty, our approach rarely extracts from the membership live (but not active) machines unjustfully. The benefit is that our procotol always terminates within a finite time. In addition, if a machine is inadvertently taken out of the membership, it can rejoin it right away using the membership protocol.

Despite the asynchrony, configuration changes are *logically* synchronized with all the regular messages in the system, and appear *virtually synchronous* to the application layer.

The protocol presented here supports partitions and merges. When partitions and merging occur, the protocol provides the application with exact information about the status of the system. It is up to the application designer to merge the partitioned histories correctly.

## 1    Introduction

We introduce a membership protocol that maintains the set of currently connected machines in an asynchronous and dynamic environment. The protocol handles both failures and joining of machines.

In such an environment, a consistent membership is a key for constructing fault tolerant distributed applications. Machines may have to keep track of other machines in the system. Knowing which machines are connected and active, and even having this knowledge consistent within the set of connected machines can be crucial. The problem of maintaining machine-set membership in the face of machine faults and joins is described in [6].

The protocol presented here is designed to implement the membership maintenance in Transis, a communication sub-system for high availability, currently developed at the Hebrew University of Jerusalem. A Transis *broadcast domain* comprises of a set of machines that can communicate via multicast messages. When sending a message inside this broadcast domain, the Transis sub-system

---

\* also at IBM Almaden Research Center

uses the network broadcast capability. Typically, only a single transmission is needed for efficient dissemination of messages to the multiple destinations.

Due to the asynchronous and dynamic properties of the environment, messages can be delayed or can be lost and machines can come up or crash. Moreover, the network itself may partition and re-connect. The *Basic* service of Transis overcomes arbitrary communication delays and message losses and guarantees fast delivery of messages at all of the currently connected destinations. The membership protocol automatically maintains the set of currently connected machines inside the broadcast domain.

The membership protocol is a careful integration of fault and join mechanisms. It preserves several important properties:

- Consensus. It maintains a consistent current configuration among the set of active and connected machines.
- Virtual-synchrony. It guarantees that members of the same configuration receive the same set of messages between every pair of configuration changes.
- Spontaneous. The fault mechanism is triggered when a machine detects that communication is broken with another machine for a certain amount of time. The join machanism is triggered when a machine detects a "foreign" message in the broadcast domain. The current set then attempts to merge with the foreign set or sets.
- Symmetric. There are no natural *joining-sides* and *accepting-sides*, and the merging is done multi-way (and not in pairs only).
- Non-blocking. It never blocks indefinitely and it allows regular flow of messages while membership changes are handled.
- Correct handling of partitions and merges. The protocol also handles failures that occur during the join.

The most challenging property of our membership protocol is handling partitions and merges. To the best of our knowledge, all of the previous membership algorithms within similar environments [12, 13, 6, 5, 15, 9] handle the joining of single machines only. However, in reality, when the network includes bridging elements, partitions are likely to occur. In this case, there are two or more sets of machines that need to be joined together. On start-ups, each machine comes up as a singleton-set, and then two or more merge into larger connected sets. Thus, we tackle all aspects of joining: re-connecting partitions, recovery or startup of a single machine, and even moving of a machine from one connected set to another (the latter being a hypothetical scenario, in our view).

Many systems do not allow partitioned execution, for the reason that system consistency might be compromised. We believe that the role of the communication sub-system is to deliver messages where possible, and provide accurate information about the success of message delivery and connection. The application designer should then decide whether execution can continue within the partitions. It is important to emphasize that the complete merging of the partitioned histories is application dependent and therefore is not handled by the membership protocol. The final section of the paper presents applications that can benefit from the support of continuous operation despite partitions.

As noted by others ([8, 7, 11]), solving the membership problem in an asynchronous environment when faults may be present is impossible. There are various approaches for circumventing this difficulty ([6, 15, 5, 13, 12]). Our approach never allows indefinite blocking but rarely extracts from the membership live (but inactive) machines unjustfully. This is the price paid for maintaining a consistent membership within the sets of connected and active machines, in an asynchronous environment, without blocking. In addition, if a machine is inadvertently taken out of the membership, it can rejoin right away using the join mechanism.

**Related Work**

Early solutions to the membership problem employed synchronous protocols ([6]). The problem with synchronous solutions is that they rely on synchronization properties that are difficult to achieve, and are not supported in standard environments.

The membership algorithm in the Isis system ([15, 5]) operates over reliable communication channels and employs a central coordinator. One of the drawbacks of their algorithm is that during configuration changes the flow of regular messages is suspended until all the previous messages are processed. In contrast, the membership protocol presented here is symmetric and does not disrupt the regular flow of messages.

Later work by Mishra *et al.* ([13]) suggests a distributed membership algorithm, based on causally ordered messages (see exact definition in the next section). In this algorithm, the machines reach eventual agreement on membership changes, but the changes are not coordinated. Our membership protocol extends their work by guaranteeing *virtually synchronous* membership changes at all the machines; in addition, we handle partitions and merges.

The approach taken by Melliar-Smith et al. ([12]) is also distributed, and uses a probabilistic algorithm. The algorithm is based on totally ordered broadcast messages, as supported by the Total algorithm ([11]). The coordinated delivery of totally ordered messages is sufficient for achieving membership consensus, and their algorithm need not send any additional messages. The main shortcoming of algorithms like the membership algorithm based on Total is that with small probability, they might block indefinitely in face of faults ([11, 12]). The protocol presented here differs from [12] in achieving consensus based on causal messages. Our approach never allows indefinite blocking but rarely extracts from the membership live (but not active) machines unjustfully.

## 2   Transis and the System Model

The system comprises of a set of machines that can dynamically crash and restart, and network(s) that might partition and re-merge. The machines communicate via asynchronous multicast messages. A multicast message leaves its source machine at once to all the machines in the system but may arrive at different times to them. Messages might be lost or delayed arbitrarily, but faults cannot alter messages' contents. Messages are uniquely identified through a pair < sender, counter > .

Transis contains the communication layer reponsible for the reliable delivery of messages in the system ([2]). Transis guarantees the *causal* (see [10]) delivery order of messages, defined as the reflexive, transitive closure of:

**(1)** $m \xrightarrow{cause} m'$ if $\mathrm{receive}_q(m) \to \mathrm{send}_q(m')$ [2]
**(2)** $m \xrightarrow{cause} m'$ if $\mathrm{send}_q(m) \to \mathrm{send}_q(m')$

In Transis, each newly emitted message contains ACKs to previous messages. The ACKs form the $\xrightarrow{cause}$ relation directly, such that if $m'$ contains an ACK to $m$, then $m \xrightarrow{cause} m'$. If a message arrives at a machine and some of its causal predecessors are missing, Transis transparently handles message recovery and re-ordering. Other environments like [5, 14] are equally suitable for providing the causality requirement. Below, we sometimes refer to the environment and messages as the Transis environment and Transis messages.

The membership protocol operates above the Transis communication layer, such that message arrival order within the protocol preserves causality. We think of the causal order as a directed acyclic graph (DAG): the nodes are the messages, the arcs connect two messages that are directly dependent in the causal order. An example DAG is depicted in Figure 1.

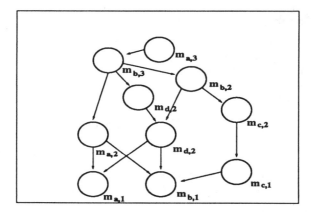

**Fig. 1.** An Imaginary DAG

The causal graph contains all the messages sent in the system. All the machines eventually see the same DAG, although as they progress, it may be "revealed" to them gradually in different orders. Whenever a message is emitted, it

---

[2] Note that '$\to$' orders events occurring at $q$ sequentially, and therefore the order between them is well defined.

causally follows all the messages in the portion of the DAG currently revealed (this results directly from the definition of $\xrightarrow{cause}$ ).

The Transis communication sub-system receives the messages off the network. It performs recovery and message handling, and at some later time, it *delivers* the messages to the upper level. Transis provides a variety of reliable multicast services. The services use different delivery criteria on the messages in the DAG. In some cases, the membership protocol interferes with the delivery of messages, as we shall see below. The paper [2] provides a detailed description of the Transis environment and services. Here is a short description of the Transis multicast services:

1. **Basic** multicast: guarantees delivery of the message at all the connected sites. This service delivers the message immediately from the DAG to the upper level.
2. **Causal** multicast: guarantees that delivery order preserves causality.
3. **Agreed** multicast: delivers messages in the same order at all sites. The ToTo algorithm implements the agreed multicast service in Transis (see [1]).
4. **Safe** multicast: delivers a message after all the active machines have acknowledged its reception.

The Transis protocols employ the network broadcast capability for the efficient dissemination of messages to multiple destinations via a single transmission.

## 3  The Membership Problem

The purpose of the membership protocol is to maintain a consistent view of the *current configuration* among all the connected machines in a dynamic environment. This view is used for disseminating reliable multicast messages among all the members. Each machine maintains locally the following view:

**CCS:** the Current Configuration Set is the set of machines in agreement.

When machines crash or disconnect, the network partitions or re-merges, the connected machines must reconfigure and reach a new agreement on the CCS. The configuration change must take place amidst continuous communication operations. Furthermore, it must indicate to the user which messages are delivered before the reconfiguration and which after. This last property is termed by Birman et al. *virtual synchrony*, and its importance is discussed in [3, 4, 5]. We define the goal of the membership protocol as follows:

**P.1** *Maintain the CCS in consensus among the set of machines that are connected throughout the activation of the membership protocol.*

**P.2** *Guarantee that any two machines that are connected throughout two consecutive configuration changes deliver the same set of messages between the changes.*

Note that our membership protocol also handles in full multi-way joining. The purpose of the protocol is to merge between two or more membership sets, and to reach an consensus decision on a joined-membership. It is possible however, that only a subset of the live machines succeed in merging their memberships, due to communication delays. This cannot be avoided, since machines might appear silent during the entire joining. Nevertheless, the joined set (or subset) will be in consensus within about its membership.

In order to clarify the discussion and focus on a single execution of the membership protocol, we add to the configuration description the following vector:

**Expected:** The *Expected* vector contains a message-id per each member of the CCS. This indicates the next message-id from this member following the last configuration change. For example, if before the configuration change, member $m$ has emitted messages up to 19, then $Expected[m] = 20$ [3].

Note that the Expected vector removes unintentional agreement on (recurring) membership sets.

## 4  Handling Faults

This section focuses on a protocol for handling departure of machines from the set of active ones.

Assume that all the machines belonging to $CCS$ initially agree on the $CCS$ contents. The Faults protocol is initiated every time the communication with any machine breaks. Each machine identifies failures separately. A machine that identifies a *communication-break* with another machine emits a FA message declaring this machine faulty.[4] The FA messages are exchanged within the flow of regular Transis messages and relate to other Transis messages in the regular causal order. The remaining machines in $CCS$ need to agree on the occurred faults. The main difficulty is to concur on the last messages received from crashed machines, because these messages may be delayed arbitrarily long.

Figure 2 depicts a simple scenario of fault handling. In this scenario, machine $A$ lost connection with machine $C$ after message $m_{c,1}$. Consequently, $A$ emits $m_{a,1}$ declaring $C$ faulty. However, machine $B$ has received further messages from $C$, up to $m_{c,3}$. Therefore, when $B$ concurs via $m_{b,1}$, the causal relations indicate that messages $m_{c,1}$ thru $m_{c,3}$ precede the fault.

---

[3] In order to provide unique message id's, message id's are pairs (incarnation, counter); Melliar Smith et al. discuss several conditions for providing this uniqueness requirement, among which is the ability to save *incarnation* numbers on nonvolatile storage, see [12]. The *Expected* message-id is therefore either within the current incarnation, or a later one.

[4] The specific method for detecting communication-breaks is implementation dependent and irrelevant to the Faults protocol. For example, in the Transis environment, each machine expects to hear from other machines in the $CCS$ set regularly. Failing this, it attempts to contact the suspected failed machine through a channel reserved for this purpose. If this fails too, it decides that this machine is faulty.

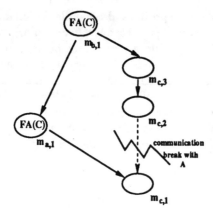

**Fig. 2.** A Simple Fault Scenario

Generally, this situation is handled as follows: When a FA message is inserted into the DAG, the faults alogrithm marks it *nondeliverable*. It releases FA messages for delivery only after reaching consensus of the *remaining* machines about *all* the faults. Messages of type FA are delivered *last* in their concurrency set (*i.e.* when a FA message causally precedes all the messages in the DAG, it is delivered). For example, in Figure 2, message $m_{a,1}$ is delivered after all of $C$'s messages, since they are all pecedent or concurrent to it. If there are multiple concurrent FA messages, they are delivered in a deterministic order. Note that each fault may be represented by more than one FA message in the DAG; only the first one delivered affects the CCS. In this way, all the machines deliver the same set of causal messages before each configuration change, which guarantees virtual synchrony. The pseudo-code of the protocol is given in Figure 3.

Each iteration of the protocol collects FA messages from other machines (or incurs a communication break with a machine). Within each iteration, a received FA message either increases the $F$ set or results in a consensus decision that shrinks it to $\emptyset$ (in the last step of the protocol). Thus, as the faults protocol is activated many times, $F$ dynamically grows and shrinks; different machines need not assent to the same $F$ set, but eventually they will assent to all the faults contained in the $F$ sets.

Recall that the upper level using Transis is provided with the representation of the current configuration set, the $CCS$. Initially, $CCS$ in the upper level contains the agreed upon membership set. After a faults set is assented to (at the end of the Faults protocol), the faults are propagated to the upper level via the FA messages in a series of *configuration changes*, and eventually the $CCS$ becomes up-to-date.

As soon as the faults protocol reaches its final step, the internal conditions that require coordination decisions are changed, even before the delivery of the FA messages that incur the configuration change. For every $f$ in the $F$ set, this internal event is called $Crash(f)$. Thus, the protocol assures that the system will not wait indefinitely for failed machines.

---

Whenever communication breaks with $q$ or a FA message is received:

- if communication breaks with $q$:
    $f\_set = \{q\}$
- if receive message $<$ FA, $f\_set$ $>$ from $r$:
    $LAST[r] = LAST[r] \cup f\_set$
    *mark the FA message non-deliverable*
- if $(f\_set \not\subseteq F)$
    $F = F \cup f\_set$
    *instruct Transis to disallow any message from $f\_set$ to enter[a]*
    *the DAG.*
    broadcast $<$ FA, $F$ $>$
- if $\forall q \in (CCS \setminus F)$ $LAST[q] = F$
    *assent to $F$*
    *mark all the FA messages of $F$ deliverable*
    *deliver FA messages last in their concurrency sets*
    $F = \emptyset$
    $LAST = \perp$

---

[a] unless it is already followed by another message in the DAG and required for recovery

---

Whenever delivering a FA message $<$ FA, $f\_set$ $>$ :

$CCS = CCS \setminus f\_set$
$\forall q \in CCS$ : set $Expected[q]$ to the message index following the last message delivered from $q$.

**Fig. 3.** The Faults Protocol

After delivering a FA message that removes a machine from the configuration, $p$ changes the *Expected* vector: For each machine in the new membership, *Expected* will contain the message id that follows the last delivered message. This id can be either the last counter $+$ 1, or a subsequent incarnation.

## 4.1 Proof of Correctness

The intuition behind the correctness proof is as follows: Each faults-set $F$ is acknowledged by all the remaining live procesors, before it is accepted and delivered. In the proof we show that this guarantees that the remaining machines achieve consensus about the messages that precede each FA change. If a machine receives a message $(m)$ before a FA message, then the acknowledgement FA it sends follows $m$ in the DAG. Therefore, all the machines that accept FA recover $m$ (if necessary). On the other hand, if $m$ arrives *after* the machine has sent its acknowledgement, $m$ will be discarded, and all the other machines will discard it, too. In this way, all the machines deliver the same messages before each FA configuration change.

First, we introduce some definitions and notations used in the proof. The data structures names are subscribed with the machine id, as in '$DAG_p$', in places where it is not obvious from the context.

- A pair of machines $p$, $q$ are in **membership consent** if

$$CCS_p = CCS_q, \text{ and}$$
$$\forall t \in CCS : Expected_p[t] = Expected_q[t]$$

- A message $m$ from $t$ causally follows the vector $Expected$, denoted $Expected \xrightarrow{cause} m$, if either it is the expected message from $t$ ($Expected[t]$), or $Expected[t] \xrightarrow{cause} m$.
- Denote $Accept_p = CCS_p \setminus F_p$. The $Accept$ set contains the (remaining) machines in $CCS$ that need to assent to $F$.
- Define:

$$Votes_p(f) = \{m \mid m \in DAG_p, \ m = <FA, F>, \ f \in F\}$$
$$Electors_p(f) = \{\text{the first message in } Votes_p(f) \text{ from each sender}\}.$$

The **Electors**$(f)$ set contains the first message from each machine that concurs on $f$'s fault.

**Lemma 4.1** *Let $p$, $q$ be machines currently in membership consent. Assume that $p$ is ready to deliver a configuration change (FA) message $CC_f$ that removes $f$ from the $CCS_p$. Let $q \in Accept_p$. Then $Electors_q(f) \subseteq Electors_p(f)$.*

**Proof:** Let $e \in Electors_q(f)$ be a message from $e_s$. Since $p$ assented to $CC_f$ and since $CC_f$ actually removes $f$ from $CCS$, $DAG_p$ currently contains FA messages that contain $f$ from all of $Accept_p$. Therefore, if $e_s \in Accept_p$, there is a FA message $e' \in DAG_p$ from $e_s$ that contains $f$. By the causality property $e$ is also in $DAG_p$, and by the definition of $Electors_p$, $e \in Electors_p(f)$.

Otherwise, $e_s \in F_p$, where $F_p$ is the faults set that $p$ assented to before delivering $CC_f$. If any of the machines in $Accept_p$ received the message $e$ before acknoweldging $F_p$, $e$ will be recovered by $p$ (if necessary), and we are done. Otherwise, all the machines in $Accept_p$ receive $e$ after sending approval to $F_p$. Therefore, the protocol indicates that they all discard it from the DAG, in contradiction to $e \in Electors_q(f)$. □

If a message follows any of the messages in $Electors_p(f)$, it is delivered only after the configuration change of $f$. All other messages are delivered before the change. Using Lemma 4.1, we show that the connected machines deliver the same set of causal messages before the configuration change of $f$.

**Lemma 4.2** *Let $p$, $q$ be machines currently in membership consent. Assume that $p$ and $q$ deliver a configuration change message $CC_f$ that removes $f$ from $CCS$. Assume that $p \in Accept_q$ and $q \in Accept_p$. Then $p$ and $q$ deliver the same set of causal messages, that follow $Expected$ and precede $CC_f$.*

**Proof:** Applying Lemma 4.1 in both directions, we get $Electors_p(f) = Electors_q(f)$. Let $m$ be a message, $Expected \xrightarrow{\text{cause}} m$, $s.t.$ $m$ is delivered by $p$ before $CC_f$. Thus, $m$ does not follow any message in $Electors(f)$. If $m$ causally precedes any message in $Electors(f)$, then by the causality property $m \in DAG_q$ and $q$ delivers it before $CC_f$.

Otherwise, $m$ is concurrent with all the messages in $Electors(f)$. Thus, $m$ was sent by a machine in $F_q$, $F_q$ being the faults set that $q$ assents to before delivering $CC_f$. If any machine in $Accept_q$ received $m$ before acknowledging $F_q$, then $q$ will recover it (if necessary) and deliver it before $CC_f$. Otherwise, $m$ arrives after all of $Accept_q$ sent their consent to all of $F_q$, and the protocol indicates that they all discard $m$.

Similarly, every message delivered by $q$ before $CC_f$ is also delivered by $p$. $\square$

**Theorem 4.3** *Let $p$, $q$ be machines currently in membership consent. If $p$, $q$ deliver the configuration change (FA) message $CC_f$, such that $p \in Accept_q$, $q \in Accept_p$, then:*

1. *$p$, $q$ deliver the same set of messages following Expected before delivering the configuration change message.*
2. *$Expected_p = Expected_q$ after the delivery.*

**Proof:** According to Lemma 4.2, the first claim holds. This immediately implies that $p$ and $q$ deliver the same configuration changes following Expected (if any) before $CC_f$. Therefore, $CCS_p = CCS_q$ after the delivery. Since $Expected$ is defined by the $CCS$ and the first item, which we have shown to be equal, the second claim holds. $\square$

The theorem shows that the state of membership consent is preserved after each change. By induction, this holds for every FA message, and the faults (configuration-changes) are delivered in the same order at the machines while preserving the virtual synchrony property.

# 5    Handling Joins

The join mechanism is trigerred when a machine detects a "foreign" message in the broadcast domain. The current set attempts to merge with the foreign set or sets. Since it operates in a broadcast domain, we expect this to typically happen at the other set(s) and the protocol works symmetrically, *i.e.* there is no joining-side and accepting-side. Note that actual simultaneity is not required for correctness. The closer the sets commence, the sooner they will complete the membership protocol.

---

Enter **Stage 0** whenever $J = \emptyset$ and intercepting a foreign message.

> broadcast < AJ, $CCS$ >
> shift to Stage 1

---

Enter **Stage 1** either from Stage 0, or whenever receiving an $AJ$ message from $CCS$.

> Set an $\alpha$ timer.
> $J = CCS$

Whenever receiving an AJ/JOIN message, or a timeout event:

- if receive a message < AJ, $j\_set$ > or < JOIN, $j\_set$ > from $q$
  > $J = J \cup j\_set$
  > if it is a JOIN message then LAST[$q$] = $j\_set$
- if $\alpha$ expires
  > broadcast < JOIN, $J$ >
  > shift to Stage 2

---

Enter **Stage 2** from Stage 1, when $\alpha$ timer has expired.

Whenever receiving a JOIN message:

- if receive message < JOIN, $j\_set$ > from $r \in J$
  > LAST[$r$] = $j\_set$
  > $J = J \cup j\_set$
  > if $J$ changed then broadcast < JOIN, $J$ >
- if $\forall q \in J$ LAST[$q$] = $J$
  > *assent to $J$*
  > $CCS = J$
  > $J = \emptyset$
  > LAST = $\bot$

**Fig. 4.** The Simplified Join Protocol, no Faults Handling

### 5.1 The Simplified Join Protocol

As a first step towards the full membership protocol, Figure 4 contains a join protocol for a faultless (asynchronous) environment.

Intuitively, Stage 0 "advertizes" the CCS in an attempt to join. Stage 1 is an optimization step, and its purpose is to collect as many "suggestions" as possible during an $\alpha$ interval. When the $\alpha$ timer expires, the $J$ set gets fixed and Stage 2 starts. In Stage 2, the machine emits a commitment JOIN message. It tries to achieve consensus on $J$, and messages from machines outside $J$ are ignored. If a member within $J$ emits an expanding suggestion, $J$ is effectively *cancelled*. The principle idea is that in this case, it is **safe** to shift to a different $J$ suggestion, since the old $J$ will never achieve consensus (because a required member will never acknowledge it). In this case, a new commitment is made. Let us first see why the simple faultless join protocol is correct. The following two claims do not constitute a full proof of correctness, and are intended only for demonstration of the main properties of the Simplified Protocol.

**Lemma 5.1** *Let $p$, $q$ be machines in membership consent. If both $p$ and $q$ emit AJ messages, then they emit the same AJ message.*

**Proof:** AJ messages are emitted only at Stage 0. Therefore, since $J$ is $\emptyset$, there are no pending joinings, and $CCS$ is agreed-on between $p$ and $q$. $\square$

We need to show that if $p, q$ are connected, they deliver the same JOIN message. The following assures this:

**Lemma 5.2** *Let $p$ be a machine, such that $p$ assents to $J_p$ in the last step of the protocol. Then $\forall q \in J_p$, $q$ assents to $J_p$.*

**Proof:** Let $r \in J_p$. Since $p$ assents to $J_p$, $r$ sent a $JOIN$ message with $J_r = J_p$. Therefore, any previous JOIN suggestion from $r$ is a subset of $J_p$ ($J$ monotonically increases at each machine). Therefore, $r$ did not send a JOIN message cancelling (expanding) $J_p$ up until it sent $J_p$. Since this is true $\forall q \in J_p$, there are no expanding suggestions from within $J_p$. But $r$ is committed to $J_p$ after sending it, and considers messages only from within $J_p$; therefore there is no message cancelling $J_p$. Since for now we assume no faults and no message losses, eventually, $r$ will receive all the JOIN messages acknowledging $J_p$. $\square$

This protocol forms the basis for the full membership protocol. The next step is to handle faults occurring during the joining.

### The Complete Membership Protocol

In the Complete Membership Protocol we address the following matters that were left out of the Simplified Join Protocol:

1. Faults handling.
2. Assimilating messages from "foreign" machines during the joining.
3. Preserving the virtual synchrony property.

**Fault Handling.** The principle idea of consensus decision on faults occurring during the membership protocol is similar to the fautls-handling protocol presented above. The difference is that there are two sets of faults: $F_{before}$ and $F_{after}$. $F_{before}$ contains fautls that are known before emitting the JOIN messages. These fautls occur effectively in the current membership, before the joining. If there are FA messages concurrent to a JOIN suggestion, a later JOIN suggestion will include them in $F_{before}$. $F_{after}$ contains faults that are repoirted after the JOIN messages. The join-set, $J$, and the faults-set, $F_{before}$, $F_{after}$, can only *increase* during the protocol, *i.e.* if a machine crashes, it is added to the faults sets and is **not** taken out of $J$ until the joining completes.

304

**Assimilating foreign messages.** The symmertical joining relies on the broadcast nature of our environment. The join mechanism is triggered when the machines intercept "foreign" messages. However, the membership protocol requires more than that: it requires reliable and causal message delivery between all the (now) connected machines. Usually this cannot be done unless all the participating machines have already been integrated into the membership [5]. For this purpose, we include a vector with a *cut-counter* for each machine in the joined set. The *cut-vector* is attached to AJ messages. The vector informs the communication system to recover messages for every foreign machine only back to this counter. Messages from machines outside the current membership are kept in a separate DAG called the *completion-DAG* (CDAG) until the membershipmembership completes. These messages cannot be delivered until the joined set is assented to. After the membership protocol terminates, some of these messages appear to belong to some past membership, and are discarded from the CDAG (see below).

**Virtual synchrony.** Another matter that is not handled by the Simplified Join Protocol in Figure 4 is the preserving of virtual synchrony. The Modified Join Protocol employs special Transis messages (AJ, JOIN, FA), that relate to all other messages in the system according to the regular causal order. The delivery of JOIN messages is delayed until they are assented to or cancelled, in order to guarantee virtually synchronous configuration changes at all the machines.

When the protocol completes, a certain join configuration message $< J, F, >$ is assented to. There are many identical JOIN messages representing $< J, F, >$ in the DAG. The machines update $CCS$ to be $J \setminus F$ upon delivery of the first assented to JOIN message. All the messages in the CDAG that do not follow the assented to JOINs are discarded from the CDAG. The DAG and CDAG are merged, and the joined membership's DAG contains only messages that follow at least one of the assented to JOIN messages.

Note that due to transient communication problems, intersecting sets may be formed. Instead of unifying the join sets of AJ messages, we actually keep a list of joining *sets* (sets are in their original transmitted form). In this way, we can handle the joining of intersecting sets correctly.

The protocol uses the following data structures per machine: $J$ contains the total set of known machines, $F_{before}$ is the set of faulty machines contained in the current JOIN suggestion, $F_{after}$ contains faulty machines that are considered active according to the current JOIN suggestion; $J\_LAST$ and $F\_LAST$ are arrays containing the most up-to-date JOIN and FA sets respectively received from each machine. We begin by introducing a series of macros in Figure 5. The Complete Membership Protocol is presented in two parts; the purpose of the first part (Figure 6, Stage 0 and 1), is to optimize, by collecting as many foreign join-attempt (AJ) messages, without committing. The second stage (Figure 7) achieves a consensus decision on the join set.

---

[5] For example, if Transis attempts to recover back messages from any detached set, it might deadlock waiting for messages that have been discarded long ago. The same problem will occur in other environments in similar forms.

---

**BROADCAST-JOIN:**

$F_{before} = F_{before} \cup F_{after}$ ; $F_{after} = \emptyset$
broadcast < JOIN, $J$, $F_{before}$ >
mark JOIN messages in the DAG that $\neq$ < $J$, $F_{before}$ > rejected

**BROADCAST-FA:**

broadcast < FA, $F_{before} \cup F_{after}$, $J$, $F_{before}$ >

**INCORPORATE-JOIN** < JOIN, $j\_set$, $f\_set$ > from $r$:

$J = J \cup j\_set$ ; $J\_LAST[r] = $ < $j\_set$, $f\_set$ >
$F_{before} = F_{before} \cup f\_set$ ; $F\_LAST[r] = F\_LAST[r] \cup f\_set$
Mark the JOIN message nondeliverable

**INCORPORATE-FA** < FA, $f\_set$, $f_J$, $f_F$ > from $r$ into $F_x$:

$F_x = F_x \cup f\_set$ ; $F\_LAST[r] = F\_LAST[r] \cup f\_set$
discard all further messages from $F_x$

---

**Fig. 5.** Macros for the Modified Join Protocol

## 5.2 Proof of Correctness

We now formulate a series of claims, whose purpose is to guarantee that connected machines do not assent to different JOIN suggestions. The principle idea shown by the following claims is that when a machine "shifts" to a new JOIN message (after committing to a previous one), it is "safe" to do so.

We will refer to the pair < $J$, $F_{before}$ > as a *suggested join configuration*. We now define *Accept* set to be $J \setminus (F_{before} \cup F_{after})$.

We employ the following two properties of the protocol:

**Property 1** During a membership protocol, the $J$ and $F_{before}$ sets at each machine are monotonically increasing.

**Property 2** If a machine emits a FA message < FA, $f\_set$, $f_J$, $f_F$ > , it has already emitted a JOIN message containing < $f_J$, $f_F$ > .

**Lemma 5.3** *If $q$ receives (at Stage 2) a JOIN message < JOIN, $j\_set$, $f\_set$ > from $r \in Accept_q$, s.t. $j\_set \not\subseteq J_q$, (similarly $f\_set \not\subseteq F_{before_q}$), then there exists a machine in $Accept_q$ that will either never acknowledge $q$'s current join configuration < $J_q$, $F_{before_q}$ > , or emit a different join configuration before acknowledging $F_{after_q}$. Therefore, the join configuration < $J_q$, $F_{before_q}$ > together with $F_{after_q}$ cannot be assented to.*

**Proof:** There are two cases: the first, $\exists s \in Accept_q$ that did not acknowledge < $J_q$, $F_{before_q}$ > and acknowledged $j\_set$ (or $f\_set$). By Property 1, $s$ will never acknowledge < $J_q$, $F_{before_q}$ > , and we are done.

Otherwise, each machine in $Accept_q$ has committed to < $J_q, F_{before_q}$ > at some point. Therefore, in order for any one of them to shift to a different join configuration, it must receive a different suggestion from within $J_q \setminus F_{before_q}$.

---

Enter **Stage 0** whenever $J = \emptyset$ and $F = \emptyset$ and intercepting a foreign message:

> broadcast < AJ, $CCS$, *cut_vector* >
> shift to Stage 1

---

Enter **Stage 1** either from Stage 0, or when receiving an $AJ$ message from $CCS$:

> Set an $\alpha$ timer.
> $J = CCS$.

Whenever receiving an AJ/JOIN message, or a timeout event:

- if receive AJ message < AJ, *j_set*, *cut_vector* >
  $J = J \cup j\_set$
  *extend CDAG recovery for Transis using cut_vector*
- if receive JOIN message
  INCORPORATE-JOIN < JOIN, *j_set*, *f_set* > from $r$
- if receive FA message
  INCORPORATE-FA < FA, *f_set*, $F_J$, $F_f$ > from $r$ into $F_{before}$
- if $\alpha$ expires or communication breaks with any machine in $CCS$
  BROADCAST-JOIN, shift to Stage 2

---

**Fig. 6.** The Modified Join Protocol: first stage

Therefore, $\exists s \in Accept_q$ that receives a different join suggestion from $F_{after_q}$. Machine $s$ receives this messages before acknowledging $F_{after_q}$ (otherwise it discards the message). Thus, before $s$ acknowledges $F_{after_q}$ it shifts to a new join configuration. Therefore, since the communication is FIFO between $s$ and $q$, $s$ never acknowledges both $J_q$, $F_{before_q}$ and $F_{after_q}$. $\square$

**Lemma 5.4** *If $q$ receives (at Stage 2) a FA message < FA, f_set, $f_J$, $f_F$ > from $r \in Accept_q$, s.t.*

(1) $J_p \neq f_J$ or $F_{before_p} \neq f_F$, and
(2) $f\_set \not\subseteq F_{before_q}$

*Then $r$ will never acknowledge $q$'s current join configuration < $J_q$, $F_{before_q}$ > .*

**Proof:** Since the communication between $r$ and $q$ is FIFO, and Property 2 holds at $r$, then $f_J \subset J_q$ and $f_F \subset F_{before_q}$ (at least one inclusion is strong). Therefore, Property 1 assures that $r$ did not acknowledge $q$'s join configuration before this FA message. Any following JOIN message from $r$ will contain $f\_set$ in its $F_{before}$ field, and will differ from $F_{before_q}$. $\square$

Lemma 5.3 and Lemma 5.4 cover all the cases in which the protocol indicates to shift to a new JOIN message (emit another JOIN message). The correctness claim is a direct consequence of this.

Enter **Stage 2** from Stage 1, when $\alpha$ timer has expired.

Whenever receiving a JOIN/FA message:

– if receive JOIN message from $q \in J \setminus (F_{before} \cup F_{after})$
    if $j\_set \not\subseteq J$ or $f\_set \not\subseteq F_{before}$
        INCORPORATE-JOIN $<$ JOIN, $j\_set$, $f\_set >$ from $q$
        BROADCAST-JOIN
    else
        INCORPORATE-JOIN $<$ JOIN, $j\_set$, $f\_set >$ from $q$
– if receive FA message from $q \in J \setminus (F_{before} \cup F_{after})$
    if $f_J = J$ and $f_F = F_{before}$
        INCORPORATE-FA $<$ FA, $f\_set$, $f_J$, $f_F >$ into $F_{after}$
        BROADCAST-FA
    else if $f\_set \not\subseteq F_{before}$
        INCORPORATE-FA $<$ FA, $f\_set$, $f_J$, $f_F >$ into $F_{before}$
        BROADCAST-JOIN
    else $F\_LAST[q] = F\_LAST[q] \cup f\_set$
– if communication breaks with $q \in J \setminus (F_{before} \cup F_{after})$
    $F_{after} = F_{after} \cup \{q\}$
    BROADCAST-FA
– let $F = F_{before} \cap CCS$
  if $\forall q \in (CCS \setminus F)$   $F\_LAST[q] \supseteq F$
    *assent to $F$*
    *mark all FA messages in $F$ deliverable*
– if $\forall q \in J \setminus (F_{before} \cup F_{after})$ :
  $J\_LAST[q] = < J, F_{before} >$ and $F\_LAST[q] \supseteq F_{after}$
    *assent to $< J, F_{before}, F_{after} >$*
    *mark all JOIN messages $< J, F_{before} >$ deliverable*
    *mark all FA messages in $F_{after}$ deliverable*
    *merge DAG and CDAG from the join point*

**Fig. 7.** The Modified Join Protocol: second stage

Whenever delivering a JOIN message $j = < f\_set, f_b, f_a >$ :

$CCS = j\_set \setminus f_b$
$\forall q \in CCS$ : set $Expected[q]$ to the message index of $q$'s message in Electors($j$).
if there is none, set $Expected[q]$ to the message index following the last message delivered from $q$.

**Fig. 8.** The Modified Join Protocol: delivery

**Theorem 5.5** *Let $p$ be a machine. If $p$ assents to $J_p \setminus (F_{before_p} \cup F_{after_p})$ (in the last step), and $q \in Accept_p$, then $q$ cannot assent to any different join configuration, other than $< J_p, F_{before_p} >$ .*

**Proof:** Since $q \in Accept_p$, there is a point in $q$'s execution when it acknowledged $< J_p, F_{before_p} >$ and $F_{after_p}$, *i.e.* it emitted a FA message $< FA, F_{before_p} \cup F_{after_p}, J_p, F_{before_p} >$ . Denote with **Situation 0** the situation comprising of $q$'s state at this point, and of $p$'s state when it assents to $J_p \setminus (F_{before_p} \cup F_{after_p})$. At Situation 0, $F_{before_p} = F_{before_q}$, $J_p = J_q$ and $Accept_p = Accept_q$. Machine $q$ is committed to this configuration at Situation 0. Trivially, $q$ could not have assented to any previous configuration, and did not emit any expanding JOIN message before Situation 0. Therefore, we need to prove that given that $p$ has assented to this configuration, $q$ will not shift to a different join configuration after situation 0. There are two possible scenarios in which $q$ might have shifted to a new join configuration:

- If $q$ received a JOIN message $< JOIN, j\_set, f\_set >$ from $r \in Accept_q$, s.t. $j\_set \not\subseteq J_q$ or $f\_set \not\subseteq F_{before_q}$.
- If $q$ received a FA message $< FA, f\_set, f_J, f_F >$ from $r \in Accept_q$, s.t. $J_q \neq f_J$ or $F_{before_q} \neq f_F$, and $f\_set \not\subseteq F_{before_q}$.

In the two cases, lemmata 5.3, 5.4 show that there exists a machine in $Accept_q = Accept_p$ that never acknowledges this join configuration (including $F_{after_p}$), in contradiction to the fact that $p$ assented to it. $\square$

## 5.3 Proof of Virtual Synchrony Property

The configuration changes that represent joining are required to preserve **P.2**, the virtual synchrony property for the higher level applications. Recall that the joining change is assented to when all the required members (excluding the faults) send identical JOIN messages . We define:

$$Electors_p = \{m \mid m = < JOIN, J_p, F_{before_p} >, m \in DAG_p\}.$$

*Electors* is the set of identical JOIN messages that promote the assentation to $< J_p, F_{before_p} >$ . The first JOIN message delivered from $Electors_p$ makes the join configuration change. The remaining JOIN messages are discarded as soon as they become deliverable. Before making the join change, $p$ delivers all the messages prior or concurrent with $Electors_p$. The merged DAG after this joining contains all the messages that follow **any one** of $Electors_p$. This is defined exactly by the *Expected* vector after the joining, $\forall q \in CCS_p$ : $Expected_p[q] = next(e_q)$, where $e_q \in Electors_p$ is the JOIN message from $q$. The merged DAG contains the messages that follow $Expected_p$.

We already proved that the join configuration $< J_p, F_{before_p} >$ is assented by all of $J_p \setminus (F_{before_p} \cup F_{after_p})$. We proceed to show they have identical *Electors* sets.

**Lemma 5.6** *Let p be a machine. Every JOIN message emitted by any machine in $J_p$ follows the cut-vector known to p.*

**Proof:** This results from the fact that each machine either sends an $AJ$ message, or shifts to Stage 1 when it receives any JOIN or AJ message within its CCS. Thus, all the JOIN messages from each set follow all the emitted cut-vectors. □

**Lemma 5.7** *Let p be a machine. If p assents to $< J_p, F_{before_p} >$ (and $F_{after_p}$), s.t. $q \in Accept_p$, then $Electors_q \subseteq Electors_p$.*

**Proof:** Let $j \in Electors_q$. If the sender of $j$ is in $Accept_p$, then surely $p$ waits for this message before delivering the join configuration change. Therefore, using Lemma 5.6 $j \in Electors_p$. Otherwise, $j$'s sender is in $F_{after_p}$. If any machine in $Accept_p$ received $j$ before acknowledging $F_{after_p}$, then $p$ will recover $j$ (if necessary) and have $j \in Electors_p$. Otherwise, all the machines in $Accept_p$ acknowledge all of $F_{after_p}$ before receiving $j$, and they all agree to discard it from the DAG, in contradiction to $j \in Electors_q$. □

**Theorem 5.8** *Let p, q be machines. Assume that p, q deliver their next JOIN configuration change message $CC_p$, $CC_q$ respectively, s.t. $p \in Accept_q$ and $q \in Accept_p$. Then:*

1. *$CC_p = CC_q$.*
2. *p and q agree on Expected after the delivery.*

**Proof:** The first claim follows directly from Theorem 5.5. Therefore, $p$ and $q$ have the same CCS set after delivering $CC$. From Lemma 5.7, we have $Electors_p = Electors_q$, which further shows that the Expected array for the $CCS$ is the same in $p$ and $q$. □

Thus, we have shown in this theorem that every two machines that merge in a join procedure, reach membership consent.

**Theorem 5.9** *Let p, q be machines in membership consent. Assume that p, q deliver their next configuration change message $CC_p$, $CC_q$ respectively, s.t. $p \in Accept_q$ and $q \in Accept_p$.*

1. *p, q deliver the same set of messages following Expected before delivering the CC message.*
2. *$CC_p = CC_q$*
3. *$Expected_p = Expected_q$ after the delivery.*

**Proof:** The proof of the first claim is identical to the proof of Theorem 4.3, replacing FA messages with general configuration-changes. We do not repeat it.

Claims 2 and 3 are contained in Theorem 5.8. □

Thus, we have shown that if $p, q$ are in membership consent and remain connected, then they deliver the same configuration changes and remain in consent. Furthermore, they deliver the same set of messages between configuration changes.

## 5.4 Proof of Liveness

The membership protocol is provably live if the following two assumptions hold:

1. The set of machines reachable in the system is finite.
2. The system produces *admissible histories* defined as follows: For each message $m$ and each machine $p$, within a finite time there is either a message from $p$ following $m$ or $p$ is *extracted* by a FA message declaring it faulty.

**Lemma 5.10** *Assume $p$ is in Stage 2 of the protocol. Then within a finite time, $p$ either assents to the join configuration $J_p \setminus (F_{before_p} \cup F_{after_p})$, or one of the sets $J_p$, $F_{before_p}$, $F_{after_p}$ increases.*

**Proof:** Let $m_j \in DAG_p$ be a JOIN or FA message containing $< J_p, F_{before} >$ , $F_{after_p}$. According to the assumptions, $p$ receives a message referring to $m_j$ from every machine in $Accept_p$ within a finite time, or a machine is declared faulty. There are a few possibilities:

1. If any message from $Accept_p$ expands the suggestion, either $J_p$ or $F_{before_p}$ increases, as required.
2. If there is any FA message following $m_j$ that contains faults from $Accept_p$, then $F_{after_p}$ increases.
3. Otherwise, the situation is that there are messages referring to $m_j$ from all of $Accept_p$, s.t. none of them extends the configuration or suggests any new faults; therefore, the configuration can be assented to. □

**Theorem 5.11** *Let $p$ be a machine that starts the membership protocol. Then $p$ completes the protocol within a finite time.*

**Proof:** Machine $p$ moves to Stage 2 in a constant $\alpha$ delay. In Stage 2, according to Lemma 5.10, $p$ either accepts its current configuration within a finite time, or increases one of the sets $J$, $F_{before}$ , $F_{after}$ . Since by the assumptions, this growths is limited, this can occur a finite number of times. □

In our implementation we use a strong extraction rule, using timeout for extraction. In this case, the liveness claim may have a definite time bound for completion. However, for purposes of the proof, it is sufficient to assume *eventual* extraction, and show eventual termination accordingly.

# 6   Discussion

The maintenance of dynamic membership in a distributed environment is essential for the construction of distributed fault tolerant applications. We exemplify this through the following list of applications.

- A general *consensus object* may be implemented over the dynamic membership in a deadlock free manner. The method is straight forward: each member machine sends a 'value' in a message. The decision value is any deterministic function of the collected values. If any of the machines should fail during the procedure, the remaining members learn about the failure within a finite time and proceed to make the decision using the subset of the values. Note that this subset is the same at all the machines, due to the virtual synchrony property. A more complicated consensus decision that utilizes the dynamic membership is given in [1].
- Fault tolerant mutual exclusion can be achieved. If the holder of a lock should fail, the remaining machines can retrieve it.
- A set of coordinated processes can provide reliable work-sharing. In this application, a certain set of tasks is distributed among replicated processes, each performing a certain portion. If one of the worker-processes should fail, the remaining machines can reclaim the portion of the work assigned to it. Note that it is imperative to have up-to-date information about the state of the failed worker in order to know which interactions (*e.g.* with clients) were completed before the failure.

Transis is a transport layer that supports partitioned operation, using the membership protocol described above. For example, assume there are 50 workstations in the computer science department that execute a distributed application. If the network is partitioned into two halves, such that each half contains exactly 25 workstations, each half will gradually remove all the machines in the other half out of its membership, and continue operation normally. When the network reconnects, the membership protocol will merge the partitions, providing the upper level with the exact point in the processing when the join occurs. It is up to the high level application designer to implement a consistent joining.

We give a few examples of applications that may benefit from the ability to operate in partitions:

- A network of ATMs that exhibits partitions should allow some transactions on tellers that are disconnected from the main computer. For example, each partition of tellers can answer to queries on balance and credit and provide the most recent information present in the partition. A partition can allow small amounts to be withdrawn in some cases.
- An airline reservation system can have a standard scheme for dividing the available tickets between partitions. When a partition occur, each partition takes a fixed pre-agreed portion of the available tickets and handles them (perhaps allowing a margin of 10% to remain free, just in case).

The applications listed above must handle re-merging carefully, in an application dependent manner. The guarantee of virtual synchrony by Transis facilitates this merging.

# References

1. Y. Amir, D. Dolev, S. Kramer, and D. Malki. Total ordering of messages in broadcast domains. Technical Report CS92-9, Dept. of Comp. Sci., the Hebrew University of Jerusalem, 1992.

2. Y. Amir, D. Dolev, S. Kramer, and D. Malki. Transis: A communication subsystem for high availability. In *FTCS conference*, number 22, pages 76–84, July 1992. previous version available as TR CS91-13, Dept. of Comp. Sci., the Hebrew University of Jerusalem.

3. K. Birman, R. Cooper, and B. Gleeson. Programming with process groups: Group and multicast semantics. TR 91-1185, dept. of Computer Science, Cornell University, Jan 1991.

4. K. Birman and T. Joseph. Exploiting virtual synchrony in distributed systems. In *Ann. Symp. Operating Systems Principles*, number 11, pages 123–138. ACM, Nov 87.

5. K. Birman, A. Schiper, and P. Stephenson. Lightweight causal and atomic group multicast. TR 91-1192, dept. of comp. sci., Conrell University, 91. revised version of 'fast causal multicast'.

6. F. Cristian. Reaching agreement on processor group membership in synchronous distributed systems. Research Report RJ 5964, IBM Almaden Research Center, Mar. 1988.

7. D. Dolev, C. Dwork, and L. Stockmeyer. On the minimal synchrony needed for distributed consensus. *J. ACM*, 34(1):77–97, Jan. 1987.

8. M. Fischer, N. Lynch, and M. Paterson. Impossibility of distributed consensus with one faulty process. *J. ACM*, 32:374–382, April 1985.

9. A. Griefer and R. Strong. Dcf: Distributed communication with fault tolerance. In *Ann. Symp. Principles of Distributed Computing*, number 7, pages 18–27, August 1988.

10. L. Lamport. Time, clocks, and the ordering of events in a distributed system. *Comm. ACM*, 21(7):558–565, July 78.

11. P. M. Melliar-Smith, L. E. Moser, and V. Agrawala. Broadcast protocols for distributed systems. *IEEE Trans. Parallel & Distributed Syst.*, (1), Jan 1990.

12. P. M. Melliar-Smith, L. E. Moser, and V. Agrawala. Membership algorithms for asynchronous distributed systems. In *Intl. Conf. Distributed Computing Systems*, May 91.

13. S. Mishra, L. L. Peterson, and R. D. Schlichting. A membership protocol based on partial order. In *proc. of the intl. working conf. on Dependable Computing for Critical Applications*, Feb 1991.

14. L. L. Peterson, N. C. Buchholz, and R. D. Schlichting. Preserving and using context information in interprocess communication. *ACM Trans. Comput. Syst.*, 7(3):217–246, August 89.

15. A. M. Ricciardi and K. P. Birman. Using process groups to implement failure detection in asynchronous environments. TR 91-1188, Dept. of Computer Science, Cornell University, Feb 1991.

# The Granularity of Waiting
## (Extended Abstract)

James H. Anderson[*1], Jae-Heon Yang[*1], Mohamed G. Gouda[2]

[1] Department of Computer Science, The University of Maryland
College Park, Maryland 20742-3255 U.S.A.
[2] Department of Computer Sciences, The University of Texas
Austin, Texas 78712-1188 U.S.A.

**Abstract.** We examine the "granularity" of statements of the form "**await** $B \rightarrow S$", where $B$ is a boolean expression over program variables and $S$ is a multiple-assignment. We consider two classes of such statements to have the same granularity iff any statement of one class can be implemented without busy-waiting by using statements of the other class. Two key results are presented. First, we show that statements of the form "**await** $B \rightarrow S$" can be implemented without busy-waiting by using simpler statements of the form "**await** $X$", "$X := y$", and "$y := X$", where $y$ is a private boolean variable and $X$ is a shared singler-reader, multi-writer boolean variable. Second, we show that if busy-waiting is not allowed, then there is no general mechanism for implementing statements of the form "**await** $B$", where $B$ is an $N$-writer expression, using only assignment statements and statements of the form "**await** $C$", where $C$ is an $(N-1)$-writer expression. It follows from these results that the granularity of waiting depends primarily on the number of processes that may write each program variable.

## 1 Introduction

Atomic operations are commonly categorized by "granularity": an operation is said to be *fine-grained* if it can be easily implemented in terms of low-level machine instructions, and is said to be *coarse-grained* otherwise. The distinction between fine- and coarse-grained atomic operations naturally arises when concurrent programs are developed in a top-down fashion; under this approach, a program is first developed using coarse-grained operations, and then each coarse-grained operation is implemented by fine-grained ones.

In this paper, we consider the latter problem, i.e., that of implementing one kind of atomic operation in terms of another. Our specific goal is to determine the extent to which such implementations can be achieved without busy-waiting. This has been recognized as an important question for many years, as evidenced by the following quote taken from a paper written by Dijkstra in 1976 [8].

---

[*] Work supported, in part, by NSF Contract CCR 9109497, and by the Center of Excellence in Space Data and Information Sciences. The first author was also supported by an award from the General Research Board at the University of Maryland.

To what extent the ideal "no unbounded repetitions in the individual programs" [busy-waiting] can be achieved in general — possibly by allowing certain *special* units of action to refer to more than one shared variable — is a question to which I don't know the answer at the moment of this writing.

The disadvantages of busy-waiting are twofold. First, programs with processes that busy-wait may suffer from performance degradation: a busy-waiting process not only wastes processor cycles, but also consumes memory bandwidth [10, 19]. Second, the use of busy-waiting often results in programs that are difficult to analyze and prove correct [5].

Recent work on wait-free synchronization has largely answered Dijkstra's question for the case of operations that only read or write shared variables; representative papers on wait-free synchronization include [1, 2, 4, 6, 11, 13, 15]. In this paper, we extend this work by considering conditional operations, i.e., operations with enabling conditions that involve shared variables. The $P$ semaphore primitive is an example of such an operation: it consists of an assignment "$X := X-1$", where $X$ is shared, that may be executed only when the enabling condition "$X > 0$" holds. We represent conditional operations by means of statements of the form "**await** $B \rightarrow S$", where $B$ is a boolean expression over program variables and $S$ is a multiple-assignment. This statement can be executed only when its enabling expression $B$ is true. It is atomically executed (when enabled) by performing its assignment $S$. We abbreviate such a statement as "**await** $B$" if its assignment is null, and as "$S$" if its enabling expression is identically true.

Because conditional operations may require processes to wait, wait-free implementations of them in general do not exist. Thus, we are left with a large gap in our understanding of the concept of "granularity". In this paper, we bridge this gap by considering the relative granularity of various classes of **await** statements. As suggested above, we consider two classes of such statements to have the same granularity iff any statement of one class can be implemented without busy-waiting by using statements of the other class. This notion of granularity extends that used in work on wait-free synchronization.

In the remainder of the paper, two key results are presented.

- First, we prove that statements of the form "**await** $B \rightarrow S$" can be implemented without busy-waiting by using simpler statements of the form "**await** $X$", "$X := y$", and "$y := X$", where $y$ is a private boolean variable and $X$ is a shared, single-reader, multi-writer boolean variable.[1] This result shows that, from a computational standpoint, operations that combine both waiting and assignment, such as the $P$ semaphore primitive, are *not* fundamental.

- Second, we show that if busy-waiting is not allowed, then there is no general mechanism for implementing statements of the form "**await** $B$", where $B$ is

---

[1] An *m-reader, n-writer variable* can be read or waited on by $m$ processes and can be written by $n$ processes. For simplicity, we do not distinguish between reading and waiting when classifying variables in this way.

an $N$-writer expression (i.e., one whose value can be changed by $N$ distinct processes) by using only assignment statements and statements of the form "await $C$", where $C$ is an $(N-1)$-writer expression.

As intermediate steps in establishing the former result, we present solutions to two synchronization problems. The first is a solution to a new synchronization problem, defined here for the first time, called the *conditional mutual exclusion problem*. The second is a new solution to the mutual exclusion problem in which processes do not busy-wait and in which only single-reader, single-writer boolean variables are used.

It follows from the two results mentioned above that the granularity of waiting depends primarily on the number of processes that can write each shared variable. Other characteristics, such as the number of processes that may read or wait on each shared variable, the size of each shared variable, and the number of shared variables that can be accessed within a single statement, are not as important. Further, these results establish that Dijkstra's ideal, "no busy-waiting", can be realized by using "special units of action" of the form "await $X$", "$X := y$", and "$y := X$", where $y$ is a private boolean variable and $X$ is a shared, single-reader boolean variable that can be written by any process.

The rest of this paper is organized as follows. In Section 2, we present our model of concurrent programs and define what it means to implement an **await** statement of one class by using **await** statements of another class. The results mentioned in the preceding paragraph are explained in more detail in Section 3 and are formally established in Sections 4 through 6. Concluding remarks appear in Section 7.

## 2 Concurrent Programs and Implementations

A *concurrent program* consists of a set of processes and a set of variables. A *process* is a sequential program consisting of labeled statements, and is specified using guarded commands [7] and **await** statements. Each *variable* of a concurrent program is either private or shared. A *private variable* is defined only within the scope of a single process, whereas a *shared variable* is defined globally and may be accessed by more than one process. Each process of a concurrent program has a special private variable called its *program counter*: the statement with label $k$ in process $p$ may be executed only when the value of the program counter of $p$ equals $k$. To facilitate the presentation, we assume that shared variables appear only in **await** statements. For an example of the syntax we employ for programs, see Figure 2.

A program's semantics is defined by its set of "fair histories". The definition of a fair history, which is given below, formalizes the requirement that each statement of a program is subject to weak fairness. Before giving the definition of a fair history, we introduce a number of other concepts; all of these definitions apply to a given concurrent program.

A *state* is an assignment of values to the variables of the program. One or more states are designated as *initial states*. If state $u$ can be reached from state $t$

via the execution of statement $s$, then we say that $s$ is *enabled* at state $t$ and we write $t \xrightarrow{s} u$. (In the case of a **do** or **if** statement, "execution of statement $s$" means the evaluation of each guard in the statement's set of guards, and the subsequent transfer of control.) If statement $s$ is not enabled at state $t$, then we say that $s$ is *disabled* at $t$. A *history* is a sequence $t_0 \xrightarrow{s_0} t_1 \xrightarrow{s_1} \cdots$, where $t_0$ is an initial state. A history may be either finite or infinite; in the former case, it is required that no statement be enabled at the last state of the history. A history is *fair* if it is finite or if it is infinite and each statement is either disabled at infinitely many states of the history or is infinitely often executed in the history. Note that this fairness requirement implies that each continuously enabled statement is eventually executed. Unless otherwise noted, we henceforth assume that all histories are fair.

When reasoning about the correctness of a concurrent program, safety properties are defined using invariants and progress properties are defined using leads-to assertions. A first-order predicate $B$ (over program variables) is an *invariant* of a program iff it is true in each state of every history of that program. Predicate $B$ *leads-to* predicate $C$ in a given program, denoted $B \mapsto C$, iff for each history $t_0 \xrightarrow{s_0} t_1 \xrightarrow{s_1} \cdots$ of the program, if $B$ is true at some state $t_i$, then $C$ is true at some state $t_j$ where $j \geq i$.

As stated in the introduction, we consider two classes of **await** statements to have the same granularity iff any statement of one class can be implemented without busy-waiting by using statements of the other class. We define this notion of an implementation precisely by defining what it means to implement one *program* by another. Our notion of an implementation is defined with respect to programs because a given **await** statement's implementation may depend on the context in which that statement appears. If program $P$ is implemented by program $Q$, then we refer to $P$ as the *implemented program*, and $Q$ as the *implementation*. (Presumably, $P$ has "coarse-grained" **await** statements, whereas $Q$ has "fine-grained" ones.)

In the full paper, we formally define the conditions required of an implementation. Informally, an implementation is obtained by replacing each **await** statement of the implemented program by a program fragment that has the same "effect" as that statement when executed in isolation. Such a program fragment is restricted to be free of unbounded busy-waiting loops. Although different program fragments in different processes may be executed concurrently (i.e., their statements may be interleaved), each program fragment must "appear" to be atomic; this condition is formalized by requiring all histories of the implementation to be *linearizable* [9].

One way to ensure linearizable execution is to use critical sections. This is the approach taken in most implementations presented in this paper. In such an implementation, each statement of the form "**await** $B \to S$" is implemented by executing the assignment $S$ as a critical section. Observe that the critical section that implements $S$ can be executed only when the enabling predicate $B$ holds. This aspect of conditional synchronization is not taken into account in traditional synchronization paradigms such as the mutual exclusion problem.

# 3  Results

In this section, we outline the results presented in the remainder of the paper. As mentioned in the introduction, our most important contribution is to show that the granularity of waiting depends primarily on the number of processes that may write each program variable. This conclusion is based on two key results, which are given in Theorems 1 and 2 below. In these theorems, we consider programs called "$k$-primitive programs".

$k$-**Primitive Programs:** A program is $k$-*primitive* iff each of its **await** statements is either of the form "**await** $X$", "$X := y$", or "$y := X$", where $y$ is a private boolean variable and $X$ is a shared, single-reader, $k$-writer, boolean variable.  □

We first consider three lemmas that are needed to establish Theorem 1.

**Lemma 1:** Any program can be implemented by a program in which each **await** statement is either of the form "**await** $B$" or "$S$".  □

We establish this lemma in Section 4 by considering a variant of the mutual exclusion problem called the *conditional mutual exclusion problem*. In the conditional mutual exclusion problem, there is a predicate associated with each process that must be true when that process executes its critical section. This problem is motivated by our desire to implement statements of the form "**await** $B \rightarrow S$" by using statements of the form "**await** $B$" and "$S$". Our solution to this problem shows that it is possible to implement any statement that combines both waiting and assignment in terms of statements that do not. The next two lemmas show that we can simplify **await** statements of the form "**await** $B$" and "$S$", respectively.

**Lemma 2:** Any program in which each **await** statement is either of the form "**await** $B$" or "$S$" can be implemented by a program in which each **await** statement is either of the form "**await** $X$" or "$S$", where $X$ is a shared, single-reader, multi-writer boolean variable.

**Proof Sketch:** We use $B_1, \ldots, B_N$ to denote the enabling predicates of statements of the form "**await** $B$" appearing in the implemented program. The implementation is obtained by replacing each statement of the form "**await** $B_k$" by a statement of the form "**await** $X_k$", where $X_k$ is a shared boolean variable that differs from any appearing in the implemented program; $X_k$ is initially true iff predicate $B_k$ is initially true. Each assignment "$S$" of the implemented program that may possibly modify $B_k$ is modified to assign $X_k := B_k$. This ensures that $X_k = B_k$ is kept invariant for each $k$.  □

**Lemma 3:** Any program in which each **await** statement is either of the form "**await** $X$" or "$S$", where $X$ is a shared, single-reader, multi-writer boolean variable, can be implemented by a $k$-primitive program for some $k$.

**Proof Sketch:** In Section 5, we prove that the mutual exclusion problem can be solved without busy-waiting using only single-reader, single-writer, boolean variables. As shown in the full paper, it is straightforward to use this solution to the mutual exclusion problem to obtain a $k$-primitive implementation. The required implementation is obtained by first implementing each assignment "$S$" as a critical section and by then modifying the program so that only single-reader boolean variables are used. (The latter is easy to do since assignments of the implemented program are executed as critical sections.) □

The preceding three lemmas establish the following theorem.

**Theorem 1:** Any program can be implemented by a $k$-primitive program for some $k$. □

According to Theorem 1, any program can be "reduced" to one in which each **await** statement is as fine-grained as possible, with the exception of multi-writer variables. In Section 6, we prove that, in general, this "multi-writer barrier" cannot be crossed. In particular, we consider a variant of the termination detection problem in which an "observer" process detects the termination of two "worker" processes. We first show that this problem can be solved without busy-waiting if the observer is allowed to wait on an expression that may be modified by both workers. We then show that such a solution is impossible if the observer can wait on only one worker at a time. This result establishes the following theorem.

**Theorem 2:** There exists a program that cannot be implemented by any 1-primitive program. □

## 4  Conditional Mutual Exclusion

In this section, we define the conditional mutual exclusion problem. We then present a program that solves this problem in which processes do not busy-wait and in which only **await** statements of the form "**await** $B$" and "$S$" are used. Our solution to this problem is used in the proof of Lemma 1 in Section 3. In the conditional mutual exclusion problem, there are $N$ processes, each of which has the following structure.

```
do true  →
        Noncritical Section;
        Entry Section;
        Critical Section;
        Exit Section
od
```

Associated with each process $i$ is an enabling predicate $B[i]$ that must be true when that process enters its critical section. An enabling predicate's value

```
process i
do true →
    Noncritical Section;
    ENTRY;
    do ¬B[i] → EXIT; ENTRY od;
    Critical Section;
    EXIT
od
```

**Fig. 1.** Using mutual exclusion to solve conditional mutual exclusion.

can be changed only by a process in its critical section. It is assumed that each process begins execution in its noncritical section. It is further assumed that each critical section execution terminates. By contrast, a process is allowed to halt in its noncritical section. No variable appearing in any entry or exit section may be referred to in any noncritical section. Also, with the exception of enabling predicates, no such variable may be referred to in any critical section. Let $ES(i)$ $(CS(i))$ be a predicate that is true iff the value of process $i$'s program counter equals a label of a statement appearing in its entry section (critical section). Let $BCS(i)$ be a predicate that is true iff the value of process $i$'s program counter equals the label of the first statement in its critical section. (For simplicity, we assume that this statement is executed once per critical section execution.) Then, the requirements that must be satisfied by a program that solves this problem are as follows.

- *Mutual Exclusion*: $(\forall i, j : i \neq j :: CS(i) \Rightarrow \neg CS(j))$ is an invariant. Informally, at most one process can execute its critical section at a time.
- *Synchrony*: $(\forall i :: BCS(i) \Rightarrow B[i])$ is an invariant. Informally, when a process first enters its critical section, its enabling predicate is true.
- *Progress*: $(\forall i :: ES(i) \mapsto CS(i) \vee \neg B[i])$ holds. Informally, if a process is in its entry section and its enabling predicate continuously holds, then that process eventually executes its critical section.

We also require that each process in its exit section eventually enters its noncritical section; this requirement holds trivially for all solutions considered in this paper, so we will not consider it further. Observe that the conditional mutual exclusion problem reduces to the mutual exclusion problem when each process's enabling predicate is always identically true.

If busy-waiting is allowed, then it is straightforward to use a solution to the mutual exclusion problem to obtain a program that solves the conditional mutual exclusion problem. In particular, consider the program given in Figure 1, which is taken from [5]. In this program, ENTRY and EXIT denote entry and exit sections from an $N$-process solution to the mutual exclusion problem. In order to execute its critical section, process $i$ repeatedly executes ENTRY and EXIT, checking $B[i]$ in between. The critical section is entered only if $B[i]$ is true;

shared var   $Q$ : array$[0..N-1]$ of $0..N$;
             $T$ : array$[0..N-1]$ of $0..N-1$;
             $B$ : array$[0..N-1]$ of boolean
initially    $(\forall\, i :: Q[i] = N)$
always       $C(u) \equiv (\forall\, p : p \neq u :: (B[p] \Rightarrow Q[p] > u.q) \wedge Q[p] \neq 0)$
             $D(u) \equiv (\exists\, v, w : v \neq u :: w = u.q \wedge v = T[w] \wedge Q[v] \neq 0)$

process  $u$          { $u$ ranges over $0..N-1$ }

private var  $u.q : 0..N$
initially    $u.q = N$

do $true$ →
      0: Noncritical Section;
      1: $Q[u],\ u.q := N-1,\ N-1$;
      2: $T[N-1] := u$;
      3: do $u.q \neq 0$ →
      4:    await $B[u] \wedge (C(u) \vee D(u))$;
      5:    $Q[u],\ u.q := u.q - 1,\ u.q - 1$;
      6:    $T[u.q] := u$
         od;
      7: Critical Section;
      8: $Q[u],\ u.q := N,\ N$
od

**Fig. 2.** Conditional mutual exclusion algorithm.

otherwise, EXIT and ENTRY are executed again. Note that when process $i$ has executed ENTRY but not EXIT, it is effectively within its "mutual exclusion critical section".

In the mutual exclusion problem, a process gets to its critical section by establishing "priority" over other processes. In the conditional mutual exclusion problem, a process may have to relinquish and establish priority over other processes an unbounded number of times before executing its critical section. To see this, observe that the enabling predicate of a given process $u$ may be repeatedly falsified and established by other processes; if $u$ is in its entry section, then in the former case, $u$ must relinquish priority over other processes, and in the latter case, $u$ must again establish priority. It is this aspect of the conditional mutual exclusion problem that makes a solution without busy-waiting problematic.

A program that solves the conditional mutual exclusion problem without busy-waiting is given in Figure 2. This program is derived from Peterson's solution to the $N$-process mutual exclusion problem given in [18]. Processes "transit" through $N+1$ levels numbered from 0 to $N$. Starting from level $N$, processes compete to enter level 0. A process at level 0 executes its critical section. $Q[u]$ represents process $u$'s current level, and $u.q$ is a private copy of $Q[u]$. $T[j]$ records the process that arrived last at level $j$. The **await** statement shown in Figure 2 allows a process at level $j+1$ to enter level $j$ only if there are at most $j$ processes in levels 0 through $j$. Observe that, if process $u$'s enabling predicate $B[u]$ is false, then process $u$'s **await** statement is disabled. The **always** section in Figure 2 is used to define two expressions $C(u)$ and $D(u)$, which appear as shorthand in the program text; in the definition of these expressions, we implicitly assume that $p$, $v$, and $w$ each range over $\{0, \ldots, N-1\}$. Roughly speaking, $C(u)$ enables process $u$ to proceed when there is no process at level 0 and $u$ is at the lowest numbered level among those processes whose enabling predicates hold. $D(u)$ enables process $u$ to proceed if there is another process $v$ that arrived later at process $u$'s current level and that process is not at level 0.

The propositions that are needed to prove Mutual Exclusion and Synchrony are as follows. In these assertions, $i@\{S\}$ holds iff the program counter of process $i$ equals some value in set $S$.

**invariant** $\quad (\forall i : 0 \leq i < N :: i@\{7\} \;\Rightarrow\; B[i])$

**invariant** $\quad (\forall i : 0 \leq i < N :: i@\{7,8\} \;\Rightarrow\; Q[i]=0)$

**invariant** $\quad (\forall j : 0 \leq j < N :: (\mathbf{N}p :: Q[p] \leq j) \;\leq\; j+1)$

Observe that the first invariant implies that Synchrony holds, and the second and third imply that Mutual Exclusion holds. To see the latter, observe that, by substituting 0 for $j$ in the third invariant, we have $(\mathbf{N}p :: Q[p] \leq 0) \leq 1$, which, by the second invariant, implies $(\mathbf{N}p :: p@\{7\}) \leq 1$.

Establishing the third invariant is the crux of the proof. Observe that process $u$ may falsify this invariant only by decrementing its level, $Q[u]$, upon executing statement 5. However, as shown in the full paper, statement 4 allows process $u$ to decrement $Q[u]$ only when $(\mathbf{N}p :: Q[p] < Q[u]) < Q[u]$ holds. This clearly implies that the third invariant is not violated. In the full paper, we give assertional proofs for the above invariants, and define a well-founded ranking to prove that the program satisfies the Progress requirement.

## 5   Fine-Grained Mutual Exclusion

In this section, we present a solution to the mutual exclusion problem in which processes do not busy-wait and in which only single-reader, single-writer boolean variables are used; we call such a solution *fine-grained*. Our solution to this problem is used in the proof of Lemma 3 in Section 3. As explained in Section 4, the mutual exclusion problem is a special case of the conditional mutual exclusion problem in which each process's enabling predicate is always identically true. For the mutual exclusion problem, the requirements given in Section 4 reduce to the following.

- *Mutual Exclusion*: $(\forall i,j : i \neq j :: CS(i) \;\Rightarrow\; \neg CS(j))$ is an invariant.
- *Progress*: $ES(i) \;\mapsto\; CS(i)$ holds for each $i$.

shared var $P, Q, T$ : array$[u, v]$ of boolean
initially $\quad P[u] = true \ \wedge \ P[v] = true \ \wedge \ Q[u] = true \ \wedge \ Q[v] = true$

| process $u$ | process $v$ |
|---|---|
| private var $u.x$ : boolean | private var $v.x$ : boolean |

| | | | |
|---|---|---|---|
| do $true \ \rightarrow$ | | do $true \ \rightarrow$ | |
| 0: | Noncritical Section; | 0: | Noncritical Section; |
| 1: | $P[u] := false$; | 1: | $P[v] := false$; |
| 2: | $Q[u] := false$; | 2: | $Q[v] := false$; |
| 3: | $u.x := T[v]$; | 3: | $v.x := \neg T[u]$; |
| 4: | $T[u] := u.x$; | 4: | $T[v] := v.x$; |
| 5: | $P[u] := u.x$; | 5: | $P[v] := \neg v.x$; |
| 6: | $Q[u] := \neg u.x$; | 6: | $Q[v] := v.x$; |
| 7: | if $u.x \ \rightarrow$ | 7: | if $v.x \ \rightarrow$ |
| 8: | await $P[v]$ | 8: | await $P[u]$ |
| | $\llbracket \ \neg u.x \ \rightarrow$ | | $\llbracket \ \neg v.x \ \rightarrow$ |
| 9: | await $Q[v]$ | 9: | await $Q[u]$ |
| | fi; | | fi; |
| 10: | Critical Section; | 10: | Critical Section; |
| 11: | $P[u] := true$; | 11: | $P[v] := true$; |
| 12: | $Q[u] := true$ | 12: | $Q[v] := true$ |
| od | | od | |

**Fig. 3.** Two-process mutual exclusion algorithm.

As shown in the full paper, an $N$-process, fine-grained solution to the mutual exclusion problem can be obtained by "nesting" $N-1$ different two-process, fine-grained solutions. The basic idea is to require each process to "compete" with each of the other $N - 1$ processes in a fixed linear order. It follows that, in order to solve the $N$-process case, it suffices to solve the two-process case. Such a solution, consisting of two processes $u$ and $v$, is depicted in Figure 3. The program is similar to the two-process solution given by Peterson in [18] and also to that given by Kessels in [12], but uses only single-reader, single-writer boolean variables.

The two variables $T[u]$ and $T[v]$ together correspond to the variable $TURN$ of Peterson's algorithm, and are used as a tie-breaker in the event that both processes attempt to enter their critical sections at the same time. Process $u$ attempts to establish $T[u] = T[v]$ and process $v$ attempts to establish $T[u] \neq T[v]$. Variables $P[u]$ and $Q[u]$ are used by process $u$ to "signal" the value of $T[u]$ to process $v$. $P[u]$ is used to signal that $T[u]$ is true and $Q[u]$ is used to signal that $T[u]$ is false. Observe that, while the value of $T[u]$ is being determined in statements 3 and 4 of process $u$, the appropriate value to signal is not known, and thus $P[u]$ and $Q[u]$ are both kept false. Also, when process $u$ is in its noncritical section (where it may halt) $P[u]$ and $Q[u]$ are both kept true; this ensures that process $v$ does not become forever blocked in its entry section. Variables $P[v]$ and $Q[v]$ are similarly used by process $v$ to signal the value of $T[v]$ to process $u$, except their roles are reversed: $P[v]$ is used to signal that $T[v]$ is false, and $Q[v]$ is used to signal that $T[v]$ is true. The algorithm ensures that both processes never simultaneously wait on variables that are false. Avoiding such a situation is the principal problem that arises when designing a fine-grained solution to the mutual exclusion problem, as busy-waiting cannot be employed to break deadlocks.

The propositions that are needed to prove Mutual Exclusion are as follows.

**invariant** $\quad u@\{10\} \;\Rightarrow\; (T[u] \;\wedge\; (P[v] \;\vee\; v@\{2,3\} \;\vee\; (\neg v.x \;\wedge\; v@\{4,5\})) \;\vee$
$\qquad\qquad\qquad\qquad \neg T[u] \;\wedge\; (Q[v] \;\vee\; v@\{3\} \;\vee\; (v.x \;\wedge\; v@\{4..6\})))$

**invariant** $\quad v@\{10\} \;\Rightarrow\; (T[v] \;\wedge\; (P[u] \;\vee\; u@\{2,3\} \;\vee\; (u.x \;\wedge\; u@\{4,5\})) \;\vee$
$\qquad\qquad\qquad\qquad \neg T[v] \;\wedge\; (Q[u] \;\vee\; u@\{3\} \;\vee\; (\neg u.x \;\wedge\; u@\{4..6\})))$

From the above two invariants, we can infer that $\neg(u@\{10\} \;\wedge\; v@\{10\})$ is an invariant; this implies that the Mutual Exclusion requirement holds. In the full paper, we give assertional proofs for these invariants, and use a well-founded ranking to prove that the program satisfies the Progress requirement.

# 6 Necessity of Multi-Writer Variables

In this section, we establish Theorem 2 of Section 3 by showing that there exists a program that cannot be implemented by any 1-primitive program. We do so by considering a variation of the termination detection problem. In our version of this problem, there are two "worker" processes $u$ and $v$ and an "observer" process $w$. The structure of each process is shown in Figure 4. The "status" of process $u$ is given by the shared variable $UB$; $u$ is "busy" if $UB$ is true and is "idle" otherwise. Process $v$'s status is given by the shared variable $VB$, which is defined similarly.

Each of the workers $u$ and $v$ executes in cycles. In the beginning of each cycle, a decision is nondeterministically made to either halt, thereby leaving the given worker's status variable forever unchanged, or to continue. Note that it is possible for a worker to halt while its status is "busy". The decision to continue can be made only if at least one of the workers is busy. If the given worker decides to continue, then its status variable is nondeterministically updated. This updating is preceded by an "initialization section" and followed by an "update section". These two program fragments are executed in order to inform the observer $w$ of a possible change in status. The observer executes its "waiting section" until it detects that both workers are idle, in which case it sets variable $w.done$ to true. (Note that it is possible that the two workers are never both idle.)

The conditions that must be satisfied by a program that solves this problem are as follows.

- *Reference*: Variables $UB$, $VB$, $u.done$, $v.done$, and $w.done$ cannot appear in any initialization, update, or waiting section.

shared var *UB*, *VB* : boolean
initially    *UB* = *true* ∧ *VB* = *true*

**process u**

private var
  *u.busy*, *u.done* : boolean
initially
  *u.busy* = *true* ∧ *u.done* = *false*

do *true* →
  0: *u.done* := ¬*UB* ∧ ¬*VB*;
  1: if *true*    → 2: halt
    ‖ ¬*u.done* → 3: skip
    fi;
  4: Initialization Section;
  5: if *true* → 6: *UB* := *UB* ∨ *VB*
    ‖ *true* → 7: *UB* := *false*
    fi;
  8: *u.busy* := *UB*;
  9: Update Section
od

**process v**

private var
  *v.busy*, *v.done* : boolean
initially
  *v.busy* = *true* ∧ *v.done* = *false*

do *true* →
  0: *v.done* := ¬*UB* ∧ ¬*VB*;
  1: if *true*    → 2: halt
    ‖ ¬*v.done* → 3: skip
    fi;
  4: Initialization Section;
  5: if *true* → 6: *VB* := *UB* ∨ *VB*
    ‖ *true* → 7: *VB* := *false*
    fi;
  8: *v.busy* := *VB*;
  9: Update Section
od

**process w**

private var *w.done* : boolean
initially    *w.done* = *false*

0: Waiting Section;
1: *w.done* := *true*

**Fig. 4.** Termination detection problem.

- *Boundedness*: Each initialization, update, and waiting section must be free of unbounded **do** loops.
- *Termination*: Each initialization and update section is guaranteed to terminate. More formally, we require $u@\{4\} \mapsto u@\{5\}$, $u@\{9\} \mapsto u@\{0\}$, $v@\{4\} \mapsto v@\{5\}$, and $v@\{9\} \mapsto v@\{0\}$.
- *Detection*: The observer is able to "detect" that both processes are idle. More formally, define *P detects Q* to hold iff $P \Rightarrow Q$ is an invariant and $Q \mapsto P$ holds. Then, we require that *w.done detects* ¬*UB* ∧ ¬*VB*. Observe that, by the Reference requirement and the program structure given in Figure 4, ¬*UB* ∧ ¬*VB* is a stable property, i.e., once it becomes true, it remains true.

The following two lemmas are used below to prove Theorem 2.

**Lemma 4:** There exists a program that solves the termination detection problem.

**Proof Sketch:** The desired program is obtained by defining the initialization, update, and waiting sections of Figure 4 as follows.

Initialization Section of $u$:
    4: $UX := false$;

Initialization Section of $v$:
    4: $VX := false$;

Update Section of $u$:
    9: **if**  $u.busy$  $\rightarrow$ 10: **skip**
      []  $\neg u.busy$  $\rightarrow$ 11: $UX := true$
    **fi**

Update Section of $v$:
    9: **if**  $v.busy$  $\rightarrow$ 10: **skip**
      []  $\neg v.busy$  $\rightarrow$ 11: $VX := true$
    **fi**

Waiting Section of $w$:
    0: **await** $UX \wedge VX$;

In the above code, $UX$ and $VX$ denote boolean shared variables that are initially false. For the resulting program, the Reference, Boundedness, and Termination requirements trivially hold. In the full paper, we prove that the Detection requirement also holds by showing that $w.done \Rightarrow \neg UB \wedge \neg VB$ is an invariant and that $\neg UB \wedge \neg VB \mapsto w.done$ holds.     □

Define a program to be $k$-*waiting* iff each of its **await** statements is either of the form "$S$" or "**await** $B$", where $B$ is a $k$-writer expression. Note that the program of Lemma 4 is 2-waiting since the **await** statement of process $w$ waits on a predicate that may be modified by both processes $u$ and $v$. Observe that a $k$-waiting program is not necessarily $k$-primitive. For example, the program of Lemma 4 has assignments that access multiple shared variables and thus is not 2-primitive. Note that such assignments are actually required by the program structure in Figure 4; this is why the following impossibility result is stated in terms of $k$-waiting programs rather than $k$-primitive ones.[2]

**Lemma 5:** The termination detection problem cannot be solved by any 1-waiting program.

**Proof Sketch:** Assume, to the contrary, that there exists a 1-waiting program $P$ that solves the termination detection problem. We derive a contradiction by showing that there exists a fair history of $P$ in which there are infinitely many statement executions of $w$. This implies that the waiting section of $w$ has an unbounded **do** loop, thus violating the Boundedness requirement.

The details of the proof are given in the full paper. The idea is as follows. First, we show that process $u$ cannot become either directly or indirectly blocked on process $v$ while $v@\{0\}$ holds. The proof is based upon the central fact that $u$ is unable to tell whether $v$ will decide to halt or continue. (If $v$ decides to halt and $u$ is blocked on $v$, then the Termination requirement will be violated.) By

---

[2] We could have defined the termination detection problem so that $UB$ and $VB$ are accessed only via statements of the form allowed by the definition of $k$-primitive programs in Section 3. Although this would have obviated the need for defining $k$-waiting programs, it would have complicated the proof of Lemma 5.

symmetry, it follows that process $v$ cannot become either directly or indirectly blocked on process $u$ while $u@\{0\}$ holds. Using these key facts, the required fair history can be constructed in a stepwise fashion: in each step, one of the workers is held at statement 0 and the other worker executes a complete cyle. This history is constructed so that each worker is idle infinitely often but both workers are never simultaneously idle. We show that in this history $w$ must repeatedly check the status of each worker, i.e., $w$ must busy-wait. □

**Proof of Theorem 2:** We show that the program given in the proof of Lemma 4 cannot be implemented by any 1-primitive program. Suppose, to the contrary, that such an implementation exists. Then, by using the initialization, update, and waiting sections of that implementation, it would be possible to construct a 1-waiting program that solves the termination detection problem. This contradicts Lemma 5. It is worth pointing out that the program of Lemma 4 *can* be implemented by a 2-primitive program by using the techniques given in Lemmas 2 and 3 in Section 3. □

## 7  Concluding Remarks

The primary objective of this paper has been to determine how programs with **await** statements should be categorized by granularity. To this end, we presented two key results. First, we showed that any program can be implemented by a $k$-primitive program for some $k$. In a $k$-primitive program, each **await** statement is as simple as possible, with the exception that $k$-writer variables are allowed. In establishing this result, we defined and solved a new synchronization problem, the conditional mutual exclusion problem. A surprising consequence of this result is the fact that **await** statements that combine both waiting and assignment can be implemented without busy-waiting in terms of those that do not.

As a second key result, we established the existence of a program that cannot be implemented by any 1-primitive program. Together, these two results give us a means for categorizing programs by granularity: the simplest programs are those that can be "reduced" to 1-primitive ones, next are those that can be "reduced" to 2-primitive ones, etc. These results also show that for $N$-process programs, simple statements of the form "**await** $X$", "$X := y$", and "$y := X$" suffice as synchronization primitives, where $y$ is a private boolean variable and $X$ is a shared, single-reader, $N$-writer boolean variable.

Our results are not merely of theoretical interest, but also have important practical consequences. On any realistic machine, any **await** statement that has a nontrivial enabling predicate must be implemented by means of busy-waiting at some level. Our results show that the required busy-waiting is simple. Specifically, our results show that any **await** statement — no matter how complicated — can be implemented by busy-waiting on single-reader, multi-writer boolean variables (as would be required by an implementation of the statement "**await** $X$" of the previous paragraph). This stands in sharp contrast to the case of previous implementations, such as that given in Figure 1, where busy-waiting on complicated "global" predicates is employed. In a recent paper by Mellor-Crummey and Scott [16], it is shown that busy-waiting on global predicates is best avoided if programs are required to be scalable, as such busy-waiting induces an unacceptable degree of memory and interconnect contention.

Our results can be generalized to allow programs with **await** statements that have multiple guards. Such statements can be represented as follows.

$$\textbf{await } B_1 \rightarrow S_1 \ [\!] \ B_2 \rightarrow S_2 \ [\!] \ \cdots \ [\!] \ B_N \rightarrow S_N$$

This statement is atomically executed by performing some assignment $S_j$ whose guard is true. If more than one guard is true, then the assignment to perform is selected nondeterministically. Such a statement can be implemented by using a solution to the conditional mutual exclusion problem, with "$B_1 \vee \cdots \vee B_N$" as the enabling predicate. Once inside its critical section, a process would simply select for execution an assignment whose guard is true.

In this paper, we have primarily limited our attention to determining those implementations that are possible and those that are impossible. Other issues, such as complexity and performance, are yet to be considered. In all of our implementations, statements are implemented by using mutual exclusion. This is partly due to the fact that in our main result, namely the implementation of statements of the form "**await** $B \rightarrow S$", no restrictions are placed upon the variables appearing in $B$ or $S$: such a statement could conceivably reference every shared variable of a program! Without such restrictions, an implementation must ensure that only one such statement is executed at a time. By imposing restrictions on variable access, it should be possible to implement **await** statements with greater parallelism. The development of such implementations is an important avenue for further research.

Another important open question is that of precisely identifying the class of programs that can be implemented by $k$-primitive programs but not $(k-1)$-primitive ones. Our results merely establish that any program can be implemented by a $k$-primitive program for *some* $k$. Characterizing the class of programs that are exactly reducible to $k$-primitive programs would allow us to precisely categorize programs by granularity. An important special case is that of identifying the class of programs that are implementable in terms of 1-primitive programs. Because any program in this class can be implemented by a program whose statements are as fine-grained as possible, one could take membership in this class as a criterion for identifying those programs with an "acceptable" grain of interleaving. Characterizing this class of programs would thus shed light on the validity of traditional atomicity criteria such as Reynolds' Rule [3, 14, 17].

# References

1. Y. Afek, H. Attiya, D. Dolev, E. Gafni, M. Merritt, and N. Shavit, "Atomic Snapshots of Shared Memory", *Proceedings of the Ninth Annual Symposium on Principles of Distributed Computing*, 1990, pp. 1-14.

2. J. Anderson, "Composite Registers", *Proceedings of the Ninth Annual Symposium on Principles of Distributed Computing*, 1990, pp. 15-30. To appear in *Distributed Computing*.

3. J. Anderson and M. Gouda, "A Criterion for Atomicity", *Formal Aspects of Computing: The International Journal of Formal Methods*, Vol.4, No.3, May, 1992.

4. J. Anderson and B. Grošelj, "Pseudo Read-Modify-Write Operations: Bounded Wait-Free Implementations", *Proceedings of the Fifth International Workshop on Distributed Algorithms*, Lecture Notes in Computer Science 579, Springer-Verlag, pp. 52-70. Expanded version to appear in *Science of Computer Programming*.

5. G. Andrews, *Concurrent Programming: Principles and Practice*, The Benjamin/Cummings Publishing Company, Inc., Redwood City, California, 1991.

6. J. Aspnes and M. Herlihy, "Wait-Free Data Structures in the Asynchronous PRAM Model", *Proceedings of the Second Annual ACM Symposium on Parallel Architectures and Algorithms*, July, 1990.

7. E. Dijkstra, *A Discipline of Programming*, Prentice-Hall, Englewood Cliffs, New Jersey, 1976.

8. E. Dijkstra, "A Personal Summary of the Gries-Owicki Theory", EWD554, March, 1976. In *Selected Writings on Computing: A Personal Perspective*, Springer-Verlag, New York, 1982.

9. M. Herlihy and J. Wing, "Linearizability: A Correctness Condition for Concurrent Objects", *ACM Transactions on Programming Languages and Systems*, Vol. 12, No. 3, 1990, pp. 463-492.

10. K. Hwang and F. Briggs, *Computer Architecture and Parallel Processing*, McGraw-Hill, 1984.

11. A. Israeli and M. Li, "Bounded time-stamps", *Proceedings of the 28th IEEE Symposium on Foundations of Computer Science*, 1987, pp. 371-382.

12. J. Kessels, "Arbitration Without Common Modifiable Variables", *Acta Informatica*, Vol. 17, 1982, pp. 135-141.

13. L. Lamport, "On Interprocess Communication, Parts I and II", *Distributed Computing*, Vol. 1, 1986, pp. 77-101.

14. L. Lamport, "*win* and *sin*: Predicate Transformers for Concurrency", *ACM Transactions on Programming Languages and Systems*, Vol. 12, No. 3, 1990, pp. 396-428.

15. M. Li, J. Tromp, and P. Vitanyi, "How to Construct Wait-Free Variables", *Proceedings of International Colloquium on Automata, Languages, and Programming*, Lecture Notes in Computer Science 372, Springer-Verlag, 1989, pp. 488-505.

16. J. Mellor-Crummey and M. Scott, "Algorithms for Scalable Synchronization on Shared-Memory Multiprocessors", *ACM Transactions on Computer Systems*, Vol. 9, No. 1, February, 1991, pp. 21-65.

17. S. Owicki and D. Gries, "An Axiomatic Proof Technique for Parallel Programs I", *Acta Informatica*, Vol. 6, 1976, pp. 319-340.

18. G. Peterson, "Myths About the Mutual Exclusion Problem", *Information Processing Letters*, Vol. 12, No. 3, June, 1981, pp. 115-116.

19. J. Peterson and A. Silberschatz, *Operating System Concepts*, Addison-Wesley, 1985.

# The Cost of Order in Asynchronous Systems

Aleta Ricciardi, Kenneth Birman[1] *, and Patrick Stephenson[2]

[1] Cornell University Department of Computer Science
Ithaca, NY 14853-7501 USA
aleta; ken@cs.cornell.edu
[2] Transarc Corporation
Pittsburgh, PA 15219 USA

**Abstract.** We consider the *Group Membership Problem* (GMP) in asynchronous systems. This problem consists of maintaining a list of processes belonging to the system, and updating it as processes join (are started) and leave (terminate or fail). Our investigations led to four independent properties that characterize instances of this problem. We closely examine three *membership services*, comparing the message cost to implement them, as well as their fault-tolerance and ability to adapt to environmental changes. We also examine their relative merits by comparing the cost to a distributed application that employs each of the membership services. We show that in typical system executions Strong GMP is less expensive to implement, is always more responsive to dynamic aspects in the environment, and allows applications to accomplish more work with less effort. As Strong GMP is the sole instance providing a *linear order* on membership changes, these results emphasize the benefits of providing Order as well as the cost of *not* providing it when it is available so cheaply.

## 1 Introduction

A *distributed system* consists of a set of independent and geographically distinct processors together with some means by which they communicate. Distributed systems offer substantial benefits over non-distributed systems, for example increased availability and performance. One obtains these benefits by exploiting replication, locality, and concurrency. Unfortunately, writing programs that take full advantage of these properties is quite difficult since there will be many

* Research supported by DARPA/NASA Ames Grant NAG 2-593, and by grants from IBM and Siemens Corporation.

independently-executing processes whose local states and possible interactions must be understood. Moreover, in many distributed systems there are no timing guarantees so that both combinatoric complexity and system asynchrony combine to prevent users from realizing the gains originally promised by distributed environments. However the appropriate formal tools can help us understand these complex interactions and how they affect the problem at hand.

Process groups have been a particularly useful and natural paradigm for programming in and reasoning about asynchronous distributed systems. Process groups arise, among other cases, whenever processes replicate to provide fault-tolerance and cooperate to execute a distributed event. The particular use of a process group determines its required behavior and semantics; in some contexts members may always need to know the exact composition of the group, while others do not require such strict coordination. The class of process *group membership problems* (GMP) describes the range of desired group semantics according to the members' level of agreement on the group's composition, the amount of coordination required to change the membership, and so forth. Given a process group membership problem, a *membership service* monitors process groups for clients and ensures that changes to these groups respect the group semantics specified by the given membership problem [5, 11, 4, 10].

A membership service should be designed fault-tolerantly, and this argues for replicating the membership service protocol at distinct processors. As a result a membership service is itself a process group – its members must be informed of each others' failures and recoveries[1] and the membership service will exhibit a characteristic group semantics.

We have explored four externally-observable consistency guarantees (i.e. characteristic group semantics) that a membership service could provide. They concern the *order* in which interested processes see changes to a group's membership, the degree of *independence* with which membership changes are made, *uniqueness* of the set of processes whose local views are identical, and eventual *convergence* of local views to a single view.

This paper examines the cost of providing totally-ordered group membership changes in asynchronous systems, as well as the cost of doing useful work with and without Order. We first describe three instances of the process group mem-

---

[1] Though we will use the term "recovered", we actually model a recovered process as completely new instance of the specified task. This simplifies our algorithms, allowing us to ignore the case of a process that fails and recovers intermittently.

bership problem for asynchronous systems[2] and their implementations. *Strong GMP* provides all four and is the sole instance providing Order. We measure the cost of providing a given service by counting the number of messages required to implement it. By proving that each of the implementations we present is minimal in this regard [12], we are able to quantify exactly the cost of providing Order. Intuitively, Strong GMP should be more expensive to implement; surprisingly, it is sometimes *less* expensive – notably when failures and recoveries are frequent – than even the weakest forms.

Our second result shows that Strong GMP permits changes of unlimited size between successive membership views. Significantly, this means a membership service characterized by Strong GMP is more fault-tolerant and that it can also reconfigure more quickly to adapt to dramatic changes in its work load.

Finally, we show that, when used as the underlying membership service for replicated data management, only Strong GMP allows operations to proceed asynchronously and does not require any operation to abort. This emphasizes both the fundamental benefits gained from Order, as well as the cost of *not* exploiting it when it can be provided cheaply. We conclude that, in the general case, providing all properties (in particular, Order) is much more useful than providing any subset.

Section 2 defines the class of asynchronous process group membership problems, discussing the environment, a logic for specifying the problems, and formalizing the four characteristic membership properties. Section 3 discusses algorithms (presented in the Appendix) that minimally implement three instances of GMP, and compares their message costs and ability to adapt to dynamic aspects of the computing environment. In Sect. 4 we compare their utility when they are the underlying membership service used for managing replicated data. We conclude in Sect. 5.

## 2 Group Membership Problems

The *Group Membership Problem* is concerned with propagating changes in a process group's composition to each of its members. There are a variety of requirements and restrictions that describe how, when, and to which processes this information is disseminated. In this section, we describe the system model specify these characteristic properties. [13] contains a formal (i.e. logical) specification.

---

[2] An instance of GMP is characterized by the consistency guarantees it ensures.

## 2.1   The Environment and Model

We consider systems in which processes communicate only by passing messages, and in which both processes and communication channels are *asynchronous*. The communication topology is assumed completely-connected and point-to-point, and its channels are assumed reliable (eventual, exactly-once delivery of uncorrupted messages) and FIFO. Processes fail by crashing, but due to communication asynchrony, such events are impossible to detect accurately [6]. However, we assume there is some means by which a process comes to *suspect* another one faulty, and require that a process receive no further messages from one it suspects (e.g. it may *disconnect* its incoming channel). Lastly, a process's belief in another's faultiness is propagated by *gossip* (e.g. through piggy-backing) to other processes in future communication, whereupon the recipient adopts the sender's belief.[3] In truth a failure suspicion is simply a one-bit descriptor one process maintains about another. We require only that the suspicion descriptor be stable (once set, it remains set), but it need not be based on any observed condition. Time-outs (together with gossip and disconnect) are one way to implement the suspector and can be a reasonably-good approximation of true failures. The gossip and disconnect properties will tend to *isolate* suspected-faulty processes among those with mutual beliefs; i.e. to partition the system into sets of processes that do not believe each other faulty. Notice that one process's beliefs affect another's behavior only if the first sends a message to the second and only if the second does not believe the first faulty.

Denote by Proc a finite[4] set of process identifiers, $\{p_1, \ldots, p_n\}$. A *history* for process $p$, $h_p$, is a sequence of events executed by $p$, and must begin with the distinct event $start_p$. Processes send and receive messages, and do internal computation. The event $send_p(q, m)$ denotes $p$ sending message $m$ to $q$, and $recv_q(p, m)$ denotes $q$'s receipt of $m$ from $p$. The distinct event $quit_p$ models the crash failure of process $p$, after which only other $quit_p$ are permitted. Process $p$ executes $faulty_p(q)$ upon suspecting $q$ to be faulty or receiving a message gossiping $q$'s faultiness, and $operating_p(q)$ upon believing $q$ has recovered.

A *cut* is an $n$-tuple of process histories, one for each process in Proc; $c = (h_{p_1}, h_{p_2}, \ldots, h_{p_n})$. An asynchronous *run* is a cut in which each history is infinite; a valid run must satisfy the model assumptions (e.g. FIFO channels, dis-

---

[3] There is no harm in a process believing itself faulty through gossip.

[4] Actually the set is infinite to model infinite executions, but at any point in time only a finite set of processes have existed. See [13] for a full discussion.

connect). We assume familiarity with Lamport's *happens-before* relation and *consistent cuts*[9]. The indexical set $\mathsf{Up}(c)$ is the subset of $\mathsf{Proc}$ whose members are functional along consistent cut $c$.

Let $\mathsf{LocalView}_p(c)$ denote $p$'s *local membership view* of the group along consistent cut $c$. The event $add_p(q)$ and $remove_p(q)$ alter $p$'s local view by adding and removing $q$. Trivially, $p \in \mathsf{LocalView}_p(c)$, and $\mathsf{LocalView}_p(c)$ is undefined when $p$ is crashed at $c$. Because $h_p$ is linear, it makes sense to talk about the $x^{th}$ version of $p$'s local view; let $\mathsf{LocalView}_p^x$ denote the $x^{th}$ distinct instance of $p$'s local view in a given run.

We extend local views to *consensus views* as follows. Given $S \subseteq \mathsf{Proc}$, and a consistent cut $c$, if the local views of all the functional processes in $S$ are identical, the consensus view is the agreed-upon local view; if $S$ has no functioning members, the consensus view is empty; and if the functioning members of $S$ have different local views, the consensus view is undefined. We say that $S$ *determines* a consensus view. Formally:

**Definition 1.** Given a consistent cut $c$ and a set of processes, $S \subseteq \mathsf{Proc}$, the *consensus view determined by $S$ along $c$* is :

$$
\mathsf{Consensus}_S(c) = \begin{cases} \emptyset & S \cap \mathsf{Up}(c) = \emptyset \\ \mathsf{LocalView}_p(c) \bigwedge \left(p, q \in S \cap \mathsf{Up}(c)\right) : \\ \qquad \left(\mathsf{LocalView}_p(c) = \mathsf{LocalView}_q(c)\right) \\ \text{undefined} & \text{otherwise.} \end{cases}
$$

Instances of GMP can be differentiated with respect to whether a consensus view need ever exist, and whether $S$ should equal $\mathsf{Consensus}_S(c)$ when it does.

## 2.2  Characteristic Membership Properties

The properties described here are broader version of those stated in [11, 13]. Since we are concerned with comparing only consistency properties, we omit explicit reference to the Liveness and Validity properties.

**Eventual Propagation** If $p$ executes $add_p(r)$ (respectively $remove_p(r)$) along cut $c$, then every process, $q$, in $\mathsf{LocalView}_p(c)$ eventually executes $add_q(r)$ (respectively $remove_q(r)$) or fails.

Eventual Propagation prevents processes from taking actions unilaterally. In fact, it implicitly forces coordination and communication between $p$ and the members of its local view *before* $p$ alters it; that is, $p$ cannot take an action independently and then hope it can propagate this action to the functional members of its local view as these process may have disconnected $p$.

**Convergence** (with respect to formula $\phi$). If eventually $\phi$ is true in a run, then eventually a consensus view exists.

Quiescence of group $S$ (QUIET($S$)), "Hereafter, neither failures nor recoveries are suspected by members of $S$", is a common example of such a $\phi$. Note, however, that Convergence with respect to QUIET($S$) is actually a restriction on the failure suspector's inaccuracy; since we require a suspector to eventually detect all true failures and recoveries, quiescence requires it not to suspect falsely when none are occurring.

**Uniqueness** For all asynchronous runs and for all consistent cuts in these runs, at most one subset, $S$, of processes satisfies $\mathsf{Consensus}_S(c) = S$.

Uniqueness is important whenever a process group is being used to simulate a single, fault-tolerant process.

**Order** All processes exhibit the same sequence of local views contemporaneously, provided the views are defined. An equivalent formulation is that processes in a consensus view proceed to the same next consensus view.

# 3 Three Membership Services

In this section we examine implementing membership services that ensure

- Convergence with respect to QUIET($S$) only,
- Eventual Propagation only,
- all four characteristic properties (Strong GMP).

Using the same knowledge-based techniques as in [14] we can show that the each algorithm we discuss is message-minimal for the membership service it implements. Message minimality gives a clean, concrete way of measuring and comparing the cost of providing Order. The three algorithms are in the Appendix.

We first show that irrespective of join and leave frequency, a membership service providing Strong GMP has very low additional overhead compared to the weaker services. Rather surprisingly, we show that when joins and leaves are frequent (as is the case in most system executions) implementing Strong GMP uses *fewer* messages overall than any of the weaker services because successive phases of S-GMP are compressed. We then show that the Strong GMP guarantees permit larger changes between consensus views than does the Eventual Propagation guarantee.

## 3.1 Virtual Partitions

The *Virtual Partitions* protocol (hereafter VP) of El Abbadi, et.al. [1], [2] is an example of a membership service providing only Convergence with respect to QUIET$(S)$. Virtual Partitions were proposed as approximations of the *can-communicate-with* relation. A process attempts to create a new virtual partition when it detects a discrepancy between (its local view of) the virtual partition to which it currently belongs and the can-communicate-with relation; for example, if it receives a message from some process not in its current virtual partition. The virtual partition to which a process actually belongs may be quite different from the one to which it believes it belongs and this has important ramifications for distributed applications. We discuss these issues in greater detail in Sect. 4. The VP protocol is a two-phase commit protocol with no minimum *approval quota.*

Convergence with respect to QUIET$(S)$ requires at least $|\operatorname{Proc}| + 2|S| - 3$ messages, and the VP protocol achieves this minimally when QUIET$(S)$ holds. There is no limit on the number of processes that can be added or removed between successive virtual partitions (local views).

## 3.2 Eventual Propagation Only

We also devised a message-minimal Eventual-Propagation-only protocol (hereafter EP). Like S-GMP it is a two-phase commit protocol that requires an initiator to block if it does not receive *majority* approval to its invitation. The majority requirement is necessary and sufficient to ensure that knowledge of the existence of any update that could have been committed will never be lost; the update's existence, because it is process-functionality information, is propagated using a gossip scheme in responses to concurrently-issued and future invitations.

As in S-GMP, at the outset of execution, no EP membership service exists. Booting the EP membership service also involves a name service and a small, initial cadre of core members. Let $\mathsf{Consensus}^0$ denote this initial set.

The *approval quota* for local view updates is the number of process from which approval to commit the update is required. Let *Sizeof-Maj(G)* denote the minimal size of a majority subset of $G$; $\textit{Sizeof-Maj}(G) = \left\lfloor \frac{|G|}{2} \right\rfloor + 1$. In EP the approval quota, $\mathcal{AQ}()$, for $p$ is a function of $\mathsf{LocalView}_p(c)$, but in contrast to S-GMP there is an *a priori* bound on the number of core members $p$ can add to or remove from $\mathsf{LocalView}_p(c)$ in any single update. Since $\mathcal{AQ}(\mathsf{LocalView}_p(c))$ must be at least a majority suppose:

$$\mathcal{AQ}(\mathsf{LocalView}_p(c)) = \textit{Sizeof-Maj}(\mathsf{LocalView}_p(c)) + k$$

where $k$ is fixed, commonly agreed upon at the beginning of each run, and no more than the size of the largest minority subset of the initial consensus view $(0 \leq k \leq \left\lceil \frac{\mathsf{Consensus}^0}{2} \right\rceil - 1)$. Then $p$ can, in any single update instance, change its view by at most $k+1$ members. Intuitively, this restriction arises from the fact that the initial condition is the only commonly-known view upon which processes agree; it provides the only source of information from which processes can base an approval quota and still be assured that the set of approving processes will always intersect.

The choice of $k$ dictates how easily a process can alter its local view – larger values of $k$ require more coordination. In practical terms the initial consensus view will typically consist of no more than three processes, so it is likely that $k \leq 1$ in most cases, preventing processes from changing successive local views by more than two processes at any time throughout an entire run.

Finally, assuming the quota rule is a simple majority then providing Eventual Propagation requires at least $|\:\mathsf{LocalView}_p(c)\:| + 2\textit{Sizeof-Maj}(\mathsf{LocalView}_p(c)) - 3$ messages; EP achieves this lower bound.

## 3.3  S-GMP

The S-GMP protocol of [11, 13] implements all four characteristic consistency properties. S-GMP uses the order it provides to rank processes and distinguish one, the *mgr*, as responsible for initiating updates to the consensus view.

With S-GMP, one subtle cost of Order is the restriction on process initiative: a lower-ranked process can initiate an update only when it believes higher-ranked processes faulty. Regarding message complexity, when *mgr* is believed faulty, the minimal cost to reconfigure depends on the degree of separation of local views and the degree of dissemination of the most recent update proposal. In only one failure scenario are three communication phases necessary, costing $2(\textit{Sizeof-Maj}(\mathsf{LocalView}_p(c)) - 1)$ extra messages. In all other circumstances, S-GMP incurs no additional message cost over EP.

An intriguing aspect of s-GMP is that when changes to the consensus view are frequent, the cost of each update is *less* than that of either the VP or EP protocols. Order, Uniqueness, and Eventual Propagation combine to force any protocol implementing them to commit an update contingent upon the future removal of members currently believed faulty. The gossipy nature of our systems has the affect of making the 'contingency', a necessary part of the second-phase commit message, equivalent to a first-phase invitation message. As a result, when changes are frequent, the cost of a single update is amortized to $n - 1$ messages, where $n = | \text{Consensus}_S(c) |$ [11]. This is cheaper than either of the other protocols.

Of course there are pathological failure scenarios in which s-GMP performs poorly. The worst case requires specific processes to fail at the most inconvenient times: *mgr* fails, then its replacement fails immediately before assuming control, then *its* replacement fails immediately before assuming control, and so forth. However, in *typical* system executions, while failures and recoveries may be frequent, that particular failure scenario is extremely improbable. In these situations s-GMP is, oddly, the least expensive of the three despite providing the strongest consistency properties.

In contrast to EP, the approval quota for s-GMP is always just a simple majority of a core member's current local view. Most significantly, there is no bound on the number of processes that can be added (obviously only a minority can be removed) between consensus views! This is indeed unexpected as it allows successive consensus views to differ wildly. Again, the Order requirement lies at the heart of the explanation since it forces reconfigurers to query the outer members for their local states. It turns out that at every point in the execution where it might be possible for two update initiators to commit disparate views, both are competing for a majority subset of the same consensus view – only one of them can 'win', thereafter blocking the other and its approval cohorts.

## 3.4  Message Complexity Comparison

Tables 1 and 2 summarize the message complexity and adaptability of the algorithms just described. While s-GMP is more costly than VP, we believe the Virtual Partitions approach is ultimately more limited since it converges only in 'quiet' systems. s-GMP is no more costly than EP for all updates except *mgr*'s removal from the core, and then only in a worst-case scenario. Moreover, we believe s-GMP will often be less expensive than EP since runs in which s-GMP can amortize its message cost (frequent joins and leaves) are far more probable than runs in which EP is cheaper (*mgr* and its replacements always failing at specific stages of the protocol).

This should seem contradictory: we are claiming that the *more* ordered protocol can be the *least* expensive and *most* productive to run. The intuition is that processes are using their knowledge of the strong ordering properties to pare down communication; the type and amount of information provided by the strong consistency guarantees allow processes to infer a great deal about the global environment independently – notably a consistent ranking of core members and the size difference and temporal distance between local views. A less powerful protocol cannot optimize in this fashion, resulting in a less-efficient scheme for performing the same updates. Thus, given an ordered protocol, a series of updates amortize message costs by exploiting knowledge of the strong ordering properties.

**Table 1.** Minimal Message Cost for a Single Update to a Local View.

| Algorithm | Consistency | Messages Required |
|-----------|-------------|-------------------|
| VP | $Conv\ wrt\ \textsc{quiet}(S)$ | $\mid \mathsf{Proc} \mid + 2\mid S \mid - 3$ |
| EP | *Limited Divergence* | $\mid \mathsf{LocalView}_p(c) \mid +$ $2(Sizeof\text{-}Maj(\mathsf{LocalView}_p(c)) - 1)$ |
| S-GMP: non-*mgr* | $Order,\ Conv\ wrt\ \textsc{true}$ | $\mid \mathsf{LocalView}_p(c) \mid +$ $2(Sizeof\text{-}Maj(\mathsf{LocalView}_p(c)) - 1)$ |
| S-GMP: *mgr* | *No Divergence,* | $\mid \mathsf{LocalView}_p(c) \mid +$ $4(Sizeof\text{-}Maj(\mathsf{LocalView}_p(c)) - 1)$ |
| S-GMP: amortized | *and Uniqueness* | $\approx \mid \mathsf{Consensus}_S(c) \mid - 1$ |

## 4  Using a Membership Service

The complexity results of the previous section address only part of the cost-comparison issue that is the goal of this paper. A second important metric is the relative *utility* these services provide higher level distributed applications. We measure utility by comparing the application's total cost when it executes on top of each of the three membership services. Thus, Order is *useful* to an application if the application is less expensive to run in an environment that

339

**Table 2.** Internal Efficiency: Maximum Size Change to Local Views.

| Algorithm | $\|Update\|$ | Approval Quota |
|---|---|---|
| VP | $\|Proc\| - 1$ | $\mathcal{AQ}(\mathsf{LocalView}_p(c)) = 1.$ |
| EP | $\leq k + 1$ | $\mathcal{AQ}(\mathsf{LocalView}_p(c)) =$ $Sizeof\text{-}Maj(\mathsf{LocalView}_p(c)) + k$ where $0 \leq k \leq \left\lceil \frac{\lfloor \|\mathsf{Consensus}^0\| \rfloor}{2} \right\rceil - 1.$ $k$ fixed throughout run. Usually $k \leq 1.$ Requires $\|\mathsf{LocalView}_p\| > k.$ |
| S-GMP | add: $\|Proc\| - 1$ <br> rem: $\left\lceil \frac{\lfloor \|\mathsf{GpView}(c)\| \rfloor}{2} \right\rceil - 1$ | $\mathcal{AQ}(\mathsf{LocalView}_p(c)) =$ $Sizeof\text{-}Maj(\mathsf{LocalView}_p(c)).$ |

provides Order than it is in an environment that does not. Since Order can be provided cheaply there would be no reason *not* to do so.

To partially address this question, we consider the problem of managing a single-copy replicated data item. This is a classical problem encountered in both distributed and database systems; arguably, it is the most important problem actually solved in current, real distributed systems. Specifically, we consider algorithms permitting *read* and *update* access to a variable shared among the members of a process group. A correct solution should present the behavior of a single-copy, non-replicated variable. We do not consider database style transactions, despite the fact that transactions may amortize certain costs over a series of update operations. Our reason for taking this approach reflects an interest in a wider range of distributed algorithms, including those cited in the introduction, which are typical of the functionality provided by a distributed programming environment (e.g. [3]). The cost of performing a single read or write to a shared variable is an accurate predictor of the cost of solving these sorts of problems. The cost of performing true database transactions, while important, is relevant primarily to a limited class of database-like applications.

For brevity, we assume the existence of a concurrency control mechanism ensuring that conflicting operations are never scheduled simultaneously (c.f. [1]). In fact, synchronization mechanisms can be layered over any of the update algorithms described below; the points made below are of general applicability. Table 3 summarizes this section.

**Table 3.** Utility to Applications of Consistency Guarantees

| Algorithm | External Efficiency:<br>Work application must do to update replicated data |
|---|---|
| VP | 2-phase commit required for EACH read and write.<br>Majority of data sites in updater's virtual partition. |
| S-GMP | Reliable multicast to Consensus($c$).<br>Flush only when Consensus($c$) changes. |

## 4.1 Virtual Partitions

Using the VP algorithm, reads can be done locally (or from any accessible copy
of a variable), but every update to a shared variable requires a two-phase commit protocol. It is not hard to understand why this is the case. The membership
consistency guarantees provided by the Virtual Partitions approach do not ensure that a process's local view of its partition represents a possible global state
in the actual system execution. In other words, a process can believe it belongs
to a virtual partition that, in reality, never existed (as a consensus view among
its partition cohorts) along any consistent cut in the execution. The first phase
of the data update protocol essentially detects whether a process's local view of
its current partition is shared by the members of it; this is necessary because
the one-copy serialization property is known to hold only if the virtual partition
accurately reflects the communication structure at the time an update is done.

## 4.2 Eventual Propagation

Similarly the EP algorithm is an inadequate base for implementing a shared
variable. Indeed, it is not at all clear that EP provides any meaningful information
for managing replicated data. Recall that within this context, membership in a
group should imply functionality and possession of a copy of a given variable.
EP emits site failure and recovery information, but guarantees neither member
agreement nor that the information is grounded in current reality: when EP tells
$p$ to add $q$, it may be because $p$ once belonged to some other process's local view
when that process added $q$. Whether $q$ is functional when $p$ adds it is, under EP,
irrelevant. In this way a process's local view provides no useful information.

As a result, it is unclear how to use EP in this context so that replicated
updates can be ordered to ensure the one-copy property. Other than a quorum replication method [7], we know of no replicated data-management scheme

that could be used to resolve this problem. Additionally, since EP provides no meaningful information, the cost of even this approach could be prohibitive: each read or write would involve interactions with multiple processes, and writes would again require some form of commit protocol. The result is that both read and write operations will be slow.

## 4.3 Strong GMP

The S-GMP algorithm, in comparison, offers an extremely lightweight environment for managing replicated data. In [15] Stephenson showed how to implement a fault-tolerant, causally-consistent, totally-ordered multicast to group $G$, using S-GMP as input, in at most $2 \times |G|$ (but usually $|G|$) messages. In [8], Joseph showed that, for a large class of concurrency control mechanisms, a $|G|$-causal multicast suffices to perform a replicated update.[5] As in VP, reads are local, but by using such a multicast, writes no longer require a coordinated commit.

To understand why this is so, recall that in contrast to VP and EP, S-GMP forces every local view to exist as a consensus view along some consistent cut in the execution. Though a process does not know precisely *when* that cut occurs, Order allows it to infer that the cut either exists 'currently' or will exist 'soon' – certainly before any other consensus view becomes defined. Consequently, every process executing an update is certain that the group upon which the update's serializability depends is well-defined both in composition and with respect to its causal-temporal place in the execution. This assurance means that any data update can be committed safely, despite changes in the underlying group. As a result, the update protocol can be asynchronous – the initiator need not delay until the data reaches other group members.

The S-GMP algorithm admits a cheaper and more asynchronous solution to the replicated data problem then either VP or EP. Of course this does not rule out the possibility of superimposing a layer on top of VP or EP that would effectively provide atomic multicast, but such a multicast would then achieve the properties of the S-GMP algorithm. The minimality proofs show that the resulting solution could never be less expensive than S-GMP.

## Remarks

One might be curious about the practical importance of the distinction we made above; after all, the cost of running one or two extra rounds in a communica-

---

[5] And to implement concurrency control if necessary.

tion protocol will surely be small. However, experience with the ISIS system has been that similar results apply when solving any of a wide variety of distributed systems problems using s-GMP as a system component. The predominant factor is the ability to issue operations asynchronously, especially beneficial in systems with bursty patterns of communication. Since operations can be emitted much faster than they can be sent they will, when issued asynchronously, queue up for transmission and can then be packaged, several to a message. This amortizes the physical cost of communication over a series of logical operations, making communication appear cheaper as the rate of operations rises. In contrast, multi-phase operation schemes are necessarily more synchronous since each successive operation involves independent communication; this required synchrony precludes the possibility of lessening the apparent cost of communication.

We conclude that the s-GMP protocol is more powerful in the properties it preserves, is generally (though not always) cheaper in terms of message complexity than the less ordered EP protocol, and is much cheaper than either VP or EP when used to solve a distributed data management problem.

## 5   Conclusions

In this paper we showed that providing linear order on process group membership changes is both inexpensive and of great utility in asynchronous systems. This involved defining characteristic consistency properties for asynchronous GMP, examining and developing protocols to build membership services providing these properties, proving the protocols message-minimal, comparing their costs (number of messages and magnitude of permissible view changes), and analyzing the ability and cost to perform some type of useful work on top of the services. Thus, reasoning from 'first principles', we have been able to make a strong case for organizing asynchronous distributed systems, at some level, around linearly ordered changes to process groups.

Practitioners of distributed computing have long looked to theory as a tool from which insight can be gained into the most appropriate way to structure distributed systems. Our results suggest that the protocols used to track membership in a distributed application can have a substantial impact on performance. Surprisingly, they also show that the s-GMP protocol, despite (or perhaps, because of) the very strong ordering properties it achieves, is in many ways the cheapest possible membership service to support. We conclude from this that

343

next generation distributed systems should routinely provide membership services, and that the s-GMP semantics represent the most appropriate ones to use for this purpose.

# References

1. A. El Abbadi, D. Skeen, and F. Cristian. An Efficient, Fault-Tolerant Algorithm for Replicated Data Management. In *Proceedings of the 5th ACM SIGACT-SIGMOD Symposium on the Principles of Database Systems*, pages 215–229. A.C.M., 1985.
2. A. El Abbadi and S. Toueg. Availability in Partitioned Replicated Databases. In *Proc. 5th ACM SIGACT-SIGMOD Symp. on Principles of Database Systems*, pages 240–251, Cambridge, MA, March 1986.
3. K. P. Birman and T. A. Joseph. Exploiting Virtual Synchrony in Distributed Systems. In *Proceedings of the Eleventh ACM Symposium on Operating Systems Principles*, 1987.
4. T. D. Chandra and S. Toueg. Unreliable Failure Detectors for Ashynchronous Systems. In *Proceedings of the Tenth Annual A.C.M. Symposium on Principles of Distributed Computing.* ACM, August 1991.
5. F. Cristian. Reaching Agreement on Processor Group Memberhsip in Synchronous Distributed Systems. Technical Report RJ 5964, IBM Almaden Research Center, August 1990. Revised from March, 1988.
6. M. J. Fischer, N. A. Lynch, and M. S. Paterson. Impossiblity of Distributed Consensus with One Faulty Process. *Journal of the Association for Computing Machinery*, 32(2):374–382, April 1985.
7. M. Herlihy. A Quorum-Consensus Replication Method for Abstract Data Types. *ACM Transactions on Computer Systems*, 1(4):32–53, 1986.
8. T. Joseph. *Low Cost Management of Replicated Data.* PhD thesis, Cornell University, 1986.
9. L. Lamport. Time, Clocks and the Ordering of Events in a Distributed System. *Communications of the A.C.M.*, 21(7):558–565, 1978.
10. J. Meyer and R. Schlichting, editors. *A Membership Protocol Based on Partial Order*, volume 6 of *Dependable Computing and Fault-Tolerant Systems*, pages 309–331. Springer-Verlag, Vienna, 1992.
11. A. Ricciardi and K. Birman. Using Process Groups to Implement Failure Detection in Asynchronous Environments. In *Procedings of the Tenth Annual A.C.M. Symposium on Principles of Distributed Computing.* A.C.M., August 19-21 1991. This is an extended abstract of Cornell University Technical Report TR91-1188, of the same name.
12. A. M. Ricciardi. Practical Utility of Knowledge-Based Analyses. In preparation, 1991.
13. A. M. Ricciardi. *The Asynchronous Membership Problem.* PhD thesis, Cornell University, September 1992.
14. A. M. Ricciardi. Practical Utility of Knowledge-Based Analyses : Optimizations and Optimality for and Implementation of Asynchronous Fail-Stop Processes. In *Fourth Conference on the Theoretical Aspects of Reasoning About Knowlege.* Morgan Kaufmann, March 22-25 1992.
15. P. Stephenson. *Fast Ordered Multicasts.* PhD thesis, Cornell University, 1991.

# Appendix

See [13] for the complete algorithms.

## The s-GMP Algorithm

Task : *mgr*
___
while (true)
  repeat
    GetUpdate($v1$);
  until ($v1$ ! = nil-id);
  *multicast*$_{mgr}$ (LocalView$_{mgr}$ , M-sub($\pm v1$));
  while ($v1$ ! = nil-id)  /* Compressed algorithm loop. */
    forall $p \in$ LocalView$_{mgr}$
      *recv*$_{mgr}$ ($p$, ack(M-sub($\pm v1$))) or *faulty*$_{mgr}$ ($p$);
    if (majority of LocalView$_{mgr}$ didn't respond) *quit*$_{mgr}$ ;
    /* Update LocalView$_{mgr}$ according to $\pm$. */
    DoCommit($v1$);
    GetUpdate($v2$);
    if (Joining new members)
      *multicast*$_{mgr}$ ($v1$, Join : State-Xfer);
      forall $p' \in v1$
        *recv*$_{mgr}$ ($v1$, ack(Join) : NextUpdate$_{p'}$) or *faulty*$_{mgr}$ ();
      $v2 =$ NextUpdate$_{v1}$;
      *multicast*$_{mgr}$ (LocalView$_{mgr}$ , M-com($\pm v1$) : M-sub($\pm v2$));
      $v1 = v2$;


Task: Outer Processes, *p*
___
  *recv*$_p$($mgr$ , M-sub($\pm v1$));
  /* Mark the processes of $v1$ faulty or operational as appropriate. */
  DoPreCommit($v1$, $\pm$);
  repeat
    *send*$_p$($mgr$ , ack(M-sub($\pm v1$)));
    *recv*$_p$($mgr$ , M-com($\pm v1$) : M-sub($\pm v2$)) or *faulty*$_p$($mgr$ );
    if (!FAULTY$_p$($mgr$ ))
      DoPreCommit($v2$);
      DoCommit($v1$);
      $v1 = v2$;
    else Wait-Reconfiguration();
  until ($v1 ==$ nil-id);


## The vp Algorithm

The following is taken from [1], but amended slightly here for clarity. The variable $VPid$ is a monotonically increasing integer.

Task : Initiator, *init*

$VPid$ = generate-unique-new-VPid();
for each processor $p$
    $send_{init}(p, \text{VP-invite}(VPid))$;
await responses;
$NewVP = \text{Acks}(init, \text{VP-invite}(VPid))$;
for each $p \in NewVP$
    $send_{init}(p, \text{VP-join}(VPid, NewVP))$;

Task: Outer Processes, $p$

$recv_p(init, \text{VP-invite}(VPid))$;
if ($VPid>$ max-VPid-seen)
    depart current virtual partition;
    $send_p(init, \text{ack}(\text{VP-invite}(VPid)))$;
    $recv_p(init, \text{VP-join}(VPid, NewVP))$;
    if ($VPid>$ max-VPid-seen) and (same-initiator)
        join $VPid$ and adopt $NewVP$;


## The EP Algorithm

As in S-GMP we do not explicitly show Disconnect, or error checking. Gossip, however, is more obvious: an outer member passes back to an initiator its local failure and recovery beliefs in the set ProcStatus$_p$.

Task: Initiator, *init*

while (ProcStatus$_{init} \neq \emptyset$)
    GetUpdate($EPvalue$, ProcStatus$_{init}$);
    $multicast_{init}(\text{LocalView}_{init}(), \text{EP-submit}(EPvalue))$;
    for each $p \in \text{LocalView}_{init}()$
        $recv_{init}(p, \text{ack}(\text{EP-submit}(EPvalue)) : \text{ProcStatus}_p)$ or $faulty_{init}(p)$;
    if (majority didn't respond) $quit_{init}$;
    for each $p$ such that ProcStatus$_p \neq \emptyset$
        ProcStatus$_{init}$ = ProcStatus$_{init} \cup$ ProcStatus$_p$;
    DoCommit($EPvalue$);
    $multicast_{init}(\text{LocalView}_{init}(), \text{EP-commit}(EPvalue))$;

Task: Outer Processes, $p$

$recv_p(init, \text{EP-submit}(EPvalue))$;
$send_p(init, \text{ack}(\text{EP-submit}(EPvalue)) : \text{ProcStatus}_p)$;
$recv_p(init, \text{EP-commit}(EPvalue))$;
DoCommit($EPvalue$);

# Efficient, Strongly Consistent Implementations of Shared Memory
## (EXTENDED ABSTRACT)

Marios Mavronicolas*     Dan Roth**

Aiken Computation Laboratory, Harvard University, Cambridge, MA 02138, USA

**Abstract.** We present linearizable implementations for two distributed organizations of multiprocessor shared memory. For the *full caching* organization, where each process keeps a local copy of the whole memory, we present a linearizable implementations of read/write memory objects that achieves essentially optimal efficiency and allows quantitative degradation of the less frequently employed operation. For the *single ownership* organization, where each memory object is "owned" by a single process which is most likely to access it frequently, our linearizable implementation allows *local* operations to be performed much faster (almost instantaneously) than *remote* ones.

We suggest to combine these organizations in a "hybrid" memory structure that allows processes to access local and remote information in a transparent manner, while at a lower level of the memory consistency system, different portions of the memory are allocated to employ the suitable implementation based on their typical usage and sharing pattern.

## 1   Introduction

The shared-memory model is an attractive paradigm of an interprocessor communication model, as it provides the programmer the illusion of a global shared memory across distributed processes. Implementations of shared memory must allow user programs to run "concurrently", i.e., to access shared data by interleaving steps or truly in parallel. However, even in the simplest cases, non-instantaneous and interleaving data accesses introduce "correctness" problems. Thus, a need arises for a *consistency mechanism* to support "correct" system behavior. Such a mechanism should allow operations to be executed concurrently on multiple copies of objects, but must still guarantee that the operations appear as if executed atomically, in some sequential order consistent with the order in which individual processes "observe" them to occur; it must also guarantee that the intended semantics of the objects is respected.

*Linearizability*, generalizing and unifying a number of earlier proposed conditions, is a strong correctness condition, in that it imposes strong ordering constraints on memory accesses performed by concurrent processes. Yet, it has been

* Supported by ONR contract N00014-91-J-1981. E-mail: mavronic@das.harvard.edu
** Supported by NSF grant CCR-89-02500. E-mail: danr@das.harvard.edu

argued quite convincingly ([7]) that only linearizability guarantees "acceptable" concurrent behavior; indeed, linearizability enjoys a number of nice properties, such as *locality* (i.e., the memory as a whole is linearizable if each individual object is), and this makes it quite attractive as a correctness condition for different applications, such as concurrent programming, multiprocessor operating systems, distributed file systems, etc., where concurrency is of primary interest.

Many authors (e.g., [1, 2, 5, 6, 8, 14]) have argued that supporting strong consistency conditions is difficult to implement efficiently. In particular, it has been claimed that although for a lot of applications a significant amount of the computation does not involve global operations, in order to maintain global consistency, all operations suffer a slowdown and the degree of concurrency achieved is limited. Capturing this intuitive tradeoff between the degree of "correctness" and concurrency, different memory systems have been suggested in order to resolve these problems. In most cases, researchers investigated different types of weaker consistency conditions, placing some of the correctness under the control of the programmer (e.g., [2, 8]). Other researchers explored the possibility of structuring the memory system as a hierarchy of caches, counting on some sort of isolation between processes that access shared data and those that do not. In some cases (e.g., [2]), a distributed shared memory was implemented by separating it at a higher level to memory accessed locally and memory accessed through ordered message passing between processes, thus losing an important advantage of shared memory abstraction in programming distributed applications, that of uniformity of accessing, without gaining anything as far as consistency control is concerned.

Most of these works suffer from that the memory consistency system was not formally defined, and there was no quantitative analysis of the performance of the implementations; thus, the tradeoff between the cost of the implementation and the strength of the consistency condition was merely qualitative. The first complexity-theoretic analysis of this tradeoff appears in [4]. There, and in subsequent papers ([3, 12]), it was quantitatively shown that weaker consistency conditions can indeed be implemented more efficiently then stronger ones, and that for strong consistency conditions the cost of implementing them (e.g., worst-case response time for performing an operation) might have to depend on the maximal message delay in the system. However, to the best of our knowledge, the problem of building a distributed shared memory system that allows for "local" operations to be performed more efficiently than "remote" ones , while still supporting strong consistency conditions, has not been quantitatively analyzed before.

In this paper, we address these two aspects of the problem; the complexity-theoretic aspect is addressed by presenting a method for developing efficient implementations of shared memory which support strong consistency conditions, and proving lower bounds on their costs; the memory-structure aspect is addressed by exhibiting a memory organization and an implementation associated with it, that achieves linearizability while allowing *local* operations to be performed much faster (almost instantaneously) than *remote* ones, and by developing the framework of the hybrid memory structure.

In most applications, significant amount of the computation does not involve global operations, but in order to maintain strong global consistency, all operations suffer a slowdown. We suggest a kind of hybrid memory structure where we can make an optimal use of all of the available local memory by combining various protocols for different variables depending on their typical usage and sharing pattern. As we develop various linearizable implementations optimized for a range of possible typical usages and since linearizability is a local consistency condition, we obtain a linearizable memory system.

We consider two aspects of a typical usage of a memory object: mostly-shared versus mostly-local memory object, and mostly-read versus mostly-write object. Objects on which a lot of global activity is anticipated are fully cached, using our *full caching* implementation that allows all processes to perform efficient global operations on them. For other objects, for which we still want to allow global access, but anticipate mostly local activity, our *single ownership* organization allows local operations to be performed almost instantaneously, at the price of a bit more expensive remote operations. Truly local objects, which are trivially linearizable, can be part of the memory system as well. The worst-case response time of fully cached objects can be furthermore "tuned" (in a precise manner, by selecting a numerical parameter) based on the more frequently anticipated operation for that object.

In this paper we develop implementations only under the continuous timing model, but it is clear that under the umbrella of the hybrid organization, different linearizable implementations that are tuned for different typical usages of the memory can be plugged in; in particular, those might assume different timing assumptions. We describe in Section 6 future work in this direction, mainly toward developing the ability to determine, in advance or dynamically, how to allocate memory objects to variables.

Due to lack of space, the details of some of our definitions, constructions and proofs are omitted here. We refer the reader to [13] for an expanded version of this paper.

## 2 The Model

The model we consider consists of a collection of application programs running concurrently and communicating through virtual shared memory which consists of read/write objects. These application programs are running in a distributed system consisting of a collection of processes located at the nodes of a complete communication network[3]. The shared memory abstraction is implemented by a *memory consistency system* (MCS), which uses local memory at the nodes, and a protocol, which defines the actions taken by processes on operation requests by the application programs. Specifically, each application program calls

---

[3] The assumption of a complete communication network is made only for clarity of presentation and can be omitted; our results extend in a straightforward way to general networks.

the corresponding MCS process in order to access shared data; the MCS process responds to such a call, possibly using information from messages sent by other MCS processes. In doing so, the MCS must provide the proper read/write semantics, with respect to the values returned to application programs, throughout the network. We make the following timing assumptions: MCS processes obtain timing information from continuous, real-time clocks that run at the same rate as real time, but might not be initially synchronized. All message delays are in the range $[d - u, d]$, for some known constants $u$ and $d$, $0 \leq u < d$.

We consider a collection of *read/write* objects and operations defined on them. An *operation* is an ordered pair of *call* and *response* events. An operation sequence is called *admissible* if it obeys the usual read/write semantics; that is, every read operation returns the value of the latest preceding write operation.

The correctness conditions we are interested in are *linearizability* and *sequential consistency*. The definitions of the correctness conditions involve, for an execution $\alpha$, the existence of an operation sequence $\tau$ which is a permutation of the operations in $\alpha$ and possesses certain properties. We say that $\alpha$ is *sequentially consistent* (cf. [9]) if there exists such an admissible $\tau$ which also *respects* $\alpha$: for each process $p_i$, the restriction of $ops(\alpha)$ ($ops(\alpha)$ denotes the sequence of call and response events appearing in $\alpha$ in real-time order) to operations of $p_i$ is equal to the restriction of $\tau$ to operations of $p_i$; that is, the sequence of call and response events in $\alpha$ can be permuted to yield a sequence that is admissible and maintains the order of events at each process. We say that $\alpha$ is *linearizable* (cf. [7]) if there exists such an admissible $\tau$ which respects $\alpha$ and, in addition, is $\alpha$-linearizable: whenever the response for operation $op_1$ precedes the call for operation $op_2$ in $ops(\alpha)$, then $op_1$ precedes $op_2$ in $\tau$; that is, the order of any two non-overlapping operations is preserved. An MCS is a *sequentially consistent implementation* if every execution of the MCS is sequentially consistent; similarly, an MCS is a *linearizable implementation* if every execution of the MCS is linearizable.

We use as our cost measure the *worst-case response time* of performing an operation in the best possible distributed implementation supporting the consistency condition. We denote by $|R|$ (respectively, $|W|$) the maximum time taken by a read (respectively, write) operation, where the maximum is taken over all executions and read/write objects.

## 3 Full Caching

In this section, we consider a *full caching* memory organization, where each process $p_i$ keeps a local copy, $X_i$, for each object $X$. We develop a family of efficient implementations of read/write objects that support linearizability. This is the first linearizable implementation, known for read/write objects[4].

We describe a family of implementations, parameterized by $\beta$, and allow for the selection of a member of that family, in order to degrade the less frequently employed (read or write) operation. These implementations, C-Linear,

---

[4] Earlier results of this research were reported in [12].

make heavy use of a novel *time slicing* technique which is of independent interest. Using this technique, each process individually "slices" time (using its local clock) and sends messages to other processes only when in an appropriate time slice. By judicious choice of the sizes of the slices, to be properly related to the message delay uncertainty $u$, this technique guarantees for each process the existence of time periods in which it does not receive any messages. Most important, it increases the amount of "common knowledge" across the system without using any control messages; thus, the event of receiving a message in the system carries with it timing information, without it being explicitly sent as part of the message. As an outcome, for any given operation, only one message is broadcasted in the system, and all messages have constant size, which does not increase with real time and depends only on the set of values used. (The message contains only the value being written or read, and one extra bit of information.)

By use of an available total order as a tie breaking mechanism, only one write operation, among possibly few occurring within a short time period becomes effective[5]; in this way, consistent local copies of memory are maintained. This common decision is an important ingredient of the correctness of the implementation.

## 3.1    A Linearizable Implementation

We start with an observation which, in a sense, gives a characterization of a caching linearizable implementation and motivates our algorithm. Consider two processes $p_i, p_j$, that perform write operations on object $X$, say, $Write_i(X, v_1)$ and $Write_j(X, v_2)$; assume it is possible for $p_i$ and $p_j$ to send messages to other processes, within time less than $u$, informing them about the values of the write operations. Due to different message delays, processes $p$ and $q$ may receive these messages in a different order. Thus, $p$ and $q$ would update their local copies of $X$ in a different way, if they use nothing but the locally available timing information. This would lead to inconsistent copies of local memory, which clearly breaks linearizability. (Since future read operations on $X$ at $p$ and $q$, that return different values, can be made to occur in an order such that no permutation of these operations can both conform to the read/write semantics and preserve the relative real-time order of non-overlapping read operations.) Thus, more information must be used to support linearizability. This motivates our linearizable implementations.

Our implementation uses a simple synchronization procedure, Synch, originally introduced and used in [12], which is run during an initialization phase of the implementation, to enable the processes achieve a certain amount of accuracy. As soon as a process enters the computation, it broadcasts a synchronization message *synch* and sets a timer $T$ for time $d$ thereafter. Each process $p_i$ sets its local time to 0 on either the first receipt of some (*synch*) message from any

---

[5] As we observe later, in a caching linearizable implementation, the decision on which value to return in a read operation may not depend solely on timing information available to the process.

other process or on expiration of $T$, whichever happens first. In [12], we show the following property of Synch [6]:

**Fact 1.** Synch *synchronizes the system within accuracy* $u$, *i.e., the maximum difference between the local times of any two processes at any real time after all processes have completed* Synch *is at most* $u$.

We assume throughout the discussion below that all processes executed Synch in a prior phase.

The main technical tool developed below is the time slicing technique (See Figure 1). An important property of our implementations is that in response to a read request, $Read_i(X)$, received by process $p_i$, the process does not necessarily return the most recent value it received; rather, it chooses and returns a possibly different one from a set of values of write operations occurring within a small period of time. It makes this decision based on information that is shown to be common to all processes, due to properties of the slicing technique. In this way, consistent local copies of memory are maintained, an important ingredient in the correctness of the implementation.

Decisions made by individual processes in this implementation, C-Linear, do not require that processes use any timing information, other than timing themselves. (That is, as part of the algorithm a process might use its local clock to "timeout" itself for a time period.) Thus, messages sent in the system do not contain any timing information. However, for clarity of presentation, we first describe the implementation C-Linear as if timing information is part of the messages, and used by processes in deciding which value to return. Later, in Subsection 3.2 we prove that this is not required and show how to modify C-Linear to avoid using any timing information.

We now describe the implementation C-Linear. First the "timings" of the algorithm are described; next, we describe how a process selects the value it returns in a read operation. In the following, $\beta$ $(0 \leq \beta < \frac{d-u}{d})$ is a parameter of the implementation and $b > 0$ is an arbitrarily small constant.

- Upon a $Read_i(X)$ event, $p_i$ sets a timer to expire at time $\beta d$ thereafter; it then returns at the earliest time possible, but at least time $u$ after it receives an update for $X$.
- A "time slicing" technique is used for handling writes; roughly speaking, $p_i$ slices each time period of $3u + b$ into an interval of length $3u$ in which actions on a write request may not be initiated, followed by an interval of length $b$ in which they may. Upon a $Write_i(X, v)$ event and when in the appropriate time interval, $p_i$ broadcasts an $update(X, v)$ message and waits for an additional $(1 - \beta)d$ time to set $X_i$ to $v$ and issue $Ack_i(X)$.

We now describe the mechanism by which $p_i$ "selects" a value to be returned in a read operation: $p_i$ considers only values that it previously set $X_i$ to, whose

---

[6] Although, by the results of Lundelius and Lynch in [11], an accuracy of $u$ is *not* optimal, our synchronization algorithm is extremely simple and an accuracy of $u$ suffices here.

local broadcasting time (for now, assumed to be part of the update message) is within $2u$ of that of the message with the currently maximal local broadcasting time. (It is shown that the most recent value received must be one of them. In particular, if no update message was received by $p_i$ since the last time it returned a value, the last returned value is the only candidate.) To do so, $p_i$ maintains a set $Pend(X)$ of "pending" update messages that it recently received. Whenever $p_i$ updates $X_i$ to $v$, either on receipt of $update(X, v)$ or as a result of a write operation $Write_i(X, v)$, it adds $(v, t)$ to $Pend(X)$, where $t$ is the local time at which $update(X, v)$ was broadcasted in the system (possibly, by $p_i$). For a $Read_i(X)$ operation, after a value $v$ has been the content of $X_i$ for time at least $u$, $p_i$ considers only those elements of $Pend(X)$ whose time component is within $2u$ of the maximal time component of elements in $Pend(X)$. Each such element defines a candidate value to be returned; $p_i$ returns the maximal (with respect to a total order defined on the values or the processes id's) of these values. Formally we show:

**Theorem 2.** C-Linear *is a linearizable implementation of read/write objects, which achieves, for each* $\beta$, $0 \leq \beta < \frac{d-u}{d}$, $|R| < \beta d + 4u + b$, $|W| = (1 - \beta)d + 3u$.

*Proof. (Outline)* As the bound on $|W|$ is clear, we only need to prove the bound on the worst-case response time for a read operation, and that the implementation is linearizable. We start with the former.

It seems as if a deadlock may occur due to successive update events; however, the time slicing technique assures that this is not the case. We show that for each process $p_i$ there exists a family of "quiet" (update-free) time intervals, $quiet_i(k)$, one for each integer $k$, with the following properties: $p_i$ receives no update messages in each $quiet_i(k)$; $quiet_i(k)$ has length at least $u$; two such consecutive intervals, $quiet_i(k)$ and $quiet_i(k + 1)$, are separated by an interval of length $< 2u + b$. These properties imply that any read operation will return before time $4u + b$ elapses from its initiation.

We proceed to show that C-Linear is a linearizable implementation. We do so by explicitly constructing, given an arbitrary timed execution $\alpha$ of C-Linear, an admissible operation sequence which respects $\alpha$ and is $\alpha$-linearizable. We outline below the construction and the main ideas used in proving its correctness.

The construction proceeds in two phases. In the first phase, we "serialize" each read and write operation in $\alpha$ to occur at the time of its response in $\alpha$, breaking ties by ordering all write operations before read ones that occur simultaneously and then using $<_V$. Clearly, by construction, the sequence $\tau'$, which results from the first phase of the construction, maintains the order of operations at each process, that is, it respects $\alpha$. Also, the order of non-overlapping operations is maintained, and $\tau'$ is $\alpha$-linearizable. However, it might not be admissible.

In the second phase, we trace all admissibility violations in $\tau'$, and fix each such violation, while still maintaining the fact that it respects $\alpha$ and is $\alpha$-linearizable, by "locally" permuting operations in the sequence. We scan the sequence $\tau'$ from its beginning, and show that by using this procedure, the index of the first operations in which a violation occurs, strictly grows as we fix a violation, and that no new violation is generated; this implies, inductively, that this procedure results in an admissible sequence $\tau$ which respects $\alpha$ and is $\alpha$-linearizable, thus proving that the implementation is linearizable.

We now elaborate on the second phase of the construction. Fix any timed execution $\alpha$ of C-Linear, and let $\tau'$ be the operation sequence resulting from the first phase. Scan $\tau'$ till a read operation $rop_1$ is reached such that a sequence of operations $wop_1, wop_2, rop_1$ is a subsequence of $\tau'$, where: all these operations are performed on some read/write object $X$; $wop_1$ and $wop_2$ stand for operations that write the values $v_1, v_2$ $(v_1 \neq v_2)$ on $X$, respectively; $rop_1$ stands for a read operation on $X$ that returns $v_1$, and $wop_2$ is the latest write operation in $\tau$ that precedes $rop_1$ in $\tau'$. We show first that this subsequence is the only possible form of an admissibility violation; this follows since a read operation can return a value only after the corresponding write operation returns.

To fix this violation we distinguish between two cases, depending on whether $wop_1$ and $wop_2$ were broadcasted in the same slice or not. In both cases, we identify a permutation that we perform on the operation sequence; we prove that the permuted sequence $\tau_1$, like $\tau'$, respects $\alpha$, is $\alpha$-linearizable, does not contain any violation that was not already in $\tau'$, but the first admissibility violation in $\tau_1$, if exists, appears in it later than in $\tau'$.

In order to prove that operations can be permuted, we prove that certain operations must overlap in time, and show that in certain cases, it is not possible for a read operation occurring in a certain time interval, to return a certain value. These hidden time constrains result from properties of the time slicing technique that we prove. In particular, we show that values can be candidates to be returned by some read operation, if and only if they were broadcasted in the "same" slice (e.g., all broadcasted in the 7-th slice, which may reflect different real times).

Since we scan $\tau'$ from the beginning to trace admissibility violations, and showed that each "fix" we make, resulting in $\tau_1$, extends the "legal" prefix of the operation sequence, without introducing new violations, by induction, this results in an admissible sequence which respects $\alpha$ and is $\alpha$-linearizable, as needed.

## 3.2 Messages with No Timing Information

In this subsection, we briefly describe how the algorithm C-Linear can be implemented so that a decision made by an individual process does not require the use of any timing information except for that of its own local clock. Thus, there is no need for timing information to be included in the messages and these have constant size that depends only on the set of values used.

We describe next the modification made to the version of C-Linear given in Section 3.1. In short, performing C-Linear without using timing information requires slightly more local computation by the deciding process. As we show, the ability to make exactly the same decisions without using timing information stems from the time slicing technique, since utilizing this technique, delivered

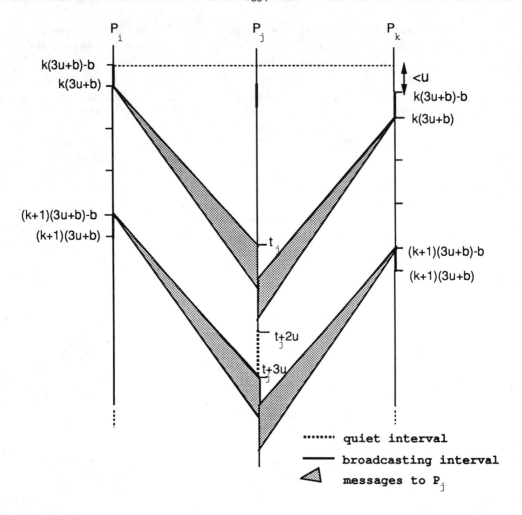

$P_i$   $P_j$   $P_k$

$k(3u+b)-b$
$k(3u+b)$

$<u$
$k(3u+b)-b$
$k(3u+b)$

$(k+1)(3u+b)-b$
$(k+1)(3u+b)$

$t_j$

$(k+1)(3u+b)-b$
$(k+1)(3u+b)$

$t+2u_j$

$t+3u_j$

········ quiet interval

—— broadcasting interval

◢ messages to $P_j$

**Fig. 1.** The slicing technique

messages carry with them timing information without it being explicitly part of them.

As described before, the message $update(X, v)$ contains a pair $(v, t)$, where $v$ is the value written, and $t$ is the reading of the local clock of the writing process at the time the update message is broadcasted. Clearly, the size of this message gets unbounded, as $t$ grows. We outline below how to implement the algorithm using only *one* extra bit (in access of the value $v$). More specifically, we show that it suffices to include in the message, instead of the local time $t$, only the parity bit of the number of the timeslice in which the message is broadcasted. (We say that $update(X, v)$, broadcasted at local time $t$, is broadcasted in the $k - th$ slice if $(3u + b)k - b \leq t \leq (3u + b)k$.)

To support this economic implementation, we prove that the time at which a process receives a message is tightly coupled with the slice in which it was broadcasted in the following way: a message that is broadcasted in the $k - th$ slice, by some process, is received by all processes before a message that is broadcasted in the $l - th$ slice, providing that $k < l$; moreover, if $l - k > 1$, it is guaranteed that there is a gap of at least $3u$ between the time at which a process receives the first message and the time it receives the second one.

Now, for each message $update((X, v), t)$, previously used in C-Linear, the writing process $p_i$ writes the value $v$ and, instead of its local clock $t$ at the time of broadcast, it writes $b_t = k \bmod 2$, such that $(3u + b)k - b \leq t \leq (3u + b)k$ (that is, the least significant bit of the slice number $k$). $p_k$ then uses an internal flag that signifies when more than $3u$ has elapsed from the time at which it received the last update to object $X$.

Clearly, due to the relation between delivery times and broadcasting times, and since different values are candidates to be returned by read operation if and only if they were broadcasted in the "same" slice, with this modification, C-Linear is implemented with constant size messages.

# 4 Single-Ownership

In this section, we consider the *single ownership* organization, in which each memory object is "owned" by a single process, the one that is most likely to perform frequent operations on that object. For this organization we develop a linearizable implementations in which local operations can be performed very efficiently, at a quite moderate price of some slowdown in performing remote operations. It is notable, though, that our implementation allows for efficient local operations, a feature sought after by other researchers as well (e.g., [2, 6]), but is still linearizable.

In the single ownership organization the owner of an object (also called the master process for that object) is the only process which keeps a local copy of it, and coordinates operations performed by other processes[7] on it. In this way, a process can access objects owned by it almost instantaneously, depending only on the uncertainty in message delays $u$. Since the underlying assumption for this organization is that variables might have different sharing patterns, a process can access an object owned by a different process, but the cost of such an access depends, naturally, on the communication latency $d$. As expected, the

---

[7] We do not assume that processes know which process "owns" each memory object. In our protocol each process, upon a read or write request, broadcasts a message, as in Section 3, but only the master process for that object takes action on this message. There is a clear trade off between the communication overhead of this protocol and the amount of storage and techniques (e.g., hashing) used for the local storage, which we do not discuss here.

cost of such a remote operation is slightly higher than that of performing a global operation in the full caching model.

Clearly, if we assume that "information" about a read/write object $X$ may flow from the master process $p^X$ to a different process only upon request, no implementation can achieve a worst-case response time for read operations which is less than $2d$. However, if this assumption is removed, this simple lower bound is no longer valid, since, for example, $p^X$ may periodically send the value it currently keeps of $X$ to all other processes. Due to communication overhead considerations, however, we choose to have information flowing from a master process to other processes only upon request.

SO-Linear is much simpler than the corresponding caching implementation; the fact that operations on a given object are coordinated by a single process allows for an efficient implementation without using the time slicing technique introduced for the full caching case. As a result, the proofs of correctness, albeit similar to their caching counterparts, are simpler.

We start with an informal description of the linearizable implementation SO-Linear:

- Upon a $Read_i(X)$ event, a process $p_i$, different from $p^X$, sends a message $read(X)$ to $p^X$ and sets a timer for time $2d + u$ thereafter. On expiration of the timer, $p_i$ returns the value it received from $p^X$. Upon receipt of $read_i(X)$ from $p_i$, $p^X$ sets a timer for time $u$ thereafter, when it sends the current value of $X$ to $p_i$.
- Upon a $Write_i(X, v)$ event, $p_i$ immediately sends a message $update(X, v)$ to $p^X$ and sets a timer for time $d$ thereafter; upon its expiration it acknowledges. On receipt of $update(X, v)$, $p^X$ sets a timer for time $u$ thereafter, when it updates $X$ to $v$.
- Let $p_i = p^X$. Upon a $Read_i(X)$ event, $p^X$ sets a timer for time $u$, when it returns the value it holds for $X$. Upon a $Write_i(X, v)$ event, $p^X$ sets a timer for time $u$, when it sets $X$ to $v$ and acknowledges.

Formally we show:

**Theorem 3.** SO-Linear *is a linearizable implementation which achieves* $|R| = u$, $|W| = u$ *for local operations and* $|R| = 2d + u$, $|W| = d$ *for remote operations.*

*Proof. (Outline)* The algorithm SO-Linear clearly achieves the stated worst-case response times. We only need to show that the implementation is linearizable. The structure of this proof is essentially the same as that of the proof of Theorem 2, so we will not repeat it here. There are two main differences between the proofs, though. One is that after characterizing the form of an admissibility violation, which, as in Theorem 2, has the form $wop_1, wop_2, rop_1$, and in order to fix this violation, we proceed by case analysis on the order in which the memory object $X$ is being *updated* to values $v_1$ and $v_2$, by the master process $p^X$. The second difference is that this time, the constraints on the ordering relationship between operations, by which we prove the required properties of the algorithm, do not result from the time-slicing, but rather from the existence of a single process that coordinates operations on an object. In particular, to prove properties of the implementation, we rely on that in all cases, the master process $p^X$ never updates or reads a value from $X$ before at least time $u$ elapses from the time of the operation request, in order to avoid possible problems due to uncertainty in message delay.

As in Theorem 2, we show that since we scan $\tau'$ from the beginning to trace admissibility violations; and show that each "fix" we make, resulting in $\tau_1$, extends the "legal" prefix of the operation sequence, without introducing new violations, by induction, this results in an admissible sequence which respects $\alpha$ and is $\alpha$-linearizable.

## 5  Lower Bounds

In this section we present lower bounds for consistent implementations under general assumptions on the pattern of sharing properties of processes.

Our main impossibility result is a lower bound of $d + \frac{u}{2}$ on the sum of the worst-case response times for read and write operations in any sequentially consistent, object-symmetric and object-independent implementation. (This implies a corresponding lower bound for linearizable implementations.) That is, we assume that read and write operations are handled by processes in a symmetric way with respect to the objects they are performed on. In particular, processes use the same algorithm for all objects. This implies that the results in Section 3 are optimal up to a small additive number of multiples of $u$.

The lower bound proof combines the use of various methods already common in the theory of distributed computing, namely, symmetry arguments and the technique of "shifting" executions (originally introduced in [11]), with a novel technique of augmenting executions to "causally link" them. The known lower bound of $d - u$ on message delay time is used in constructing the executions, to achieve non-availability of knowledge to processes. As part of this proof, we derive a property of any sequentially consistent implementation which is of independent interest and might be used for verifying correctness of such implementations. In the following, we only sketch the constructions and the proofs.

**Theorem 4.** *In any sequentially consistent, object-symmetric and object-independent implementation of at least three objects using at least four processes, $|R| + |W| \geq d + \frac{u}{2}$.*

*Proof. (Outline)* Assume, by way of contradiction, that there exists a sequentially consistent, object-symmetric and object-independent implementation of such objects for which $|R| + |W| < d + \frac{u}{2}$. We construct an execution in which two different processes, $p$ and $p'$, performing successive read operations on an object $X$ are "forced" by symmetry to return values $v_1$ and $v_2$ in different order; this, clearly, violates sequential consistency. We appropriately choose massage delay times in our construction to achieve such symmetry. Specifically, we consider two write operations that write $v_1$ and $v_2$, and make $p$ "learn" quickly about the write of $v_1$, but not about the write of $v_2$. (The roles of $v_1$ and $v_2$ are reversed for $p'$.) Hence, assuming rapid completion of successive read and write operations (i.e., $|R| + |W| < d + u/2$) forces the read operations by $p$ and $p'$ to return different values and establishes the contradiction. Two technical claims facilitate our main construction.

Our first claim (inspired by a result in [10]) shows that by carefully choosing message delays, and using the shifting technique, a non-symmetric configuration "looks" totally symmetric to the processes. Specifically, let $p_i$, starting at time 0, write $v_1$ on $Y$, and immediately read $X$ and, $p_j$, starting at time $\frac{u}{2}$, write $v_1$ on $X$, and immediately read $Y$. (Assume that both $X$ and $Y$ are initialized to $v_0$). We show that in this case, the read operation by $p_i$ returns $v_1$.

We then provide a necessary condition that sequentially consistent implementations must satisfy. Consider an execution in which there are only two write operations on $X$, which write different values $v_1$, $v_2$. Then:

**Claim 5.** *Let processes $p_i, p_j$ perform a read operation on $X$, after both writes on $X$ are completed and $p_i$ and $p_j$ "learn" about them. Then, both read operations return the same value.*

We prove this claim by contradiction. The main tool used in the proof is that of "interrupting" two sequences of reads by $p_i$ and $p_j$ and augmenting them by adding operations to causally link these two sequences, thus contradicting the assumption that the processes can return different values.

We now informally describe our main construction. Processes $p$ and $p'$, starting at time 0, write $v_1$ on $Y$, read $X$, write $v_2$ on $Y$ and read $X$ again. Processes $q$ and $q'$, starting at time $\frac{u}{2}$, write $v_1$ and $v_2$ on $X$, respectively, and then read $Y$. Messages from $q$ to $p$ and from $q'$ to $p'$ take time $d - u$, while messages from $q'$ to $p$ and from $q$ to $p'$ take time $d$.

Applying our first claim to $p$, $q$ and to $p'$, $q'$ implies, by symmetry, that the first read operation of $p$ on $X$ returns $v_1$, while the first read operation of $p'$ on $X$ returns $v_2$. (The delays, along with the assumption $|R| + |W| < d + u/2$, guarantee that the behavior of $p$ is not affected by writes of $v_2$, and likewise for $p'$ and $v_1$.) By the symmetry in our construction, the second reads of $X$ by $p$ and $p'$ must return different values. Claim 5 implies that it cannot be the case that the second read by $p$ returns $v_1$, while the second read by $p'$ returns $v_2$. It follows that they return $v_2$ and $v_1$, respectively. This, however, violates sequential consistency.

Since linearizability implies sequential consistency, we immediately have:

**Theorem 6.** *In any linearizable, object-symmetric an object-independent implementation of at least three objects using at least four processes, $|R| + |W| \geq d + \frac{u}{2}$.*

We remark that the previous lower bounds do not apply to the single-ownership implementation presented in Section 4, where different processes may run different algorithms for different objects. Also, under the hybrid memory structure described in Section 1 this lower bound holds only for objects of the same type (e.g., allocated to the full-caching organization) and processes uniformly accessing them.

Our next impossibility result is a lower bound of $\frac{u}{2}$ on the worst-case response time for a read operation in any linearizable implementation. The proof makes use of the "shifting" technique to improve upon a lower bound given in [4].

**Theorem 7.** *In any linearizable implementation of a read/write object $X$ that can be accessed by at least two processes, $|R(X)| \geq \frac{u}{2}$.*

# 6 Discussion and Future Research

This paper continues the complexity-theoretic study of the costs of implementing memory objects under various correctness conditions for shared-memory multiprocessor systems, initiated in [4, 10] and further pursued in [3, 12]. Furthermore, we suggested a new kind of memory organization, which combines all the advantages of a global strong consistency condition with the ability to efficiently perform local operations. Under this hybrid memory framework, we presented two different shared memory organizations and implementations associated with them, which show that it is possible to support strong correctness conditions efficiently under different sharing patterns and anticipated typical usage of memory objects. In particular, our results show that when a lot of local activity is anticipated for some of the memory objects, it is possible to implement shared memory so that it still allows for global operations, but local operations are performed more efficiently than remote ones, as it should be, while still providing the strong correctness guarantees of linearizability.

We believe that these results contribute to the understanding of the relation between the cost of implementing distributed shared memory systems that obey consistency conditions, and the more practical question of efficiently and correctly supporting concurrency in a system which, naturally, performs some blend of local and global operations.

Our lower and upper bounds shed more light on the conditions under which each of the consistency conditions we discuss, sequential consistency and linearizability, is more cost-effective. In particular, the lower bound for sequential consistency together with the upper bound for linearizability, not only show that our full-caching implementation is essentially optimal, but suggest a narrow gap between these two consistency conditions with respect to the sum of the worst-case response times for read and write operations. Since we show that this sum depends identically on $d$ for both sequentially consistent and linearizable caching implementations, this implies that for "balanced" applications, i.e., applications in which frequencies of read and write operations are quite comparable, and for sufficiently small $u$, supporting linearizability is more cost-effective. This is not the case, however, for "non-balanced" applications, as suggested by the nonzero lower bound on the worst-case response time for any operation ([4]) in any linearizable implementation, and the corresponding sequentially consistent implementations also presented in ([4]).

It can be easily seen that our full caching implementation allows the possibility of *self-stabilization* against clock faults which might cause messages to be sent by processes at inappropriate times: by using properties of the time-slicing technique, a process can easily detect the fault, by monitoring the presence and rate of the "quiet" intervals, and lead the system to normal operation by re-running the initial synchronization procedure Synch. Consequently, we believe that the methods developed in this paper can be used in a wider context; in particular, our algorithms and synchronization methods (more specifically, the time-slicing technique) should be applicable to other problems in distributed computing, in particular, to more general broadcasting and deadlock resolution problems.

The most intriguing research area suggested by this paper is that of further investigating the hybrid memory organization. We have considered two aspects of typical usage that one might want to take advantage of in building hybrid memory structure. In the case of sharing pattern, it seems quite plausible that in some cases, one can determine in advance major trends in the sharing pattern of the variable, but it would be interesting to investigate how to determine this dynamically, and how to dynamically adapt to these changes. Similar questions might be asked with respect to the frequency of read and write operations on a given memory object; some advantage can clearly be gained by determining an appropriate $\beta$ in advance, but it is intriguing to investigate how to dynamically adapt $\beta$ in such situations.

While capturing the typical usage trade-off (i.e., different frequencies of read and write operations) by developing a continuum of implementations, we only dealt with two extreme cases of the sharing pattern of a variable. It would be interesting to investigate the existence of intermediate linearizable protocols, that might provide a *group* of processes some advantage in accessing a memory object, while still allowing other processes to perform remote operations on them, less efficiently, and maintain linearizability.

## Acknowledgments:

We would like to thank Hagit Attiya and Roy Friedman for useful discussions and comments. We would also like to thank the WDAG committee members for their helpful remarks.

# References

1. Y. Afek, G. Brown and M. Merritt, "A Lazy Cache Algorithm," in *Proceedings of the 1st ACM Symposium on Parallel Algorithms and Architectures*, pp. 209–222, July 1989.
2. M. Ahamad, P. Hutto and R. John, *Implementing and Programming Causal Distributed Shared Memory*, TR GIT-CC-90-49, Georgia Institute of Technology, December 1990.
3. H. Attiya, "Implementing FIFO Queues and Stacks," in *Proceedings of the 5th Workshop on Distributed Algorithms*, pp. 80–94, Lecture Notes in Computer Science (Vol. 579), Springer-Verlag, October 1991.
4. H. Attiya and J. Welch, "Sequential Consistency versus Linearizability," in *Proceedings of the 3rd ACM Symposium on Parallel Algorithms and Architectures*, pp. 304–315, July 1991.
5. Jean-Loup Baer and Weu-Hann Wang, "Multilevel Cache Hierarchies: Organizations, Protocols and Performance," in *Journal of Parallel and Distributed Computing*, 6, pp. 451–476, 1989.
6. G. Brown and M. Merritt, "Hierarchical Lazy Caching," in *Proceedings of the 28th Annual Allerton Conference on Communication, Control and Computing*, pp. 548–557, October 1990.
7. M. Herlihy and J. Wing, "Linearizability: A Correctness Condition for Concurrent Objects," *ACM Transactions on Programming Languages and Systems*, Vol 12, No. 3, pp. 463–492, July 1990.
8. P. Hutto and M. Ahamad, *Slow Memory: Weakening Consistency to Enhance Concurrency in Distributed Shared Memories*, TR GIT-ICS-89/39, Georgia Institute of Technology, October 1989.
9. L. Lamport, "How to Make a Multiprocessor Computer that Correctly Executes Multiprocess Programs," *IEEE Transactions on Computers*, Vol. C-28, No.9, pp. 690–691, September 1979.
10. R. Lipton and J. Sandberg, *A Scalable Shared Memory*, Technical Report CS-TR-180-88, Princeton University, September 1988.
11. J. Lundelius and N. Lynch, "An Upper and Lower Bound for Clock Synchronization," *Information and Control*, Vol. 62, No. 2/3, pp. 190–204, August/September 1984.
12. M. Mavronicolas and D. Roth, "Sequential Consistency and Linearizability: Read/Write Objects," in *Proceedings of the 29th Annual Allerton Conference on Communication, Control and Computing*, October 1991. Expanded version: "Linearizable Read/Write Objects,", Technical Report TR-28-91, Aiken Computation Laboratory, Harvard University, 1991. Submitted for publication.
13. M. Mavronicolas and D. Roth, *Efficient, Strongly Consistent Implementations of Shared Memory*, Technical Report TR-05-92, Aiken Computation Laboratory, Harvard
14. Weu-Hann Wang, Jean-Loup Baer and Henry M. Levy, "Organization and Performance of a Two-level Virtual-Real Cache Hierarchy," in *Proceedings of the 16th International Symposium on Computer Architecture*, pp. 140–148, June 1989.

# Optimal Primary-Backup Protocols

Navin Budhiraja*, Keith Marzullo*, Fred B. Schneider**, Sam Toueg***

Department of Computer Science, Cornell University, Ithaca NY 14853, USA

**Abstract.** We give primary–backup protocols for various models of failure. These protocols are optimal with respect to degree of replication, failover time, and response time to client requests.

## 1  Introduction

One way to implement a fault-tolerant service is to employ multiple sites that fail independently. The state of the service is replicated and distributed among these sites, and updates are coordinated so that even when a subset of the sites fail, the service remains available.

A common approach to structuring such replicated services is to designate one site as the *primary* and all the others as *backups*. Clients make requests by sending messages only to the primary. If the primary fails, then a *failover* occurs and one of the backups takes over. This service architecture is commonly called the *primary-backup* or the *primary-copy* approach [1].

In [5] we give lower bounds for implementing primary-backup protocols under various models of failure. These lower bounds constrain the degree of replication, the time during which the service can be without a primary, and the amount of time it can take to respond to a client request. In this paper, we show that most of these lower bounds are tight by giving matching protocols.

Some of the protocols that we describe have surprising properties. In one case, the optimal protocol is one in which a non-faulty primary is forced to relinquish control to a backup that it knows to be faulty! However, the existence of such a scenario is not peculiar to our protocol. As shown in [5], relinquishing control to a faulty backup is indeed necessary to achieve optimal protocols in some failure models. Another surprise is that in some protocols that achieve optimal response time, the site that receives the request (*i.e.* the primary) is not the site that sends the response to the clients. We show that this anomaly is not idiosyncratic to our protocols—it is necessary for achieving optimal response time.

* Supported by Defense Advanced Research Projects Agency (DoD) under NASA Ames grant number NAG 2–593 and by grants from IBM and Siemens.
** Supported in part by the Office of Naval Research under contract N00014-91-J-1219, the National Science Foundation under Grant No. CCR-8701103, DARPA/NSF Grant No. CCR-9014363, and by a grant from IBM Endicott Programming Laboratory.
*** Supported in part by NSF grants CCR-8901780 and CCR-9102231 and by a grant from IBM Endicott Programming Laboratory.

The rest of the paper is organized as follows. Section 2 gives a specification for primary-backup protocols, Sect. 3 discusses our system model, Sect. 4 summarizes the lower bounds from [5], and Sect. 5 summarizes our results. Sections 6, 7 and 8 describe the protocols that achieve our lower bounds, and Sect. 9 describes a protocol in which the primary is forced to relinquish control to a faulty backup. We conclude in Sect. 10. Due to lack of space, the description of some of the protocols and all proofs are omitted from this paper. See [4] for a complete description and proofs.

## 2 Specification of Primary-Backup Services

Our results apply to any protocol that satisfies the following four properties, and many primary-backup protocols in the literature (*e.g.* [1,2,3]) do satisfy this characterization.

Pb1: There exists predicate $Prmy_s$ on the state of each site $s$. At any time, there is at most one site $s$ whose state satisfies $Prmy_s$.

Pb2: Each client $i$ maintains a site identity $Dest_i$ such that to make a request, client $i$ sends a message (only) to $Dest_i$.

For the next property, we model a communications network by assuming that client requests are enqueued in a message queue of a site.

Pb3: If a client request arrives at a site that is not the primary, then that request is not enqueued (and is therefore not processed by the site).

A request sent to a primary–backup service can be lost if it is sent to a faulty primary. Periods during which requests are lost, however, are bounded by the time required for a backup to take over as the new primary. Such behavior is an instance of what we call *bofo (bounded outage finitely often)*. We say that an *outage* occurs at time $t$ if some client makes a request at that time but does not receive a response[1]. A $(k, \Delta)$-*bofo server* is one for which all outages can be grouped into at most $k$ periods, each period having duration of at most $\Delta$.[2] The final property of the primary–backup protocols is that they implement a bofo–server (for some values of $k$ and $\Delta$).

Pb4: There exist fixed and bounded values $k$ and $\Delta$ such that the service behaves like a single $(k, \Delta)$–bofo server.

Clearly, Pb4 can not be implemented if the number of failures is not bounded. In particular, if all sites fail, then no service can be provided and so the service is not $(k, \Delta)$ for any finite $k$ and $\Delta$.

---

[1] For simplicity, we assume in this paper that every request elicits a response.

[2] Therefore, as well as being finite, the number of such periods of service outages can occur is also bounded (by $k$).

# 3 The Model

Consider a system with $n_s$ sites and $n_c$ clients. Site clocks are assumed to be perfectly synchronized with real time[3]. Clients and sites communicate through a completely connected, point-to-point, FIFO network. Furthermore, if processes (clients or sites) $p_i$ and $p_j$ are connected by a (nonfaulty) link, then we assume for some *a priori* known $\delta$, a message sent by $p_i$ to $p_j$ at time $t$ arrives at $p_j$ at some time $t' \in (t..t + \delta]$.

We assume that all clients are non-faulty and consider the following types of site and link failures: *crash failures* (faulty sites may halt prematurely; until they halt, they behave correctly) [4], *crash+link failures* (faulty sites may crash or faulty links may lose messages), *receive–omission failures* (faulty sites may crash or omit to receive some messages), *send–omission failures* (faulty sites may crash or omit to send some messages), *general–omission failures* (faulty sites may fail by send-omission, receive-omission, or both). Note that link failures and the various types of omission failures are different only insofar as a message loss is attributed to a different component. Link failures are masked by adding redundant communication paths; omission failures are masked by adding redundant sites. As we will see, the lower bounds for the two cases are different.

Let $f$ be the maximum number of components that can be faulty (*i.e.* $f$ is the maximum number of faulty sites in the case of crash, send–omission, receive–omission and general–omission failures, whereas $f$ is the maximum number of faulty sites and links in the case of crash+link failures).

# 4 Lower Bounds

In Tab. 1, we repeat the lower bounds from [5] for the degree of replication, the blocking time and the failover time for the various kinds of failures. Informally, a protocol is *C-blocking* if in all failure–free runs, the time that elapses from the moment a site receives a request until a site sends the associated response is bounded by $C$.[5] Failover time is defined to be the longest duration (over all possible runs) for which there is no primary. However, the failover time bounds only hold for protocols that satisfy the following additional (and reasonable) property.

**Pb5:** A correct site that is the primary remains so until there is a failure.

---

[3] The protocols can be extended to the more realistic model in which clocks are only approximately synchronized [7].

[4] The lower bounds are also tight for fail-stop failures [10] except for the bound on failover time.

[5] We assume that it takes no time for a site to compute the response to a request.

**Table 1.** Lower Bounds—Degree of Replication, Blocking Time and Failover Time

| Failure type | Replication | Blocking time ($C$) | Failover Time |
|---|---|---|---|
| Crash | $n_s > f$ | 0 | $f\delta$ |
| Crash+Link | $n_s > f+1$ | 0 | $2f\delta$ |
| Send–Omission | $n_s > f$ | $\delta$ if $f=1$<br>$2\delta$ if $f>1$ | $2f\delta$ |
| Receive–Omission | $n_s > \lfloor\frac{3f}{2}\rfloor$ | $\delta$ if $n_s \leq 2f$ and $f=1$<br>$2\delta$ if $n_s \leq 2f$ and $f>1$<br>$0$ if $n_s > 2f$ | $2f\delta$ |
| General–Omission | $n_s > 2f$ | $\delta$ if $f=1$<br>$2\delta$ if $f>1$ | $2f\delta$ |

## 5  Summary of Results

We first present a primary-backup protocol schema that will be used to derive the protocols for all the failure models. This schema is based on the *properties* of two key primitives, **broadcast** and **deliver**, that sites use to exchange messages. We show that the schema satisfies Pb1—Pb5 by only using these properties independent of the particular failure model. Each failure model—crash, crash+link, send–omission, receive–omission and general–omission—is handled with a different implementation of **broadcast** and **deliver**, and in all but one case optimal protocols are constructed.

The protocols for crash and crash+link failures show that all the corresponding lower bounds are tight. The protocol for general-omission failures uses a translation technique similar to [8], and demonstrates that our lower bounds for general-omission failures are tight, except for the bound on blocking time when $f = 1$. However, for this special case we have derived a different protocol (not described in this paper) having optimal blocking time . In all failure free runs of this protocol, the site that receives the request (*i.e.* the primary) is not the site that sends the response to the client. We show that this behavior is necessary in this paper.

We do not show the protocols for send-omission and receive-omission failures in this paper because they are similar to the protocol for general-omission failures. These protocols establish that the bounds for send-omission failures are tight. For receive-omission failures, the lower bound on blocking time when $n_s > 2f$ and the lower bound on failover time are also tight. However, our protocol does not have optimal replication, as it requires $n_s > 2f$ (rather than $n_s > \lfloor\frac{3f}{2}\rfloor$).

Finally, in [5] we proved that all receive-omission protocols having $\lfloor\frac{3f}{2}\rfloor < n_s \leq 2f$ necessarily exhibit a scenario in which a non-faulty primary is forced to relinquish control to a faulty backup. In Sect. 9, we describe such a protocol: it uses two sites and tolerates a single receive-omission failure. In addition, this protocol is $\delta$-blocking and so it demonstrates that our lower bound on blocking time is tight for $n_s \leq 2f$ and $f = 1$. As in the protocol for general omission when $f = 1$, it is the backup that sends responses to clients. This behavior is shown to be necessary for an important class of protocols.

## 6  Protocols for the Clients and the $(k, \Delta)$–bofo server

Property Pb4 requires that the primary–backup service behave like some $(k, \Delta)$–bofo server. Figure 1 gives such a canonical $(k, \Delta)$–bofo server (say $s$), and Fig. 2 gives the protocol for client $i$ interacting with $s$. As with any other bofo server, a client will not receive the response to a request if either the request to $s$ or the response from $s$ is lost.

```
initialize()
cobegin
  || inform–clients("Dest = s")
  || do forever
        when received request from client c
        response := Π(state, request)
        state = state ∘ response
        send response to client c
     od
coend

procedure initialize()
  state := ε

procedure inform–clients(ic)
  send (ic) to all clients
```

Fig. 1. Protocol run by a single $(k, \Delta)$ bofo–server $s$

In Fig. 2, *response-time* corresponds to the amount of time the client has to wait in order to get the response from $s$, which is just the round trip message delay. The exact value for *response-time* depends on the failure model being assumed.

## 7  The Primary–Backup Protocol Schema

We first make the simplying assumption that the links between the clients and the sites are non–faulty and there are no omission failures between the clients and the sites (i.e. only the links between sites can be faulty for crash+link failures,

```
cobegin
  || do forever
      if received "Dest = s" then
          Dest_i := s
    od
  || do forever
      ⋮

      if want to send request
        send request to Dest_i
        if not received response by response-time then
            recover() /* call some recovery procedure, which might retry */
        else
      ⋮

    od
coend
```

**Fig. 2.** Protocol run by client $i$ interacting with server $s$

and omission failures can occur only between sites for omission failures). We
show in Sect. 7.1 how this assumption can be removed.

In order to emulate the server $s$ (and consequently satisfy property Pb4), our
primary–backup protocol consists of $n_s$ sites $\{s_1, \ldots, s_{n_s}\}$, each of which runs
the protocol in Fig. 3. The protocol for the clients remains the same.

```
initialize(i)
cobegin
  || if i = 0 then primary(i) else backup(i)
  || delivery-process(i)
  || failure-detector(i)
coend
```

**Fig. 3.** Protocol run by site $s_i$ to emulate server $s$

The procedures **primary** and **backup** (shown in Fig. 4) are the same for all
the failure models. On the other hand, the implementation of the procedures **initialize, broadcast**(used in Fig. 4), **delivery–process** and **failure–detector**
change depending on the particular failure model. However, we ensure that these
different implementations always satisfy a set of properties, called B1—B11 below. We extracted these properties in order to make our proofs modular. In
particular we proved that, independent of the failure model, the protocol in
Figs. 3 and 4 satisfies Pb1–Pb5, as long as the remaining procedures satisfy
B1—B11. As a result, we could then prove Pb1–Pb5 for any other failure model

by just ensuring that the implementation of **broadcast, delivery–process** and **failure–detector** for that failure model satisfied B1–B11.

---

**procedure primary**($j$)
  **cobegin**
    || inform–clients(*"Dest = $s_j$"*)
    || broadcast((mylastlog, $s_j$, $last(state_j)$), $j$) /* to all sites */
      **do forever**
        **when** received *request* from client $c$
          *response* := $\Pi(state_j, request)$
          $state_j$ := $state_j$ o *response*
          broadcast((log, $s_j$, *response*), $j$)
          **send** *response* **to** client $c$
      **od**
  **coend**

**procedure backup**($k$)
  **do forever**
    $((tag, s_j, r), j)$ := **Deq**($Rqueue_k$)
    /* assume that dequeueing an empty queue
    does not return any sensible value of *tag* */

    /* synchronizing with the new primary */
    **if** $tag$ = mylastlog **then**
      **if** $r \in state_k$ **then**
        **if** $r = last(state_k)$ **then skip**
        **else** $state_k$ := $state_k \setminus last(state_k)$
      **else** $state_k$ := $state_k$ o $r$

    /* logging *response* from primary */
    **if** $tag$ = log **then** $state_k$ := $state_k$ o $r$

    /* becoming the primary */
    **if** $\forall j < k : Faulty_k[s_j]$ **then primary**($k$)
  **od**

**Fig. 4.** The procedures **primary** and **backup**

---

We now give the properties B1—B11. In these properties, $d, C$ and $\tau$ are some constants whose values depend on the failure model. Intuitively, $d$ corresponds to the amount of time that can elapse from the time a message is broadcast to the time it is dequeued by the receiver, $C$ corresponds to the blocking time and $\tau$ corresponds to the interval between successive "I am alive" messages that sites send to each other (as we will see in the implementation of **failure–detector**).

When we say that a site "halts", we mean that either the site has crashed or has stopped executing the protocol by executing a **stop**. The array of booleans $Faulty_k$ indicates which servers $s_k$ believes has halted: $Faulty_k[s_j]$ being true implies $s_k$ believes that $s_j$ has halted. Finally, we define a broadcast by a site to be *successful* if the site does not halt during the execution of **broadcast**.

The properties can be subdivided according to the procedures to which they relate:

Properties of **broadcast** and **delivery–process**:

**B1:** If $s_j$ initiates a broadcast $b'$ after broadcast $b$, then no site dequeues $b'$ before $b$.

**B2:** If $s_j$ initiates a broadcast $b$ at time $t$, then no site dequeues $b$ after time $t + d$.

**B3:** If $s_j$ initiates a broadcast at time $t$ and does not halt by time $t + C$, then the broadcast is successful. Furthermore, no broadcast takes longer than $C$ to complete.

Properties of **failure–detector**:

**B4:** If $Faulty_j[s_k]$ becomes true, then it continues to be true, unless $s_j$ halts.

**B5:** The value of $Faulty_j[s_k]$ can only change at time $t = l\tau + d$ for some integer $l \geq 0$.

**B6:** If $Faulty_j[s_k] = true$ at time $t$ then $s_k$ has halted by time $t$.

**B7:** If $s_j$ has not halted by time $t_1$, and $s_i$, $i < j$ has halted by time $t_2$ where $t_1 = t_2 + \tau + d$, then $Faulty_j[s_i] = true$ by time $t_1$.

Properties of **broadcast** and **delivery–process** interacting with **failure–detector**:

**B8:** No correct site halts in procedures **initialize, broadcast, delivery–process** or **failure–detector**.

**B9:** If $s_j$ initiates a successful broadcast at time $t$, then for all non–halted sites $s_k$, $k > j$, $Faulty_k[s_j] = false$ through time $\lceil \frac{t}{\tau} \rceil \tau + d$.

**B10:** If $s_j$ initiates a successful broadcast $b$, then for every non–halted site $s_k$: $(Faulty_k[s_j] = true) \Rightarrow (s_k$ has dequeued $b)$.

**B11:** If $s_j$ initiates a broadcast $b$ at time $t$ and $s_k, k > j$ broadcasts $b'$, then either no site dequeues $b$ after $b'$, or $Faulty_k[s_j] = false$ through time $t + d$.

## 7.1 Outline of the Proof of Correctness

We now informally argue that the protocol in Figs. 3 and 4 satisfies Pb1–Pb5 as long as the procedures **initialize, broadcast, delivery–process** and **failure–detector** satisfy B1—B11.

Define: $Prmy_{s_j}$ at time $t \equiv s_j$ has not halted by time $t$

$$\wedge \ \forall k < j : Faulty_j[s_k] = true \text{ at time } t.$$

From the above definition, Pb1 can now be seen from B6 and the backup protocol in Fig. 4. Pb2 trivially follows from Fig. 2. Pb3 follows from Fig. 4 as no request is sent to a site $s_j$ before $s_j$ becomes the primary. Also, Pb5 holds (from B8 and Fig. 4) as a correct primary continues to be the primary. We now show Pb4.

In order to show Pb4, we need to show two things–the state of the new primary is consistent with the state of old primary; and all outages are bounded. We first show that the states are consistent.

Starting at the top of Fig. 4: when a site $s_j$ becomes the primary, it first informs the clients of its identity by calling **inform–clients**. For now, ignore the broadcast of (`mylastlog`,$s_j$,–) by primary $s_j$.

Whenever $s_j$ gets a request from a client, it computes the response, changes state, broadcasts the log to the backups and sends the response back to the client. It can be seen from Fig. 4 that if primary $s_j$ sends a response $r$ to the client, then $s_j$ must have executed a successful broadcast of (`log`, $s_j$, $r$). This fact and properties B1,B2,B9 and B10 imply that (`log`, $s_j$, $r$) must also have been dequeued by any backup $s_k$ before $s_k$ becomes the primary. Thus, the state of $s_k$ will continue to be consistent with the state of $s_j$ iff the states were consistent when $s_j$ became the primary. We show this as follows.

Informally, the states of $s_j$ and $s_k$ could be inconsistent when $s_j$ becomes the primary for the following reason. Consider a scenario in which some primary $s_i$ crashes during the broadcast of (`log`,$s_i$, $r$) for some $r$. It is possible that $s_k$ received (`log`, $s_i$, $r$) and $s_j$ did not. As a result, the states of $s_j$ and $s_k$ now differ. It is for this reason that $s_j$ broadcasts (`mylastlog`, $s_j$, $r'$) where $r' = last(state_j)$ on becoming the primary. On receiving this, $s_k$ sees that $r' \neq last(state_k) = r$ and removes $r$ from its state. As a result, $state_j$ and $state_k$ become equal. Similarly, $s_k$ would add $r$ to its state had $s_j$, and not $s_k$, received (`log`, $s_i$, $r$).

In the scenario described in the last paragraph, response $r$ is never sent to the client (*i.e.* there is a service outage). We now show that such outages are bounded. $s_i$ did not send the response, and so by B3, must have halted by time $t$ (say). Now from B7 either $s_{i+1}$ halts or becomes the primary by time $t + \tau + \delta$. Since no correct site halts (by B8 and Fig 4), and the number of faulty sites are bounded by $f$, there eventually will be a time when there is a correct primary and no more outages occur.

From B3, the protocol $C$–blocking. Furthermore, it can be shown from B7, B8 and Fig. 4 that the failover time of the protocol is $f(d + \tau)$ for arbitrarily small and positive $\tau$.

However, the **primary** procedure in Fig. 4 does not work if there are message losses between the clients and the sites (due to link or omission failures). For example, a non–faulty primary might omit to receive all requests from a client due to a failure, violating Pb4. Similarly, **inform–clients** might omit to inform some of the clients. However, it is relatively easy to account for these failures when clients are non-faulty. Assume that there is an upper bound (say $G$) between any two requests from a client and that requests carry sequence numbers. If the primary does not receive any requests from a client during an interval of length $G$ or if the primary receives some request with a sequence number gap, then the primary halts. Similarly, the primary can detect that a response was lost by having clients acknowledge responses. If such an acknowledgement is not received, then again the primary halts. Properties Pb1–Pb5 can again be shown to be true if we make the above modification in Figs. 2 and 4.

# 8 Implementation for the various Failure Models

In this section, we show how to implement B1—B11 for the various failure models.

## 8.1 Crash Failures

The procedures implementing B1—B11 for crash failures are given in Fig. 5. Whenever we say that a site "delivered $M$", we mean that the procedure **deliver** has been called with $M$. **Enq** adds an element to the head of a queue and **Deq** dequeues an element from the tail.

---

**procedure initialize**($k$)
    $state_k := Rqueue_k := \epsilon$
    $\forall i : Faulty_k[s_i] := false$

**procedure broadcast**($M, k$)
    send $M$ to all sites

**procedure deliver** ($M, k$)
    Let $M$ be of the form $(tag, -, -)$
    if $tag \in \{\text{log}, \text{mylastlog}\}$ then **Enq**($Rqueue_k, (M, k)$)

**procedure delivery–process**($k$)
    **do forever**
        if received $M$ then **deliver**($M, k$)
    **od**

**procedure failure–detector**($k$)
    **cobegin**
        || **for** $i := 0$ to $\infty$
            **when** $current\text{-}time = i\tau$: send $(\text{alive}, s_k, i\tau)$ to all sites
        || **for** $i := 0$ to $\infty$
            **when** $current\text{-}time = i\tau + d$:
                $\forall j :$ **if** not delivered $(\text{alive}, s_j, i\tau)$ then $Faulty_k[s_j] := true$
    **coend**

**Fig. 5.** Procedures for crash failures

---

We now informally argue that B1–B11 hold for this implementation if $d = \delta$ and $C = 0$. B1 holds as channels are FIFO and, B2 holds as $d = \delta$ and the maximum message delivery time is also $\delta$. B3, B4 and B5 can be seen trivially. B6 and B7 can be seen from **failure–detector** as there are no message losses and message delivery time is atmost $\delta$. B8 holds trivially. It can be shown that if $s_j$ halts at time $t$, then no site sets $Faulty[s_j]$ to true before time $t + \delta$. B9, B10 and B11 now follow.

The procedures in Fig. 5 require $n_s > f$, and so the lower bound on the degree of replication is tight. Since $C = 0$ and $d = \delta$, from Sect. 7.1, the lower bounds on blocking time and failover time are tight as well.

## 8.2  Crash+Link Failures

The procedures in Sect. 8.1 do not work if links can fail. For example, if $s_j$ sends a message to $s_k$ then the message might not reach $s_k$ due to a link failure (which will violate B6 and B10). We therefore replace the implementation in Fig. 5. with the one in Fig. 6, except that **deliver** is the same as before. For this implementation, $d = 2\delta$ and $C = 0$. These procedures use **fifo–broadcast** and **fifo–deliver** in Fig. 7 which ensure that intermittent link failures become permanent failures: if $s_j$ fifo–broadcasts a message $m$ to $s_k$ and $s_k$ omits to fifo–deliver $m$, then $s_k$ will not fifo–deliver any subsequent message from $s_j$.

It can be shown (proof omitted) that this new implementation again satisfies B1–B11 if $n_s > f + 1$. Informally, this is true because of the following reason. Whenever $s_j$ initiates a broadcast of $M$ at time $t$, it sends $M$ to all sites, and the sites then relay $M$ to all other sites. Since $n_s > f + 1$, there is always at least one non-faulty path between any two non-crashed sites, where a path consists of zero or one intermediate sites. Therefore, if $s_j$ does not crash during the broadcast, then all non-crashed sites will deliver $M$ by time $t + 2\delta$. Furthermore B1 will be satisfied because of the FIFO properties of fifo–broadcast and fifo–deliver.

This crash+link protocol requires $n_s > f + 1$, is 0–blocking (since $C = 0$), and has a failover time of $f(2\delta + \tau)$ (since $d = 2\delta$). Thus, all lower bounds for crash+link failures are tight.

## 8.3  General–Omission Failures

The implementation of the procedures for general-omission failures is given in Figs. 8 and 9, except **delivery–process** which is the same as Fig. 6. Whenever, we say that a site "fifo-delivered $M$", we mean that the procedure **fifo–deliver** was called with $M$. These procedures were developed using a technique similar to [8] (although modified to work in our non-round-based model) which requires $n_s > 2f$ and $d = 2\delta$.

```
procedure initialize(k)
    state_k := Rqueue_k := Dqueue_k := ε
    ∀i : Faulty_k[s_i] := false
    last-sent_k := ∀j : expected_k[j] := 0

procedure broadcast(M, k)
    time := current-time
    fifo-broadcast(init, M, s_k, time)

procedure delivery-process(k)
    cobegin
      || fifo-delivery-process(k)
      || do forever
            (tag, M, −, t) := Deq(Dqueue_k)
            if tag = init then fifo-broadcast (echo, M, s_k, t)
            if tag = echo and not dequeued (tag, M, −, t) before then deliver (M, k)
         od
    coend

procedure failure-detector(k)
    A^i_j = (alive, s_j, iτ)
    cobegin
      || for i := 0 to ∞
            when current-time = iτ: fifo-broadcast(init, A^i_k, s_k, iτ)
      || for i := 0 to ∞
            when current-time = iτ + d:
               ∀j : if not delivered A^i_j then Faulty_k[s_j] := true
    coend
```

**Fig. 6.** Procedures for crash+link failures

```
procedure fifo-broadcast(tag, M, s_k, t)
    send (tag, M, s_k, t, last-sent_k) to all
    last-sent_k := last-sent_k + 1

procedure fifo-deliver (tag, M, s_j, t)
    Enq(Dqueue_k, (tag, M, s_j, t))

procedure fifo-delivery-process (k)
    do forever
       if received (tag, M, s_j, t, last_j) then
          if (last_j ≠ expected_k[j]) then skip
          else
             expected_k[j] := expected_k[j] + 1
             fifo-deliver (tag, M, s_j, t)
    od
```

**Fig. 7.** Procedures for crash+link failures

```
procedure initialize(k)
    state_k := Rqueue_k := Dqueue_k := ε
    ∀i : Faulty_k[s_i] := false
    current-primary:=last-sent_k := ∀j :expected_k[j] := 0

procedure broadcast(M, k)
    time := current-time
    fifo-broadcast(init, M, s_k, time)
    if by time + d fifo-delivered (echo, M, s_j, time)
        for at least n_s − f different j then return
    else stop

procedure deliver (M, k)
    Let M be of the form (tag, s_j, −)
    if tag ∈ {log, mylastlog} then
        if j <current-primary then return
        else
            current-primary:= j
            Enq(Rqueue_k, (M, k))
```

**Fig. 8.** Procedures for general–omission failures

We now briefly argue that these procedures satisfy B1—B11. The detailed proof is omitted from this paper. Had we used the implementation of broadcast in Fig. 6, B10 (in particular) would be violated because a faulty primary $s_j$ might omit to send the logs to the backups. Therefore, in Fig. 8, $s_j$ stops in the broadcast of a response (say $r$) if less than $n_s − f$ sites fifo–deliver and subsequently fifo–broadcast $r$. However, even if $s_j$ does not stop in the broadcast, a faulty (but non-crashed) site $s_k$ might still omit to deliver $r$, due to a receive-omission failure, and later become the primary were $s_j$ to fail. To prevent this, $s_k$ ensures (in procedure **failure–detector**) that it fifo–delivers some message (say $m'$) from at least one of the above $n_s − f$ sites that had earlier fifo–broadcast $r$. If $s_k$ does not receive such an $m'$, then $s_k$ stops. Now, if $s_k$ omitted to fifo–deliver $r$, then by the properties of fifo–broadcast and fifo–deliver, $s_k$ cannot fifo–deliver $m'$ and would stop (and, therefore, cannot become the primary). Property B6 is similarly satisfied by ensuring that sites detect their own failure to send or receive **alive** messages and therefore stop.

These procedures require $n_s > 2f$, $d = 2\delta$ and $C = 2\delta$. Furthermore, we have developed a protocol for $f = 1$ (omitted in this paper) that is $\delta$–blocking. Thus, we establish that all lower bounds for general-omission failures are tight.

As mentioned earlier, the $\delta$–blocking protocol for $f = 1$ has scenarios in which the site that receives the request is not the site that responds to the clients. This is in fact necessary. Define a protocol to be "pass the buck" if in any failure–free run of the protocol, the site that receives a request is not the site that sends the corresponding response.

```
procedure failure-detector(k)
   ∀i, j : Aʲⱼ := (alive, sⱼ, iτ)
   ∀i, j : Fʲⱼ := (fault, sⱼ, iτ)
   cobegin
      ‖ for i := 0 to ∞
         when current–time = iτ: fifo-broadcast(init, Aⁱₖ, sₖ, iτ)
      ‖ for i := 0 to ∞
         when current–time = iτ + δ:
            ∀j : if not fifo–delivered (init, Aʲⱼ, sⱼ, iτ) then
               fifo-broadcast (echo, Fʲⱼ, sₖ, iτ)
      ‖ for i := 0 to ∞
         when current–time = iτ + d:
            witnessₖ[k] := {sⱼ|fifo–delivered (echo, Aⁱₖ, sⱼ, iτ)}
            ∀j ≠ k : witnessₖ[j] := {sᵢ|fifo–delivered  (echo, Aʲⱼ, sᵢ, iτ) or
                                    fifo–delivered (echo, Fʲⱼ, sᵢ, iτ)}
            if ∃j : |witnessₖ[j]| < nₛ − f then stop
            if ∃j : not delivered Aʲⱼ then Faultyₖ[sⱼ] := true
   coend
```

**Fig. 9.** Procedures for general–omission failures

**Theorem 1.** *Any C–blocking protocol, where C < 2δ, for send–omission failures is "pass the buck".*

*Proof.* Omitted in this paper. See [4]. □

## 8.4  Other Failure Models

The implementations of the procedures for send-omission and receive-omission failures are similar to those for general-omission failures and so are omitted from this paper. For receive-omission failures, the lower bound on the degree of replication and the lower bound on blocking time when $n_s \le 2f$ and $f > 1$ are *not* tight. Finding optimal protocols remains an open problem. However, the lower bound on failover time for receive-omission failures, and all lower bounds for send-omission failures are tight.

## 9  A Surprising Protocol

We now describe a δ–blocking protocol tolerating receive-omission failures for the special case of $n_s = 2$ and $f = 1$. This protocol is complex, and so we omit the detailed description and only outline the protocol's operation here. This protocol shows that our lower bound on blocking time when $n_s \le 2f$ and $f = 1$ is tight. The protocol has the odd (yet necessary as shown in [5]) property that a non-faulty primary is forced to relinquish to a faulty backup. Furthermore, the protocol is "pass the buck". We, however, show that most δ–blocking protocols tolerating receive omission failures have to be "pass the buck".

Informally, let $\Gamma$ be the maximum time between any two successive client requests (possibly from different clients), and let $D$ be such that if some site $s$ becomes the primary at time $t_0$ and remains the primary through time $t \geq t_0 + D$ when a client $i$ sends a request, then $Dest_i = s$ at time $t$. We write $D < \Gamma$ to mean that $D$ is bounded and $\Gamma$ is either unbounded or bounded and greater than $D$. Then

**Theorem 2.** *Any $C$-blocking protocol, where $C < 2\delta$, for receive-omission failures with $n_s \leq 2f$ and $D < \Gamma$ is "pass the buck".*

*Proof.* Omitted from this paper. □

Whether a protocol has to be "pass the buck" when the relation $D < \Gamma$ does not hold is an open question.

We now describe the protocol. There are two sites $s_0$ and $s_1$. They communicate with each other using **fifo–broadcast** and **fifo–deliver** shown in Fig. 7. Henceforth, when we say that a site sends a message to the other, we will mean that the message is sent with **fifo-broadcast** and other site receives it with **fifo-deliver**.

In a failure-free run of this protocol, since the backup responds to the client, the primary forwards any response to the backup (with a **green** tag as we see below) and the backup sends this response to the client. However, if there is a failure, then the primary responds to the clients. In this case, the primary forwards a response to the backup with a **red** tag. The backup does not forward a response to the client if the response has a **red** tag.

Let $s_0$ initially be the primary. Whenever $s_0$ receives a request from the client, it computes a response $r$, changes state, and sends (**green**,$r$) to $s_1$. Upon receiving this message, $s_1$ updates its state, acknowledges to $s_0$, and then sends $r$ to the client. Because it is the backup that responds to the client, the protocol is $\delta$-blocking. Site $s_0$ processes a new request only after receiving the acknowledgement from $s_1$ for the previous request. Finally, $s_0$ periodically sends **alive** messages to $s_1$, and $s_1$ acknowledges these messages.

Suppose that $s_0$ does not get $s_1$'s acknowledgement for some message, say, (**green**,$r$) (the argument is similar if no acknowledgement is received for an **alive** message). There are three possibilities: (1) $s_1$ has crashed, (2) $s_1$ omitted to receive (**green**,$r$) and so did not send the acknowledgement, (3) $s_0$ omitted to receive the acknowledgement. $s_0$ now waits until it is supposed to send the next **alive** message. $s_0$ sends this **alive** message and waits for an acknowledgement. We now consider the above three cases separately.

**Case 1:** $s_1$ has crashed. As a result, $s_0$ does not receive the acknowledgement to the **alive** message. $s_0$ continues as the primary. From then on, whenever $s_0$ receives a request from the client, it computes the response $r$, sends (**red**,$r$) to $s_1$, and then sends the response back to the client. Also, $s_0$ continues to send **alive** messages. Since $s_0$ is correct, it can continue like this forever.

**Case 2:** $s_1$ is faulty and omitted to receive (**green**,$r$). By the property of fifo–broadcast and fifo–deliver, $s_1$ will not receive the **alive** messages that $s_0$ sends.

$s_1$ concludes that $s_0$ has crashed, sends ("$s_1$ is primary") to $s_0$ and becomes the primary. After that, it behaves like $s_0$ in case 1 above (including sending **alive** messages to $s_0$). Since $s_0$ is correct, it receives ("$s_1$ is primary") (as opposed to case 1) and so it becomes the backup. Also, since $s_0$ is correct it will not omit to receive (**red**,$r$) messages that $s_1$ sends and so $s_0$ keeps its state consistent with $s_1$. Subsequently, if $s_0$ stops receiving **alive** messages from $s_1$, then $s_1$ has crashed and $s_0$ becomes the primary once again.

**Case 3:** $s_0$ is faulty. Since $s_1$ is correct, it receives the **alive** message from $s_0$, sends the corresponding acknowledgement and remains the backup (as opposed to case 2). However, by the property of fifo–broadcast and fifo–receive, $s_0$ will not receive this acknowledge to the **alive** message (or the ("$s_1$ is primary") message), and so it behaves as in case 1 and continues as the primary. Similar to case 2, $s_1$ receives all (**red**,$r$) messages that $s_0$ sends and so its state is consistent with $s_0$. Finally, $s_1$ becomes the primary if it stops receiving **alive** messages from $s_0$.

Case 2 in the protocol is the odd scenario in which the correct primary $s_0$ is being forced to relinquish to $s_1$, known to be faulty. However, this scenario is not something peculiar to our protocol. We showed in [5] that relinquishing to a faulty backup is necessary when $n_s \leq 2f$.

# 10   Discussion

In [5], we present lower bounds for primary–backup protocols which constrain the degree of replication, the failover time, and the amount of time it can take to respond to a client request. In this paper, we derive matching protocols and show that all except two of these lower bounds are tight. Furthermore, we show that in some cases the optimal response time can only be obtained if the site that receives the request is not site that sends the response to the clients.

We have attempted to give a characterization of primary-backup that is broad enough to include most synchronous protocols that are considered to be instances of the approach. There are protocols, however, that are incomparable to the class of protocols we analyze as these protocols were developed for an asynchronous system [6,9]. We are currently studying possible characterizations for a primary-backup protocol in an asynchronous system and expect to extend our results to this setting.

# References

1. P.A. Alsberg and J.D. Day. A principle for resilient sharing of distributed resources. In *Proceedings of the Second International Conference on Software Engineering*, pages 627–644, October 1976.
2. J.F. Barlett. A nonstop kernel. In *Proceedings of the Eighth ACM Symposium on Operating System Principles, SIGOPS Operating System Review*, volume 15, pages 22–29, December 1981.

3. Anupam Bhide, E.N. Elnozahy, and Stephen P. Morgan. A highly available network file server. In *USENIX*, pages 199–205, 1991.

4. Navin Budhiraja, Keith Marzullo, Fred B. Schneider, and Sam Toueg. Optimal primary–backup protocols. Technical report, Cornell University, Ithaca, N.Y., 1992. In preparation.

5. Navin Budhiraja, Keith Marzullo, Fred B. Schneider, and Sam Toueg. Primary–backup protocols: Lower bounds and optimal implementations. In *Proceedings of the Third IFIP Working Conference on Dependable Computing for Critical Applications*, 1992. To Appear.

6. Timothy Mann, Andy Hisgen, and Garret Swart. An algorithm for data replication. Technical Report 46, Digital Systems Research Center, 1989.

7. Gil Neiger and Sam Toueg. Substituting for real time and common knowledge in asynchronous distributed systems. In *Sixth ACM Symposium on Principles of Distributed Computing*, pages 281–293, Vancouver, Canada, August 1987. ACM SIGOPS-SIGACT.

8. Gil Neiger and Sam Toueg. Automatically increasing the fault-tolerance of distributed systems. In *Proceedings of the Seventh ACM Symposium on Principles of Distributed Computing*, pages 248–262, Toronto, Ontario, August 1988. ACM SIGOPS-SIGACT.

9. B. Oki and Barbara Liskov. Viewstamped replication: A new primary copy method to support highly available distributed systems. In *Seventh ACM Symposium on Principles of Distributed Computing*, pages 8–17, Toronto, Ontario, August 1988. ACM SIGOPS-SIGACT.

10. Richard D. Schlichting and Fred B. Schneider. Fail-stop processors: an approach to designing fault-tolerant computing systems. *ACM Transactions on Computer Systems*, 1(3):222–238, August 1983.

# List of Referees

Afek, Y.

Attiya, H.

Bar Noy, A.

Bougé, L.

Budhiraja, N.

Cahn, R.S.

Chandra, T.

Coan, B.

Dolev, D.

Dolev, S.

Dwork, C.

Garay, J.

van Haaften, P.

Jayanti, P.

Kirousis, L.

Kosa, M.

Kutten, S.

Kumar, S.

Mansour, Y.

Mayer, A.

Merritt, M.

Moran, S

Moses, Y.

Orda, A.

Papatriantafillou, M.

Patt Shamir, B.

Peleg, D.

Rhee, I.

Sandoz, A.

Santoro, N.

Schiper, A.

Schoone, A.

Smith, D.

Spirakis, P.

Taubenfeld, G.

Tel, G.

Toueg, S.

Tsigas, P.

Welch, J.

Zaks, S.

# List of Authors

Afek, Y. ....... 1,85
Amir, Y. ...... 292
Anagnostou, E. 203
Anderson, J.H. 313
Attiya, H. ..... 35
Awerbuch, B. .. 185
Bar-Ilan, J. .... 277
Bazzi, R. ...... 166
Berman, P. .... 221
Birman, K. .... 329
Budhiraja, N. .. 362
Cidon, I. ....... 264
Dolev, D. ...... 292
El-Yaniv, R. ... 203
Gafni, E. ...... 85
Garay, J.A. .... 153,221
Garofalakis, J. . 110
Gouda, M.G. .. 313
Greenberg, D.S. 54
Hadzilacos, V. . 203
Herlihy, M. .... 35
Israeli, A. ...... 95,136
Jayanti, P. ..... 69
Kortsarz, G. ... 238
Kramer, S. .... 292
Kranakis, E. ... 253
Lubitch, R. .... 11
Malki, D. ...... 292
Mansour, Y. ... 185

Marzullo, K. .... 362
Mavronicolas, M. 346
Moran, S. ....... 11
Neiger, G. ...... 166
Peleg, D. ........ 238,277
Perry, K.J. ...... 153,221
Pinhasov, M. .... 95
Pinter, S. ....... 136
Ponzio, S. ....... 120
Rachman, O. .... 35
Rajsbaum, S. ... 110
Ricciardi, A. .... 329
Ricklin, M. ...... 1
Roth, D. ........ 346
Santoro, N. ..... 253
Schneider, F. .... 362
Shavitt, Y. ...... 264
Spirakis, P. ..... 110
Stephenson, P. .. 329
Strong, R. ...... 120
Tampakas, B. ... 110
Taubenfeld, G. .. 54
Toueg, S. ....... 69,362
Tromp, J. ....... 85
Vitanyi, P.M.B. . 85
Wang, D.-W. ... 54
Yang, J.-H. ..... 313
Zamsky, A. ..... 136

# Lecture Notes in Computer Science

For information about Vols. 1–559
please contact your bookseller or Springer-Verlag